MW01717387

street art
characters
personajes

STREET ART: CHARACTERS
STREET ART: PERSONAJES

Editor
Josep María Minguet

Art Direction, design, layout, text
an all photographs by
Louis Bou @ Monsa

Translation
Babyl Traducciones

©INSTITUTO MONSA DE EDICIONES
Gravina 43 (08930)
Sant Adrià de Besòs
Barcelona
Tlf. +34 93 381 00 50
Fax.+34 93 381 00 93
www.monsa.com
monsa@monsa.com

ISBN10 84-96823-21-0
ISBN13 978-84-96823-21-1
D.L B-32266-2.007

Printed in Spain by
Indústrias Gráficas Mármol

"tiPod Typography Designed by Ipsum Planet for Neo2 <www.neo2.es>"

"La tipografía tiPod ha sido diseñada por Ipsum Planet para la revista Neo2 <www.neo2.es>".

street art
characters
personajes

monsa

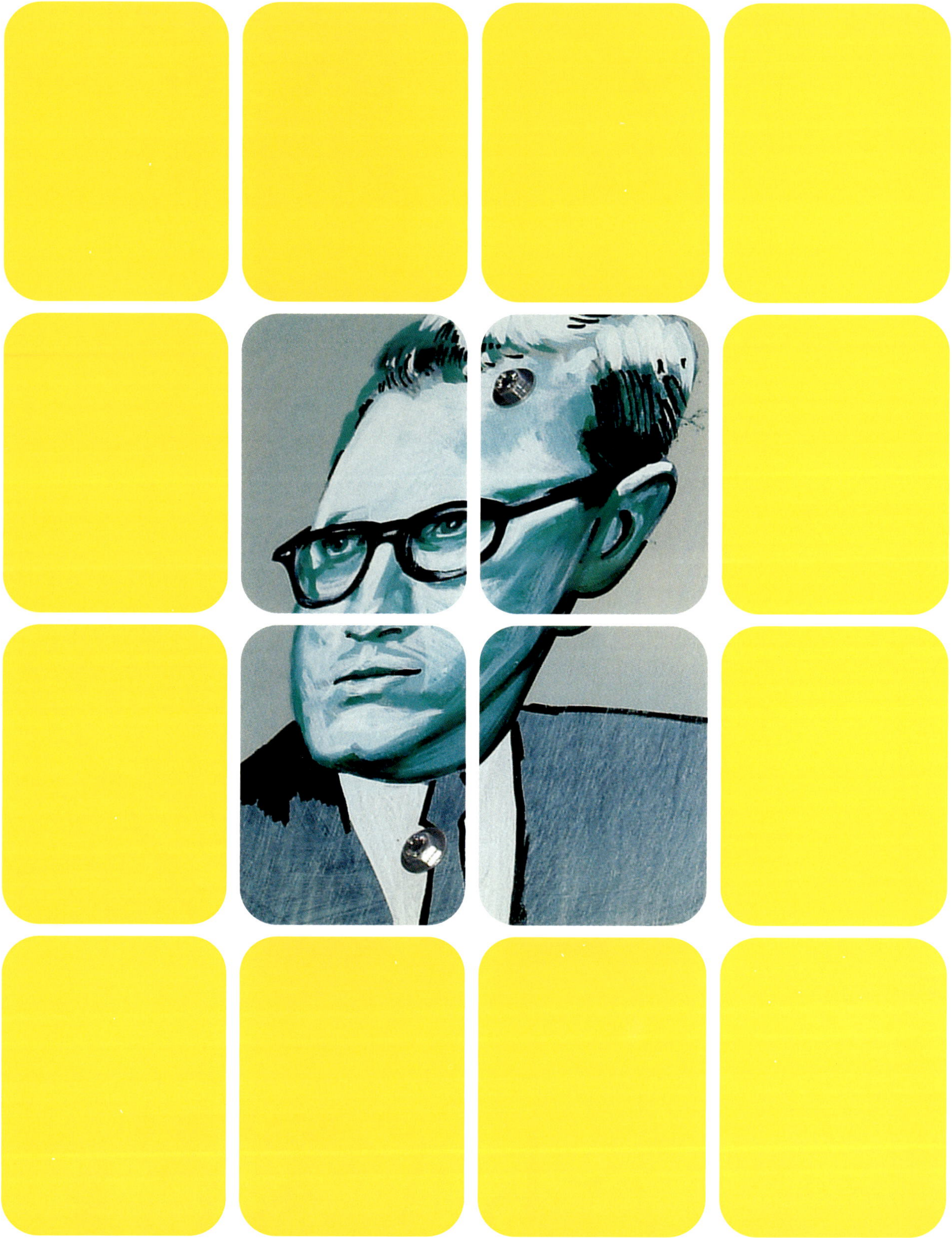

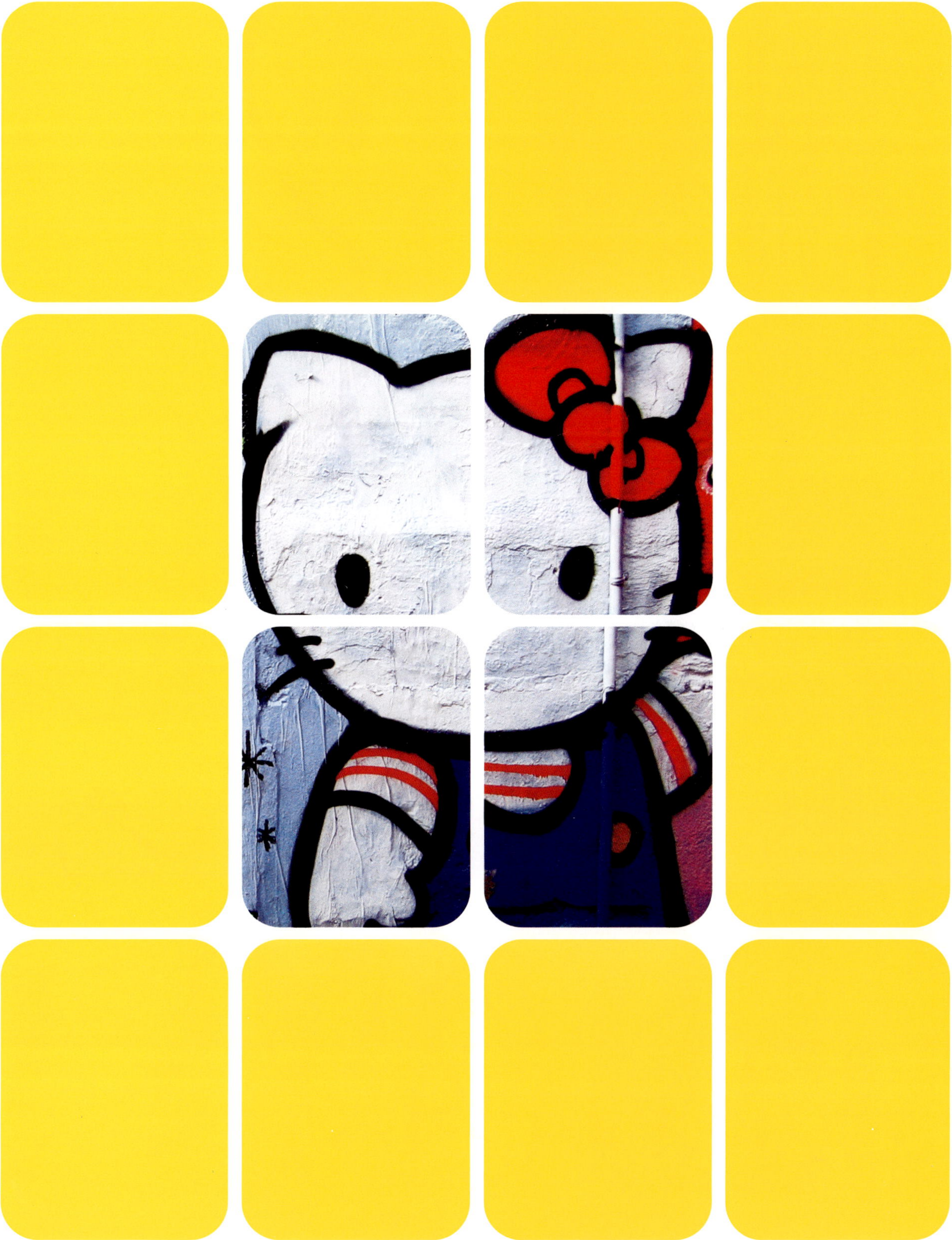

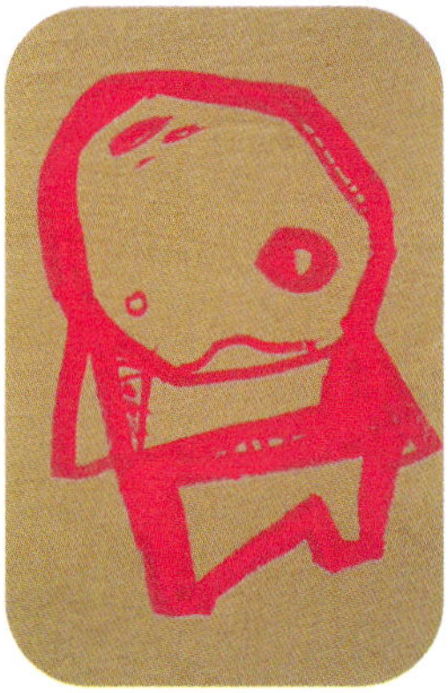

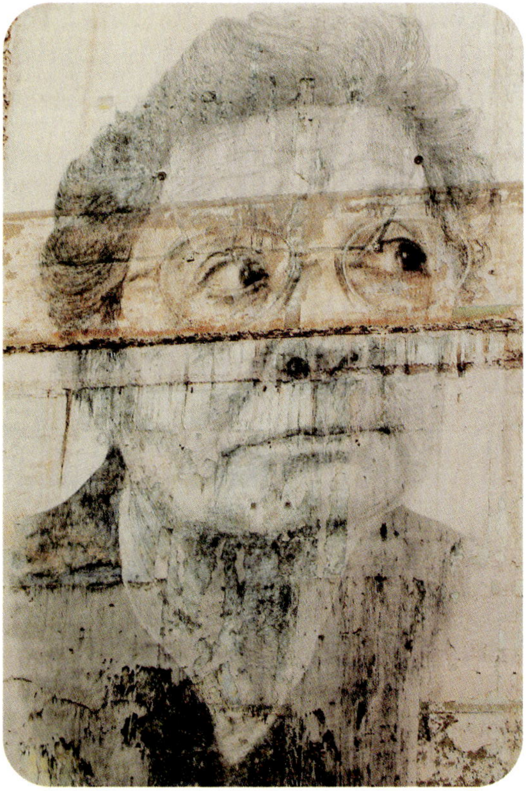

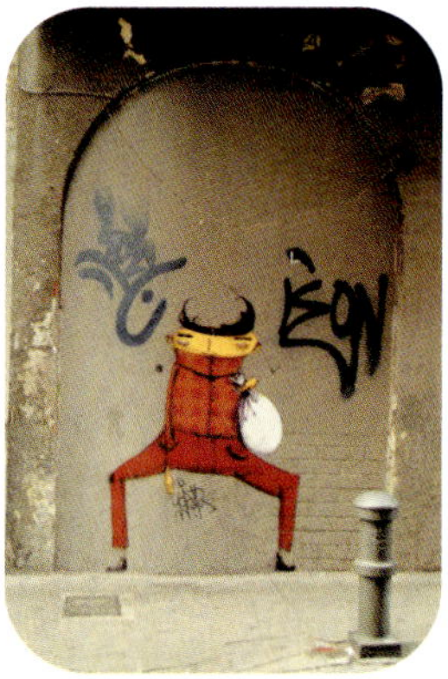

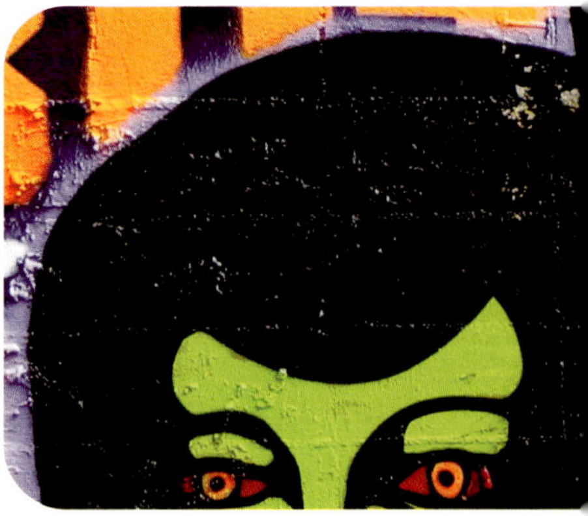

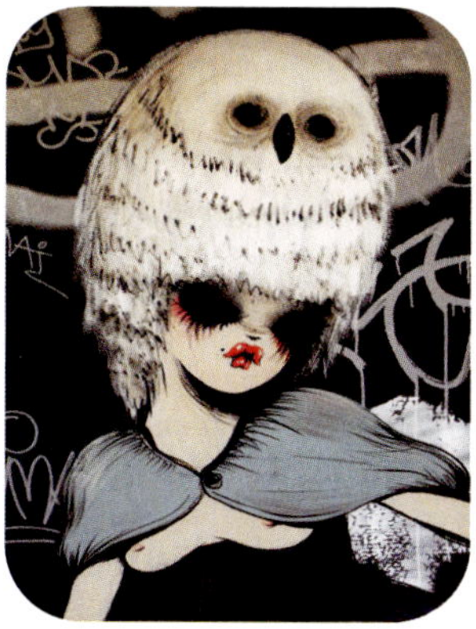
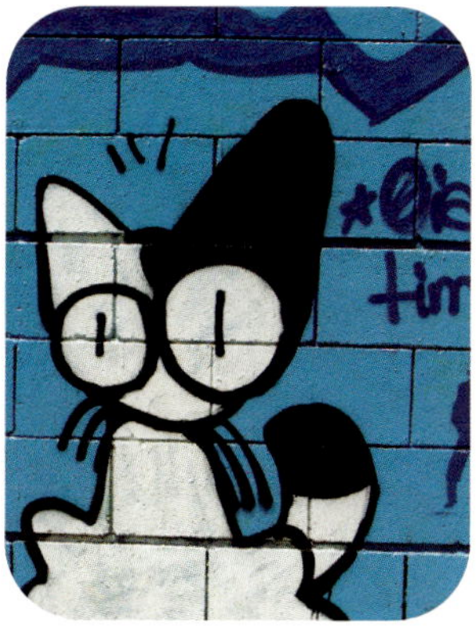
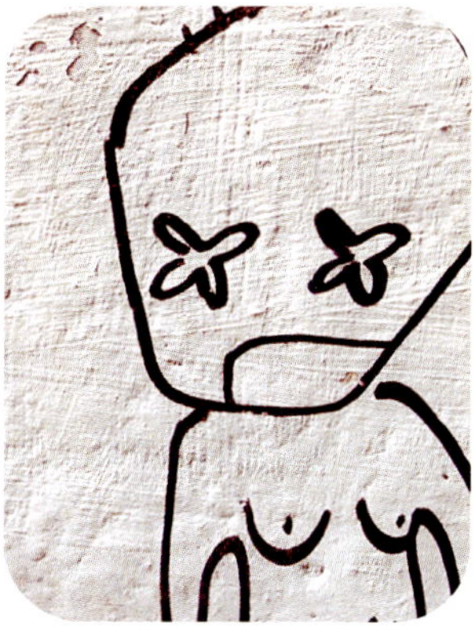

Street art is any art done on a public space and the term include traditional graffiti, stencils, sticker art, video projection and street installations. Characters are fundamental in the contemporary street art world and we can find all sort of caricatures made of spray, charcoal, acrylic, markers and also in posters and stickers. This book shows celebrities, monsters, animals, outer space visitors, divas and tramps, the villains and the heroes drawn on the walls of cities such as New York, London and Barcelona.

Street art es cualquier obra de arte realizada en un espacio público y el término incluye desde el graffiti tradicional, las plantillas, stickers y hasta vídeo proyecciones. Los personajes son fundamentales en el street art contemporáneo y podemos encontrar un amplio abanico de caricaturas hechas con spray, tiza, acrílico o rotulador. En este libro econtraremos animales, monstruos, celebridades, divas, héroes y villanos dibujados en las paredes de ciudades como Nueva York, Londres, París o Barcelona.

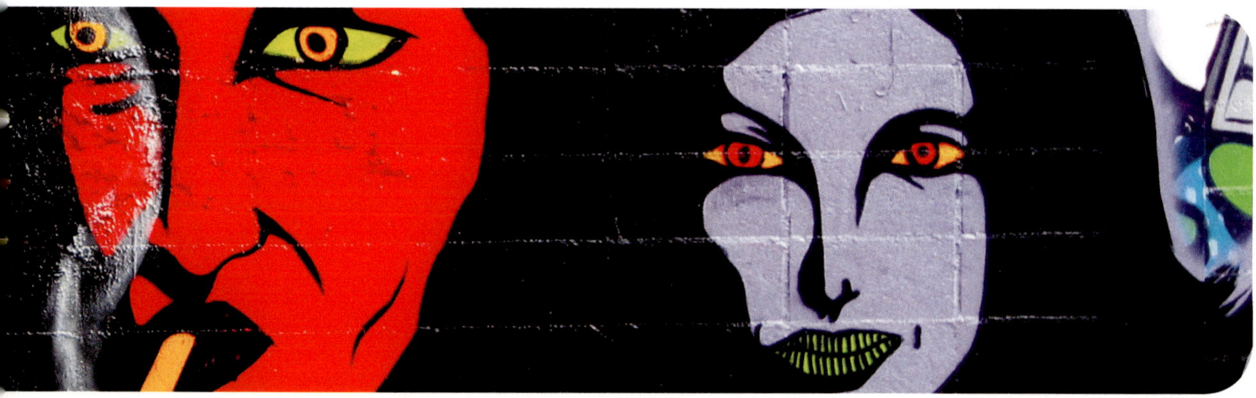

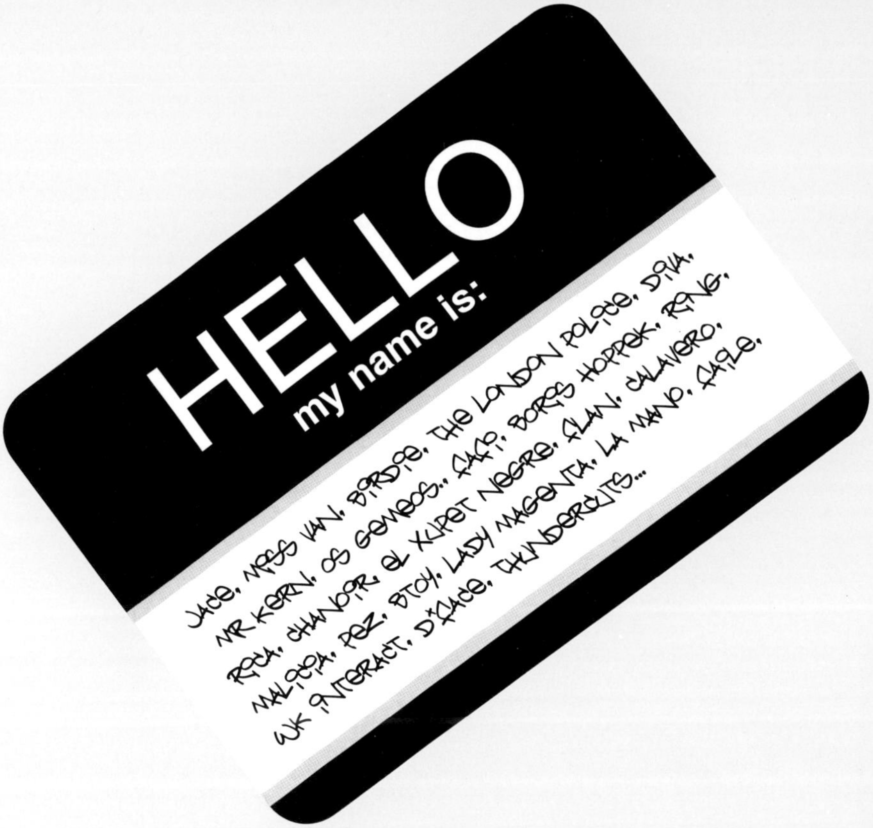
HELLO
my name is:
JACE, MISS VAN, BIRDIE, THE LONDON POLICE, DIVA,
MR KERN, OS GEMEOS., FAFI, BORIS HOPPEK, RING,
ROCA, CHANOIR, EL XUPET NEGRE, FLAN, CALAVERO,
MALICIA, PEZ, BTOY, LADY MAGENTA, LA MANO, FAILE,
WK INTERACT, D*FACE, THUNDERCUTS...

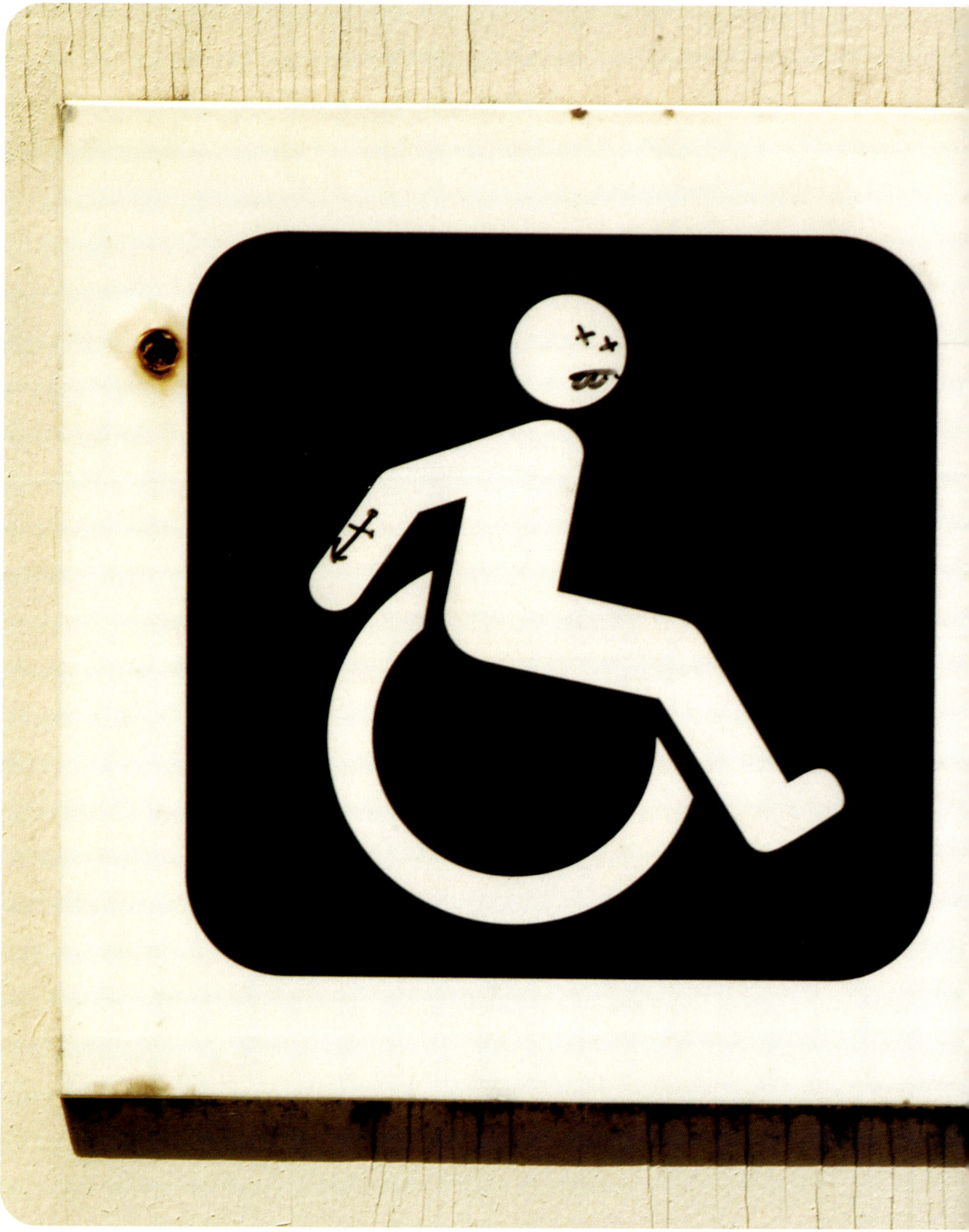

new york

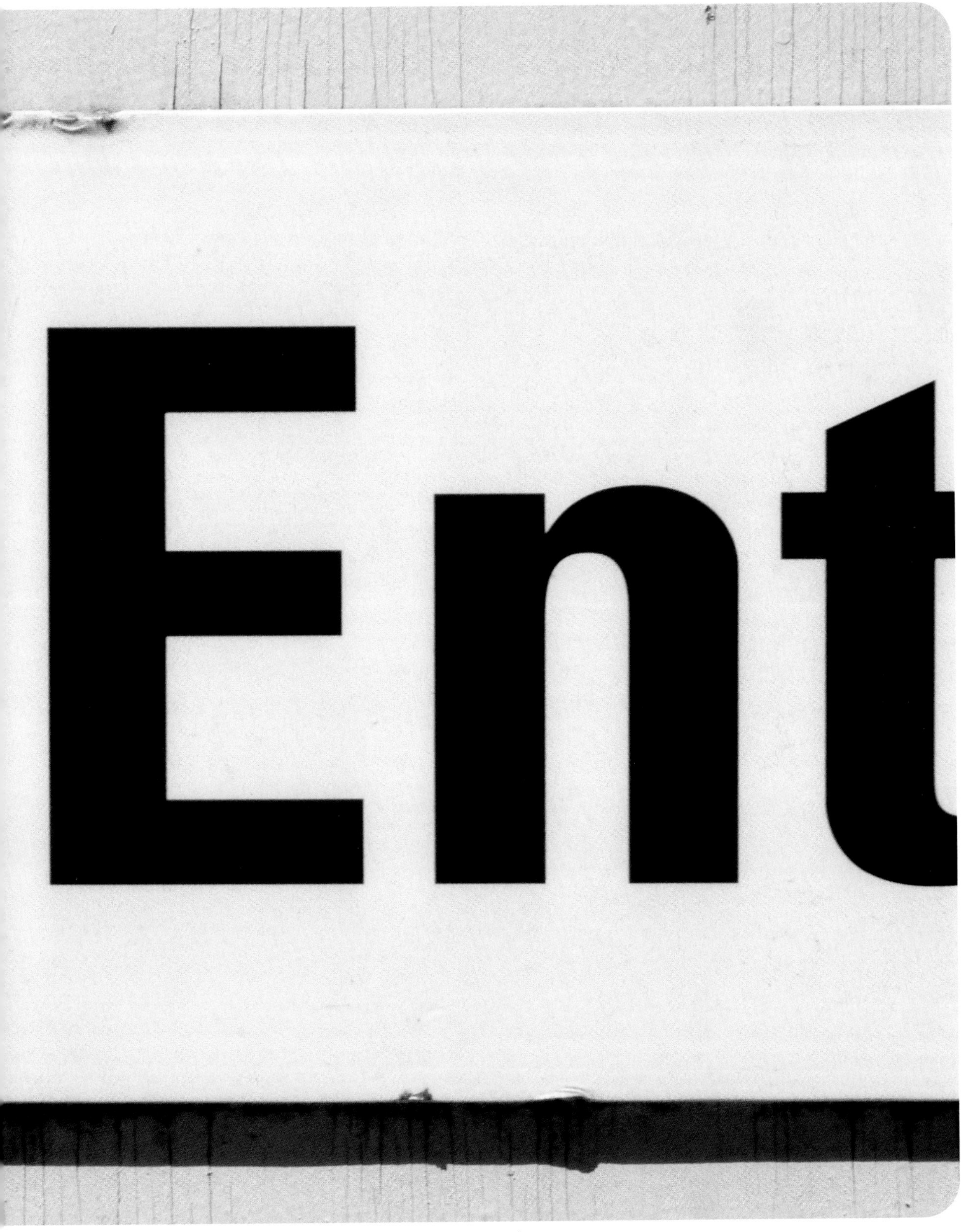

new york

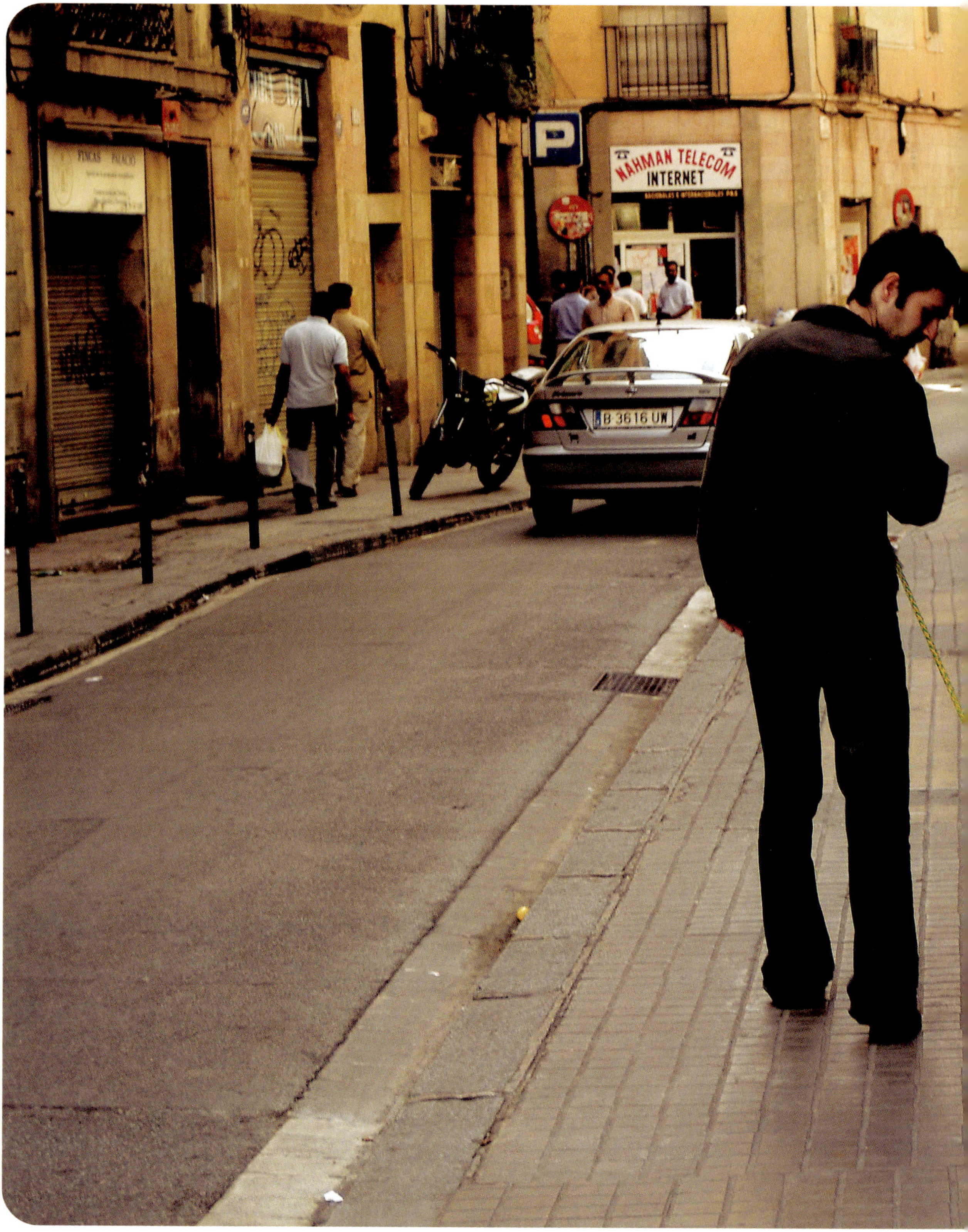
P
NAHMAN TELECOM
INTERNET
B 3616 UW

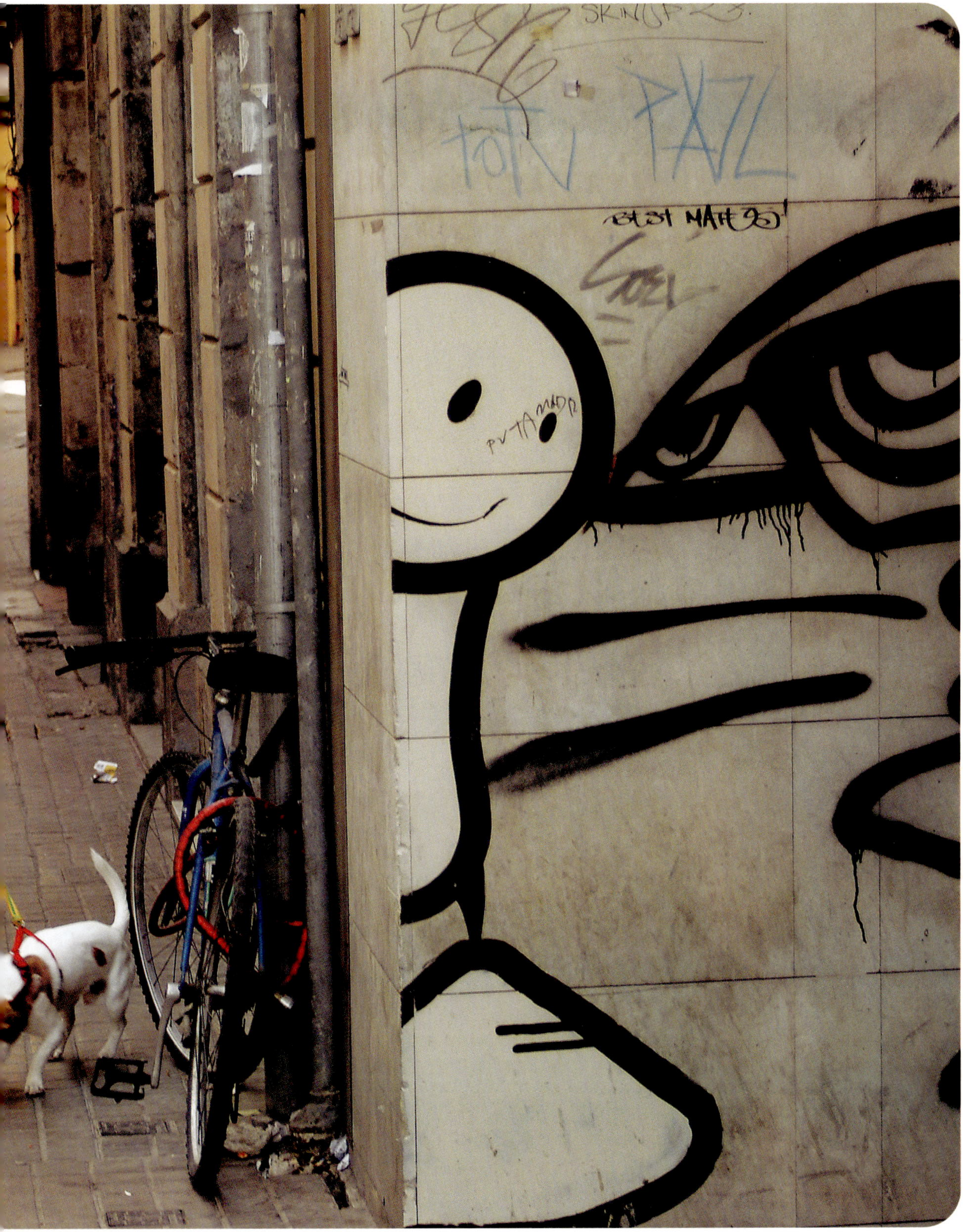

barcelona

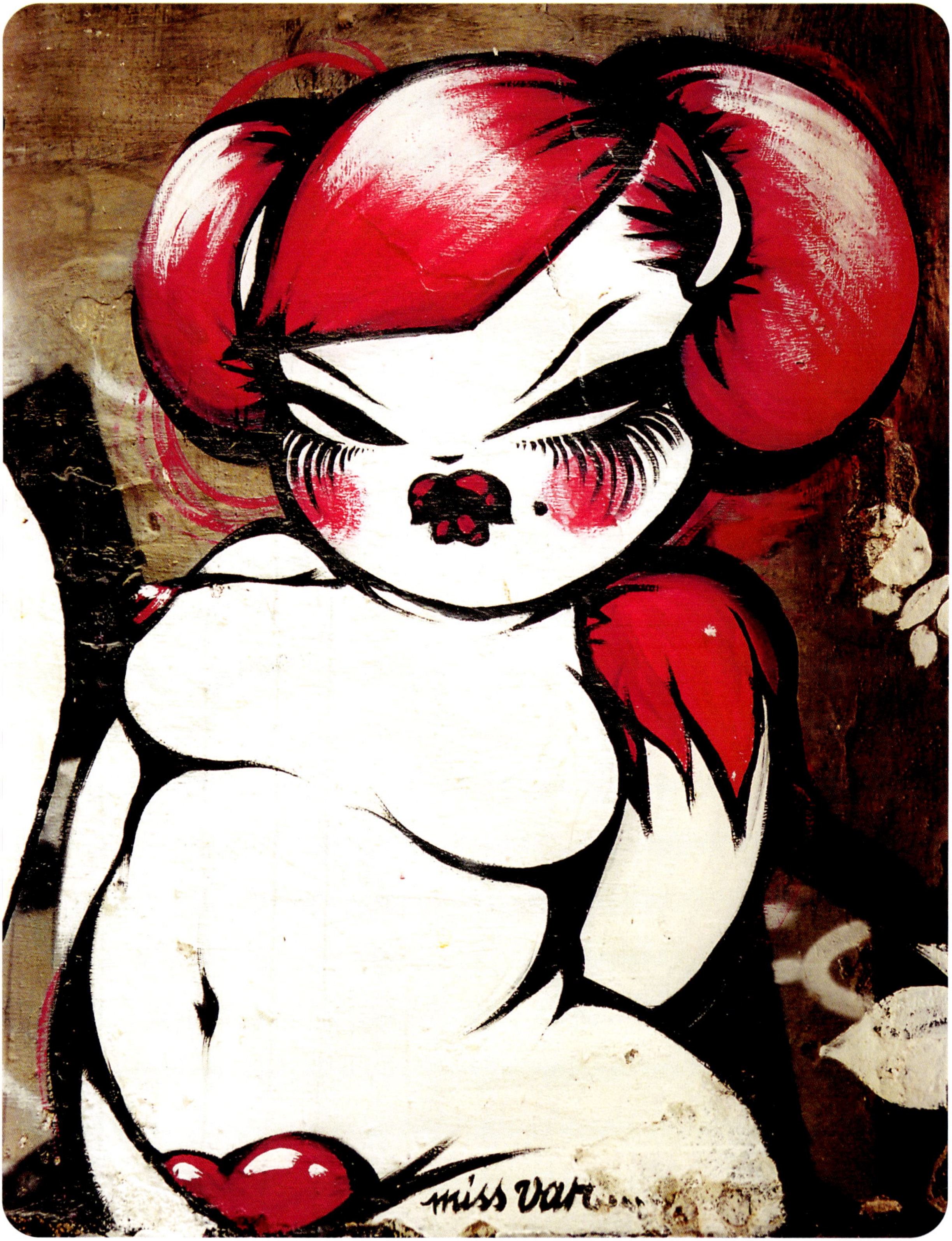

barcelona

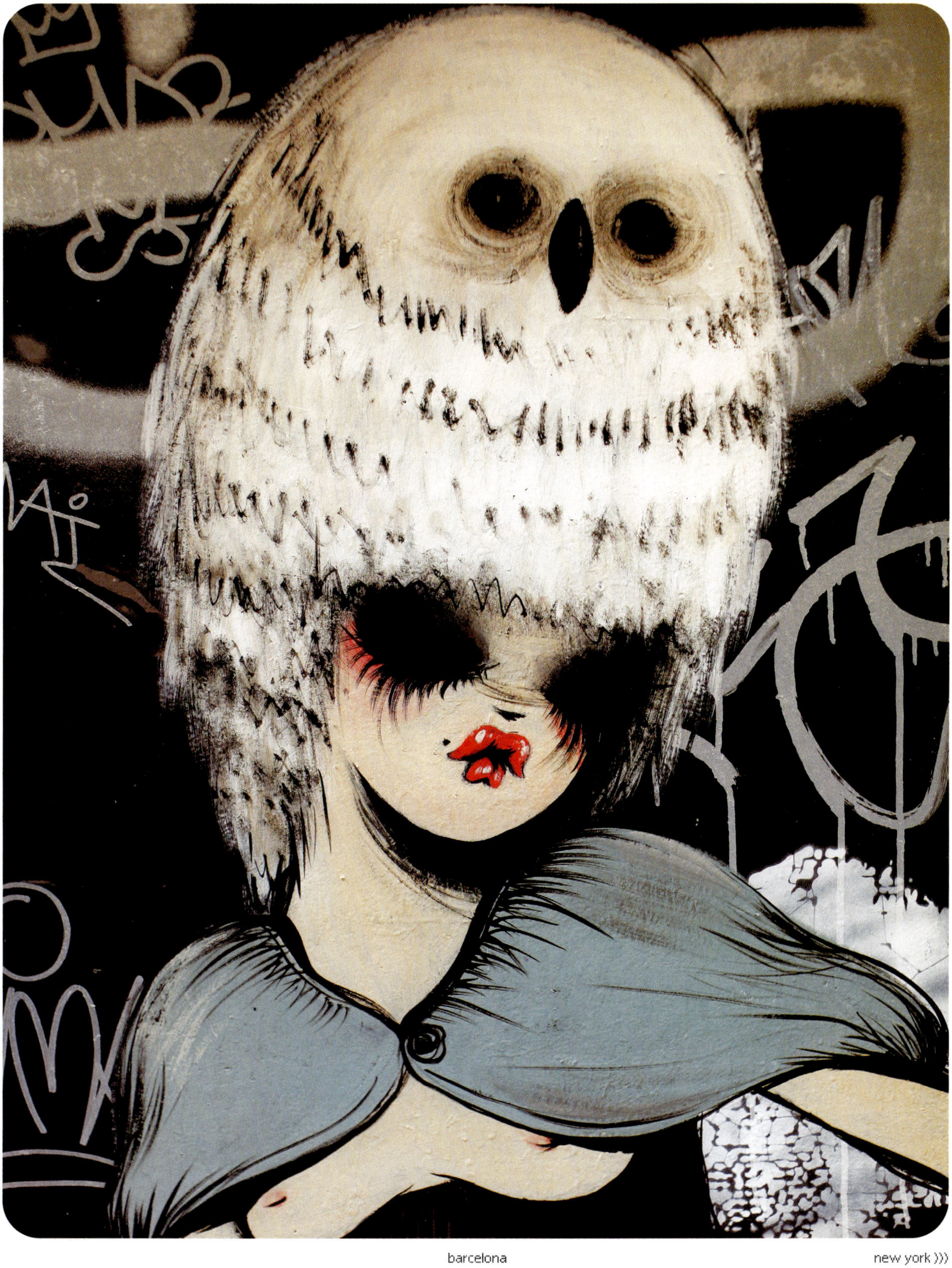

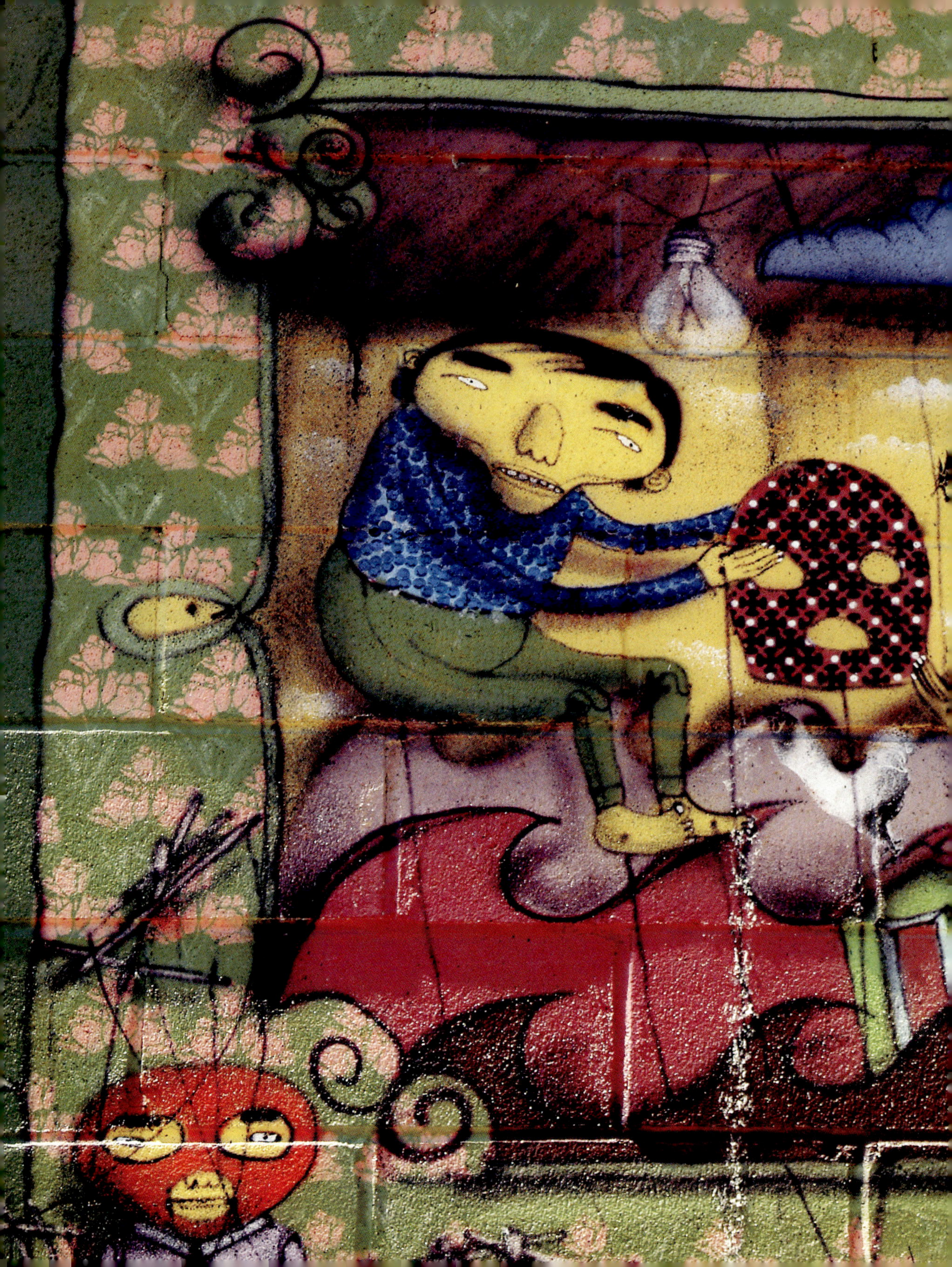

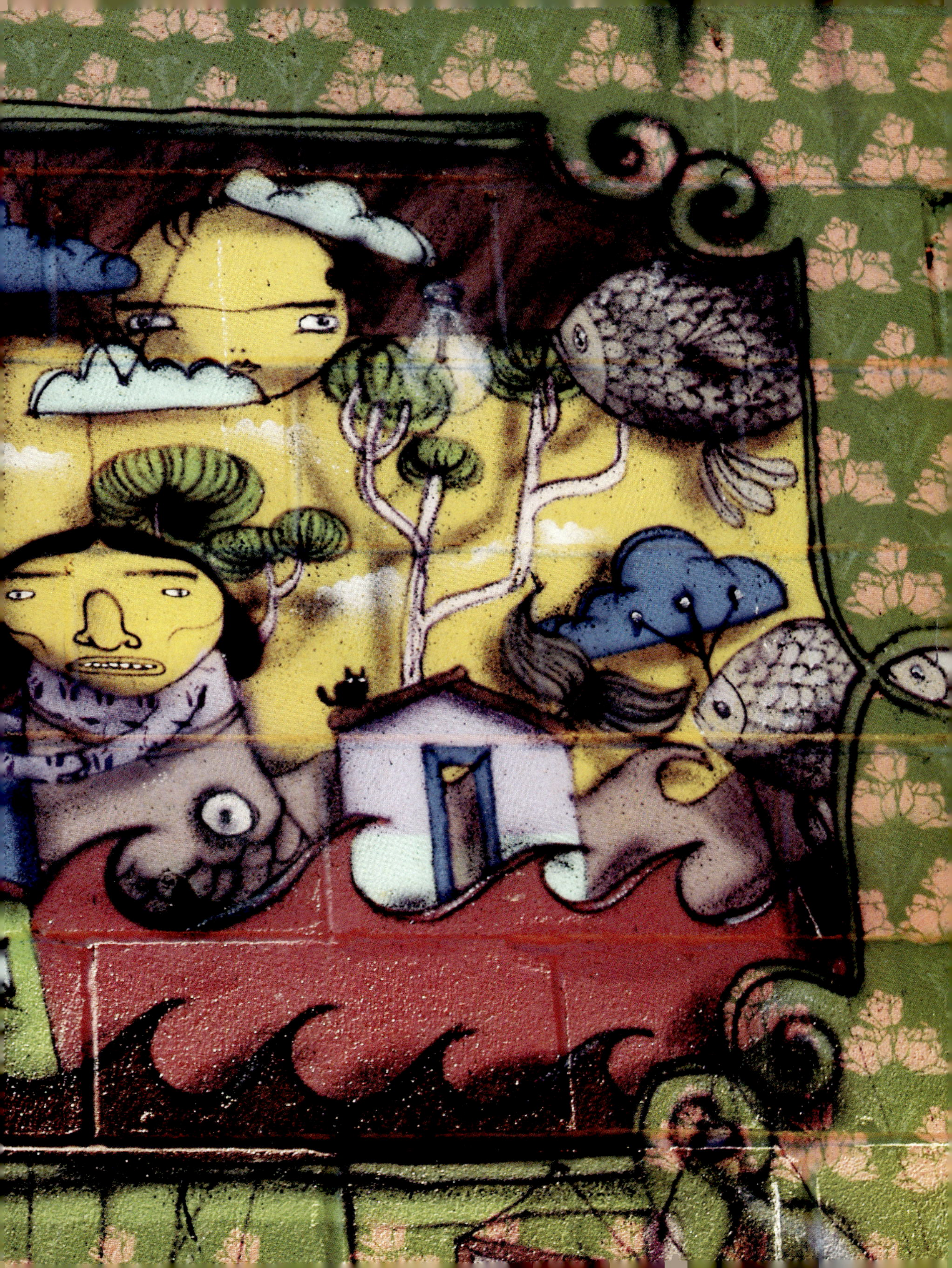

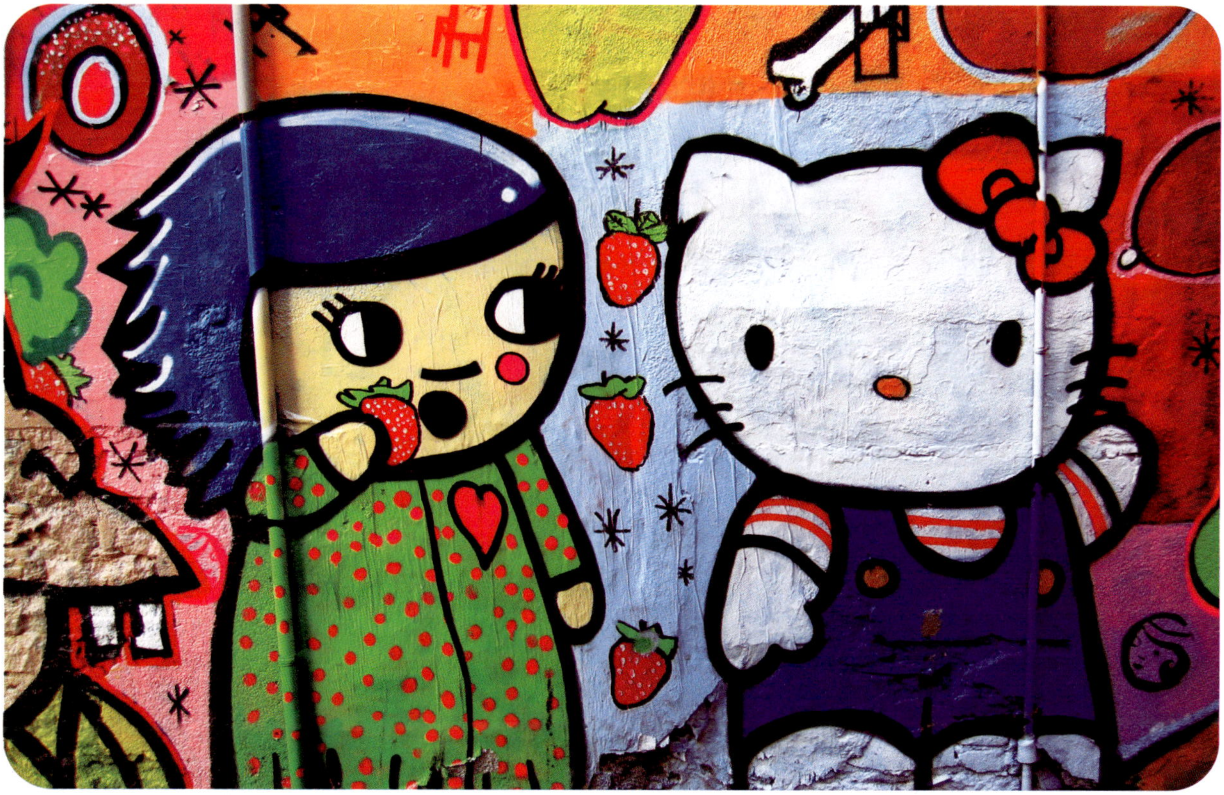

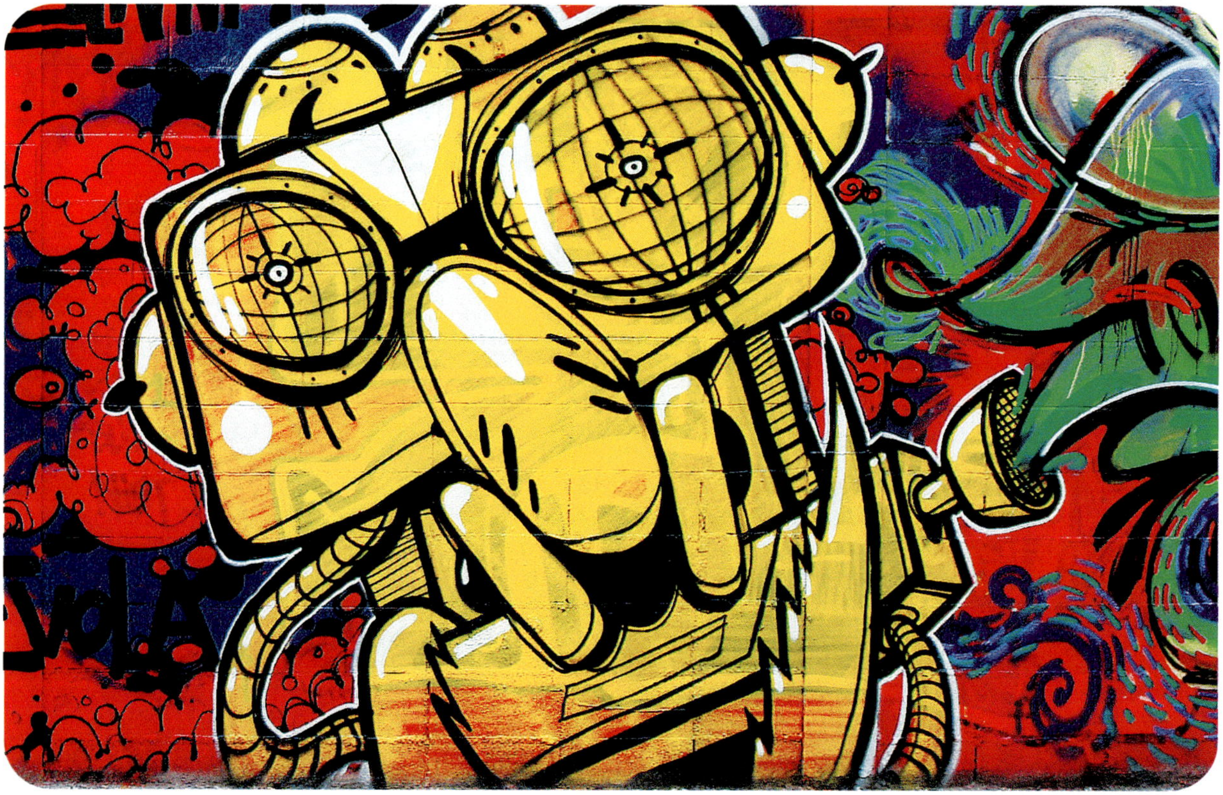

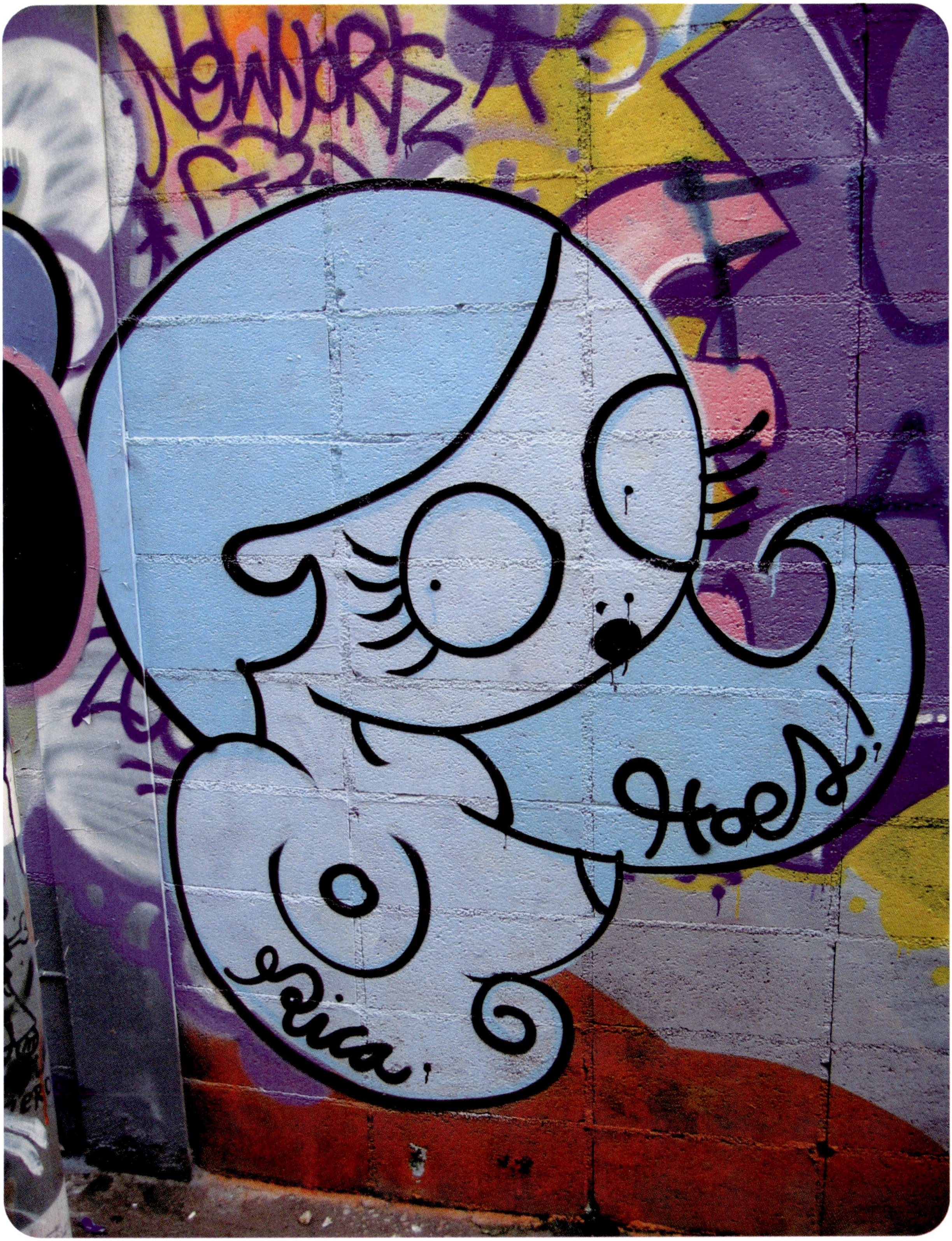

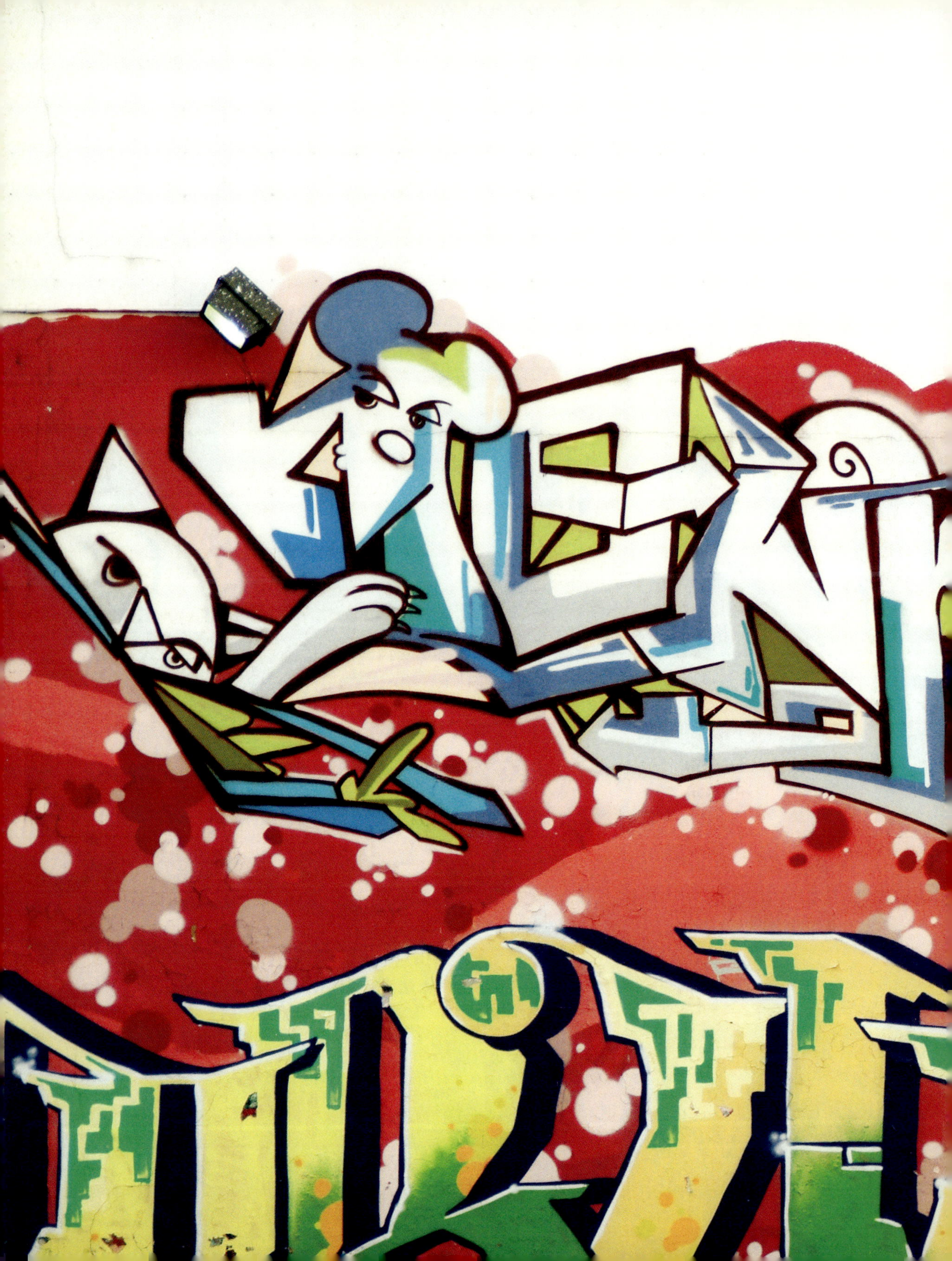

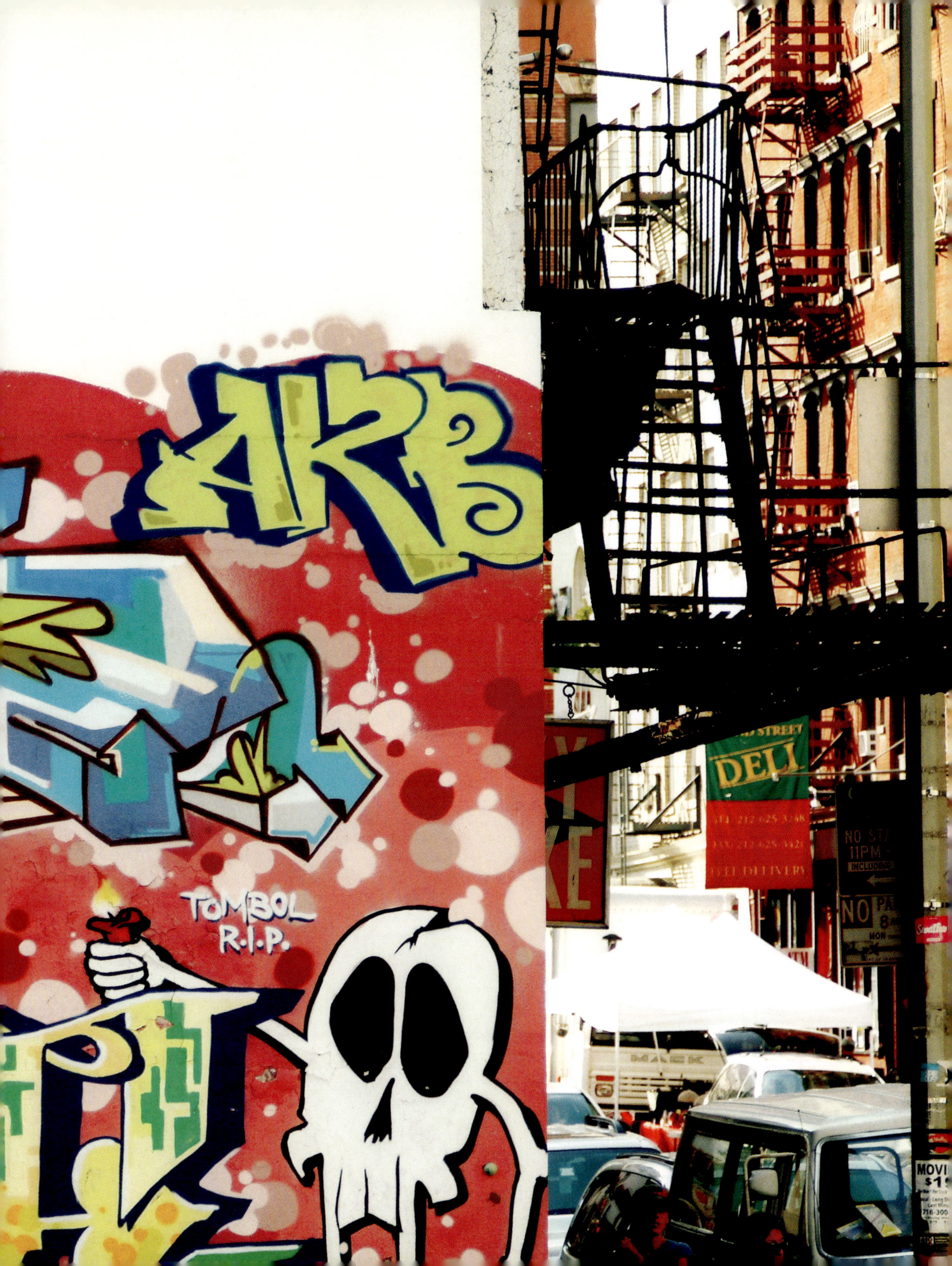
TOMBOL
R.I.P.
DELI

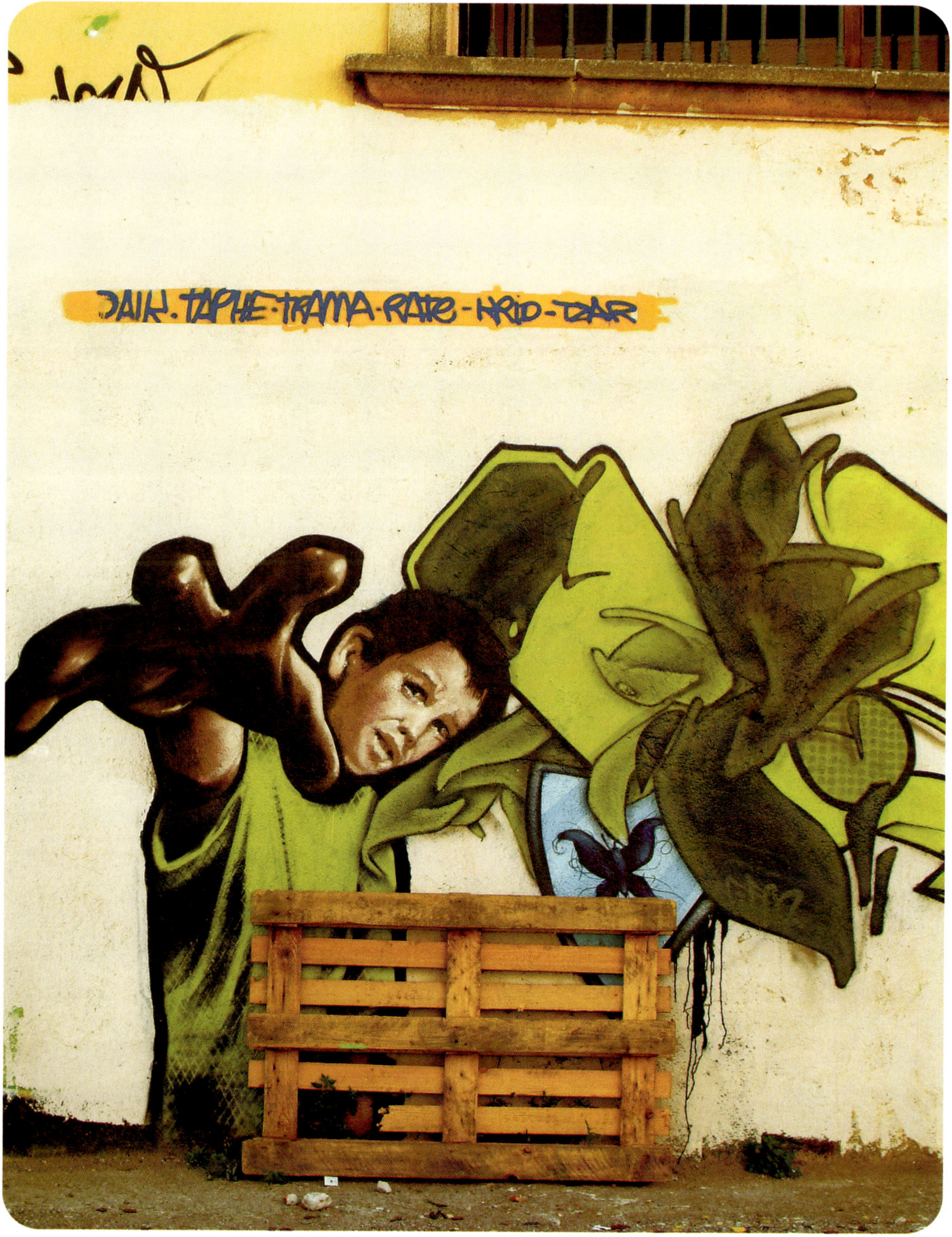

barcelona

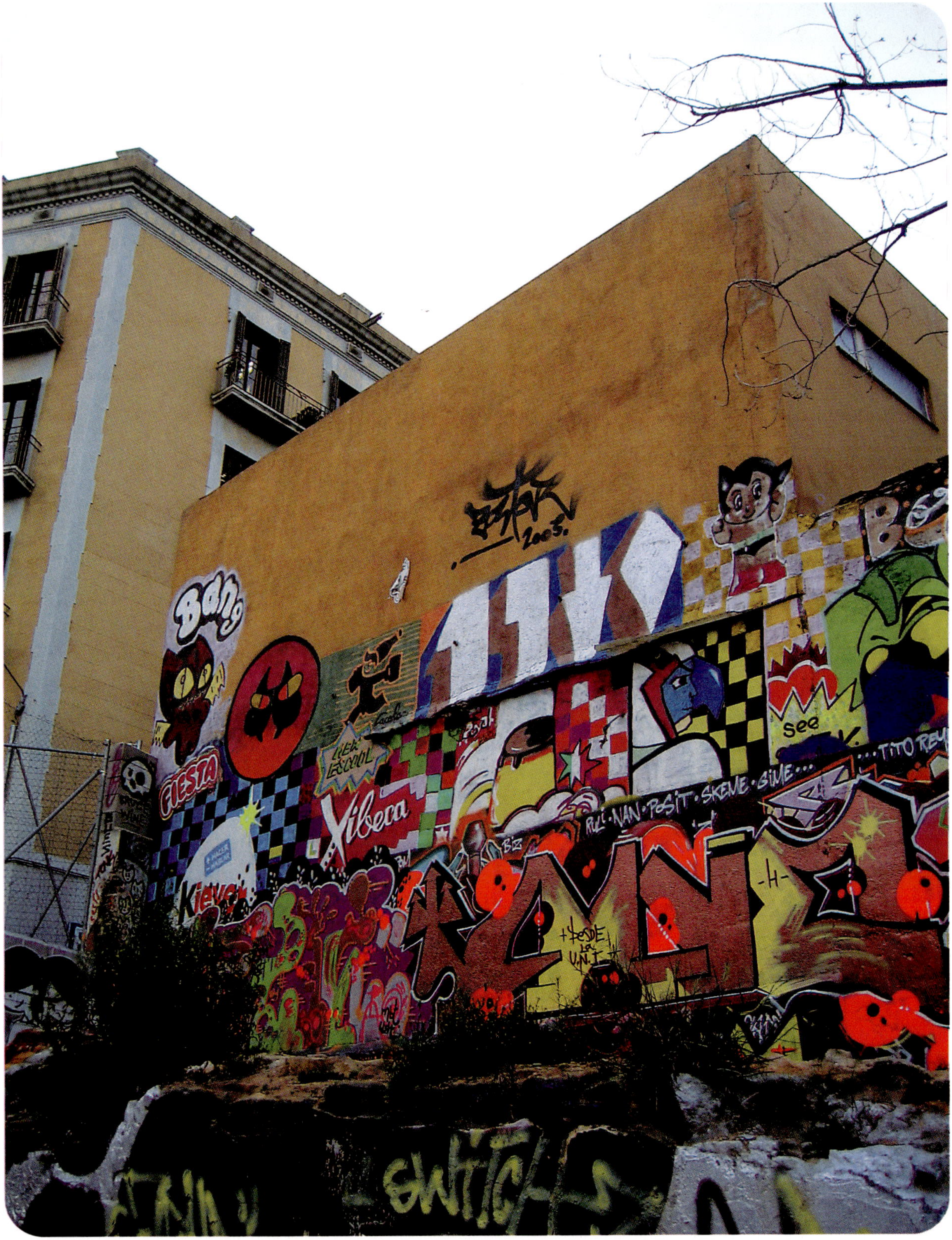

barcelona

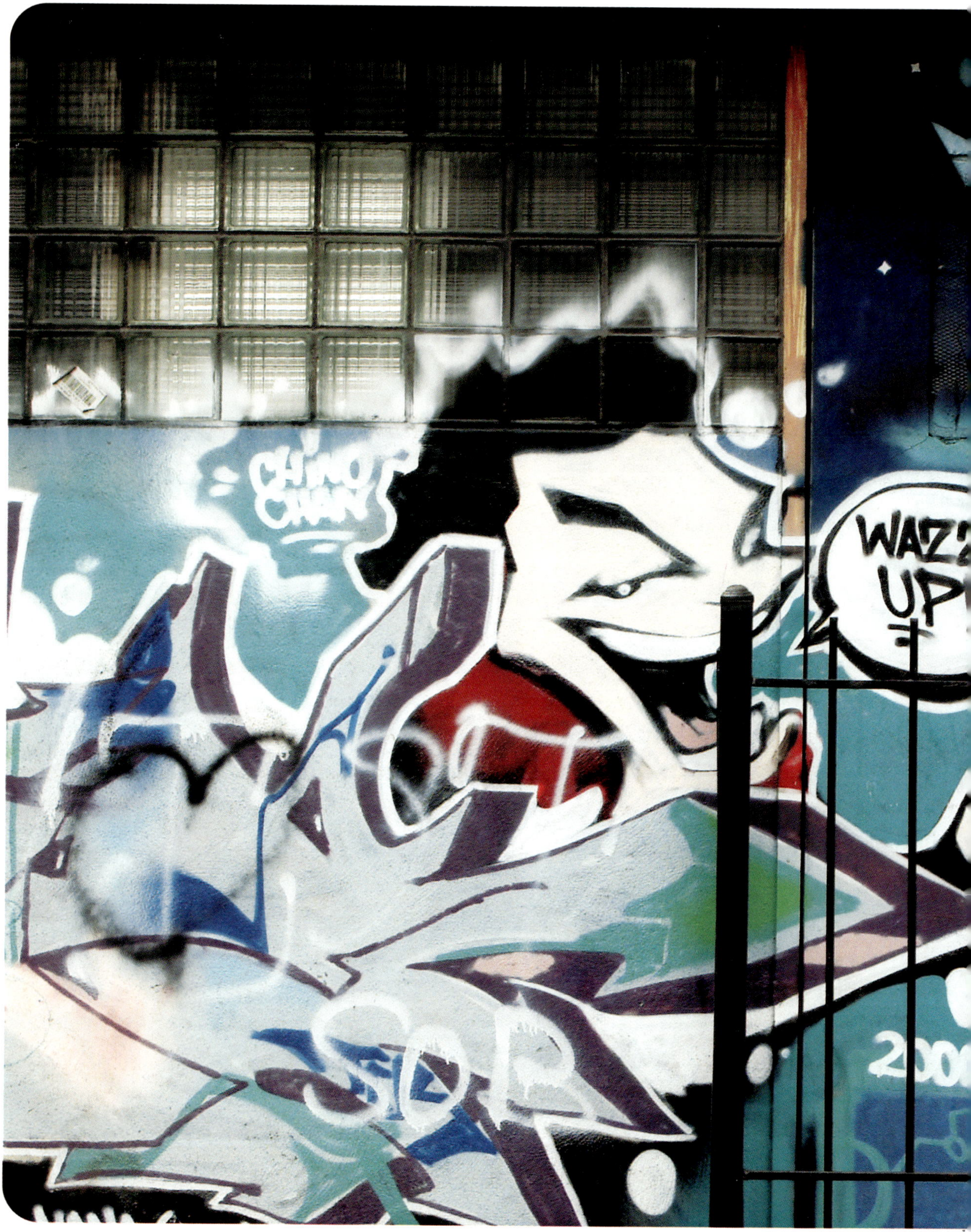
CHINO CHAN

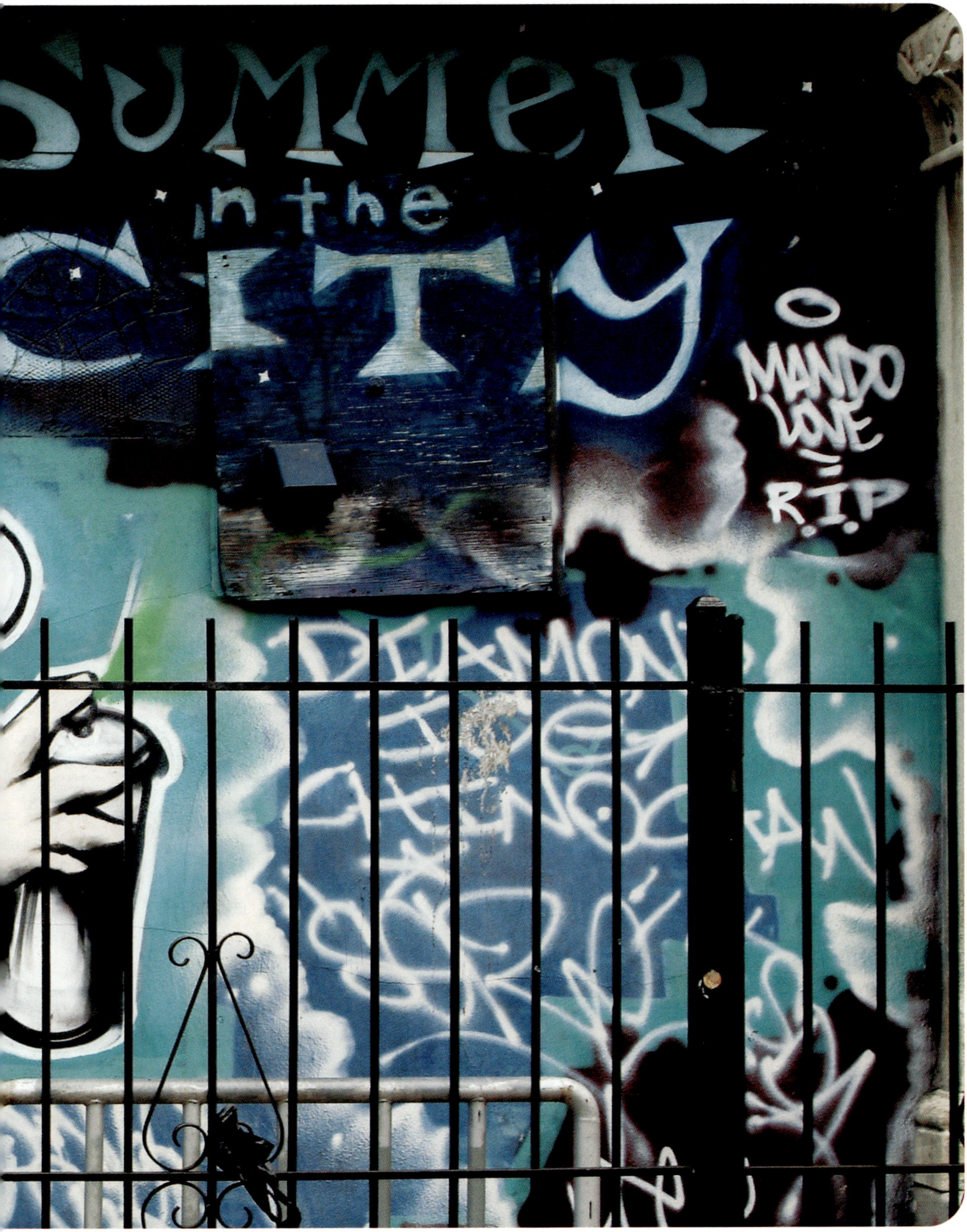
SUMMER
in the
CITY
MANDO
LOVE
R.I.P

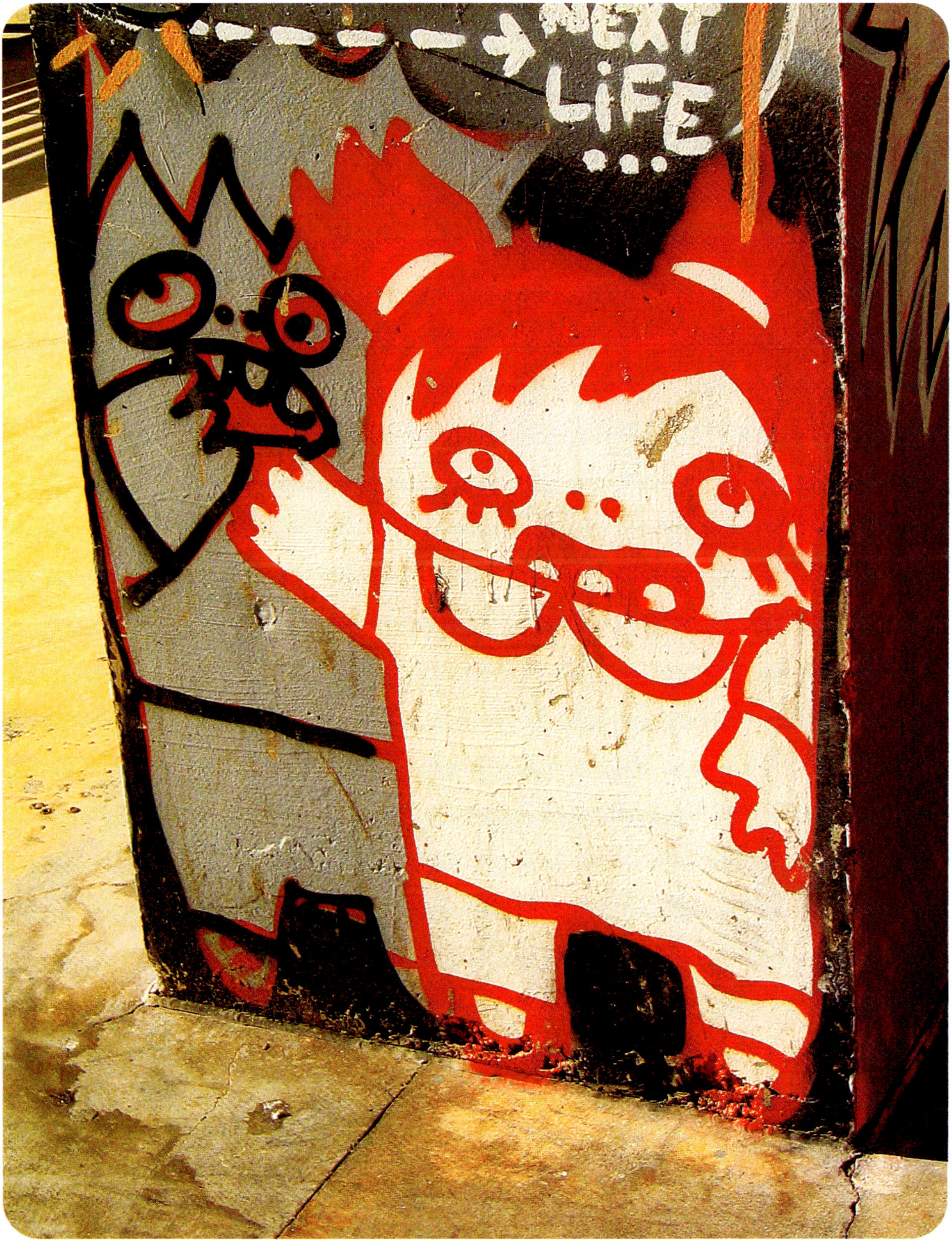

barcelona

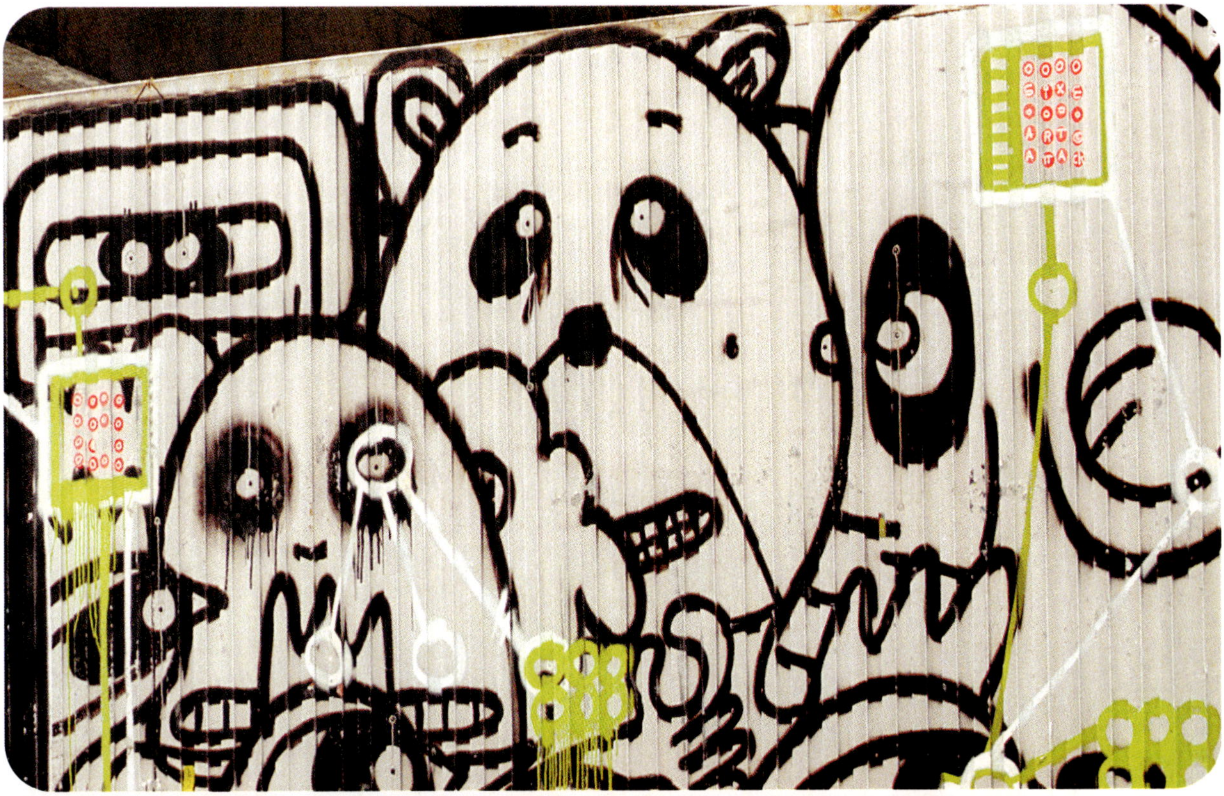

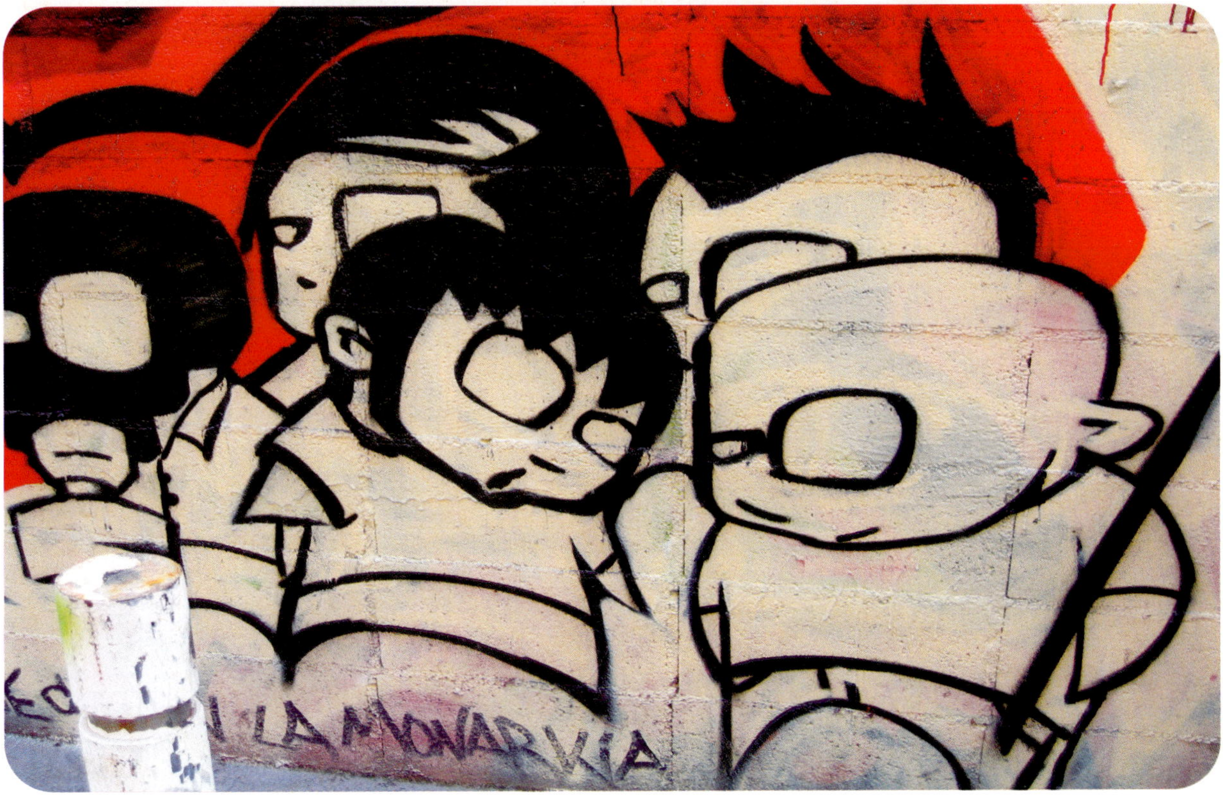
LA MONARKIA

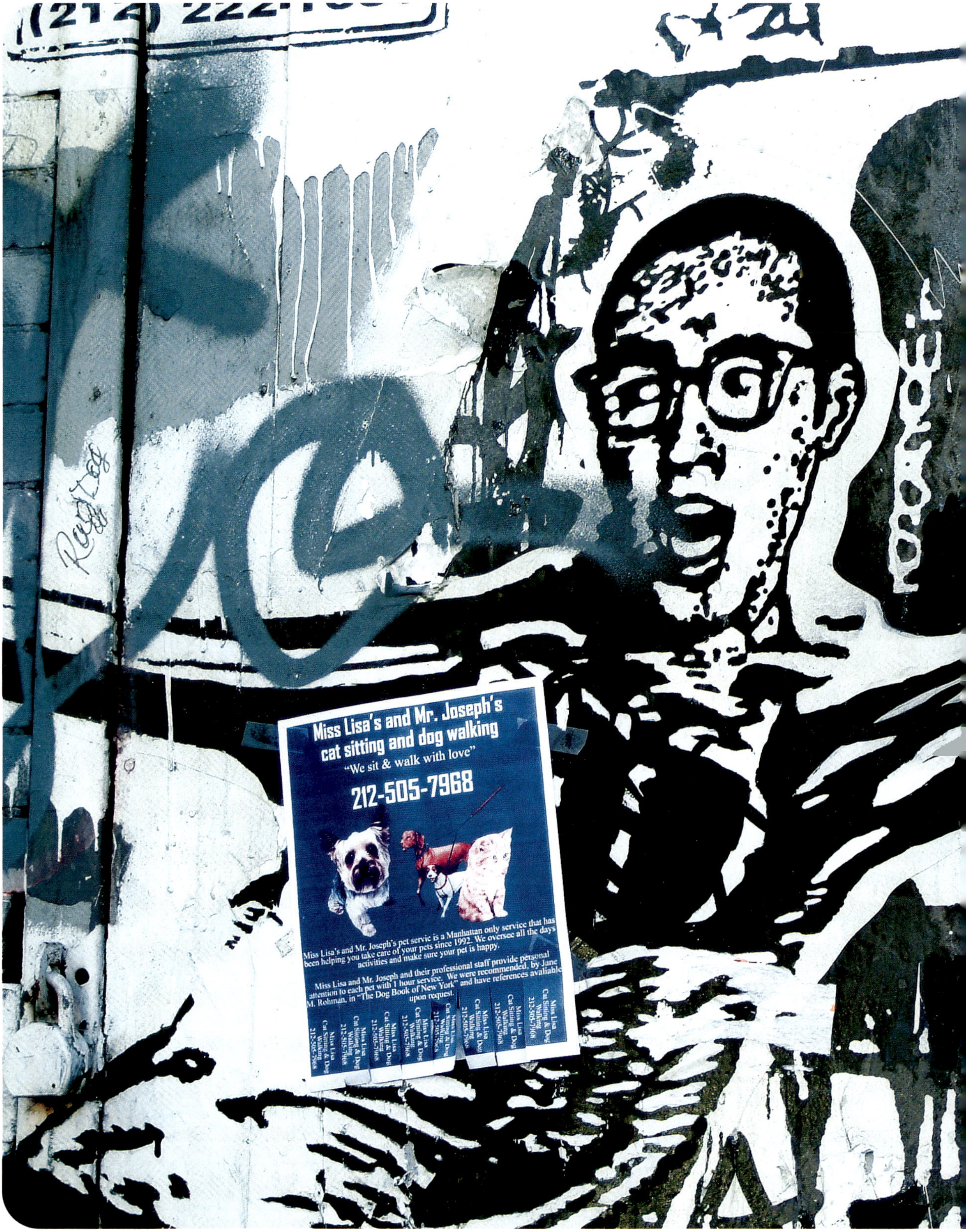
(212) 222-
Miss Lisa's and Mr. Joseph's cat sitting and dog walking
"We sit & walk with love"
212-505-7968
Miss Lisa's and Mr. Joseph's pet servic is a Manhattan only service that has been helping you take care of your pets since 1992. We oversee all the days activities and make sure your pet is happy.
Miss Lisa and Mr. Joseph and their professional staff provide personal attention to each pet with 1 hour service. We were recommended, by Jane M. Rohman, in "The Dog Book of New York" and have references avaliable upon request.
Miss Lisa Cat Sitting & Dog Walking 212-505-7968

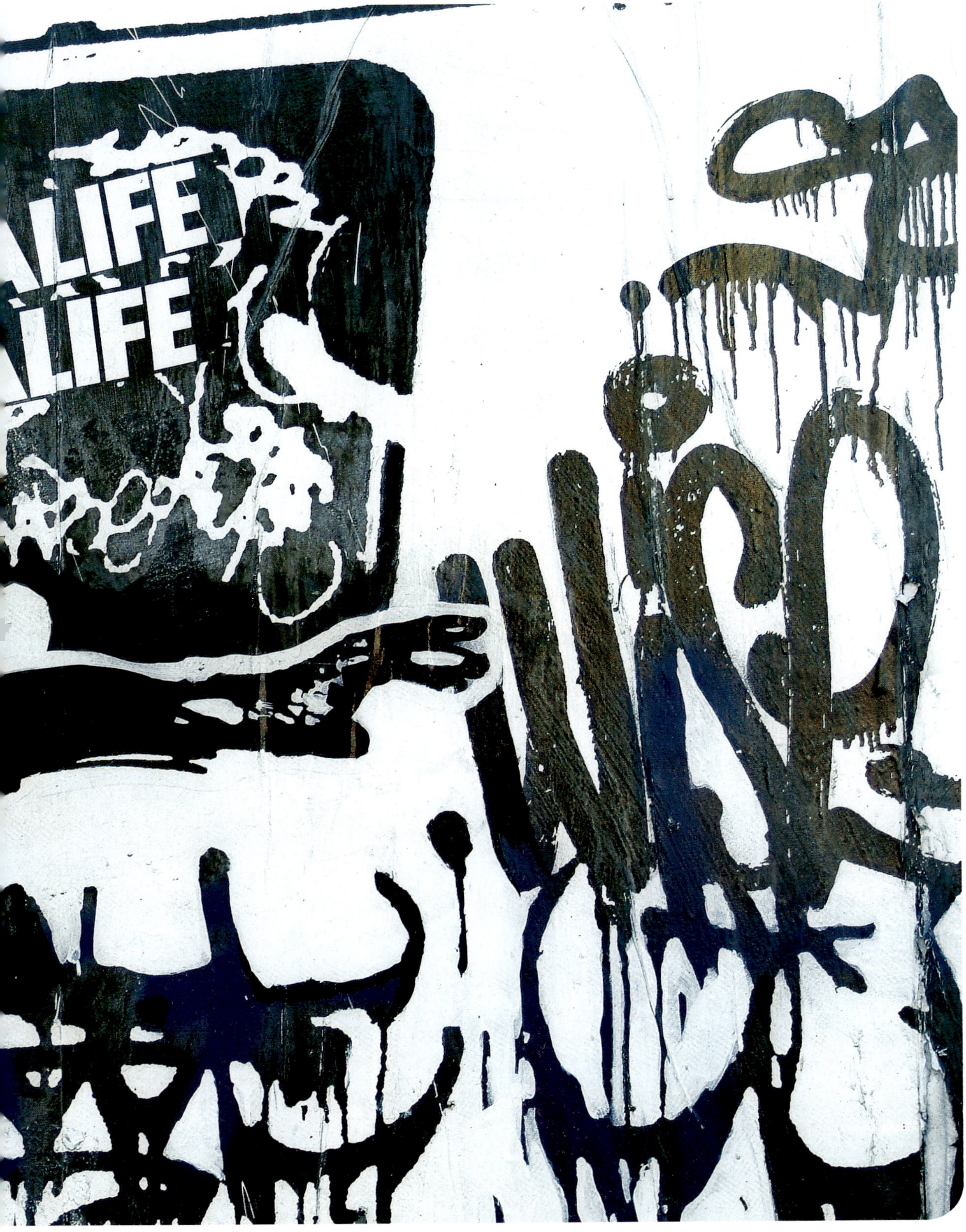
ALIFE
ALIFE

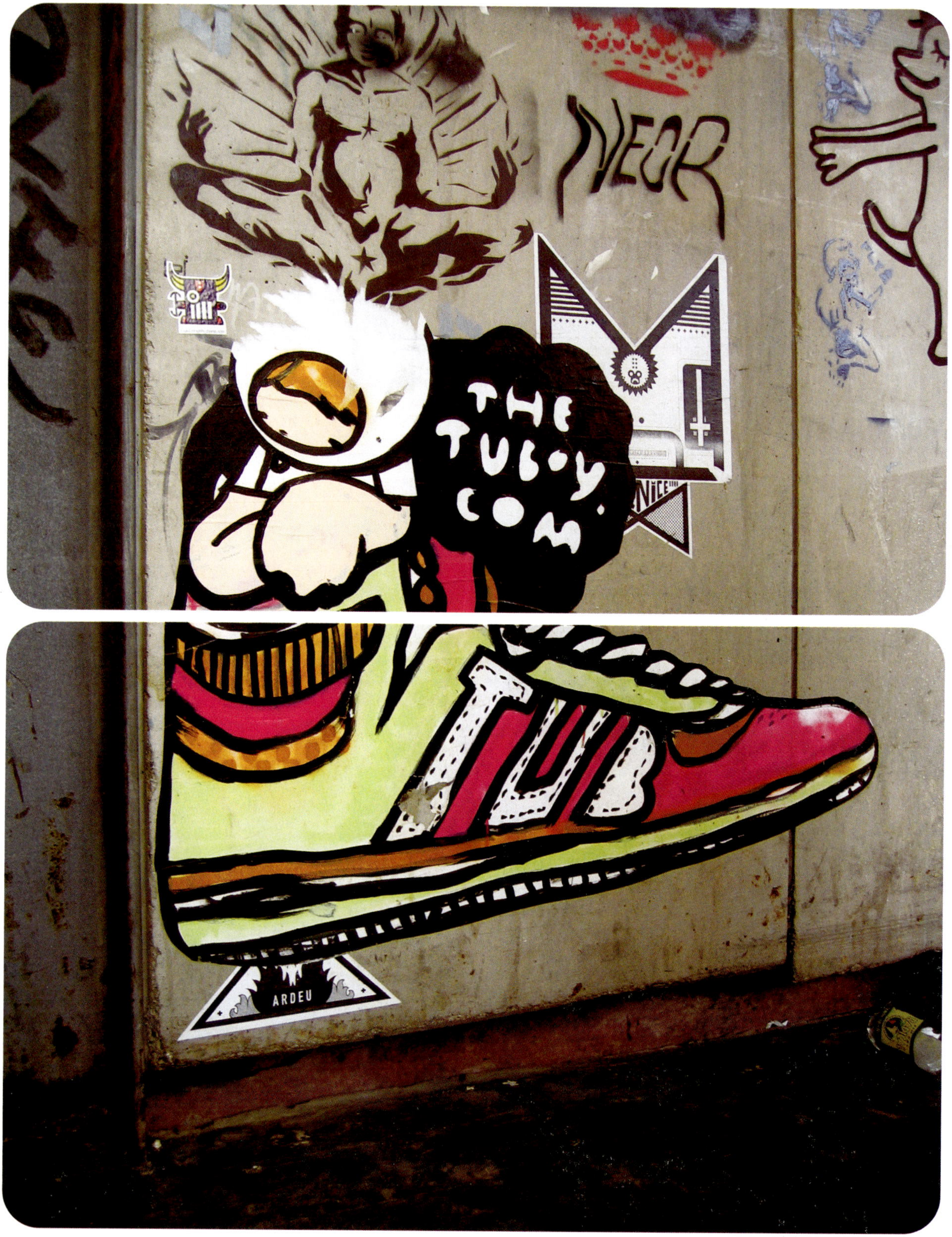
THE
TUBOY.
COM
ARDEU

OPTIK
SOY
FOLLADORA
SARDINILLAS
AL
OLEO

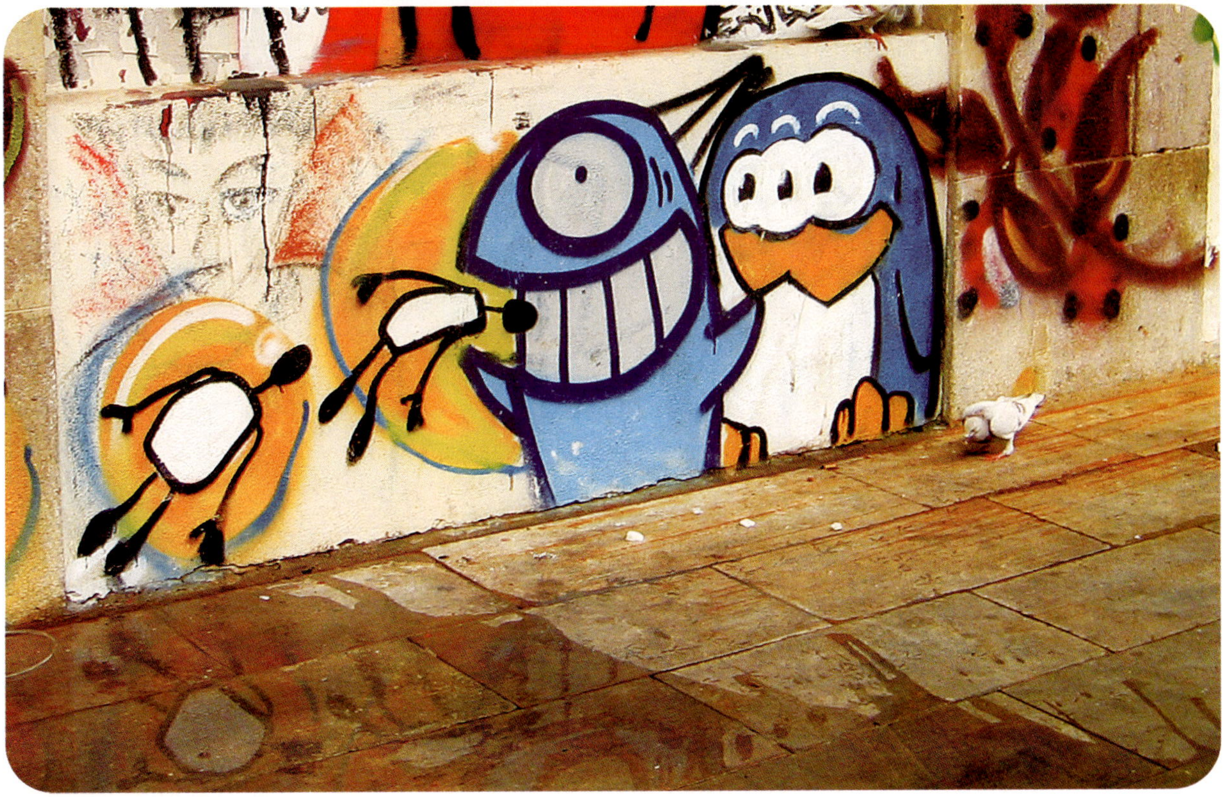

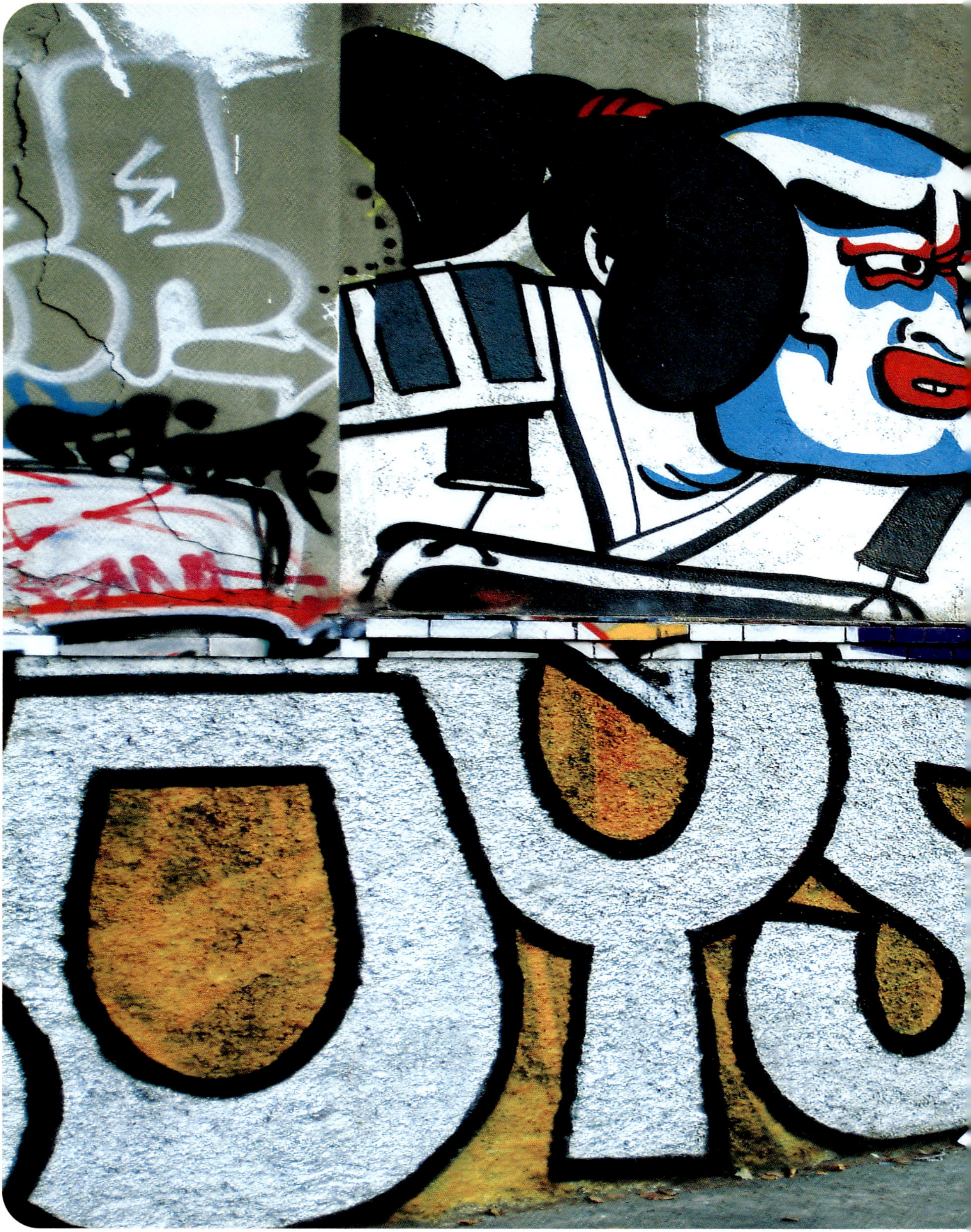

barcelona

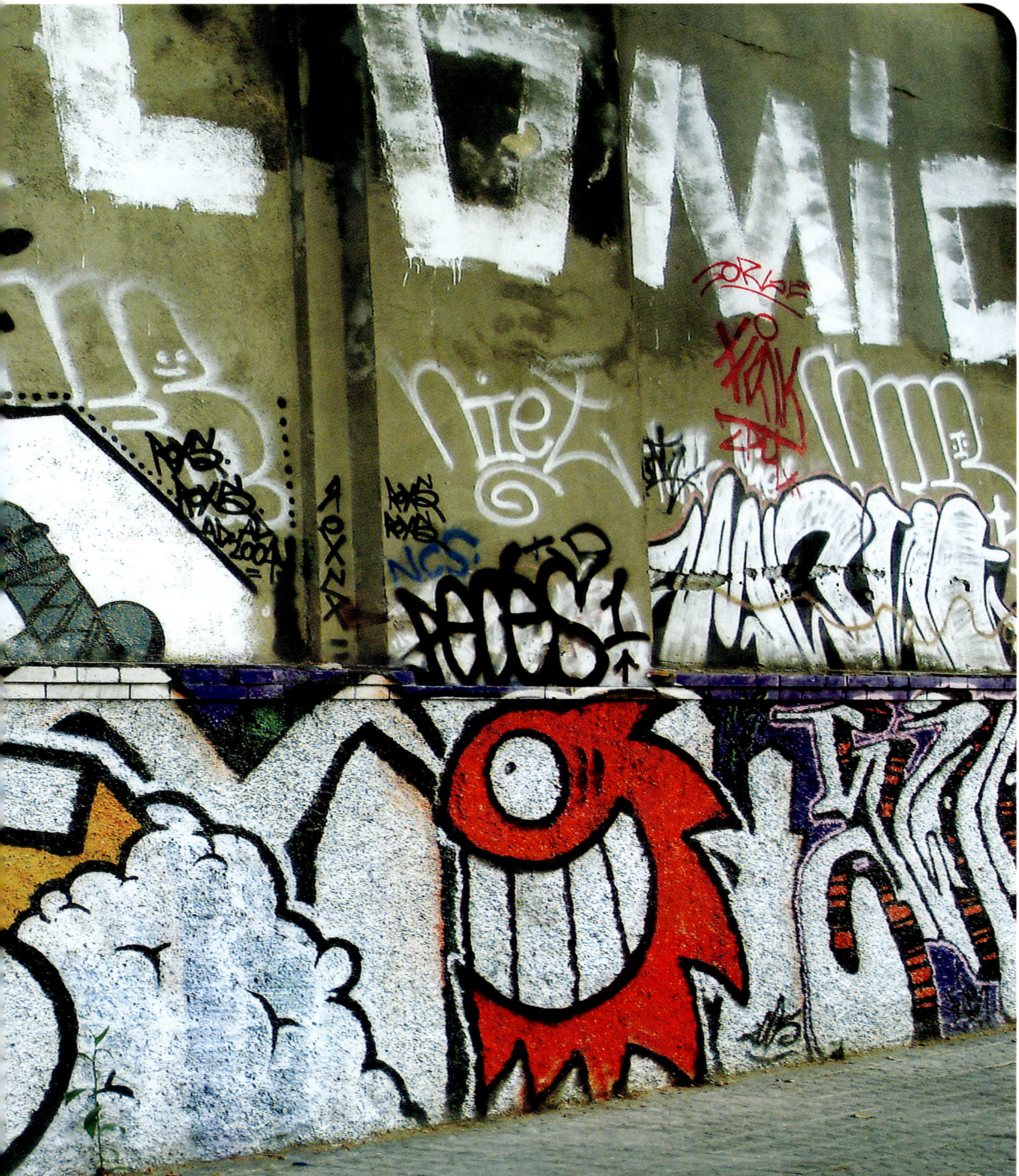

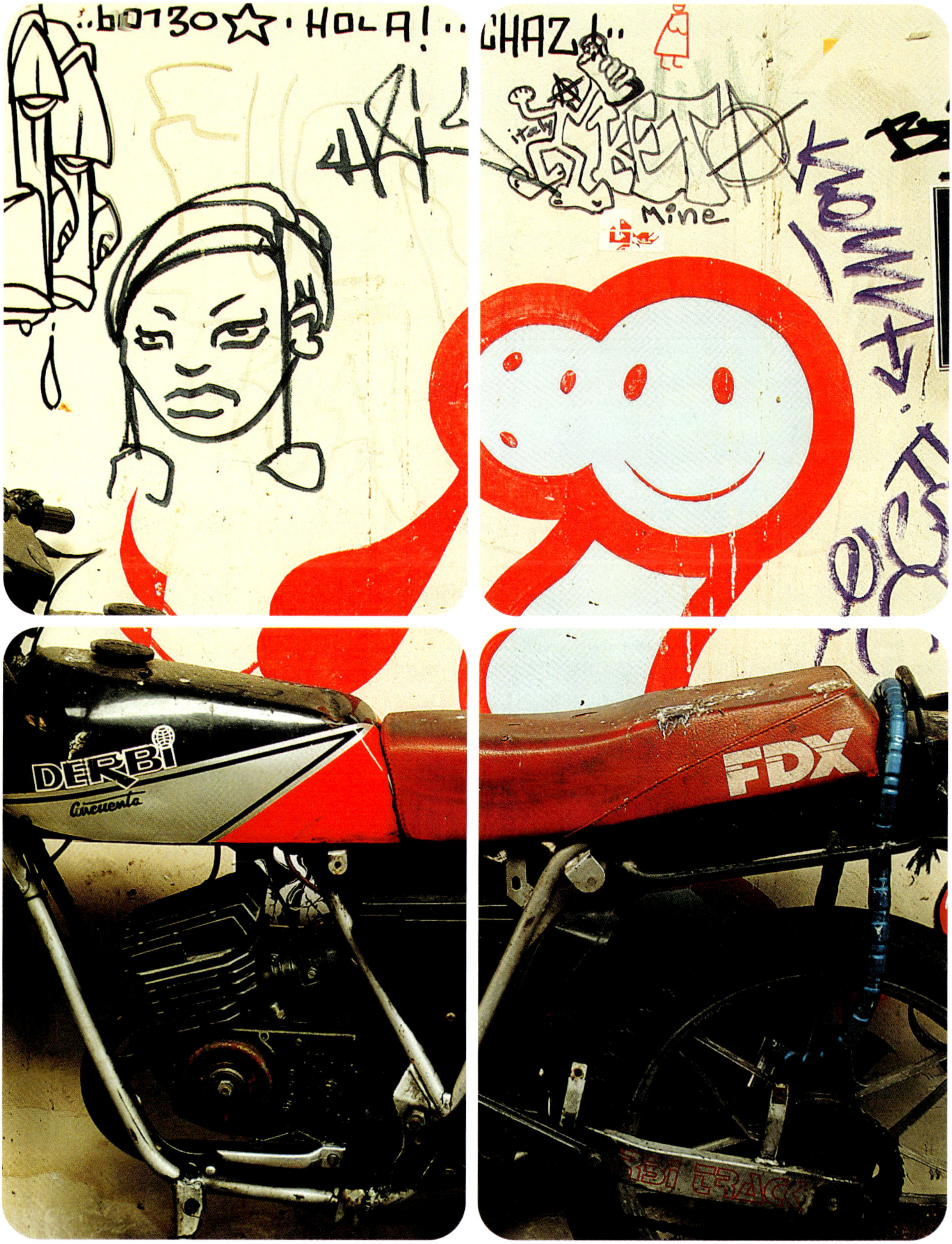
HOLA!
Mine
DERBI
Cincuenta
FDX

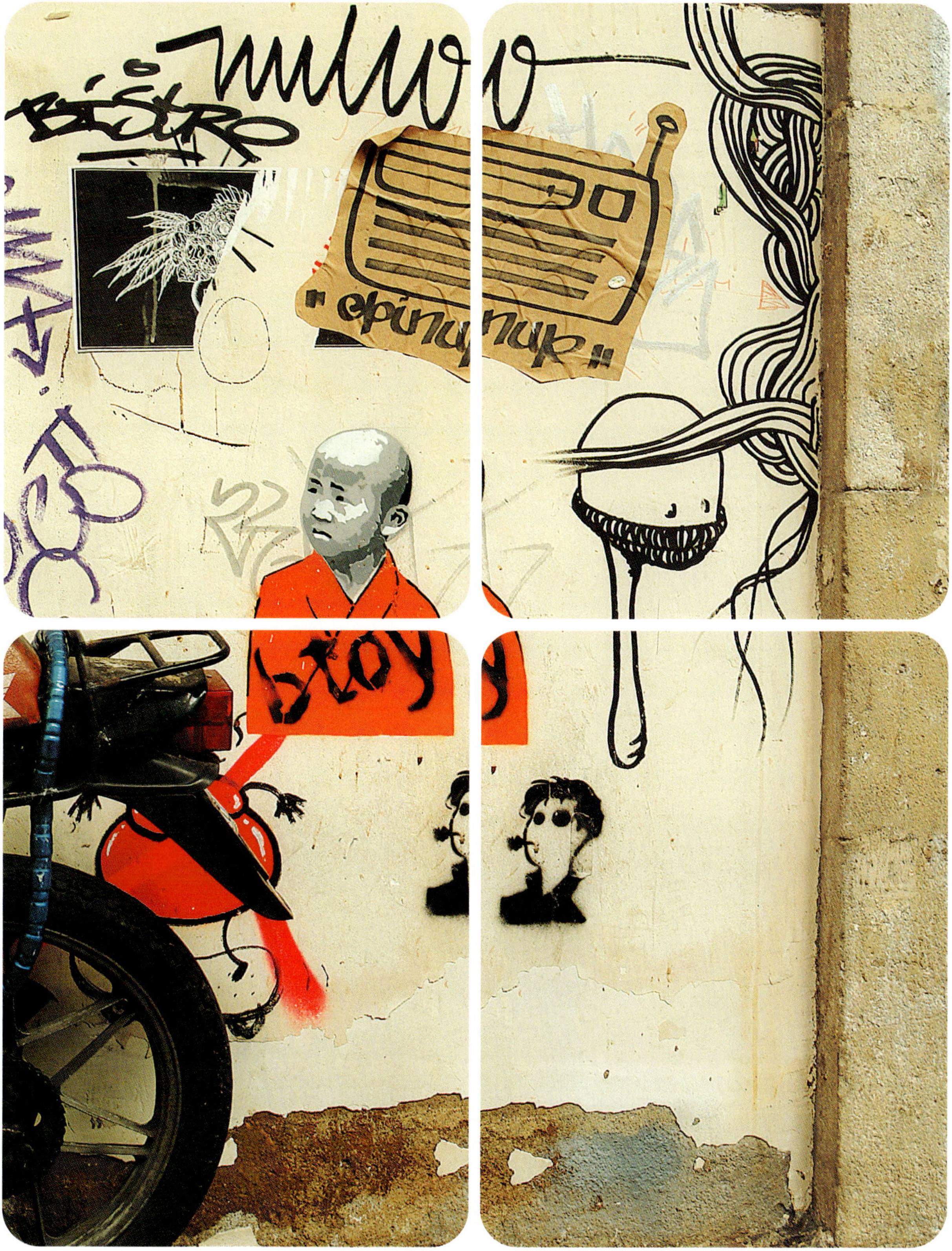
btoy

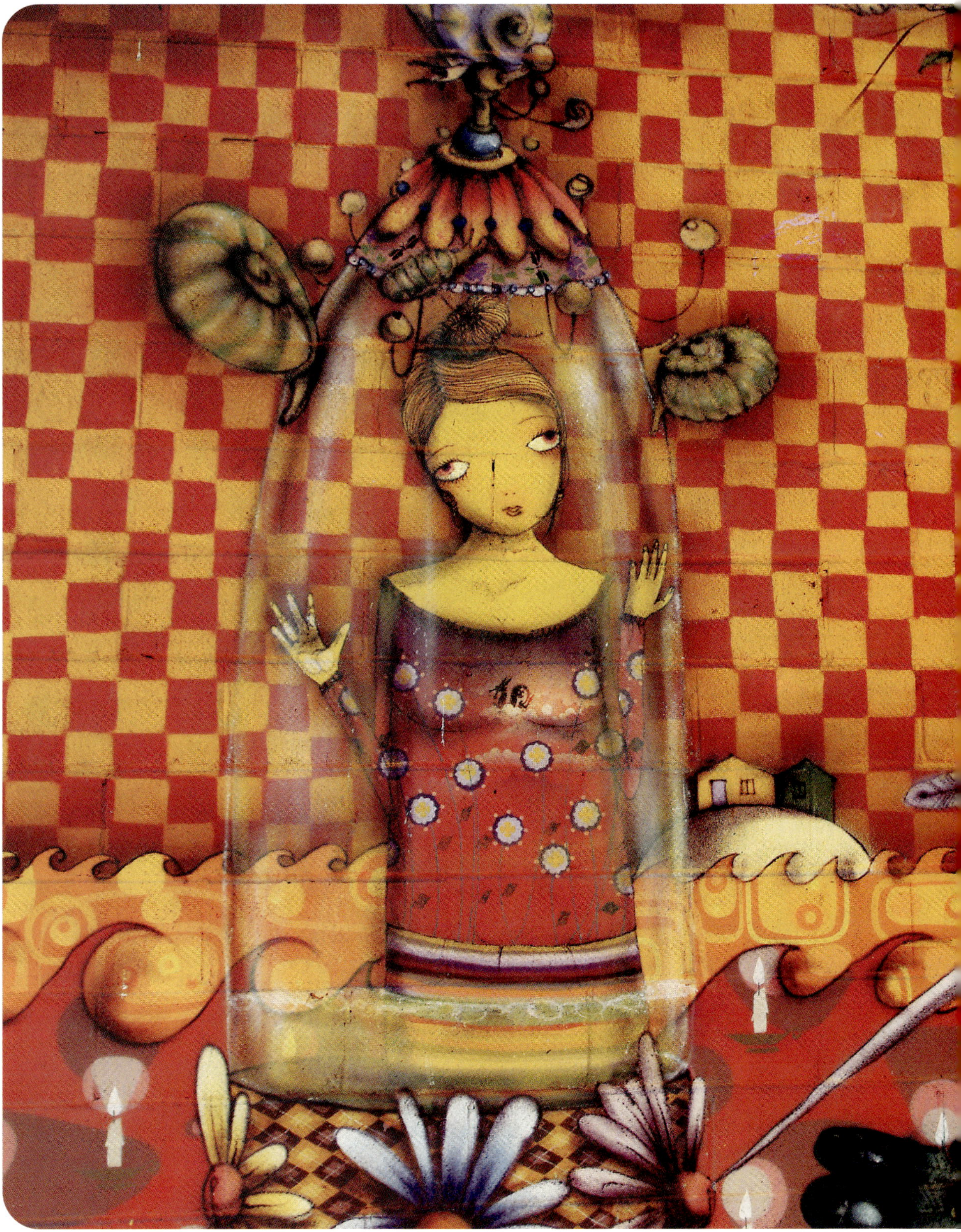

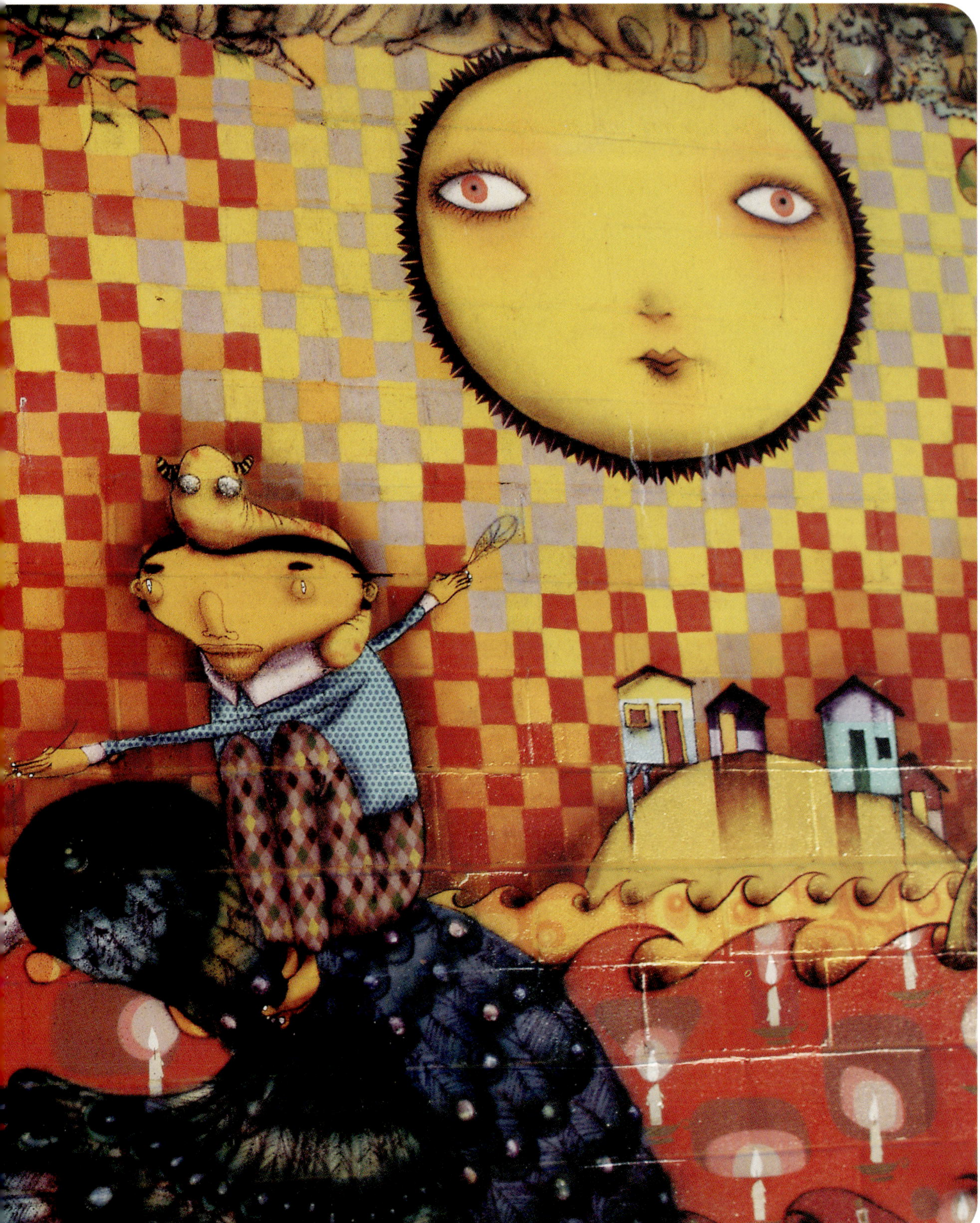

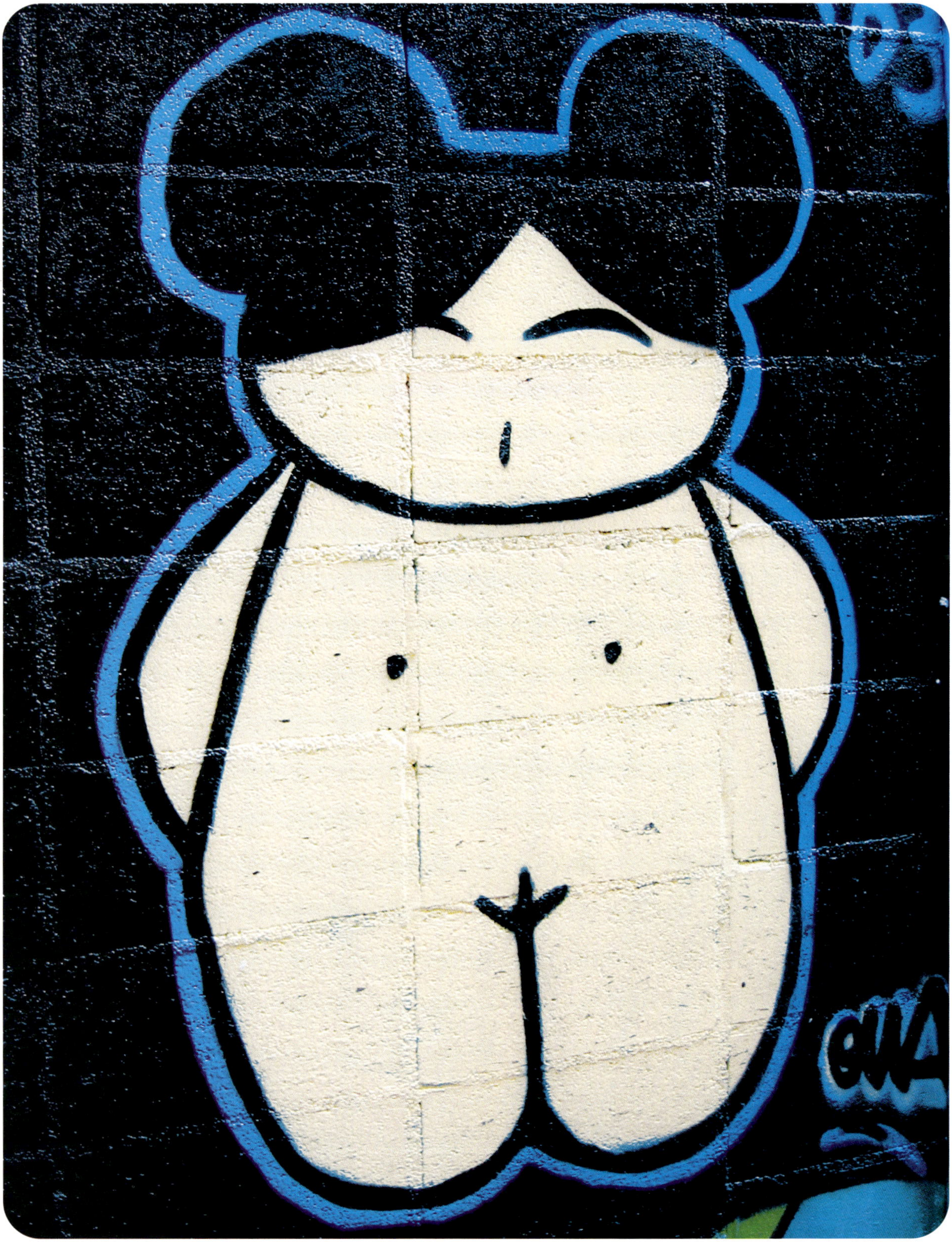

barcelona

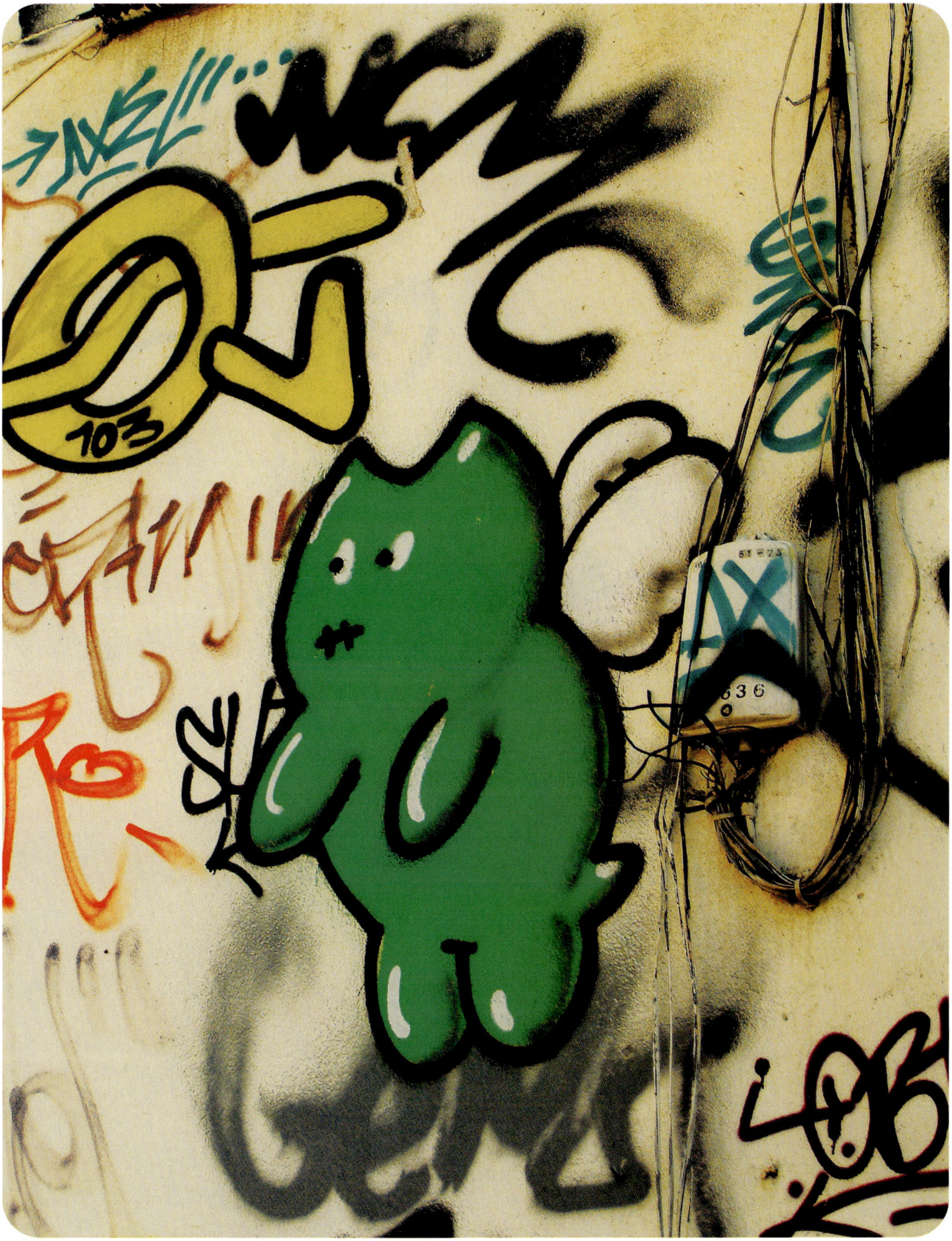

barcelona

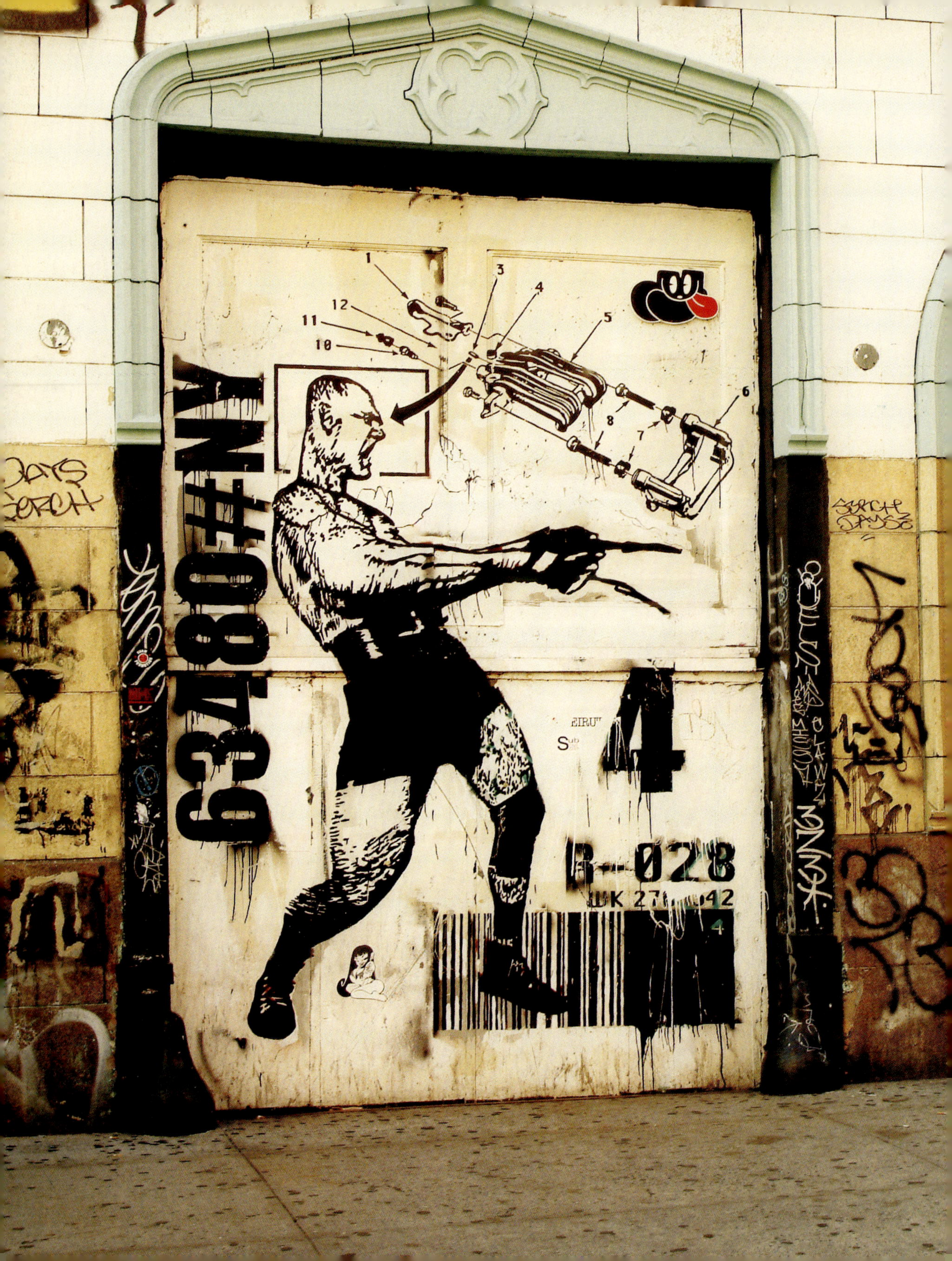
4
R-028

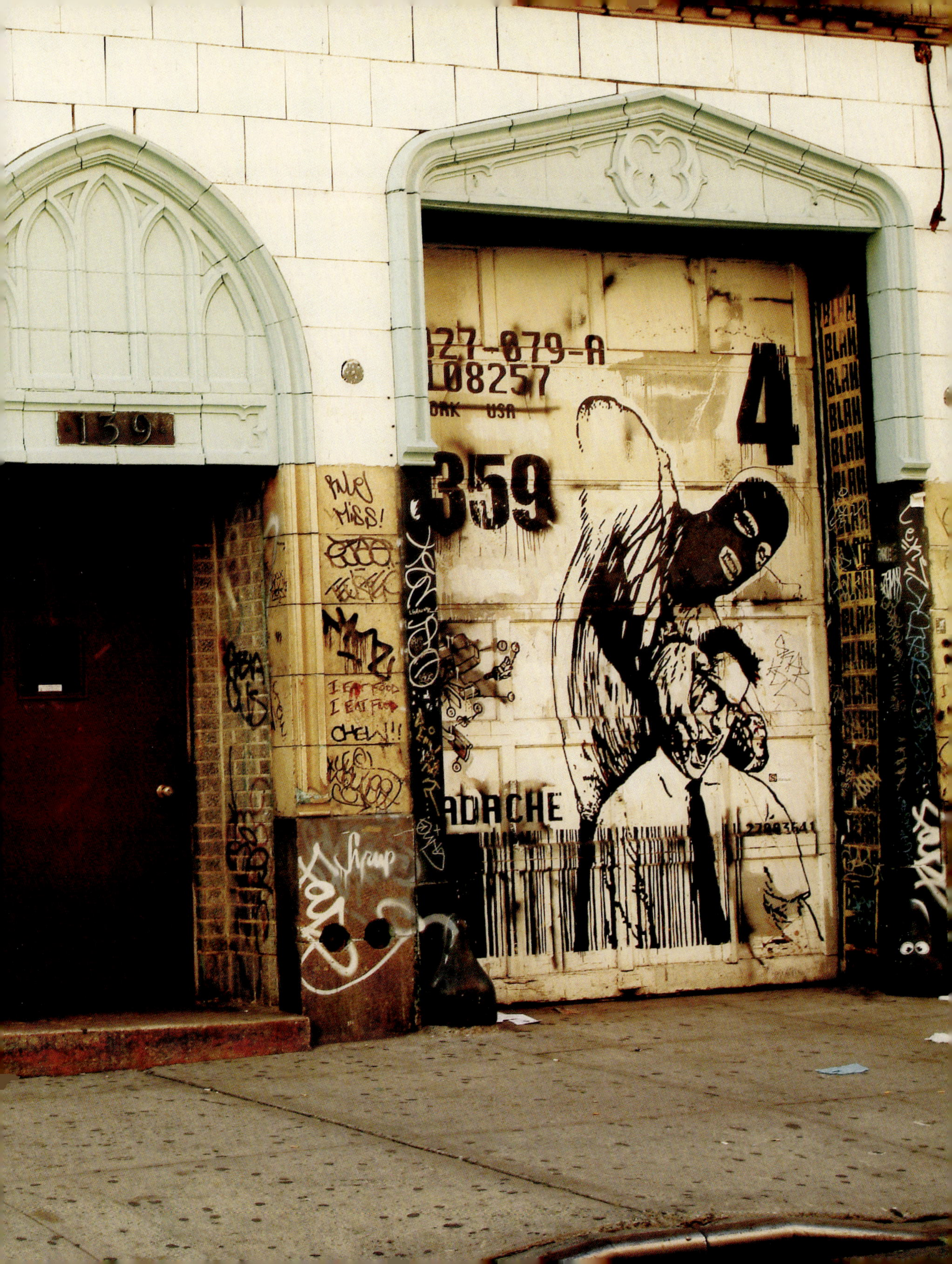
139
27-079-A
L08257
USA
359
4
BLAH
I EAT FOOD
CHEW!!!
ADACHE

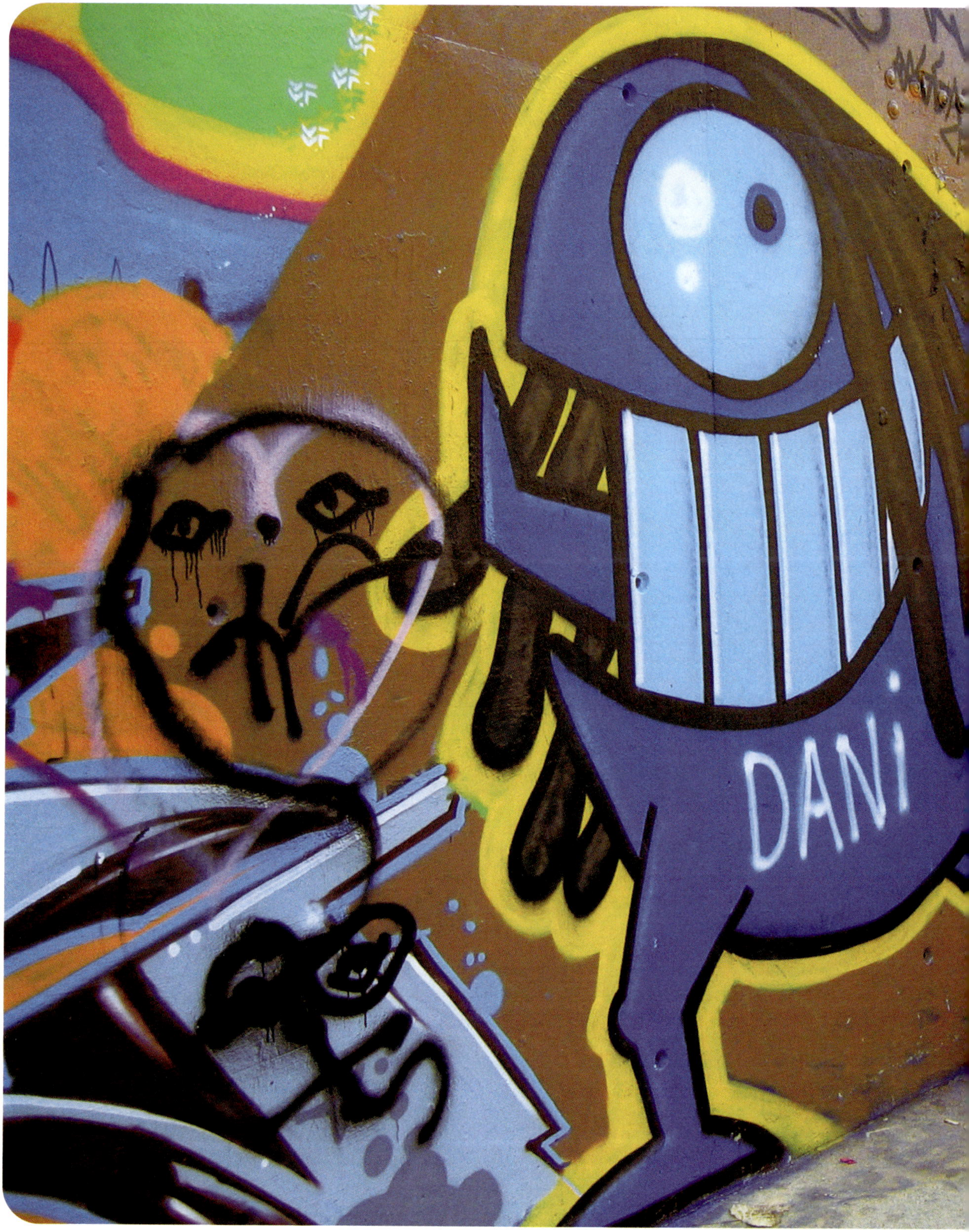
DANI

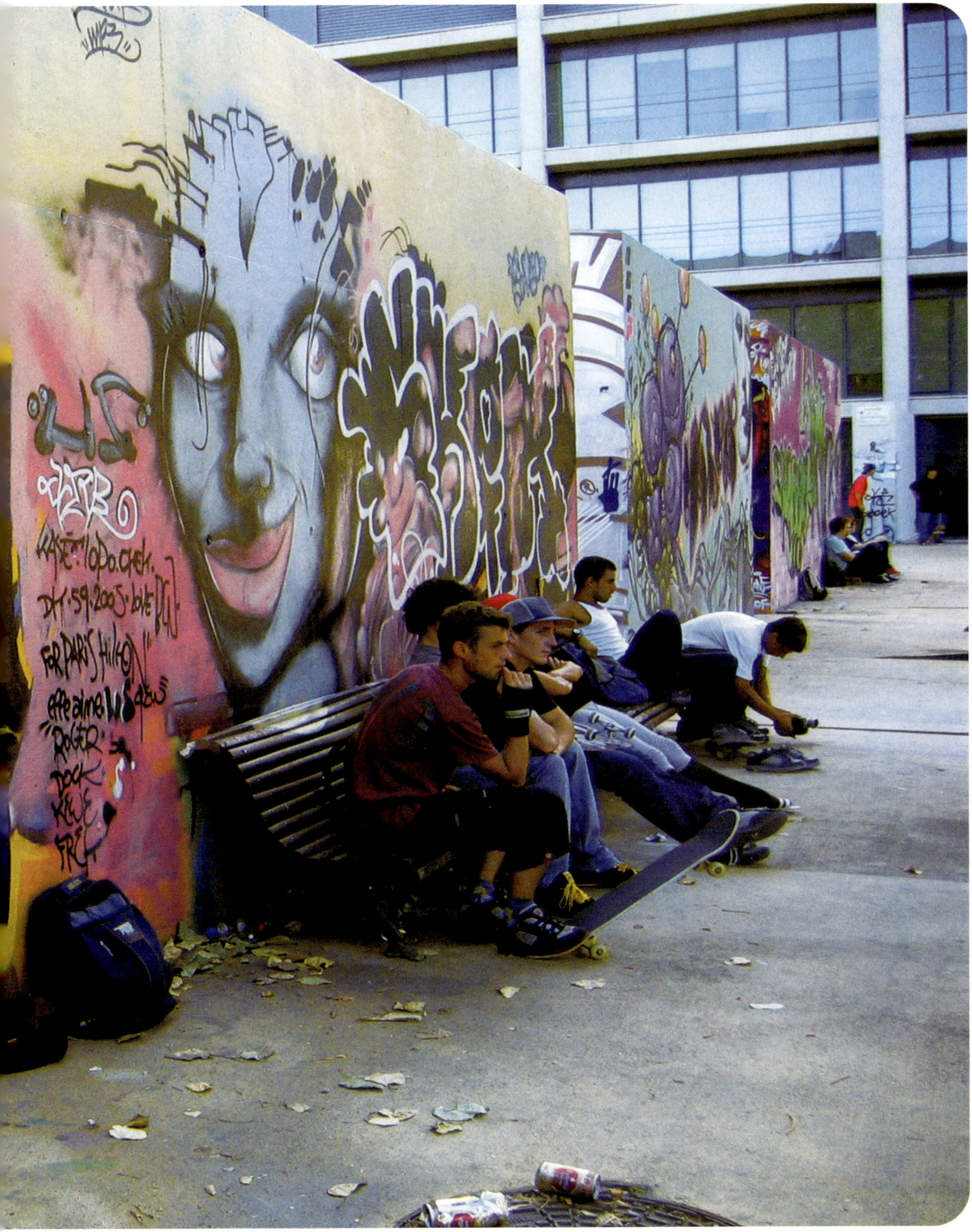

barcelona

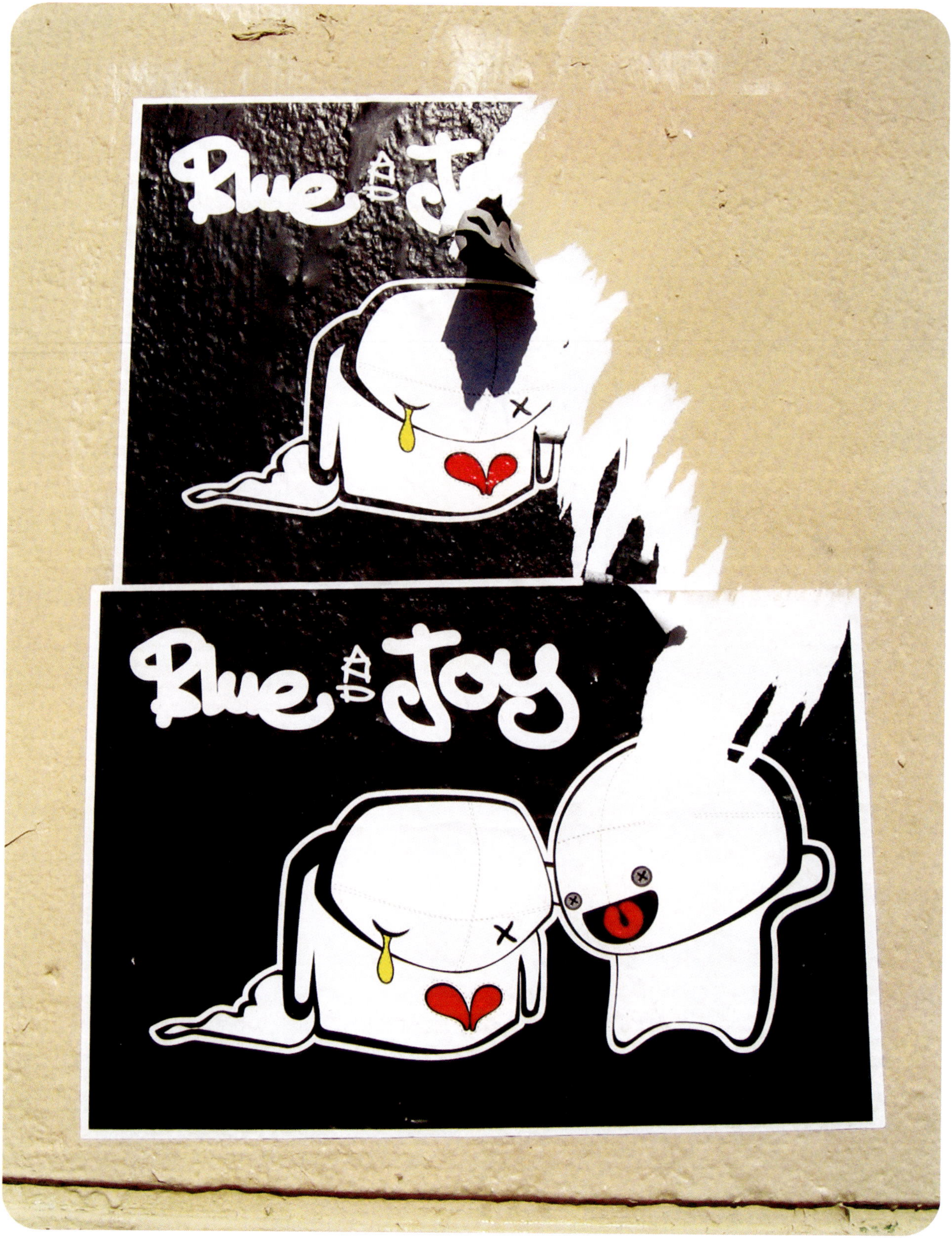

barcelona

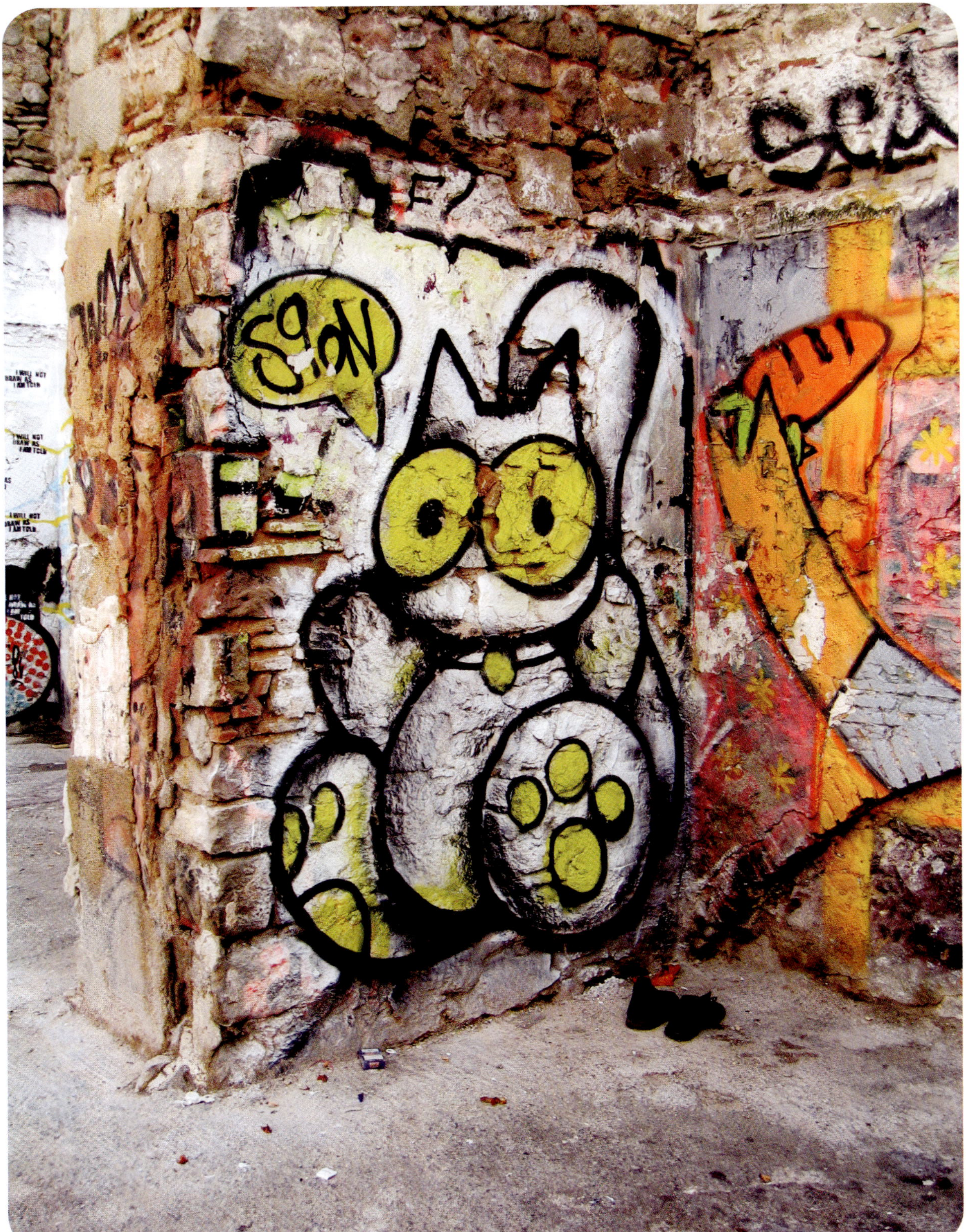

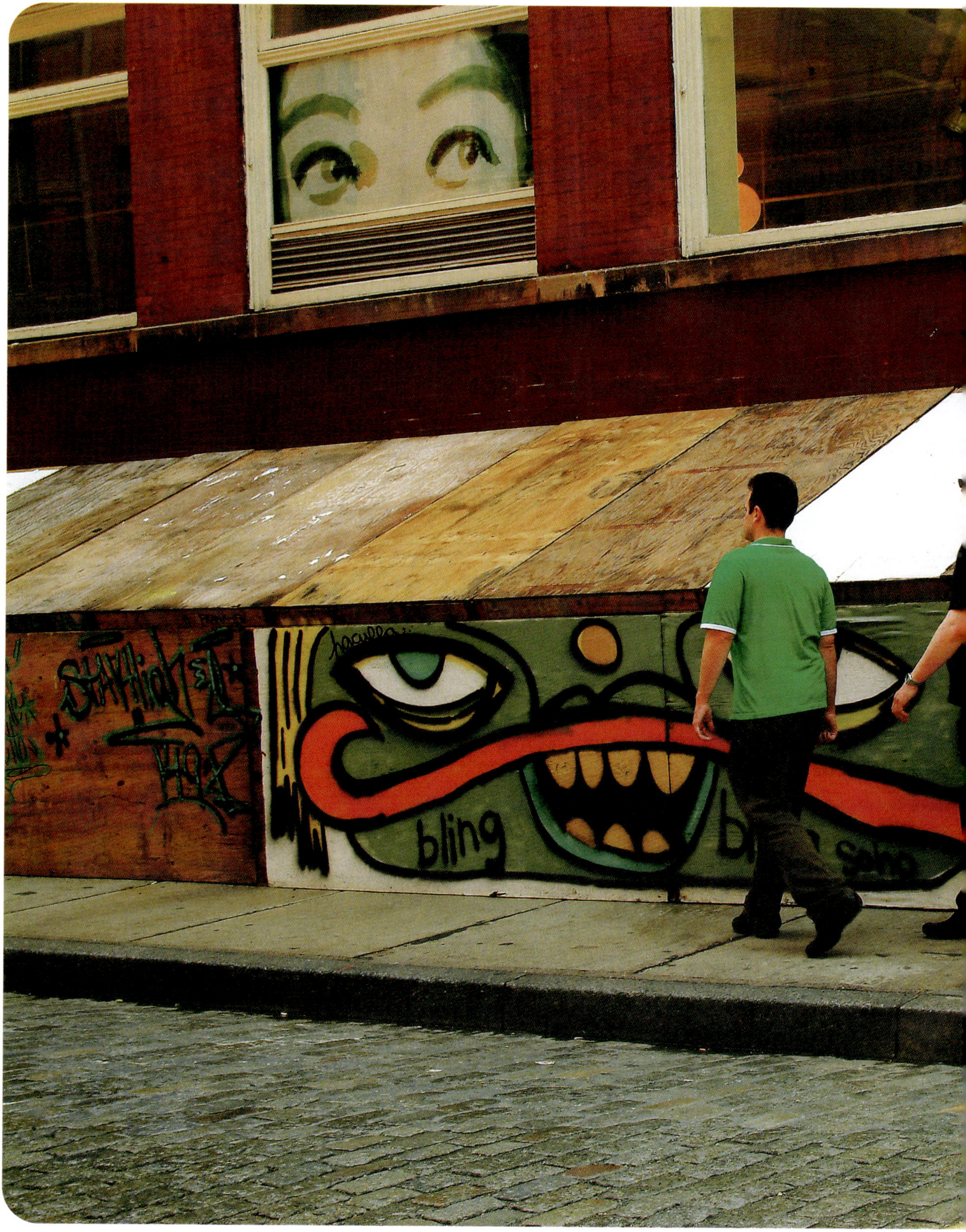
bling

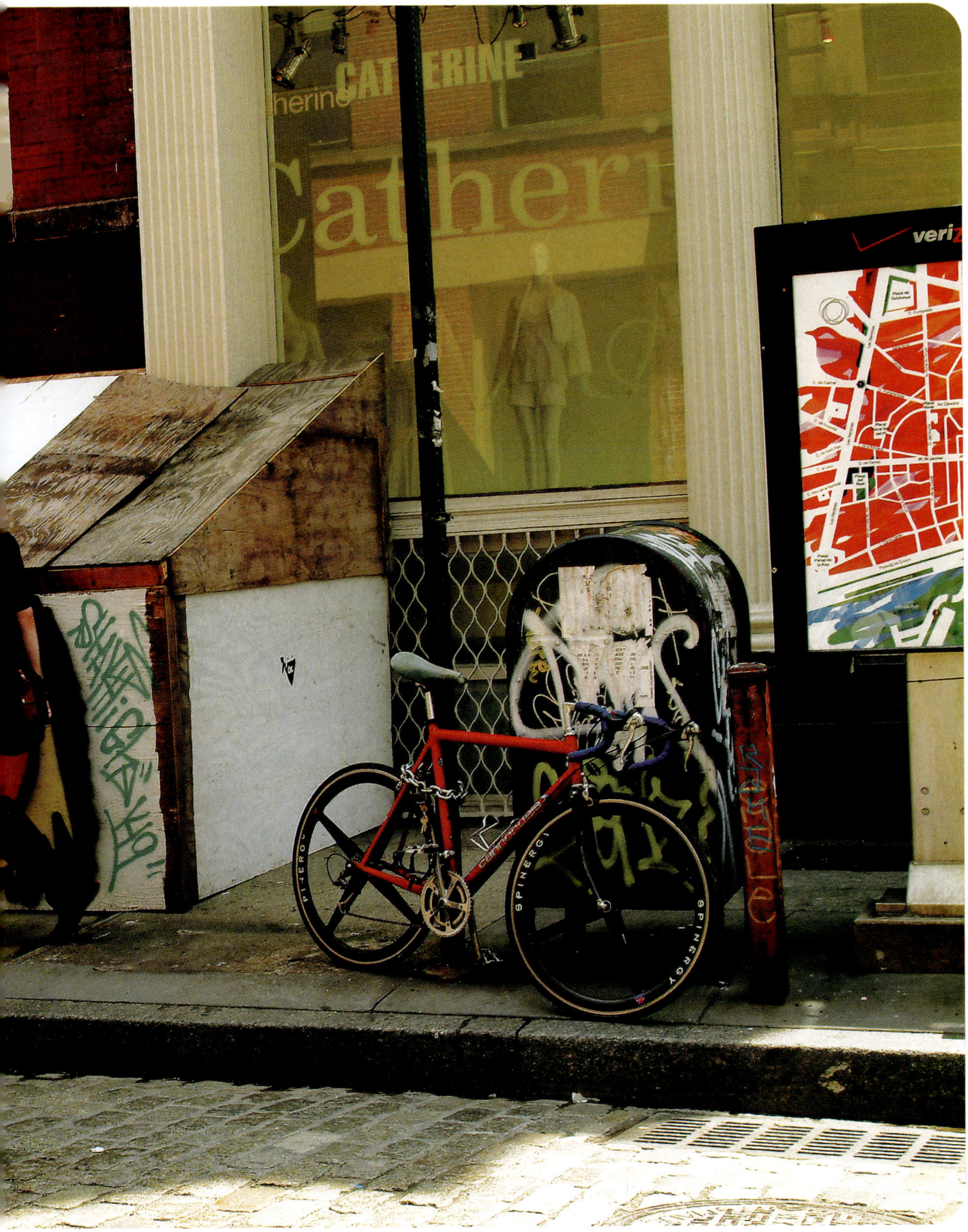
CATHERINE
herine
Catheri
veriz
SPINERGY

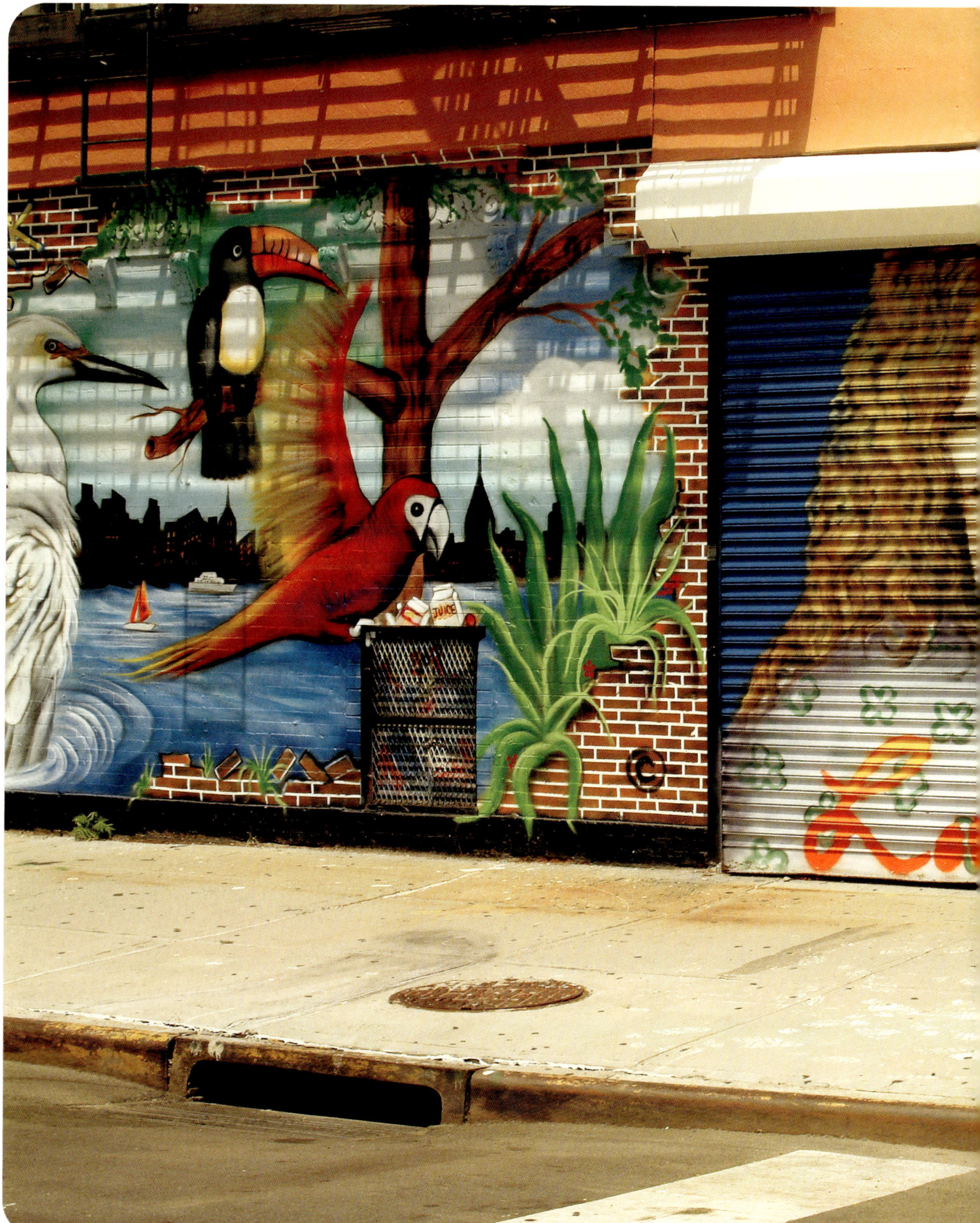
JUICE

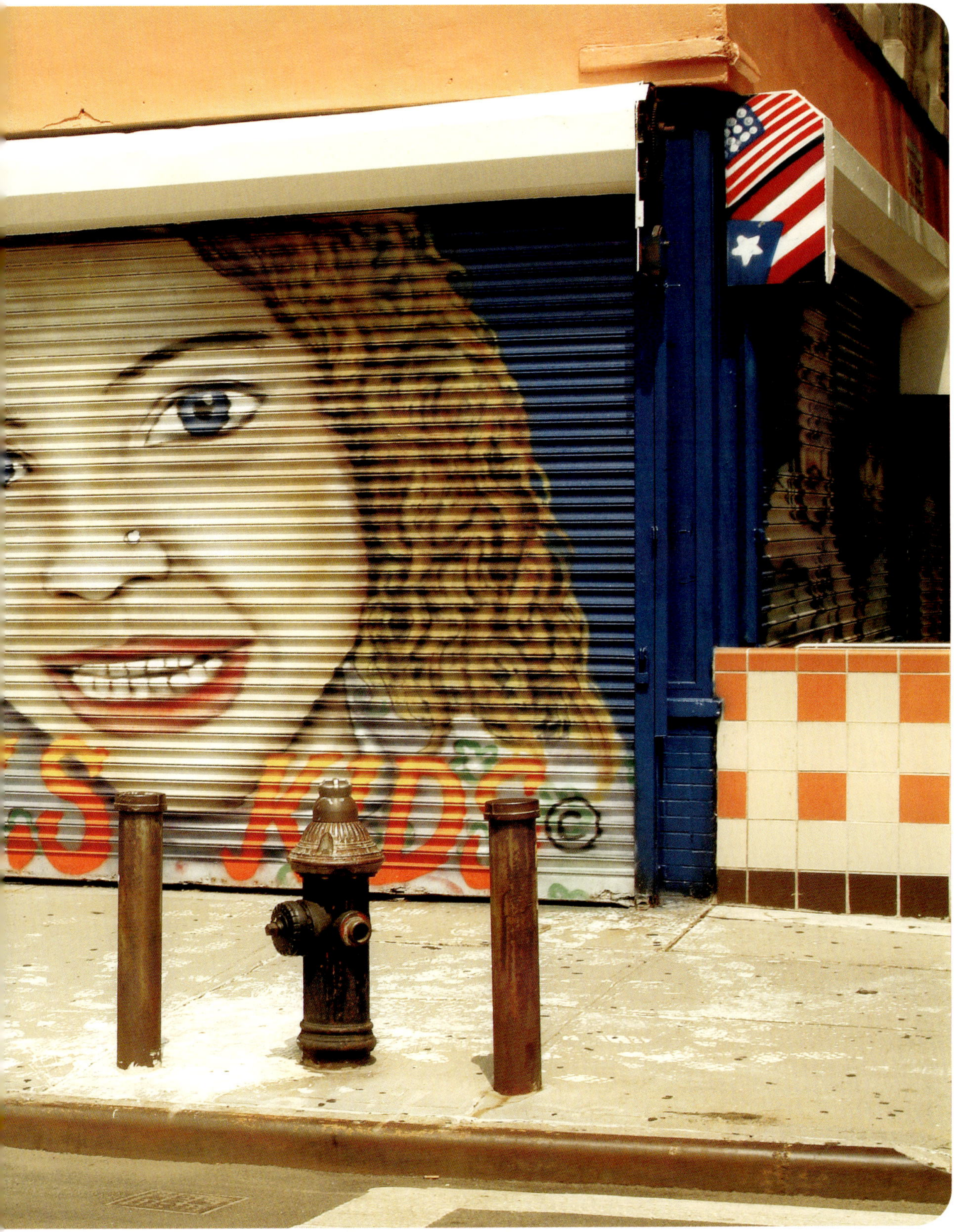

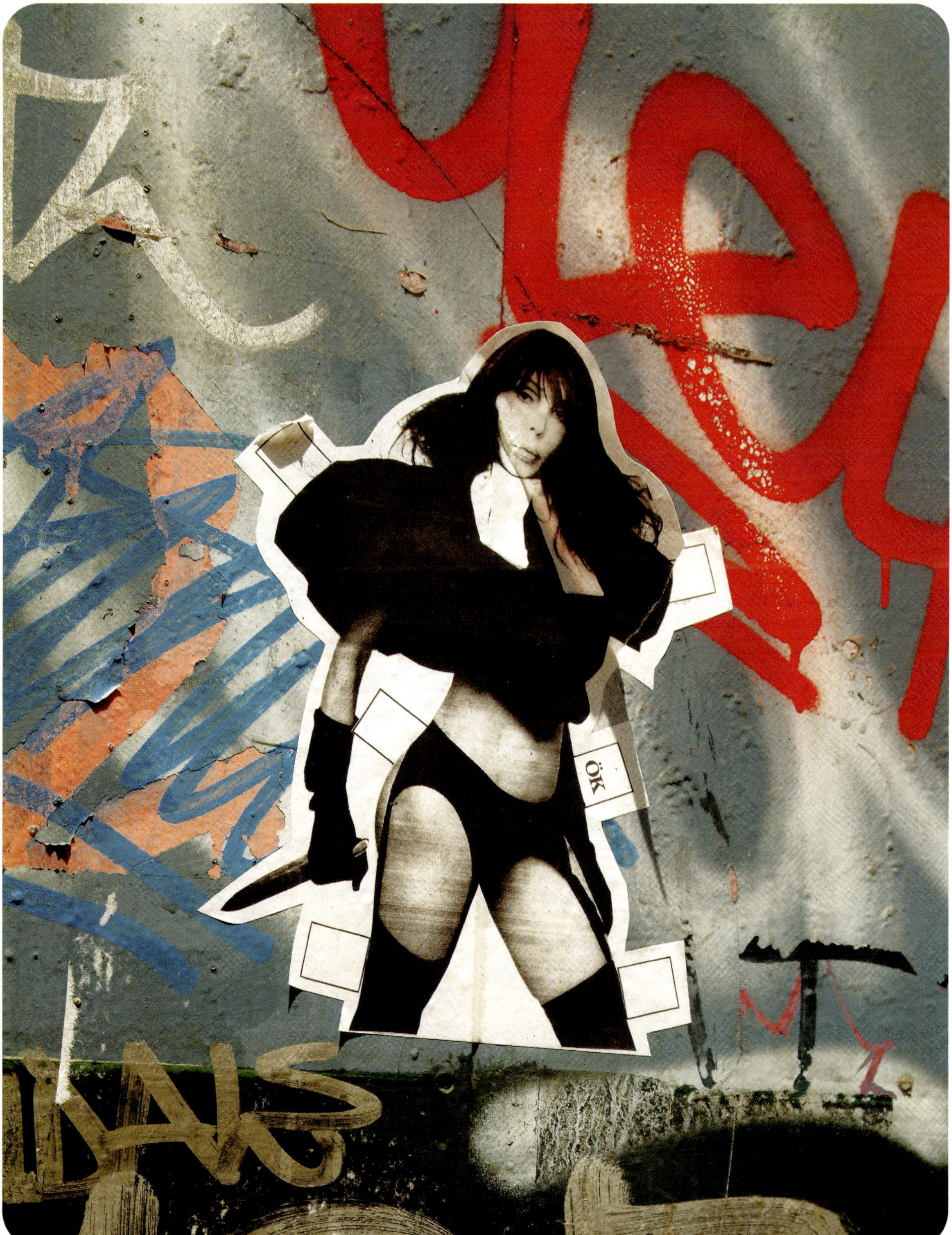
ÖK

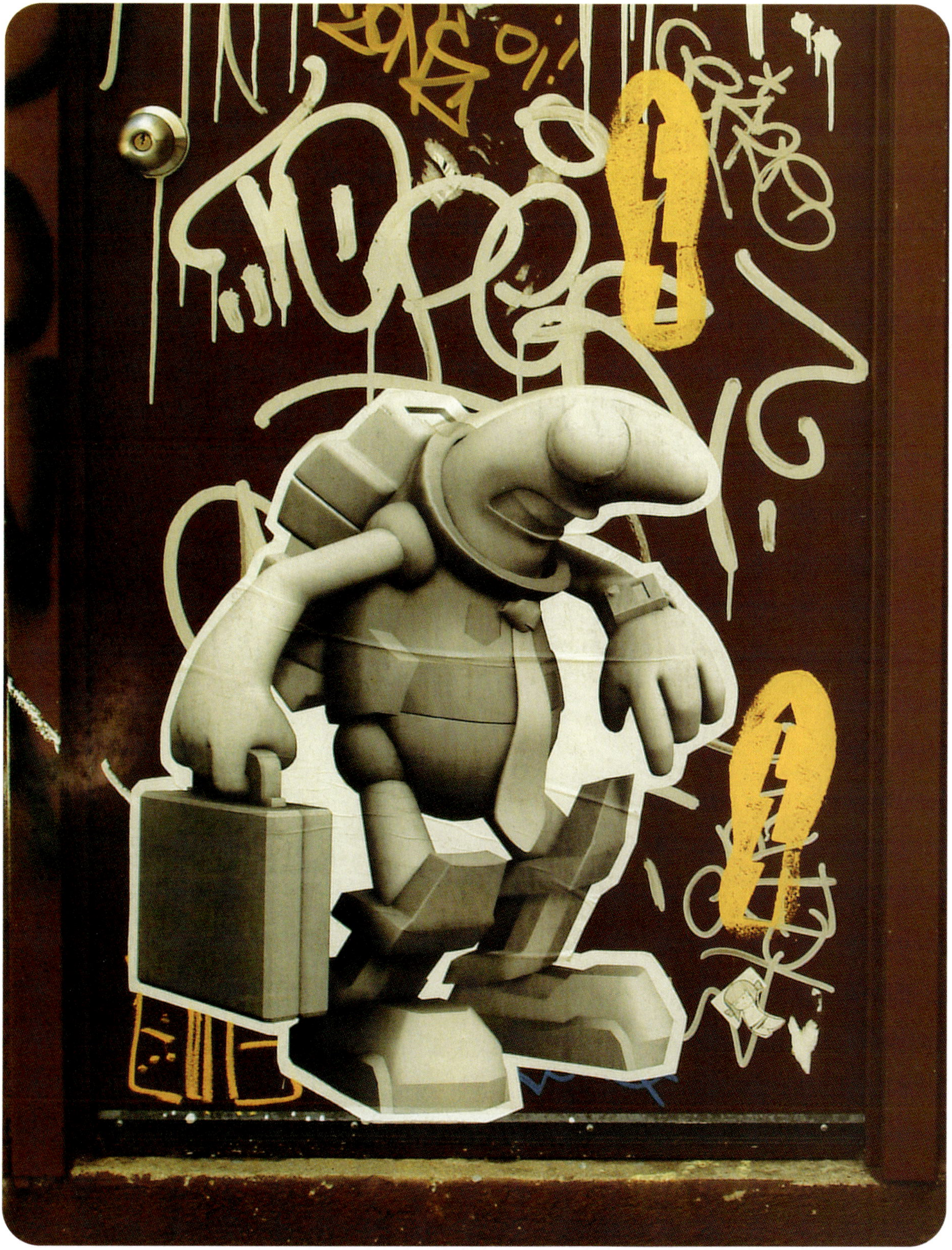

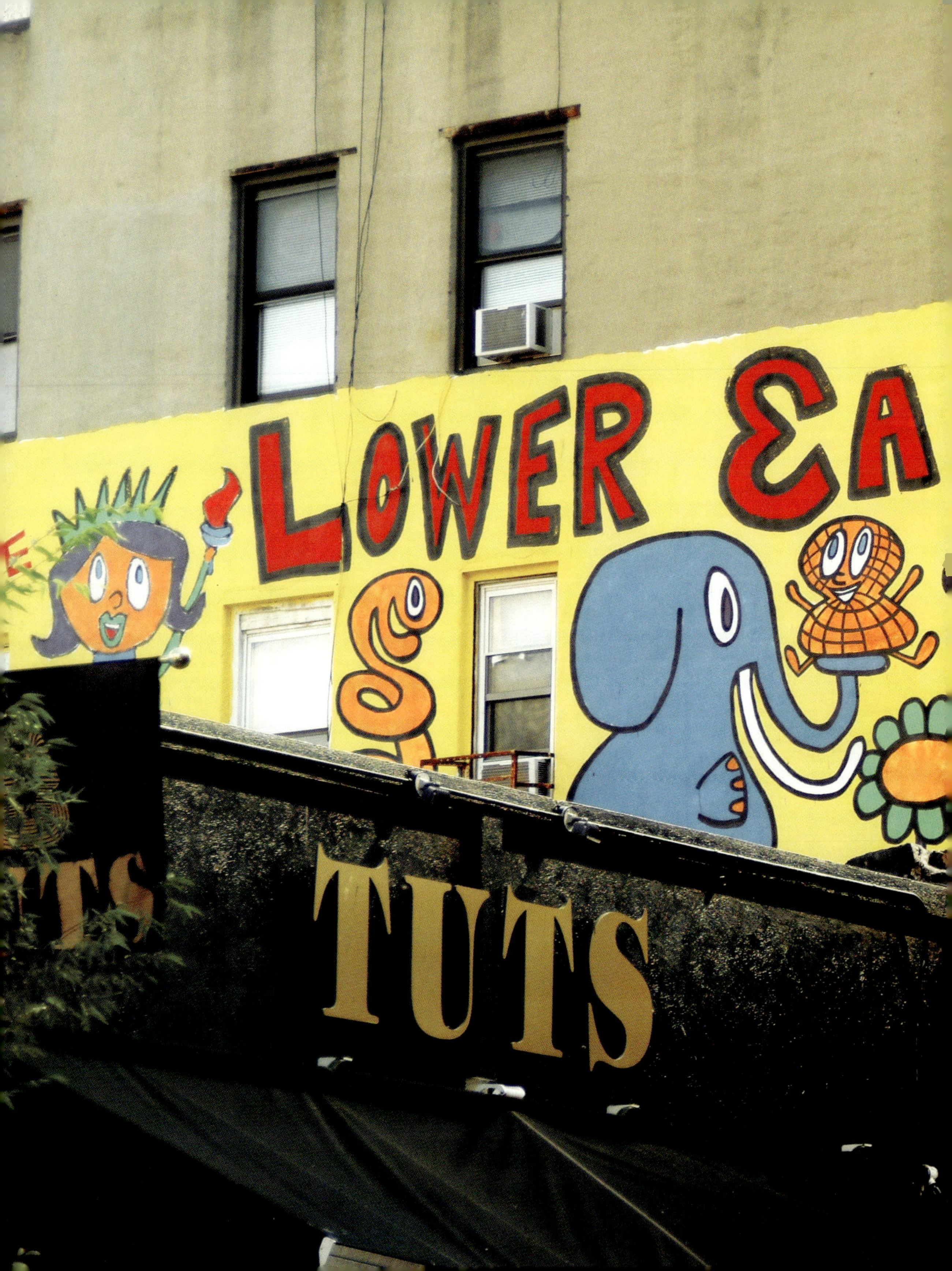
LOWER EA
TUTS

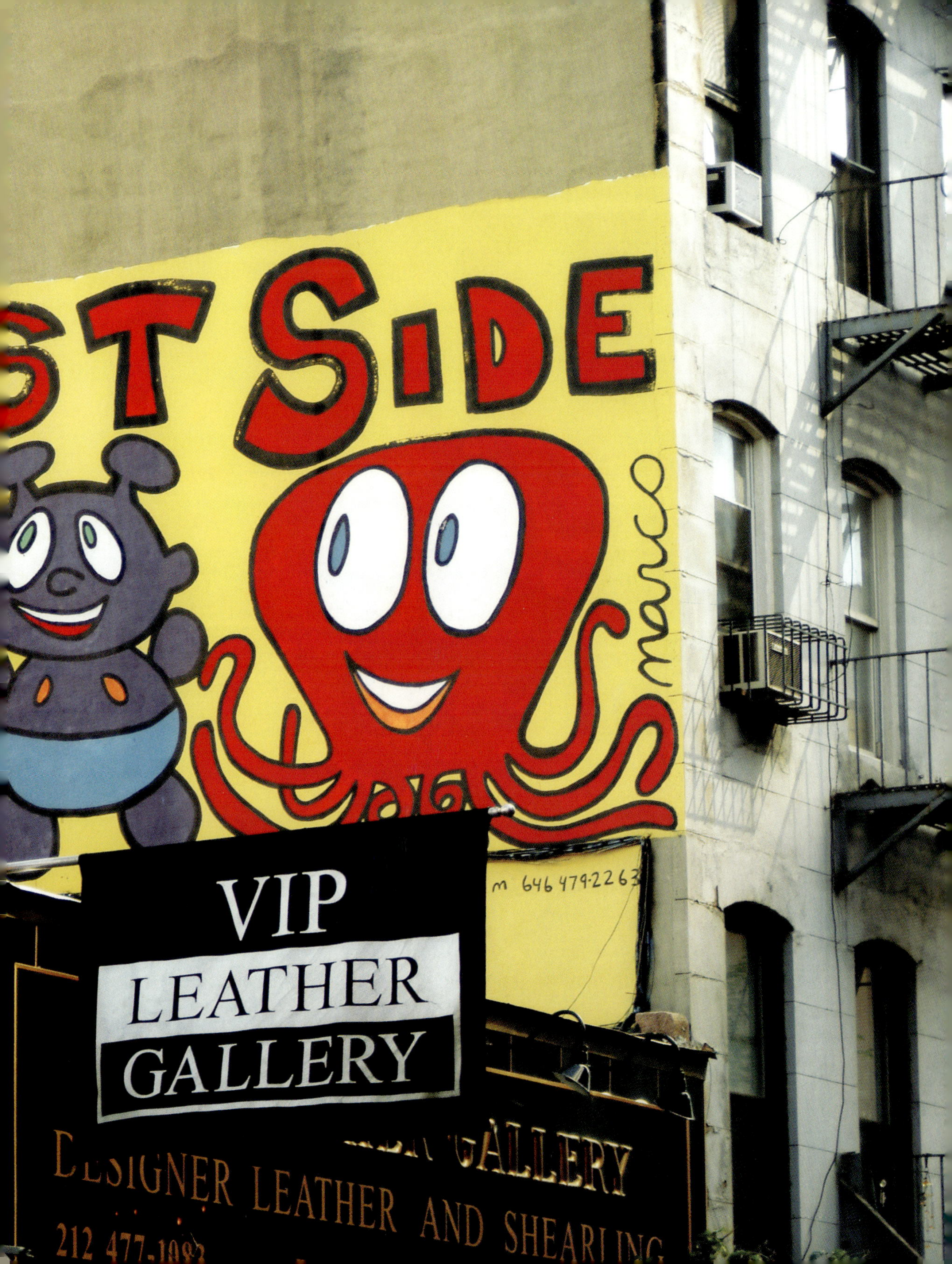
ST SIDE
marco
646 479-2263
VIP
LEATHER
GALLERY
GALLERY
DESIGNER LEATHER AND SHEARLING

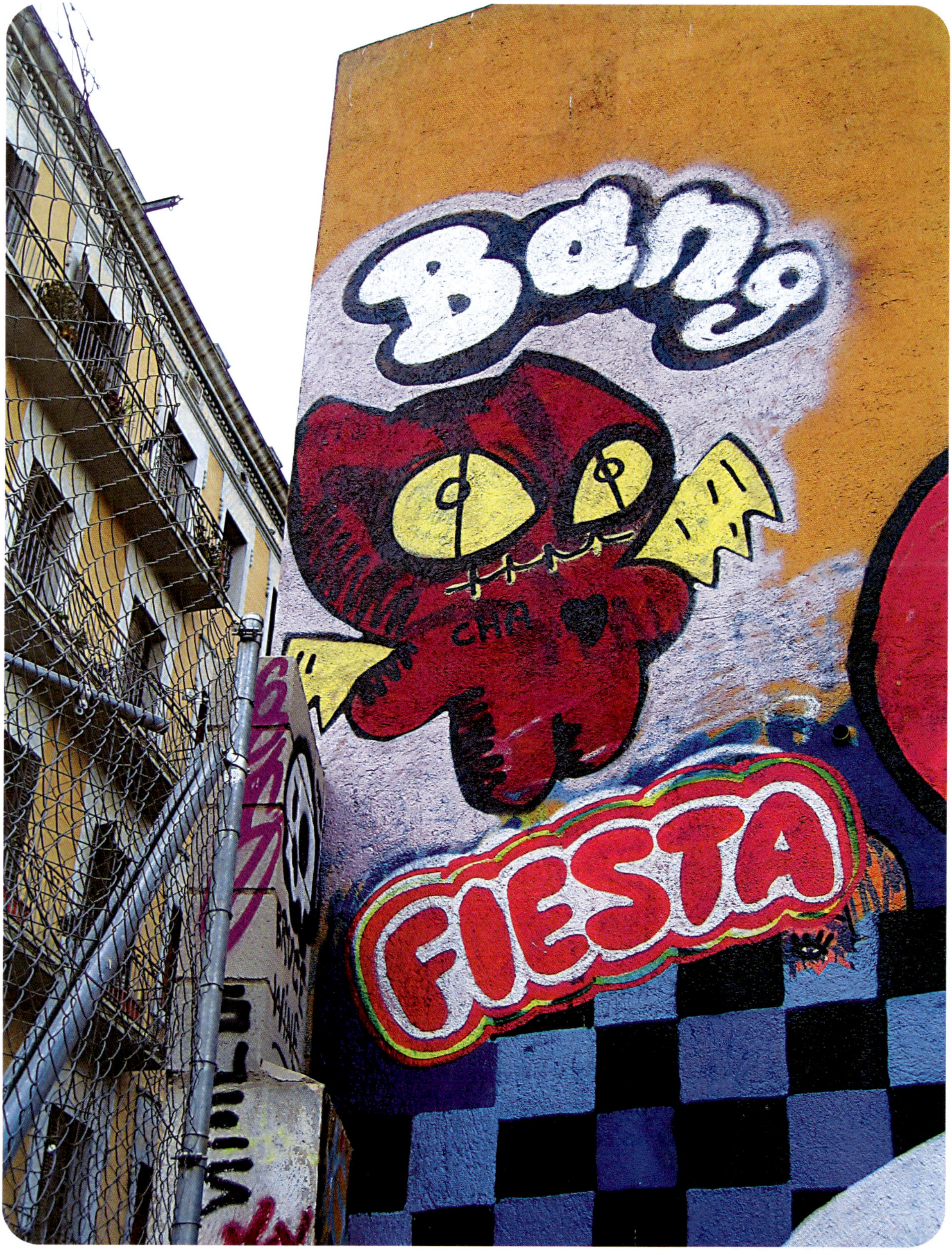
Bang
CHA
FIESTA

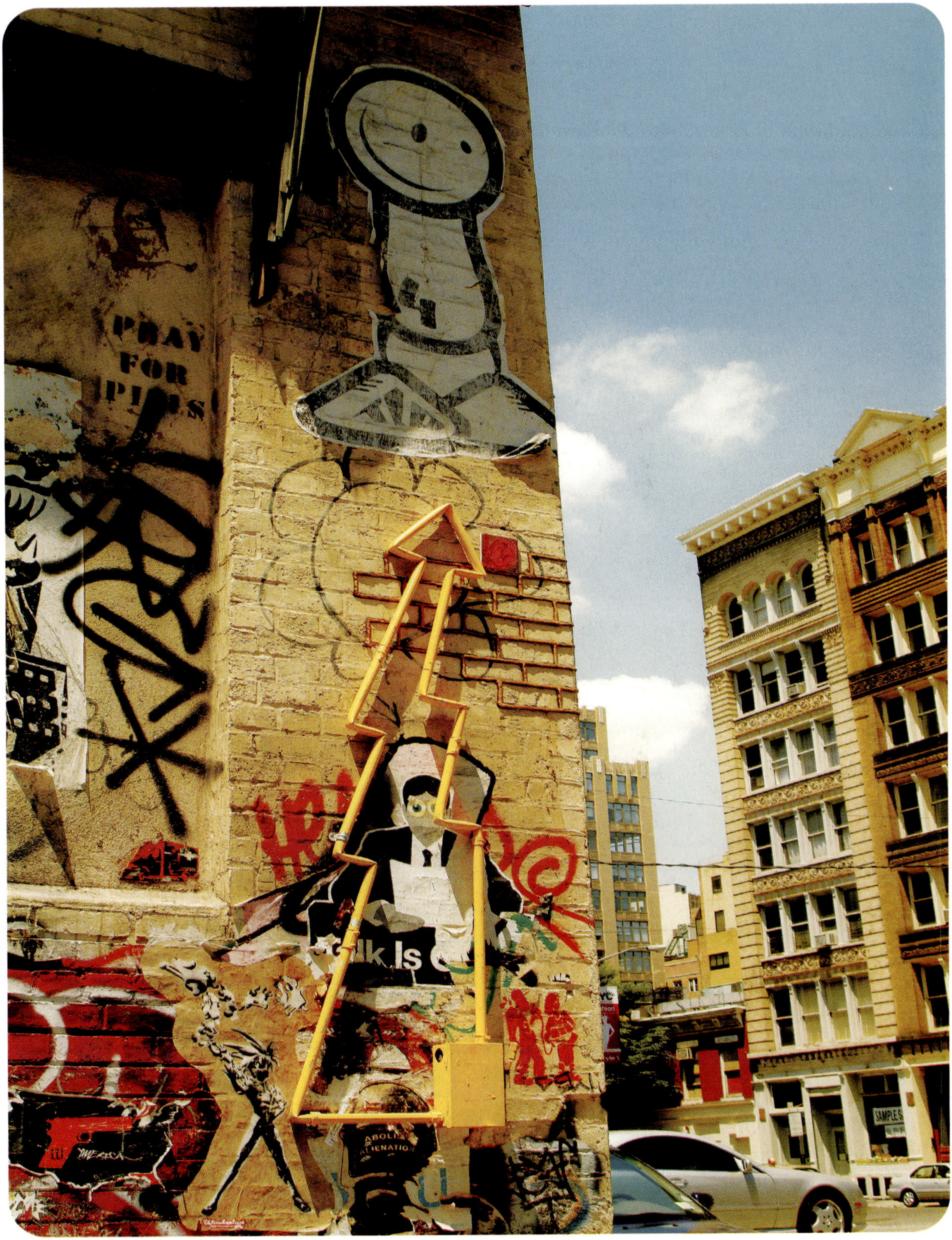
PRAY
FOR
PI S

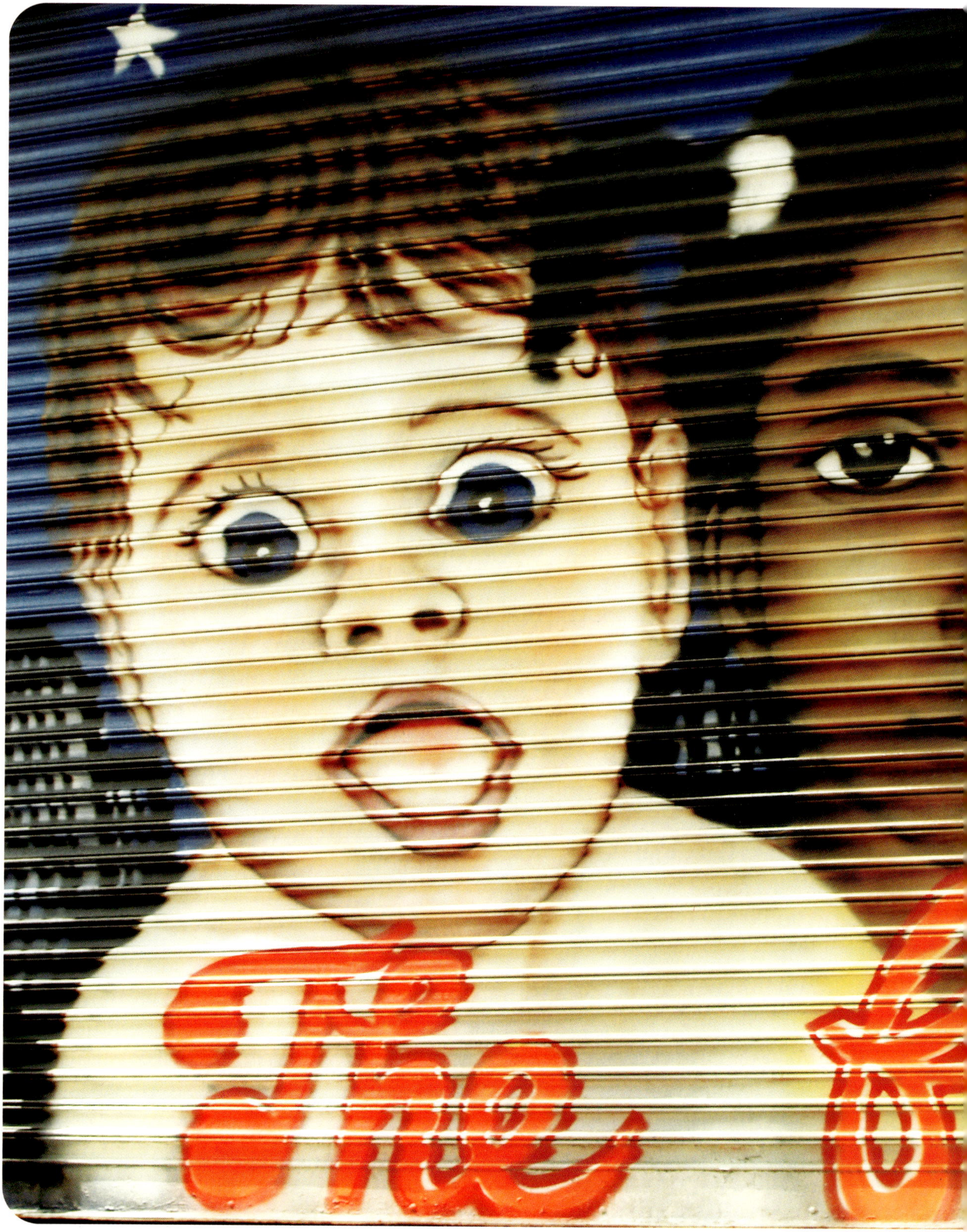
The

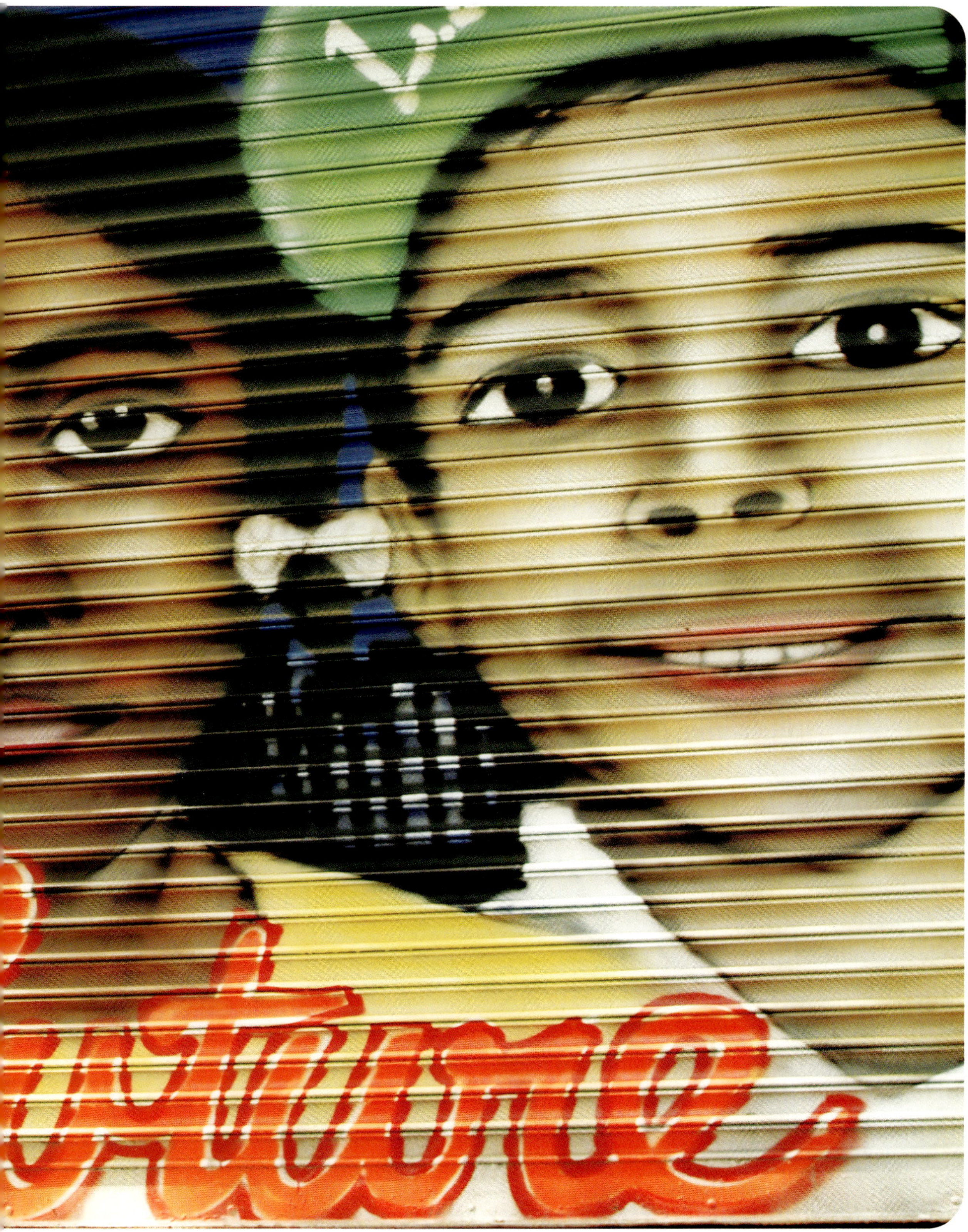

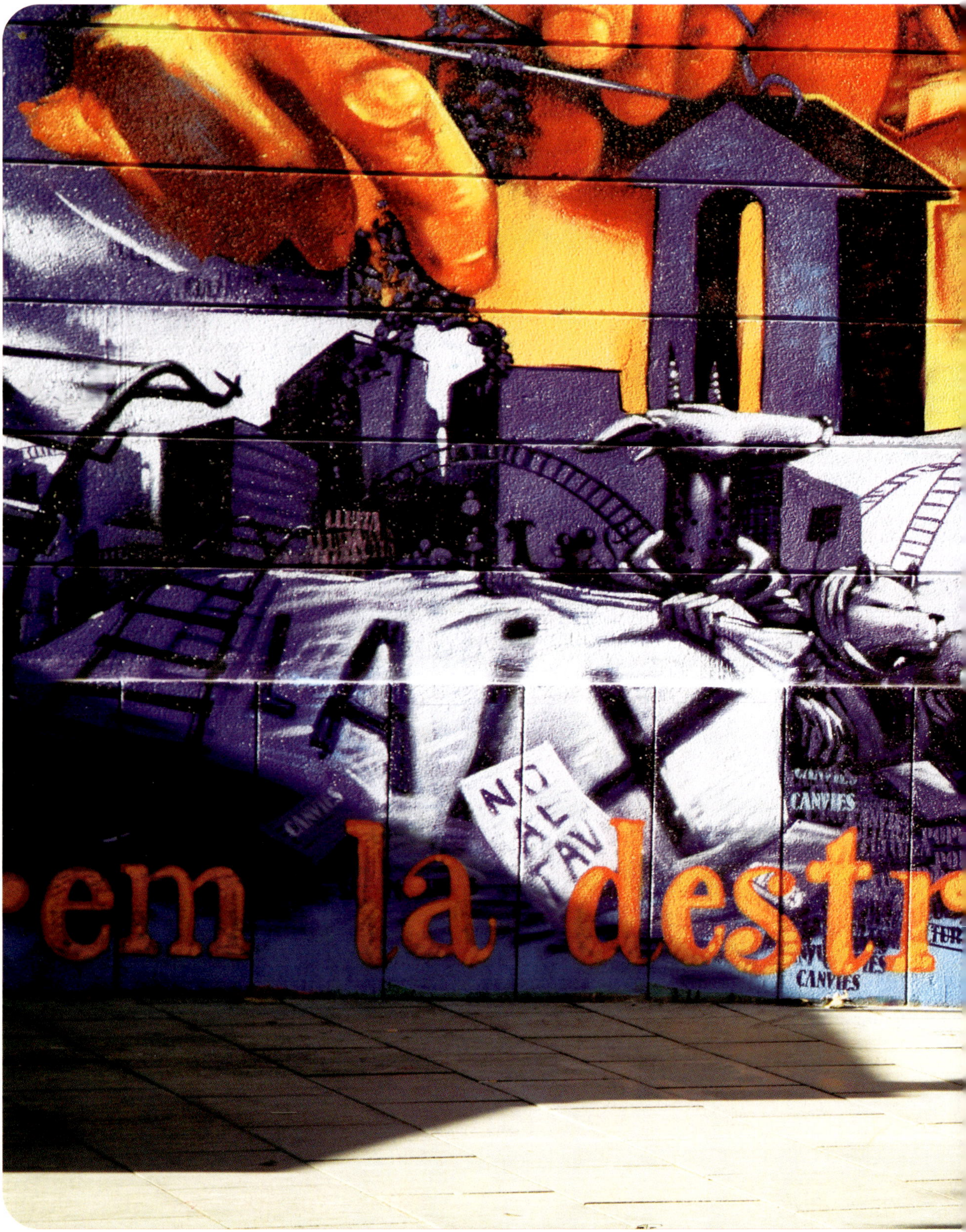
em la destr
CANVIES

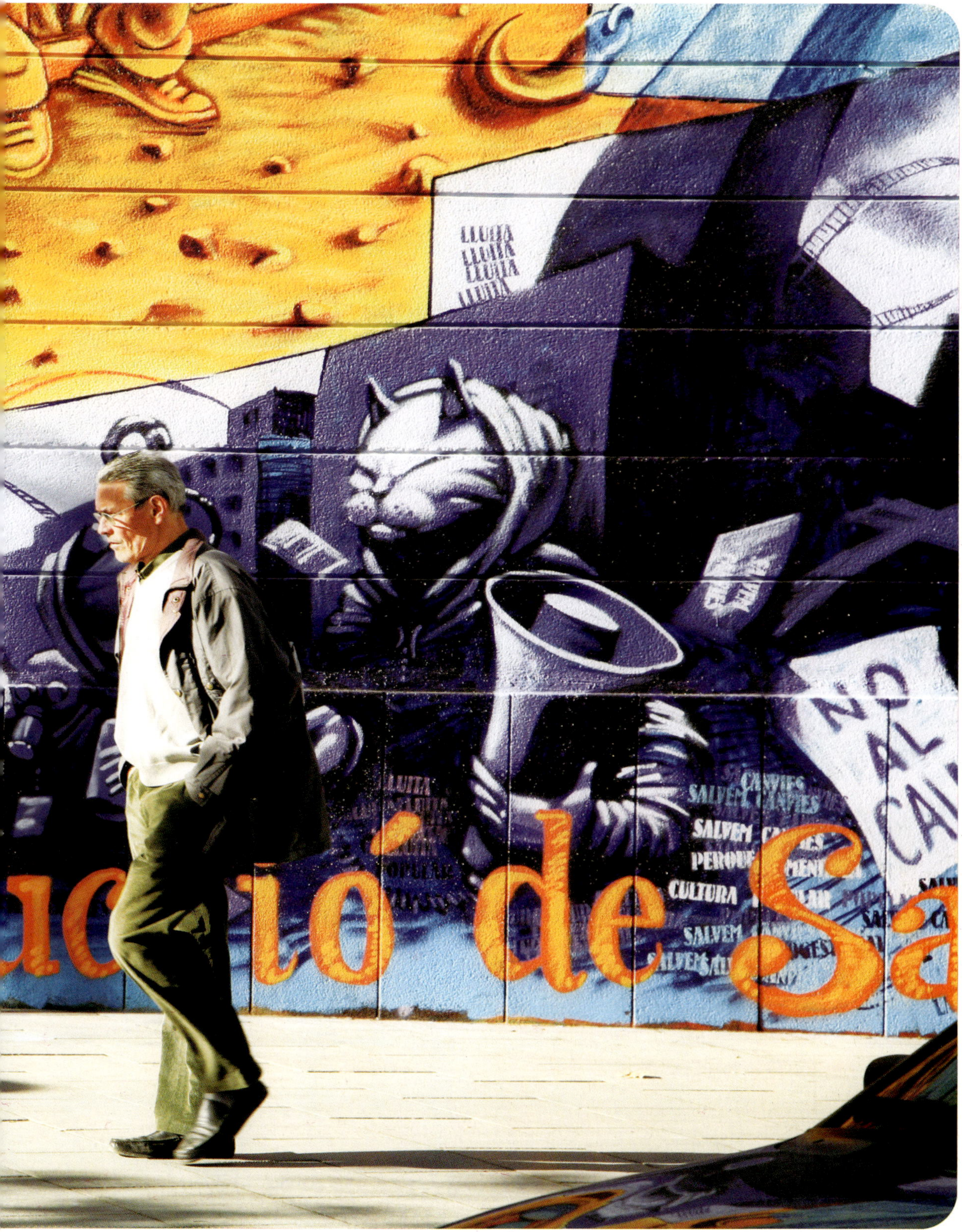
LLUITA
LLUITA
LLUITA
NO
AL
de
SALVEM
CULTURA
SALVEM

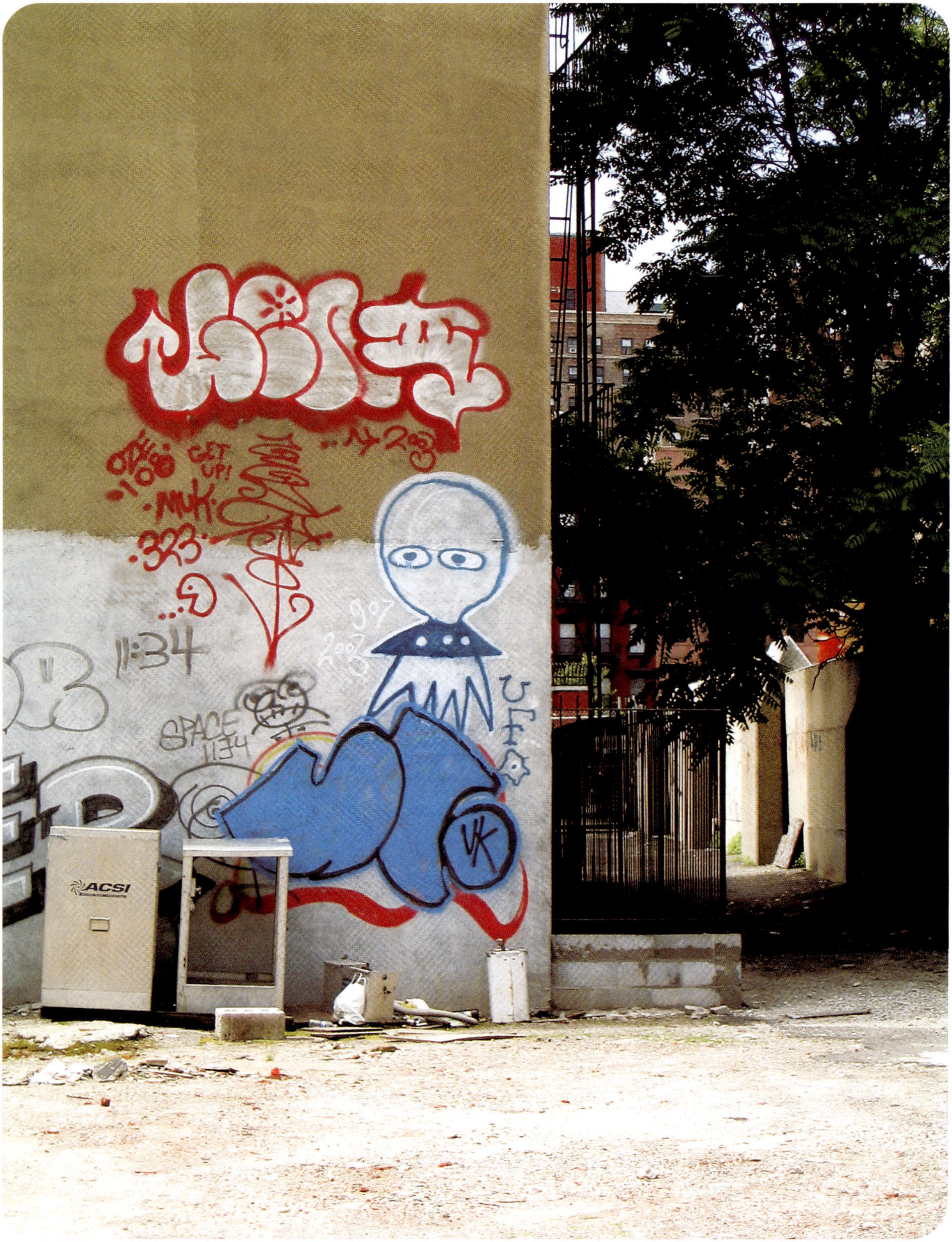
GET UP!
MUK
323
11:34
SPACE
ACSI

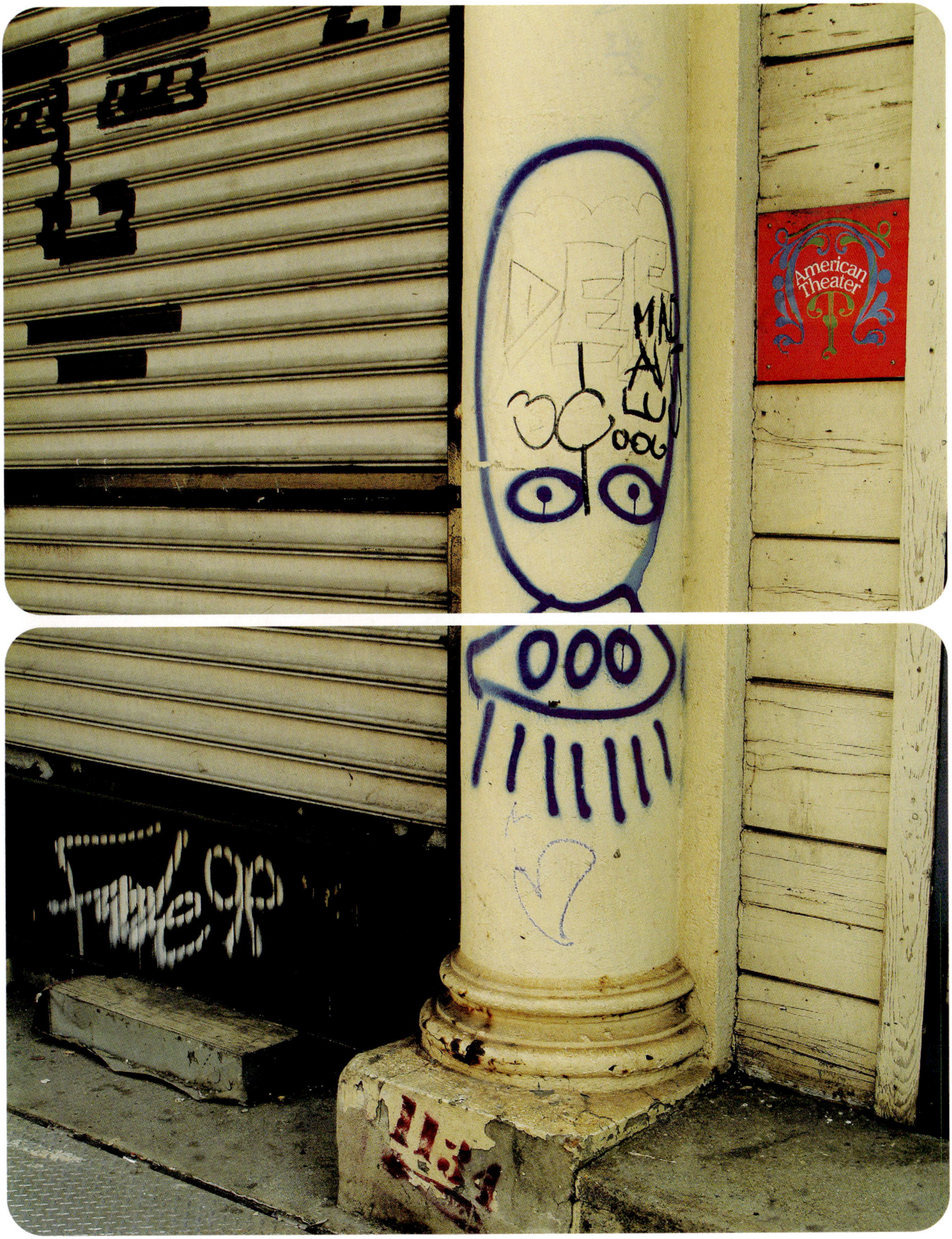
American
Theater

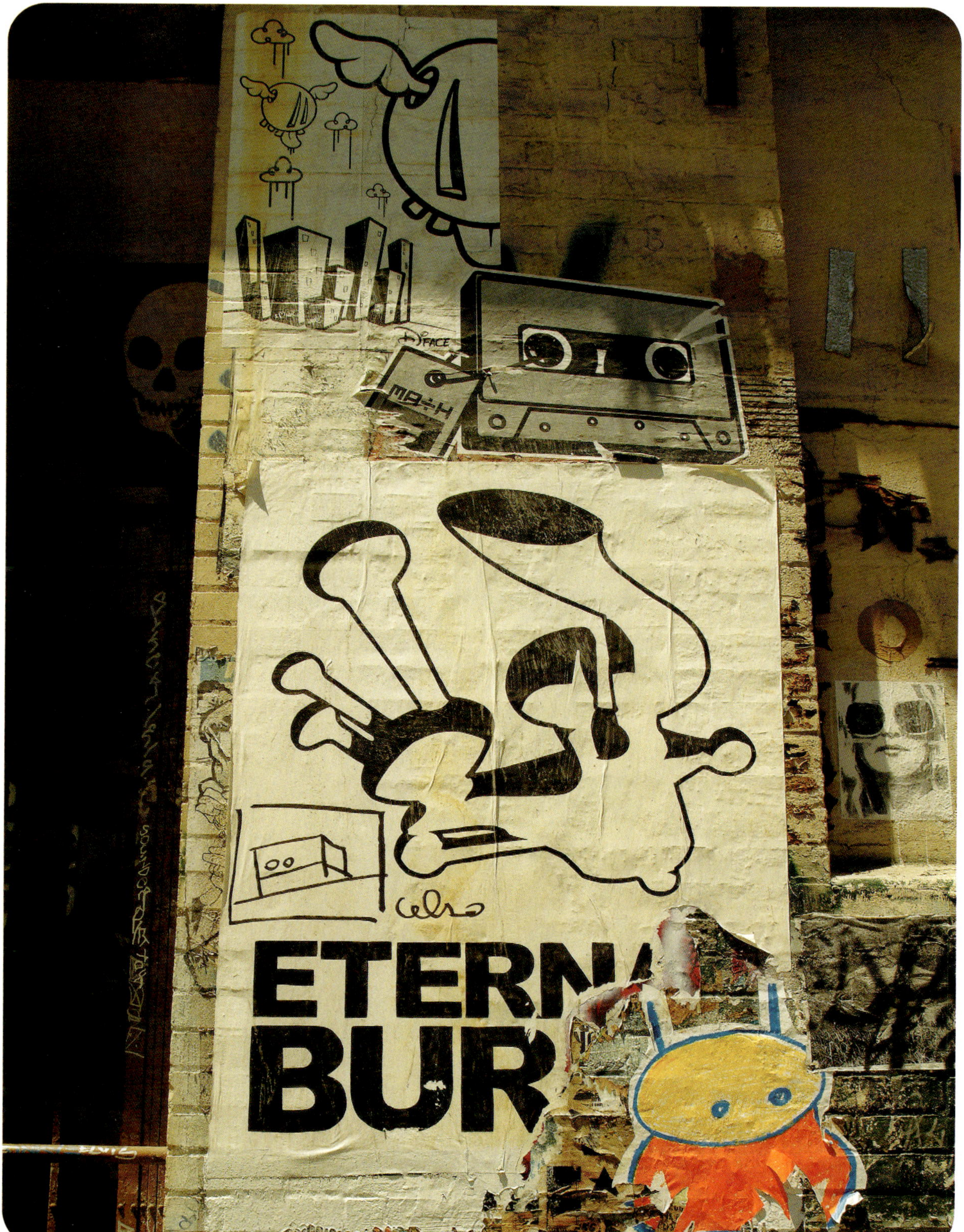
D*FACE
ETERN
BUR

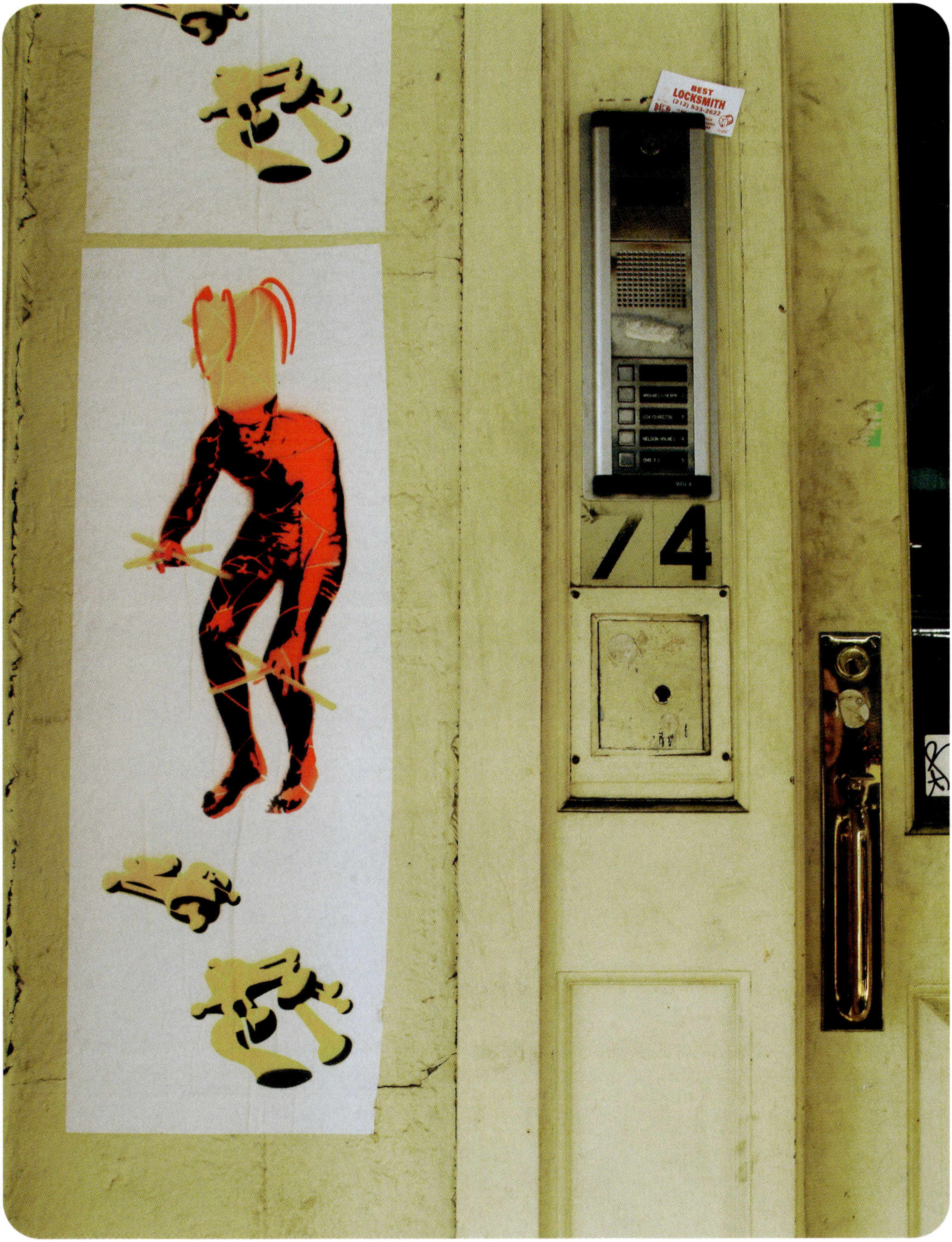
BEST
LOCKSMITH
74

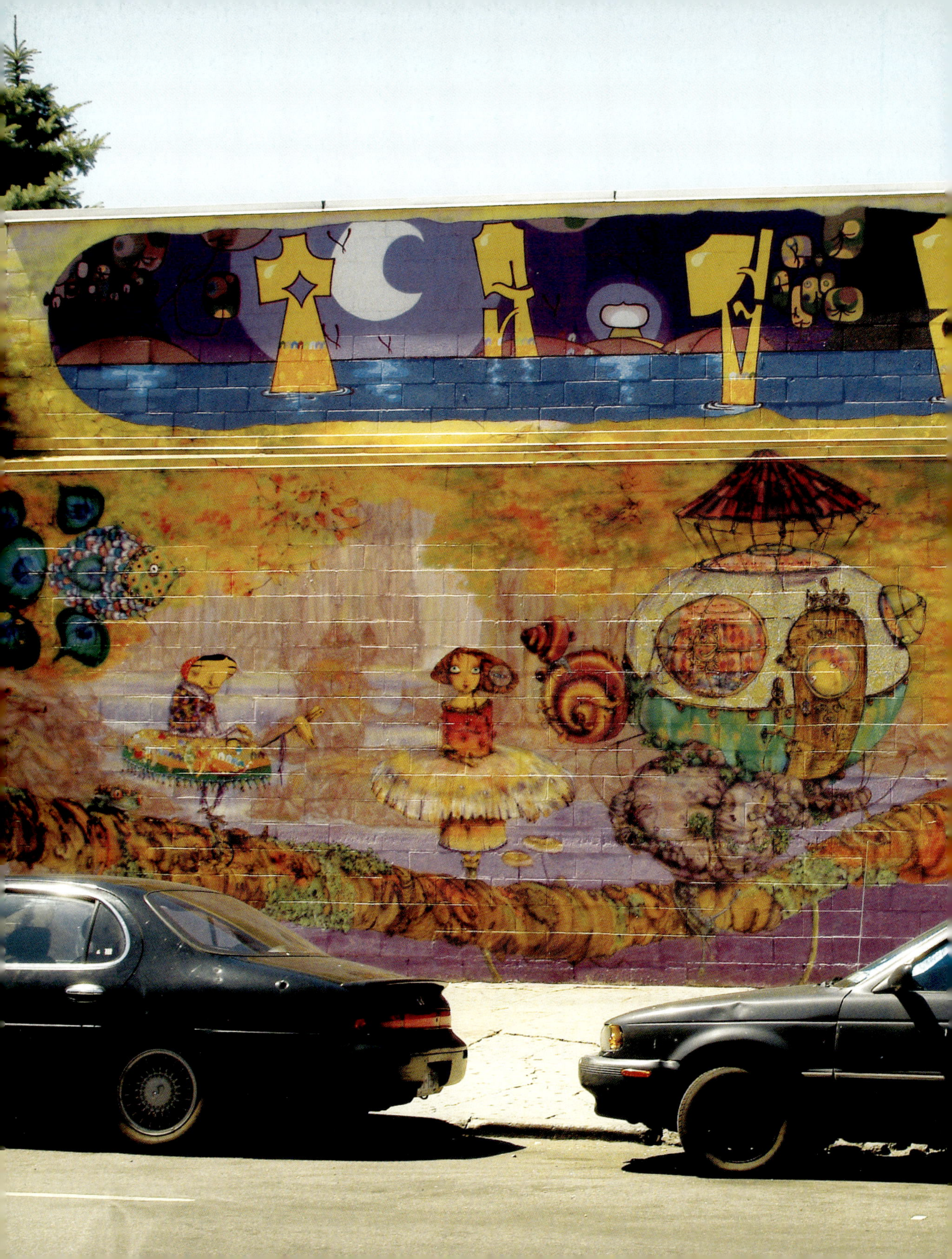

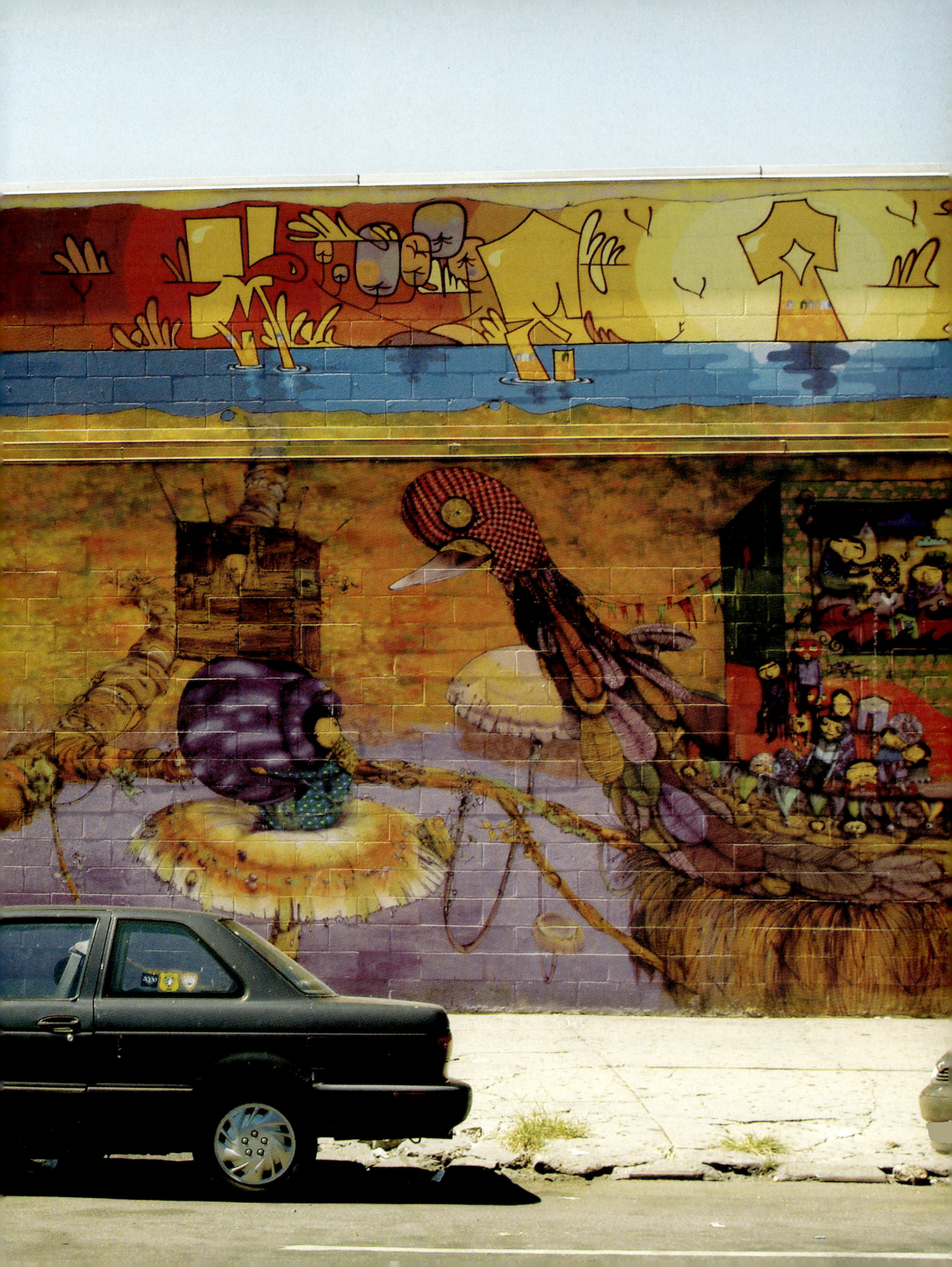

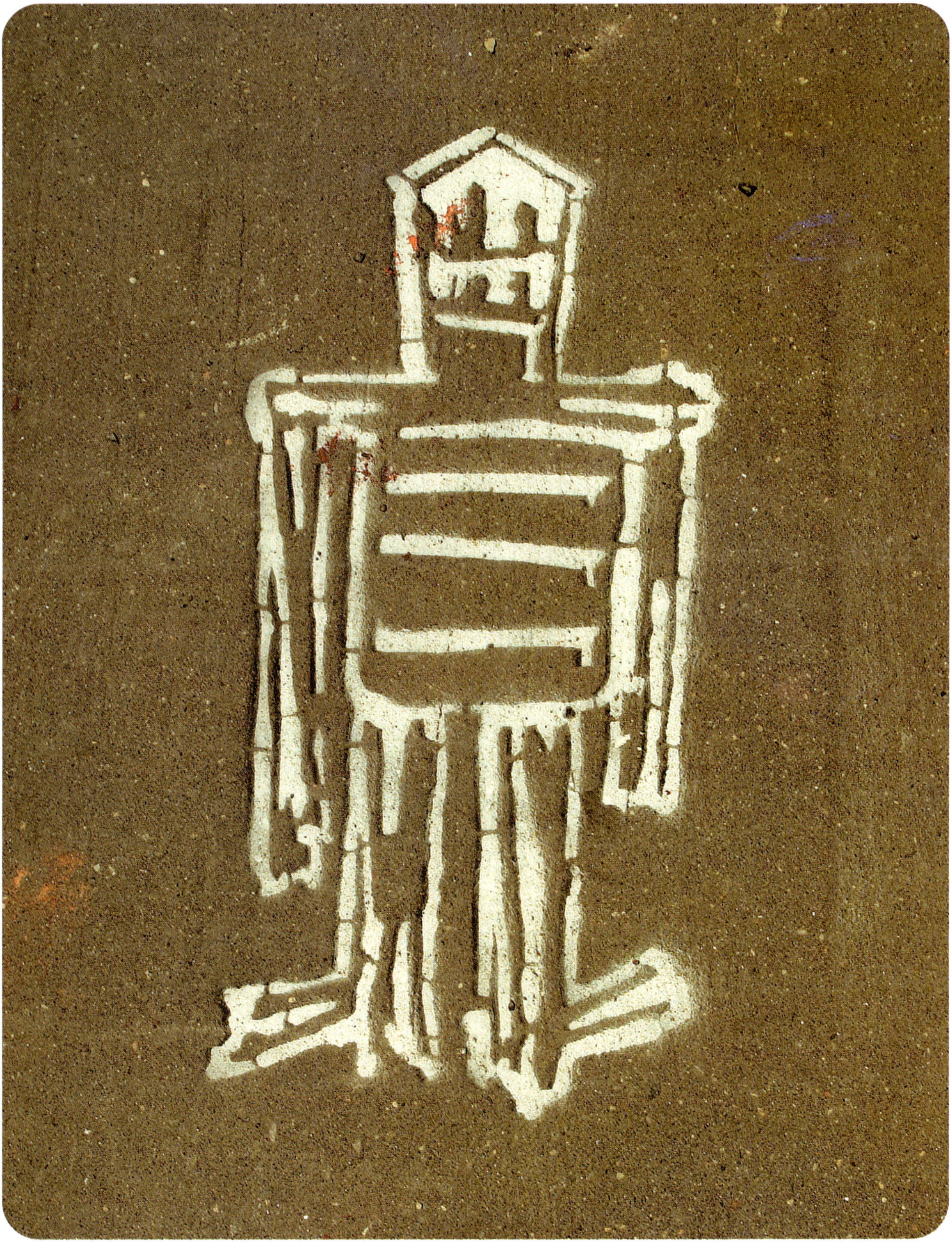

new york

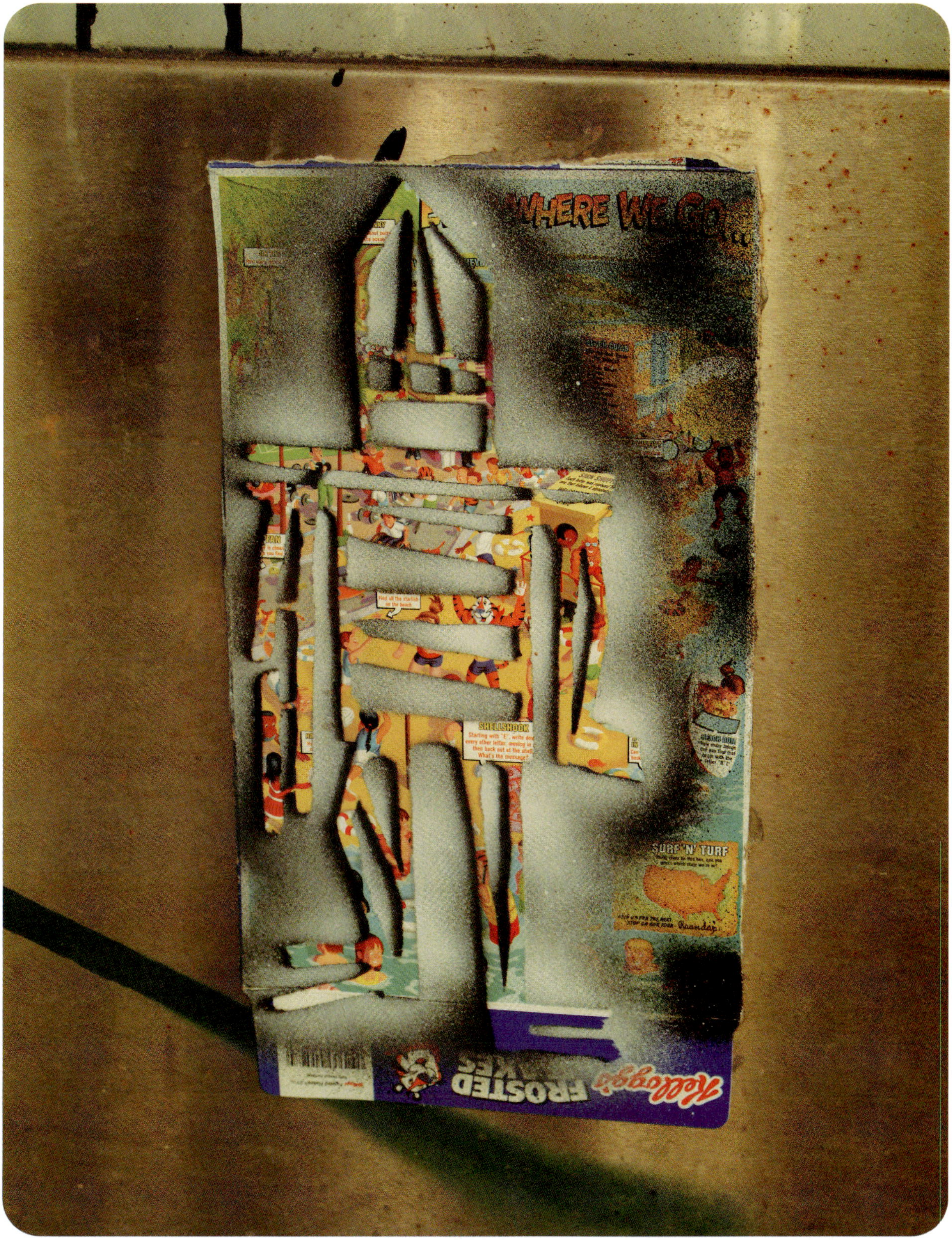

new york

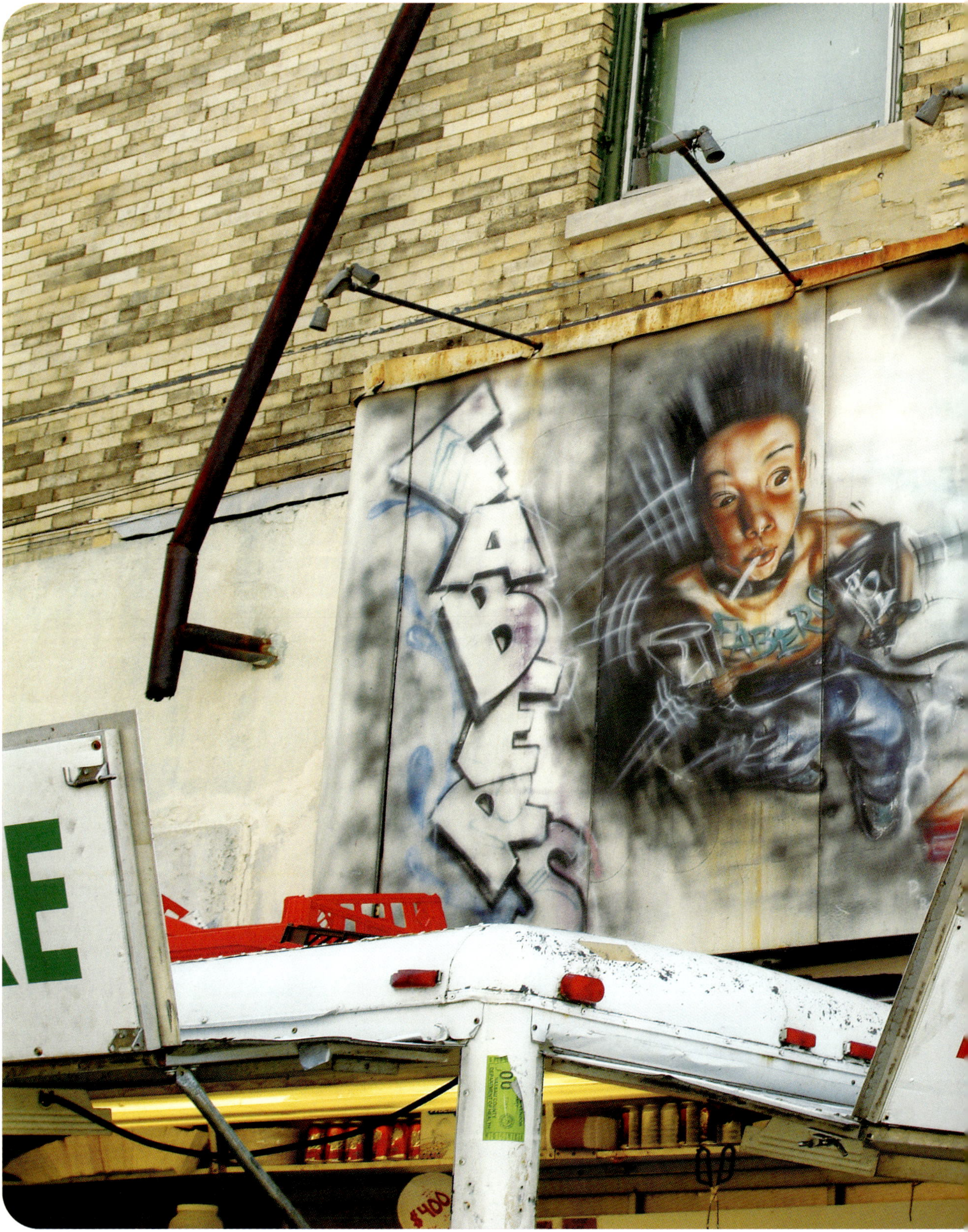
FABERS
$400

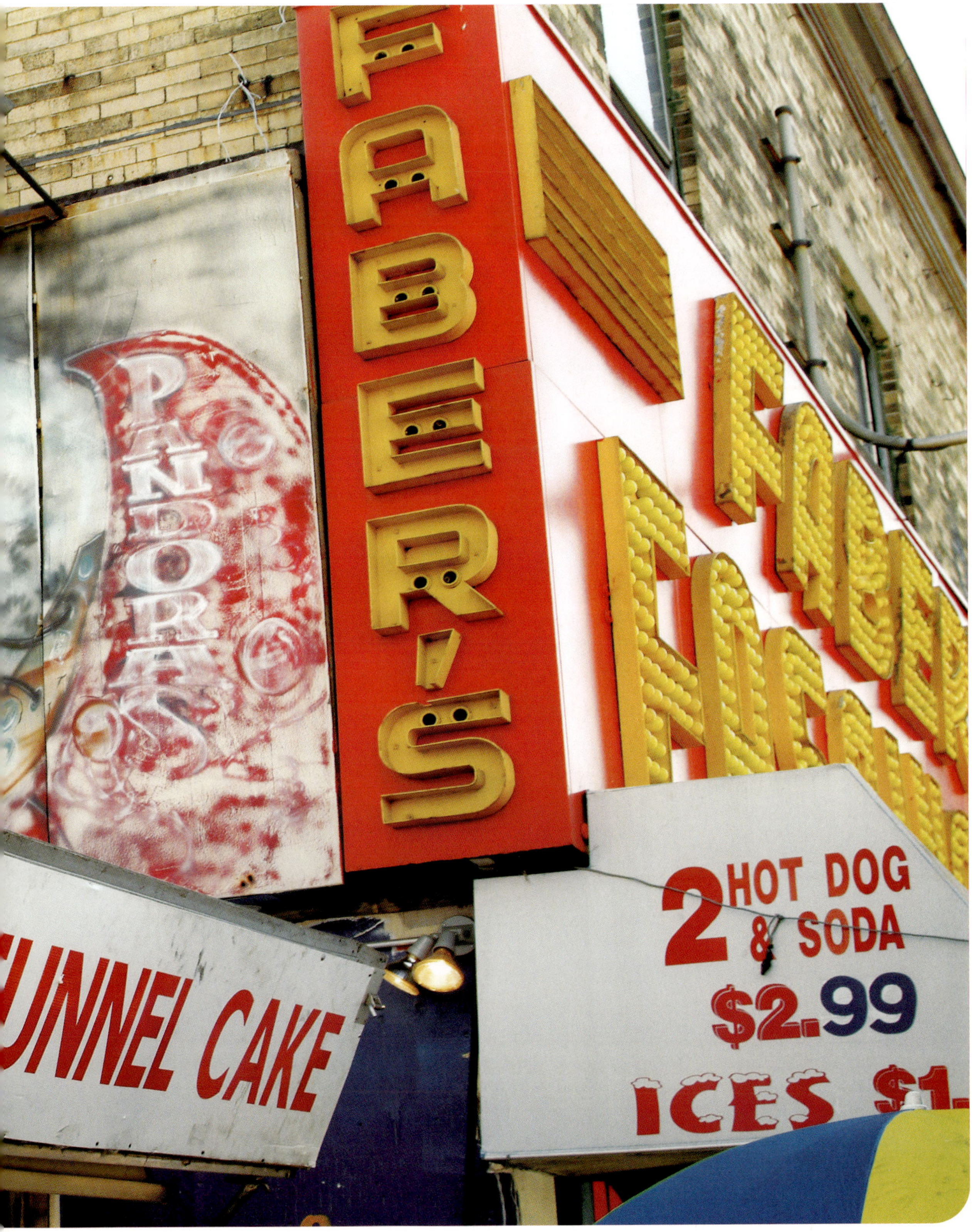
FABER'S
PANDORA'S
2 HOT DOG & SODA
$2.99
ICES
CAKE

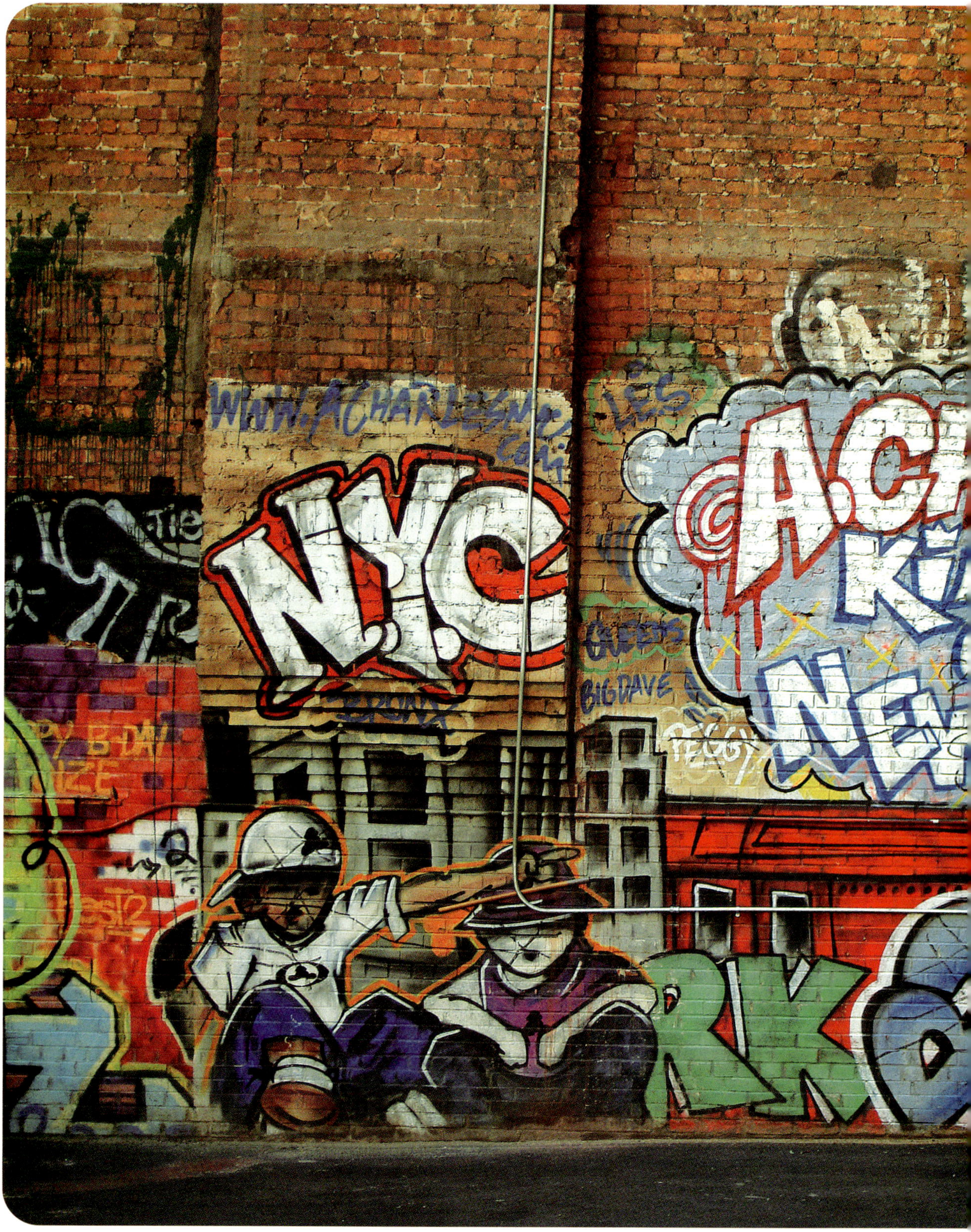
N.Y.C
BIG DAVE

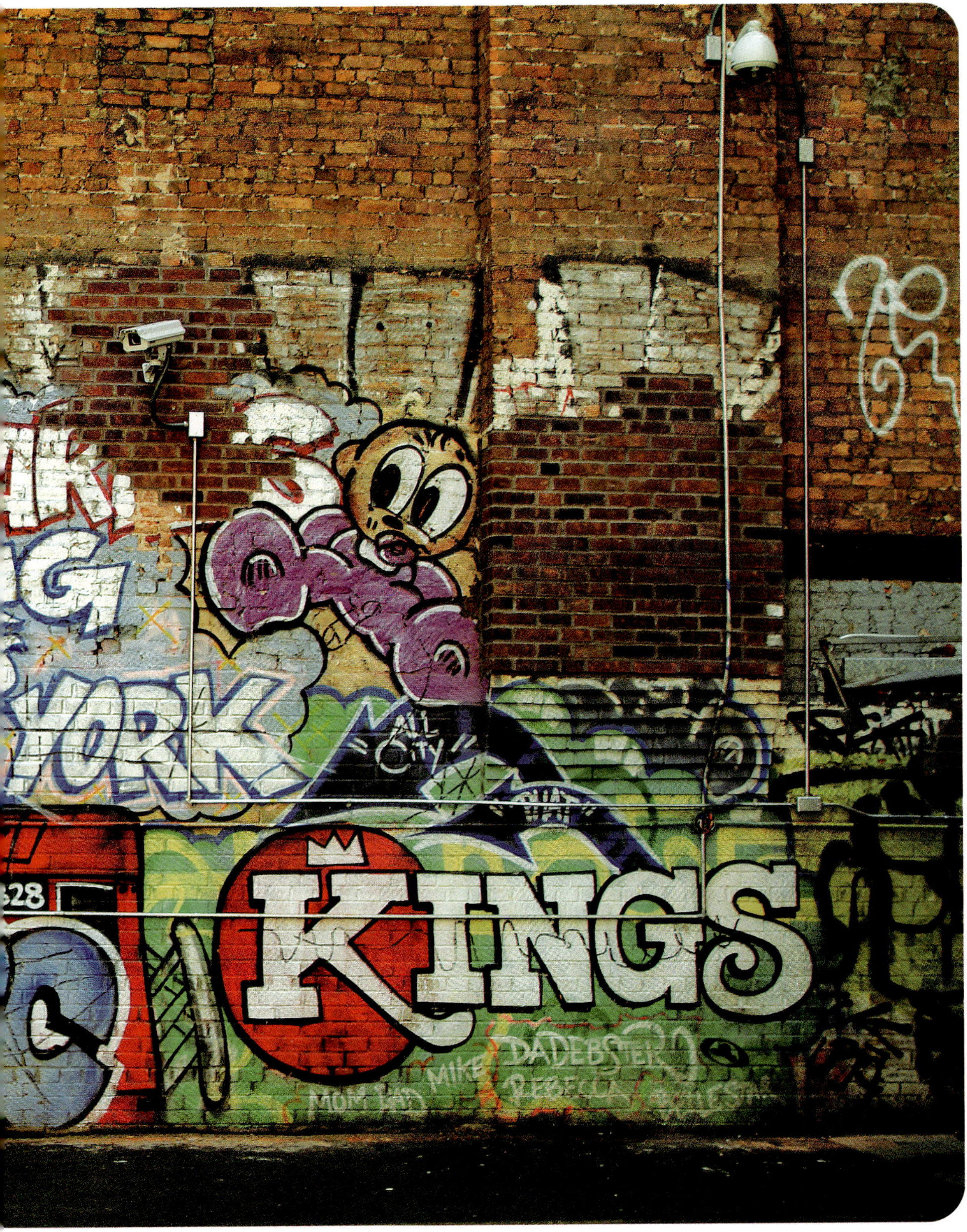
YORK
KINGS
MIKE
MOM DAD

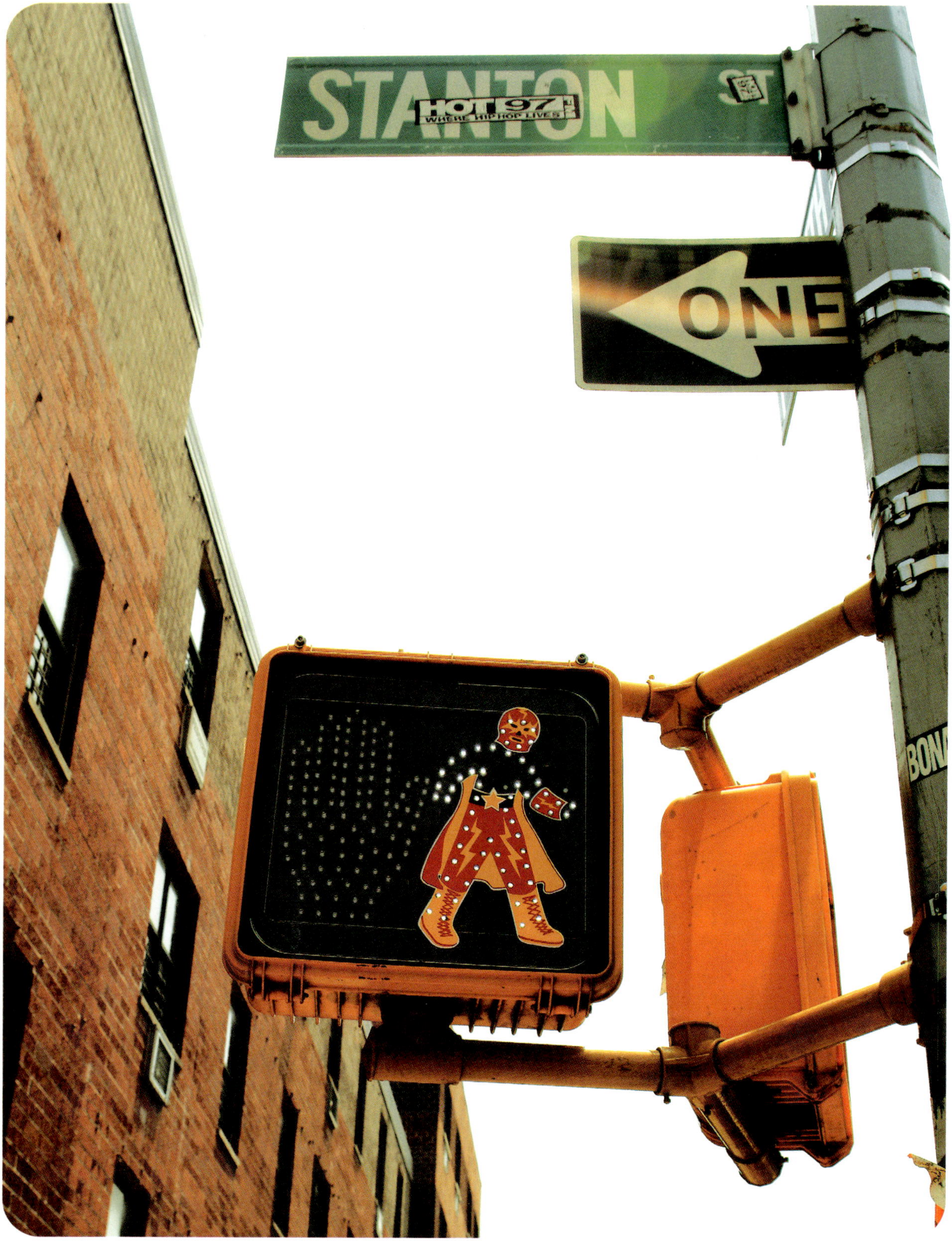

new york

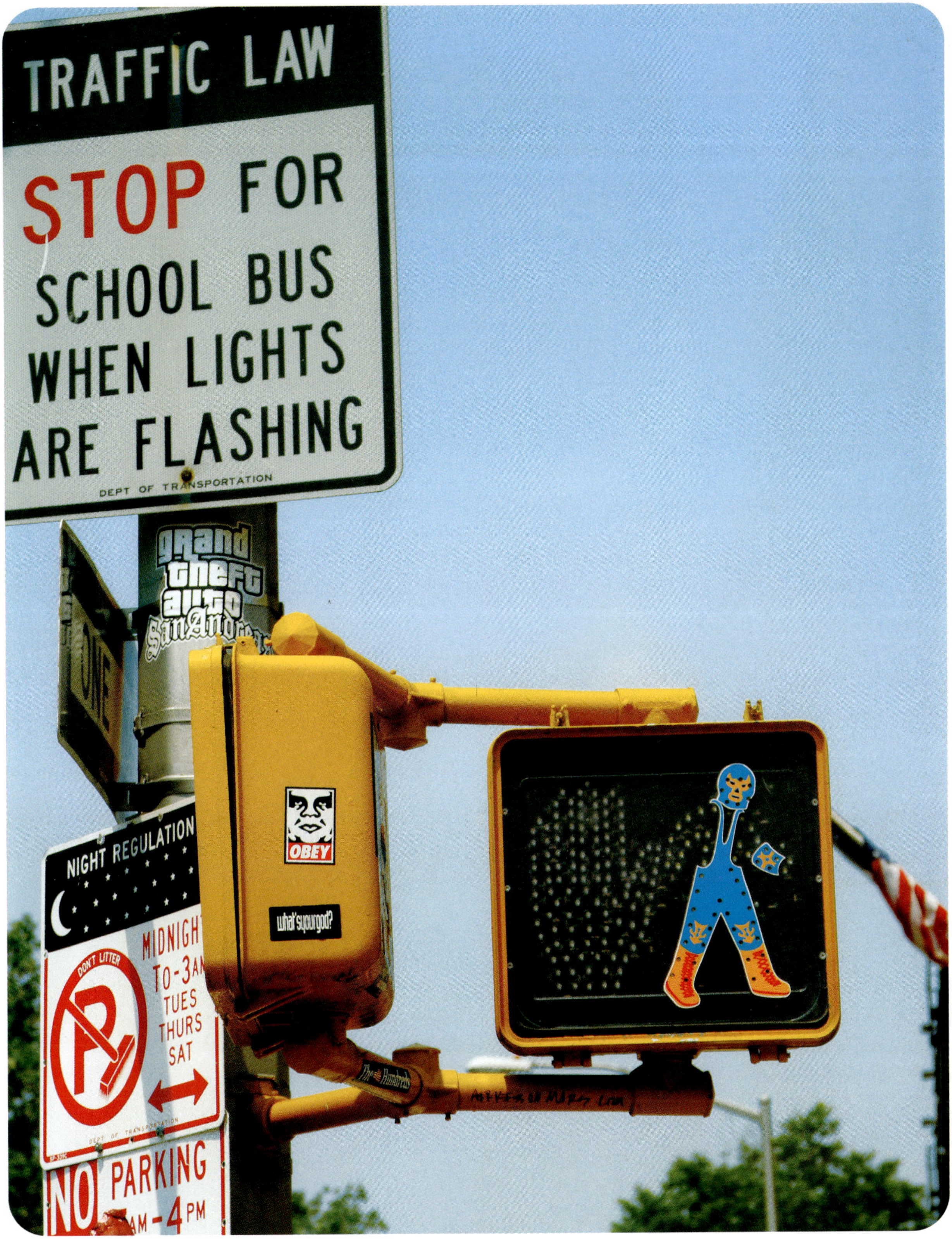
TRAFFIC LAW
STOP FOR SCHOOL BUS WHEN LIGHTS ARE FLASHING
DEPT OF TRANSPORTATION
grand theft auto
ONE
NIGHT REGULATION
DON'T LITTER
TUES
THURS
SAT
OBEY
what'supurgod?
PARKING

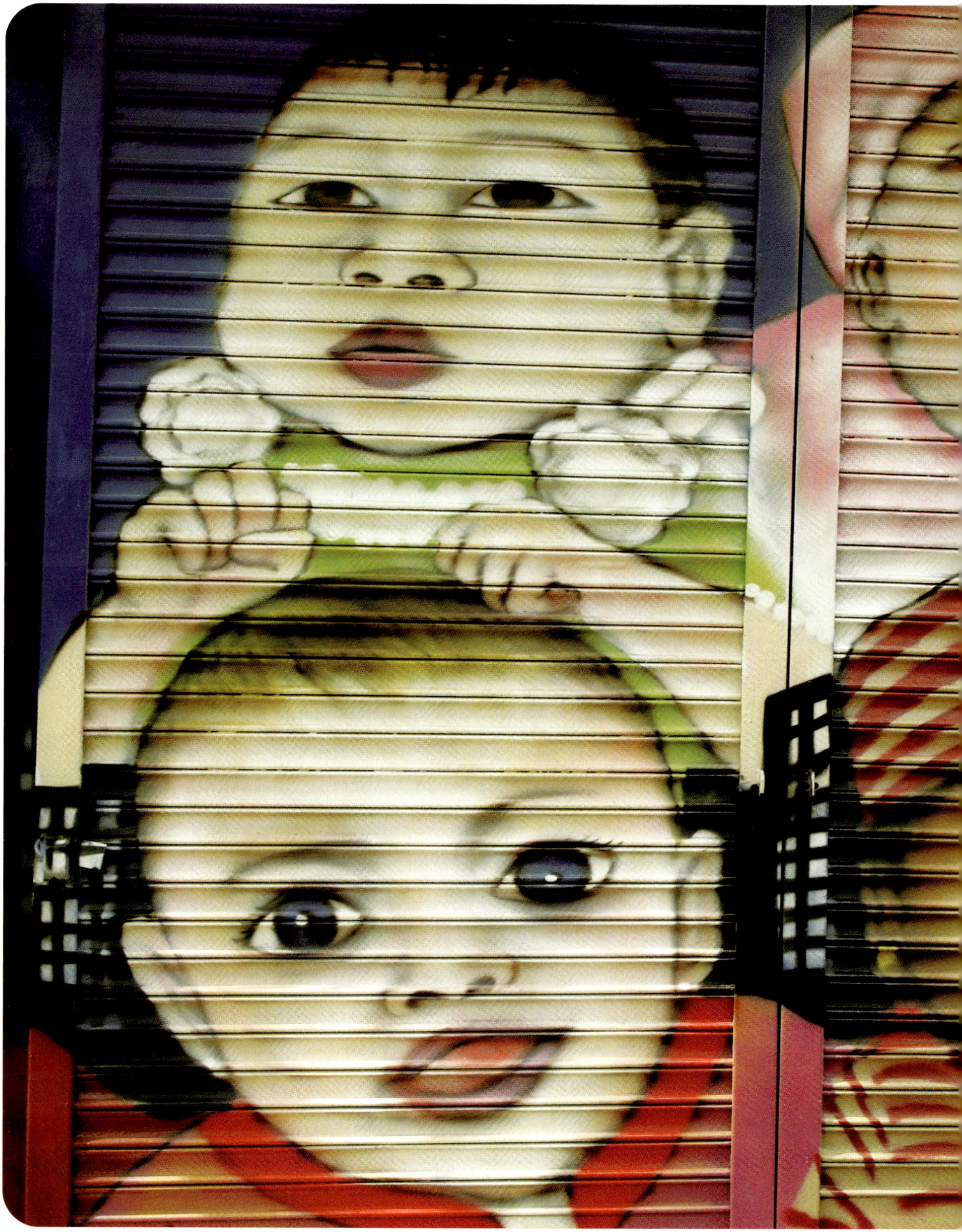

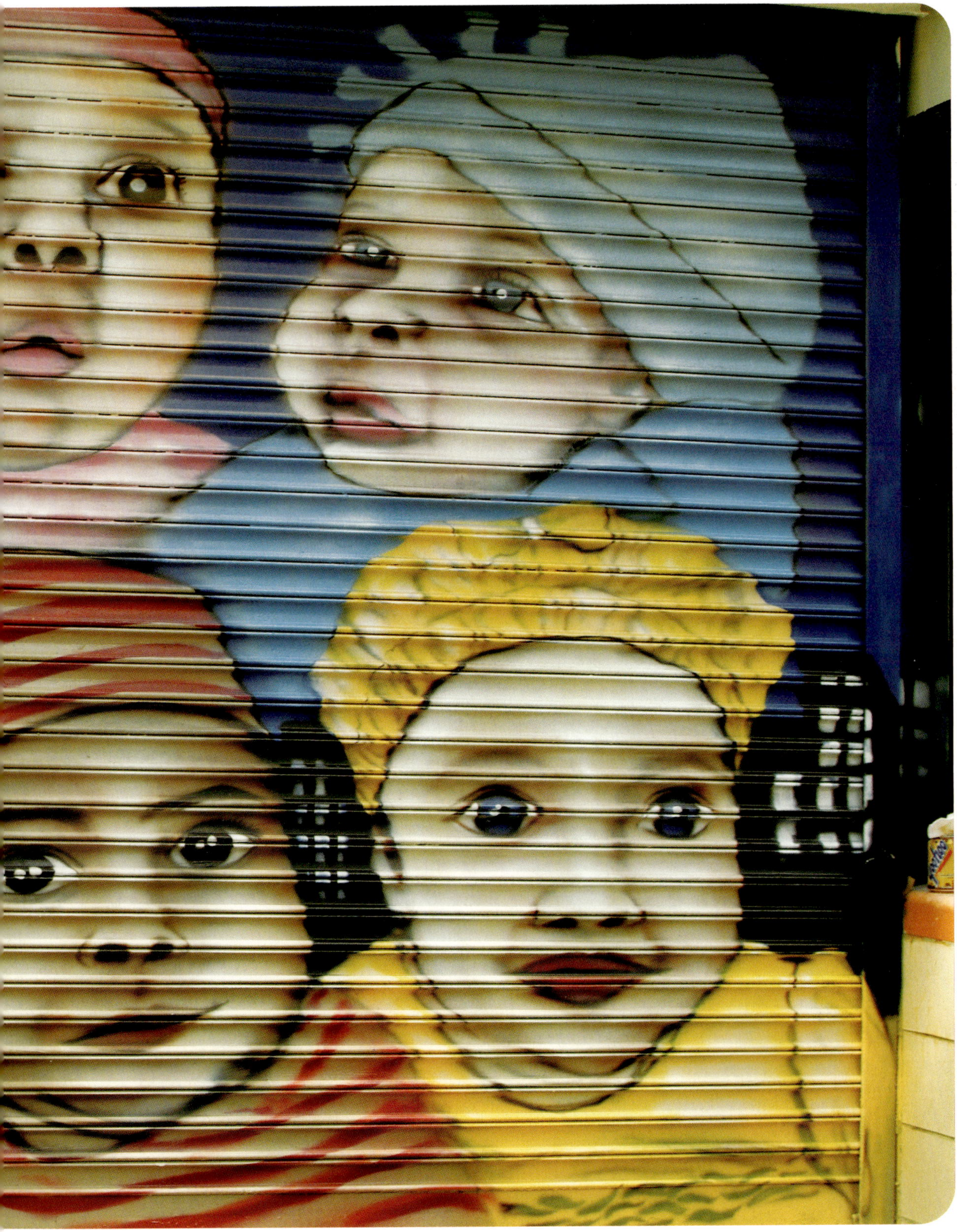

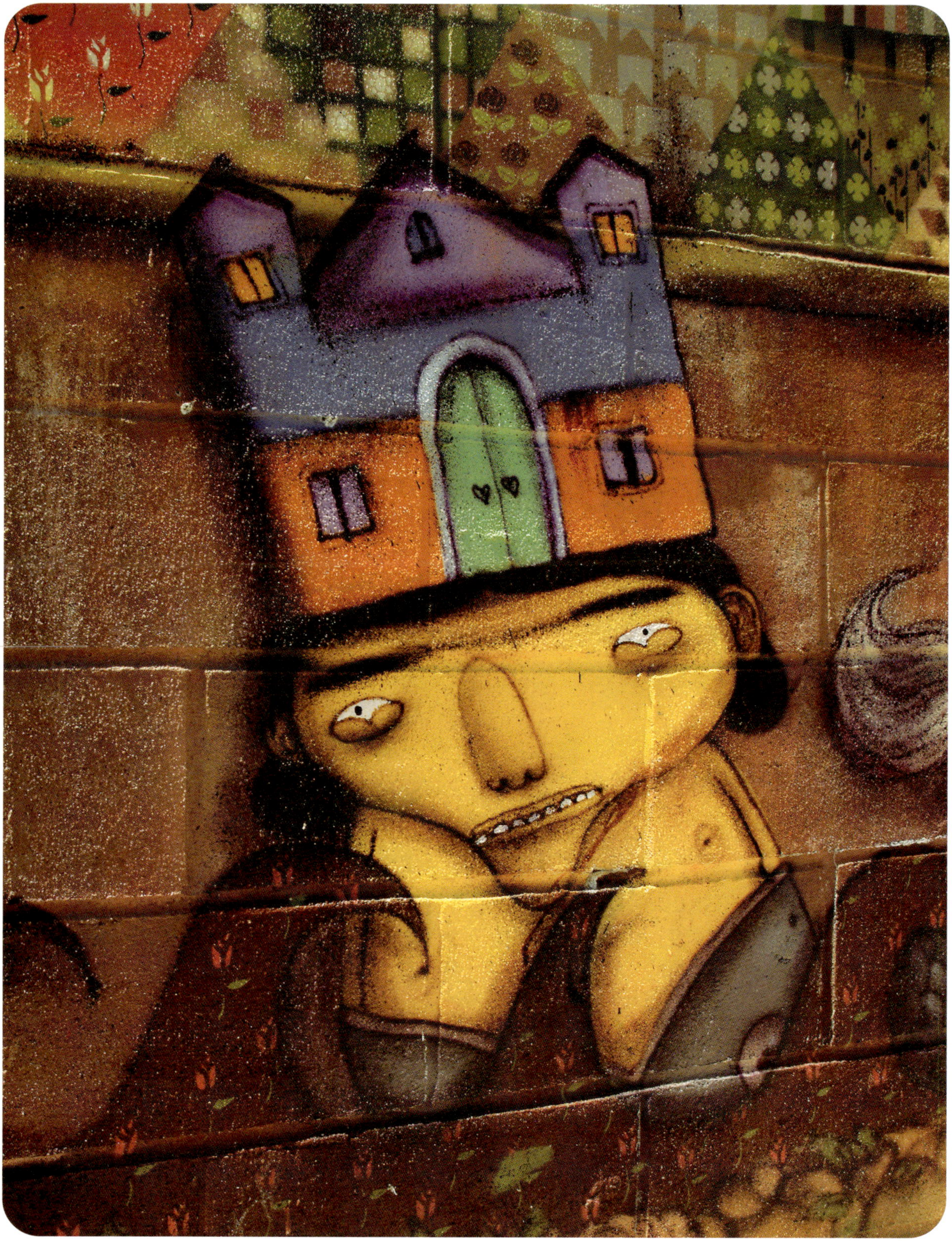

new york

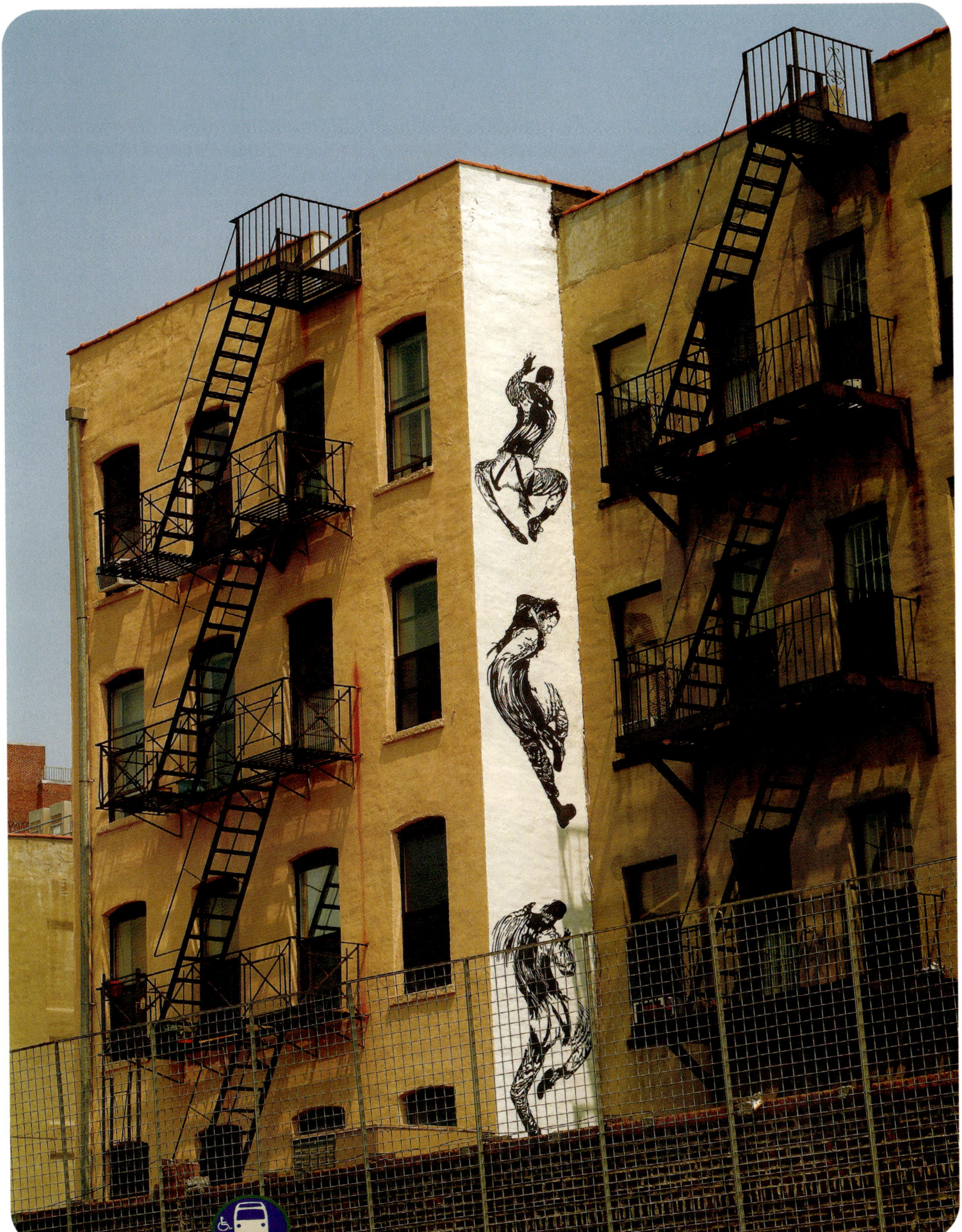

new york

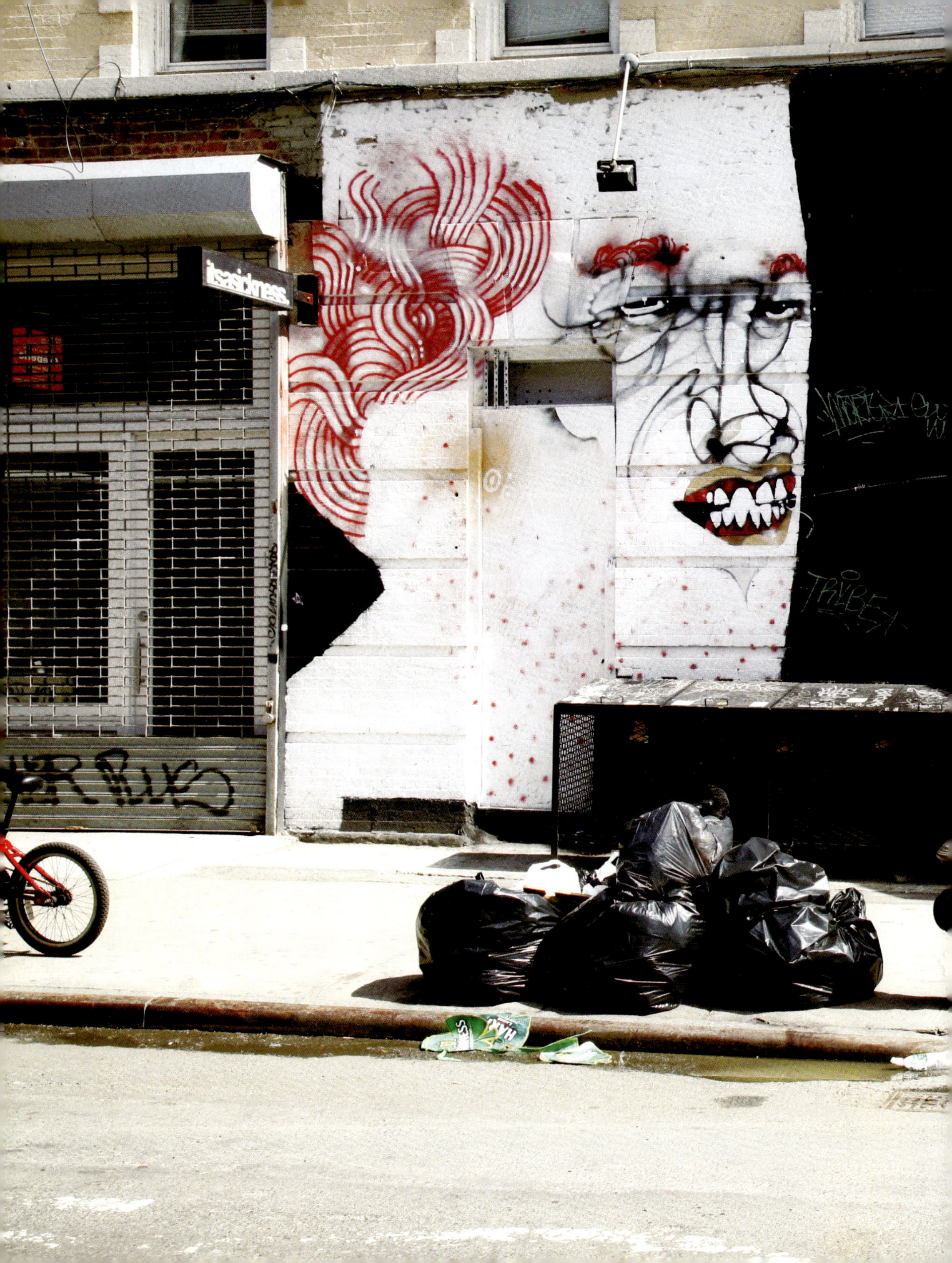
itsasickness.

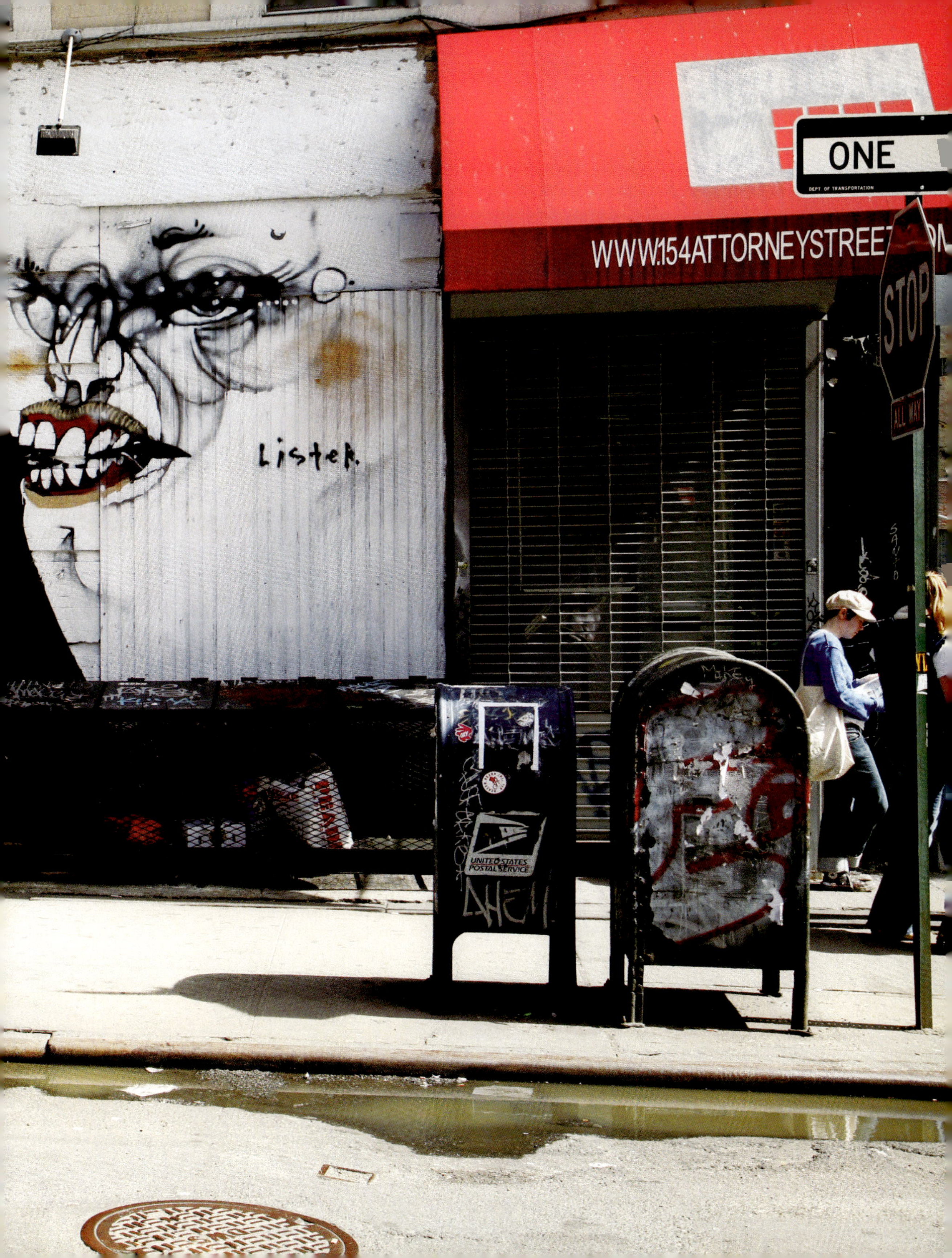
ONE
DEPT OF TRANSPORTATION
WWW.154ATTORNEYSTREET
STOP
ALL WAY
Lister
UNITED STATES POSTAL SERVICE

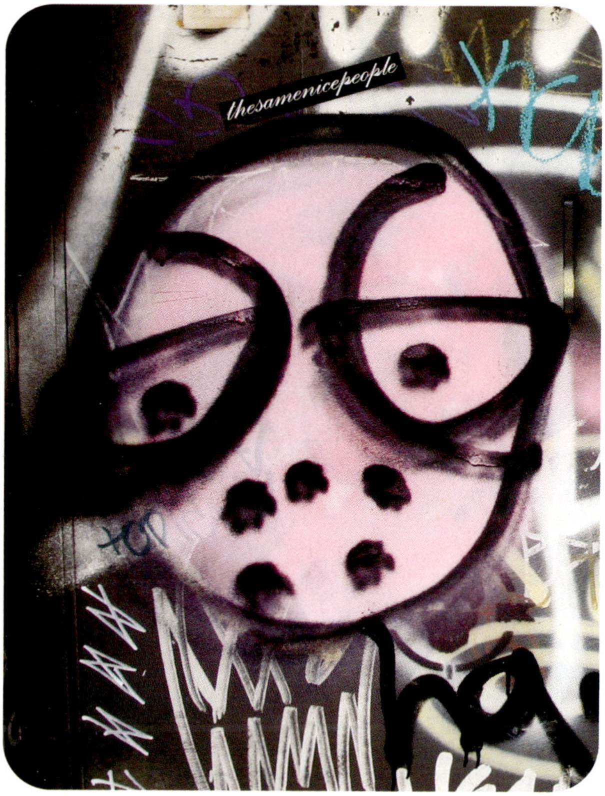

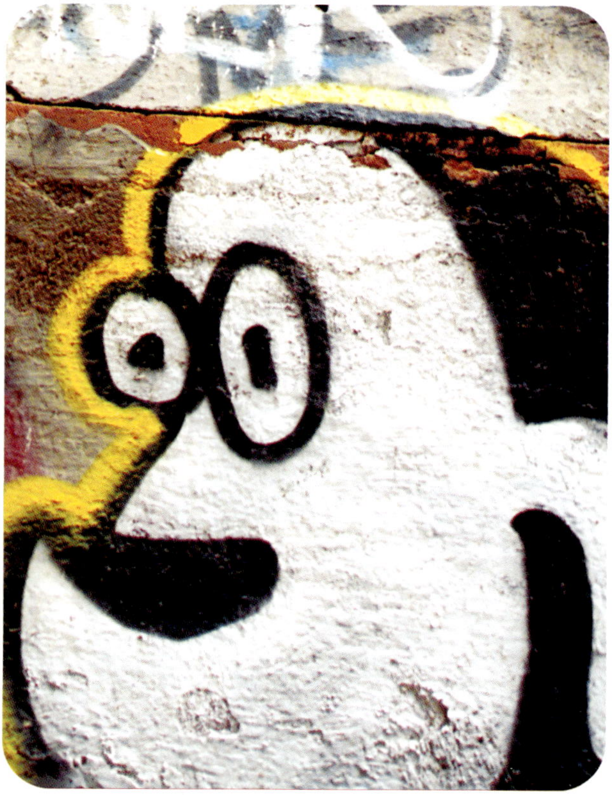

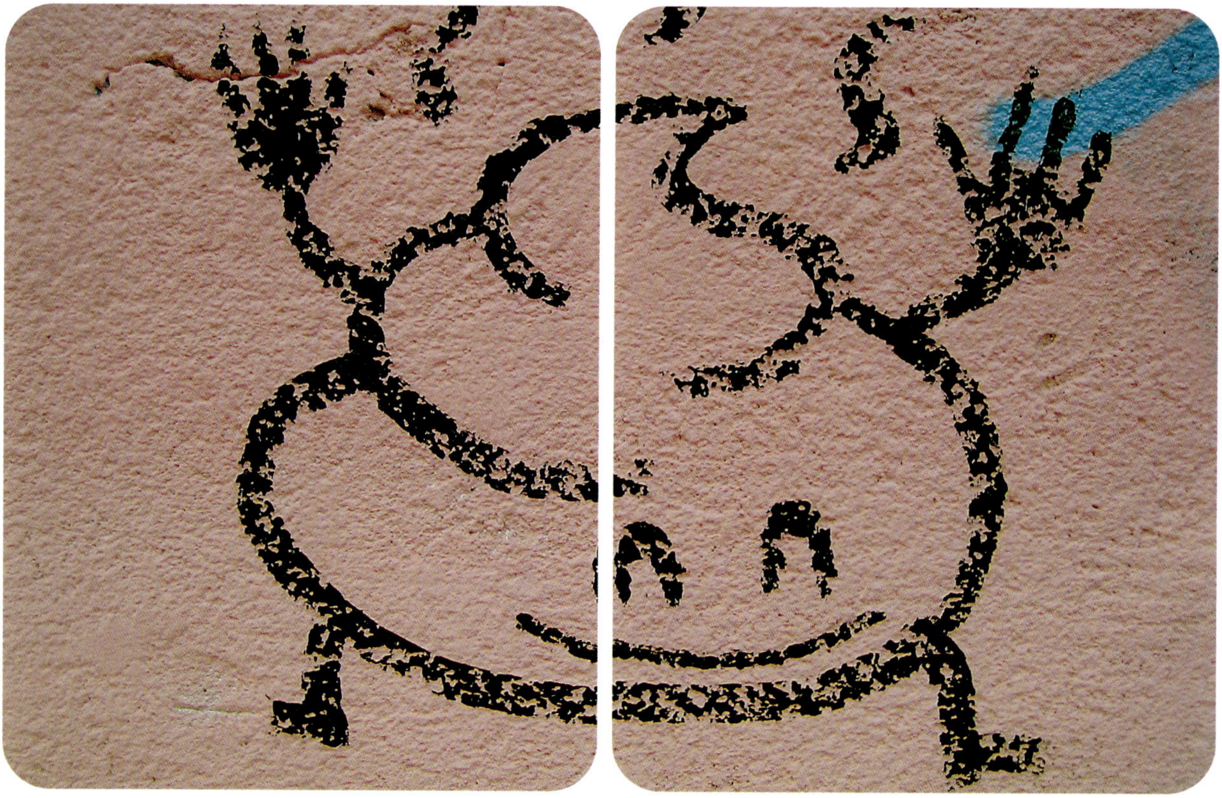

new york + barcelona

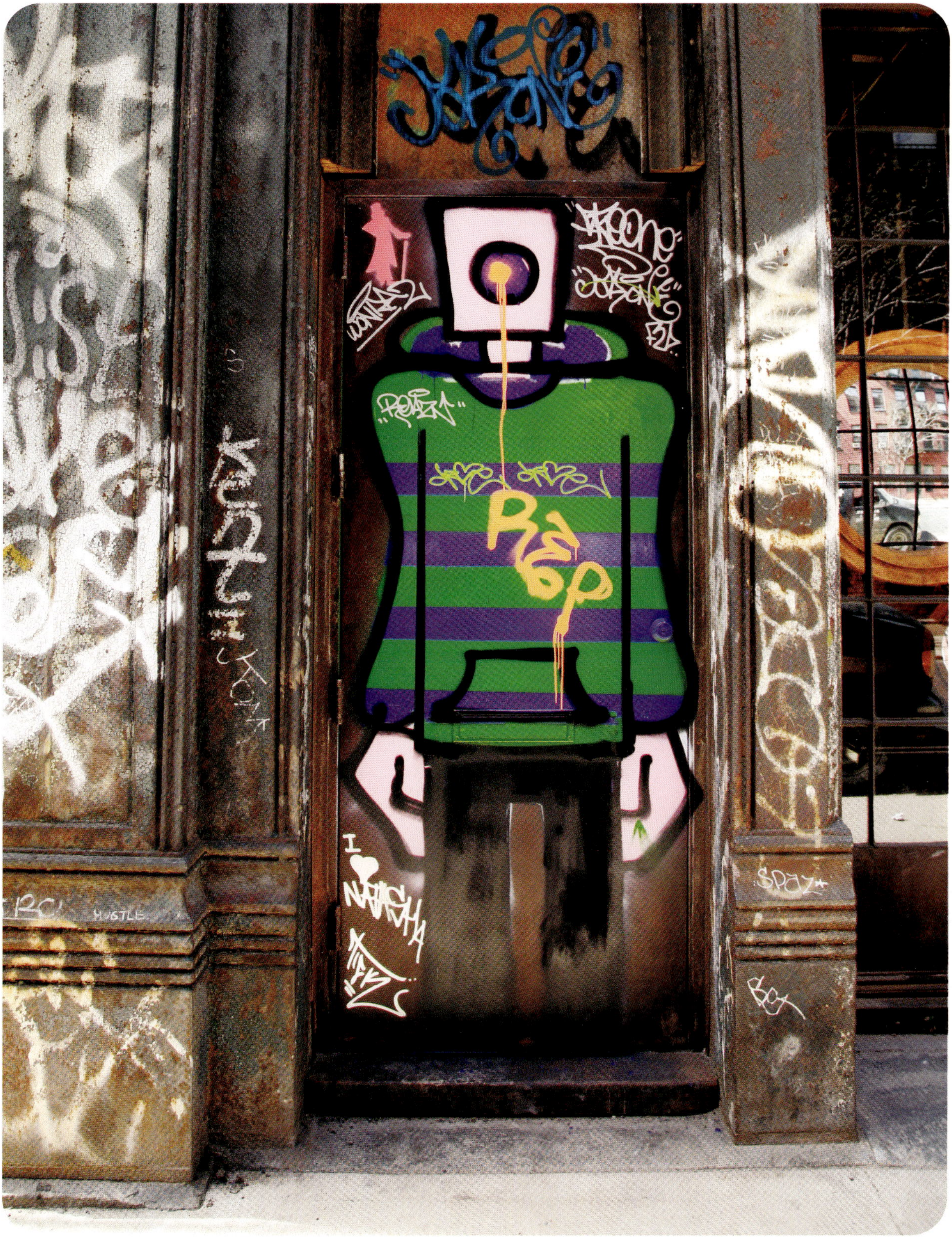
HUSTLE
SPAZ

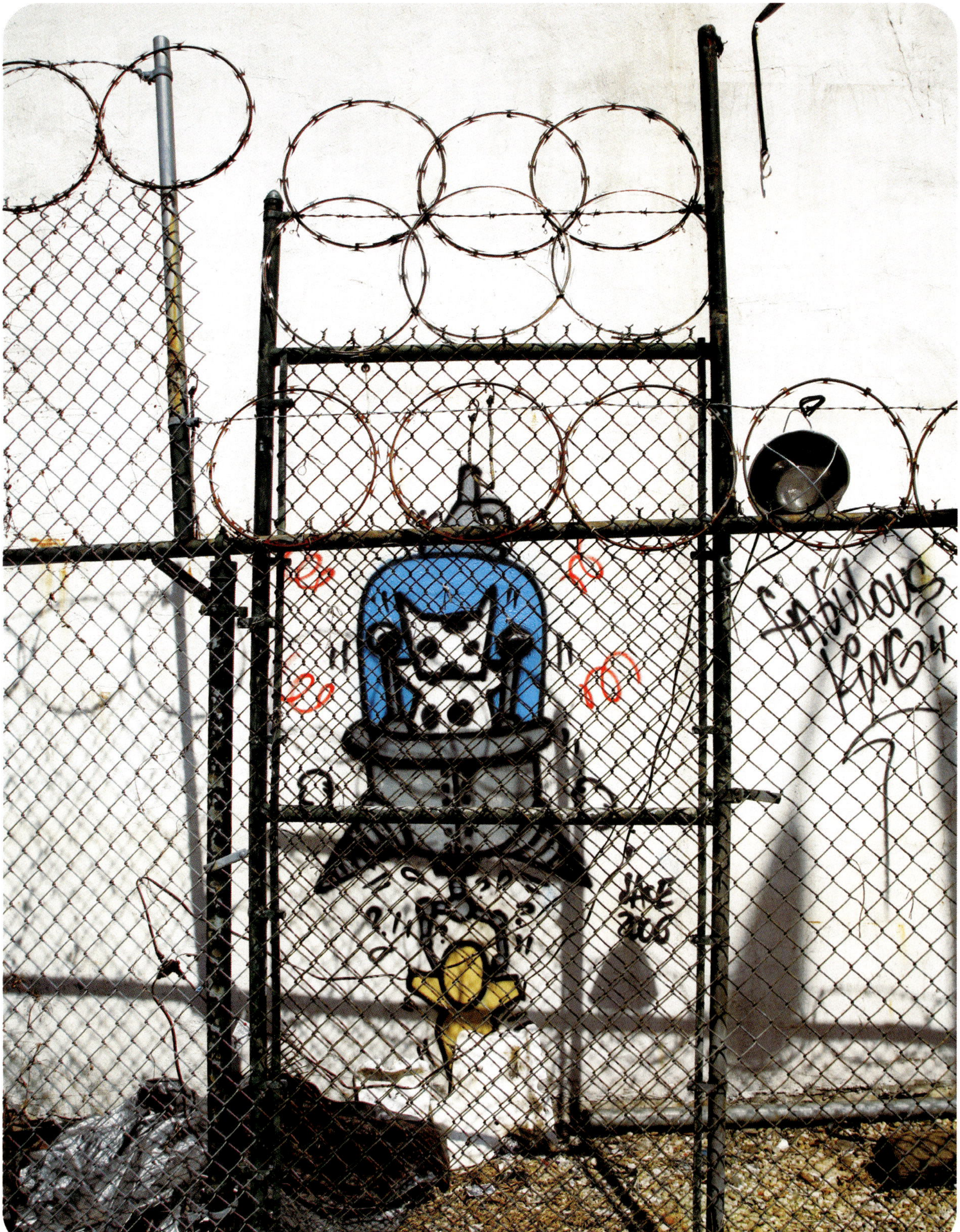

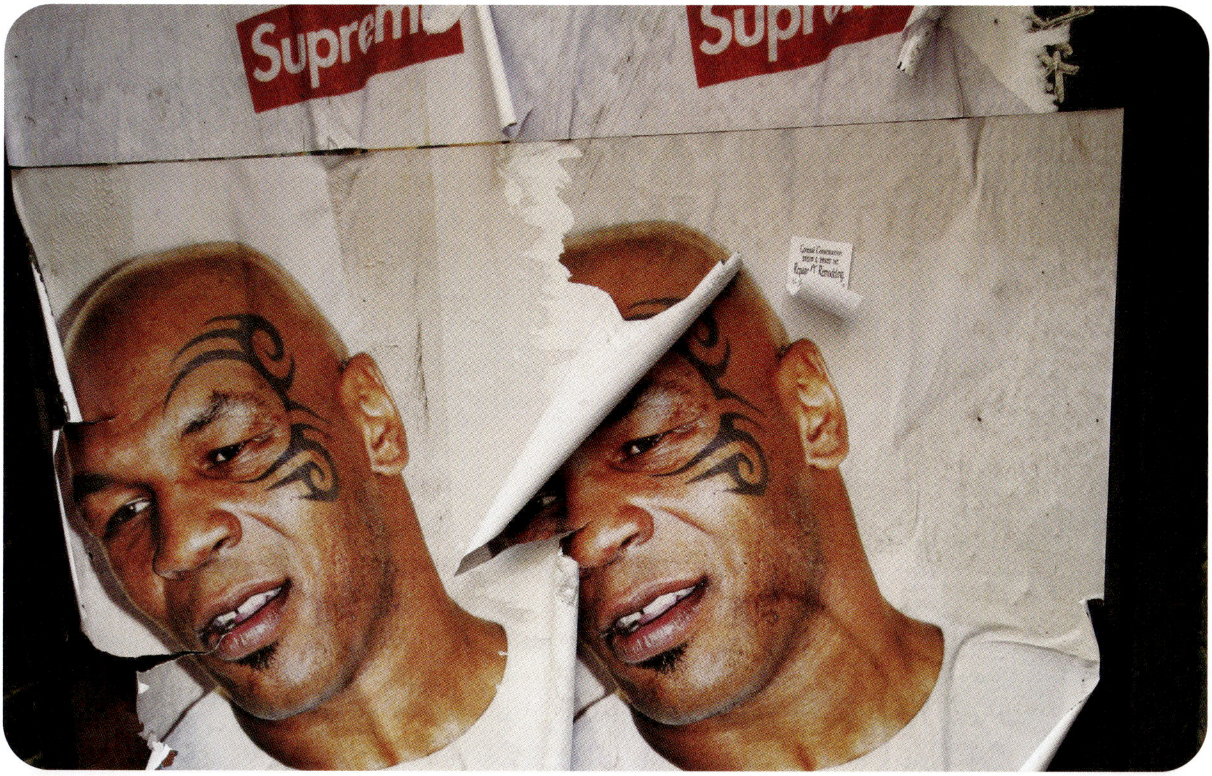
Suprem
Supr

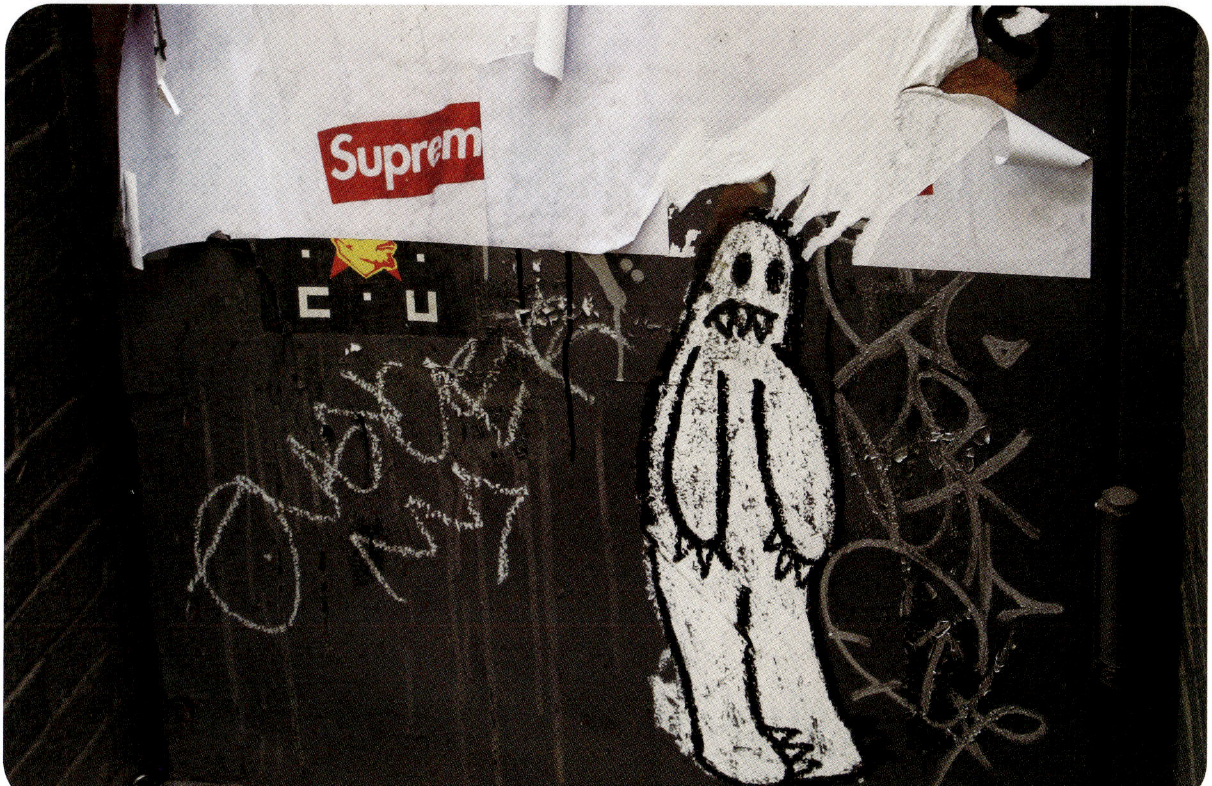
Suprem

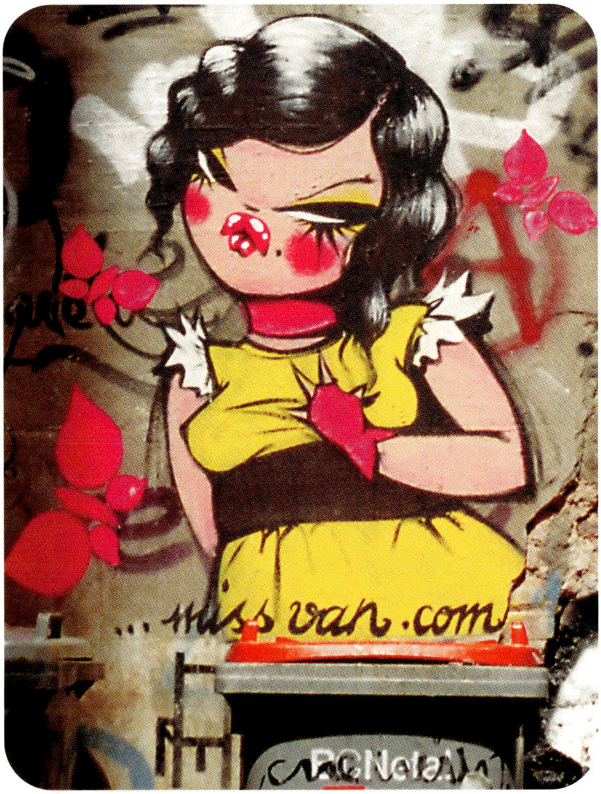
...miss van.com

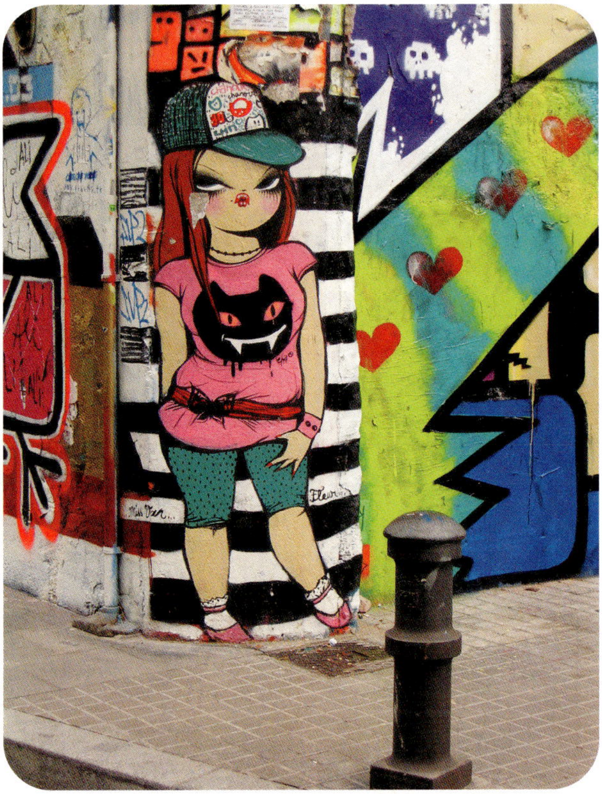

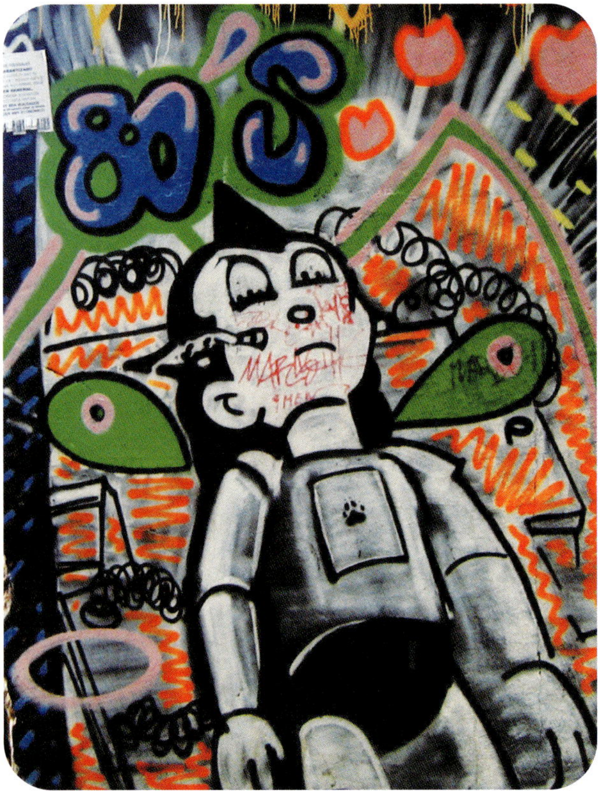
80'S

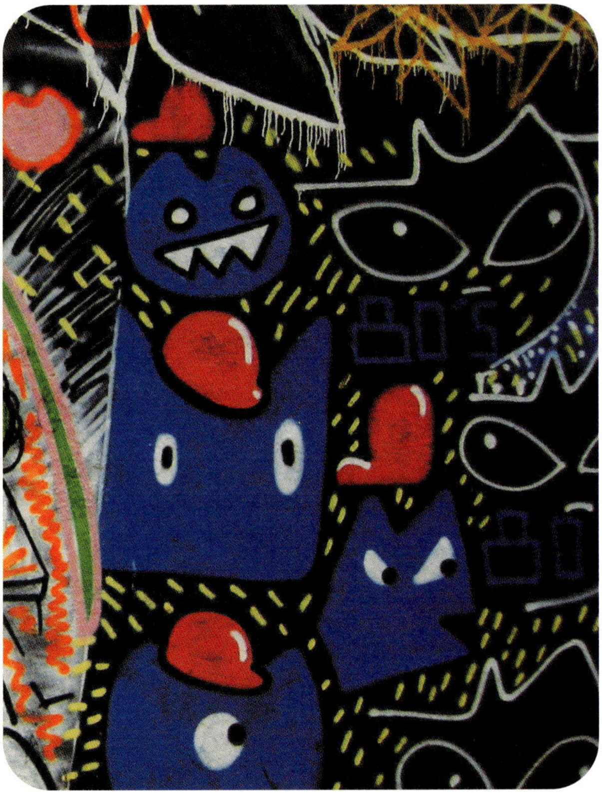

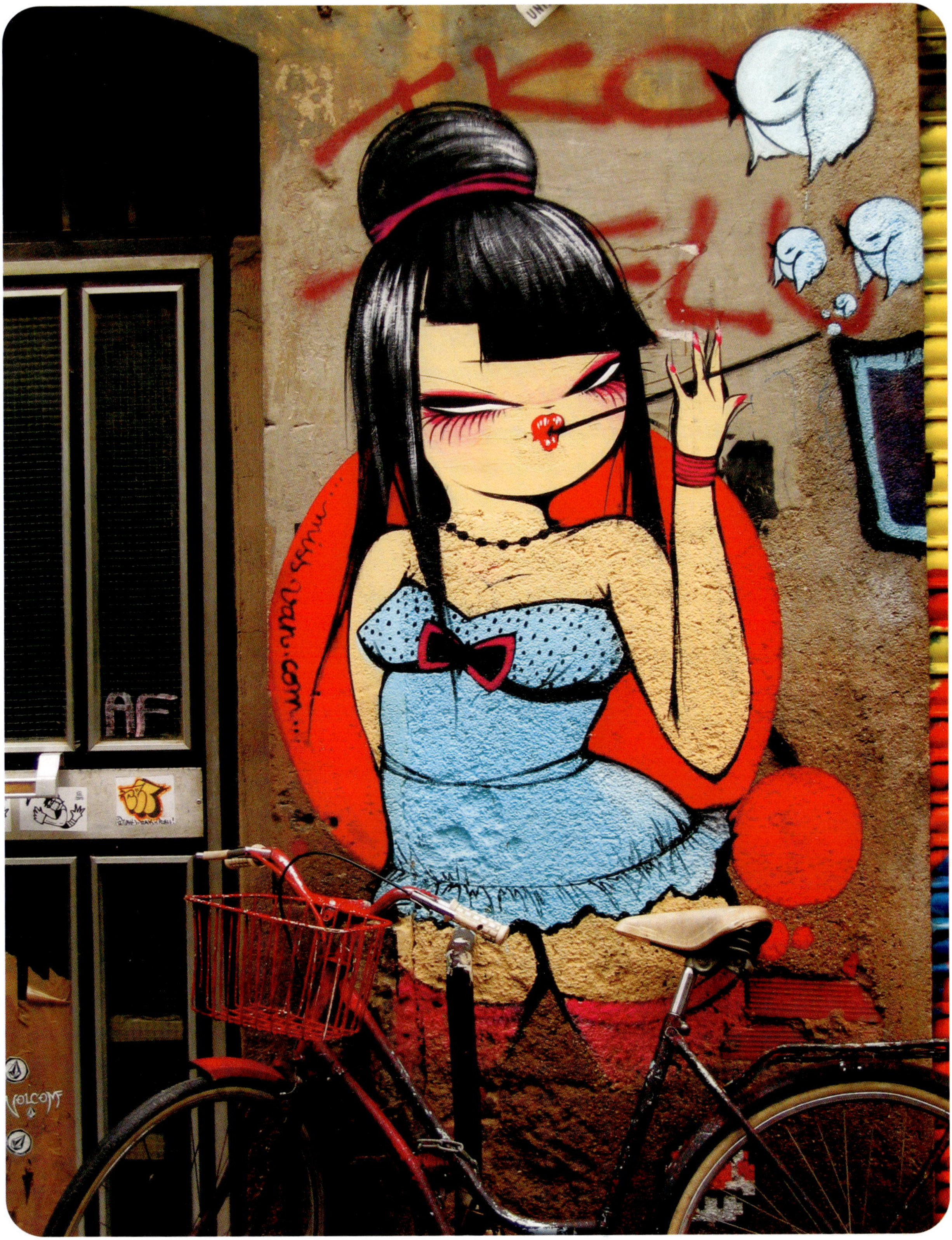
AF

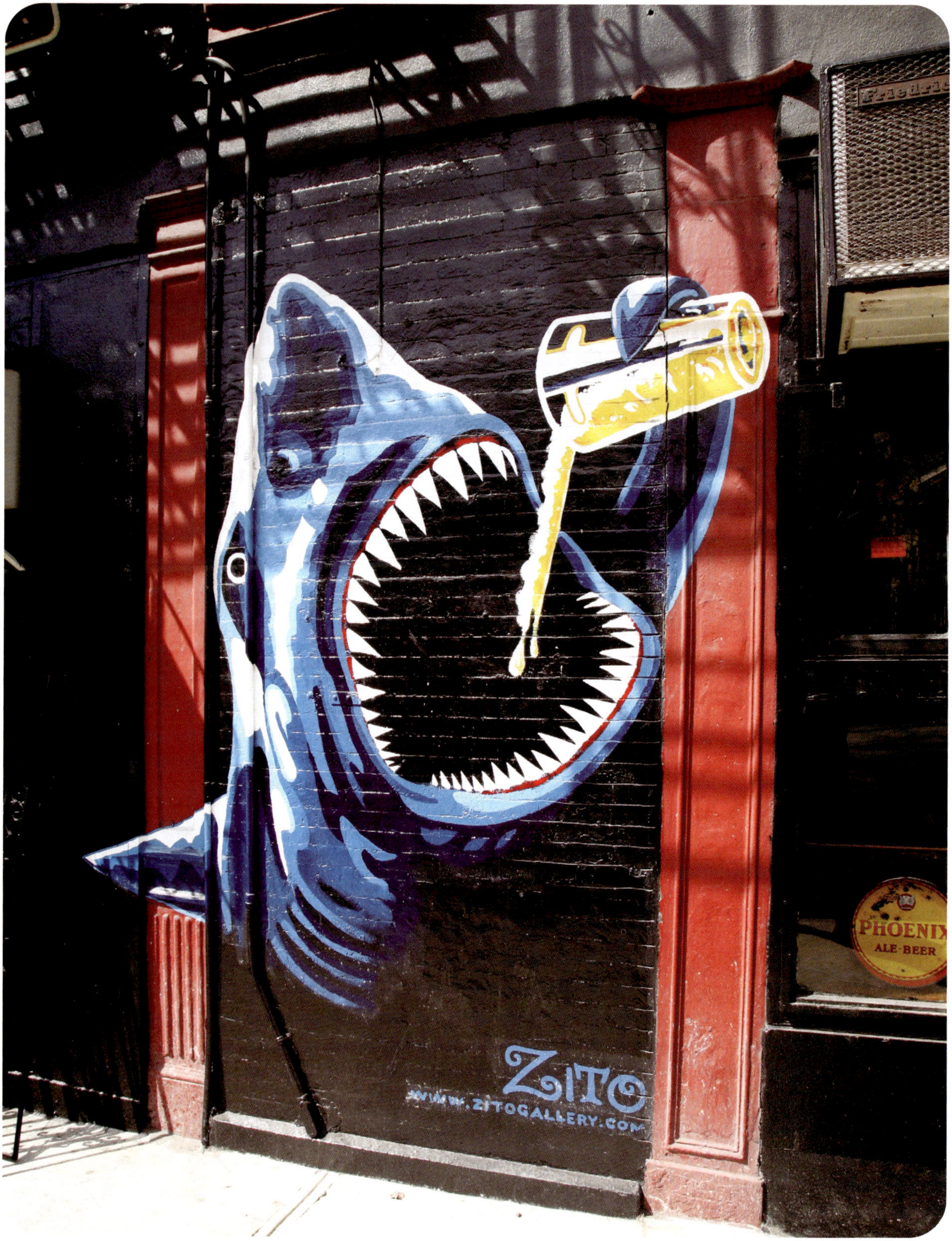
ZITO
WWW.ZITOGALLERY.COM
PHOENIX
ALE-BEER

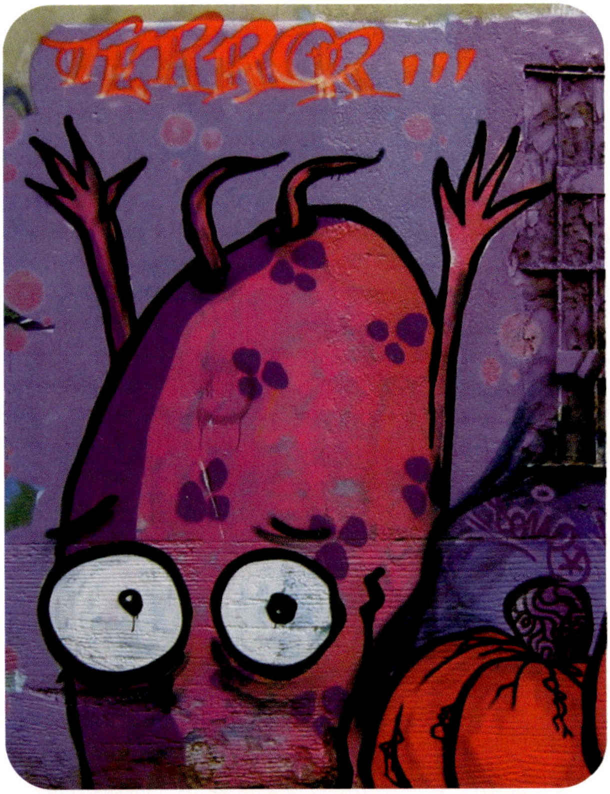
TERROR

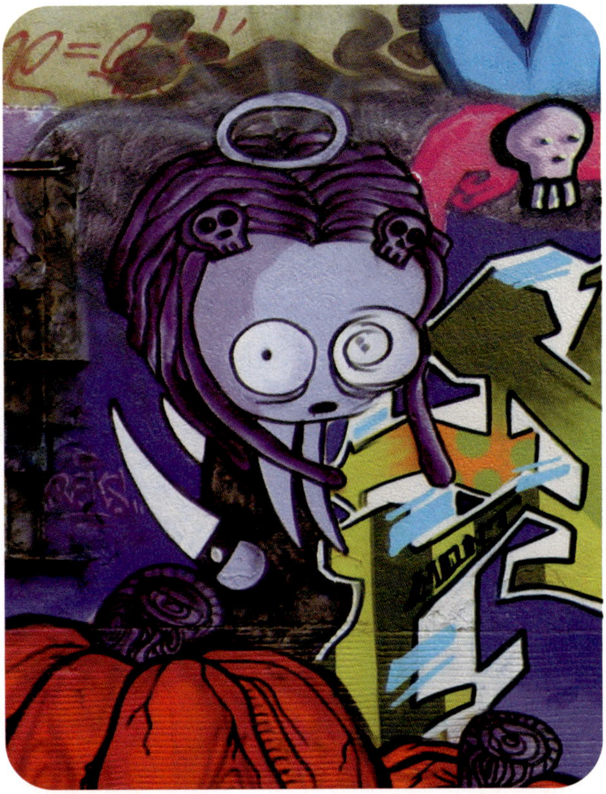

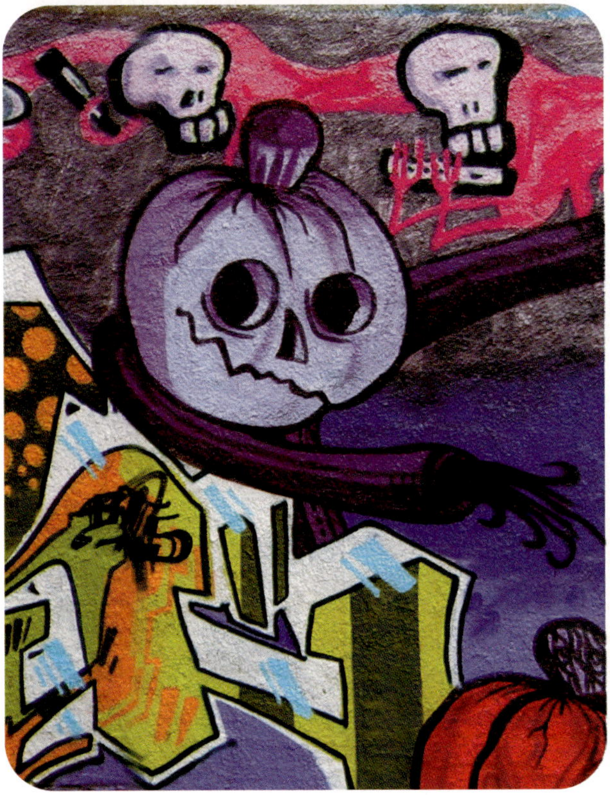

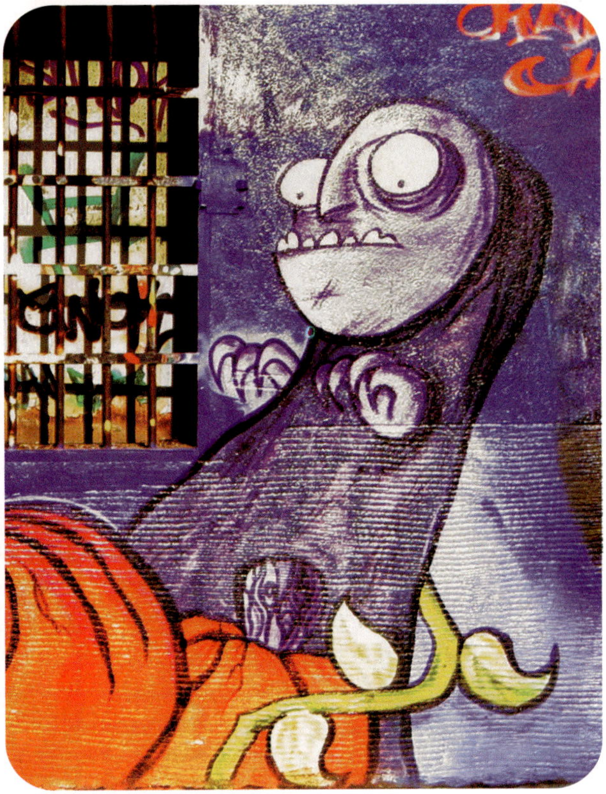

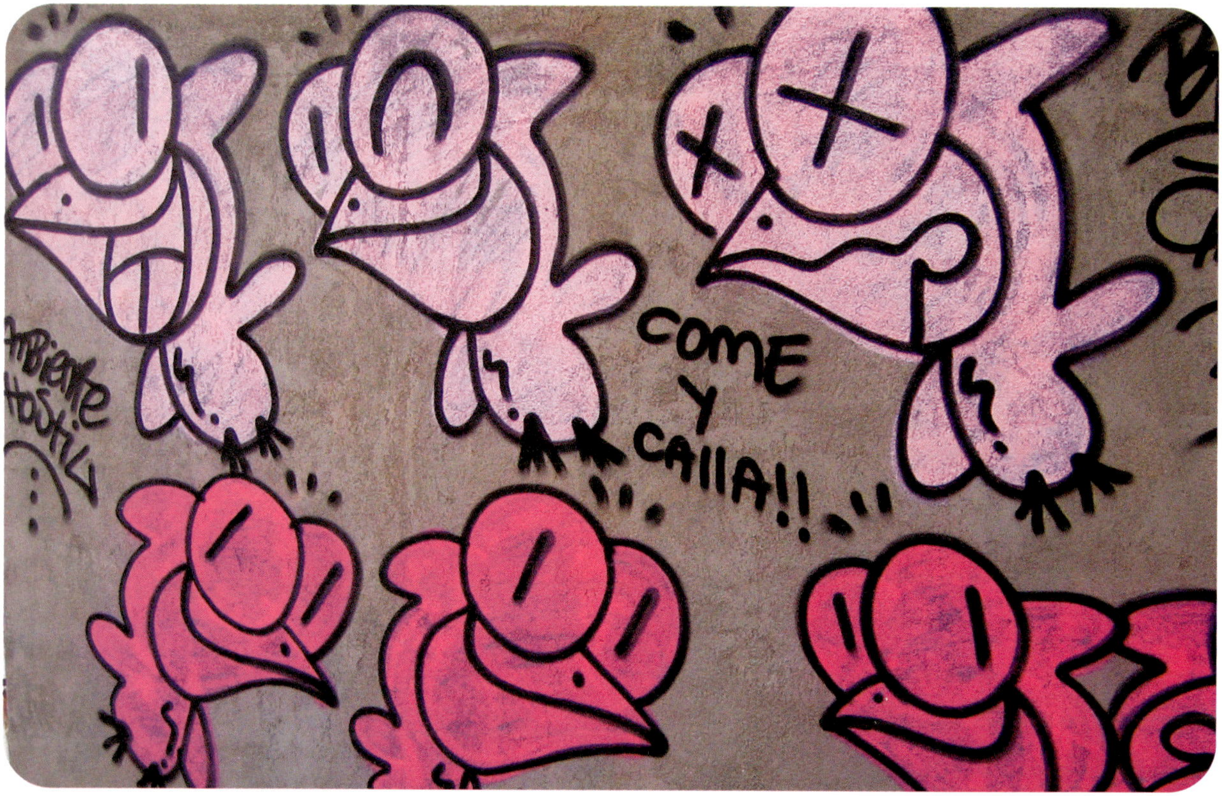
COME
Y
CALLA!!

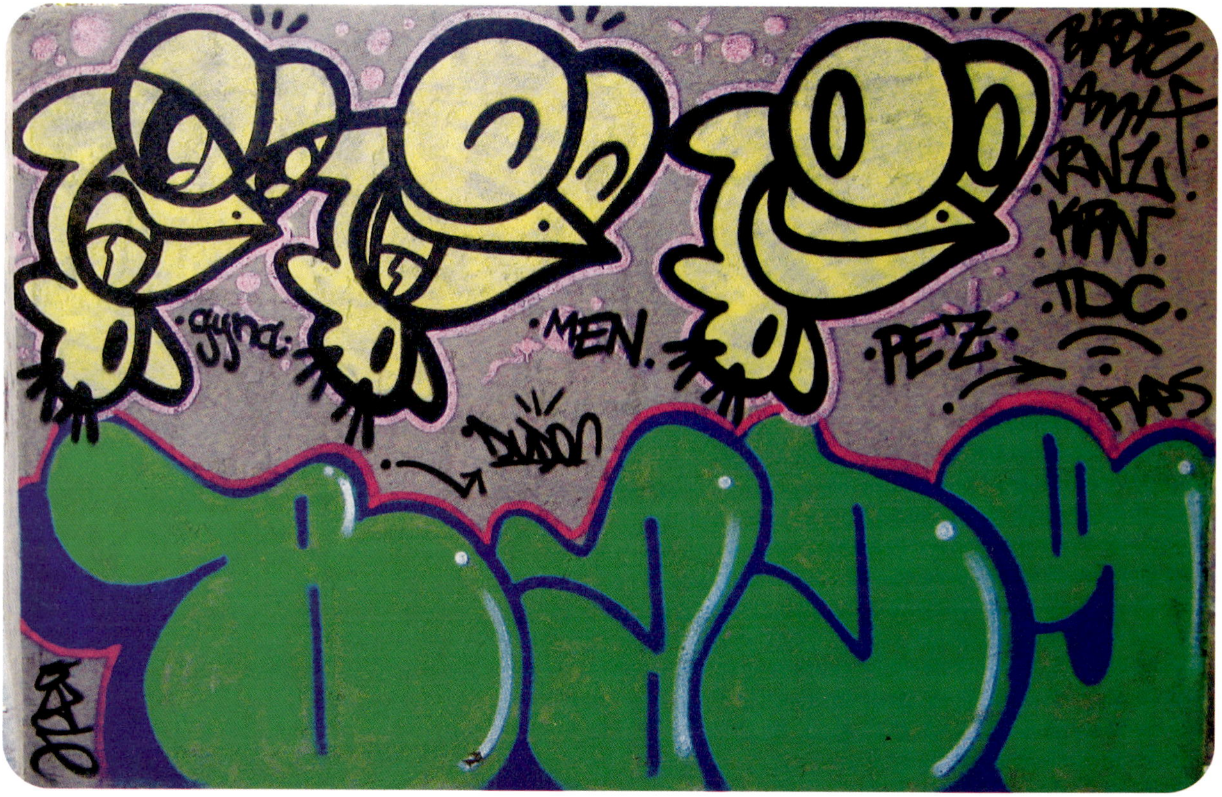
MEN.
PEZ
TDC

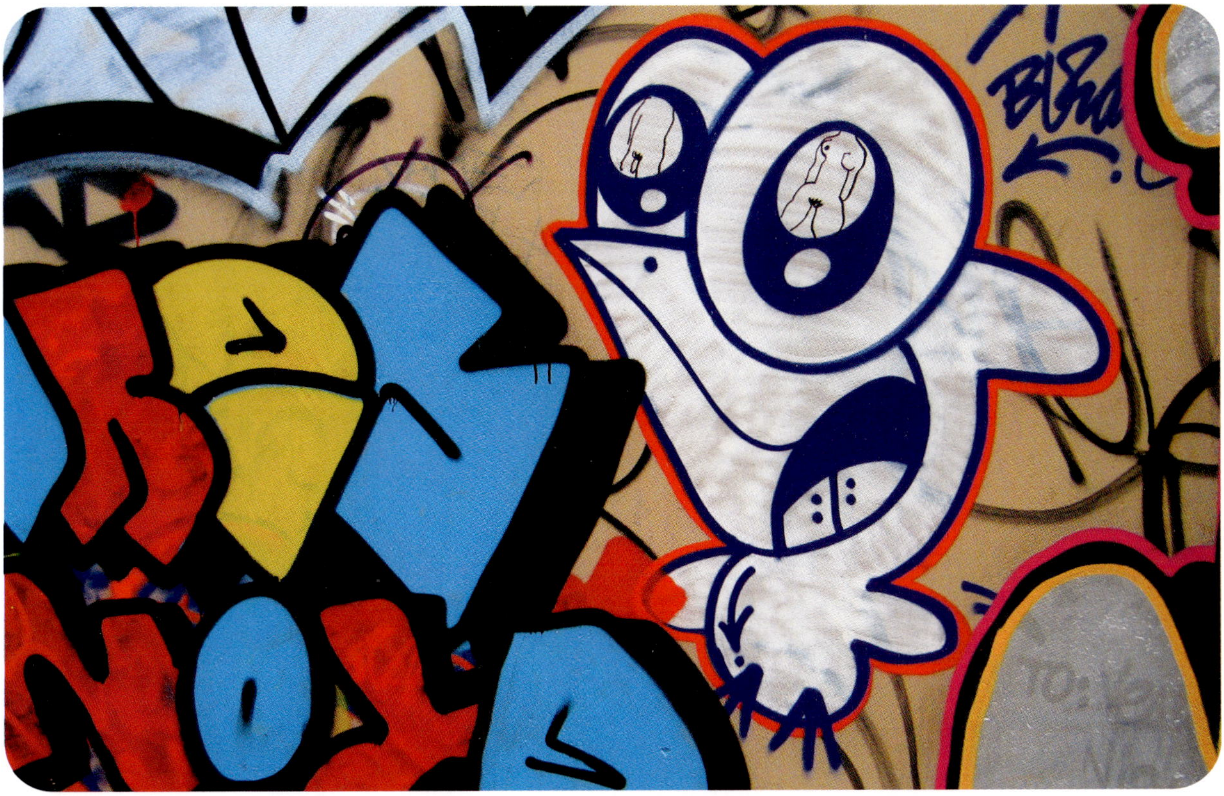

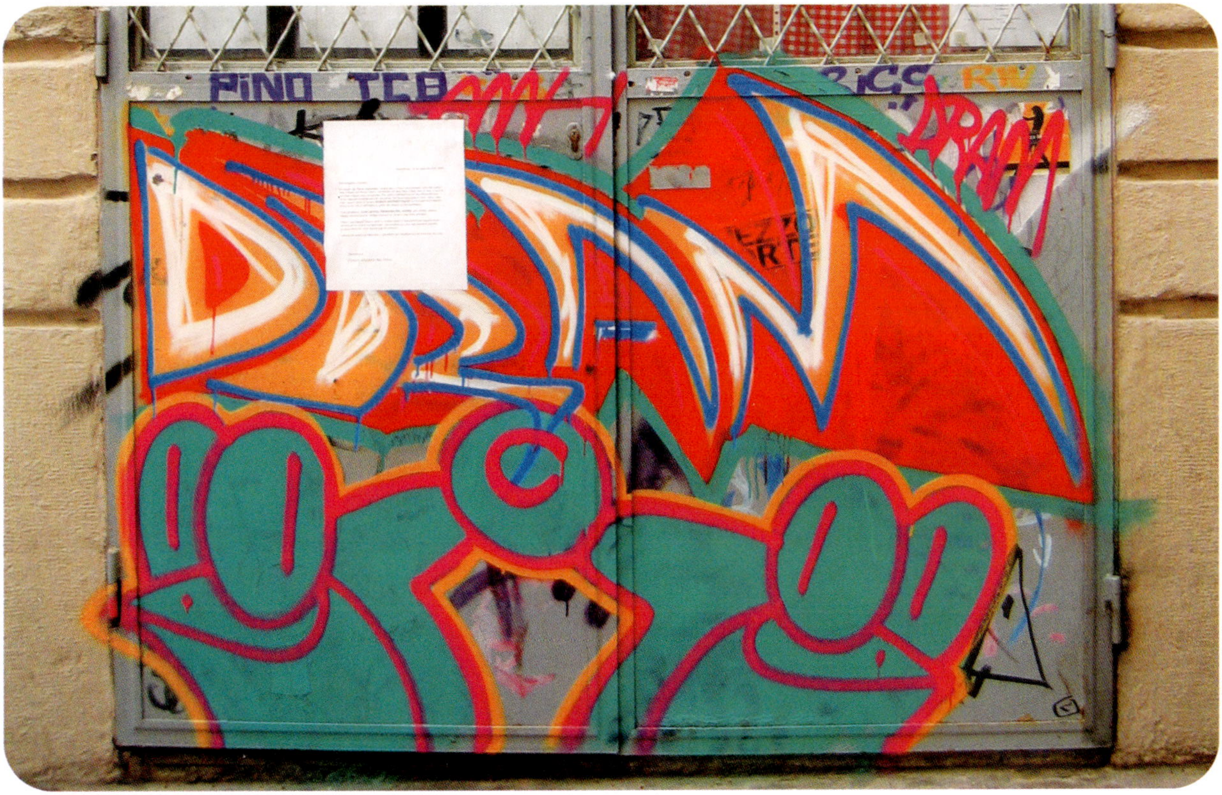
PINO
DRAM

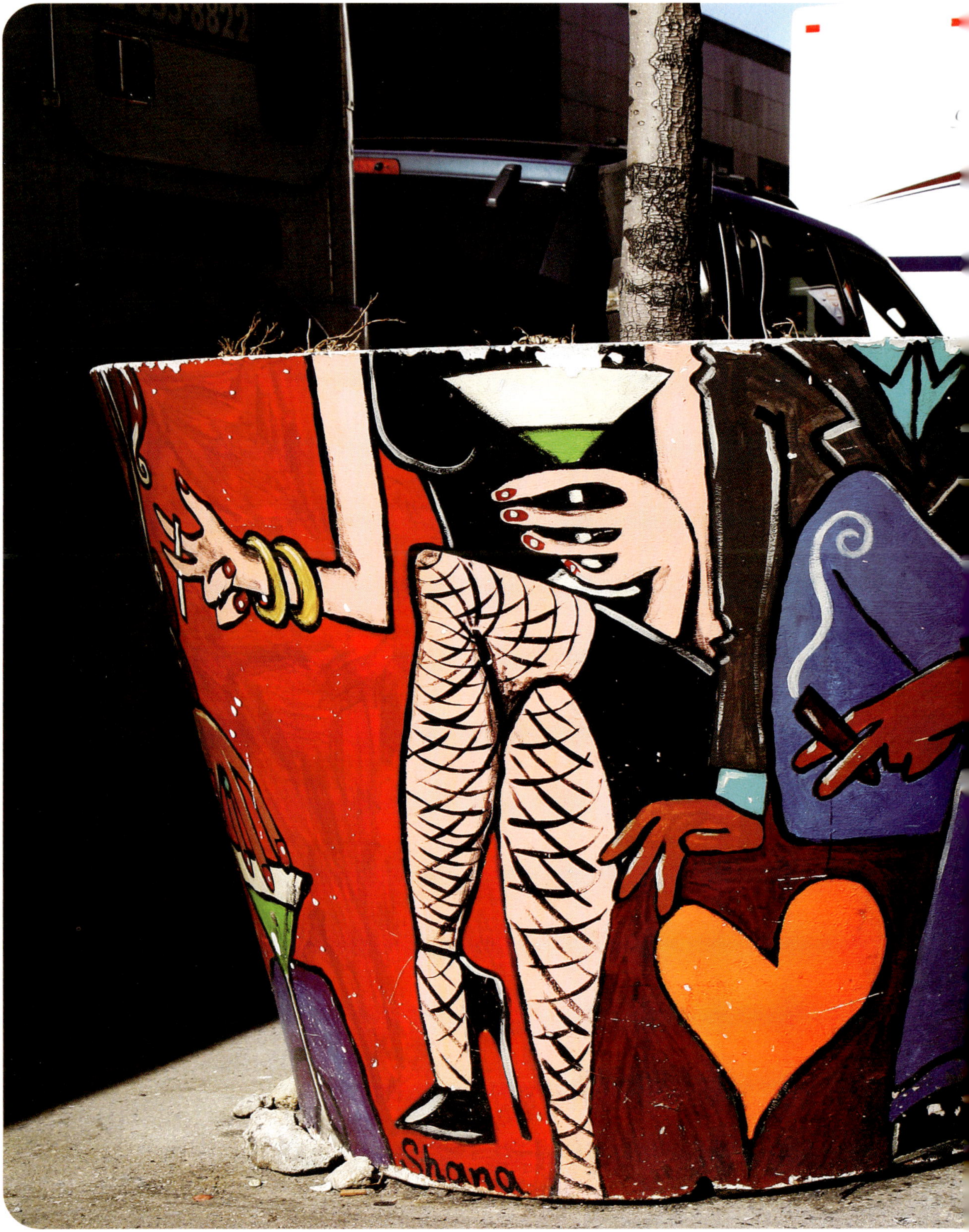
Shana

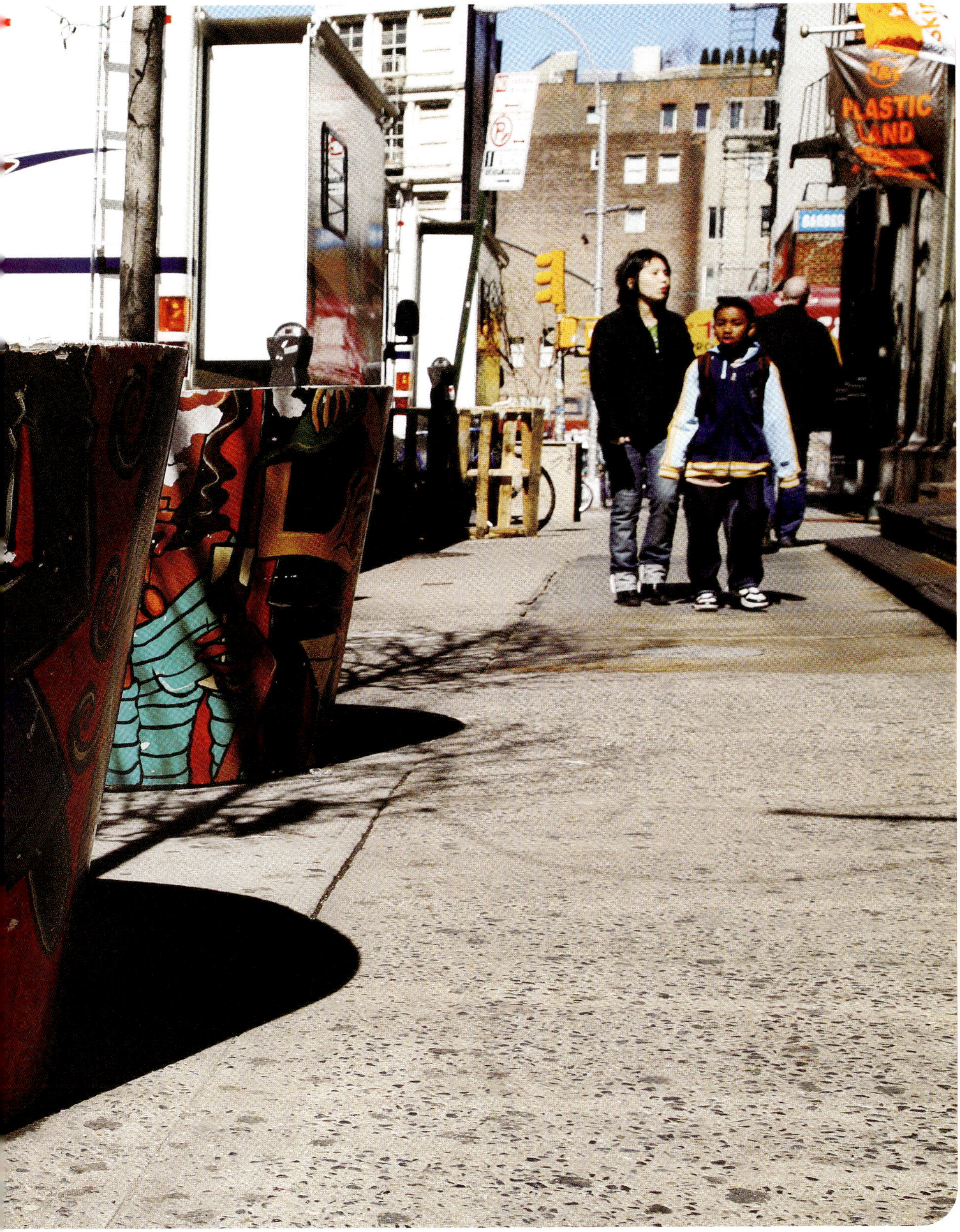
PLASTIC
LAND
BARBER

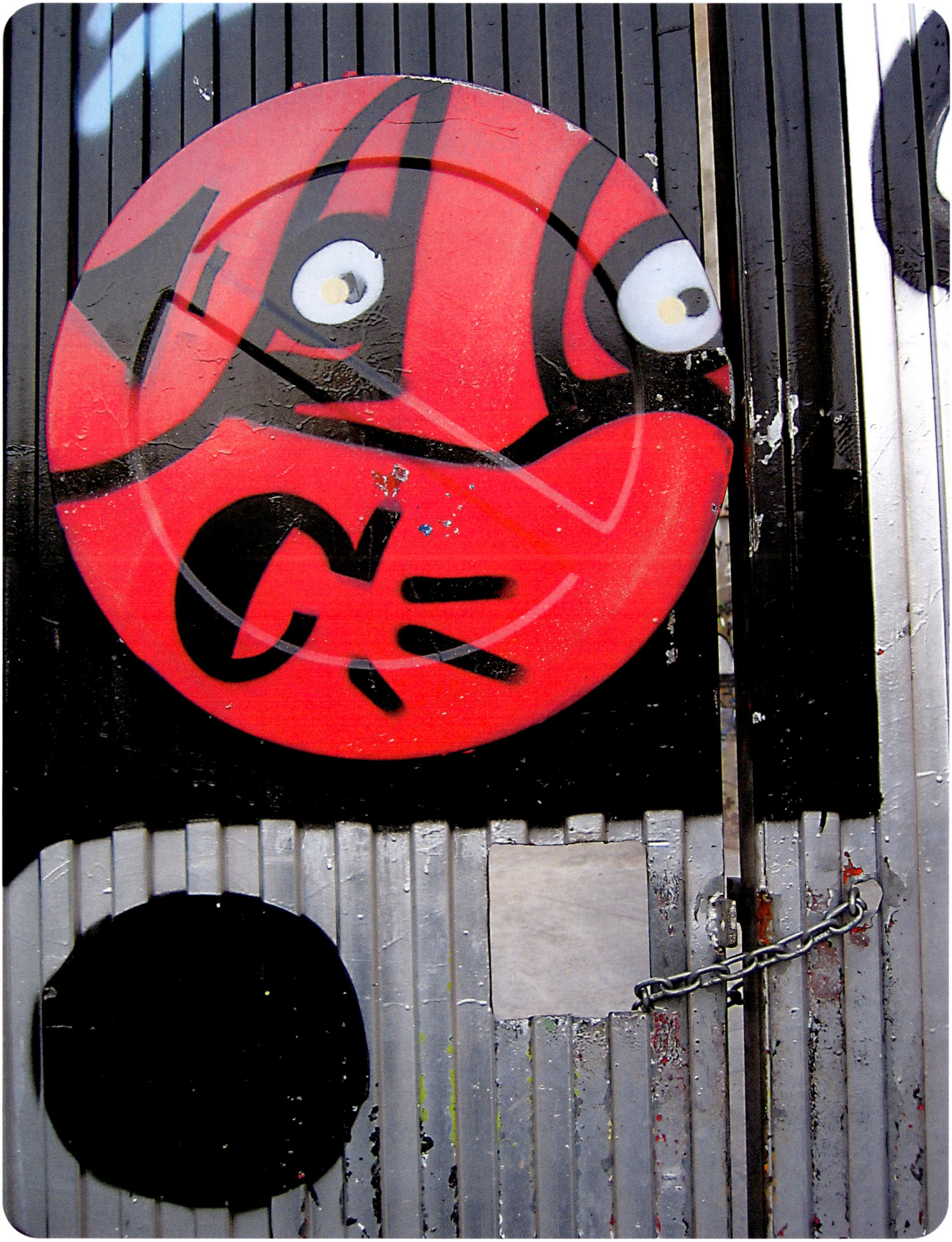

barcelona

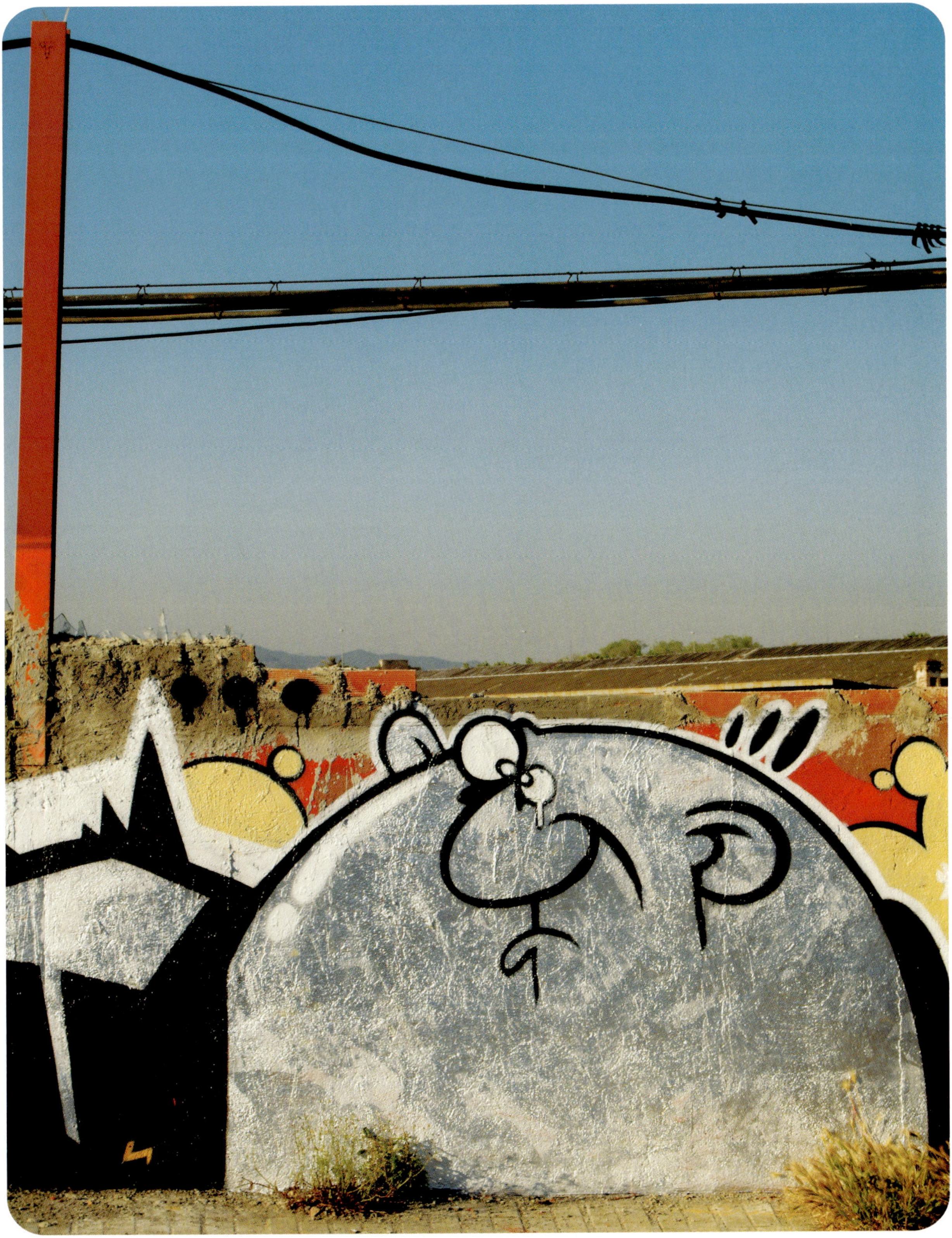

barcelona

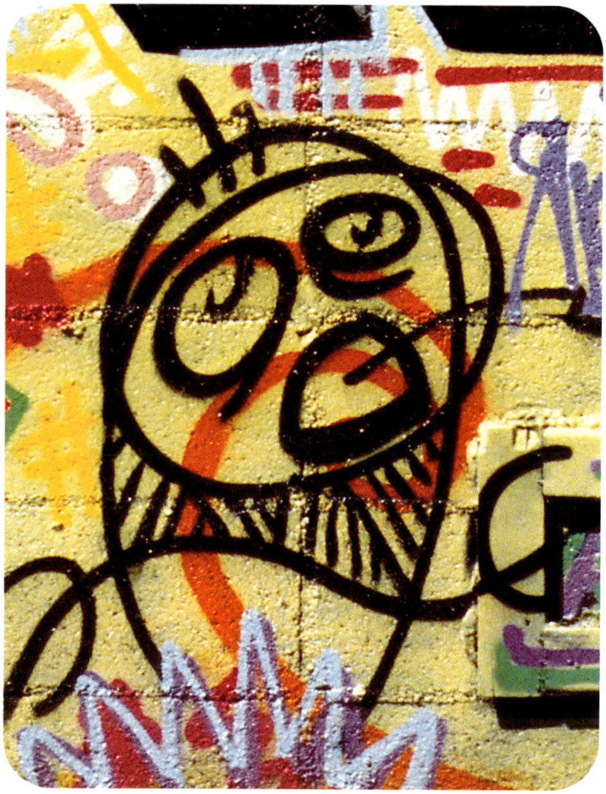

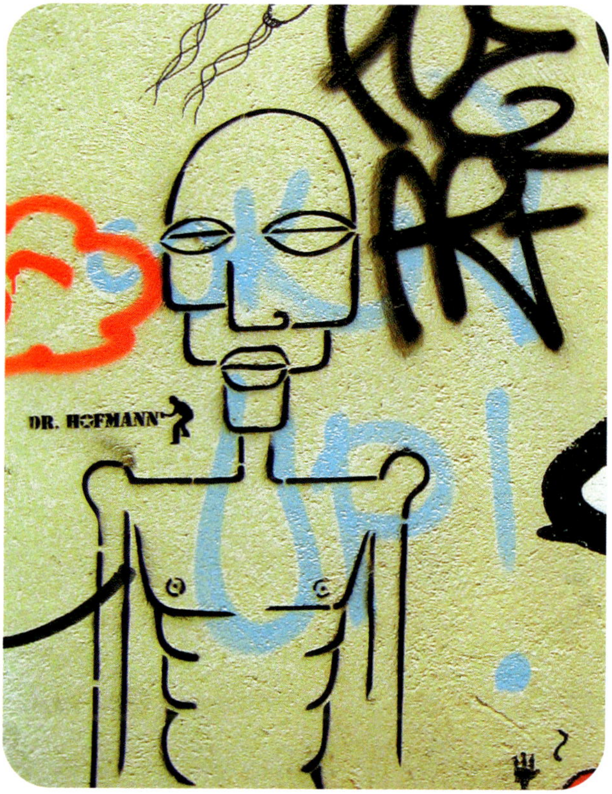
DR. HOFMANN

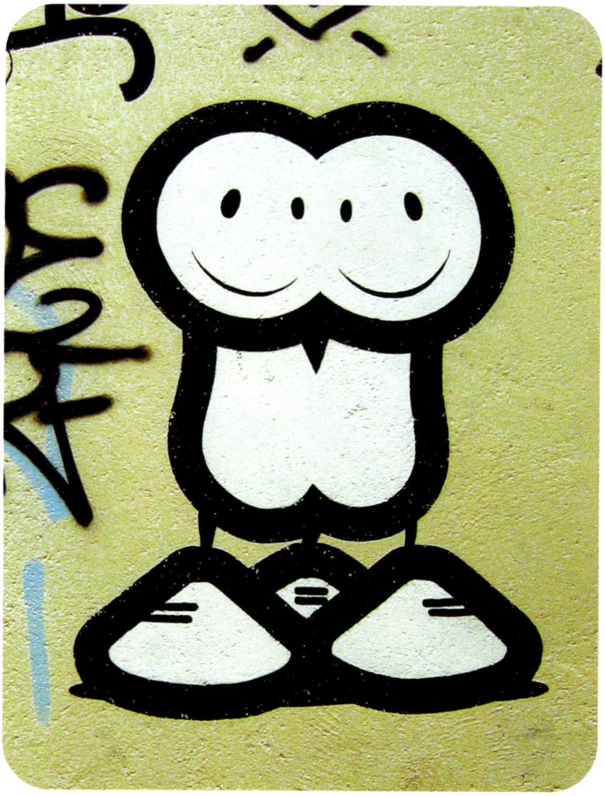

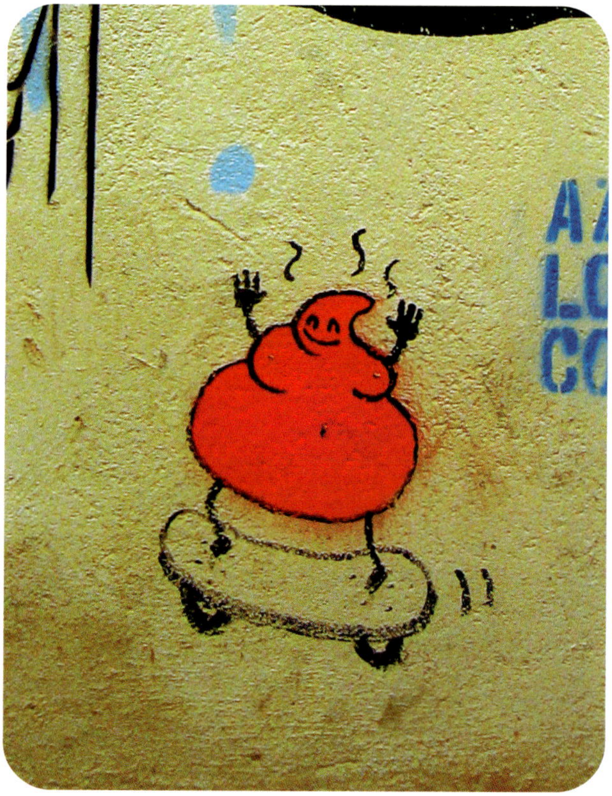

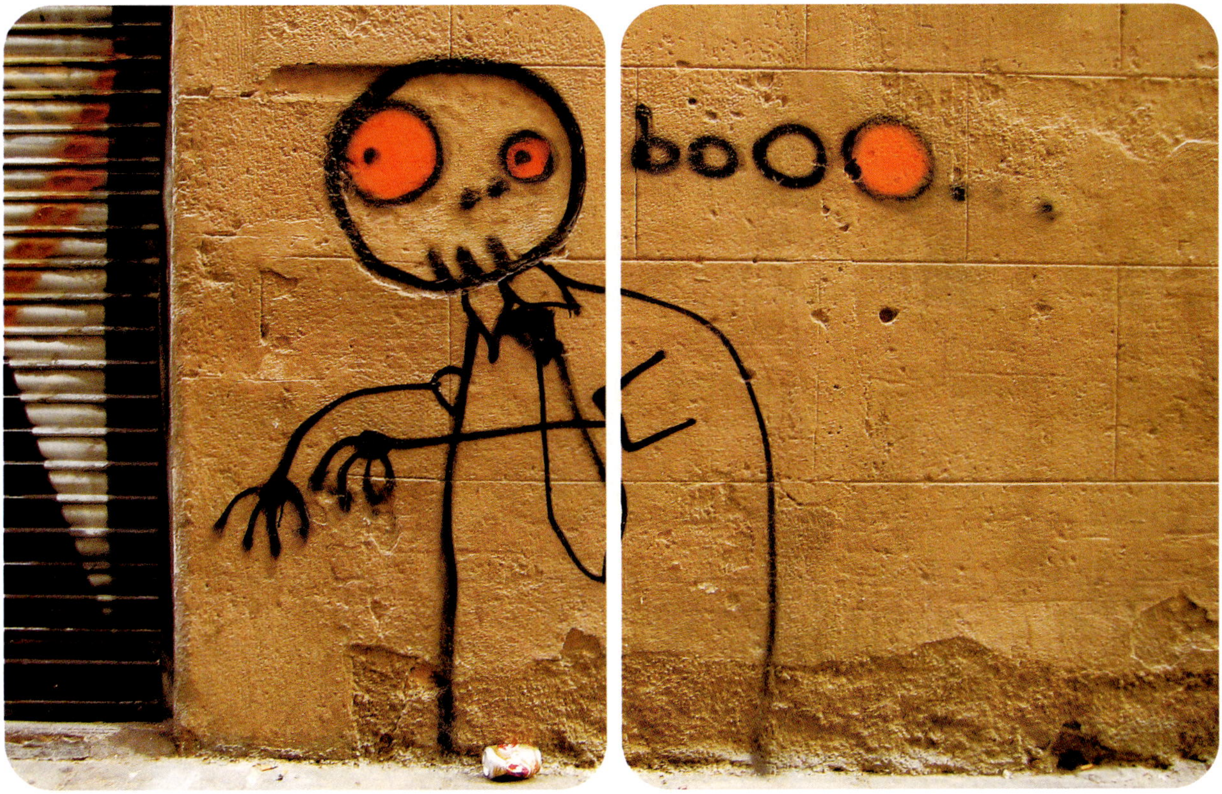

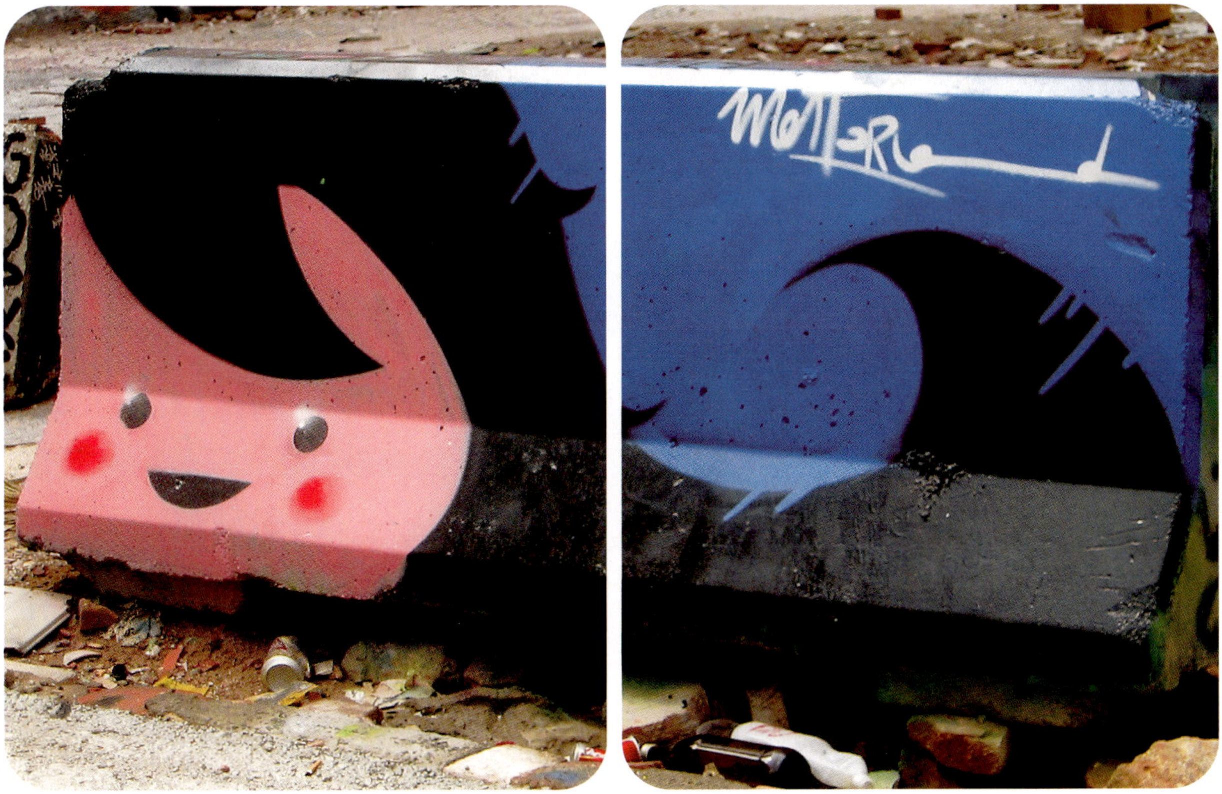

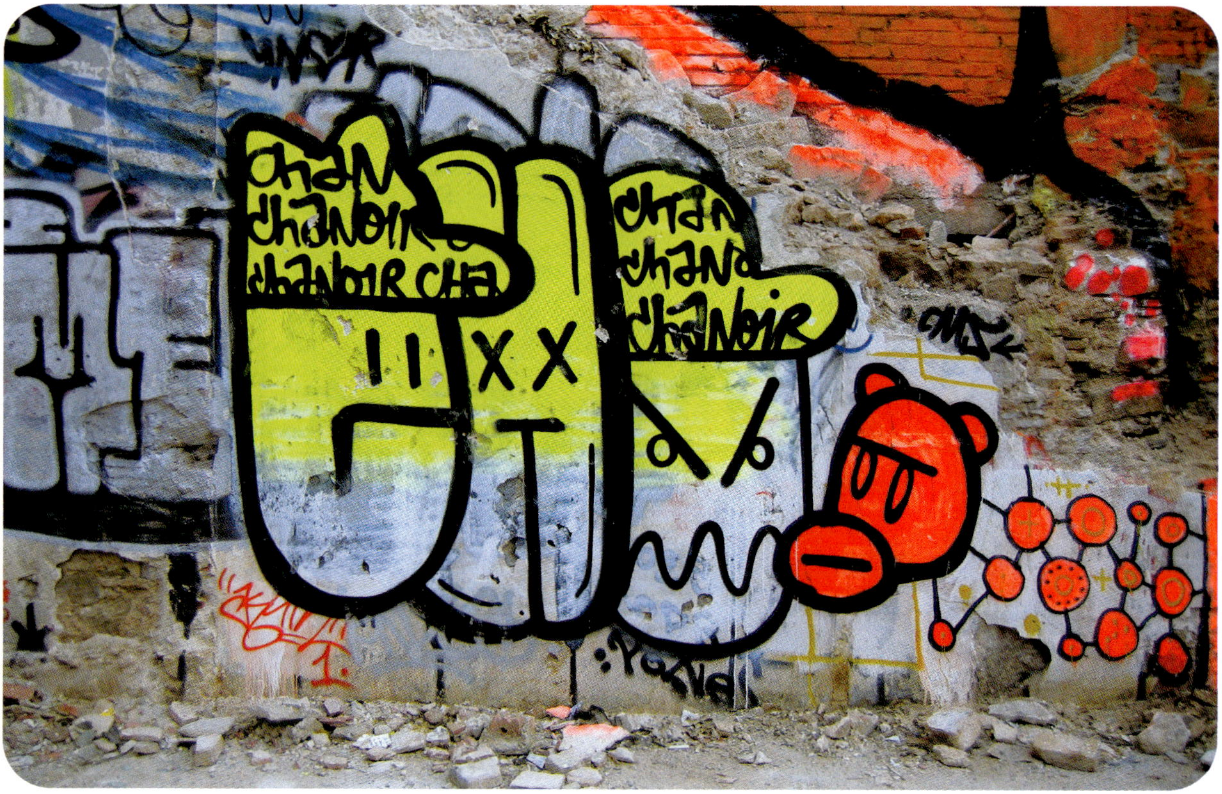
chan
chanoir
chanoir cha
chan
chana
chanoir

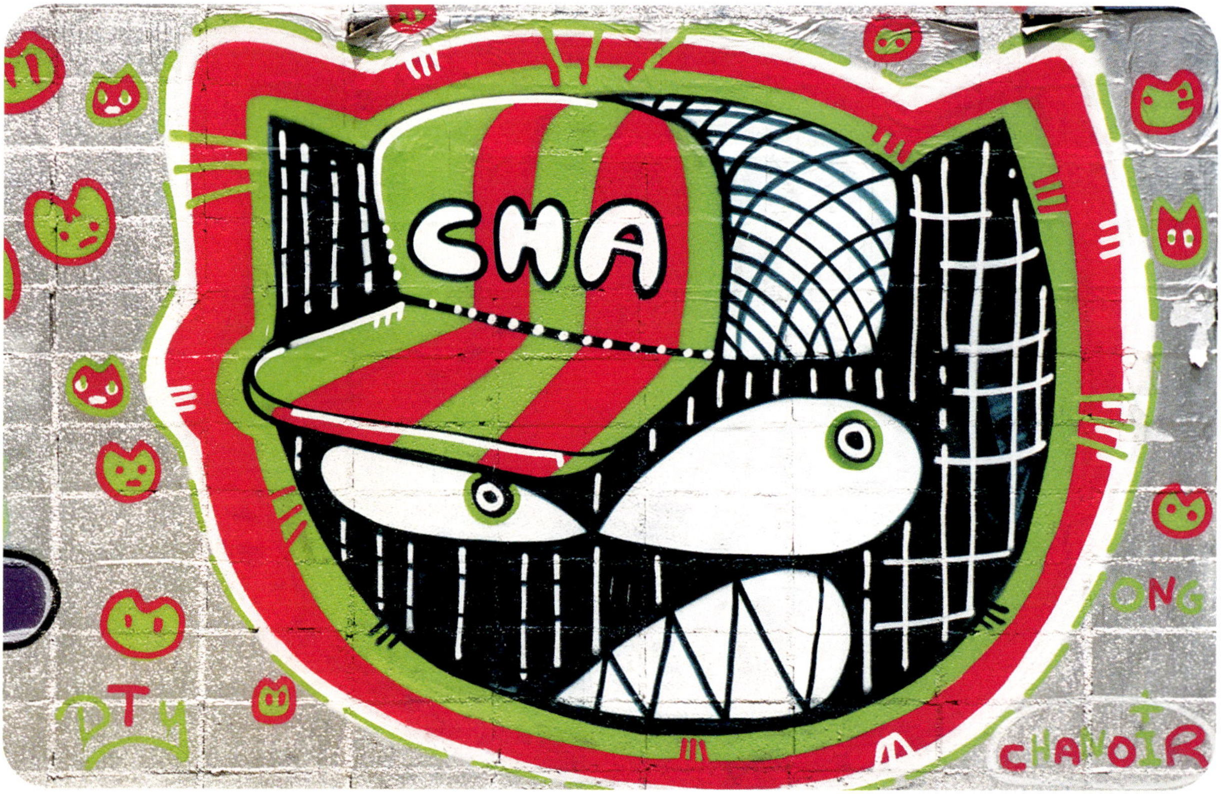
CHA
ONG
DTY
CHANOIR

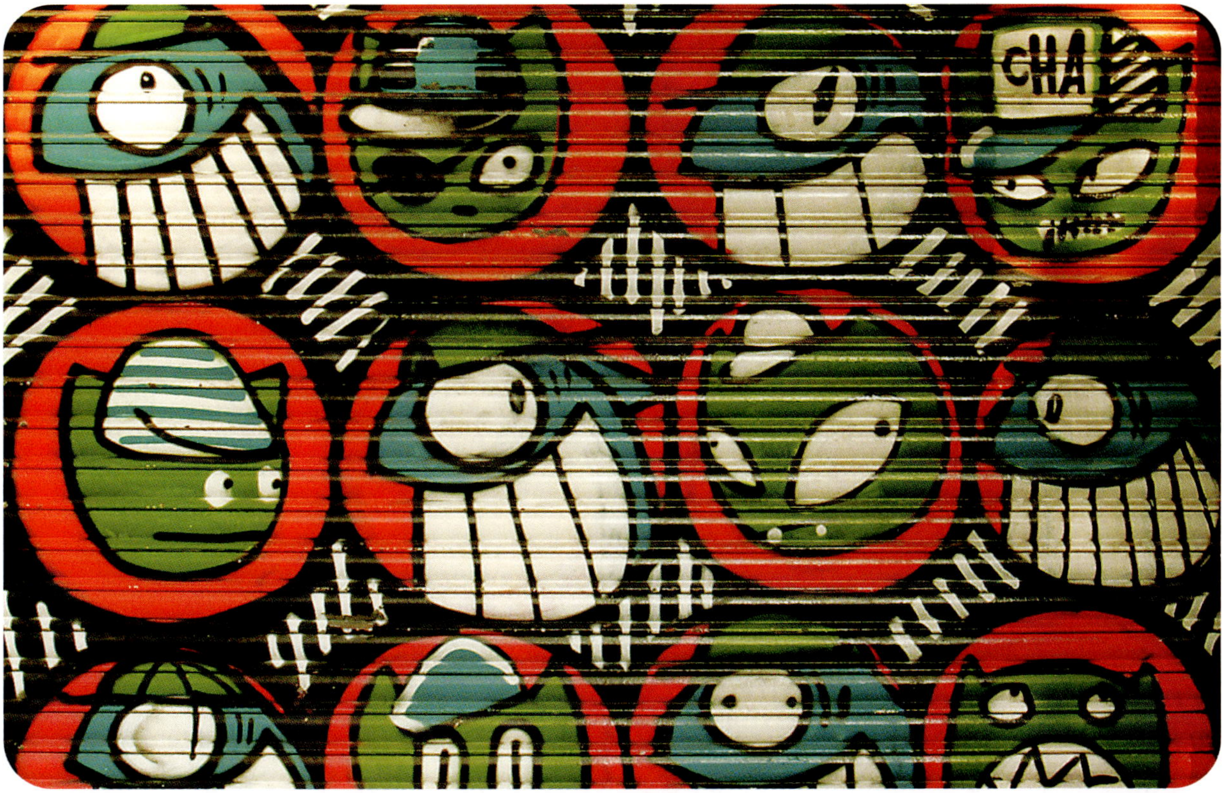
CHA

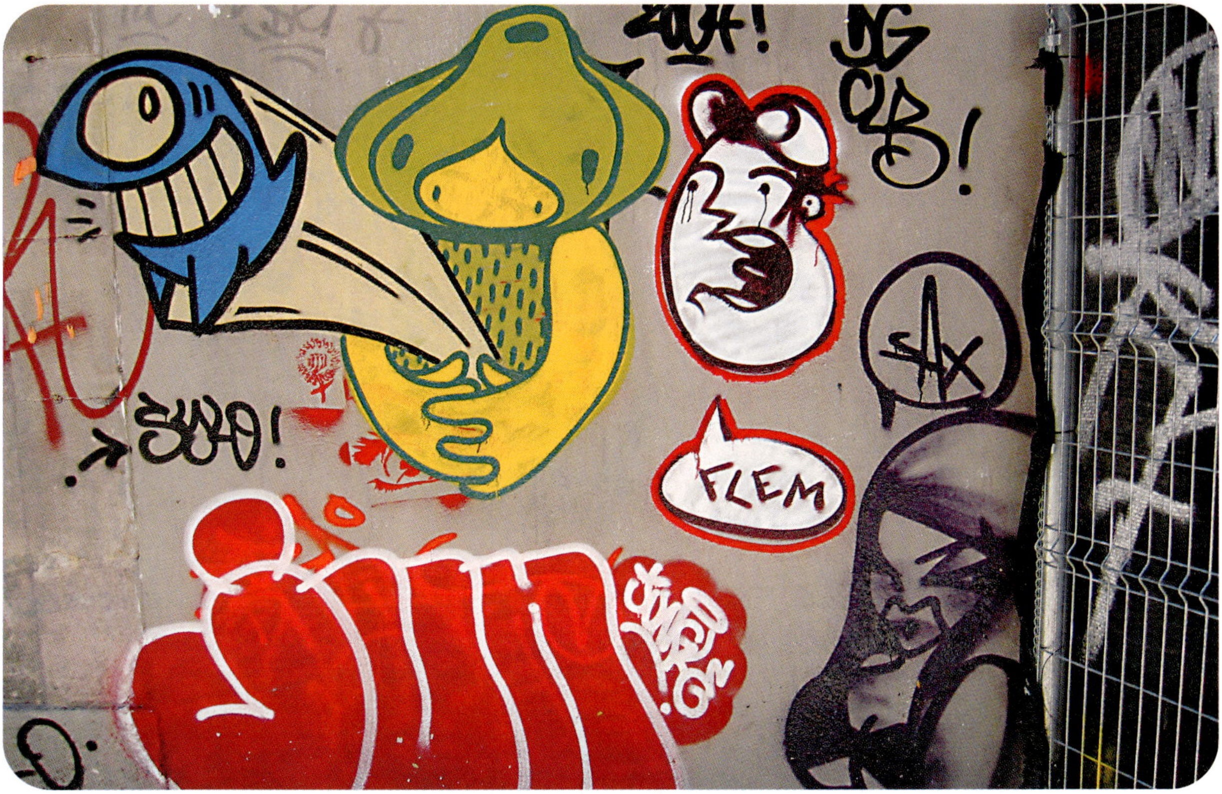
FLEM

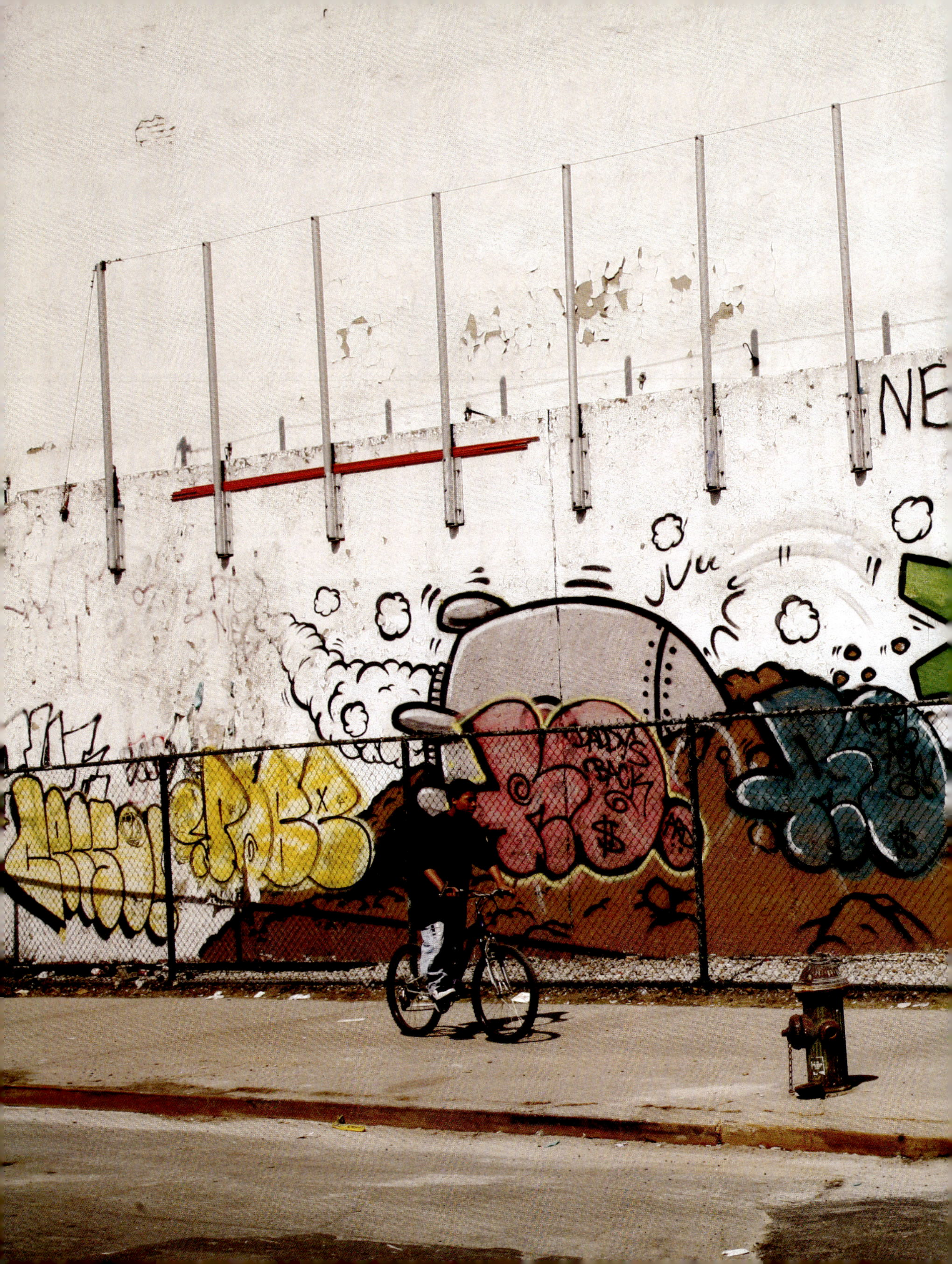
NE

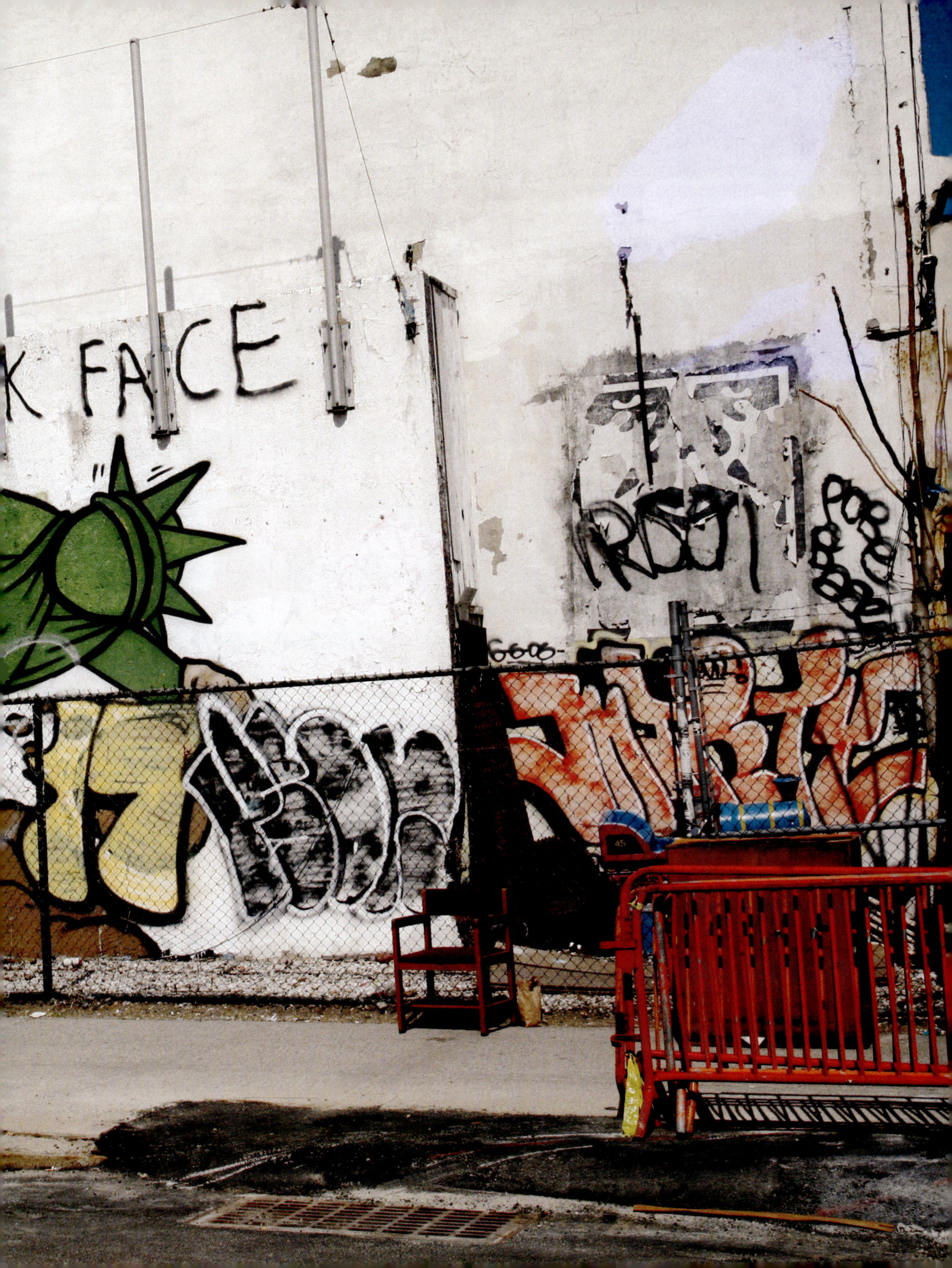
K FACE

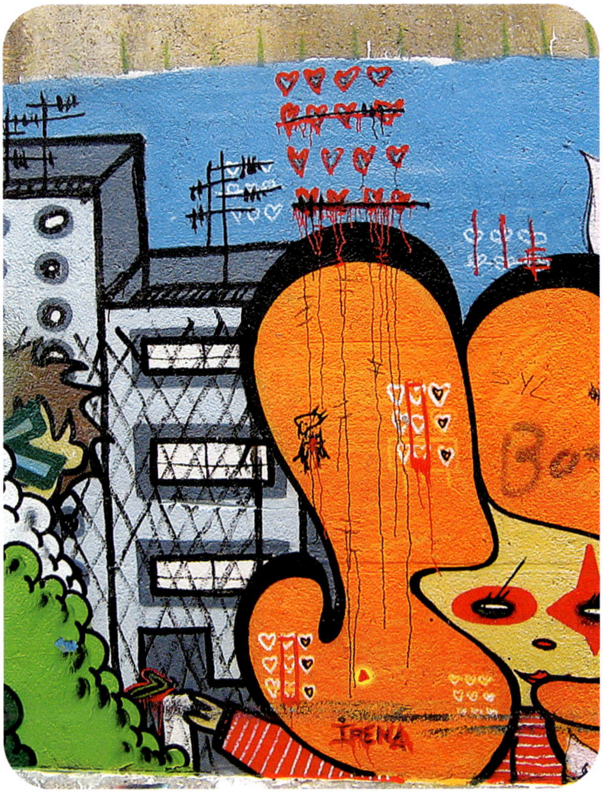
IRENA

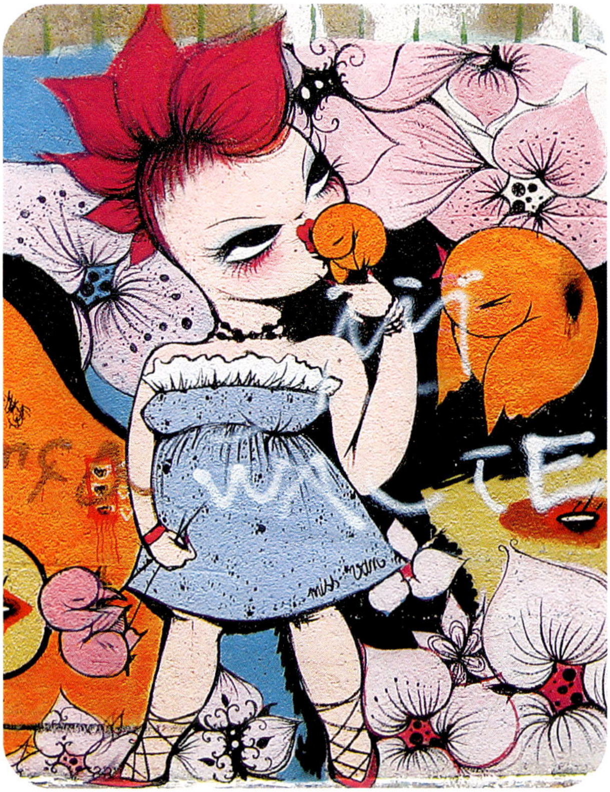

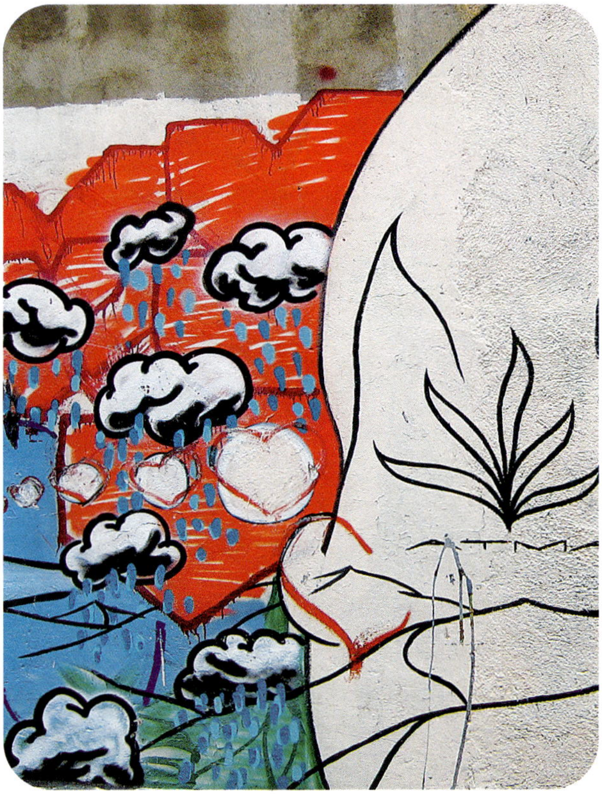

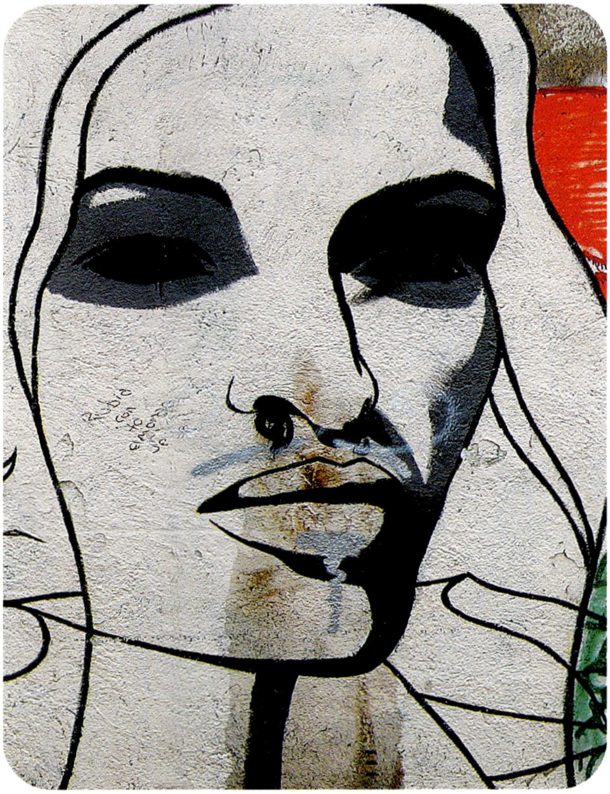

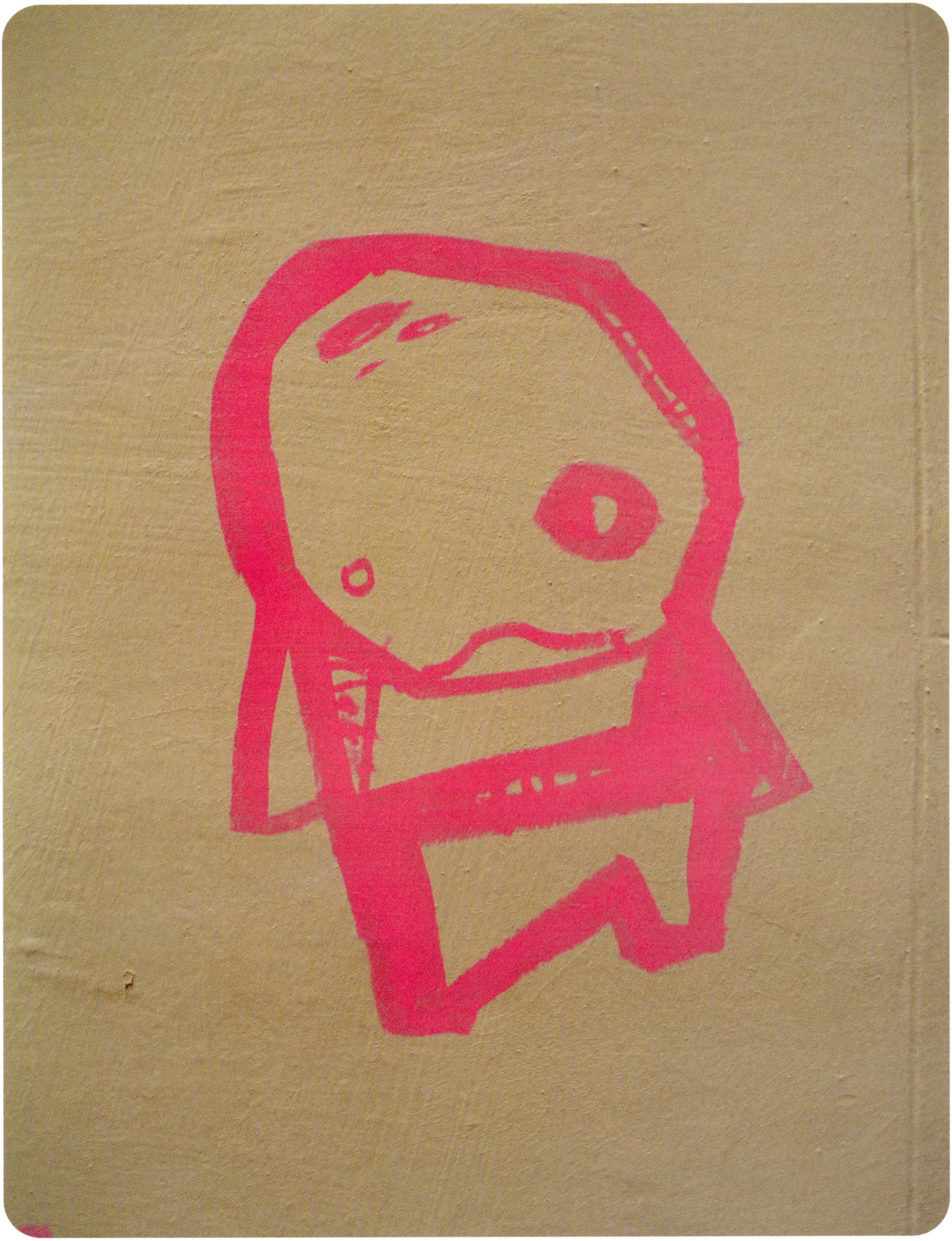

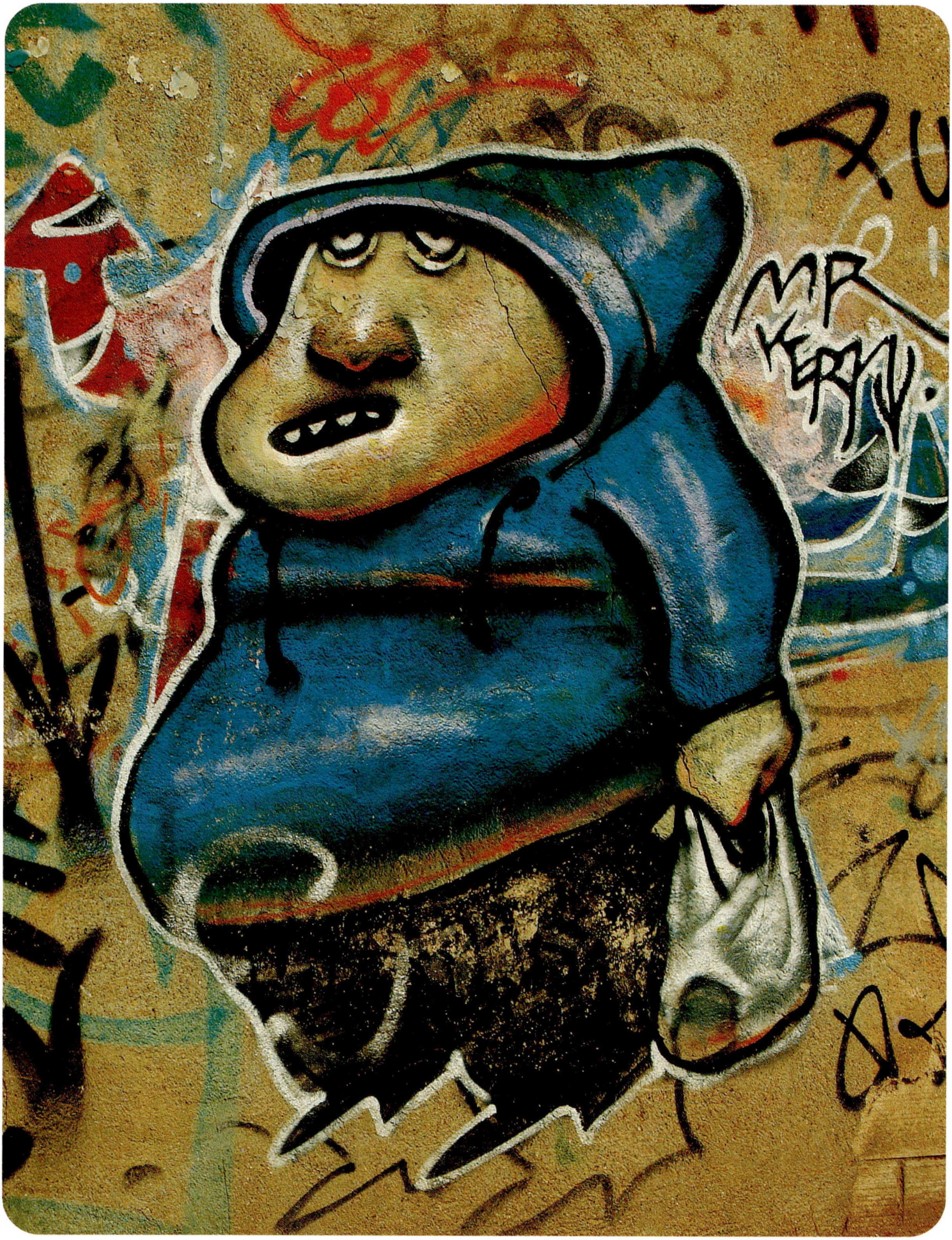

barcelona

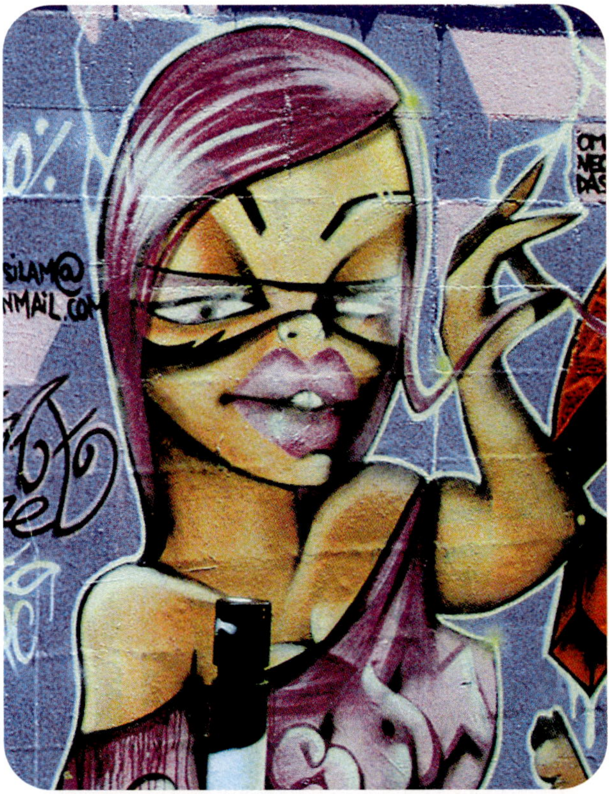

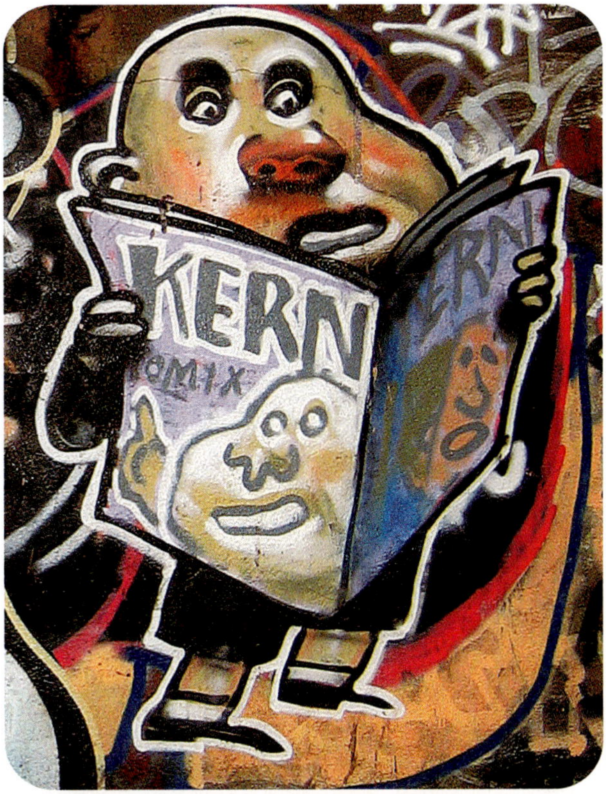
KERN

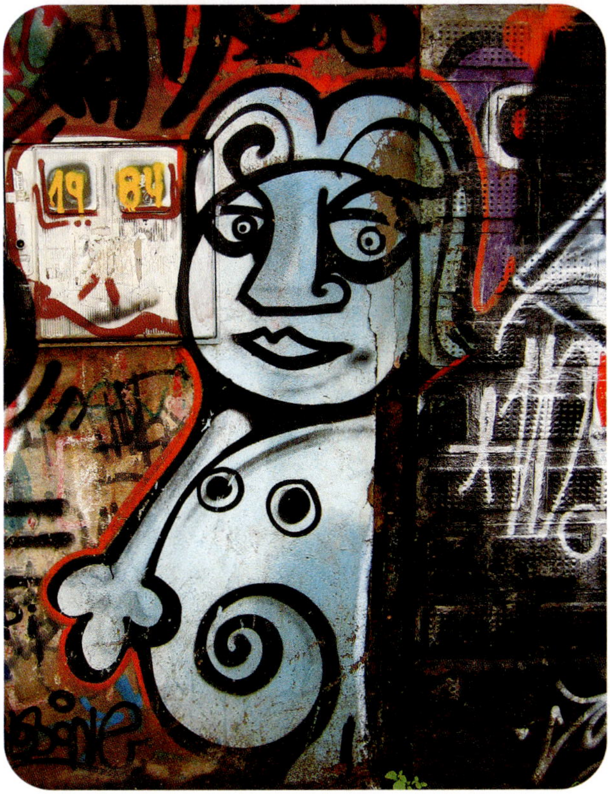
19 84

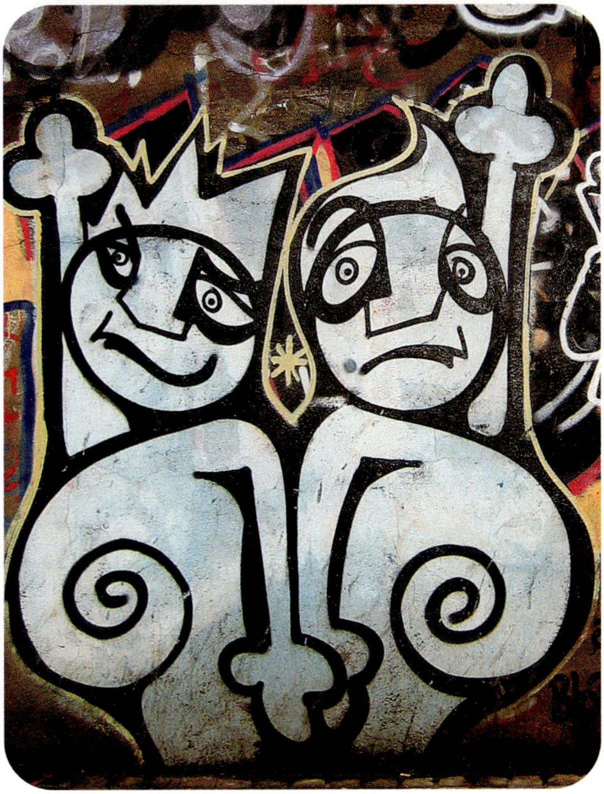

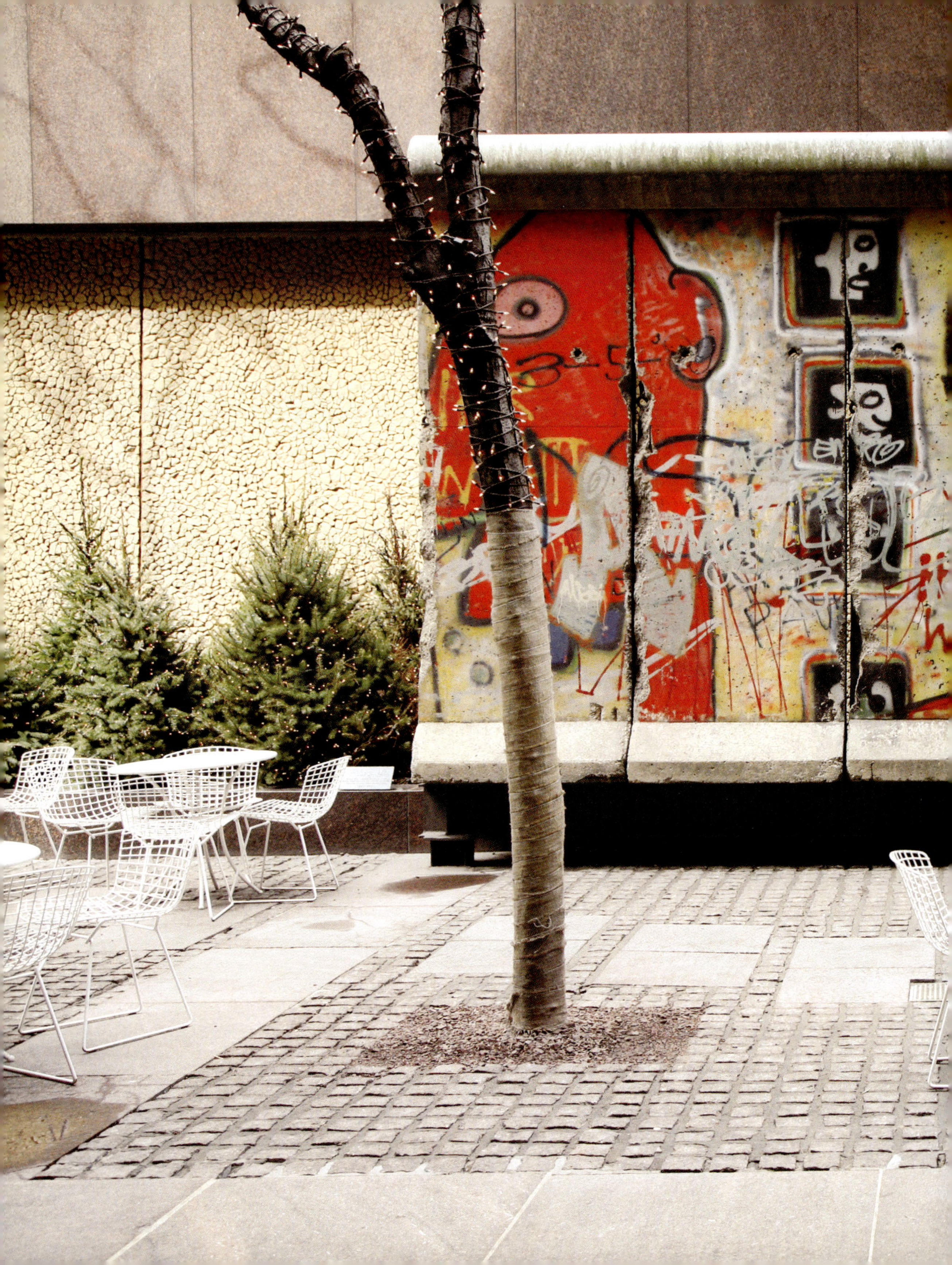

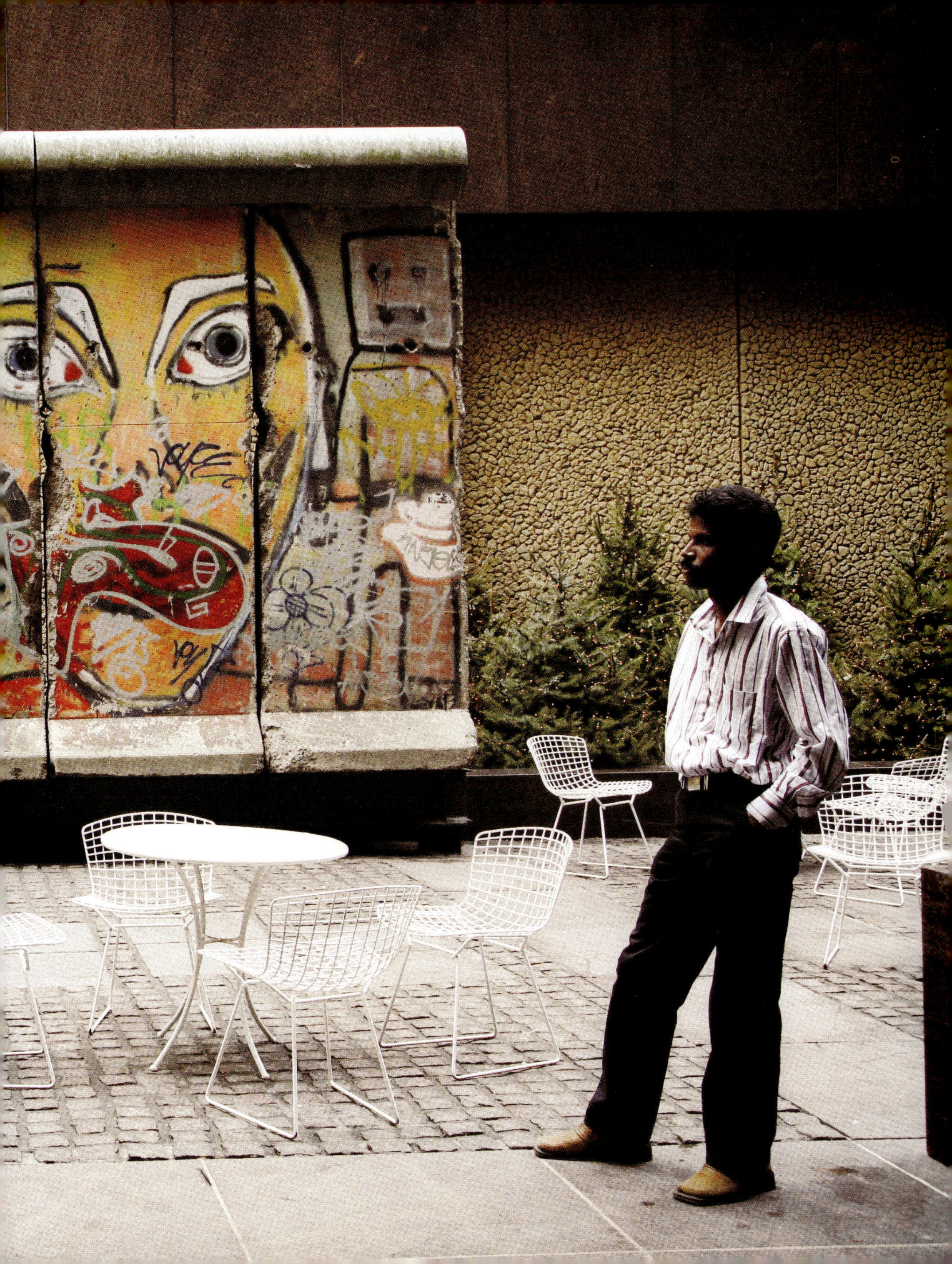

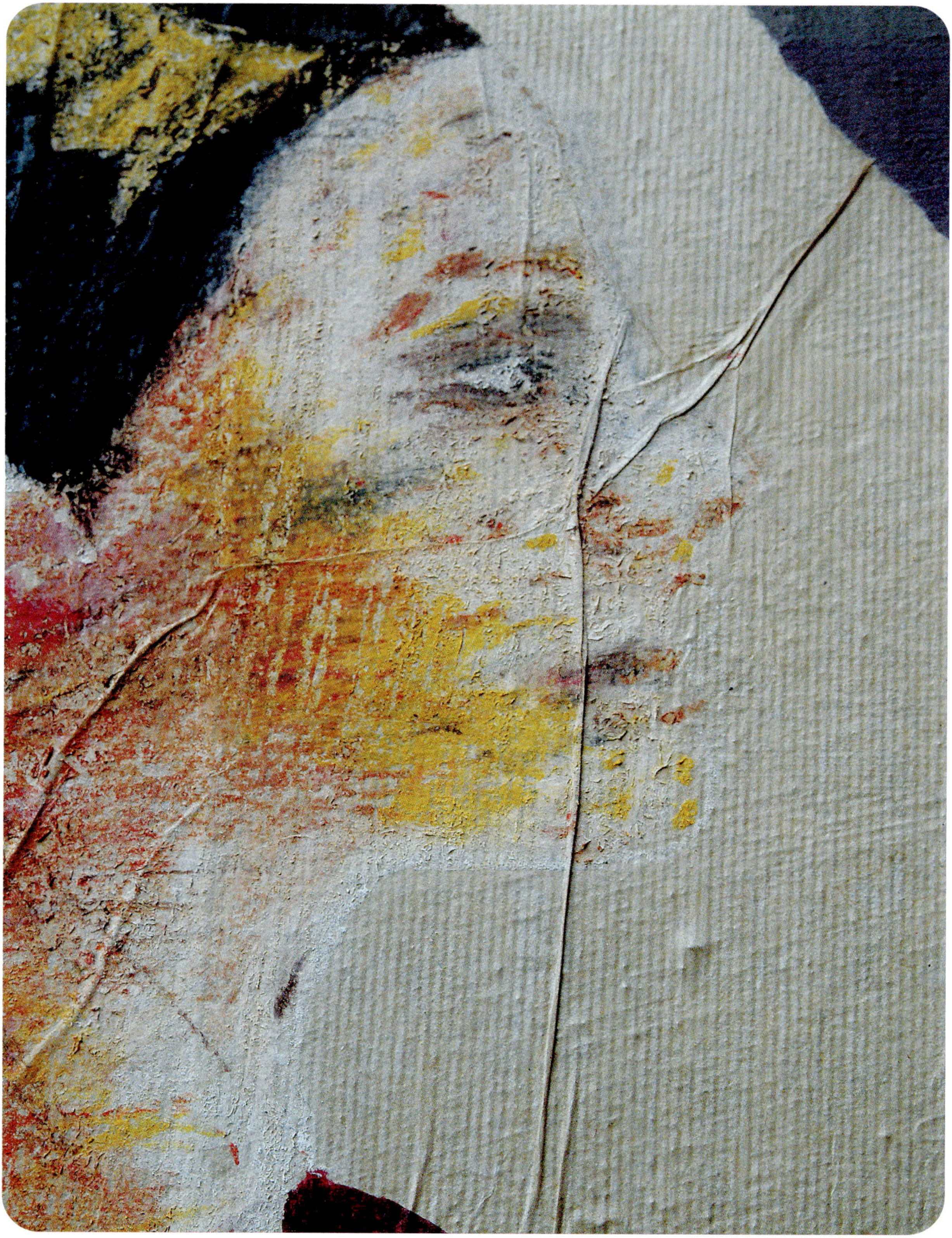

barcelona

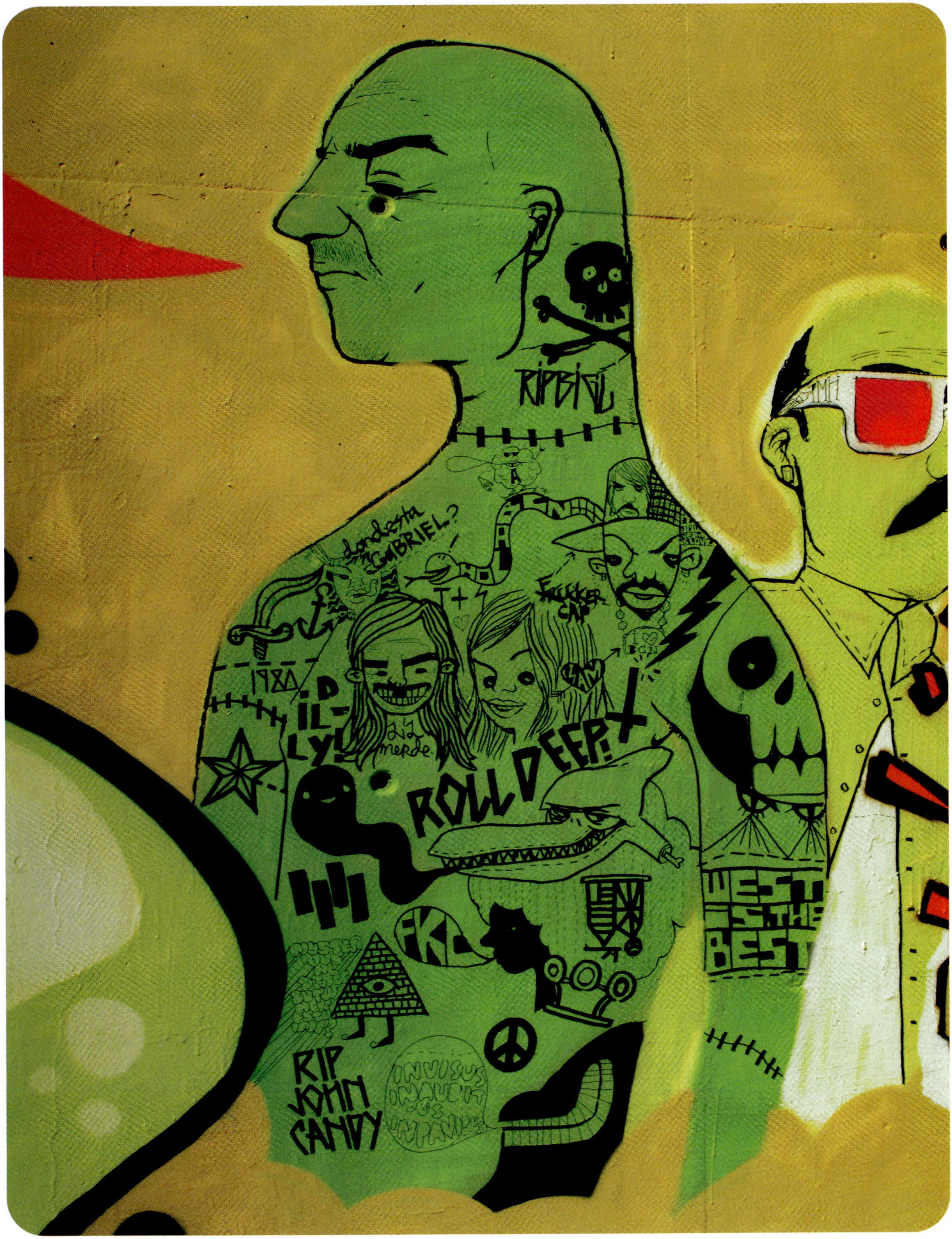
dondesta GABRIEL?
1980
ROLL DEEP!
RIP JOHN CANDY

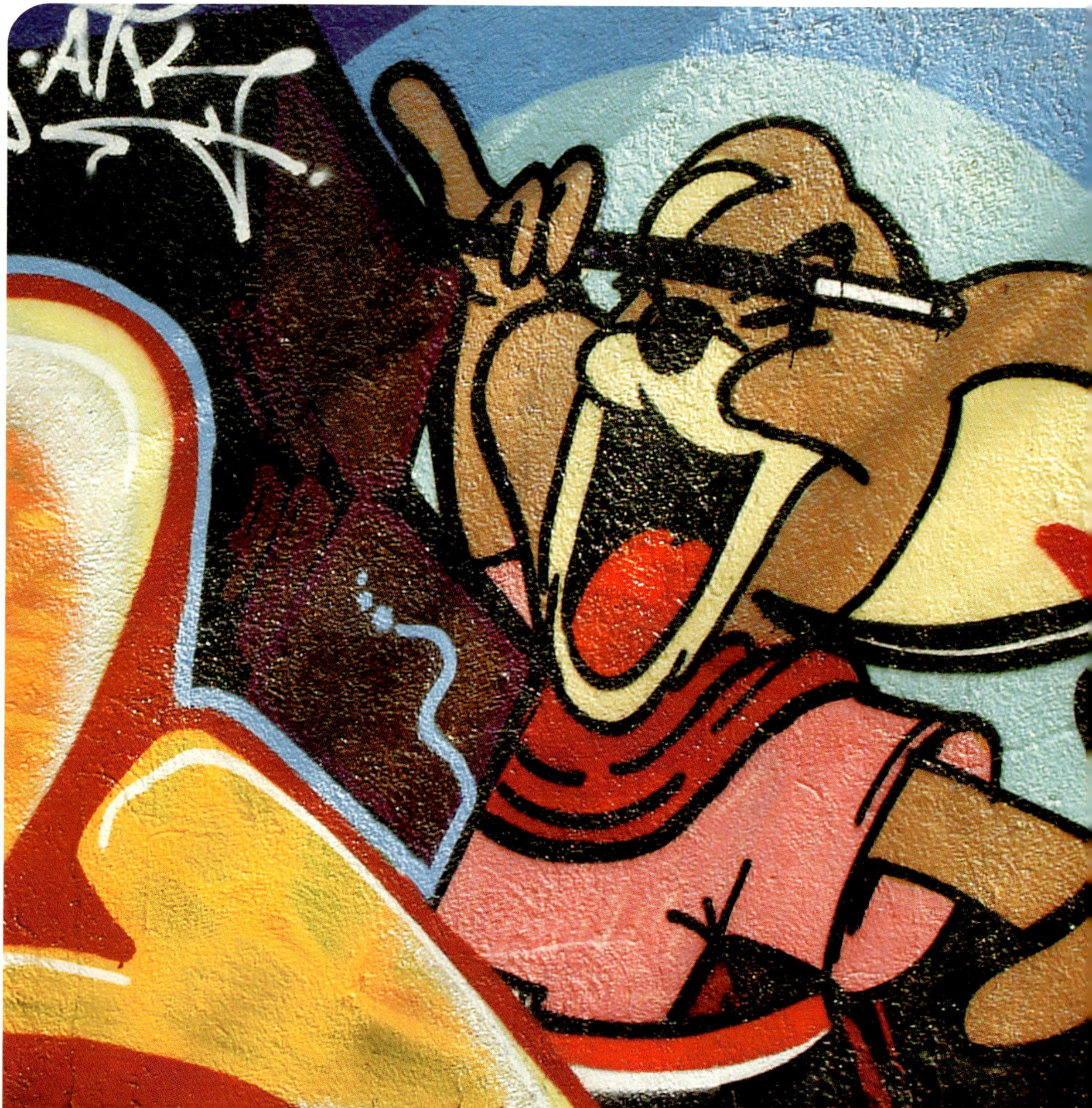

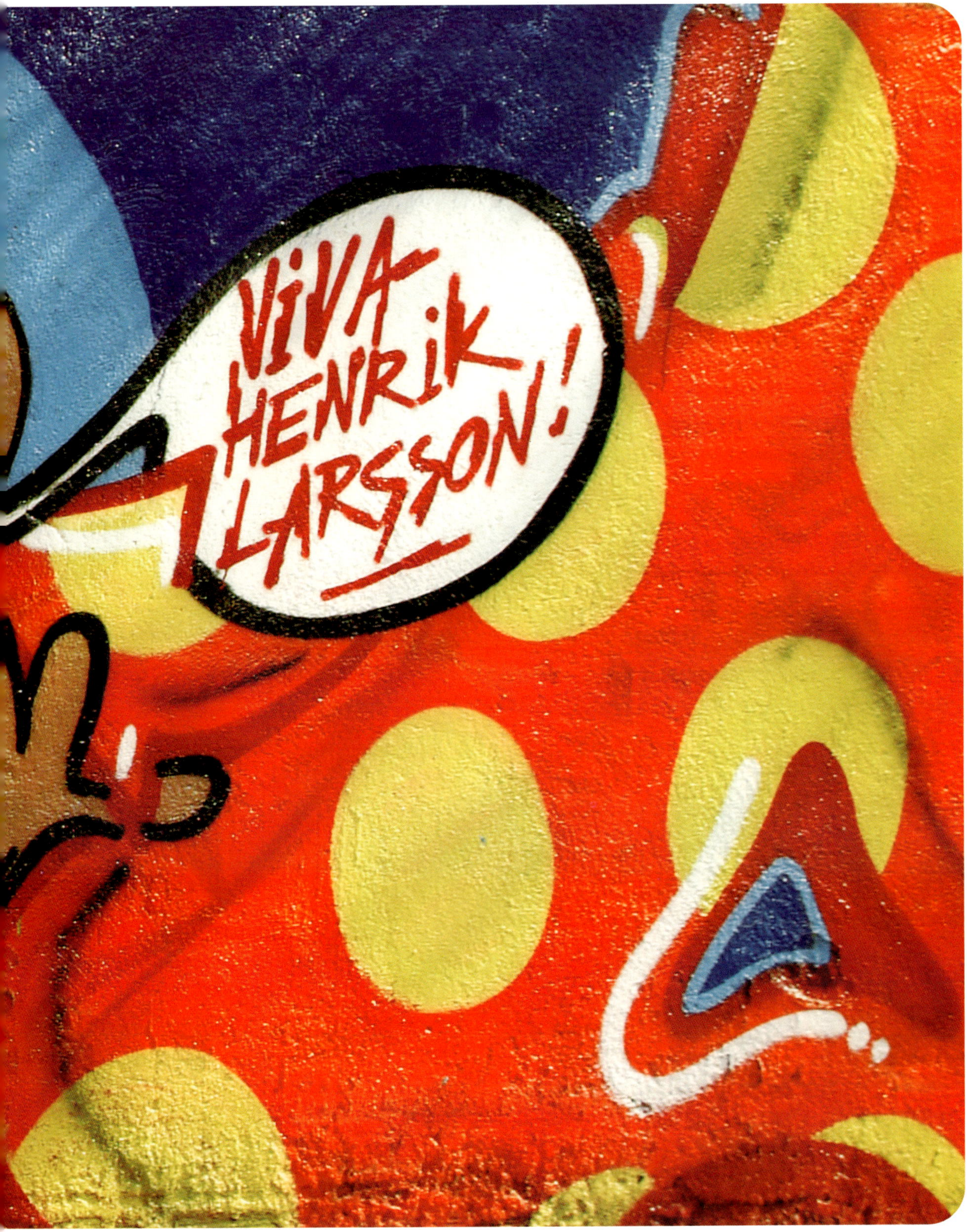
VIVA
HENRIK
LARSSON!

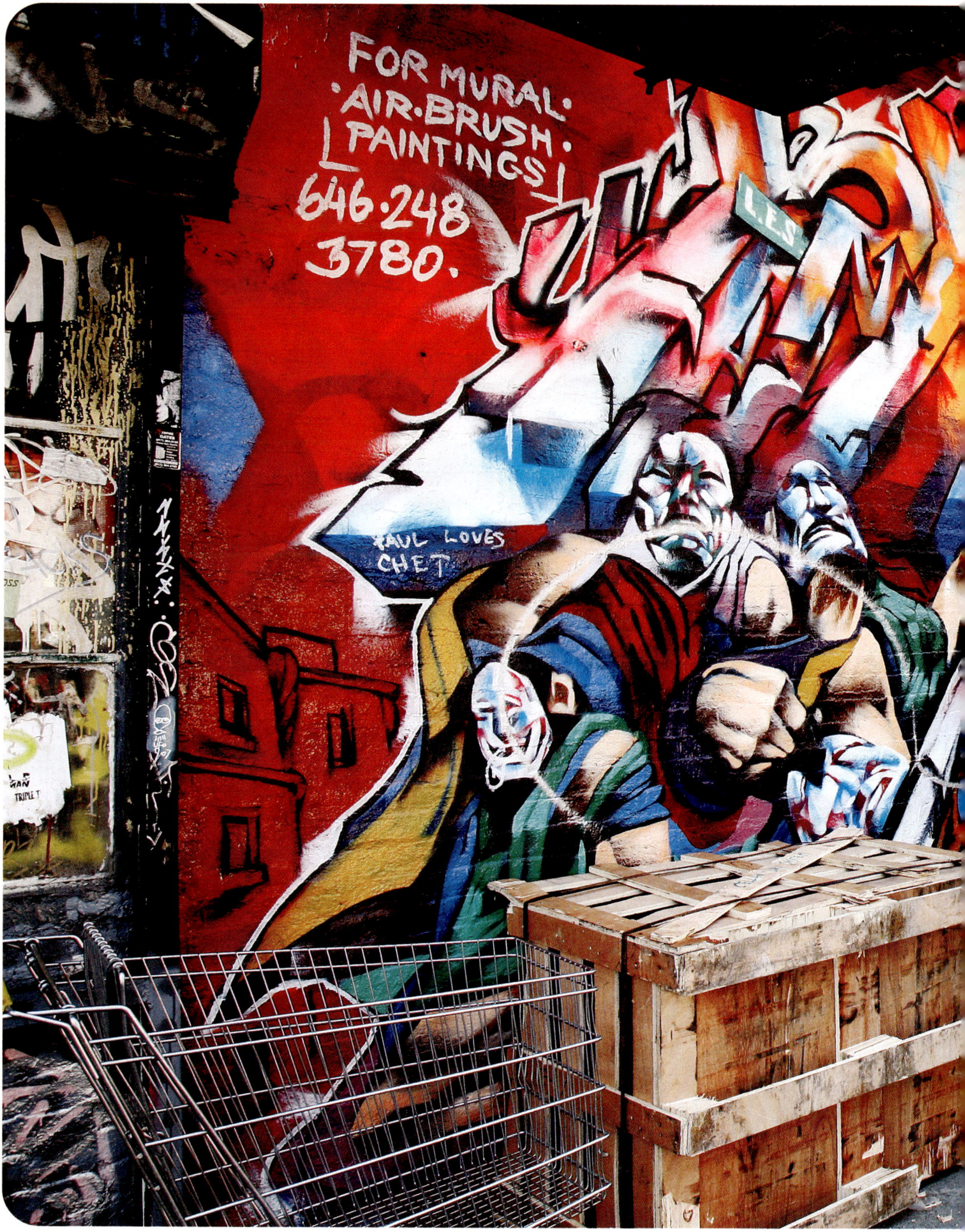
FOR MURAL
AIR·BRUSH
PAINTINGS
646·248
3780.
L.E.S
PAUL LOVES
CHET

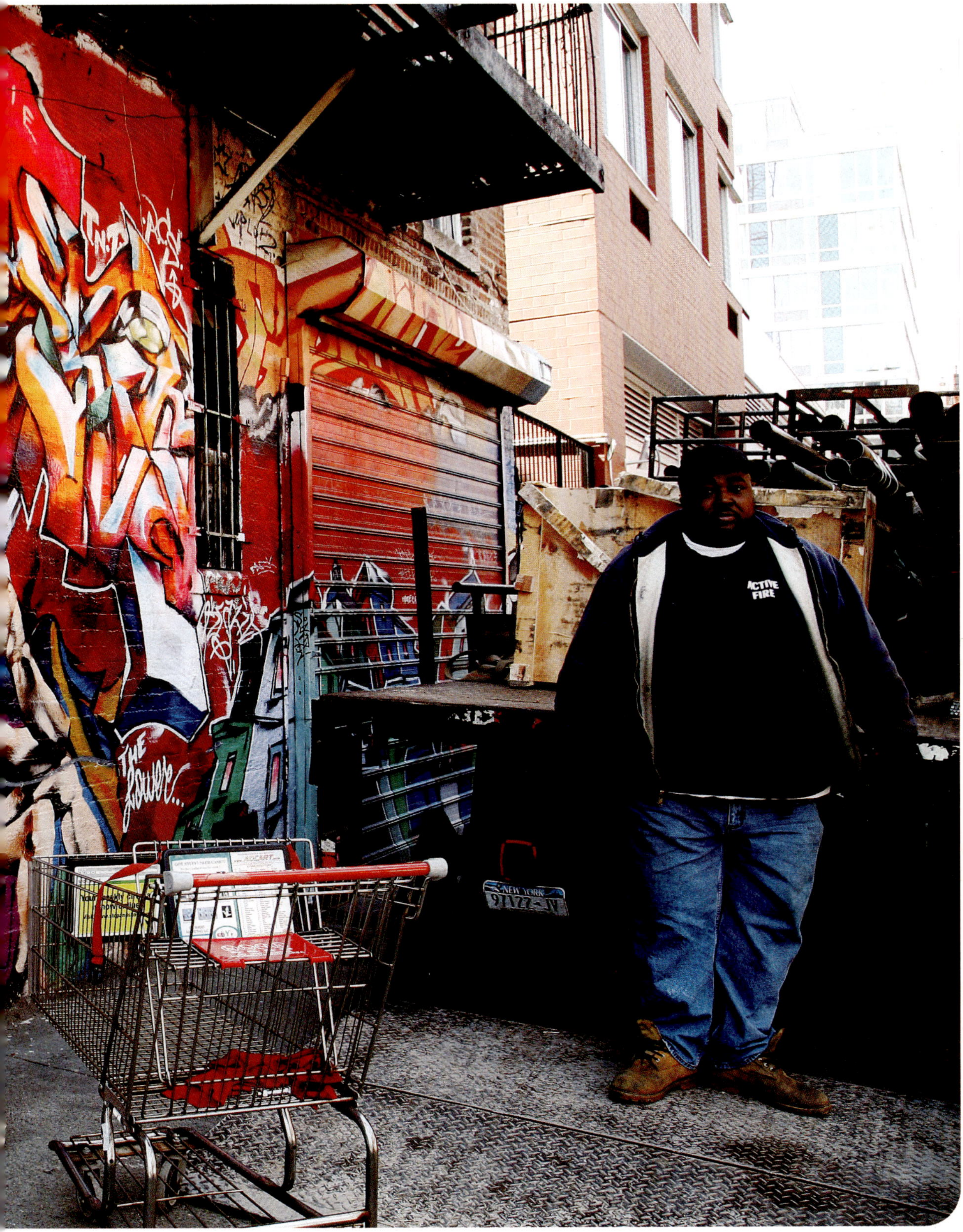
ACTIVE
FIRE
The Power...
NEW YORK
97122-JV

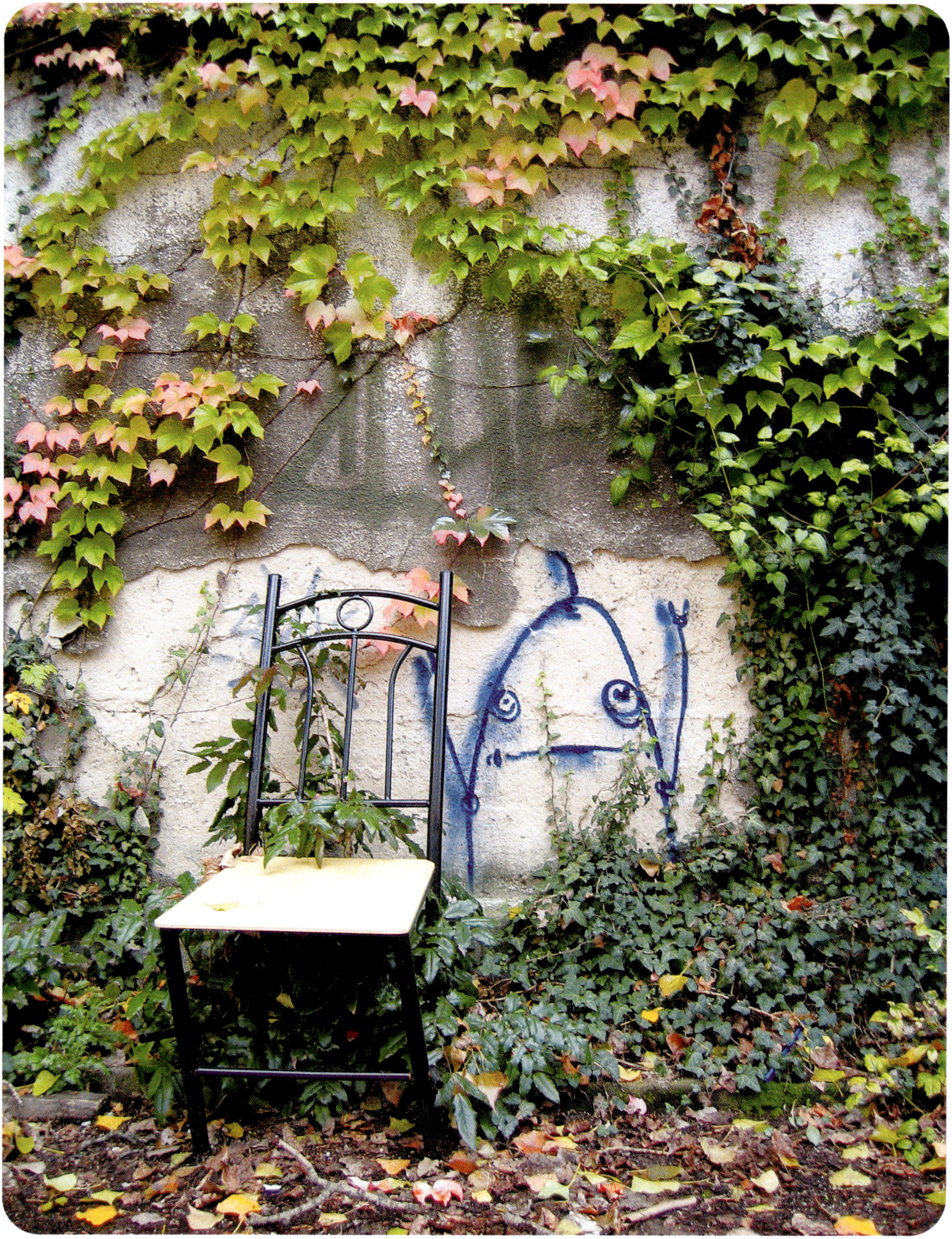

frankfurt

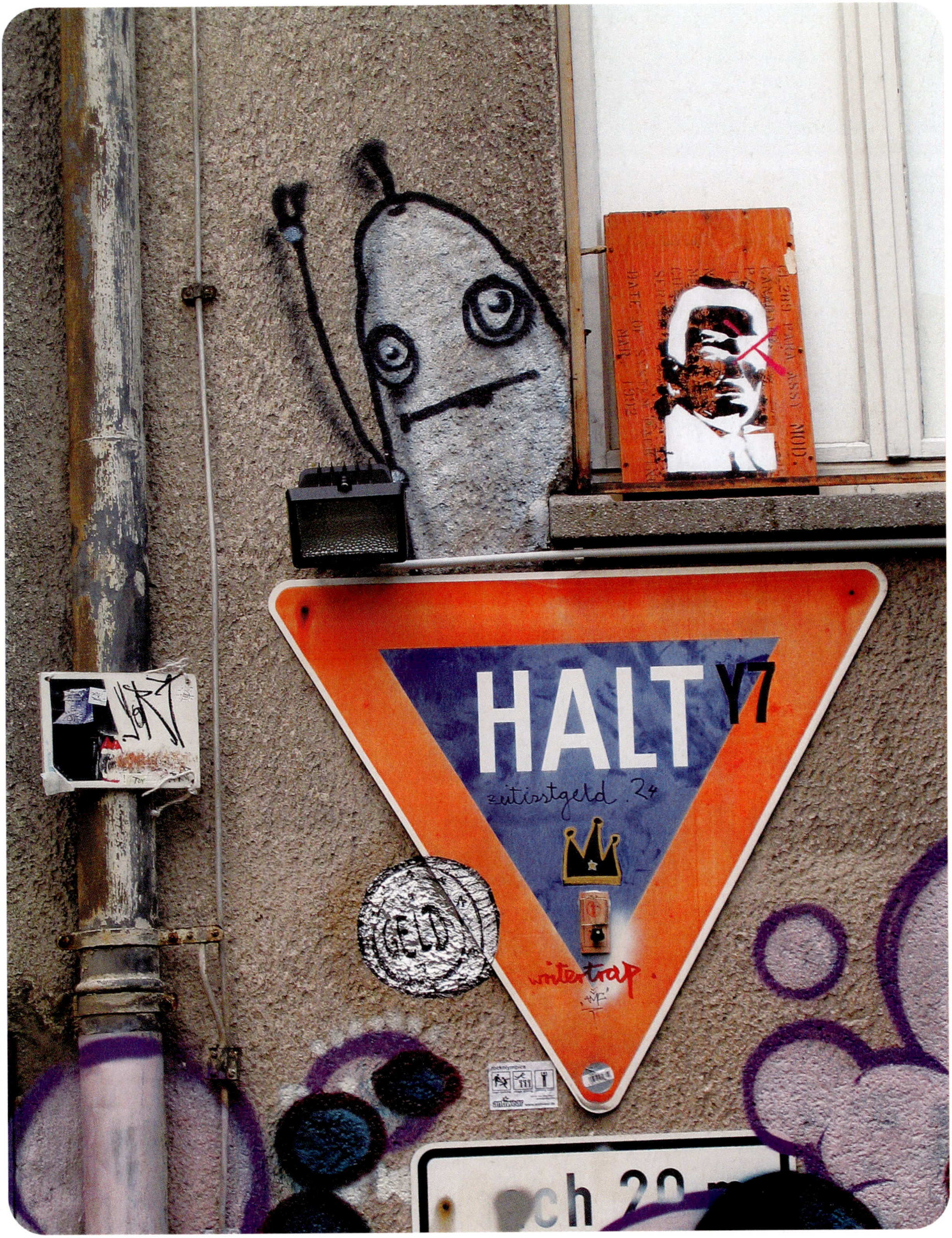
HALT
Y7
zeitistgeld .24
wintertrap

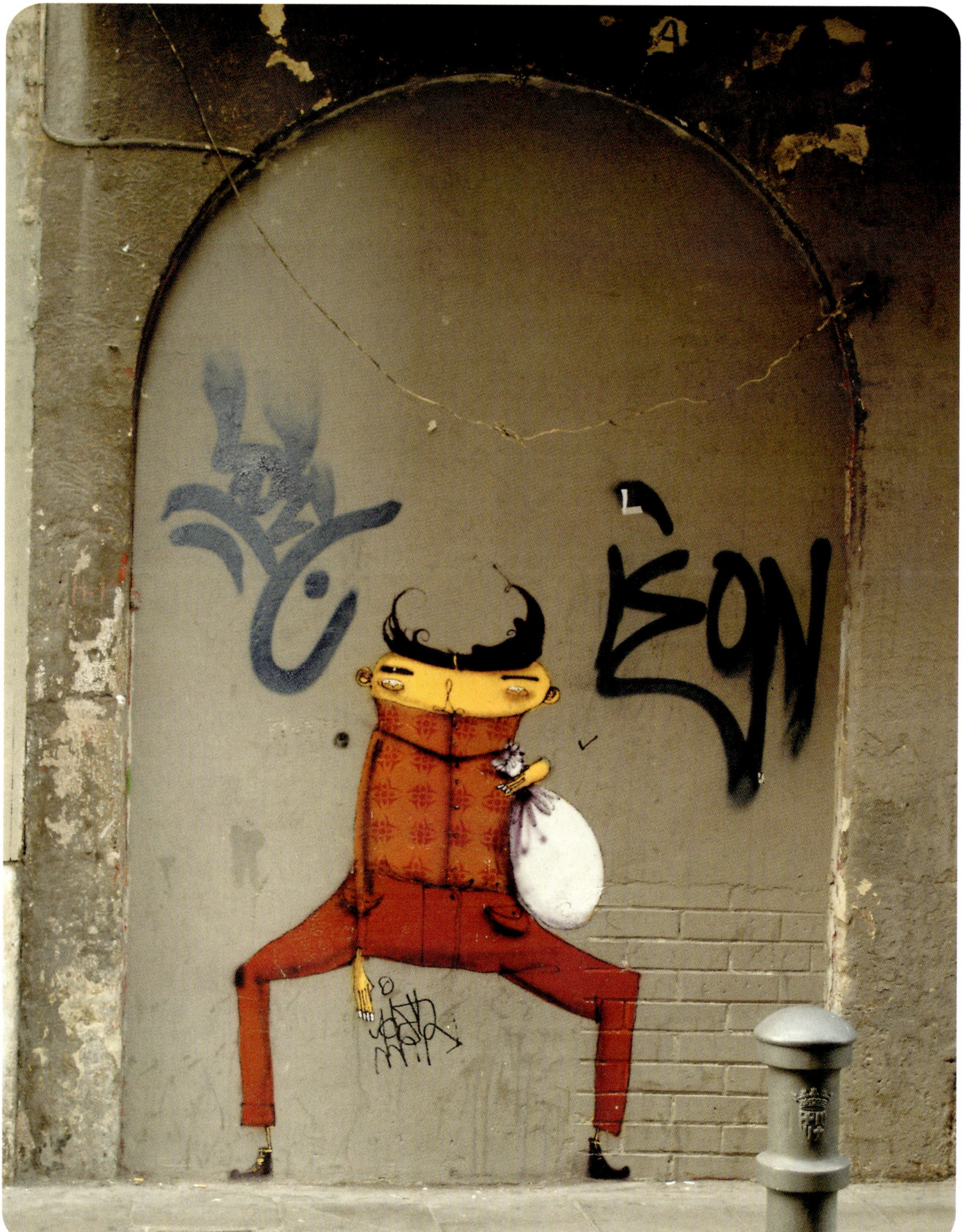

barcelona

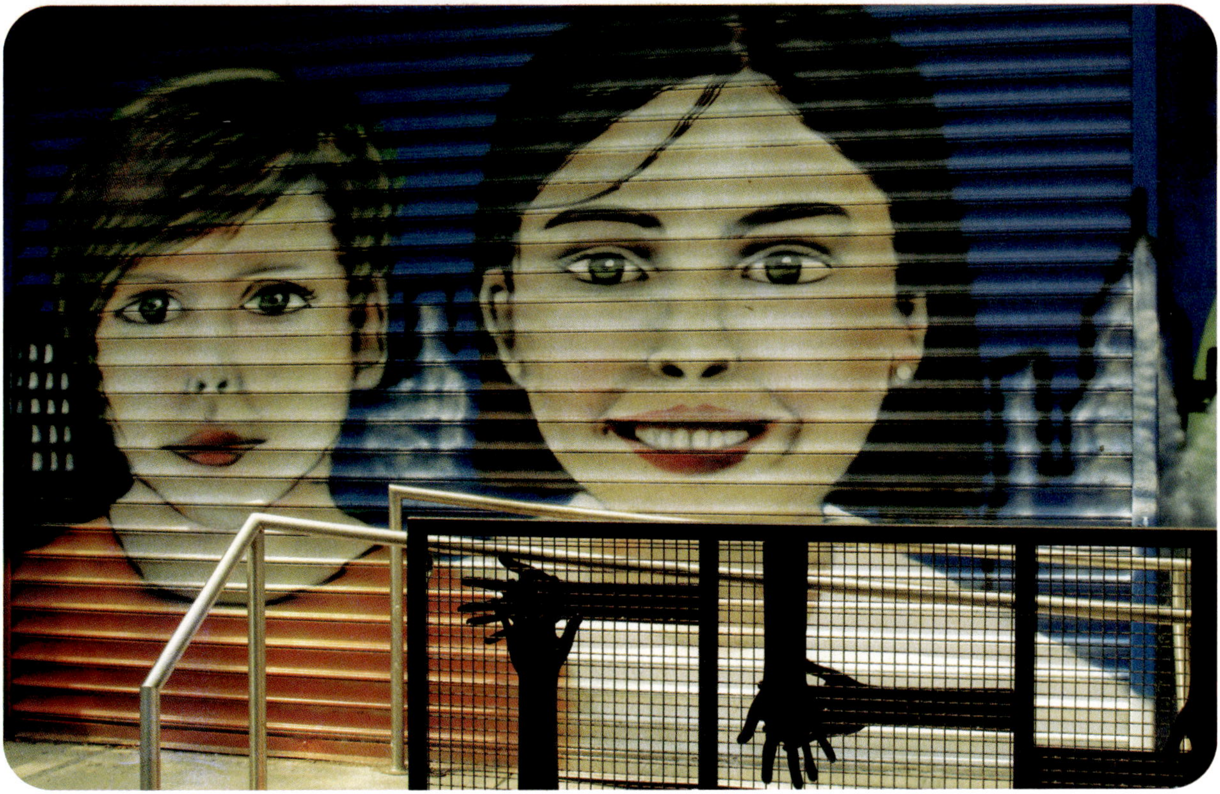

barcelona + new york

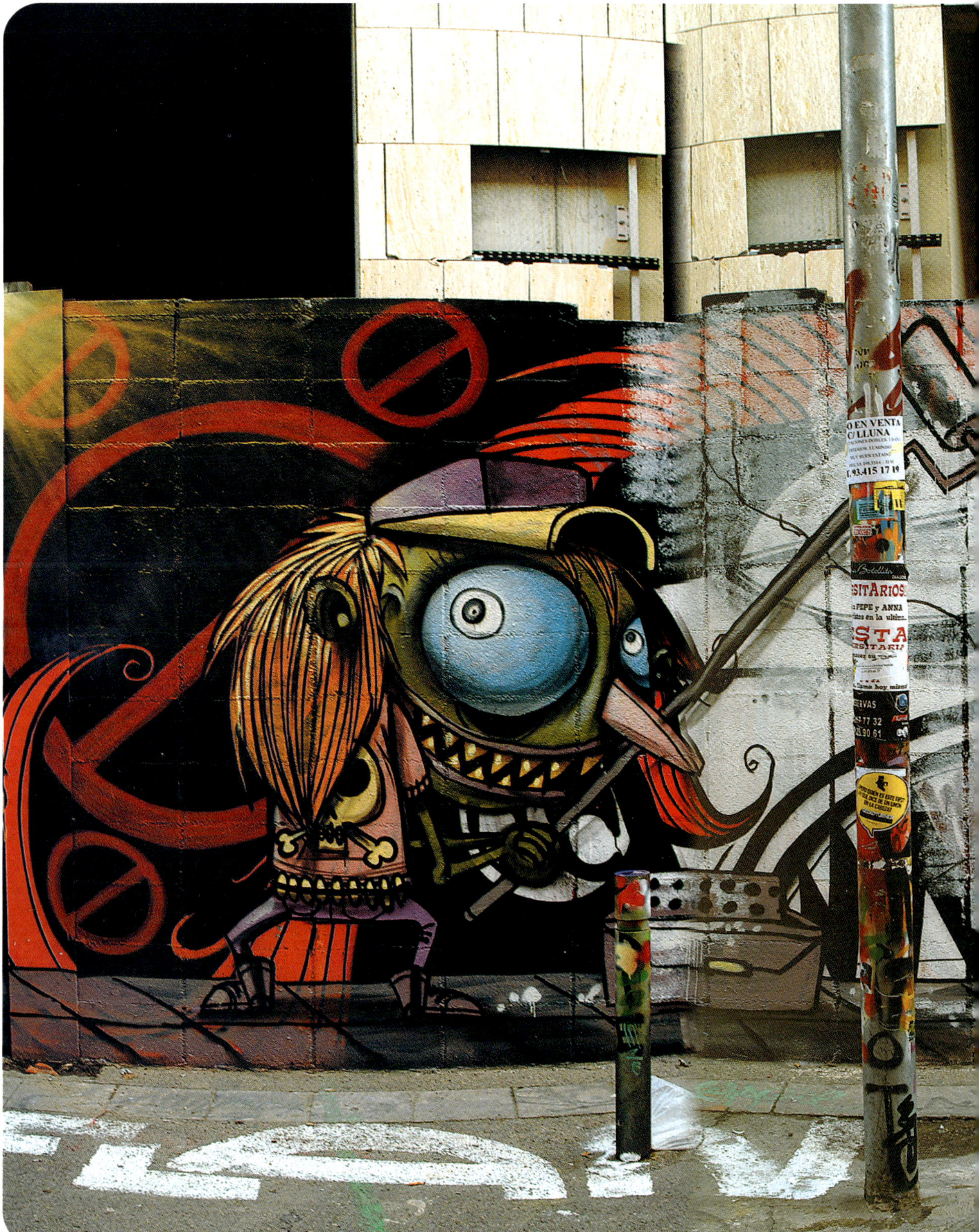
EN VENTA
LLUNA
93.415 17 19
PEPE y ANNA

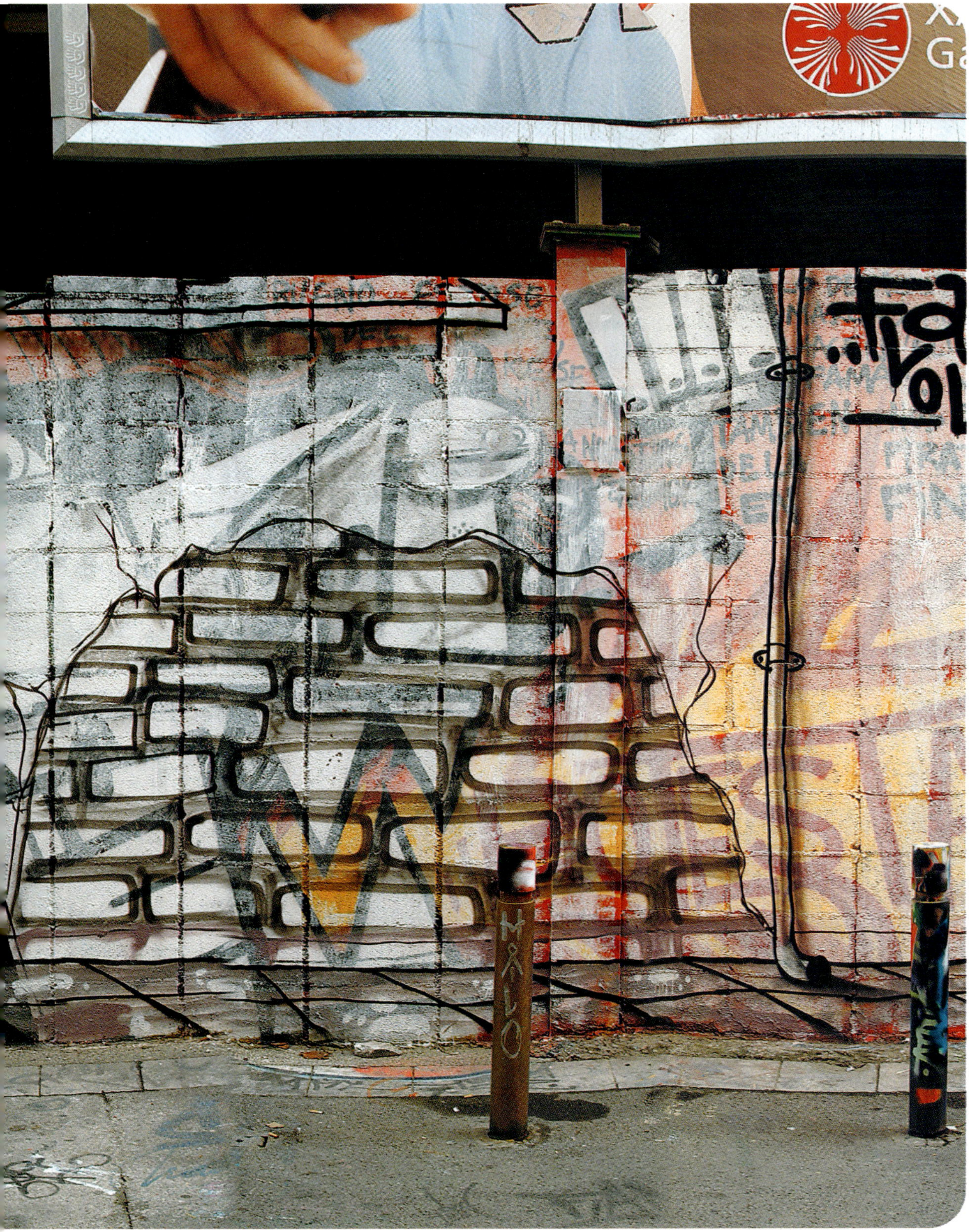

barcelona

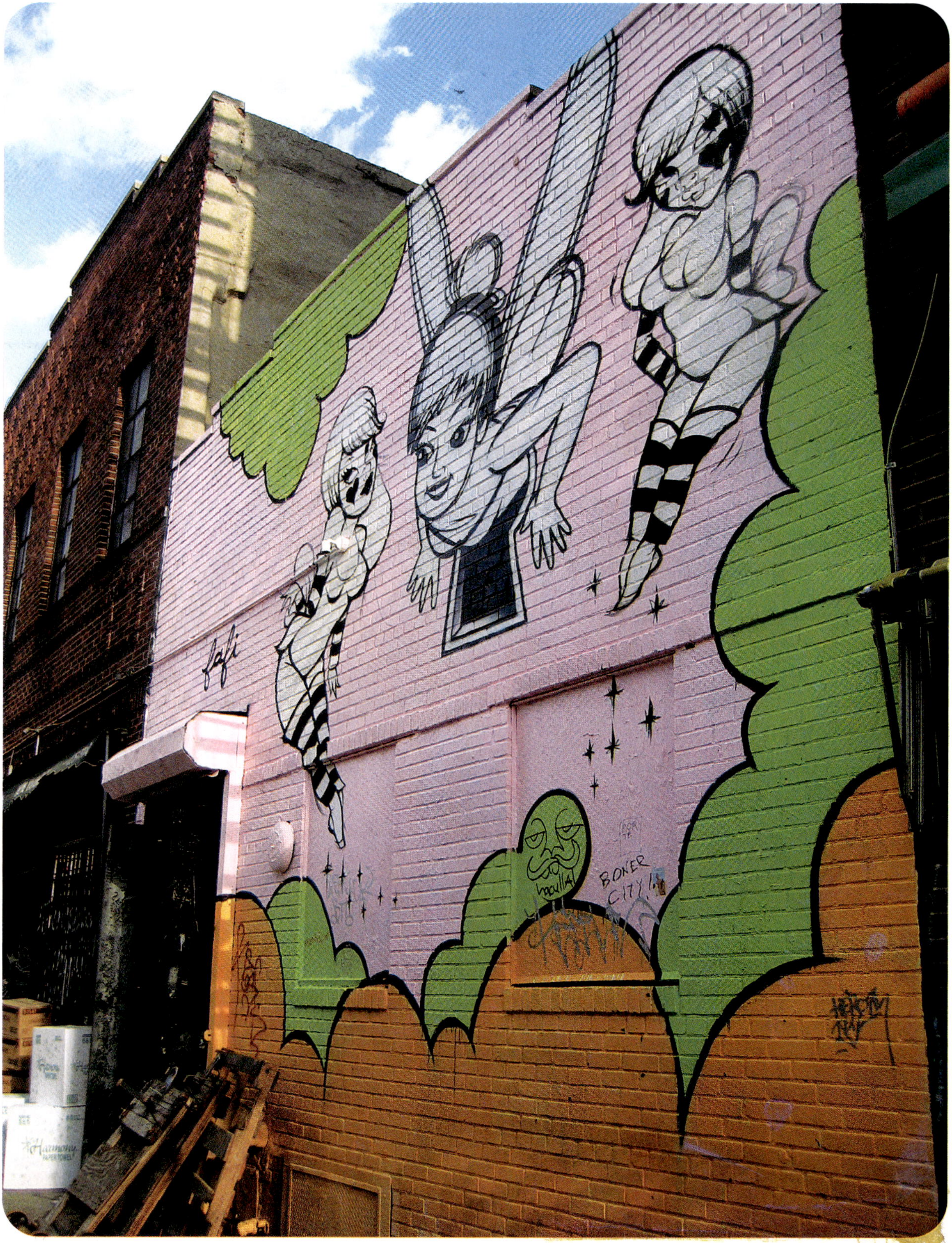
fafi
BONER CITY!

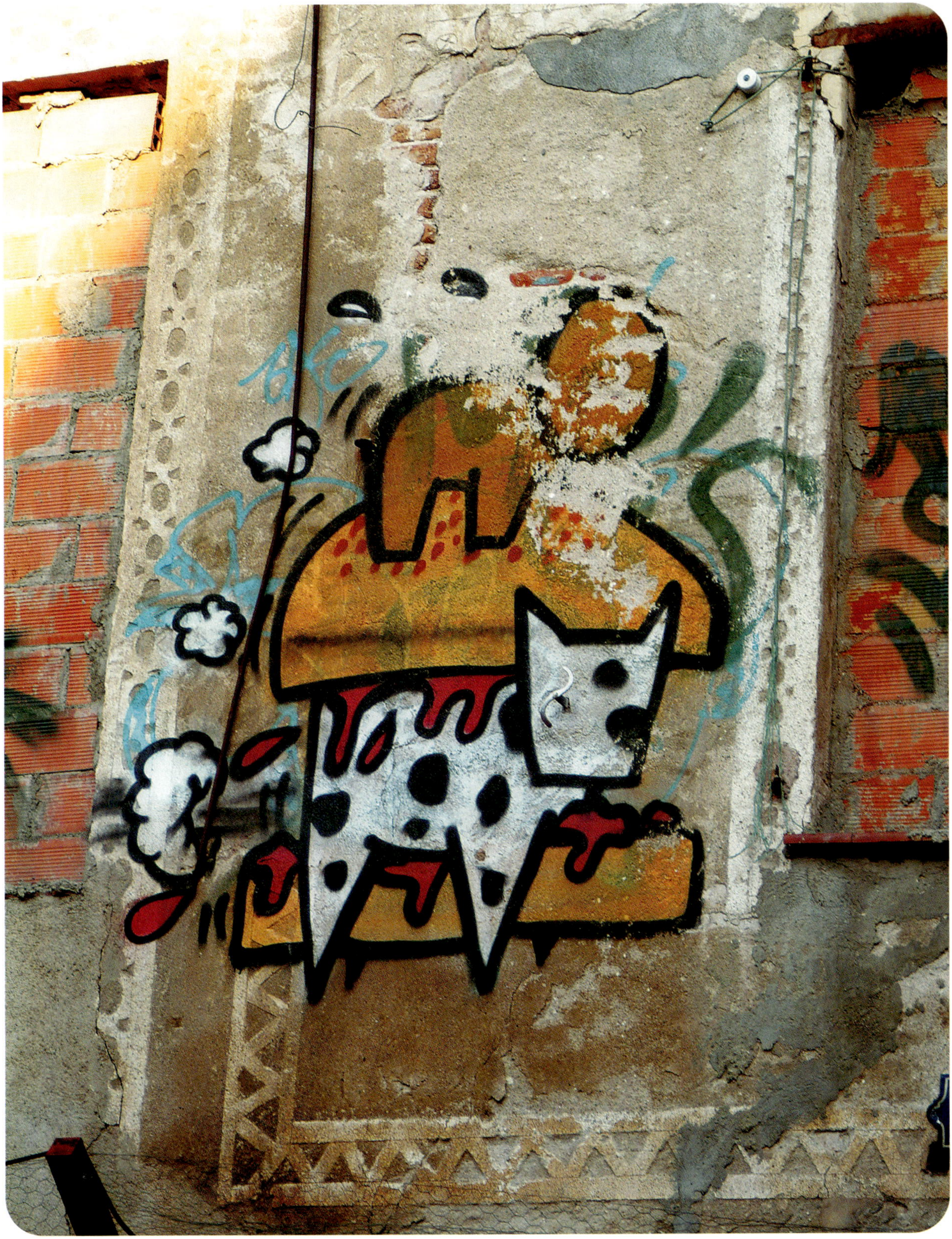

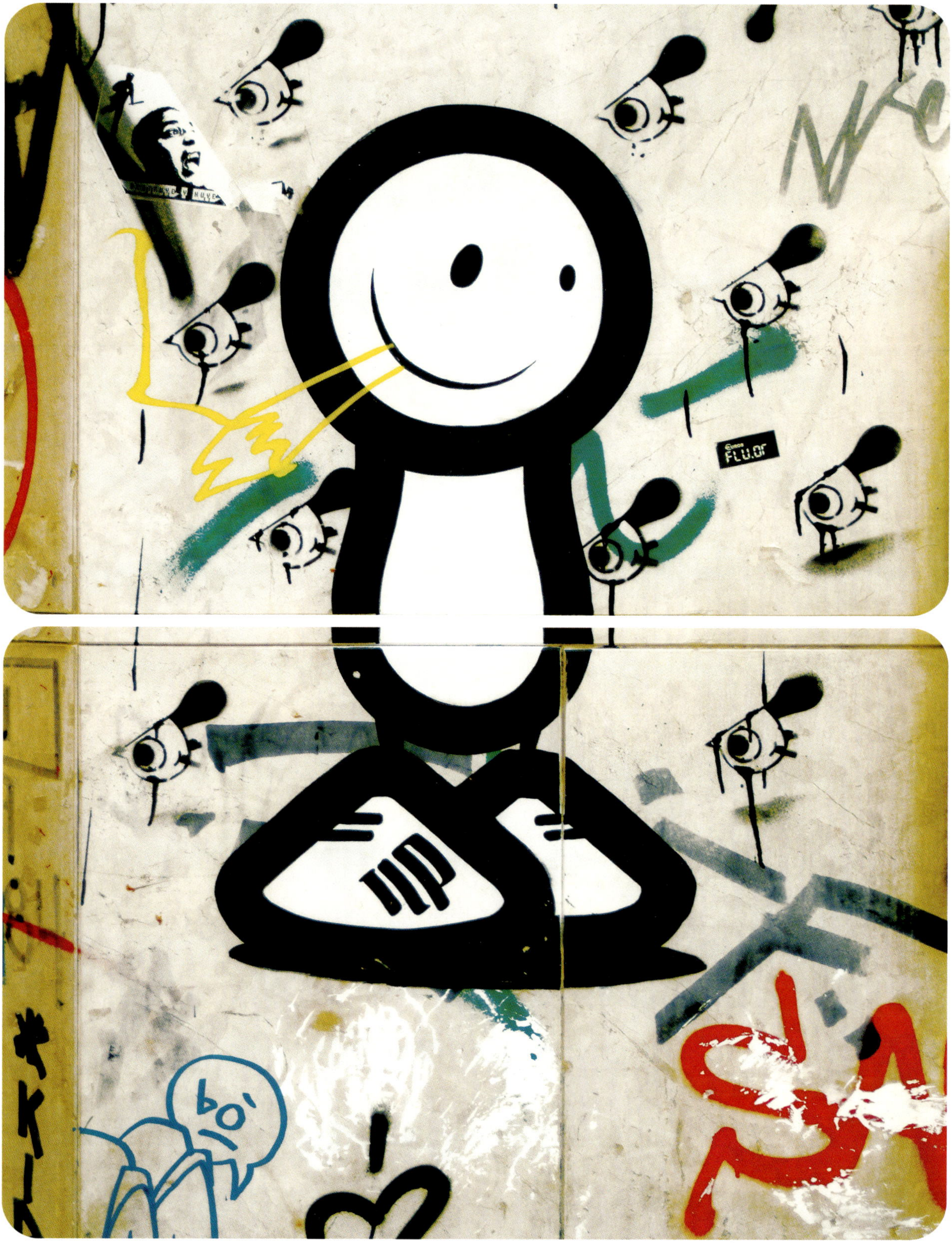

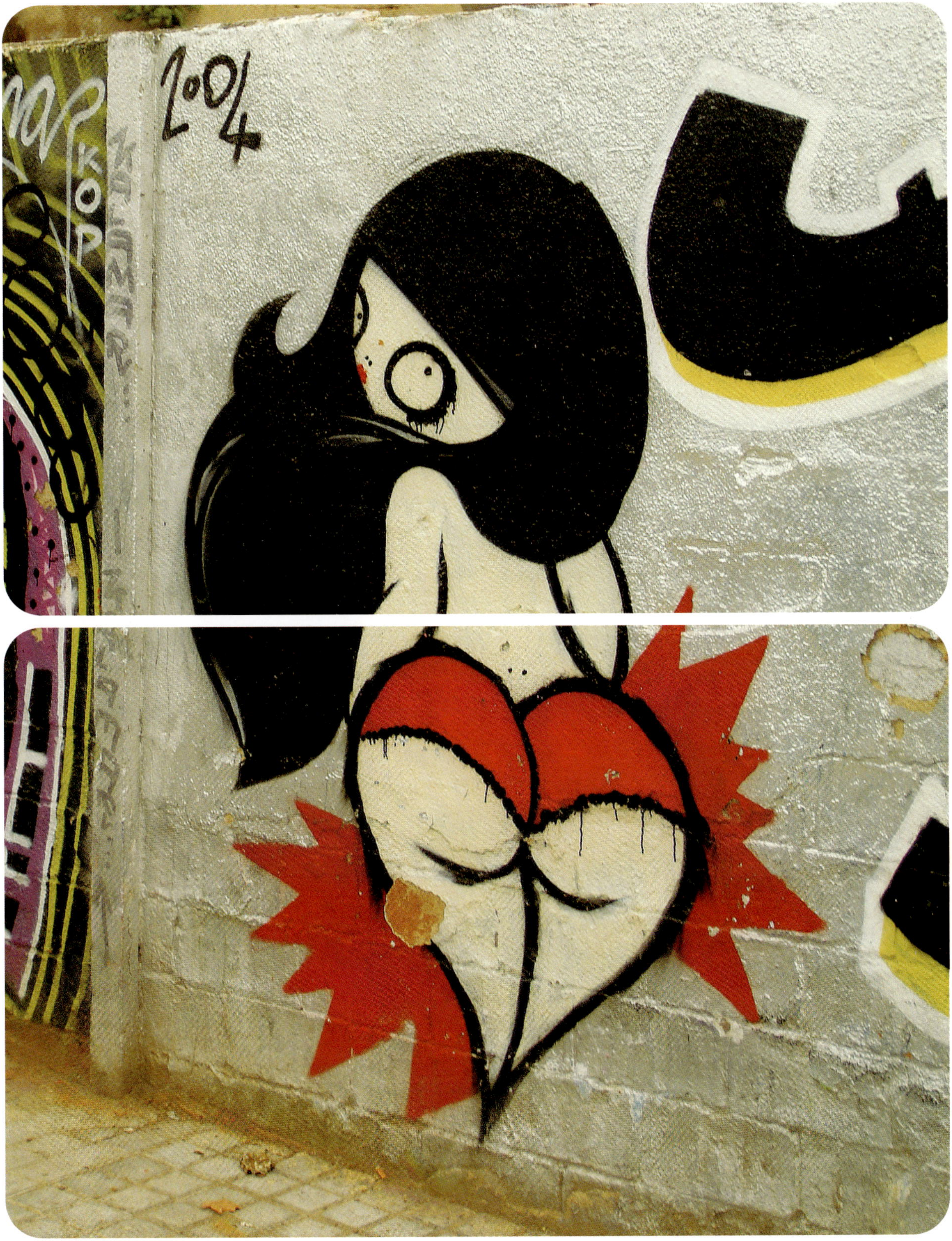

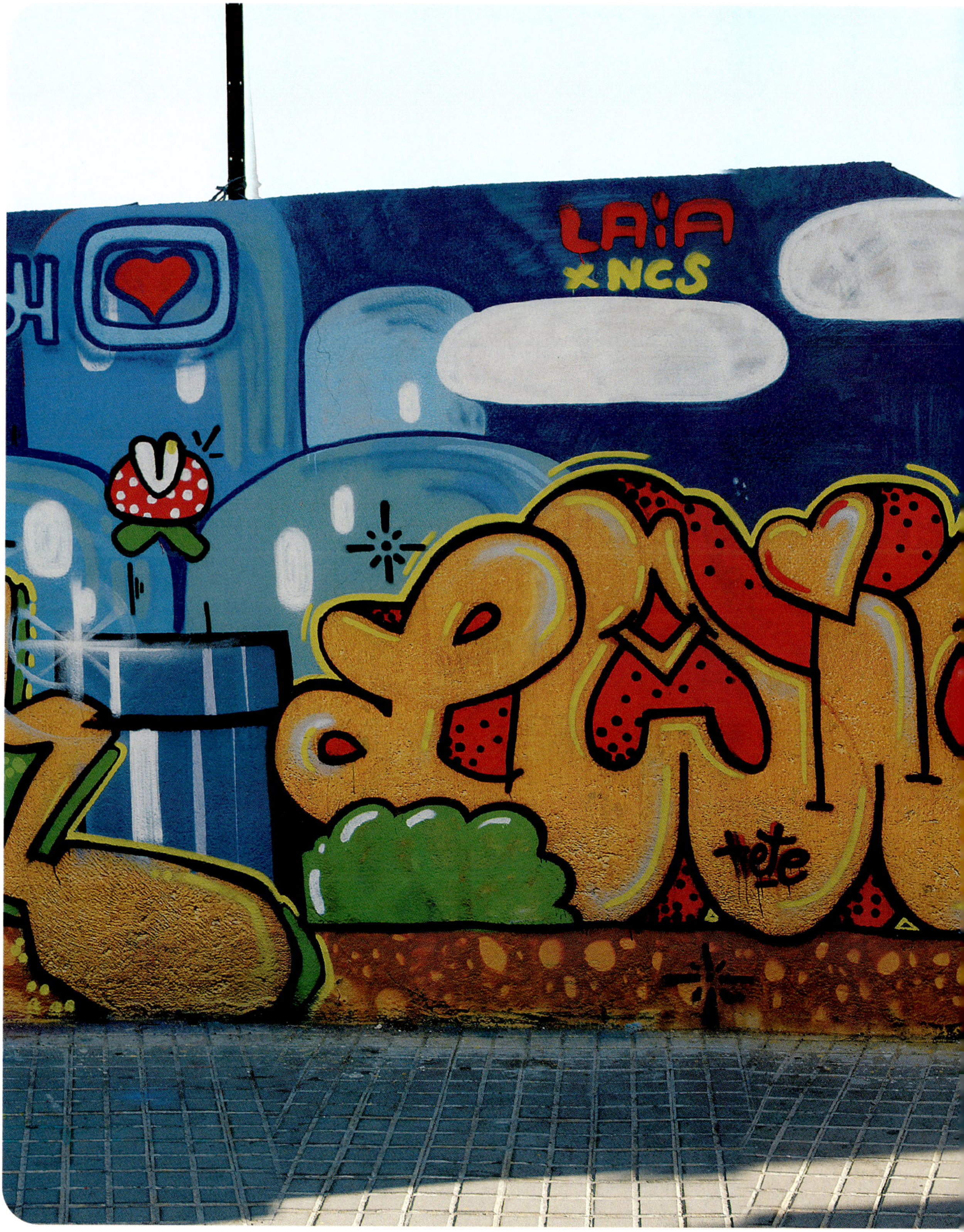
LAiA
xNCS
hete

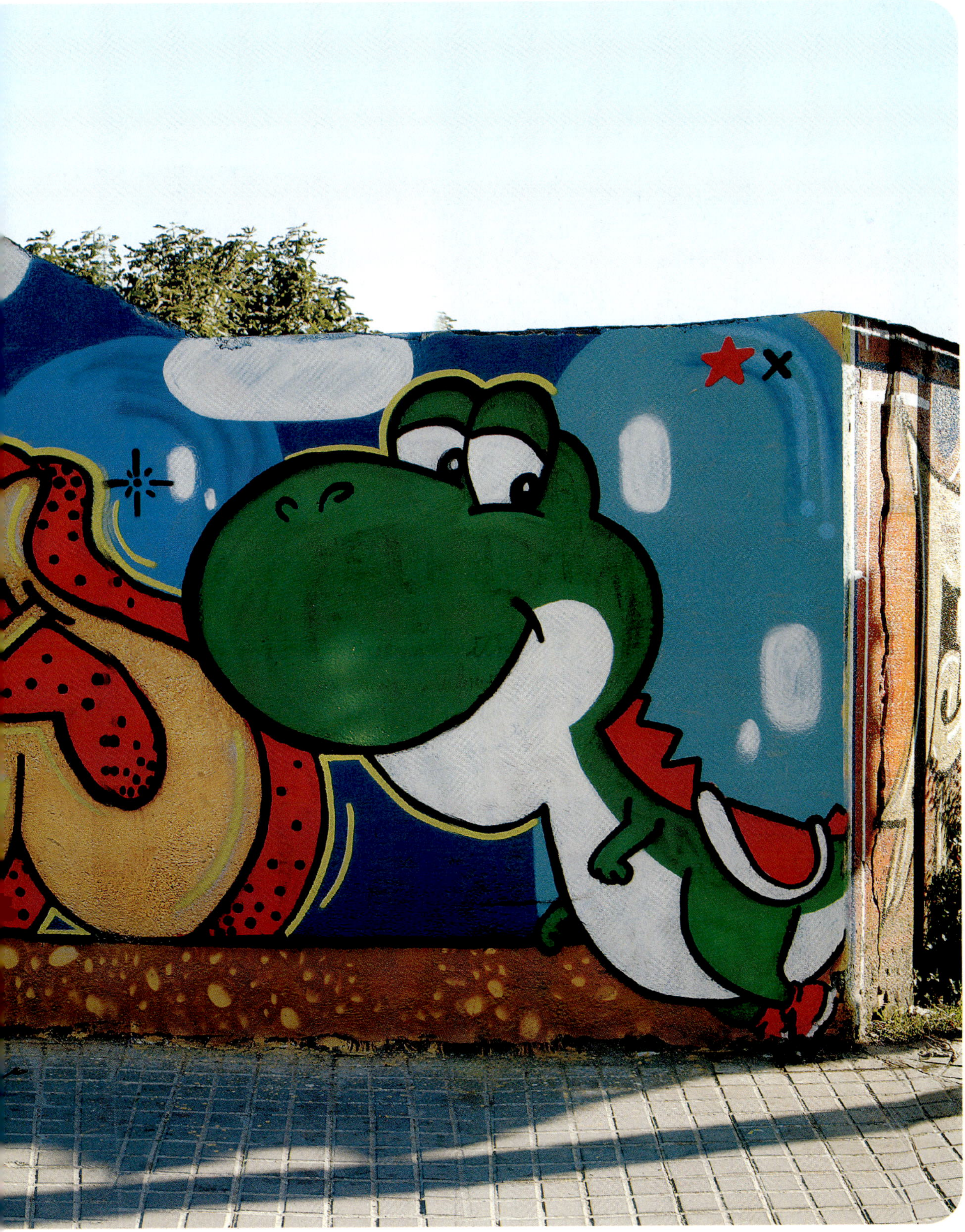

barcelona

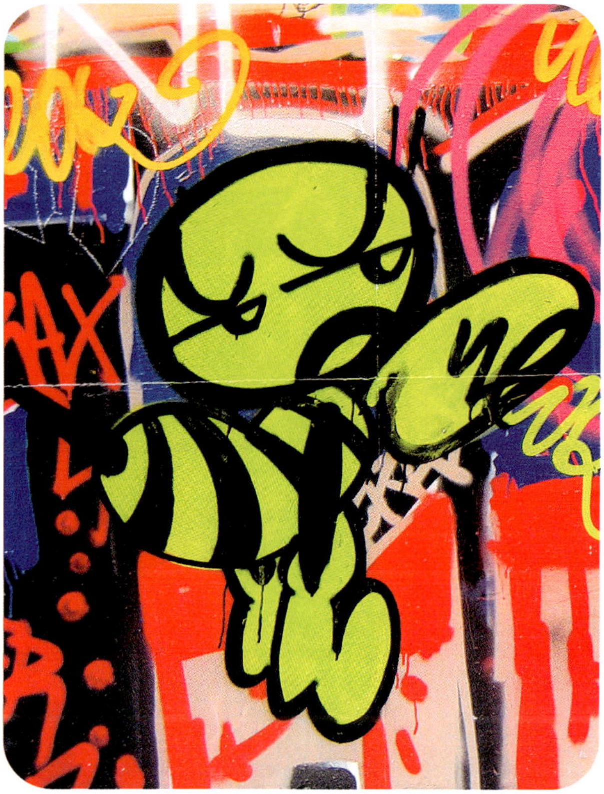

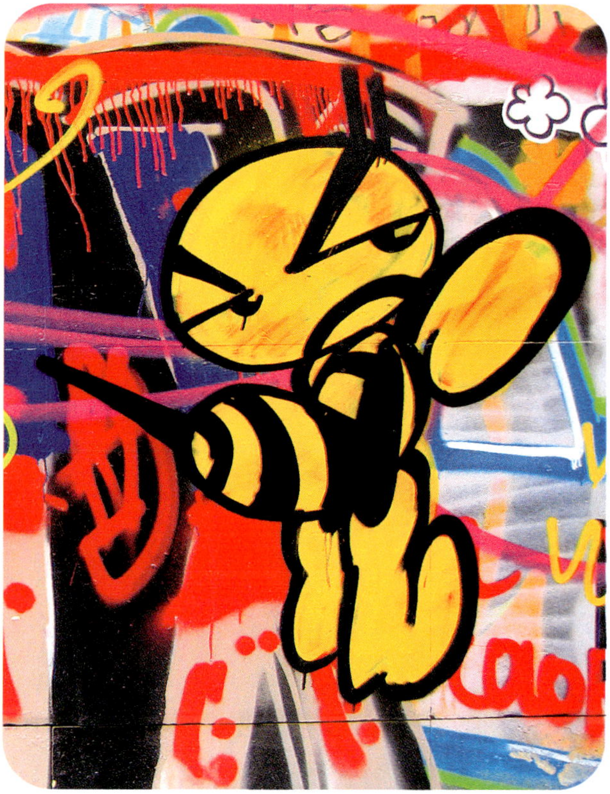

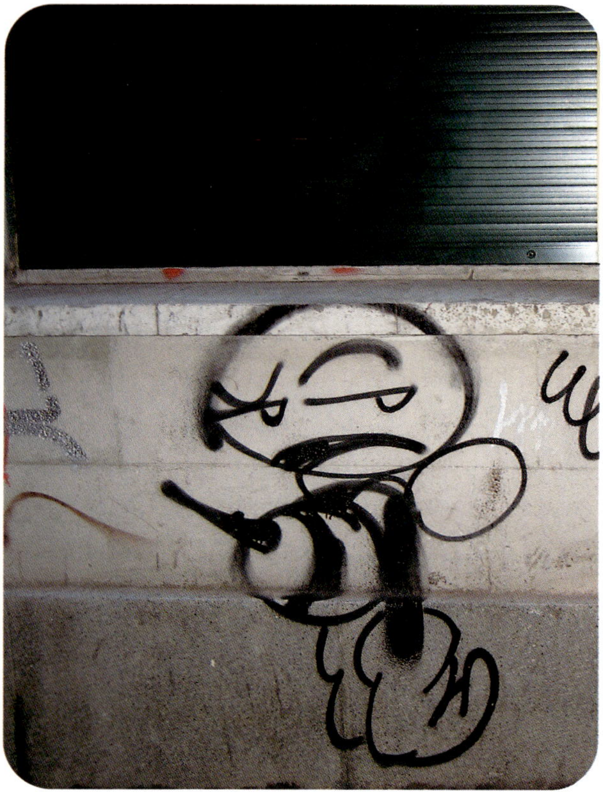

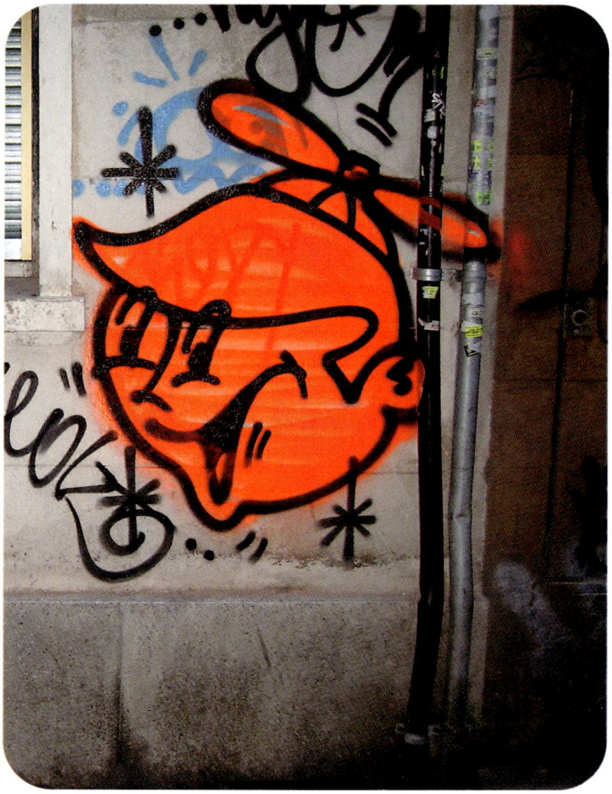

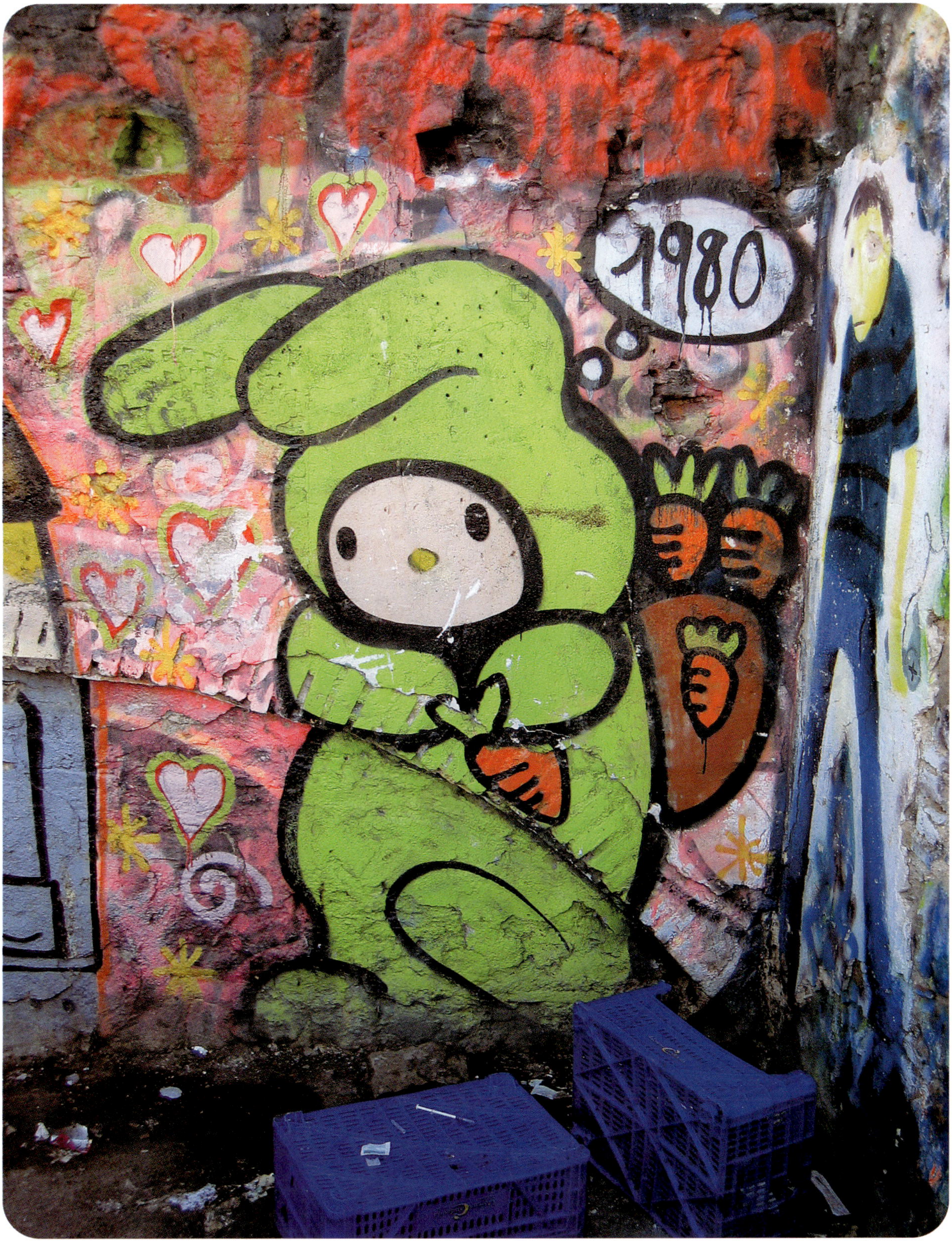
1980

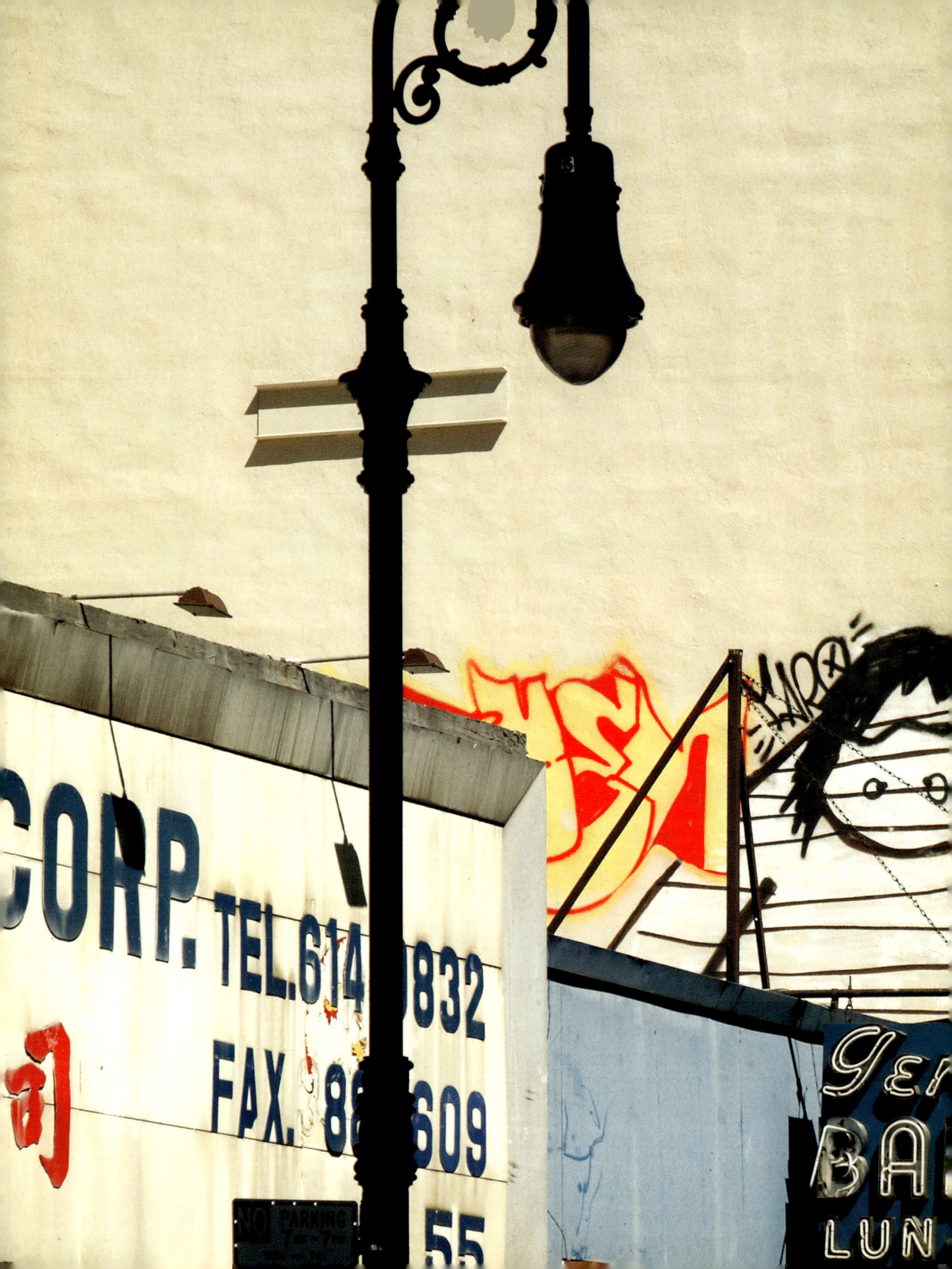
CORP.
TEL. 614 832
FAX. 8 609
55
NO PARKING

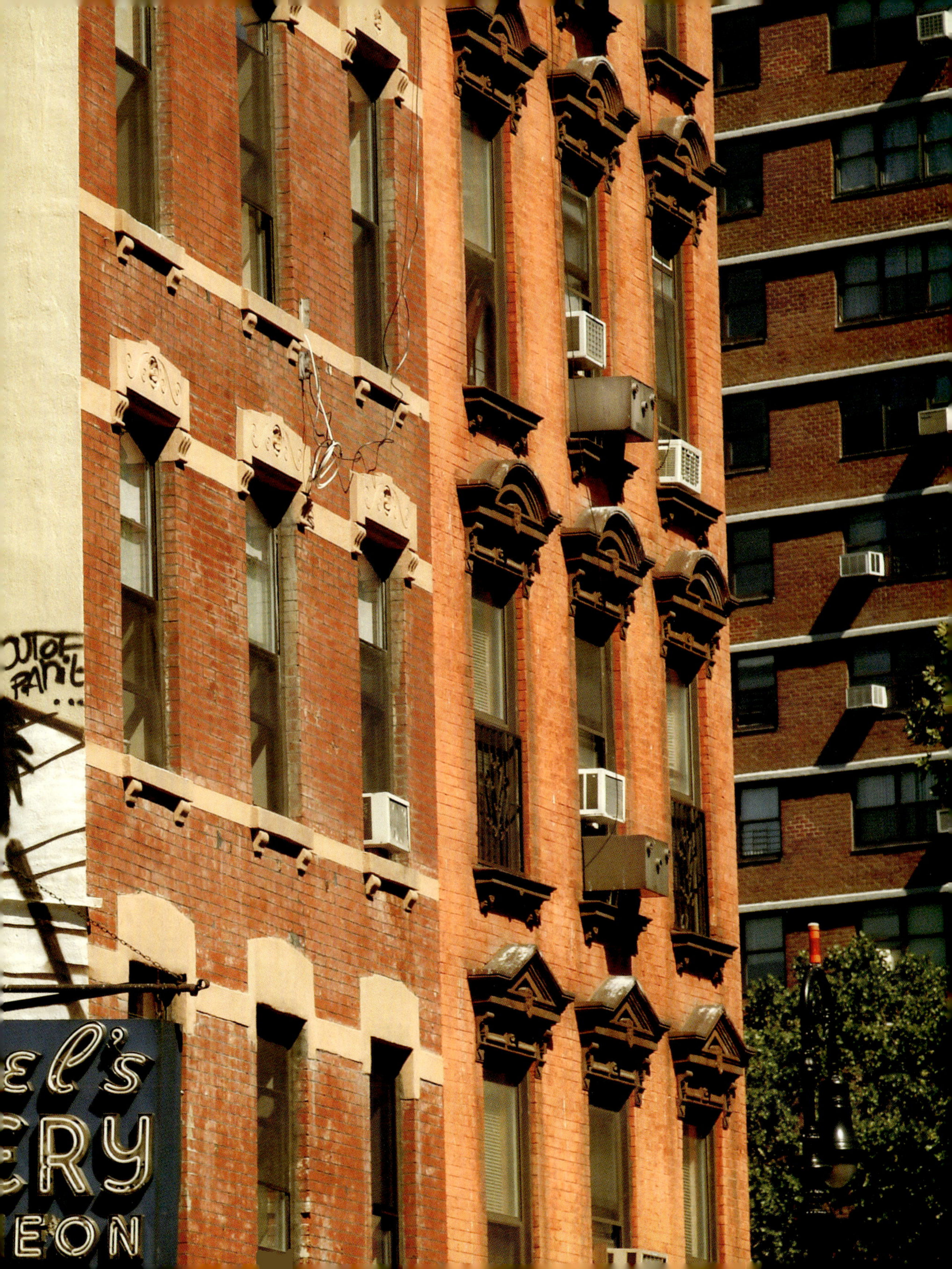
el's
ERY
EON

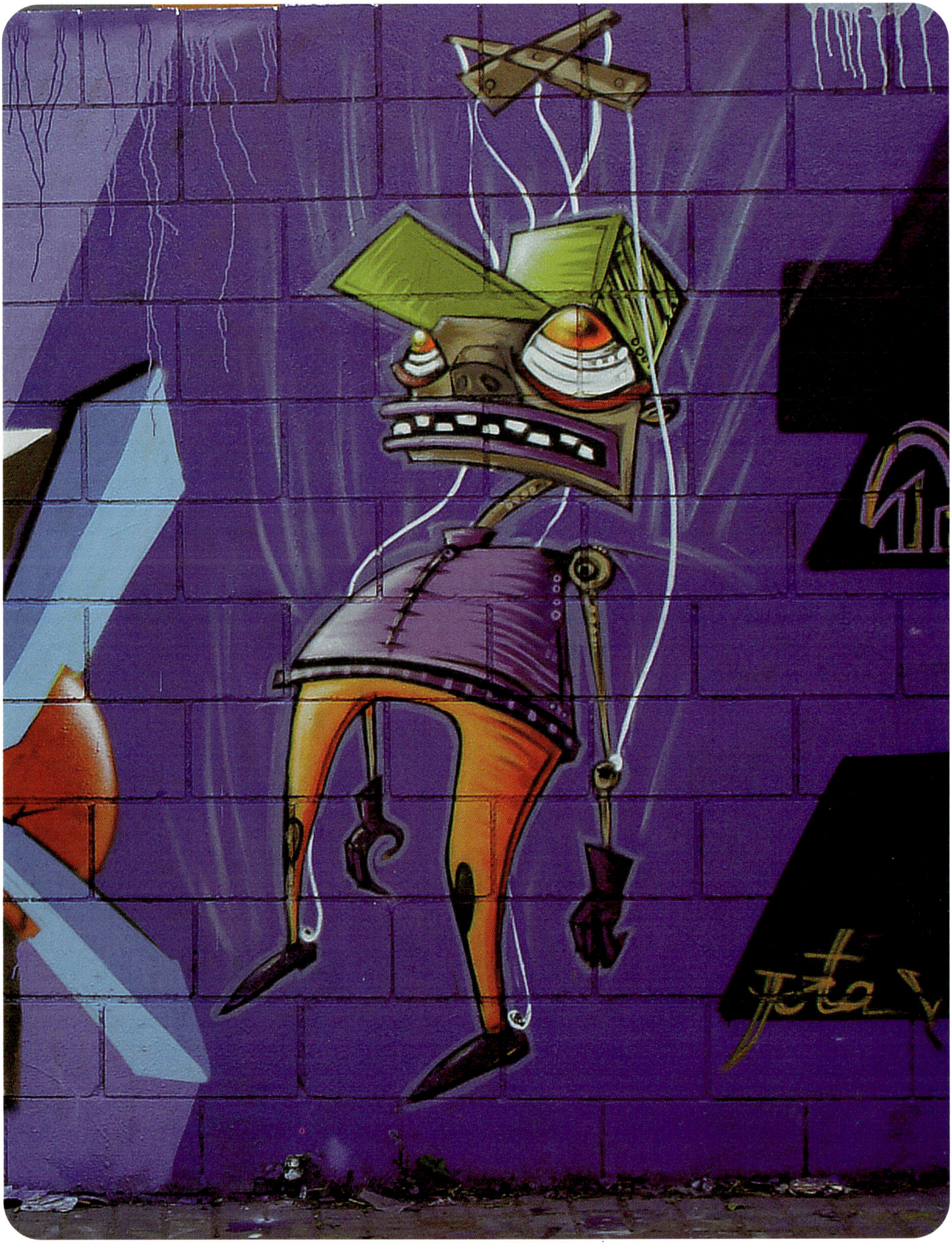

barcelona

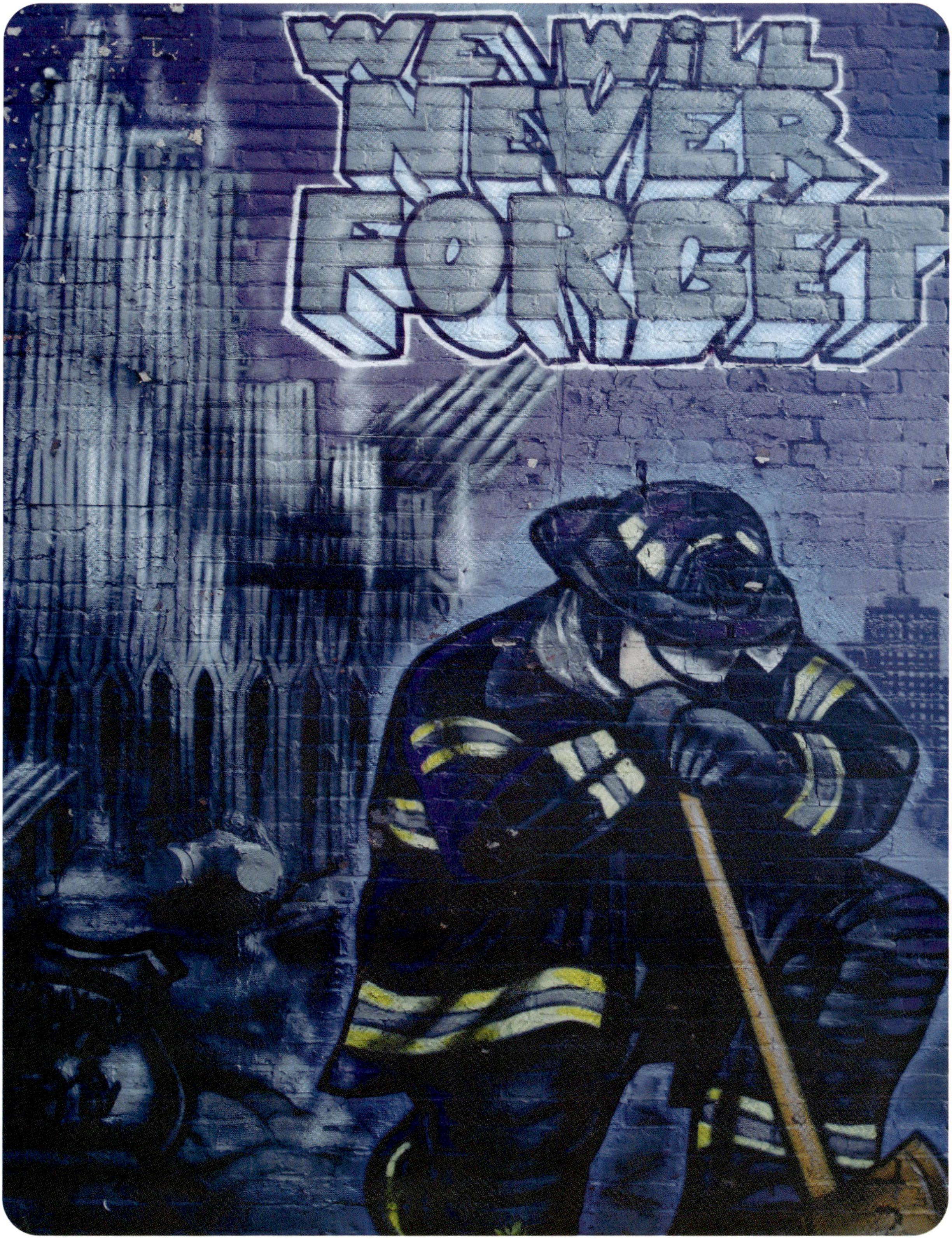
WE WILL NEVER FORGET

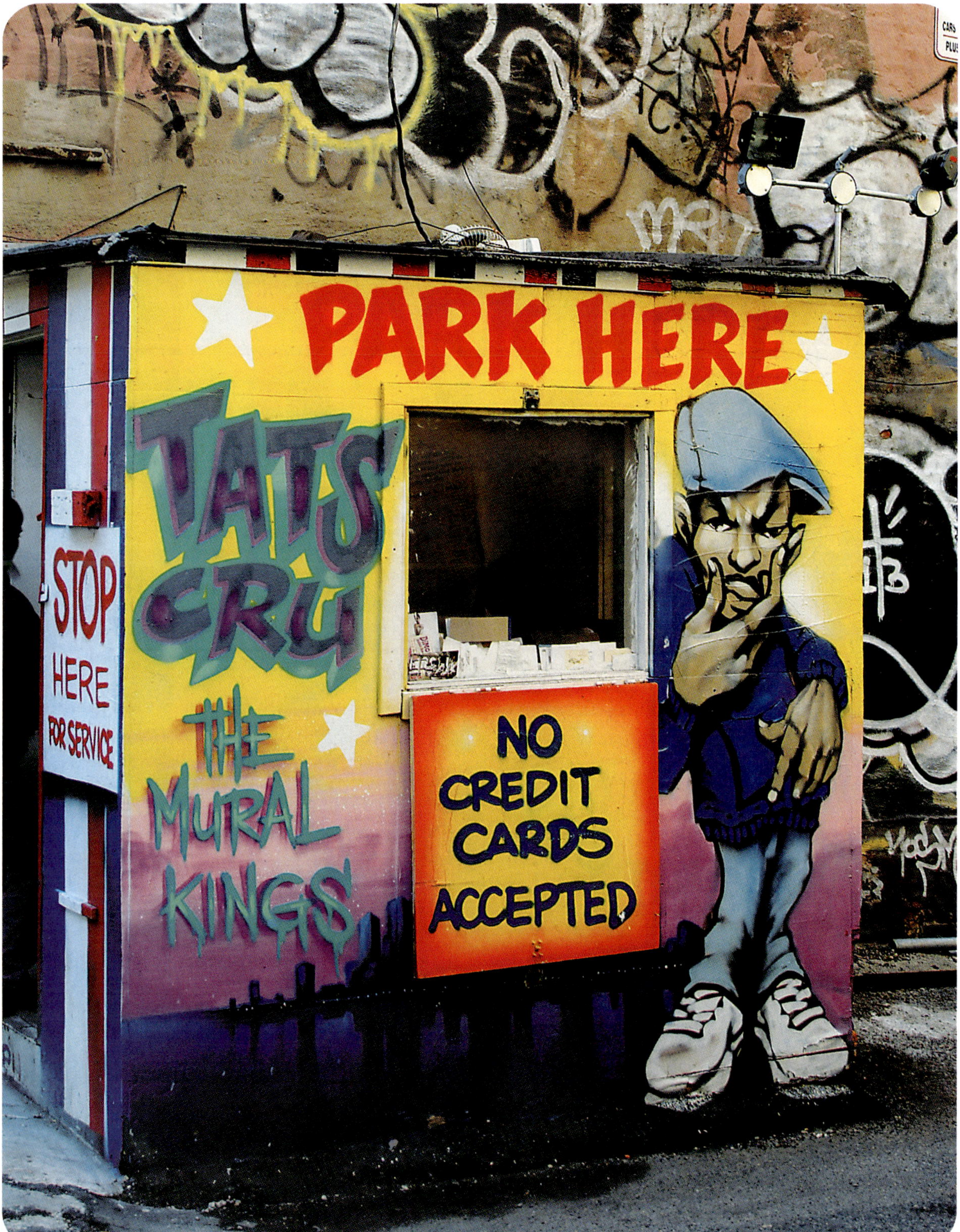
PARK HERE
TATS CRU
THE MURAL KINGS
NO CREDIT CARDS ACCEPTED
STOP HERE FOR SERVICE

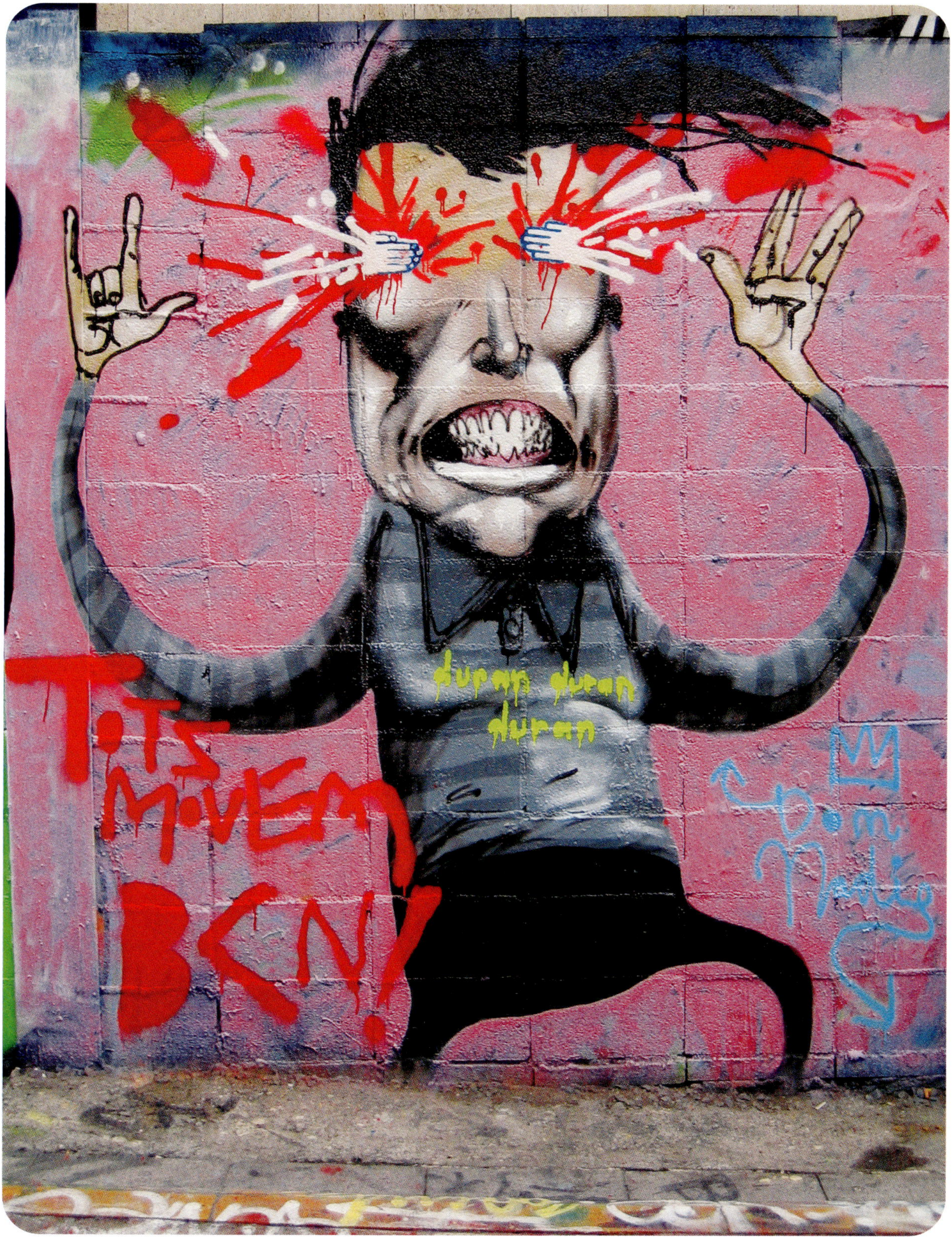

barcelona

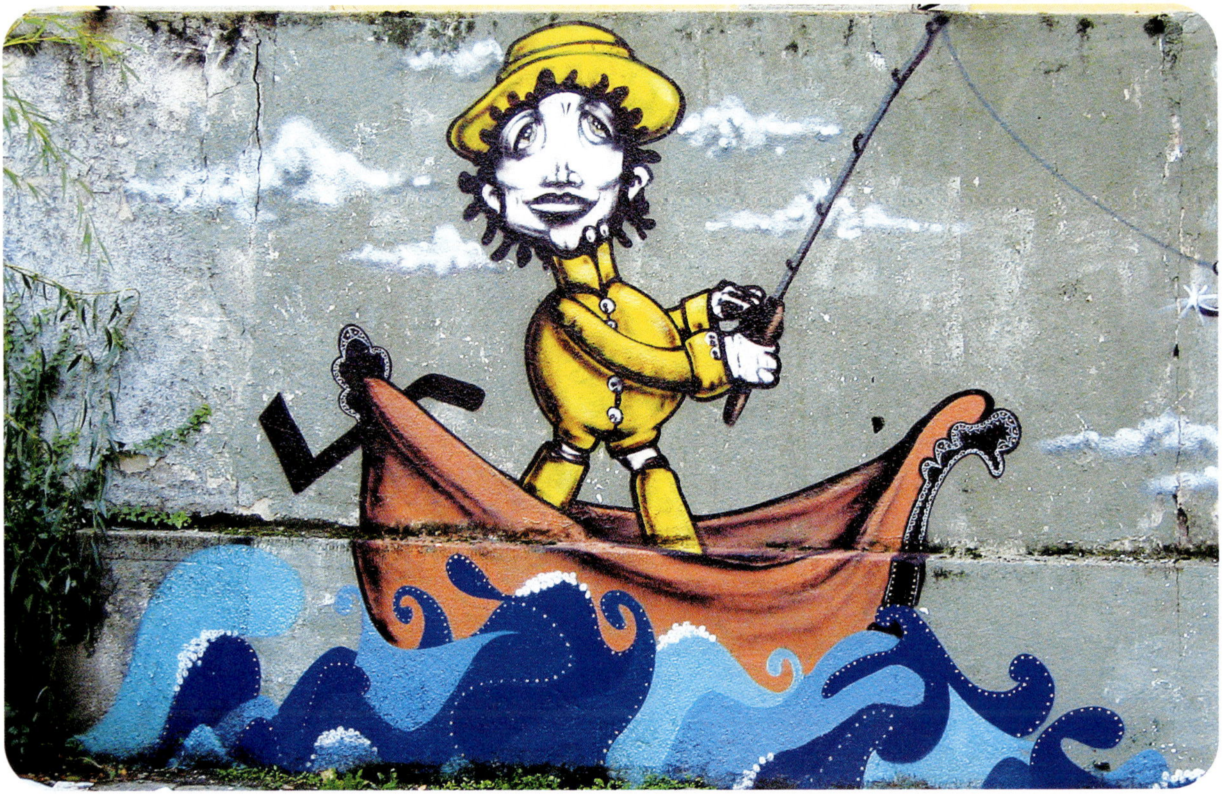

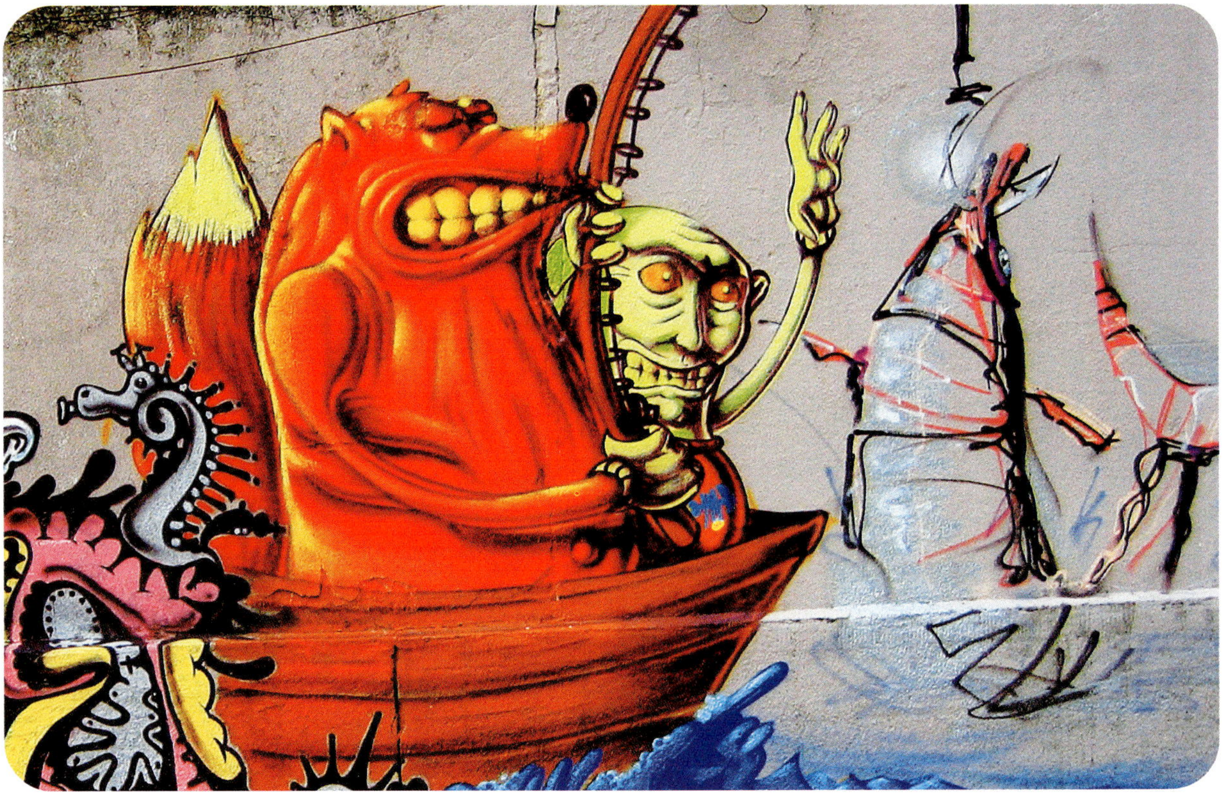

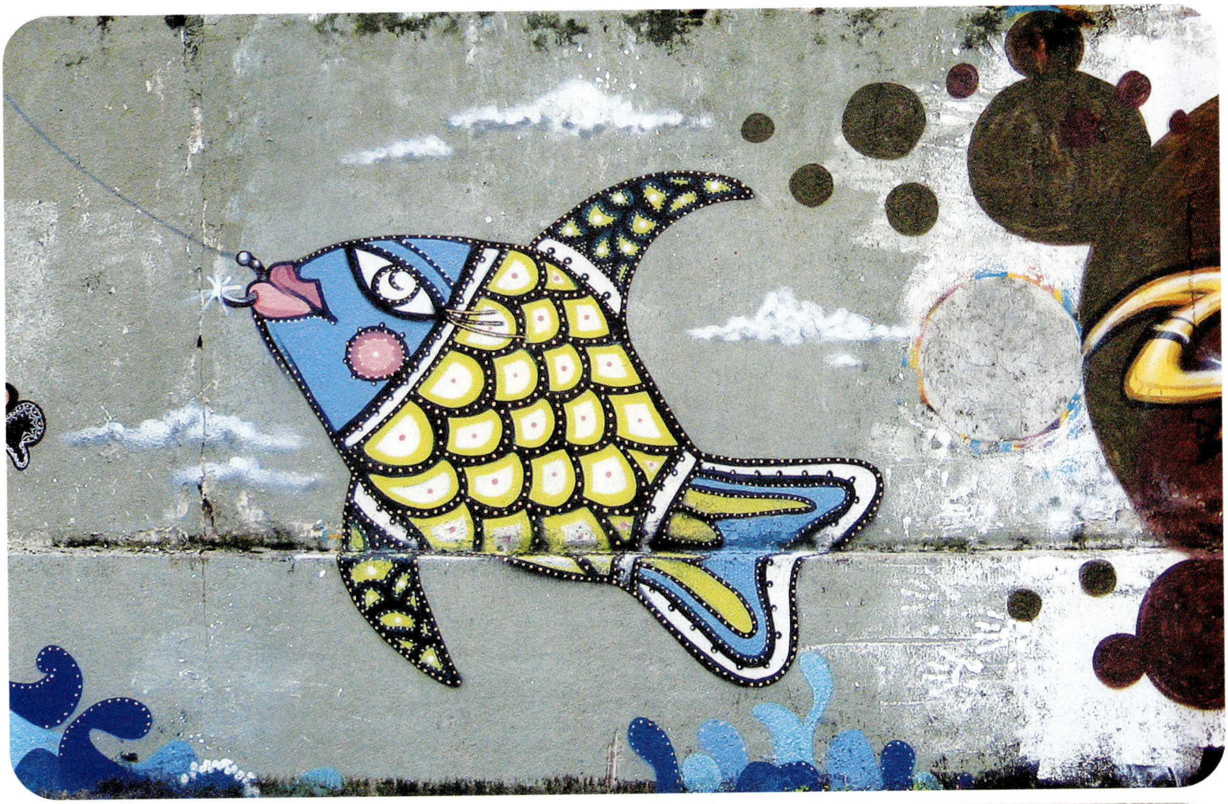

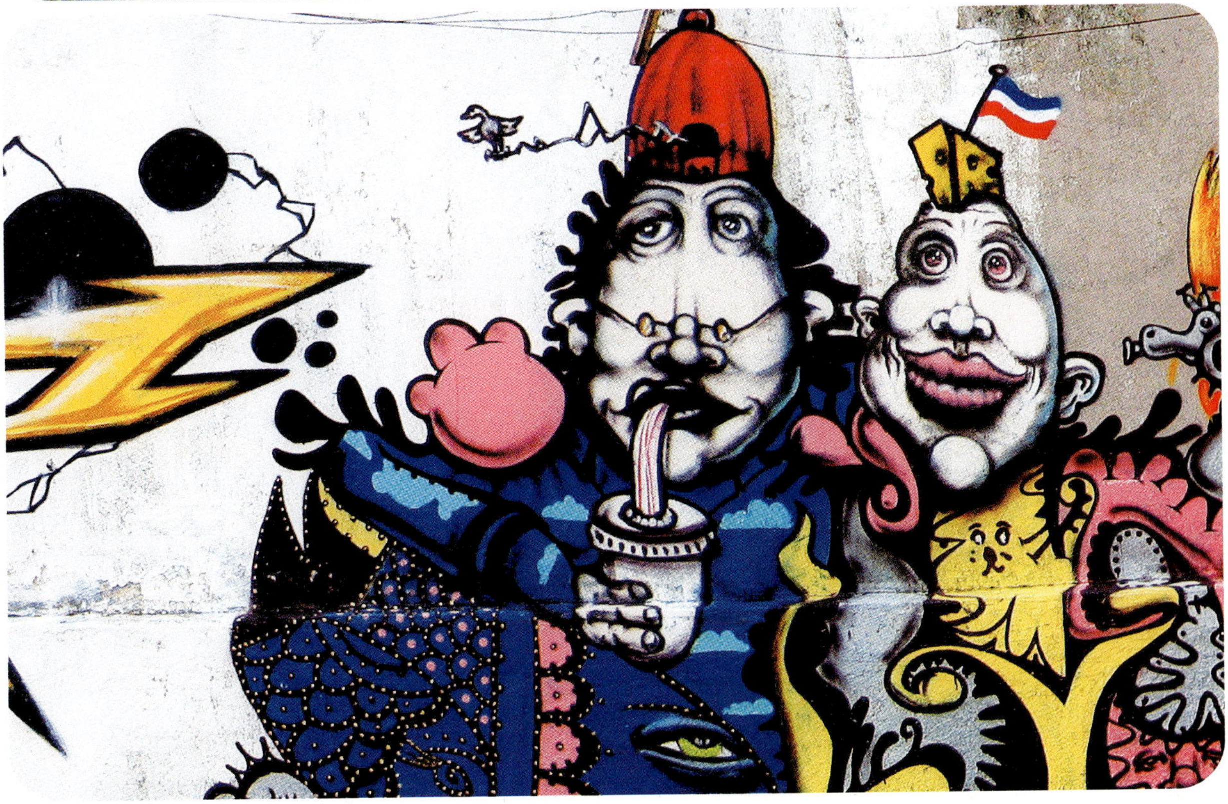

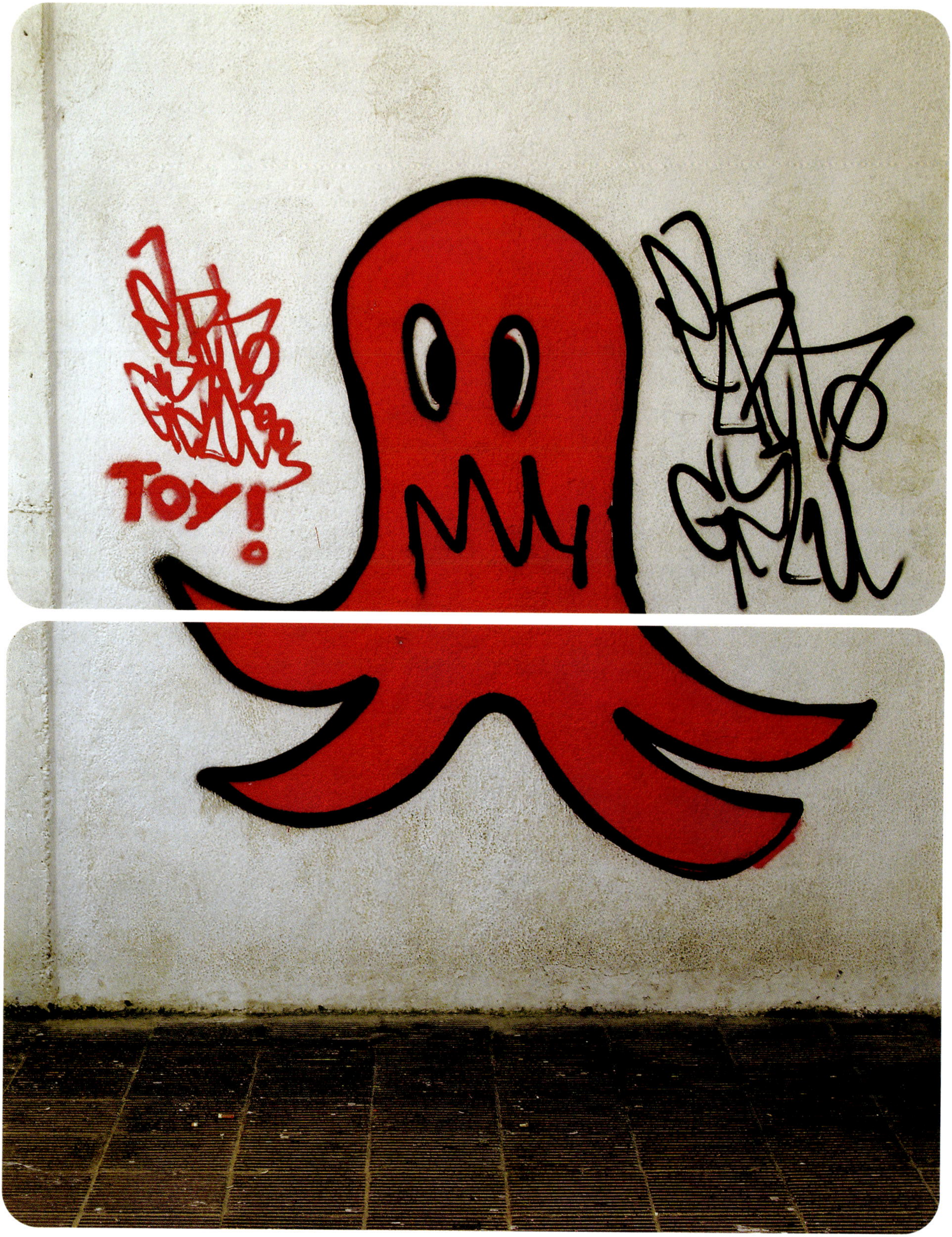

barcelona

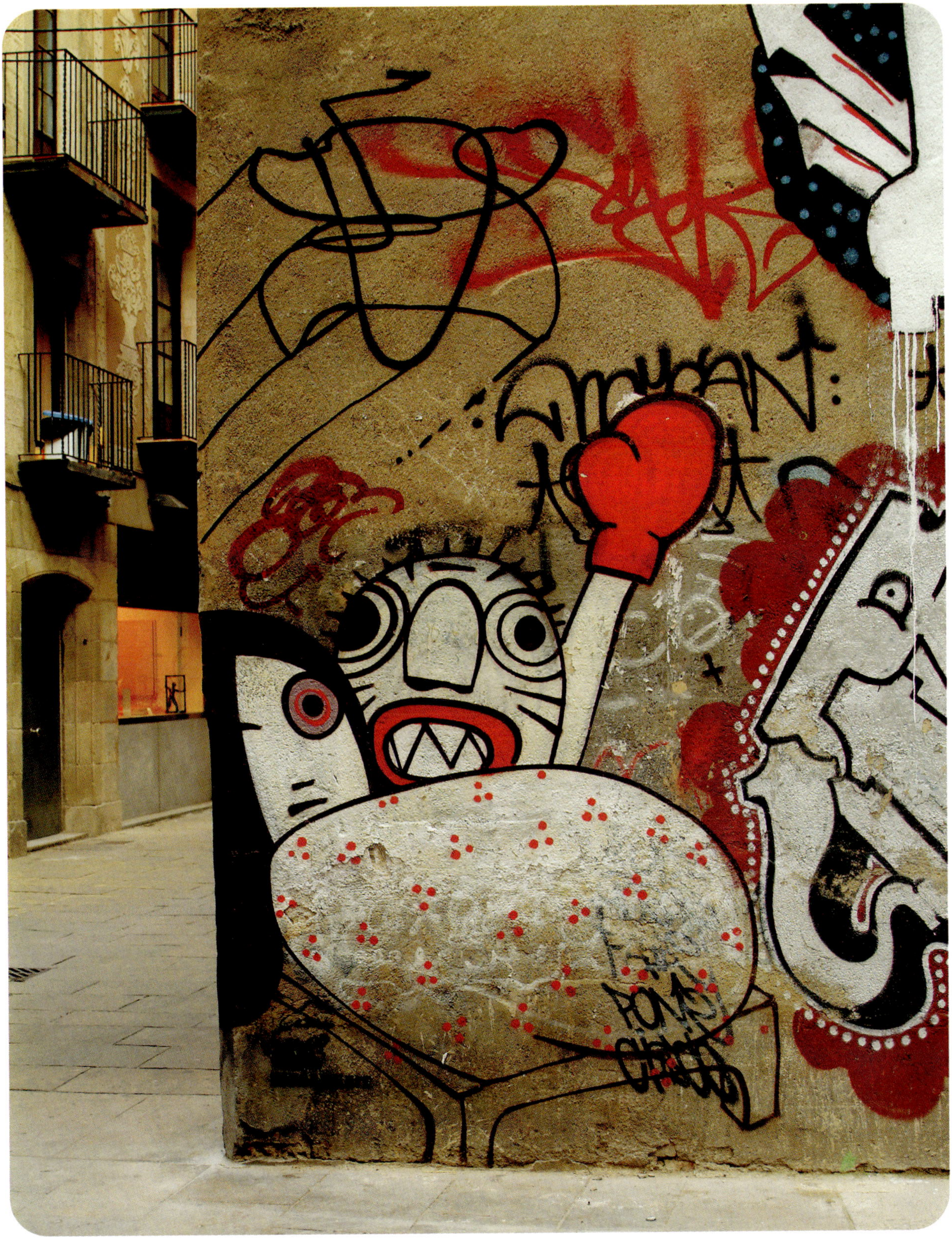

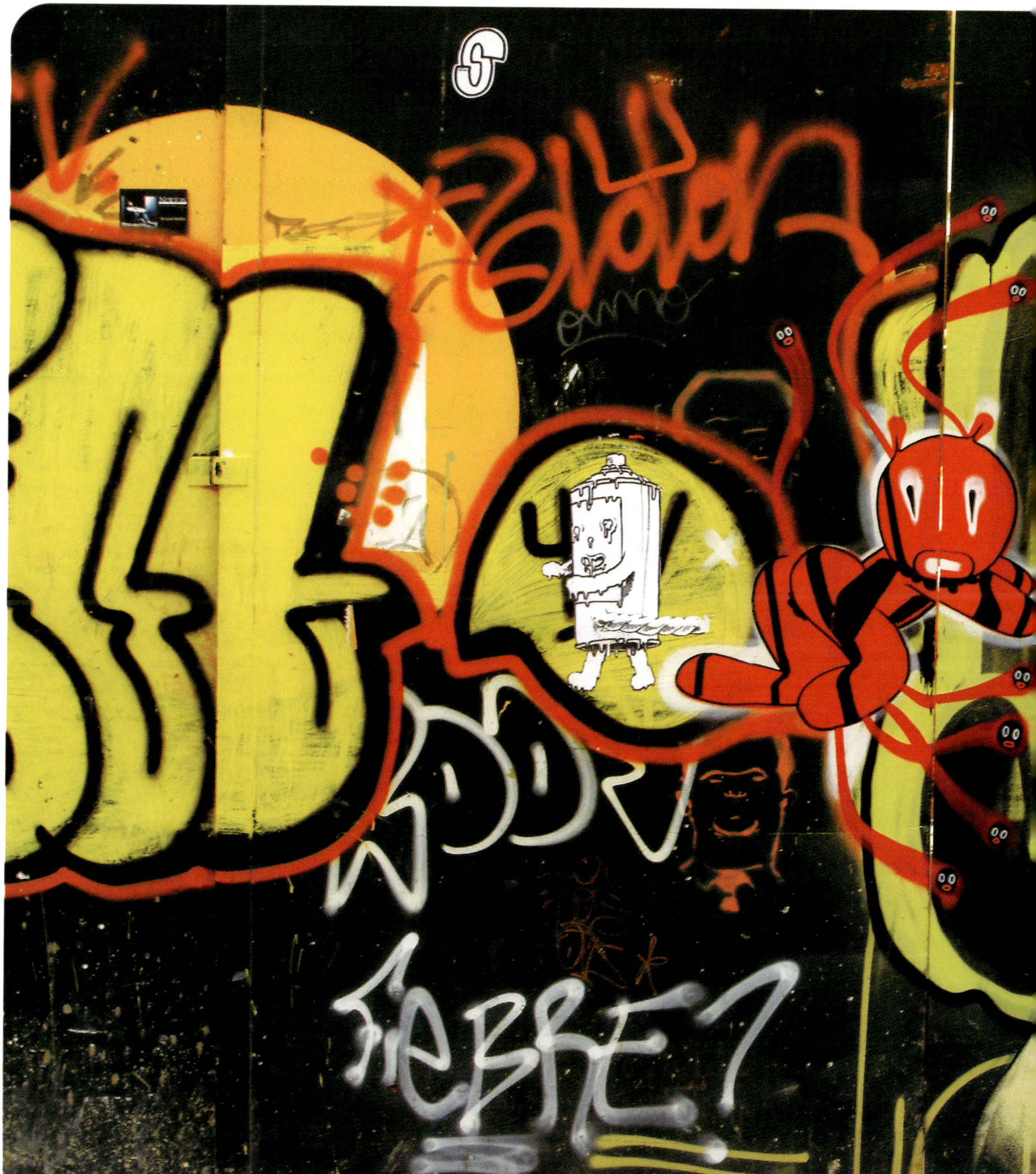

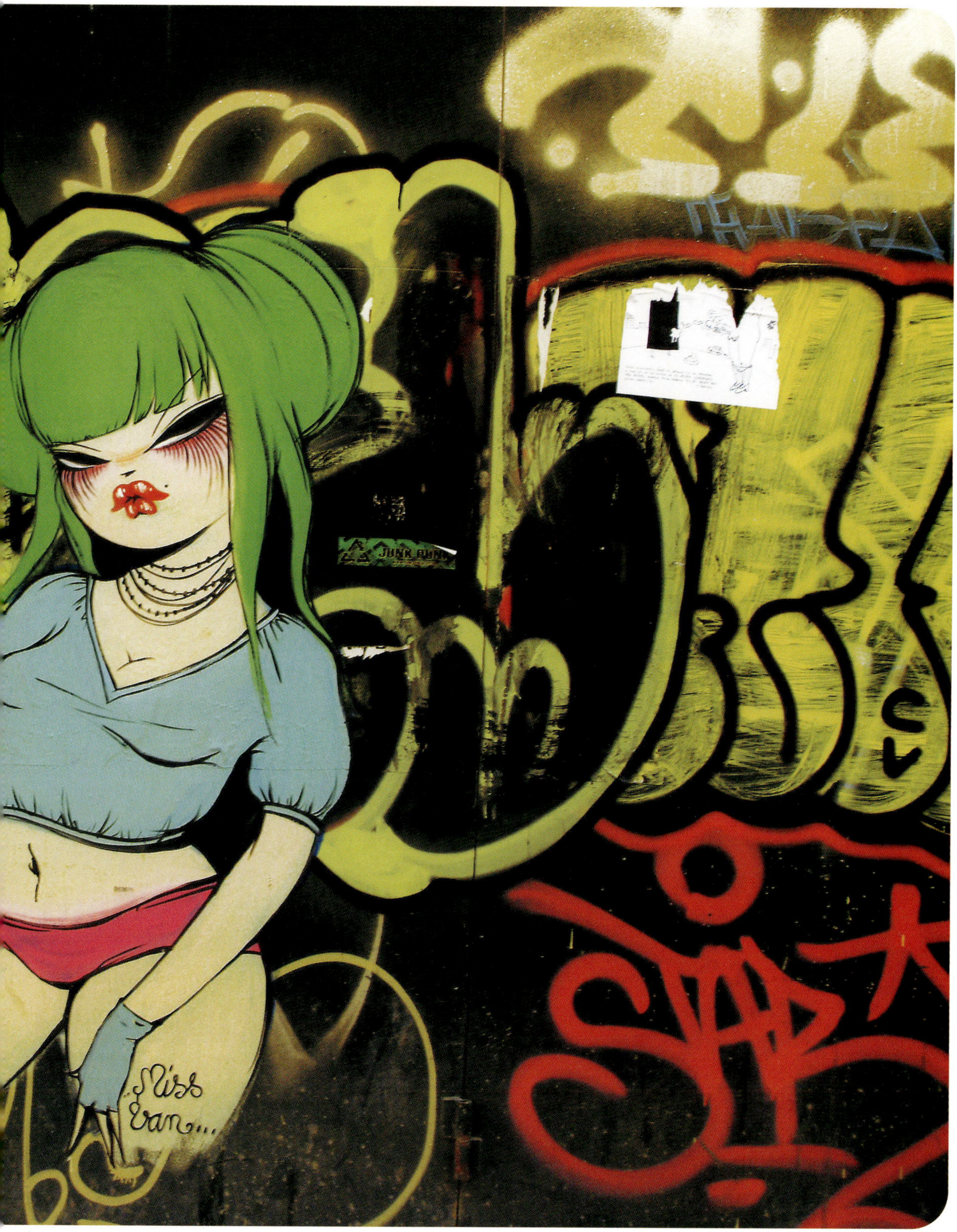

barcelona

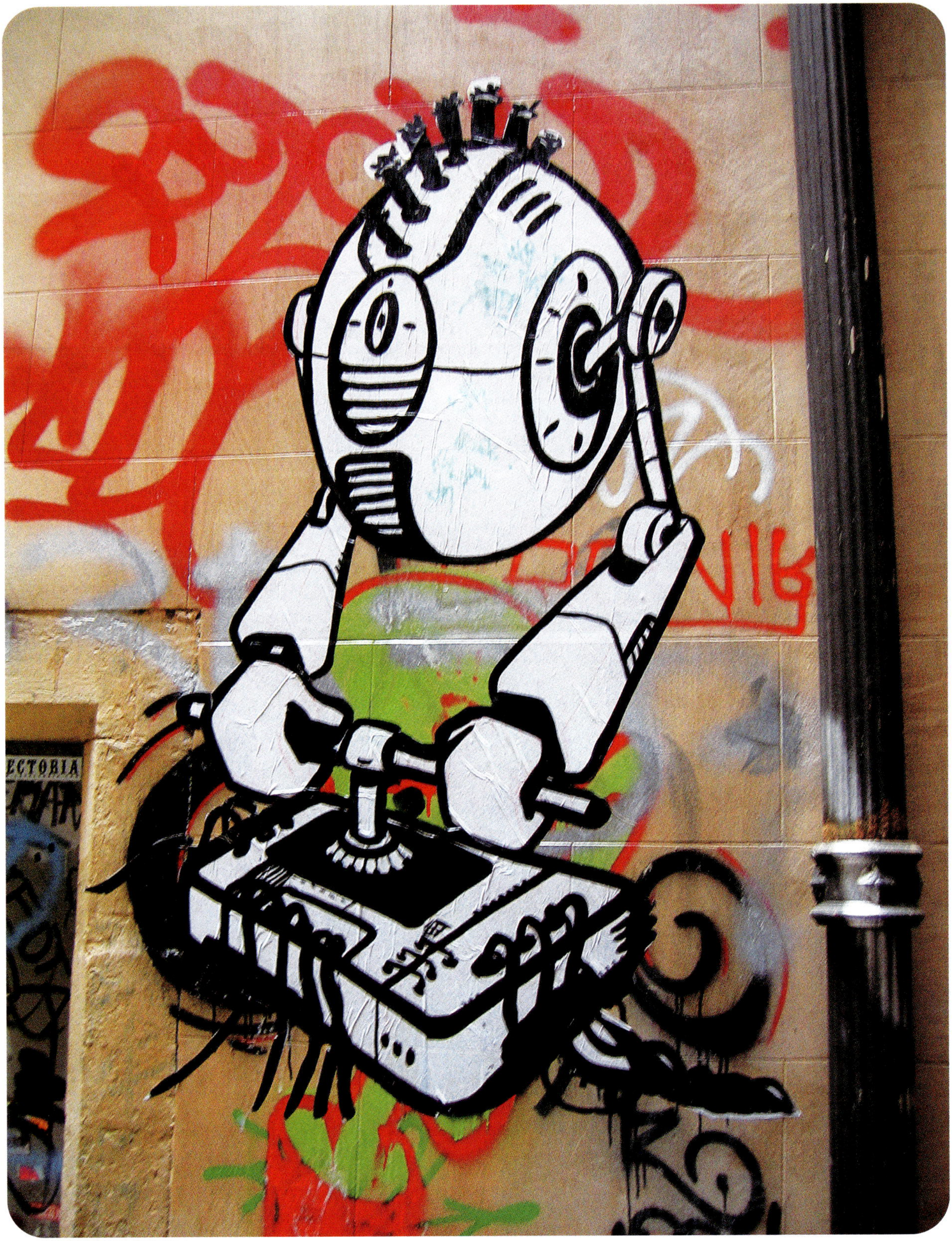

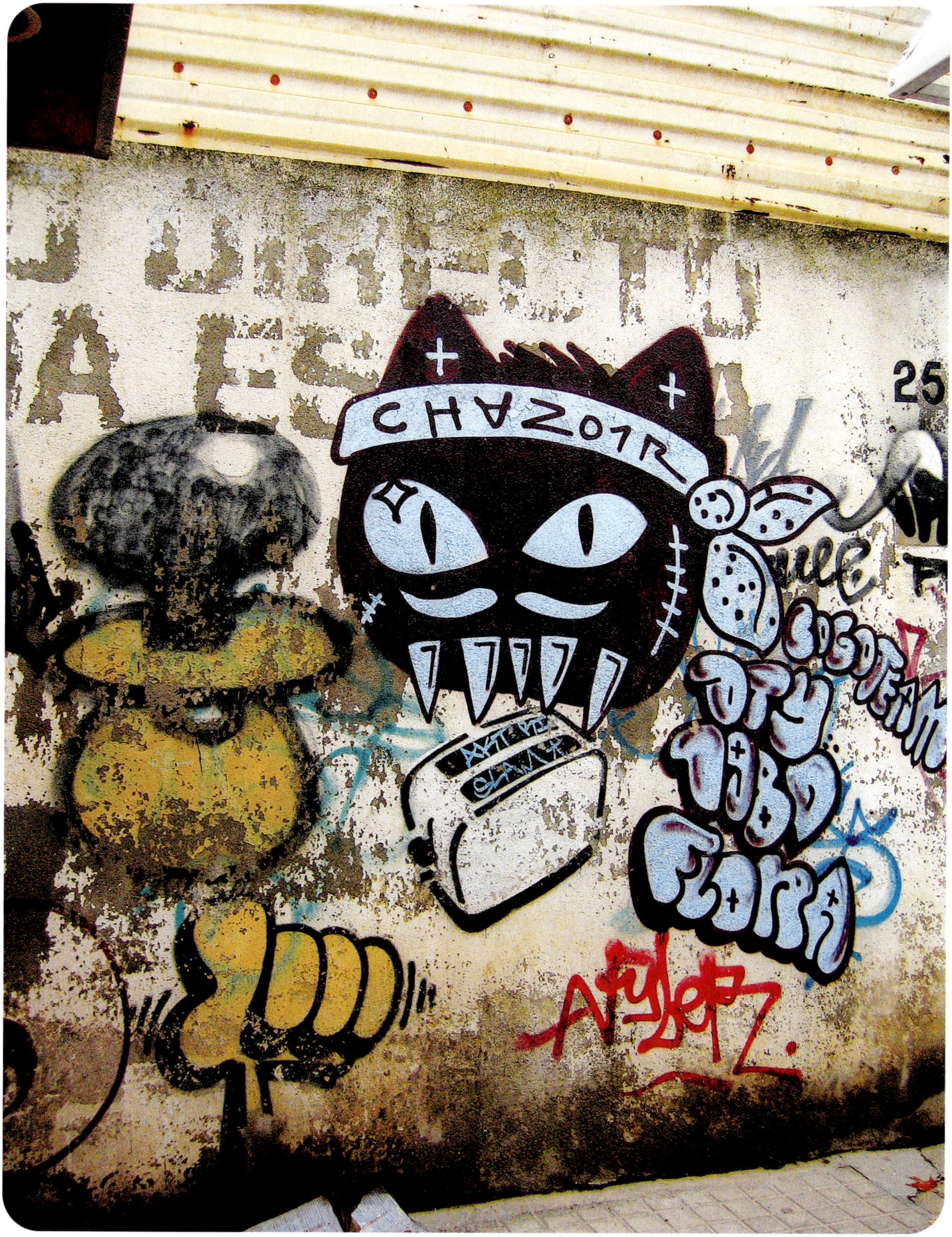

barcelona

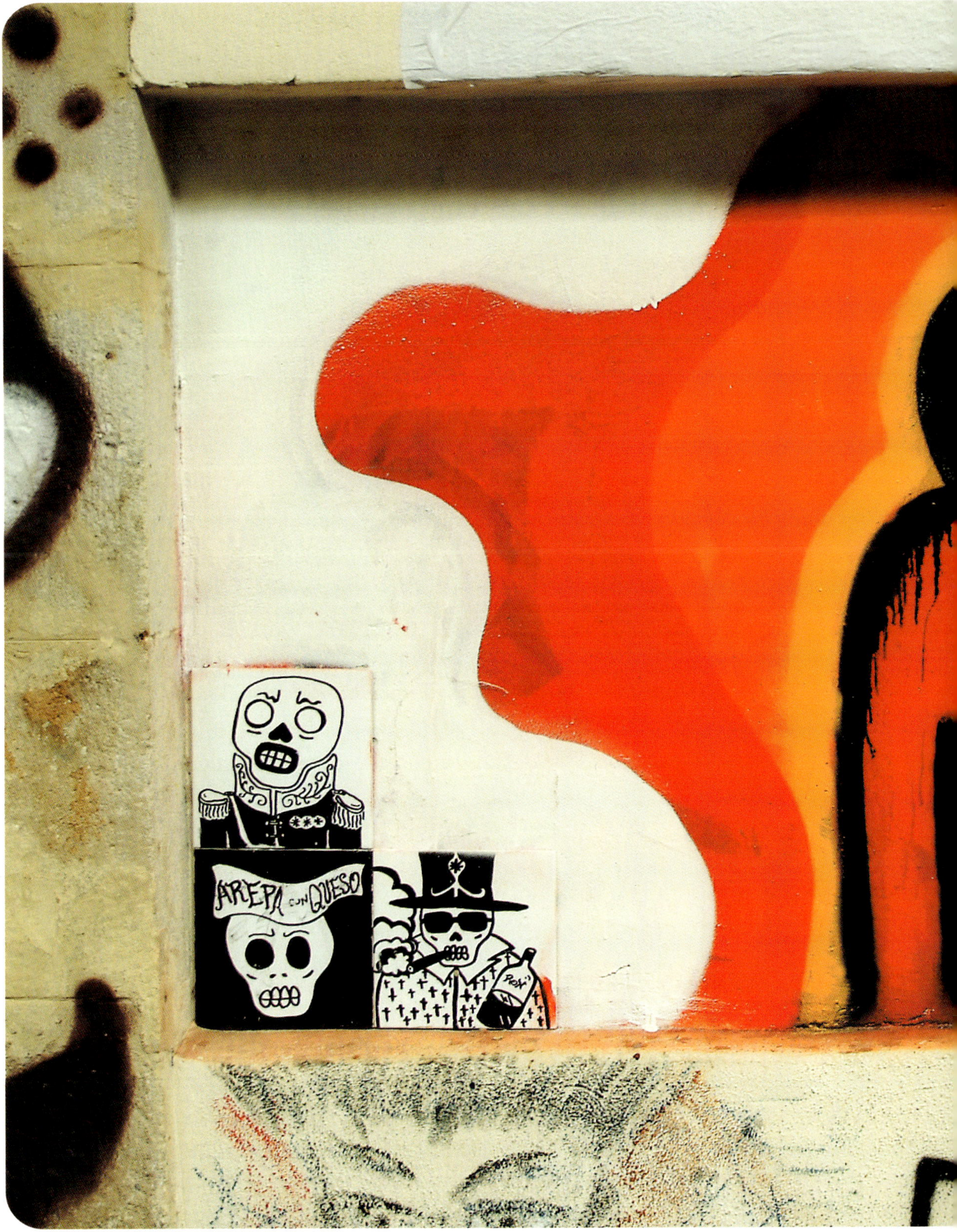
AREPA CON QUESO

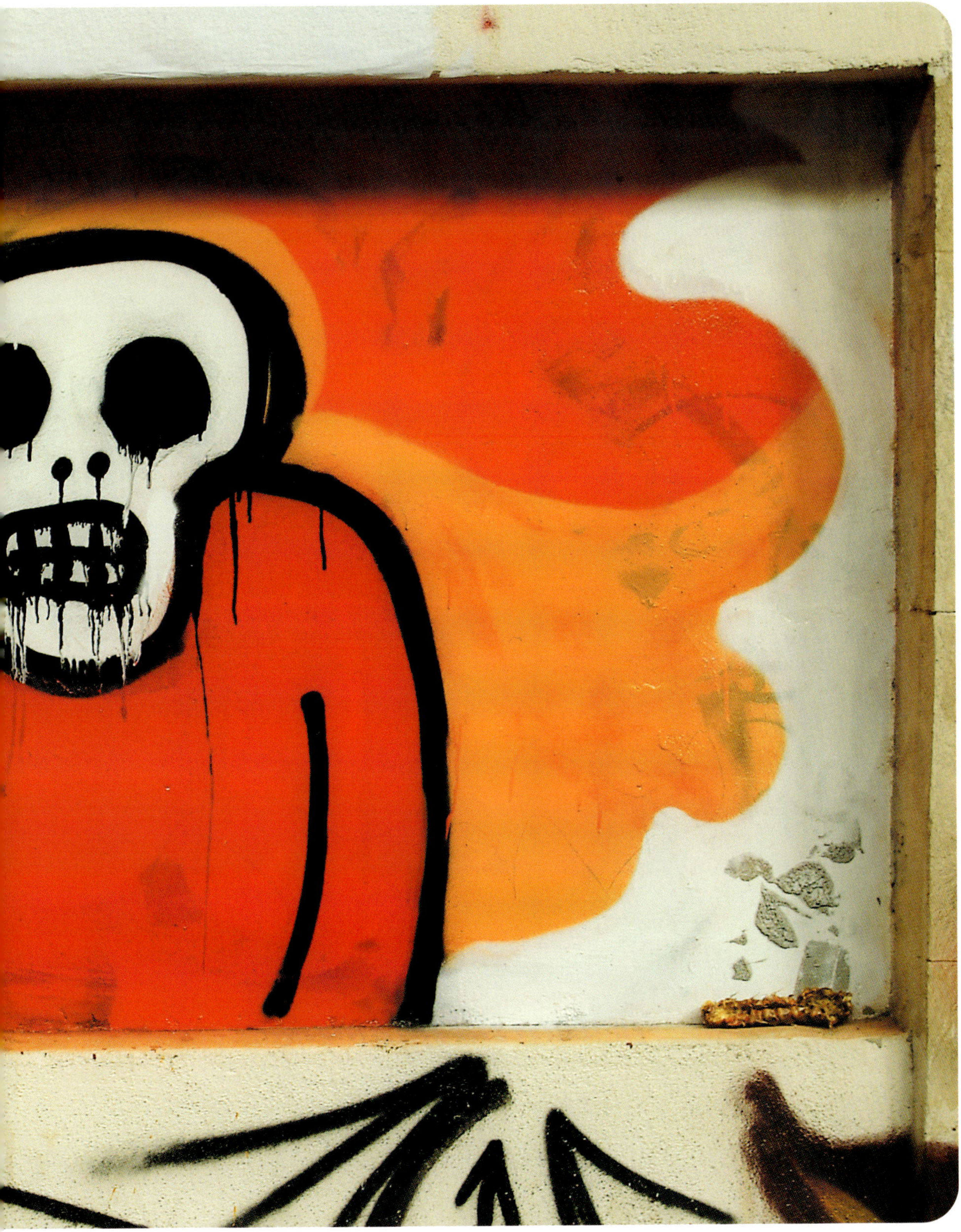

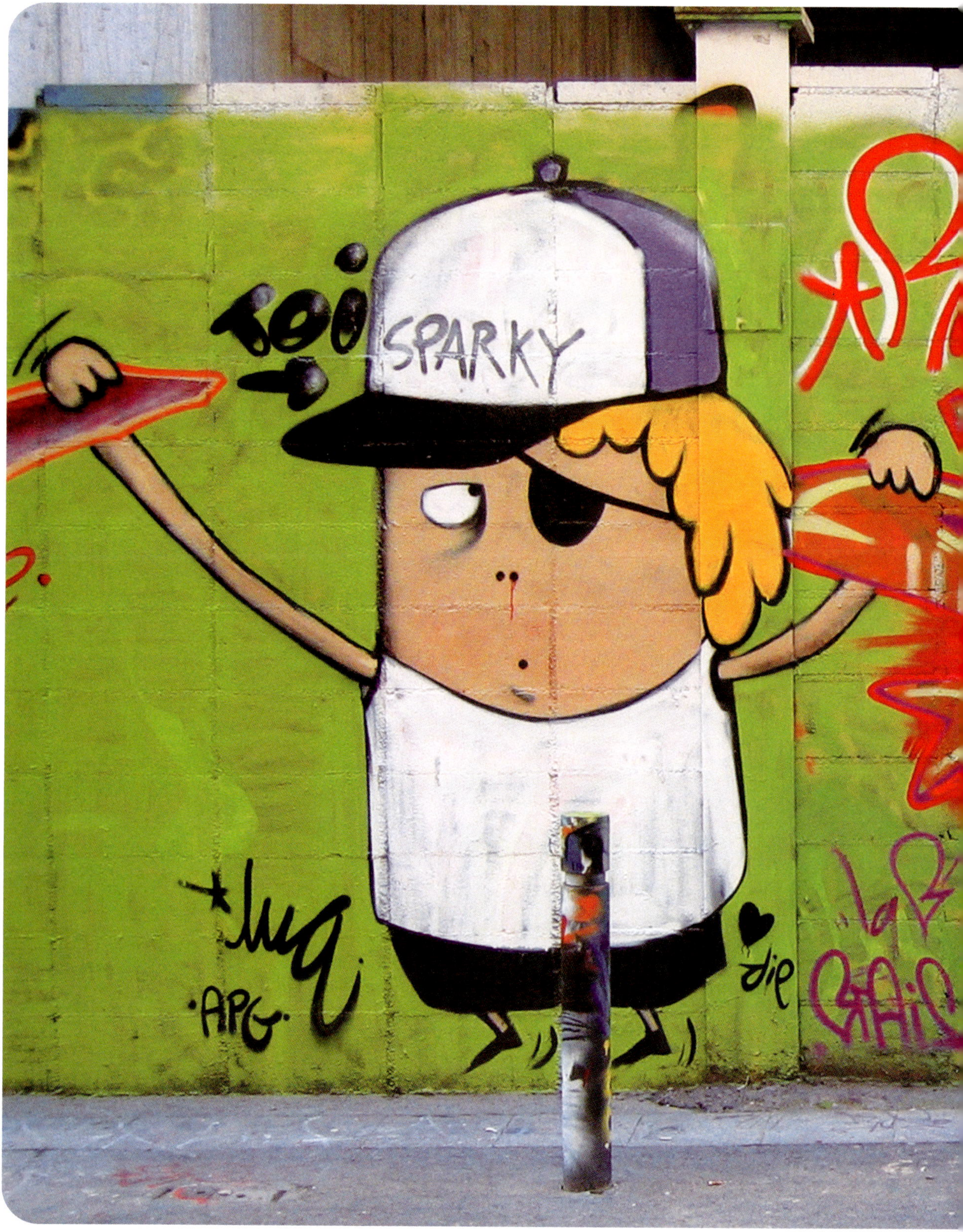
SPARKY

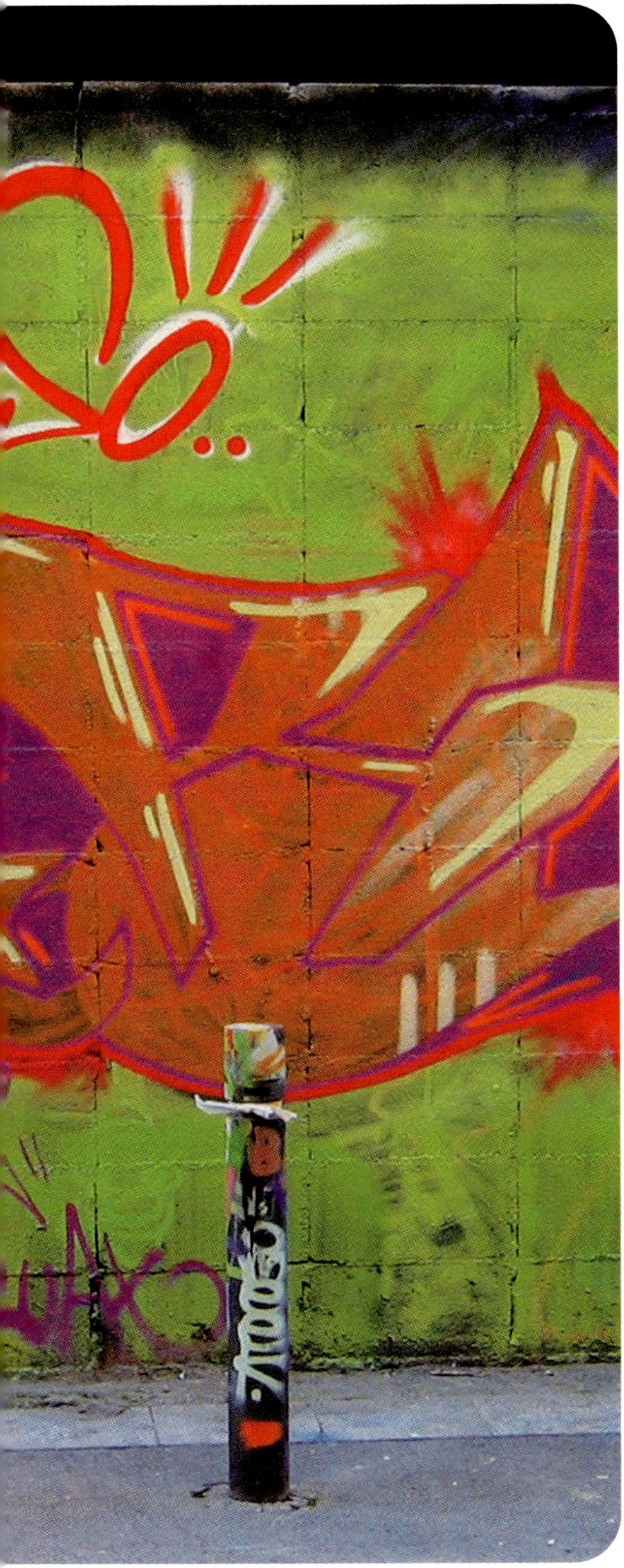

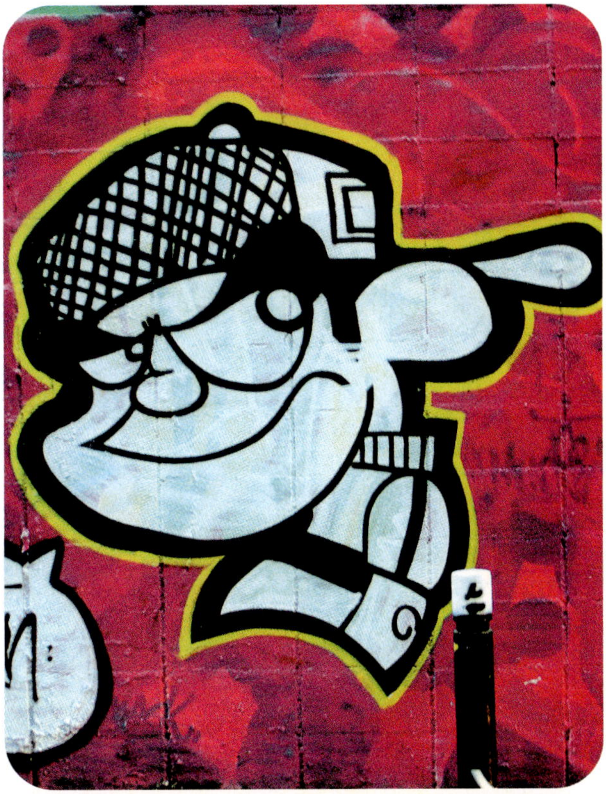

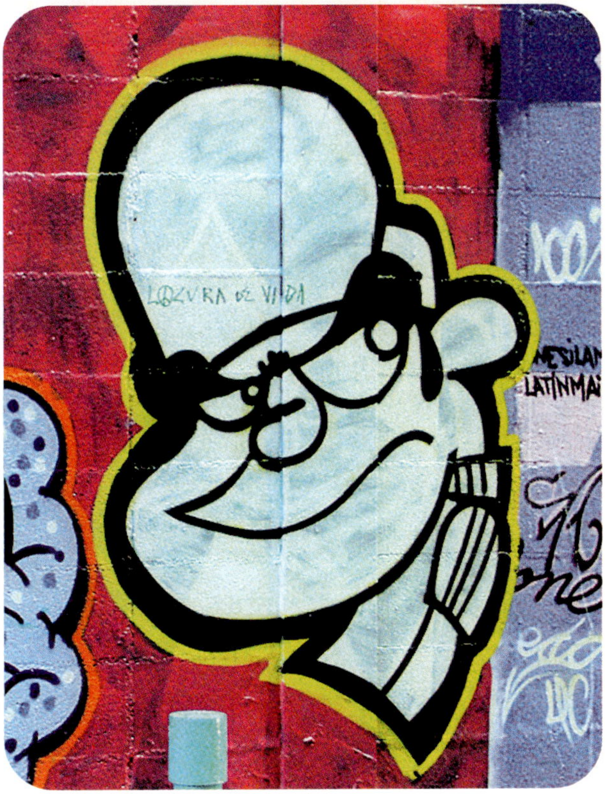
LOCURA DE VIDA

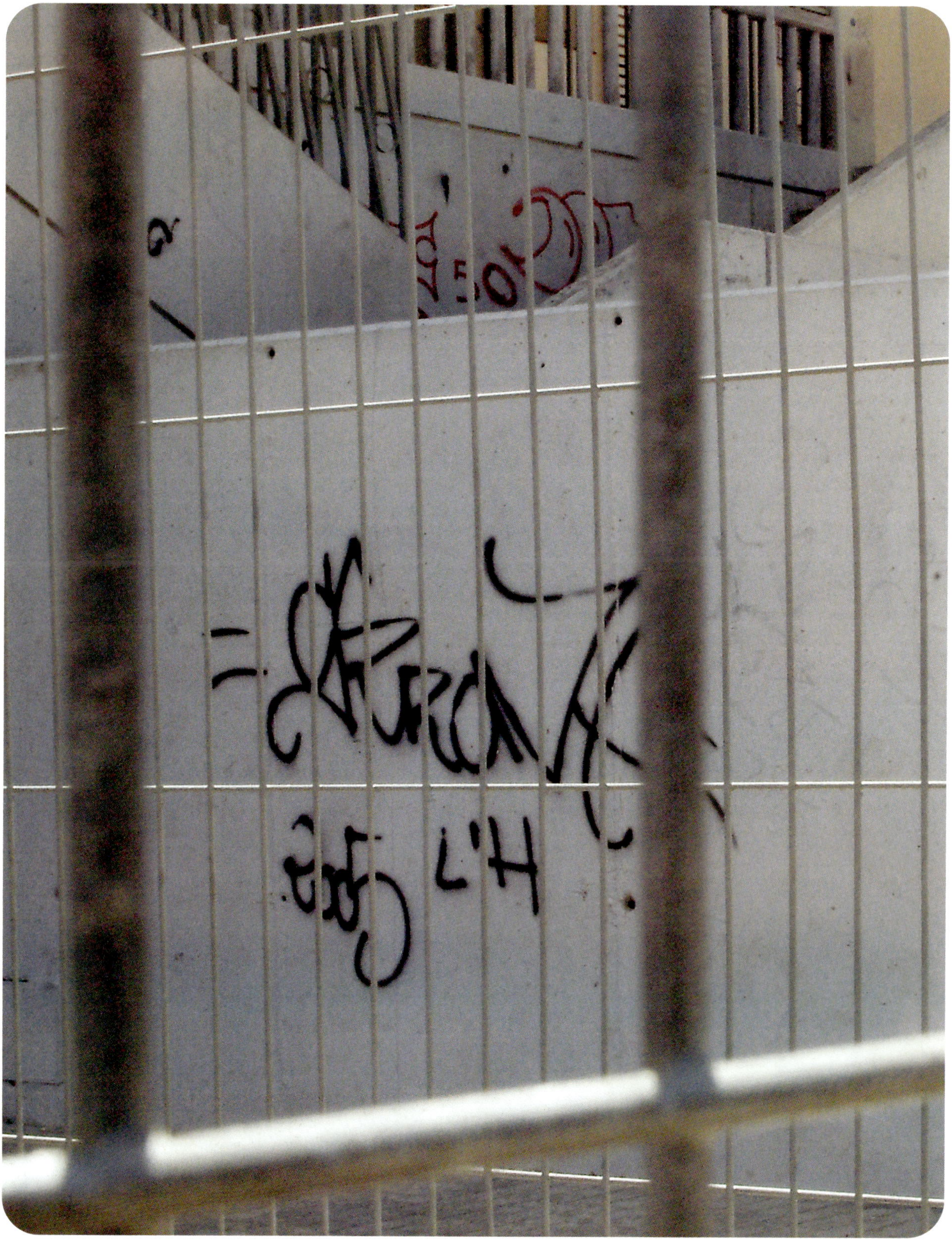

barcelona

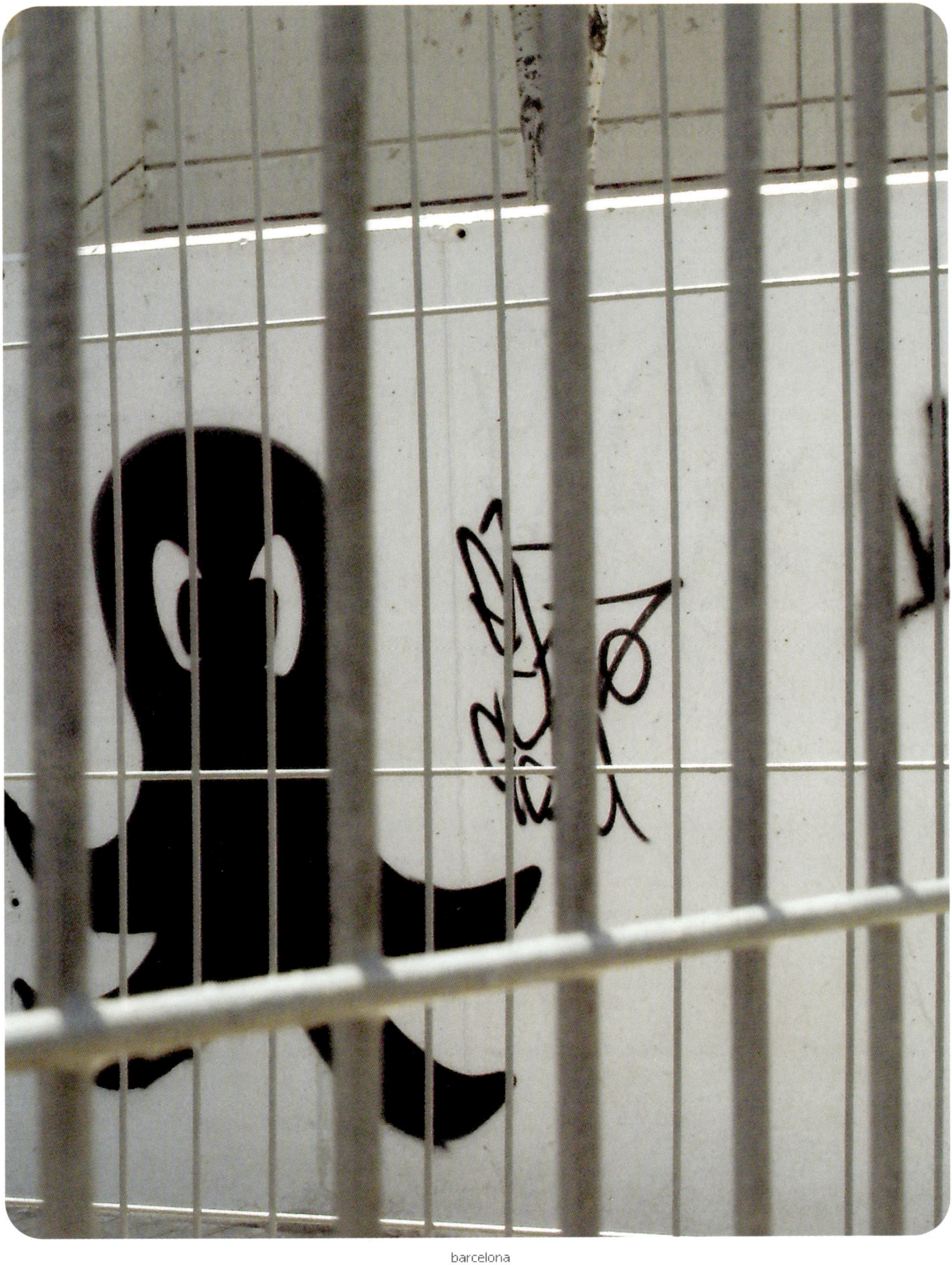

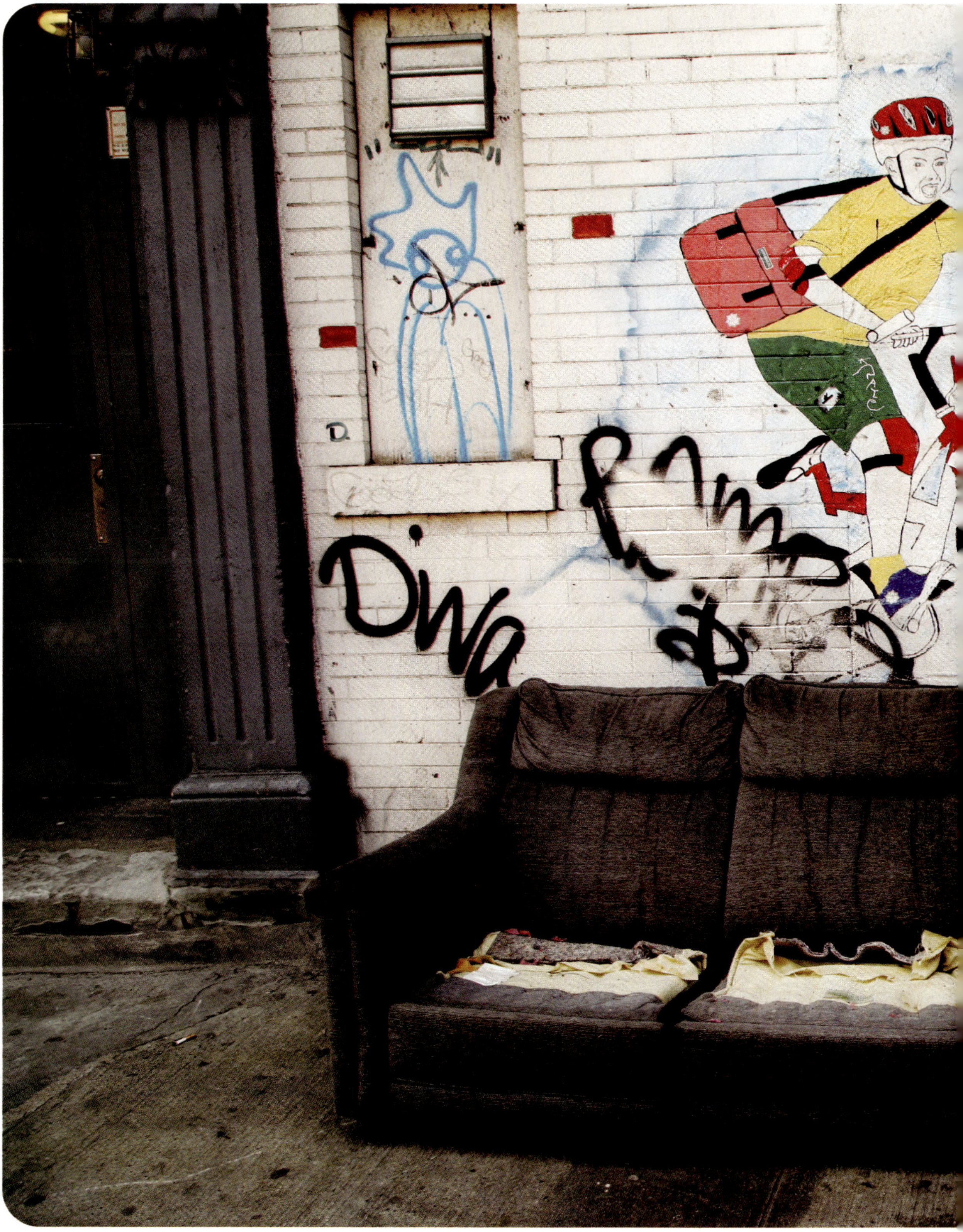
Diva

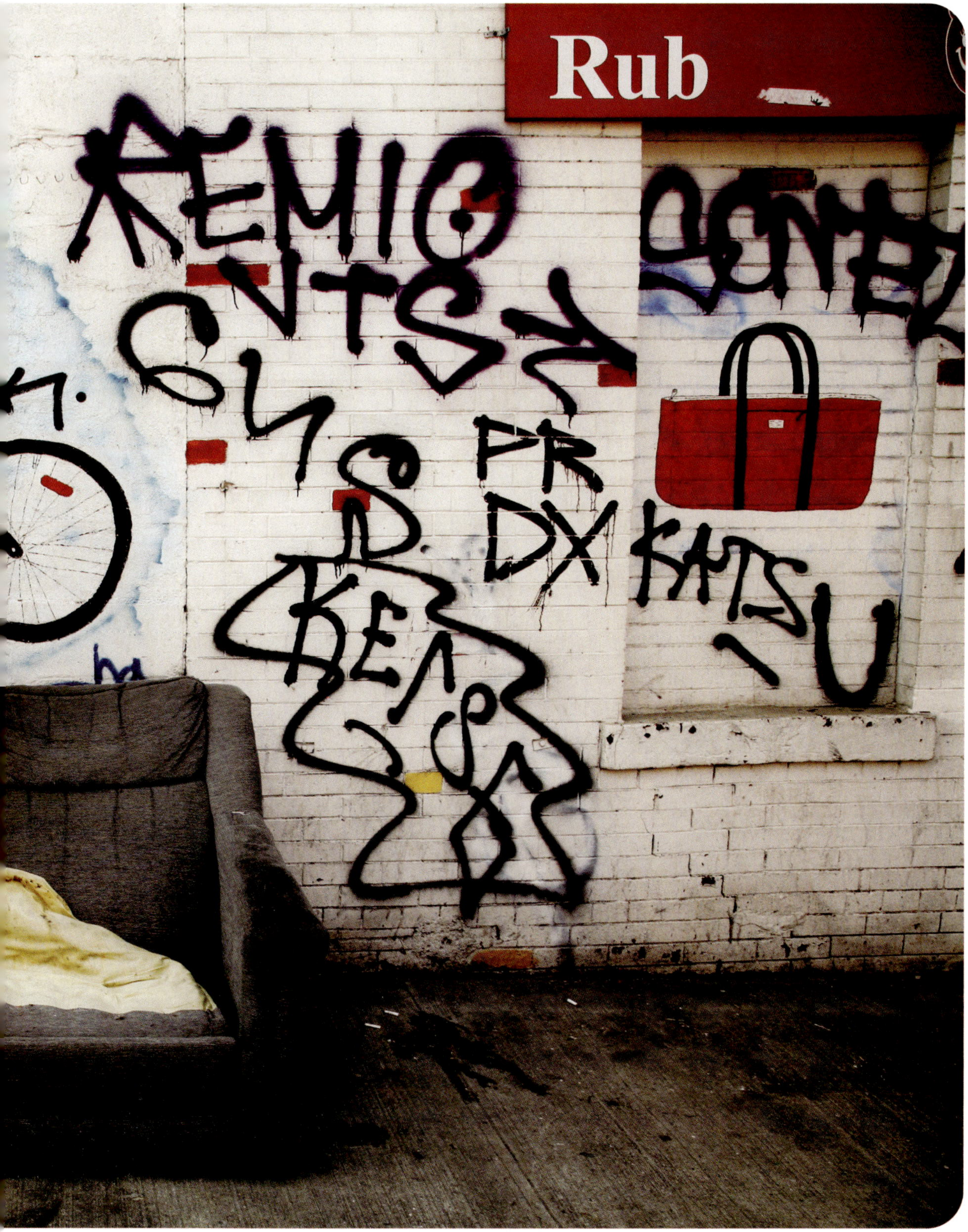
Rub

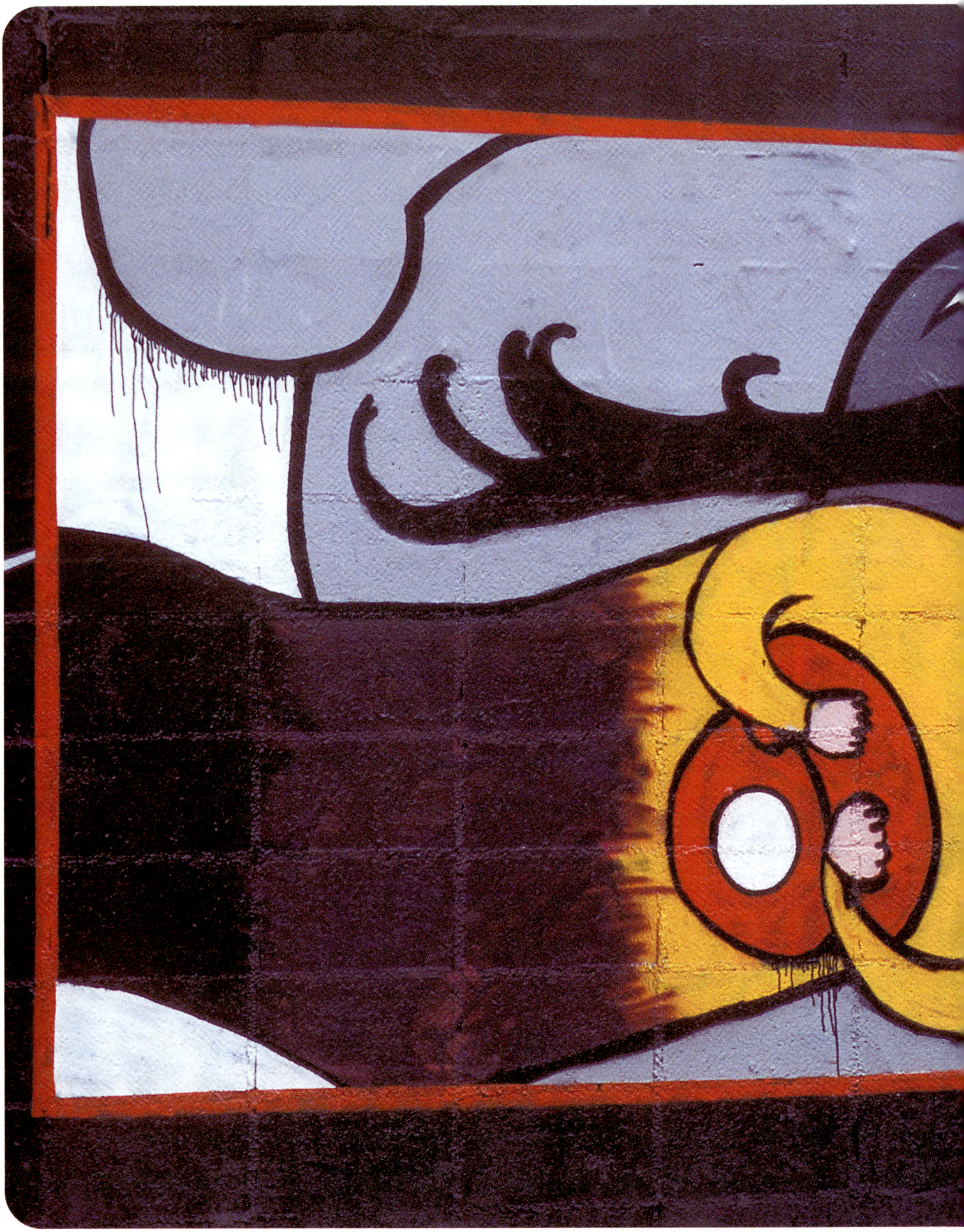

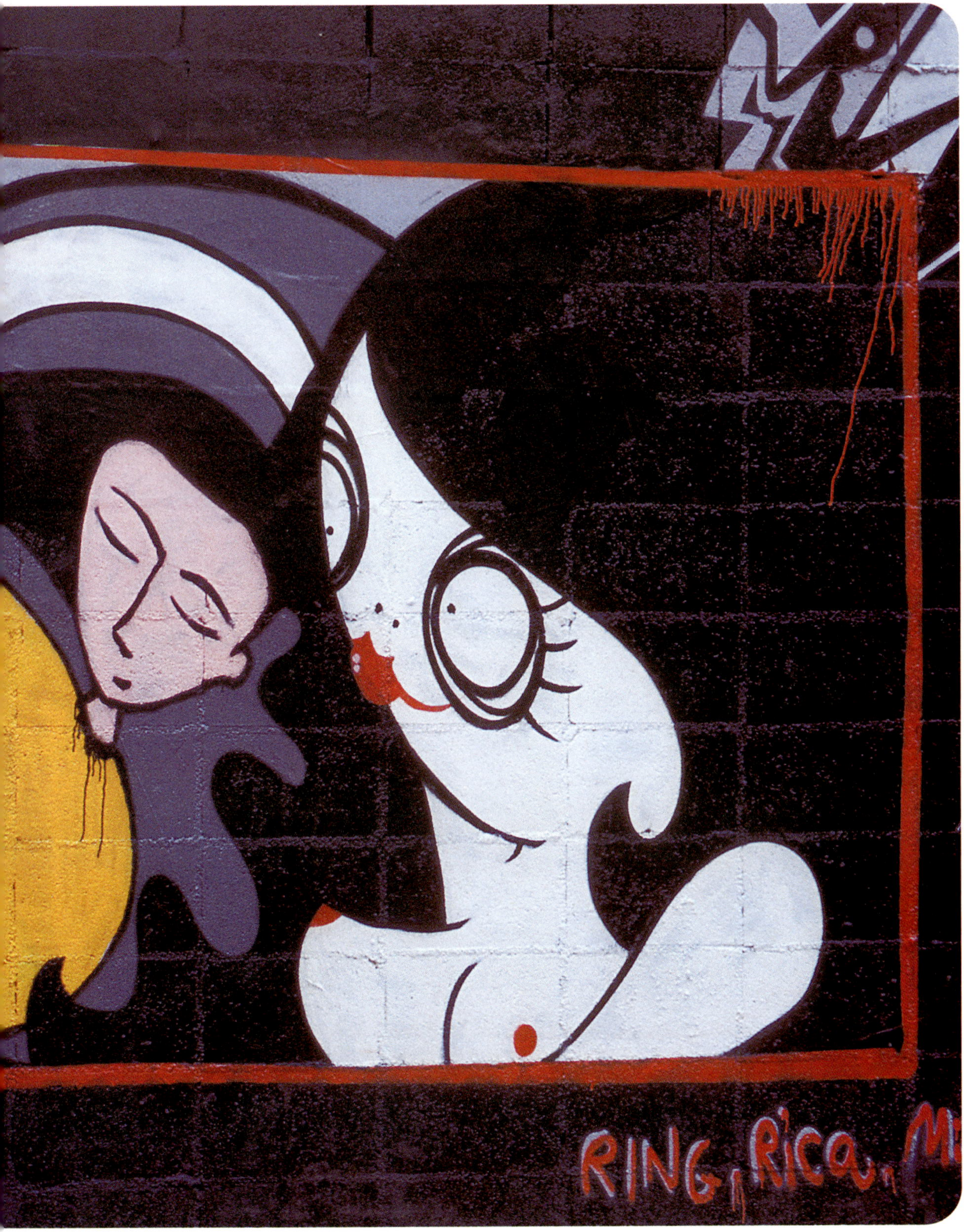
RING, Rica, M

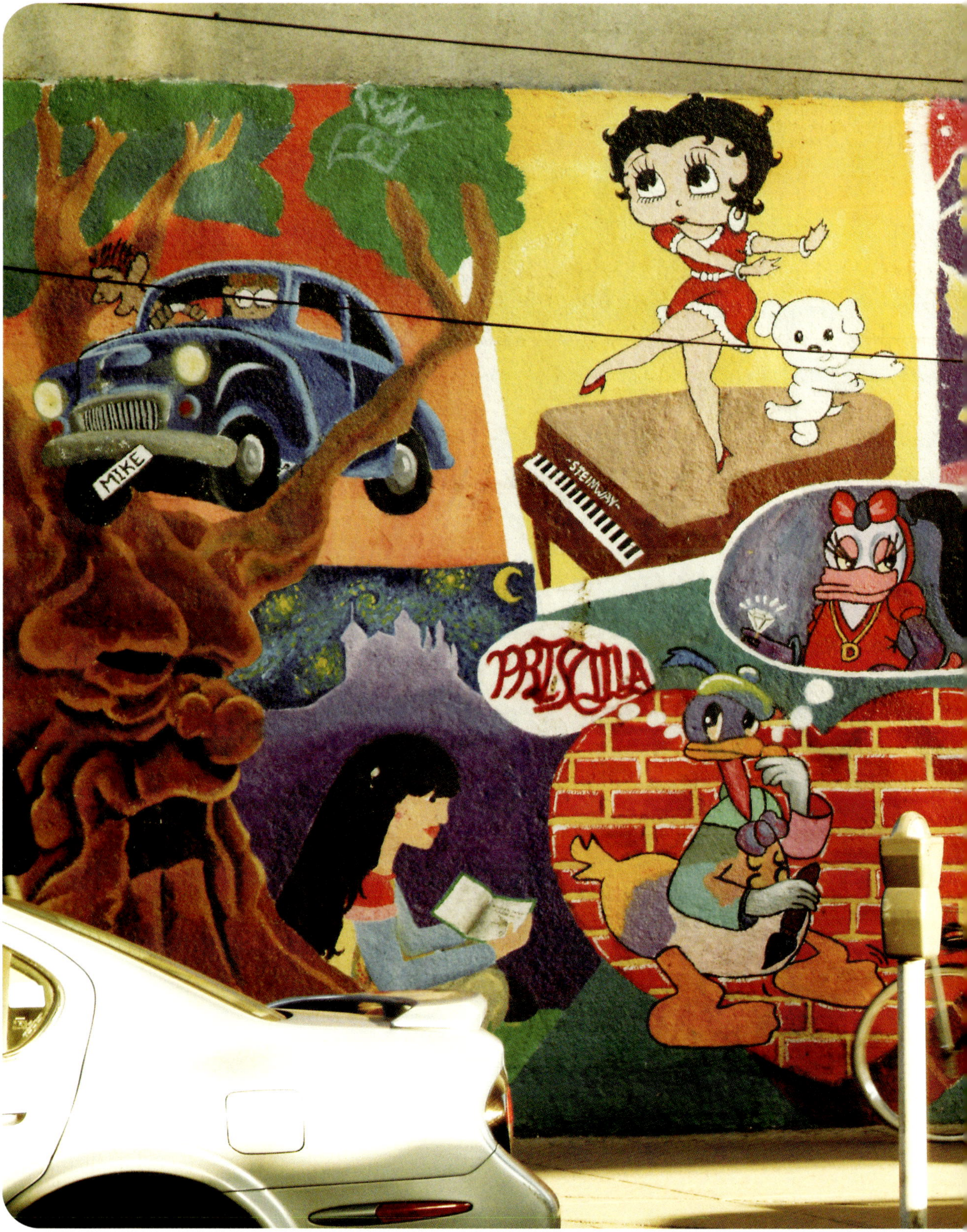
MIKE
STEINWAY
PRISCILLA

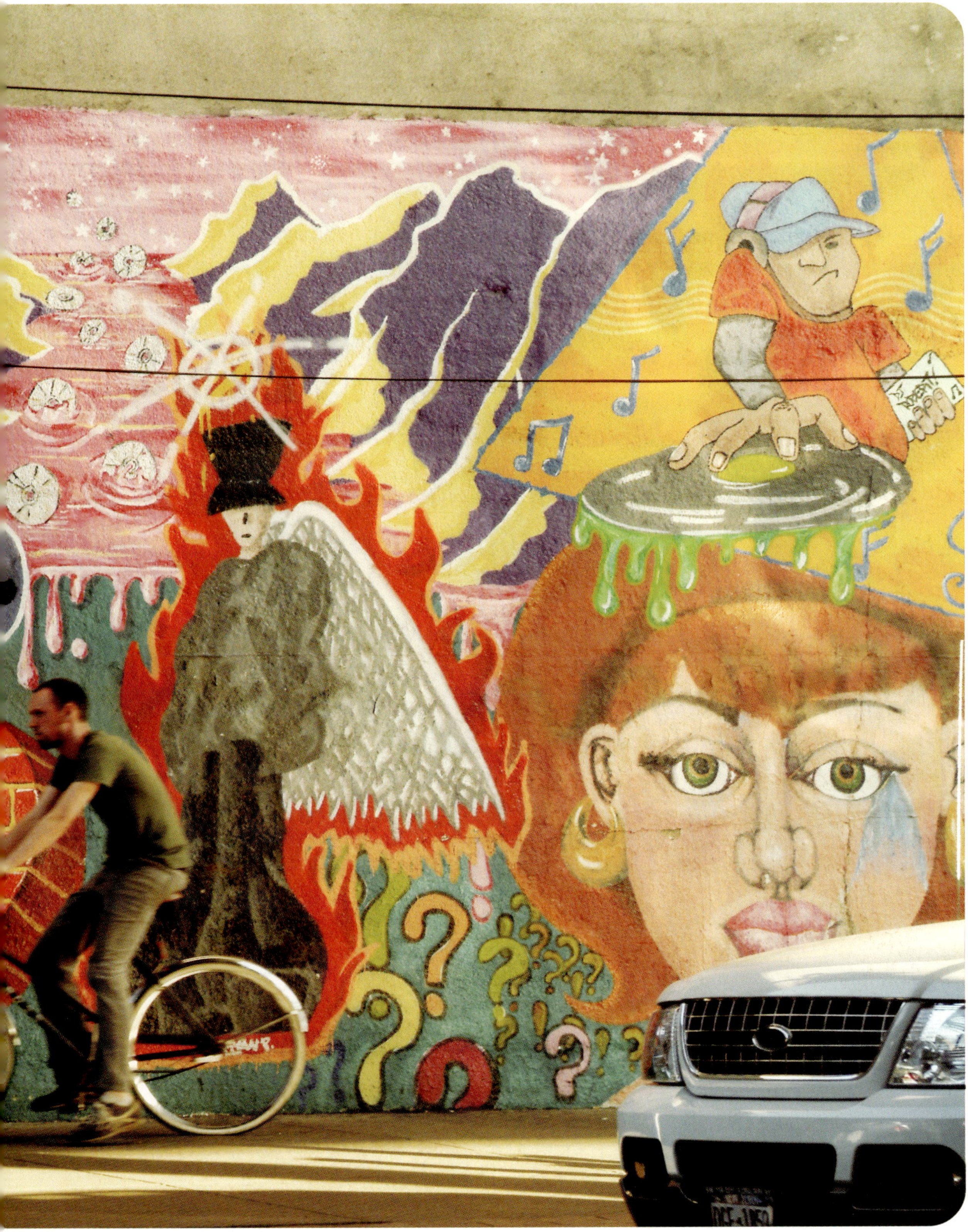

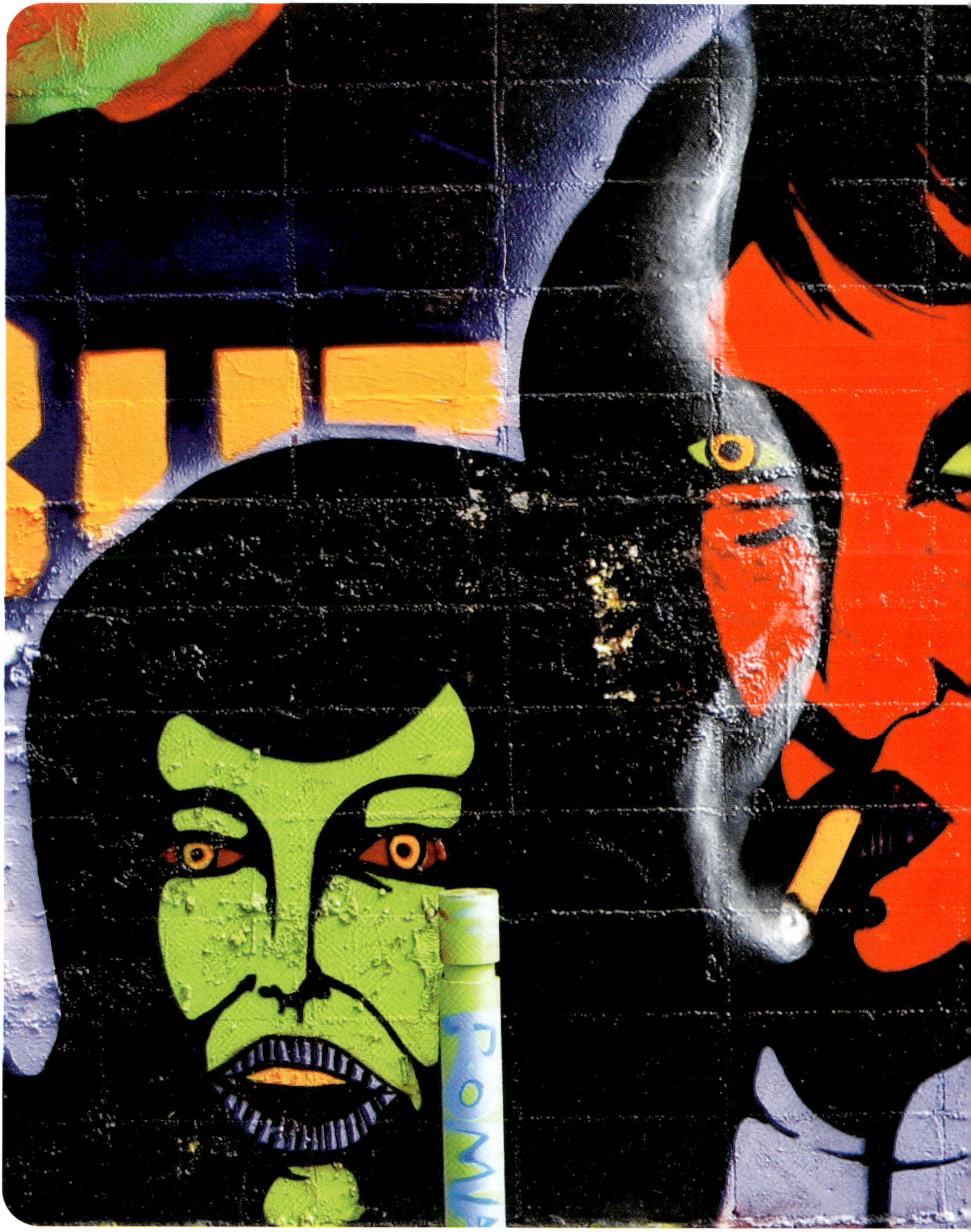

barcelona

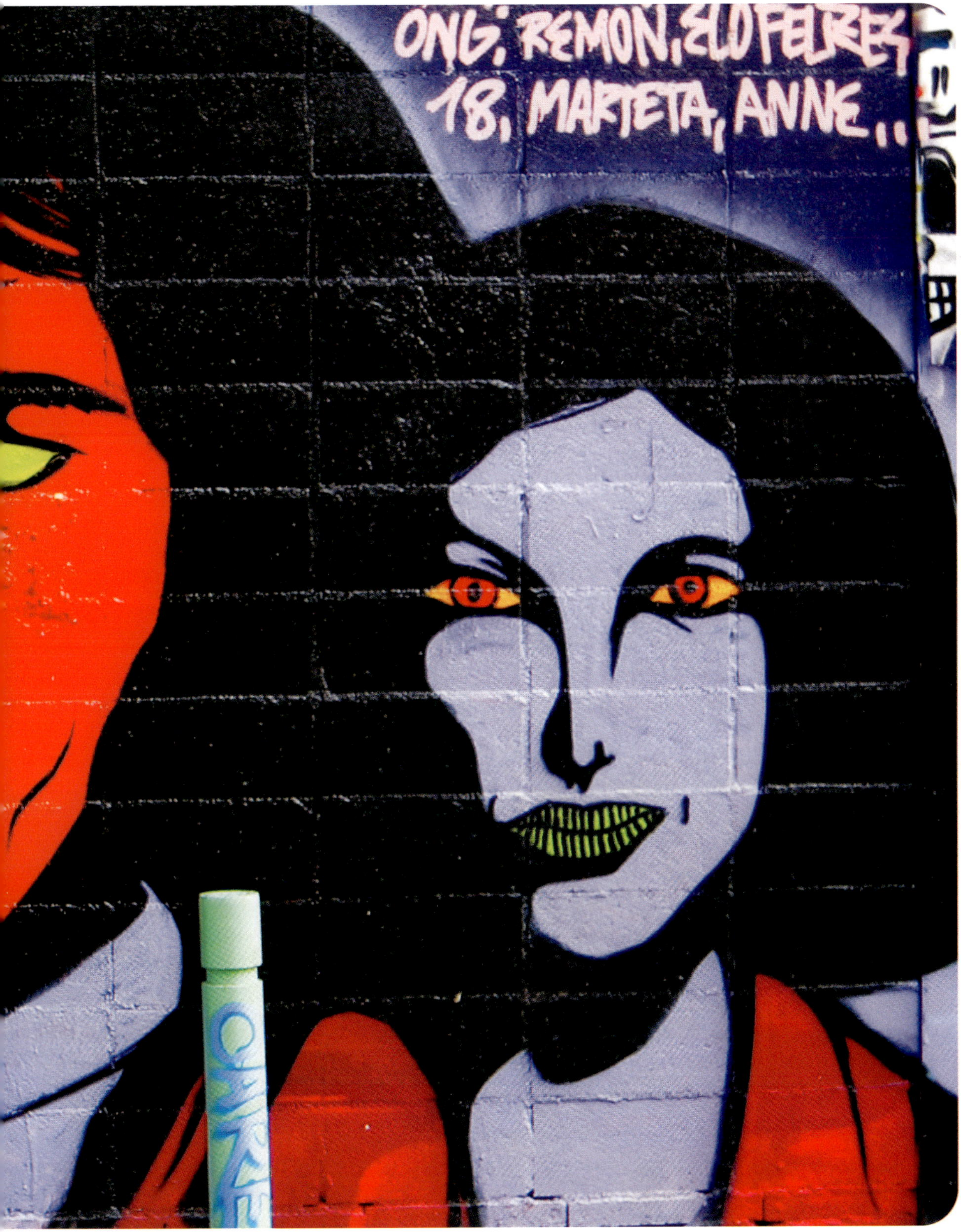
ONG, REMON,
18, MARTETA, ANNE..

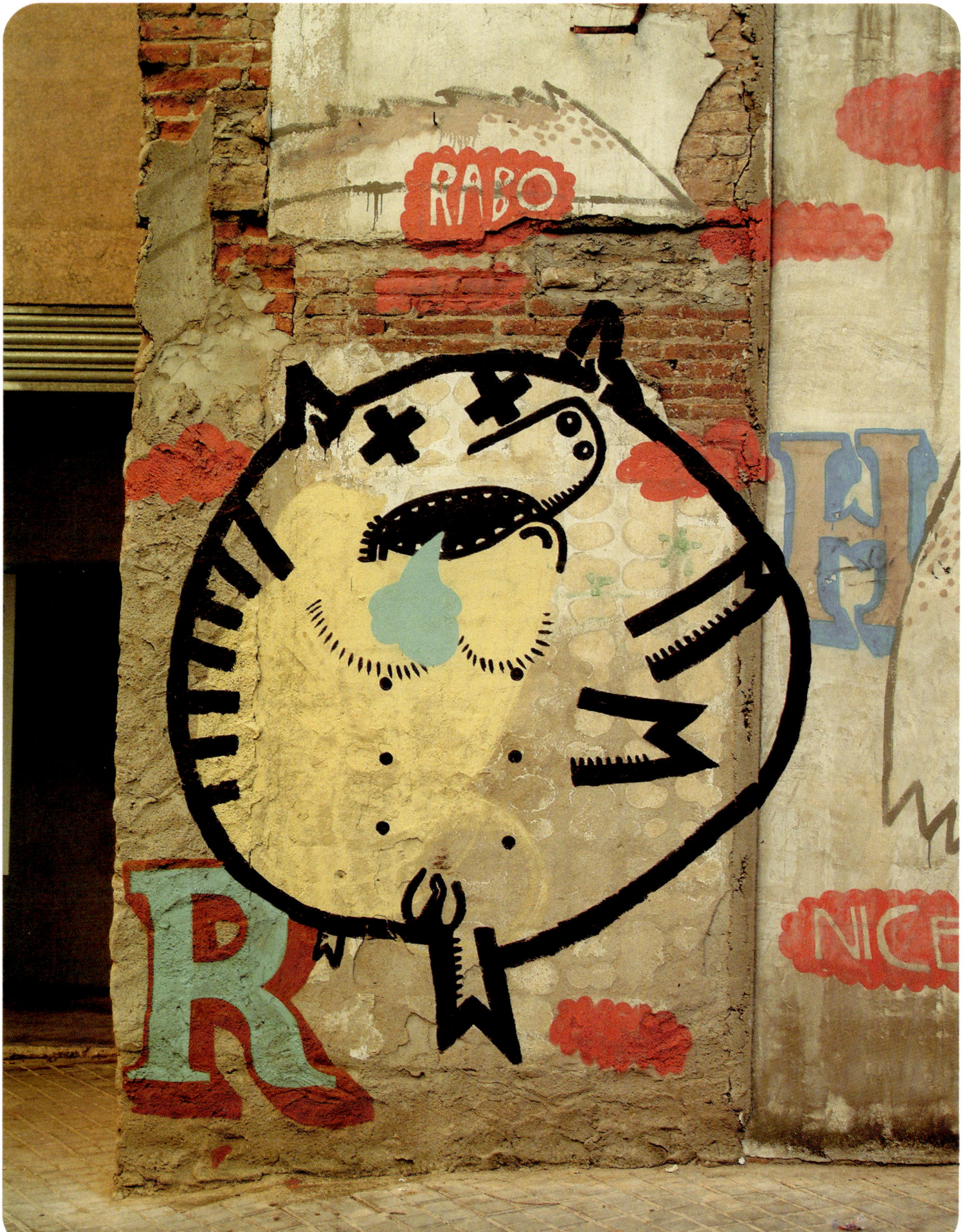

barcelona

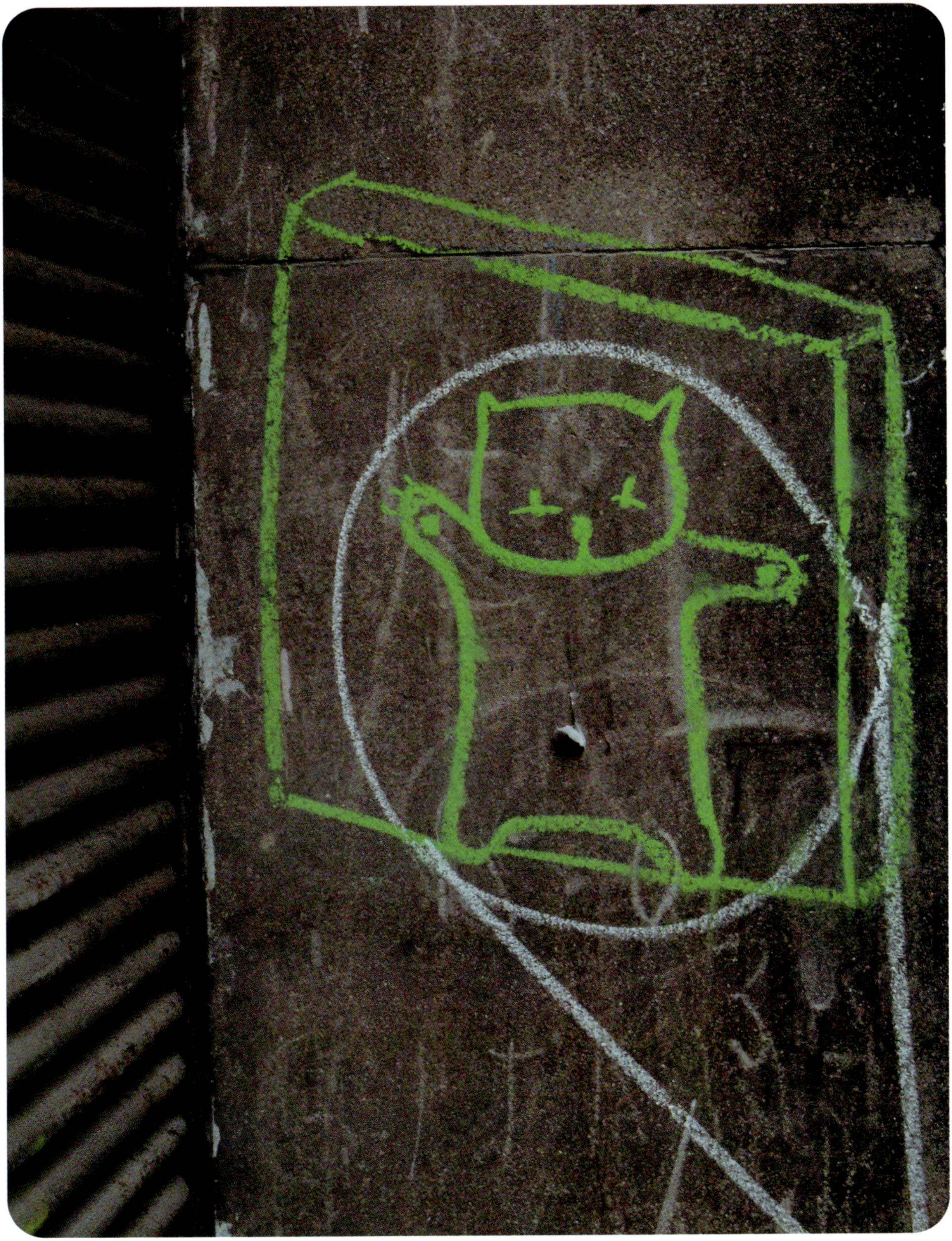

barcelona

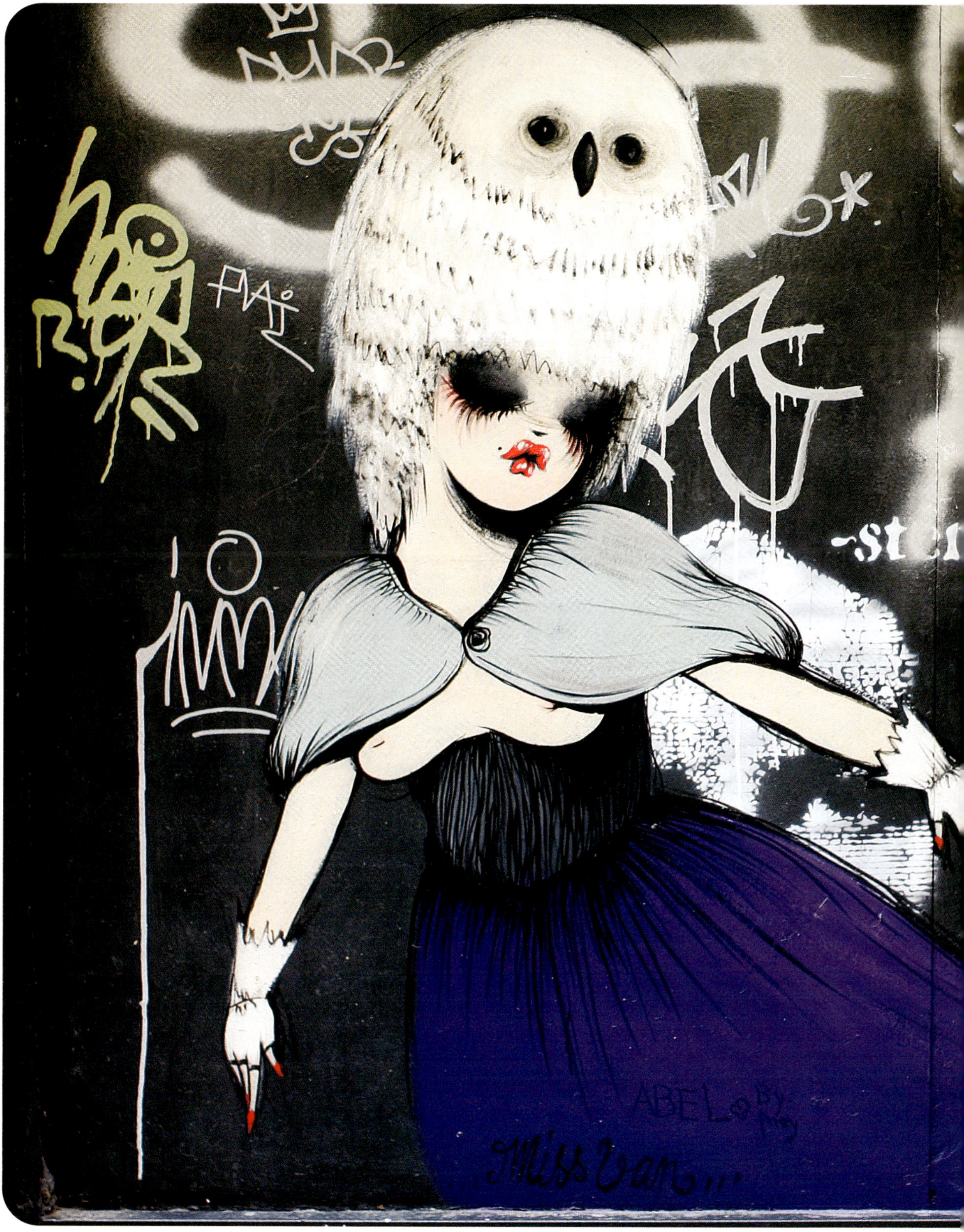
ABEL
Miss Van...

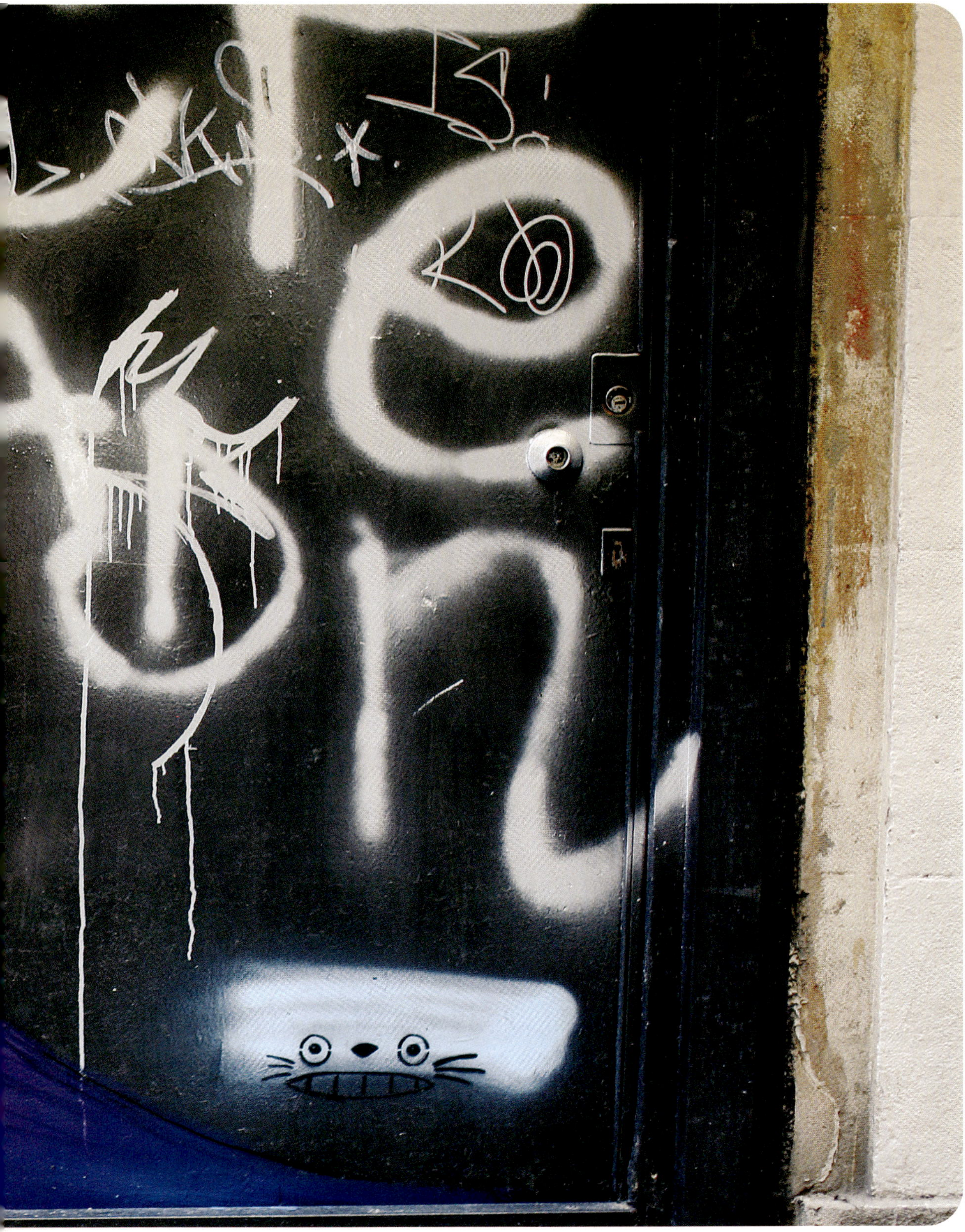

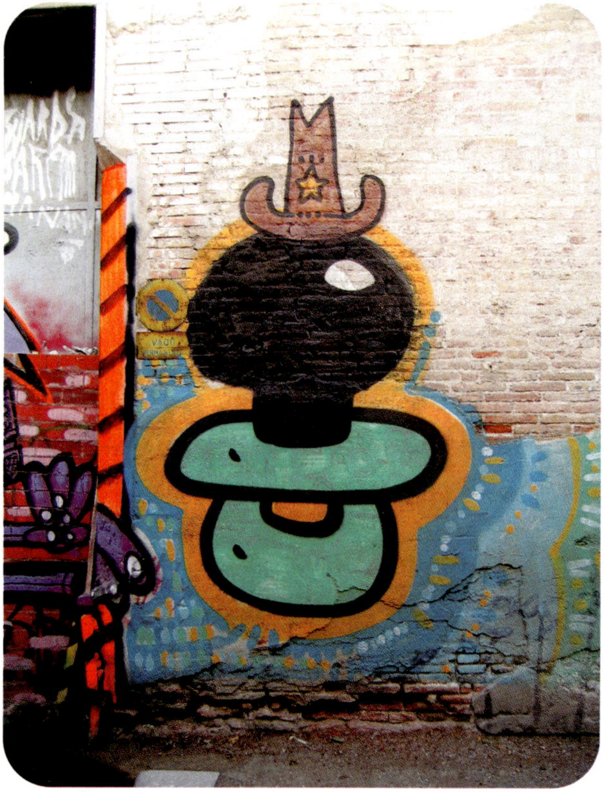

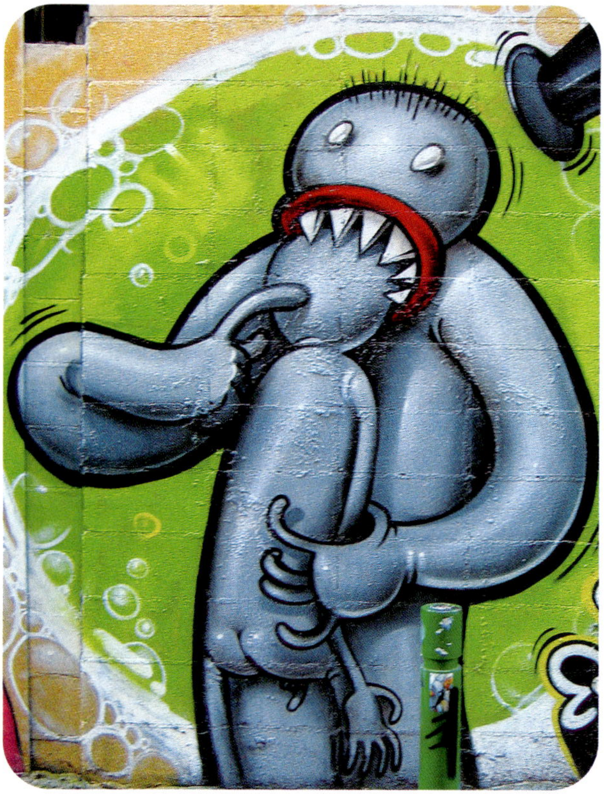

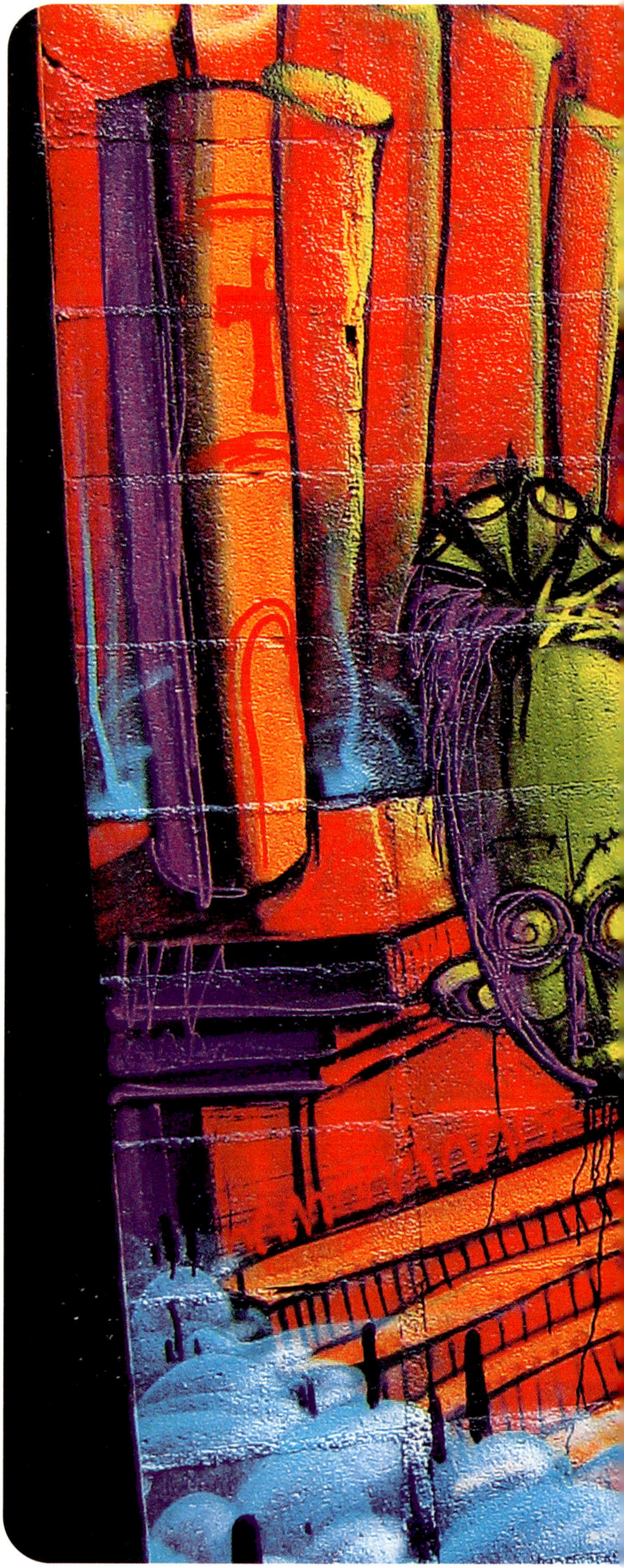

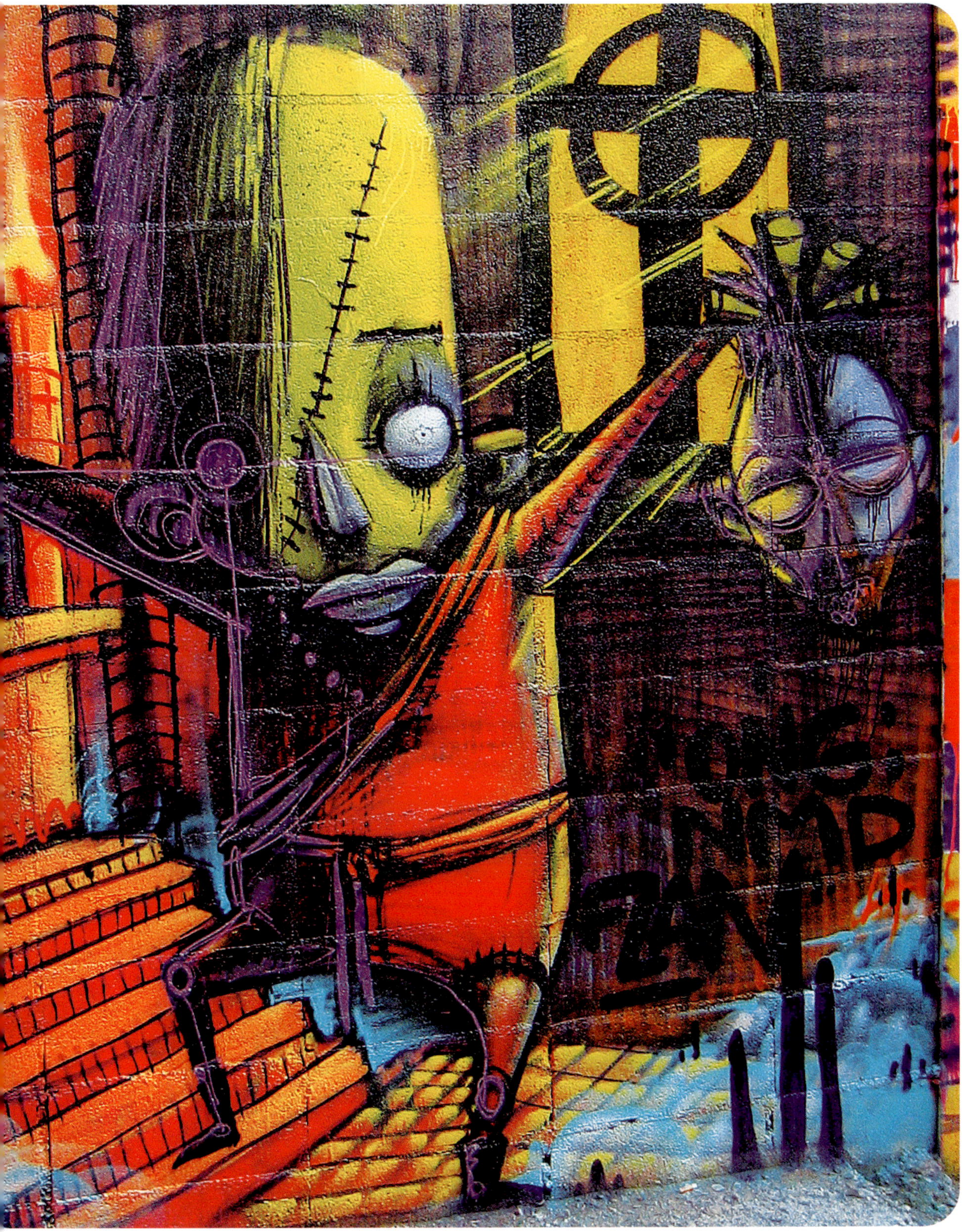

barcelona

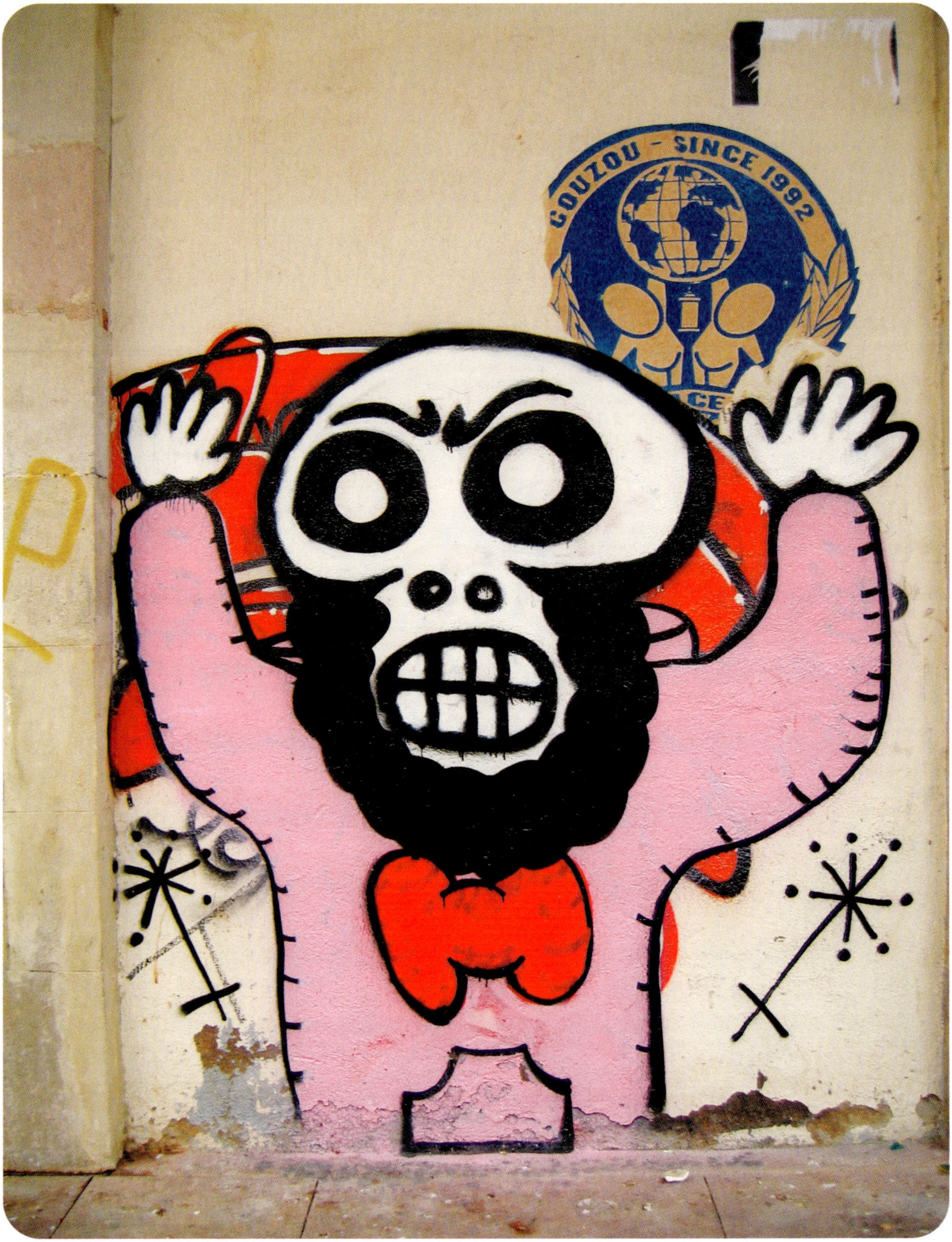

barcelona

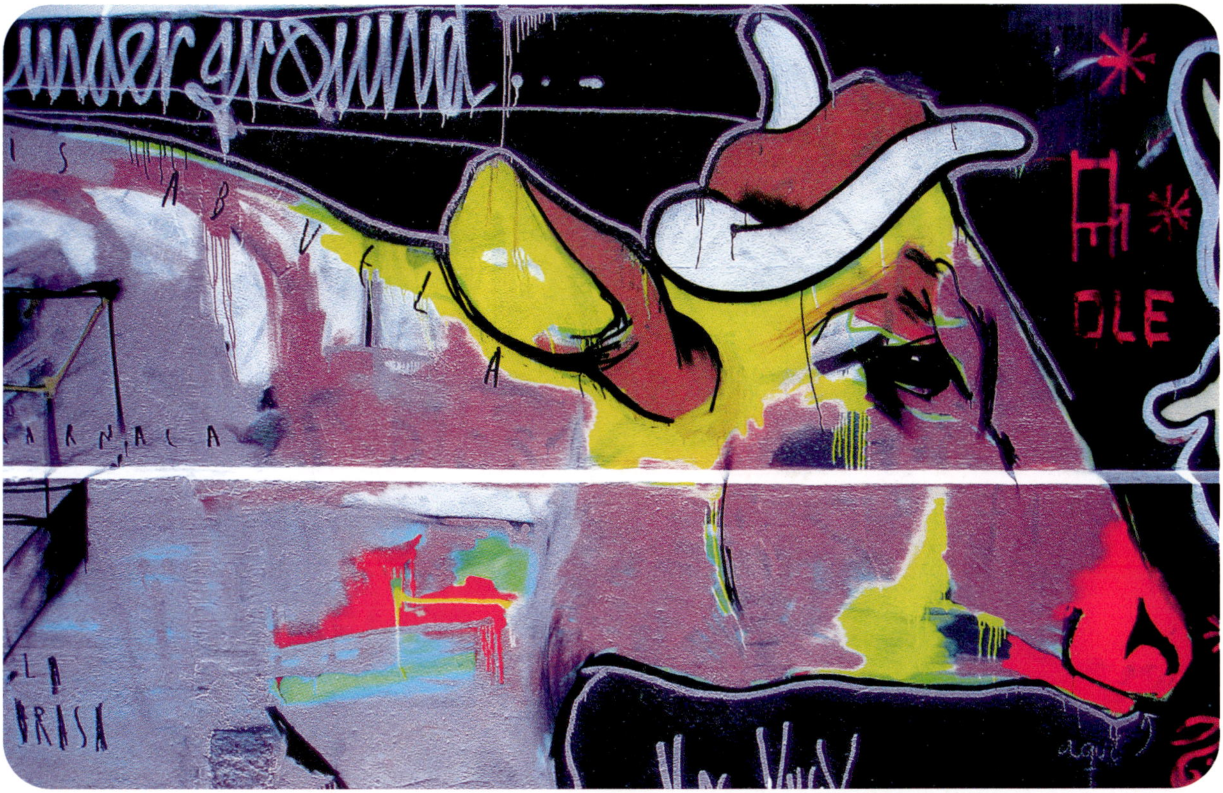
underground...
OLE
LA
BRASA

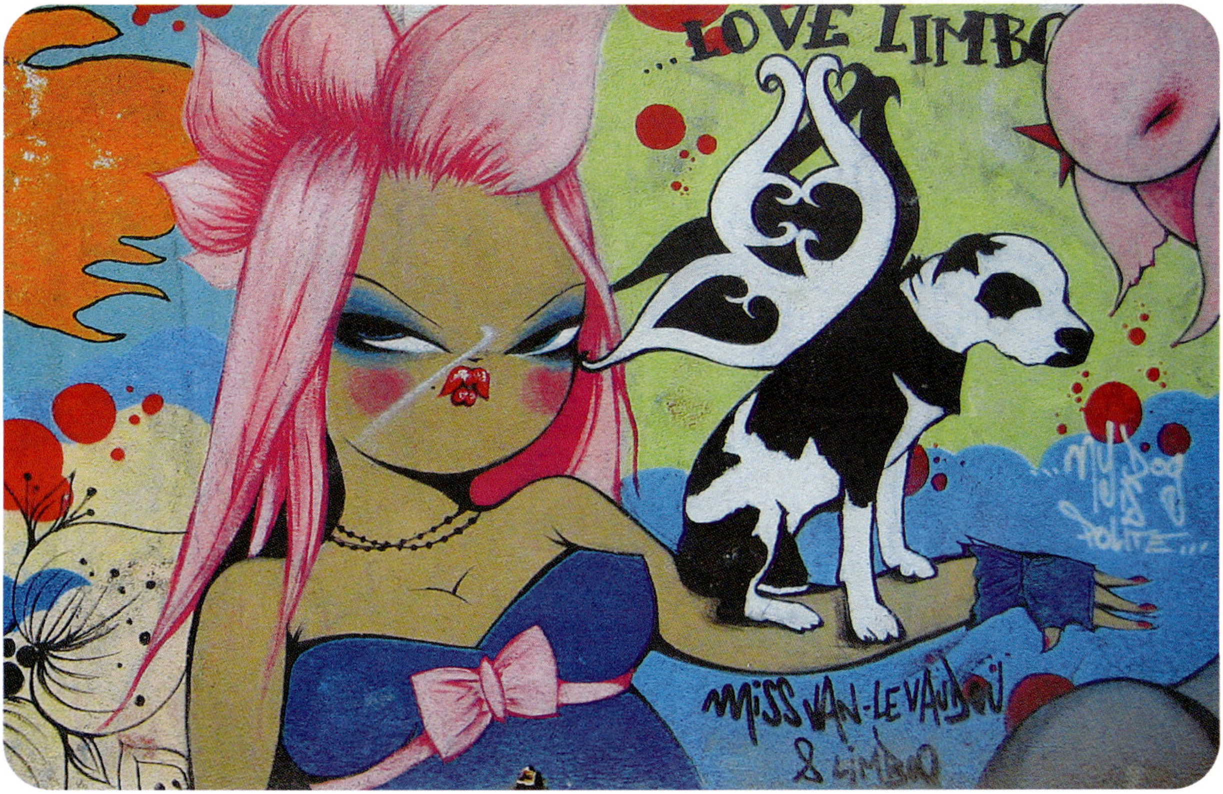
...LOVE LIMB
MISS VAN-LE VAUDOU
& LIMBO

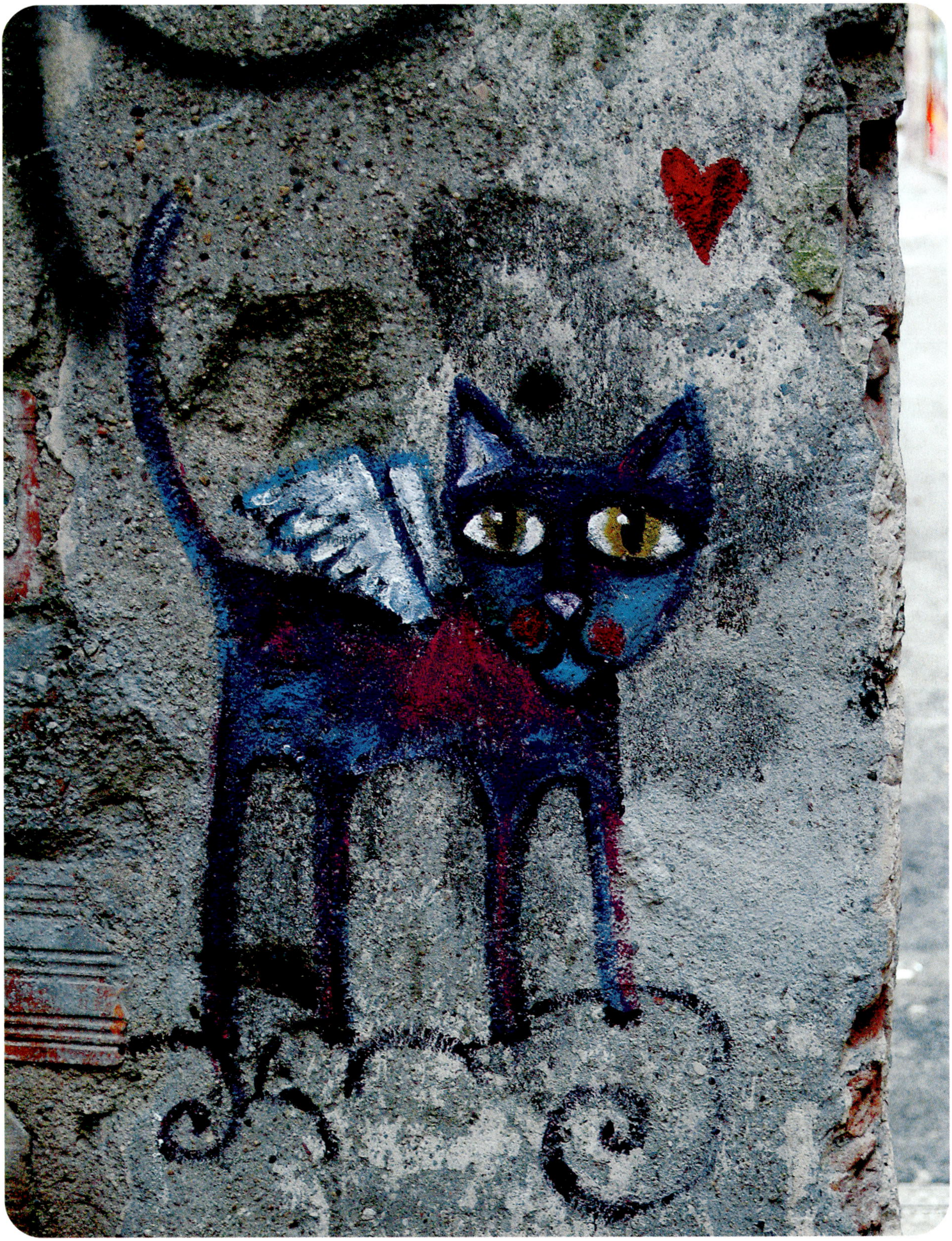

barcelona

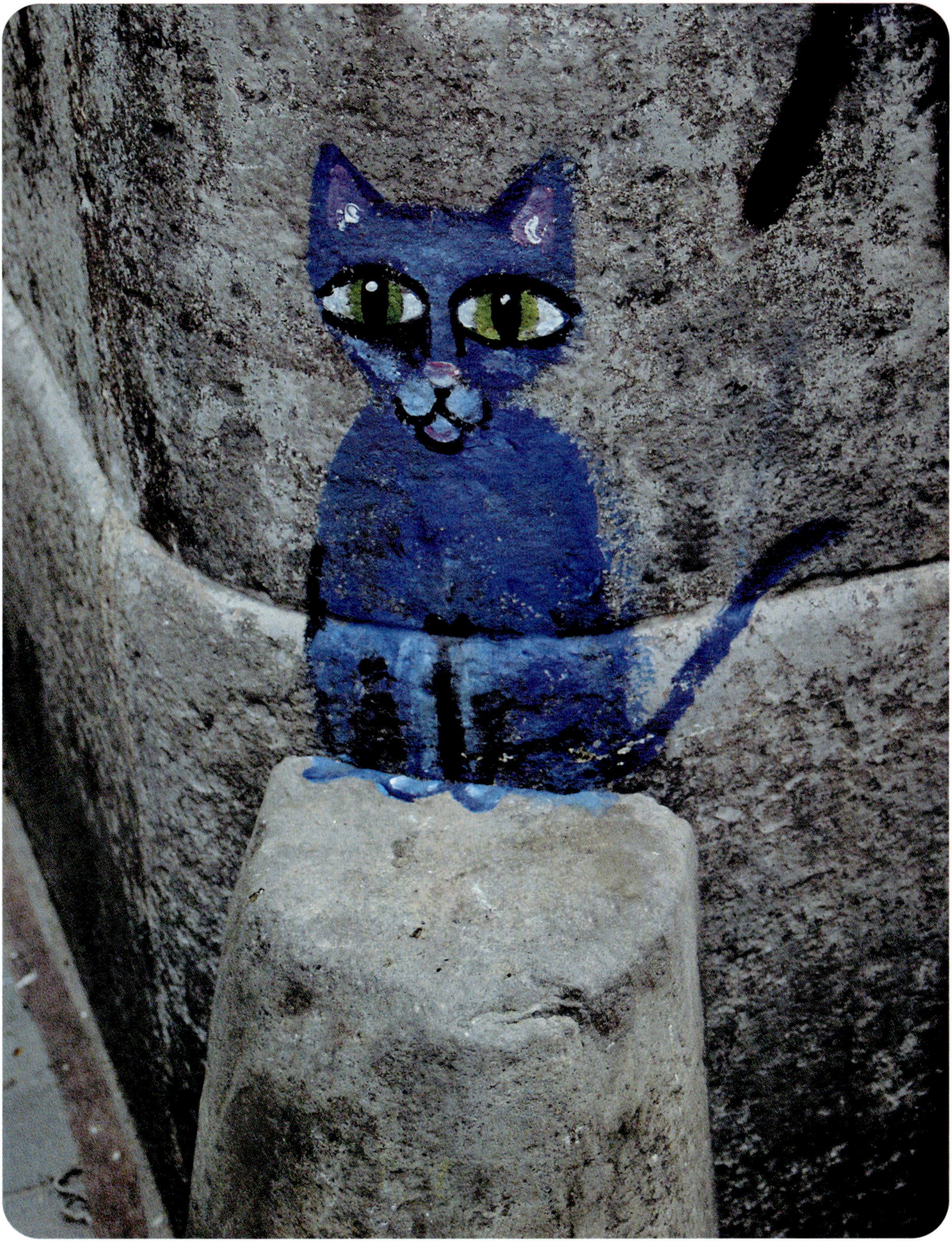

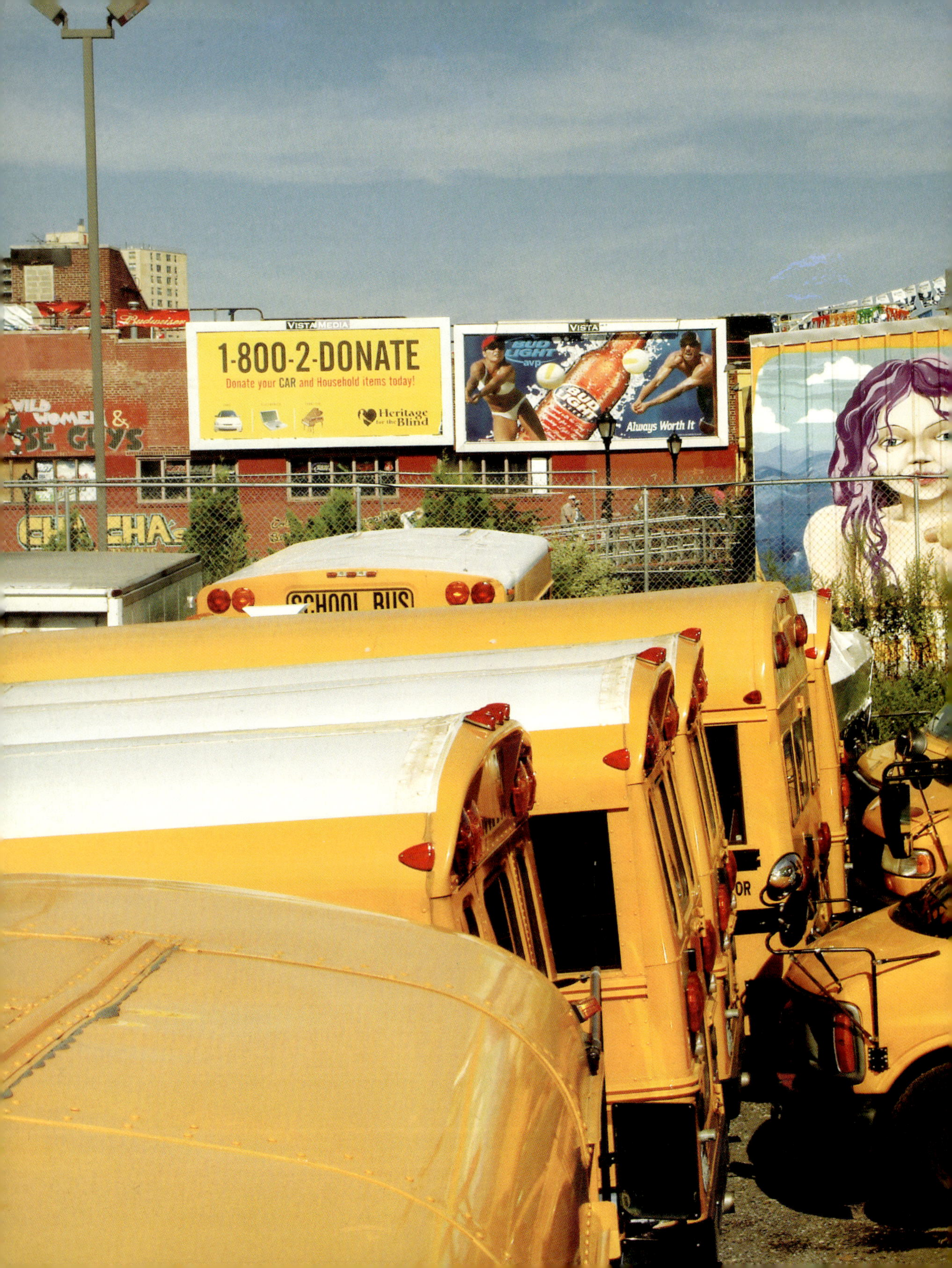
VISTA MEDIA
1-800-2-DONATE
Donate your CAR and Household items today!
Heritage for the Blind
VISTA
BUD LIGHT
Always Worth It
SCHOOL BUS

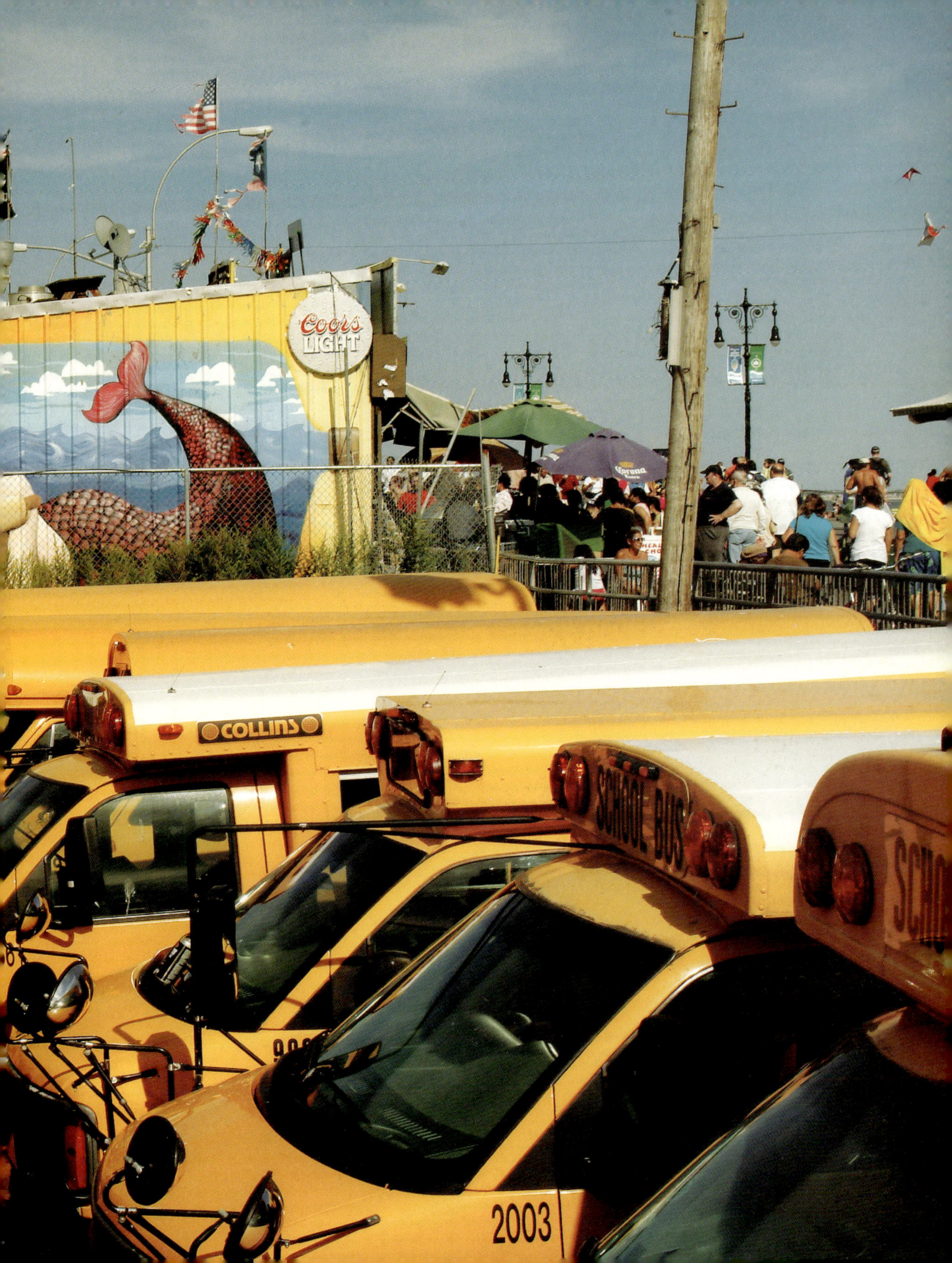
Coors LIGHT
Corona
COLLINS
SCHOOL BUS
2003

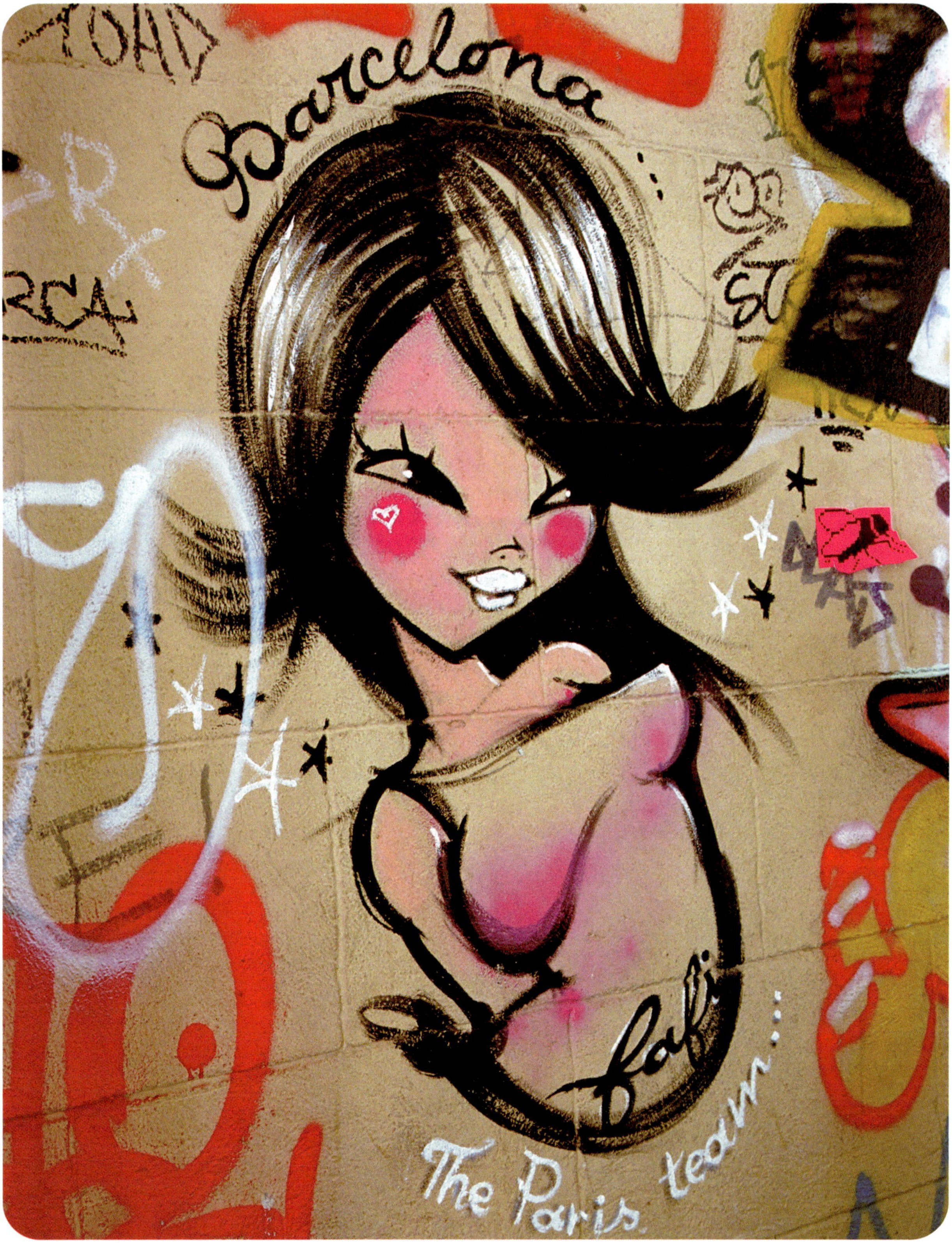
Barcelona
fafi
The Paris team...

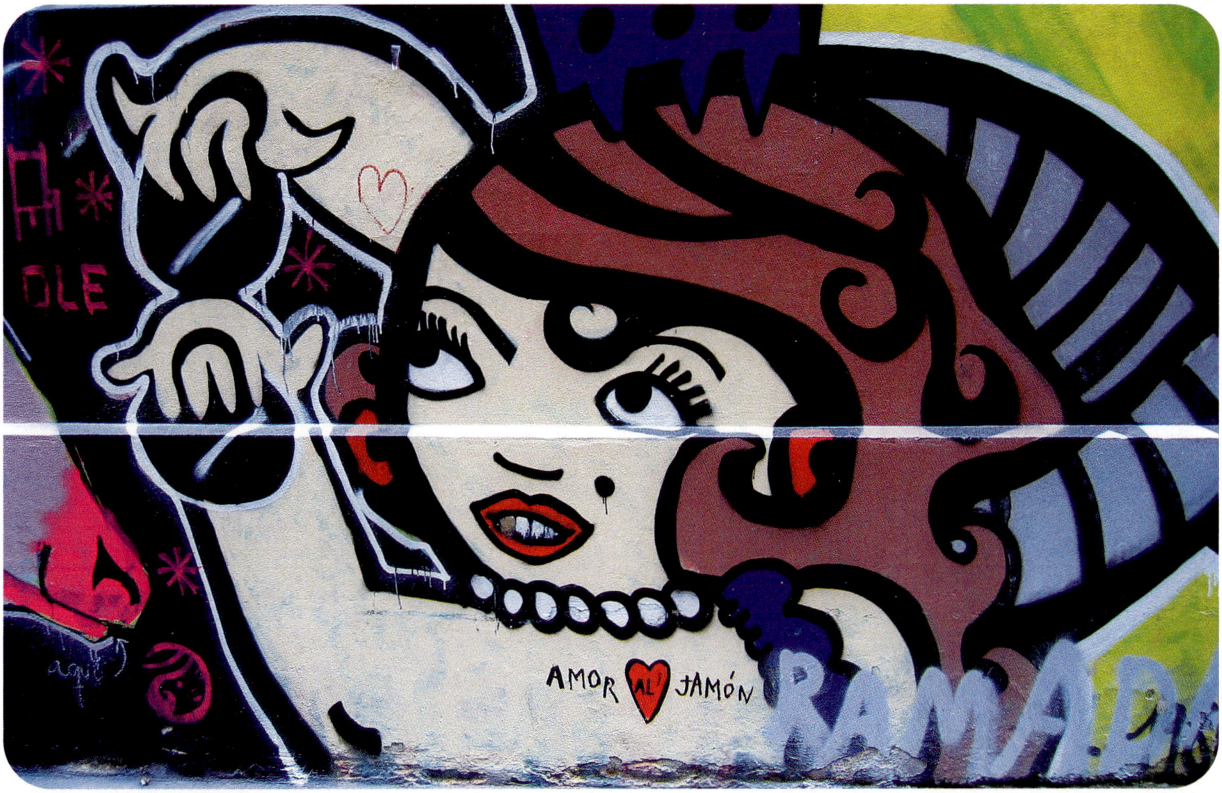
OLE
AMOR AL JAMÓN
RAMADA

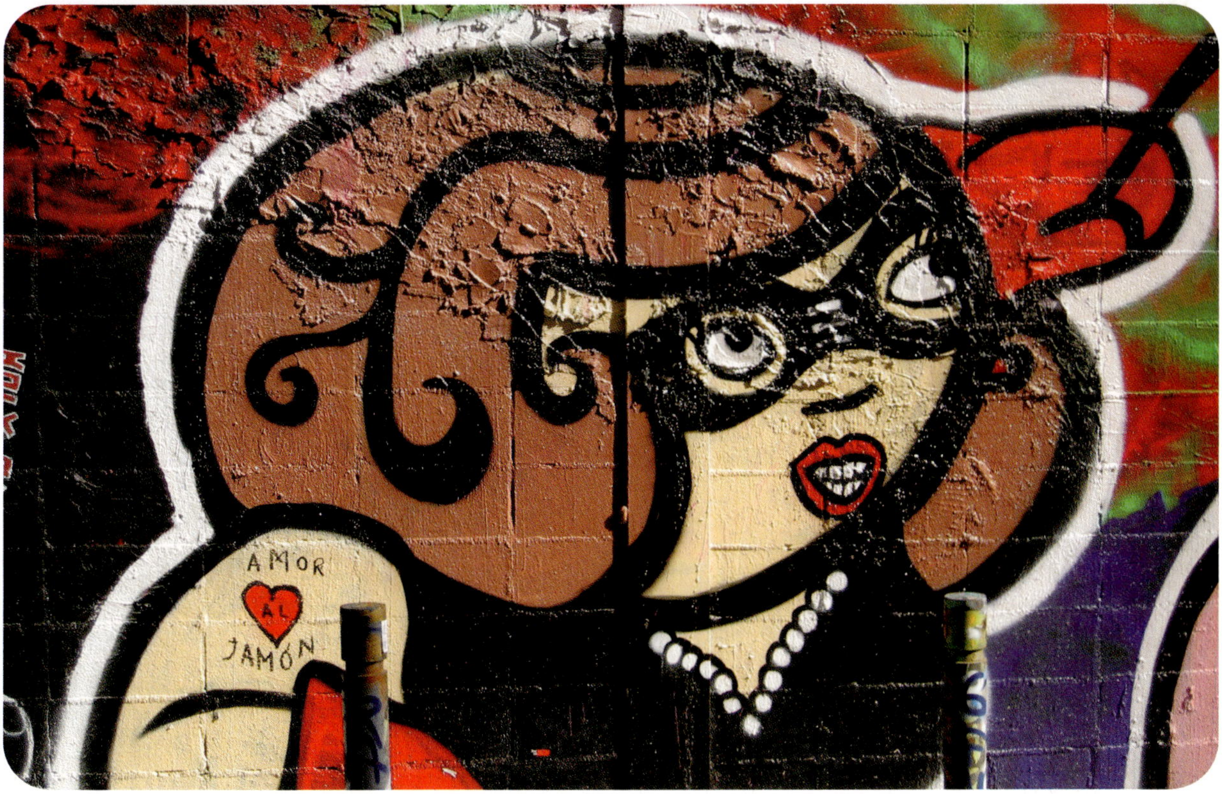
AMOR
AL
JAMÓN

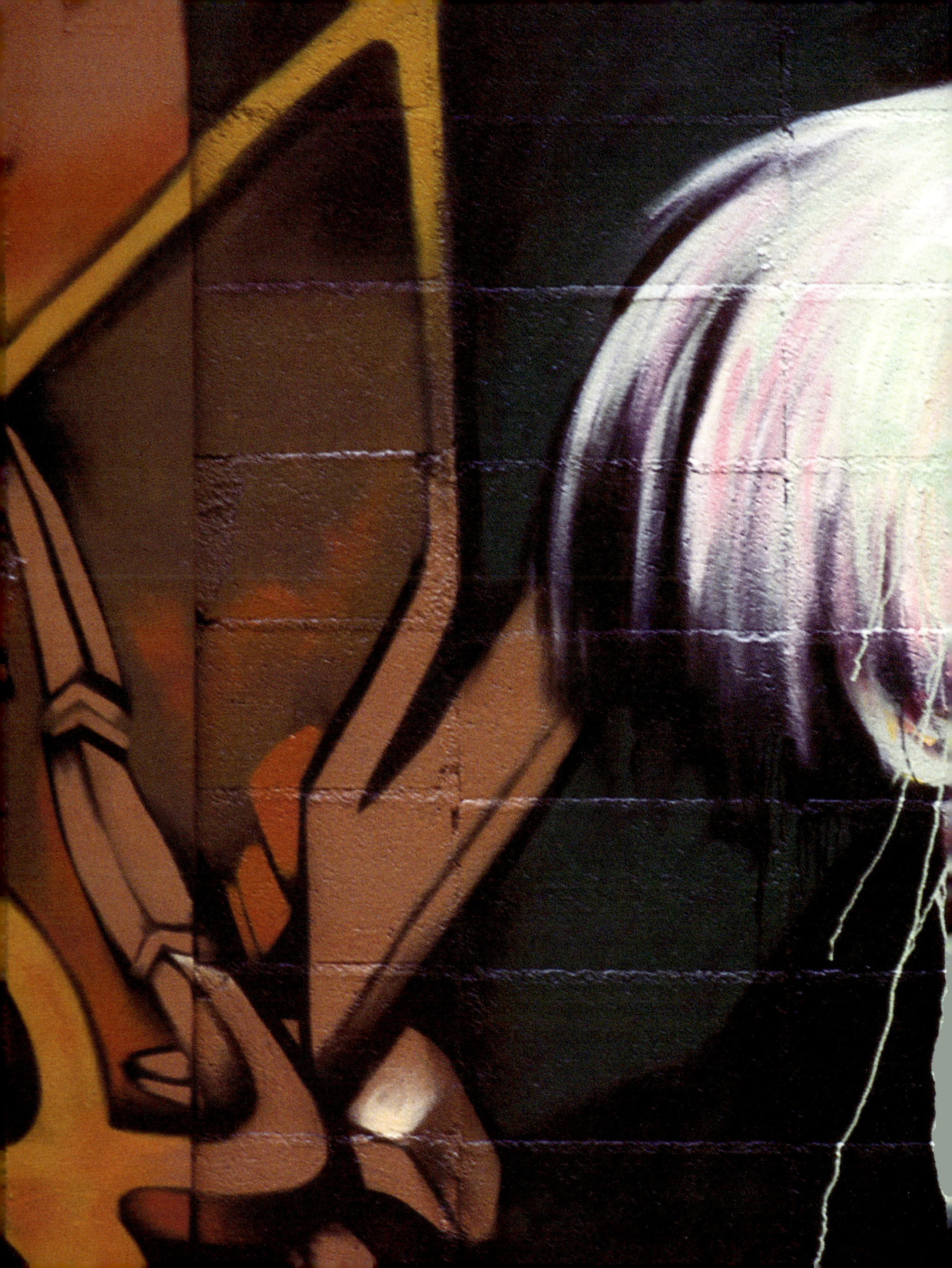

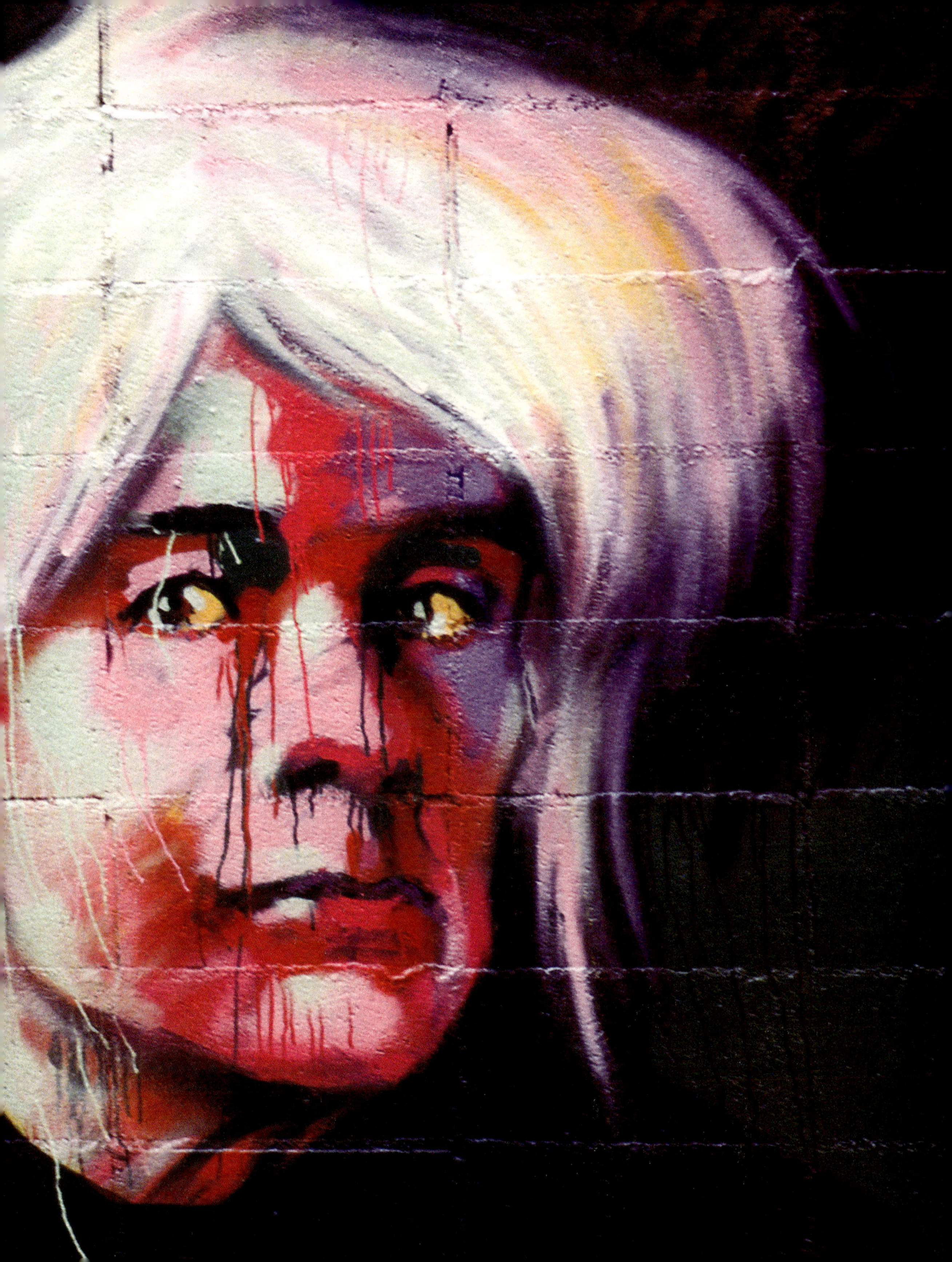

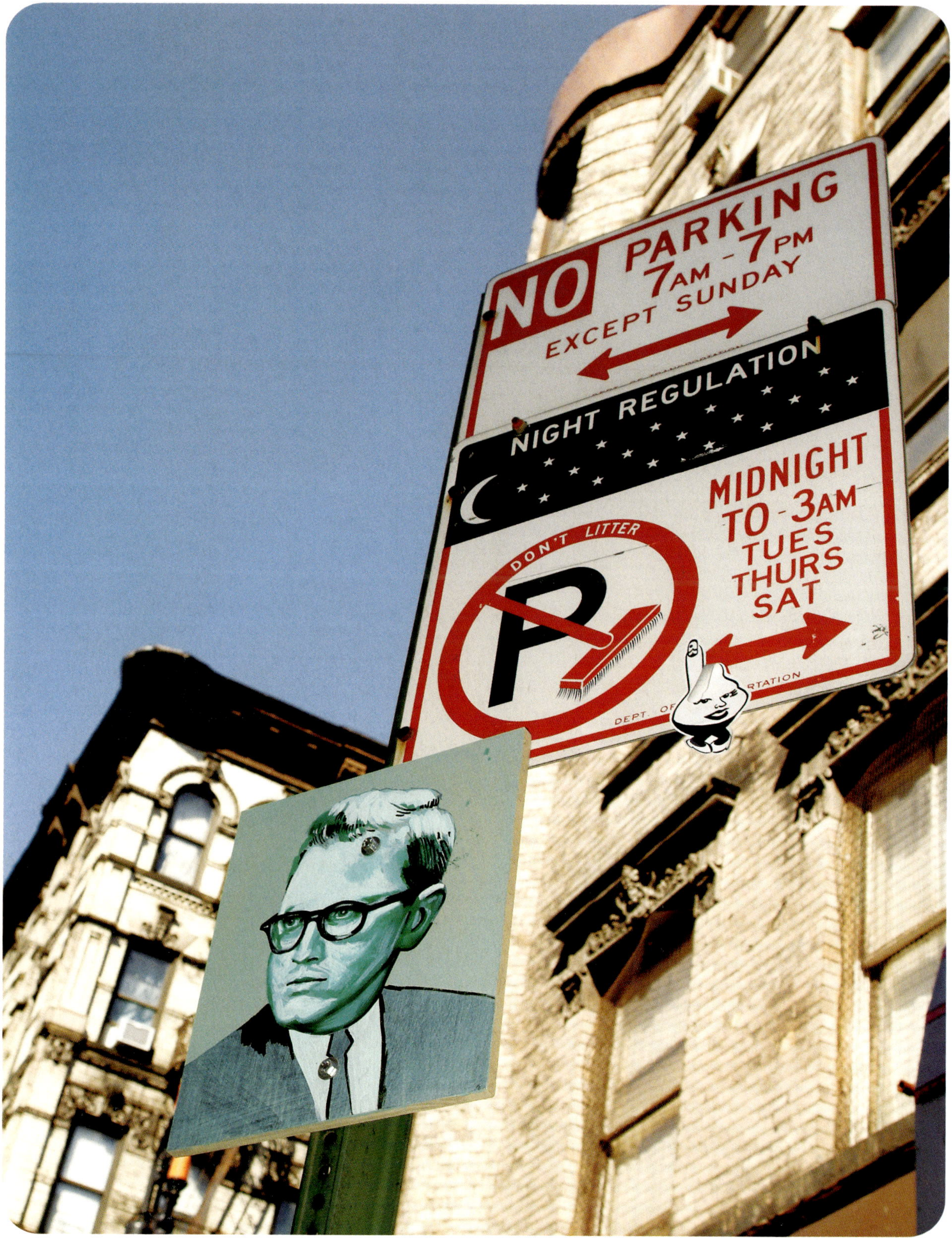
NO PARKING
7AM - 7PM
EXCEPT SUNDAY
NIGHT REGULATION
MIDNIGHT
TO - 3AM
TUES
THURS
SAT
DON'T LITTER

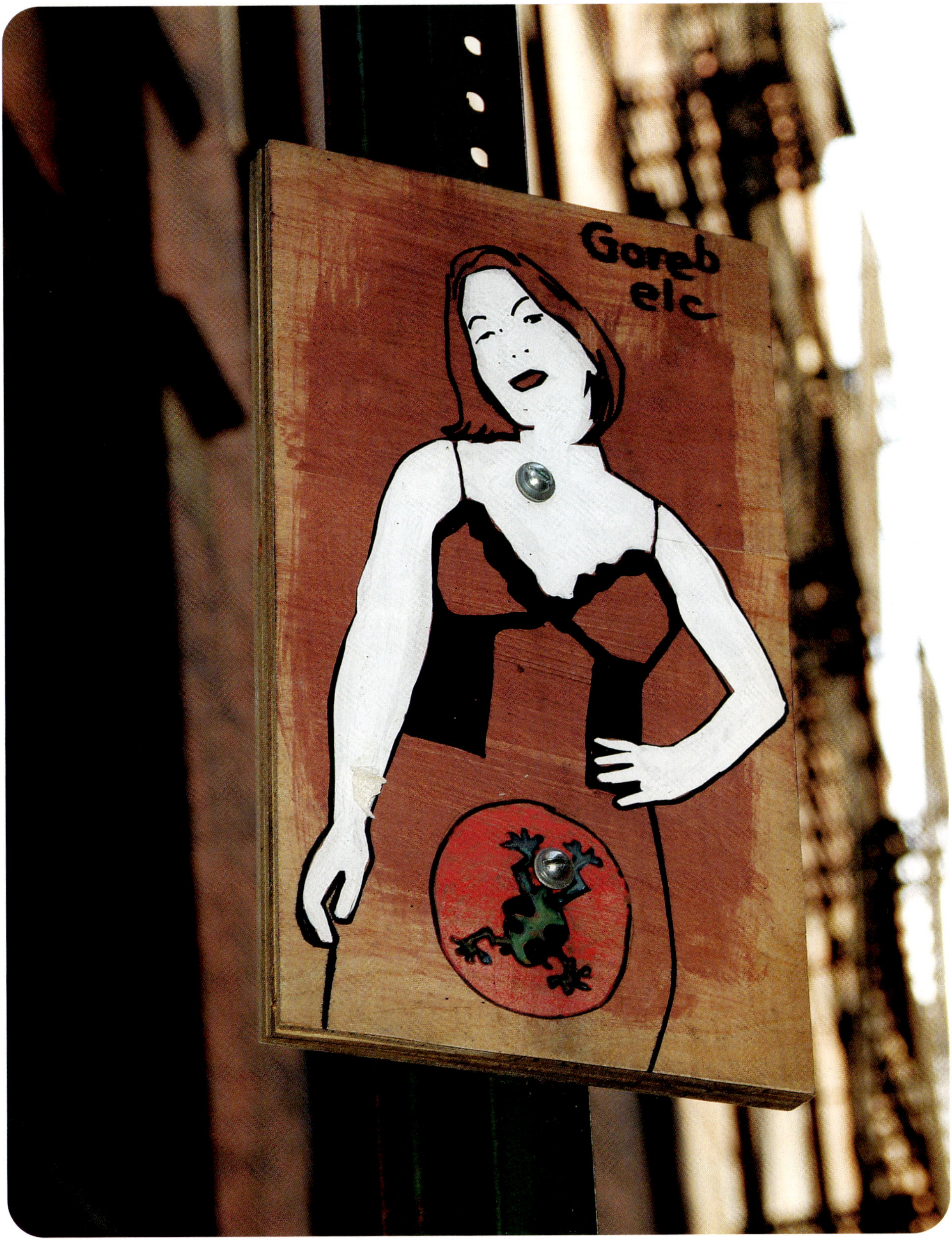
Goreb
elc

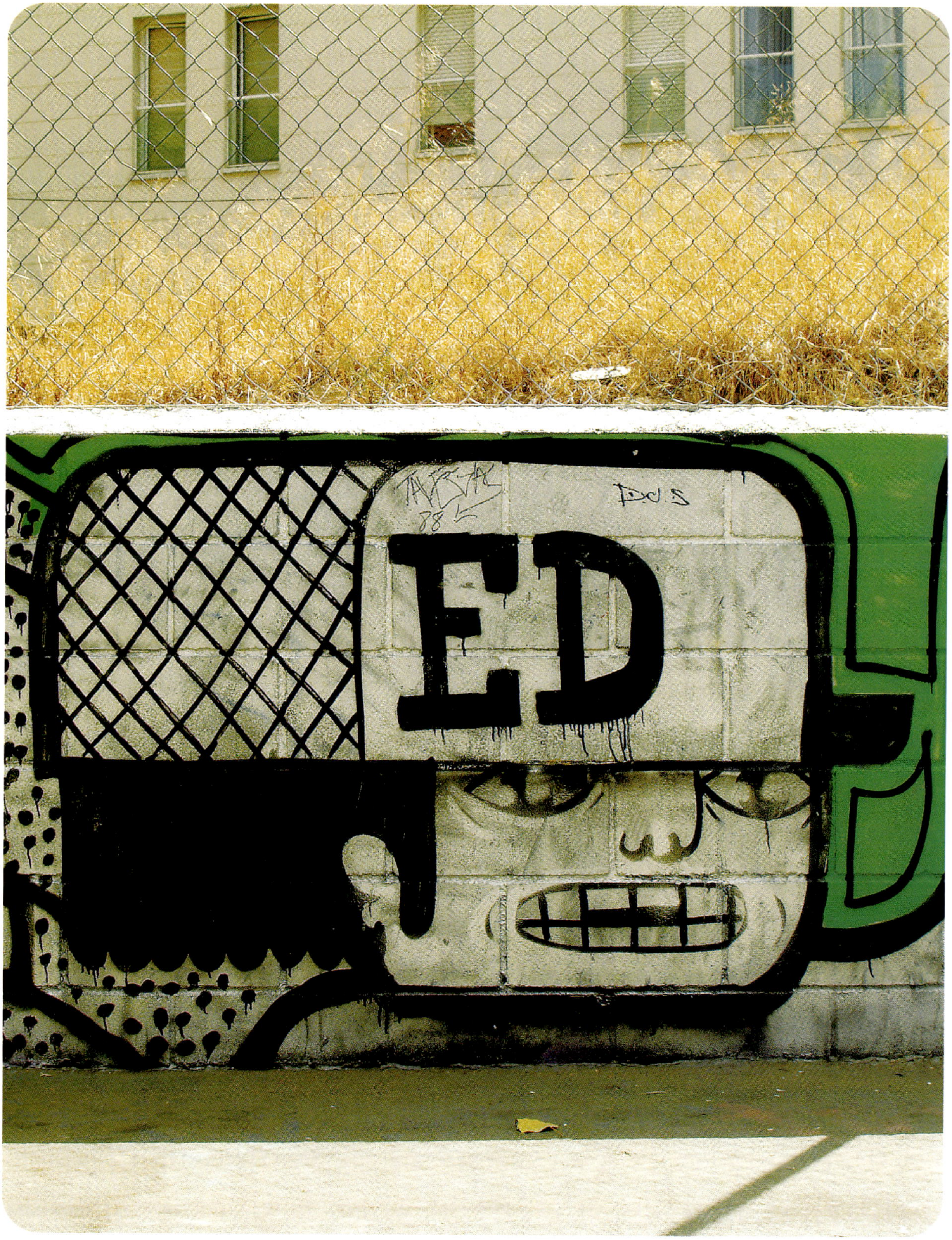
ED

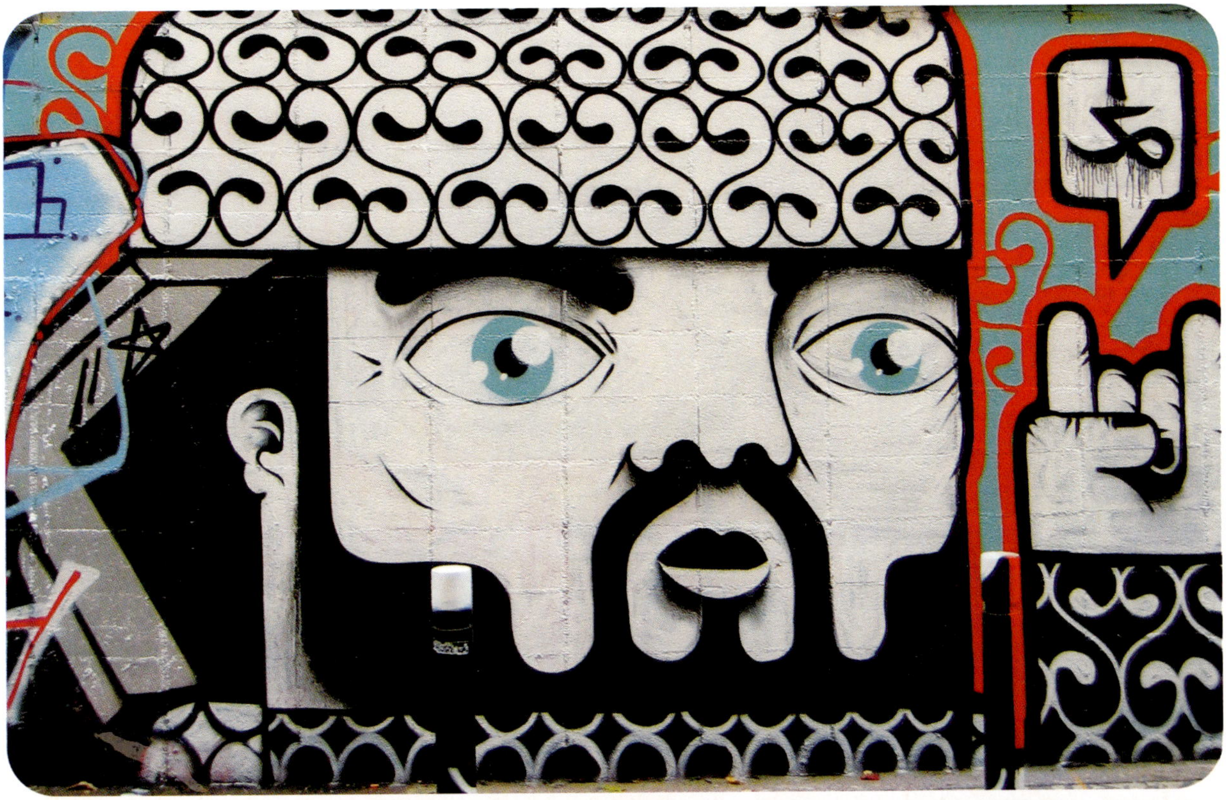

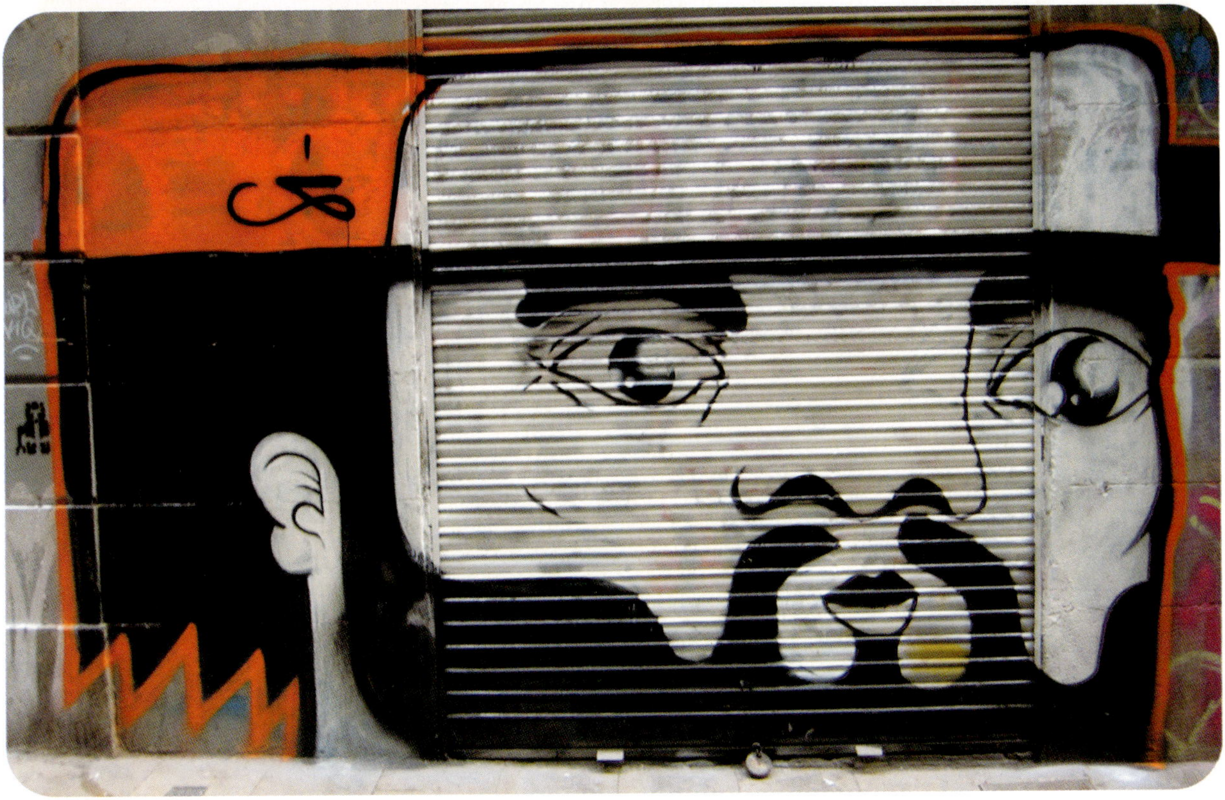

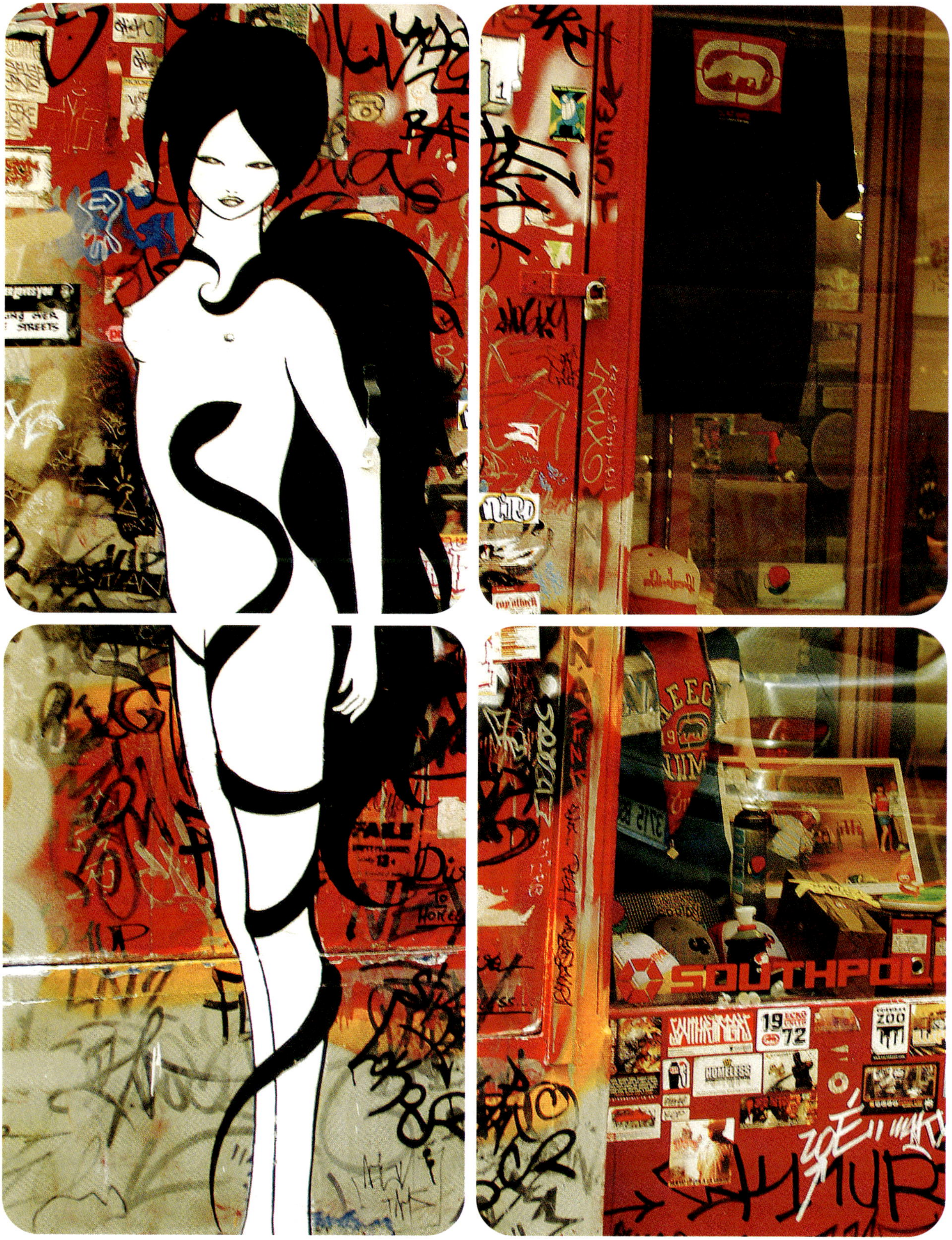
STREETS
HOMELESS
19
72
ZOO

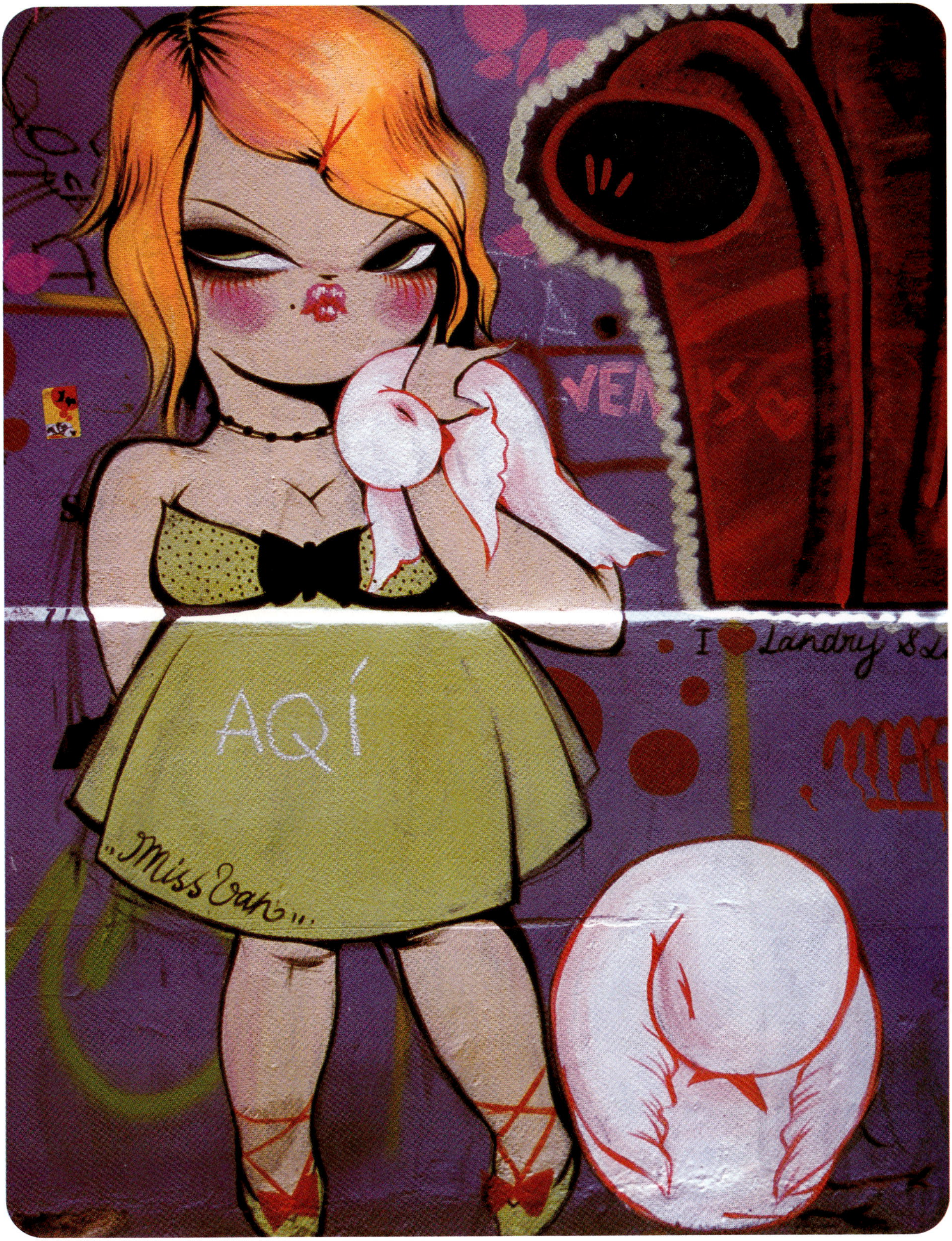
AQÍ
Miss Van

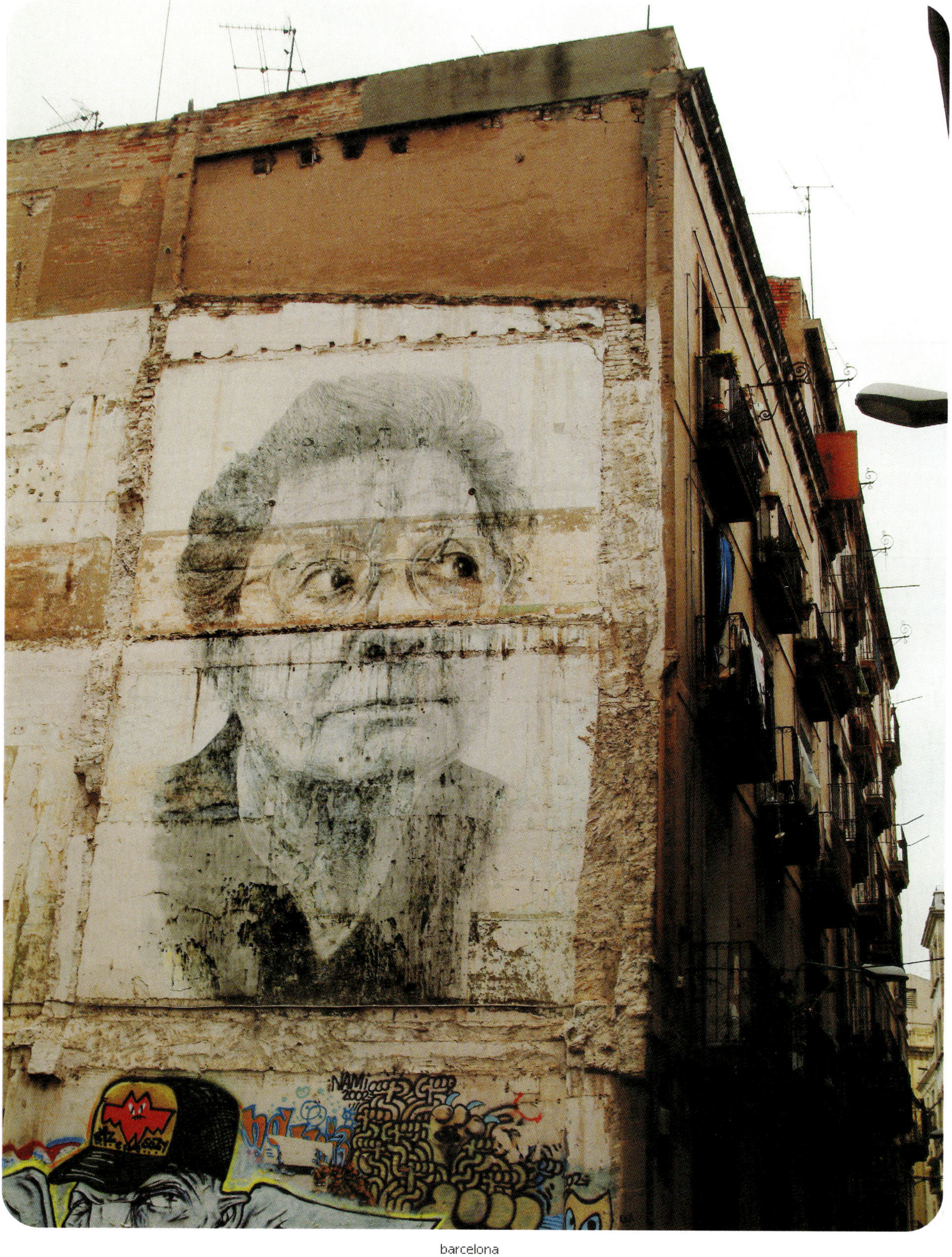
NAMI

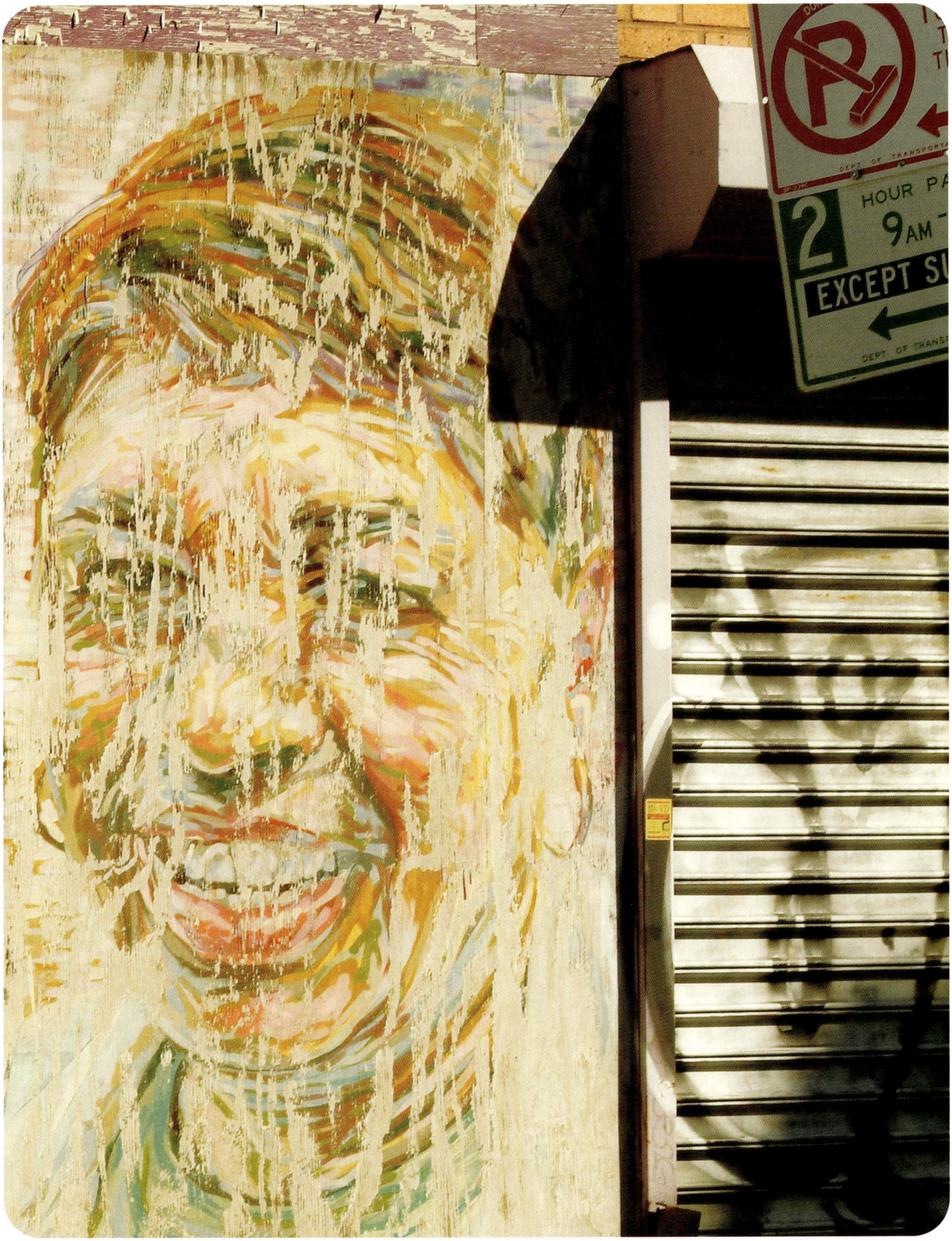
2
HOUR
9AM
EXCEPT

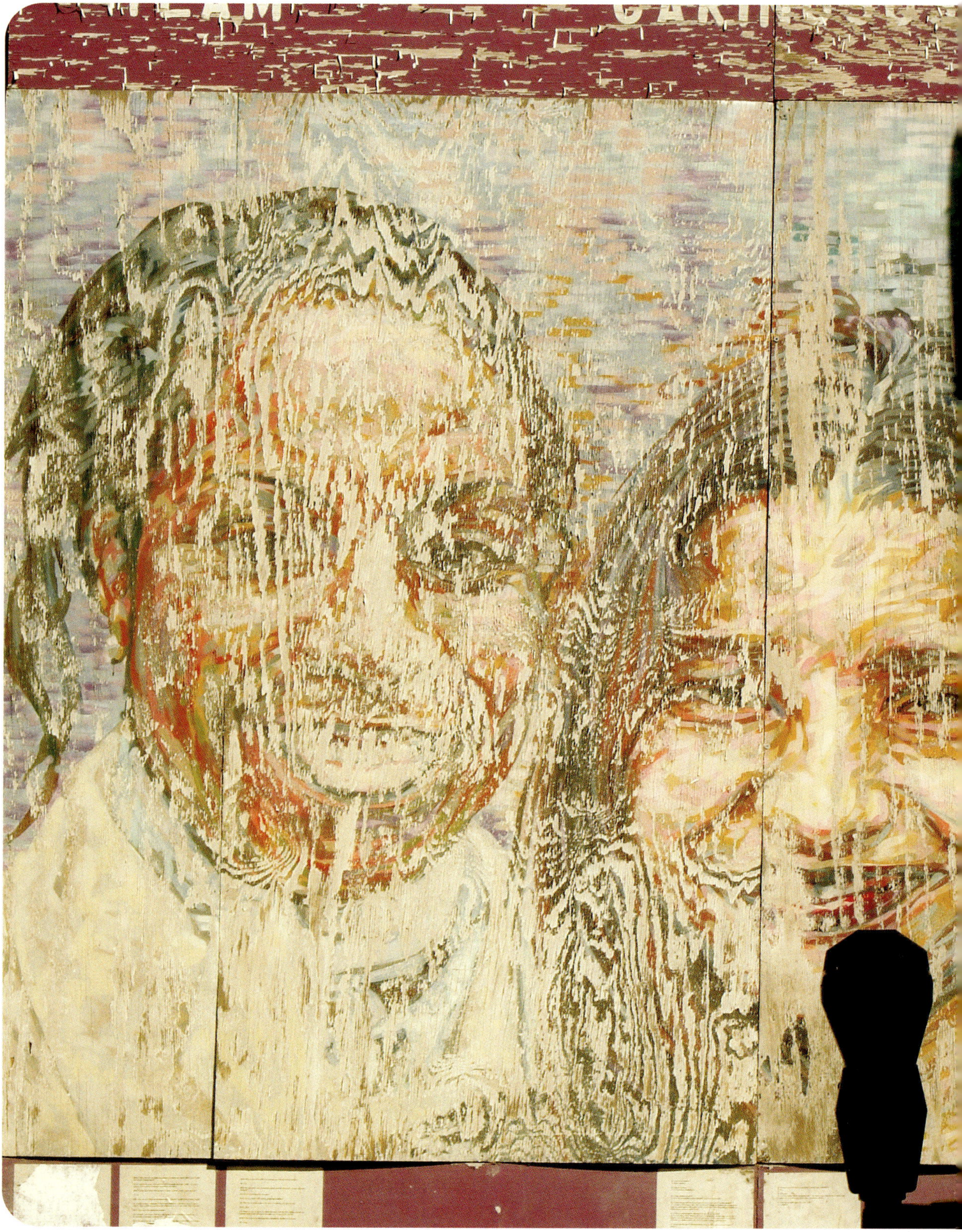

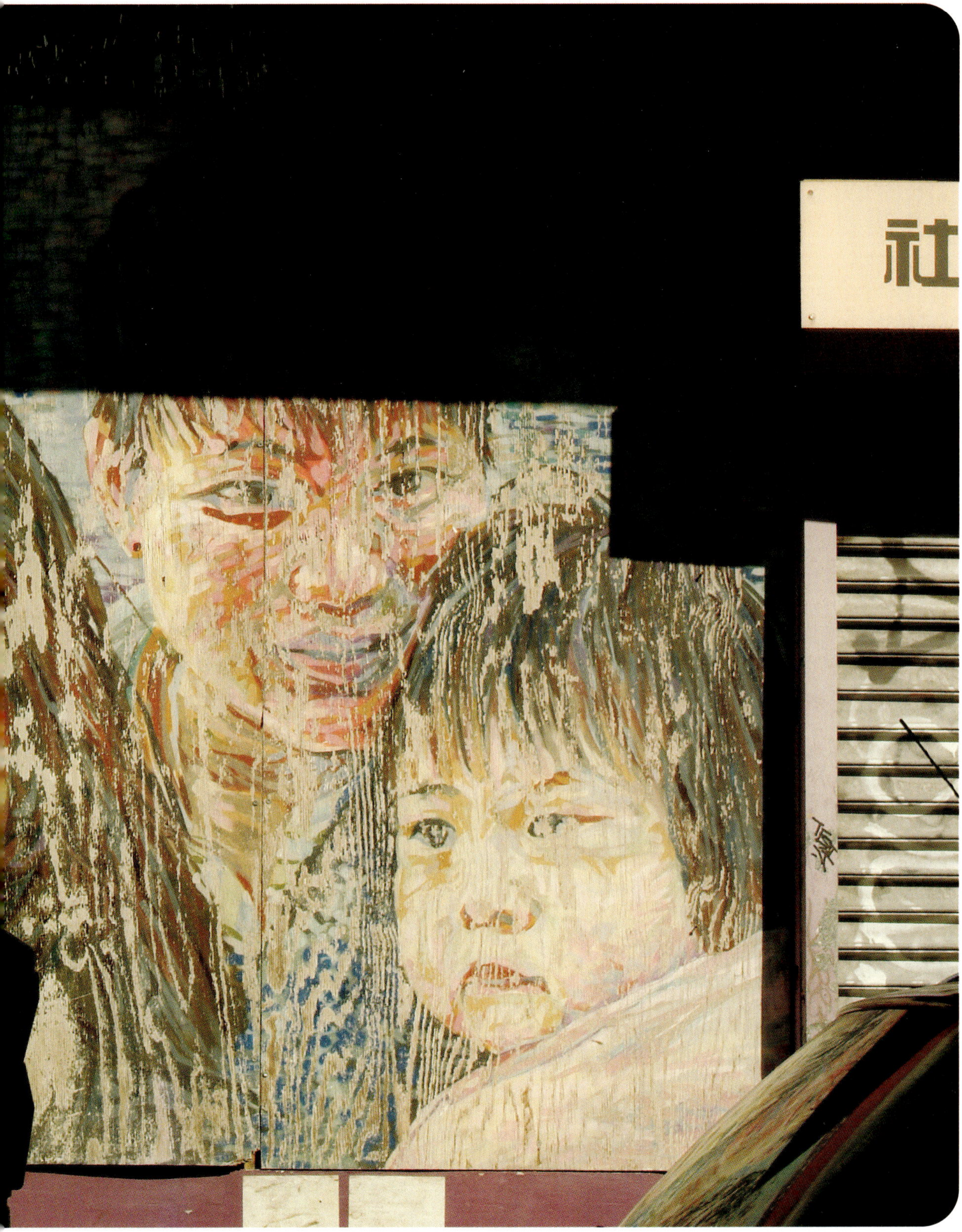
社

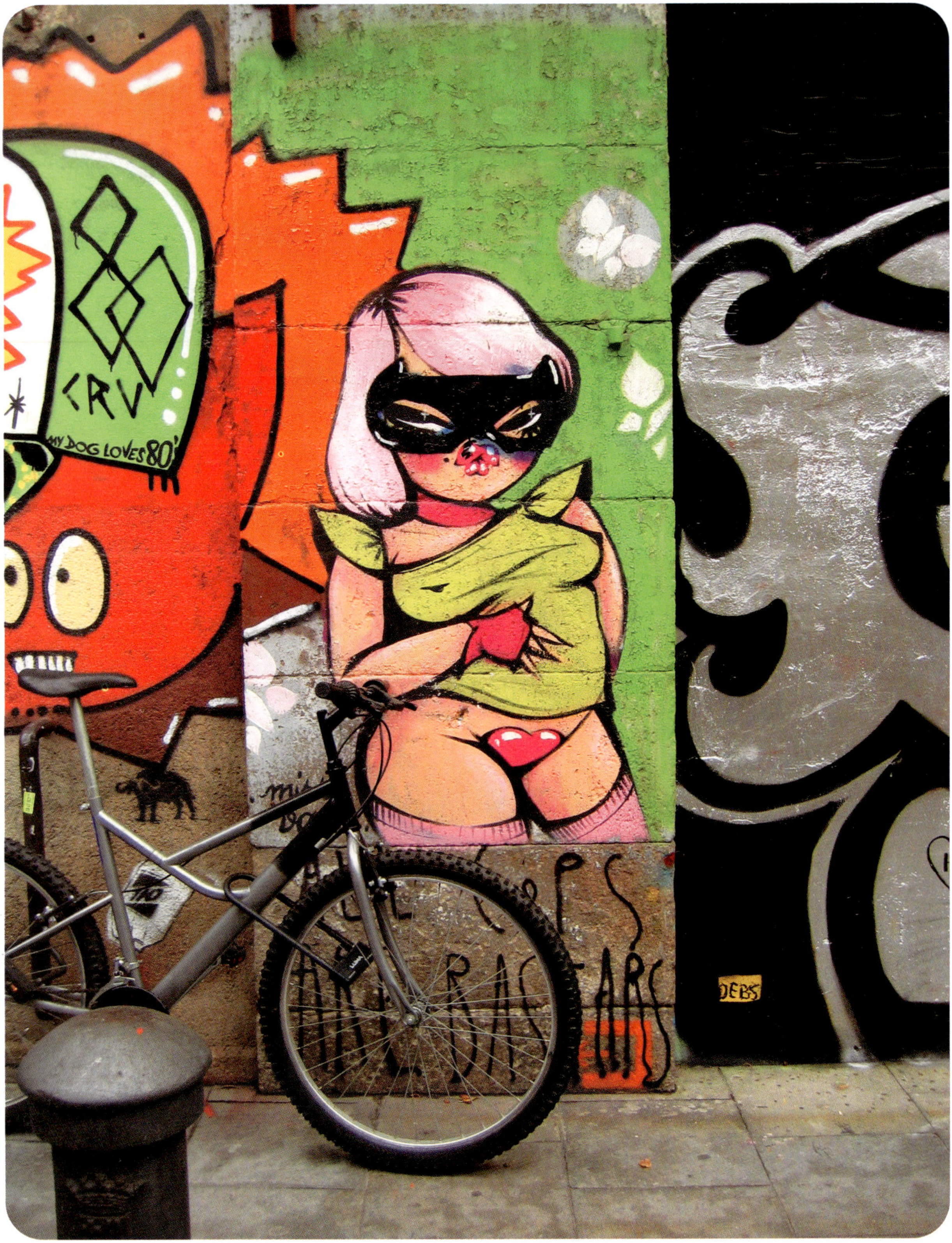
CRV
MY DOG LOVES 80'
DEBS

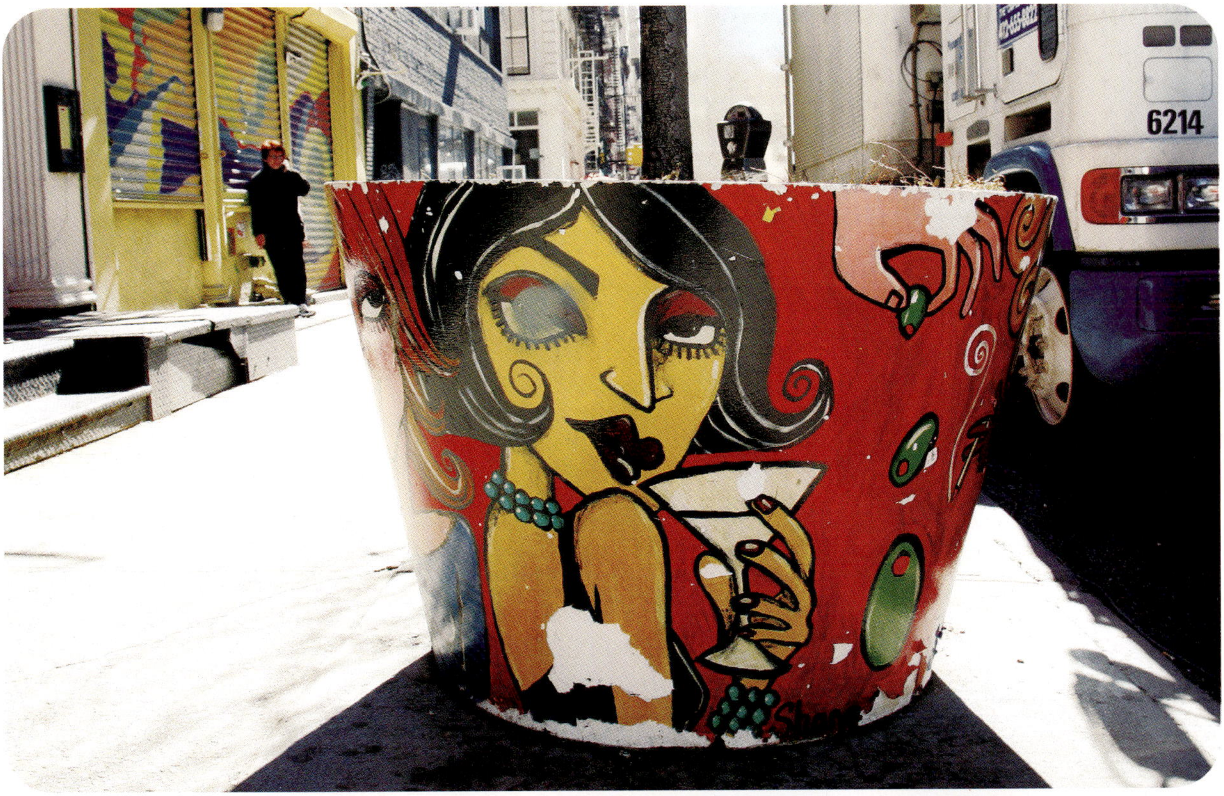
6214

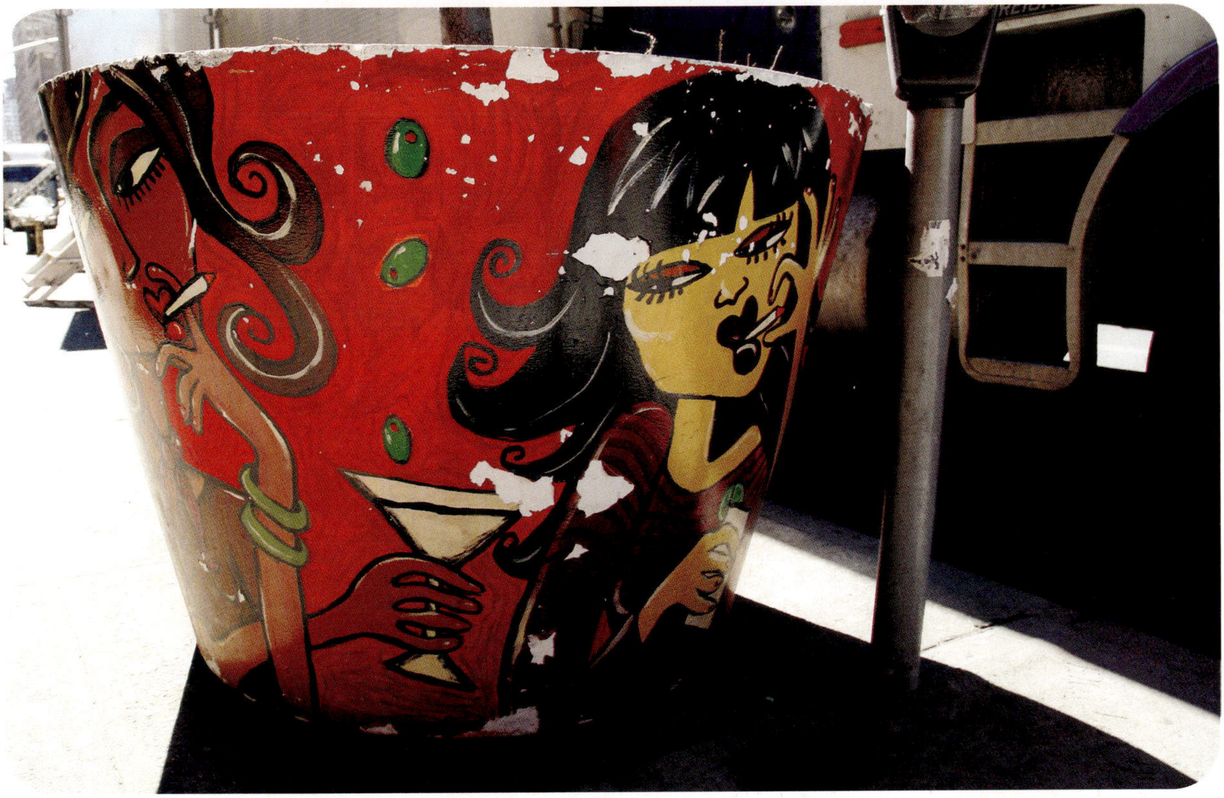

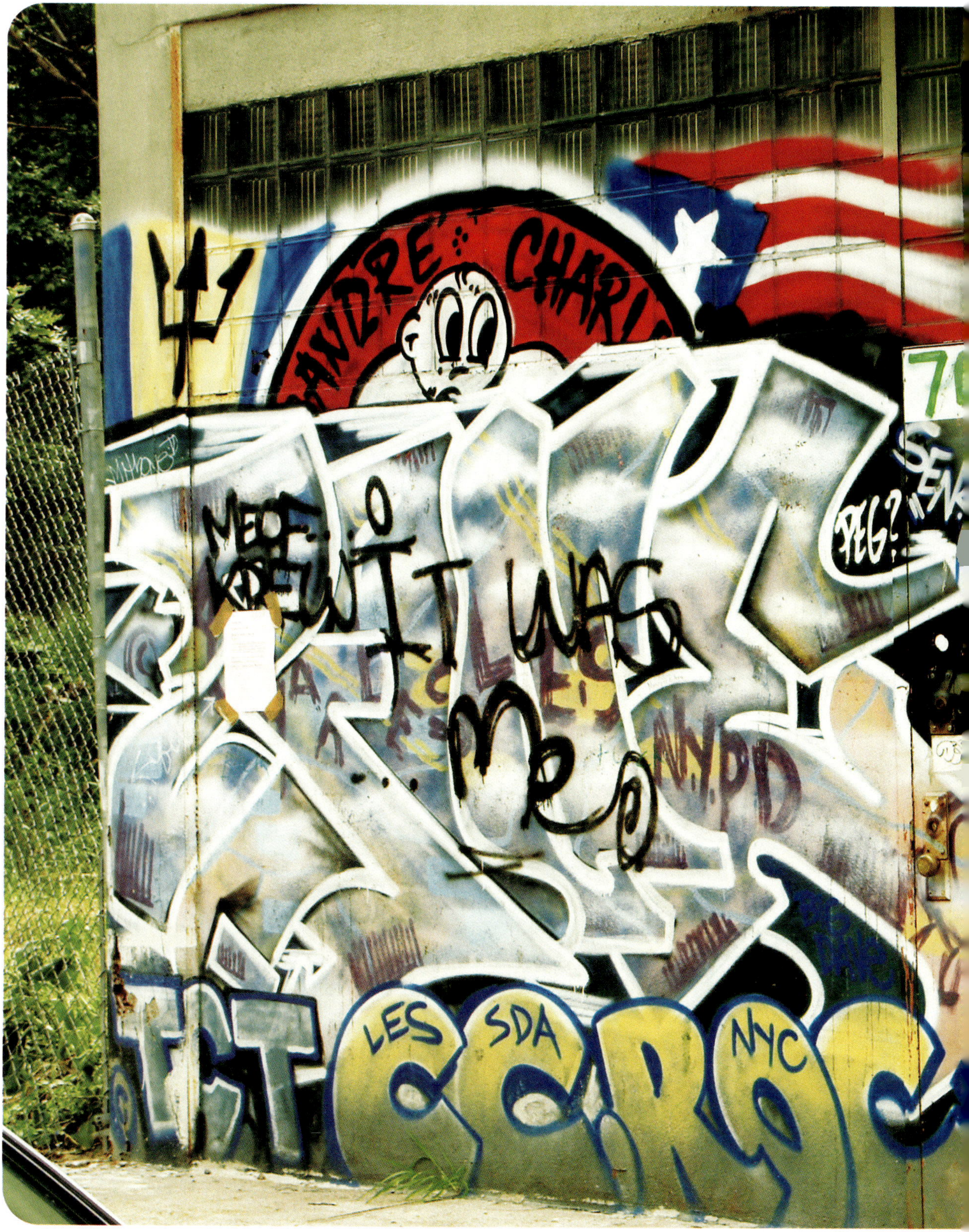
ANDRE
N.Y.PD
LES
SDA
NYC

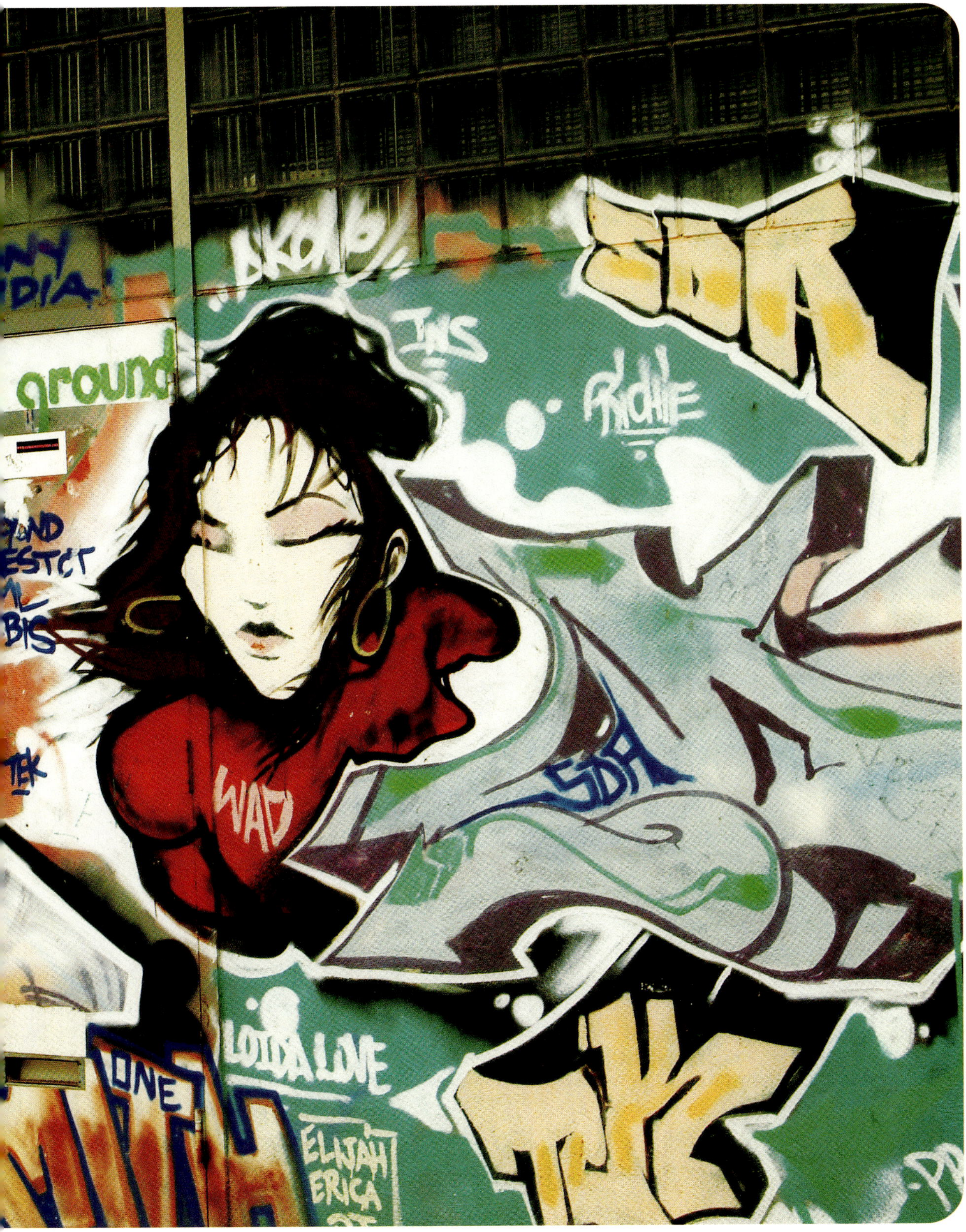
ground
RICHIE
SDA
WAD
LOIDA LOVE
ONE
ELIJAH
ERICA

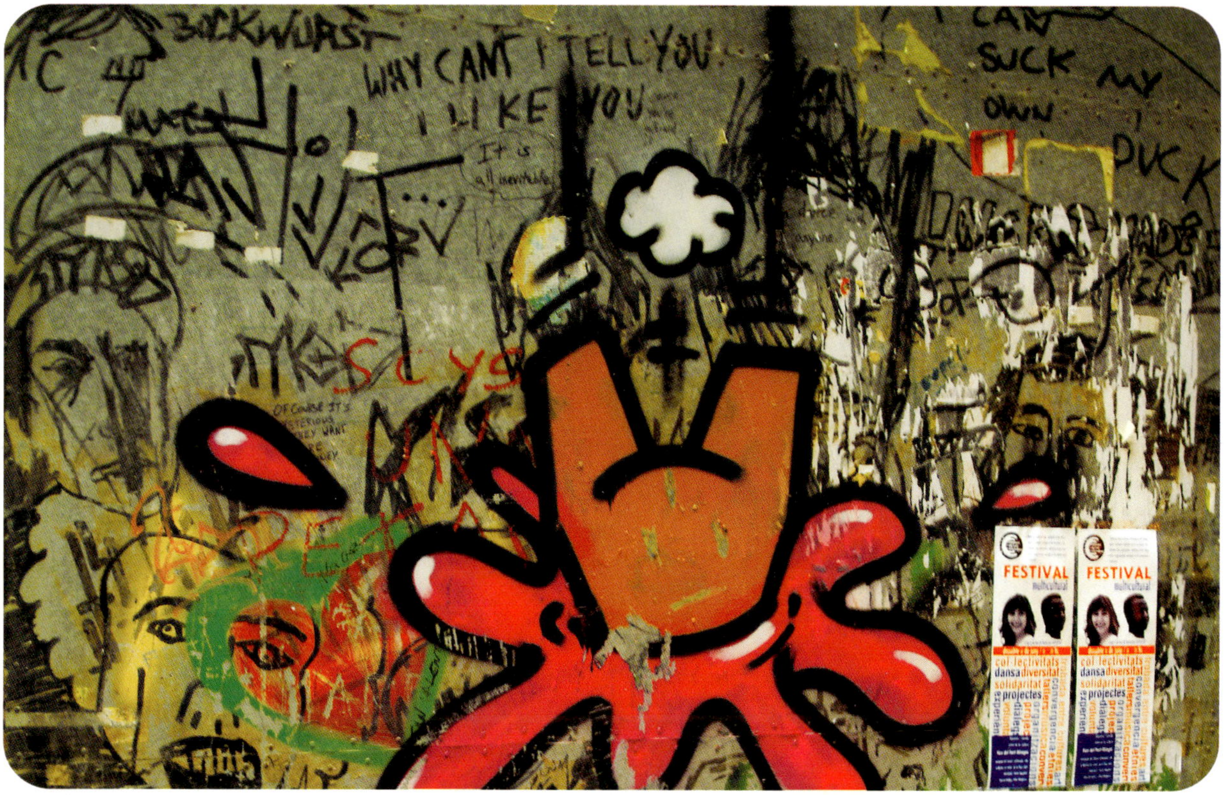
BOCKWURST
WHY CANT I TELL YOU I LIKE YOU
It is all inevitable
SUCK MY OWN DUCK
FESTIVAL
multicultural
col·lectivitats
dansa
diversitat
solidaritat
projectes
FESTIVAL
multicultural
col·lectivitats
dansa
diversitat
solidaritat
projectes

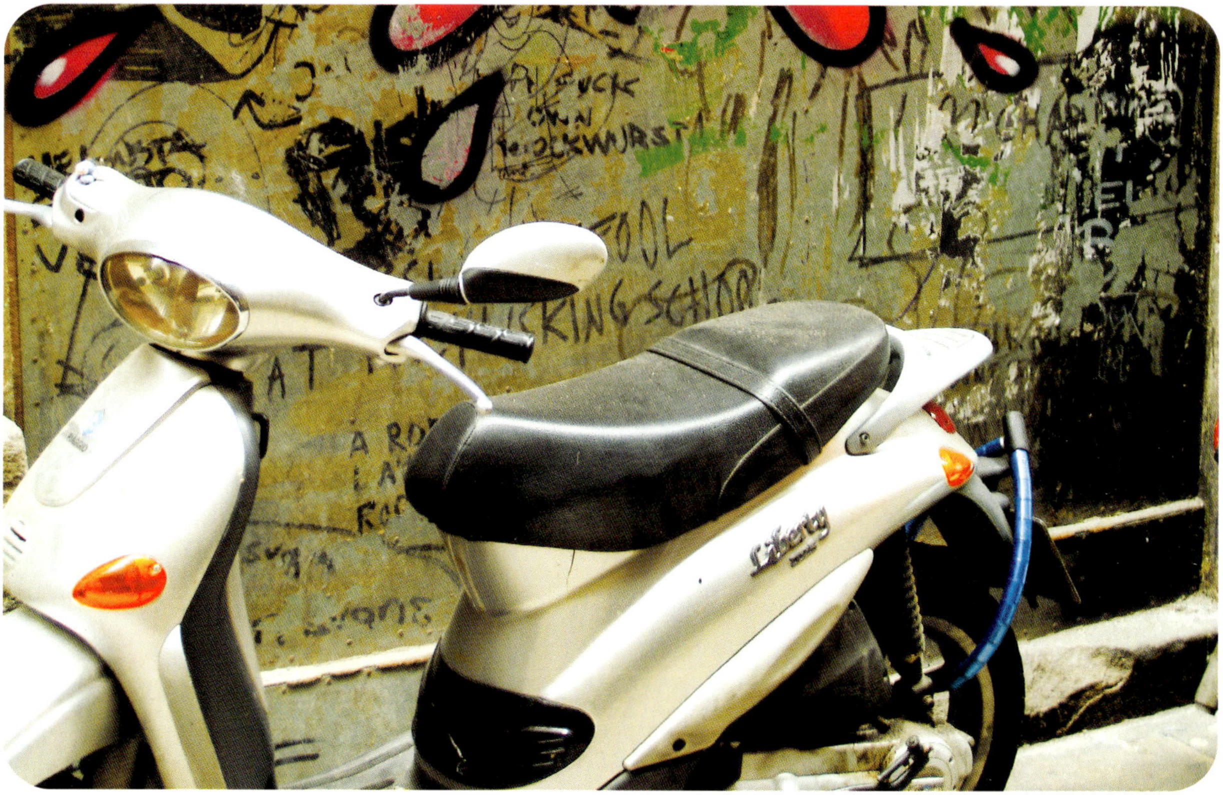
SUCK OWN BOCKWURST
FUCKING SCHOO
Liberty

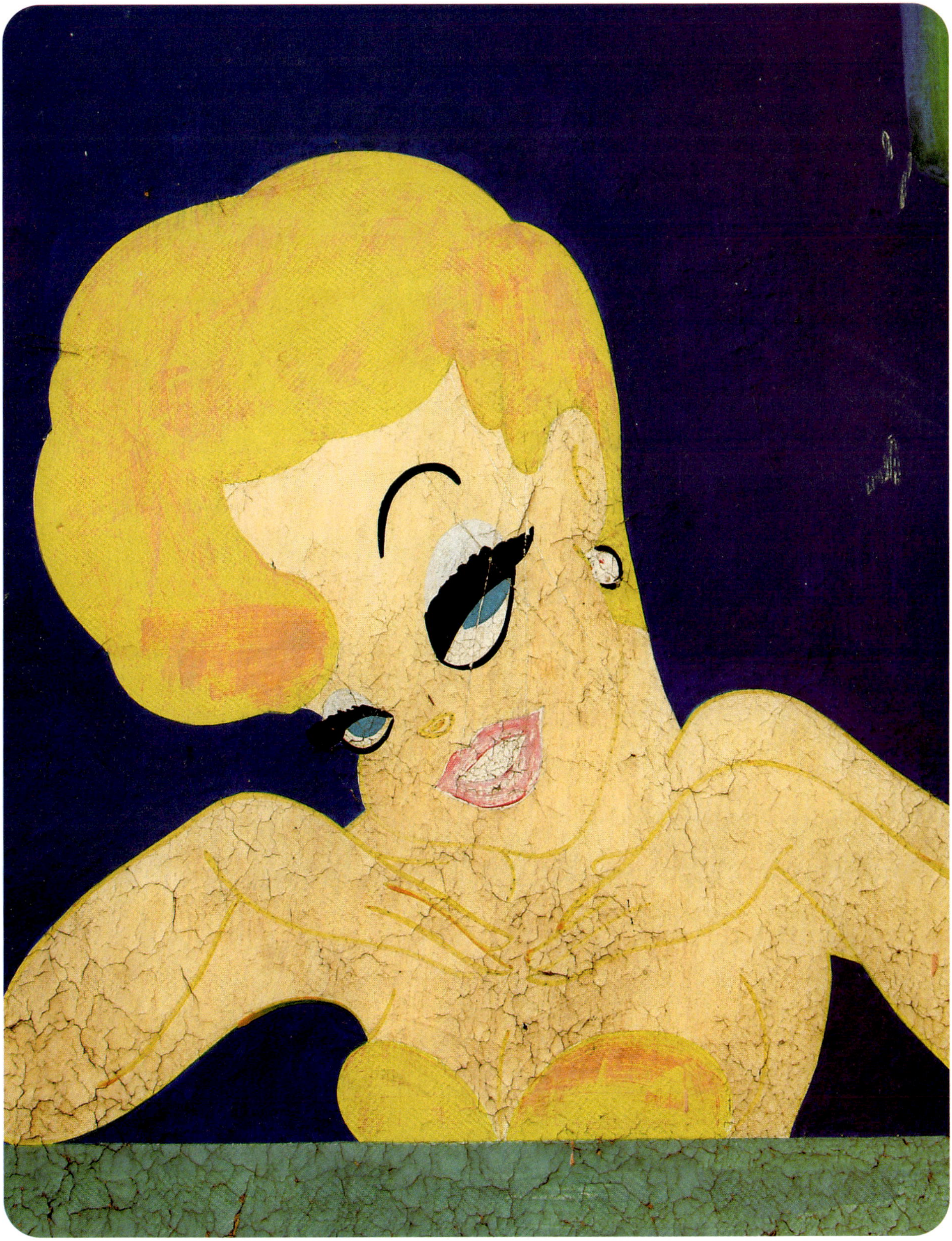

barcelona

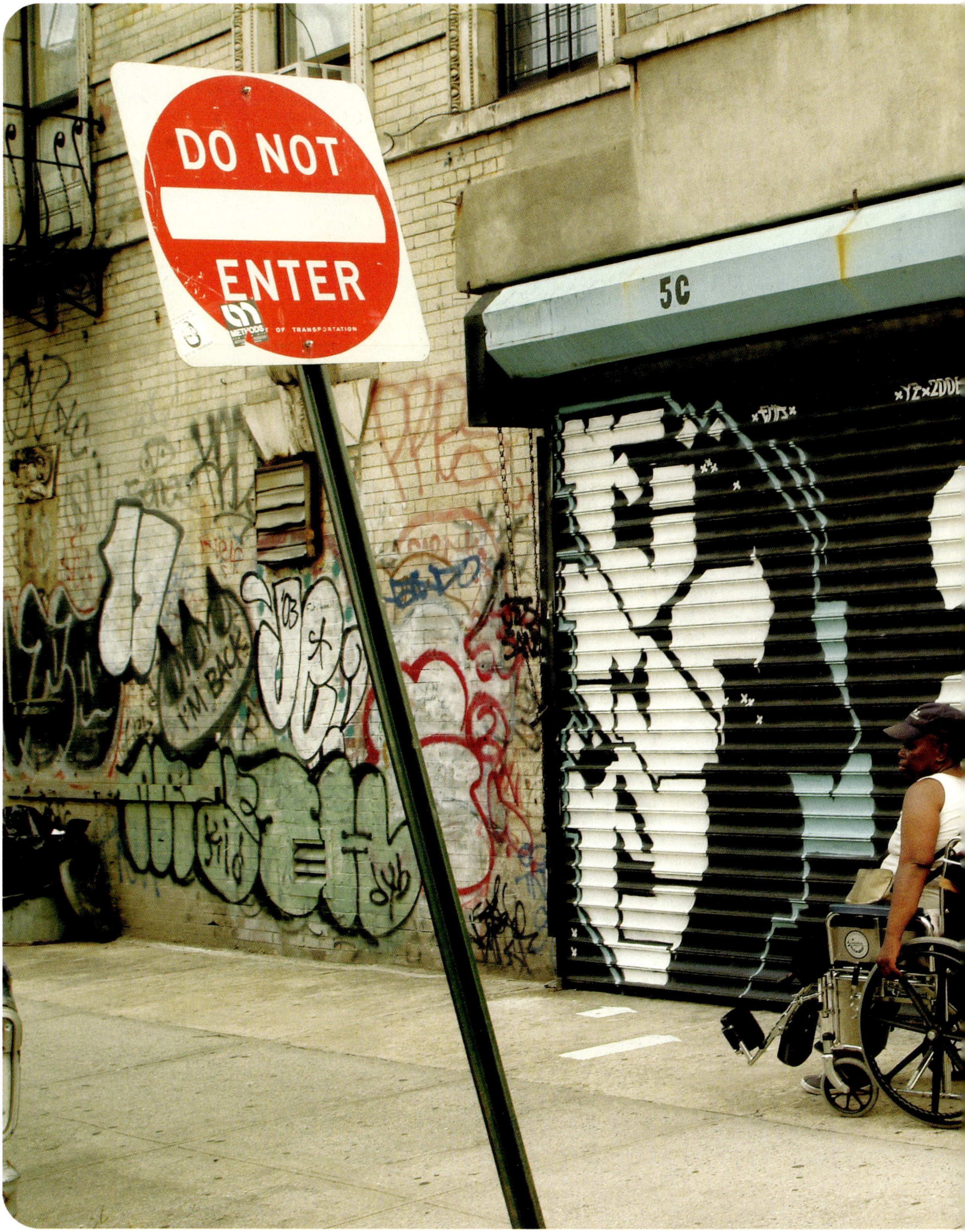
DO NOT
ENTER
5C

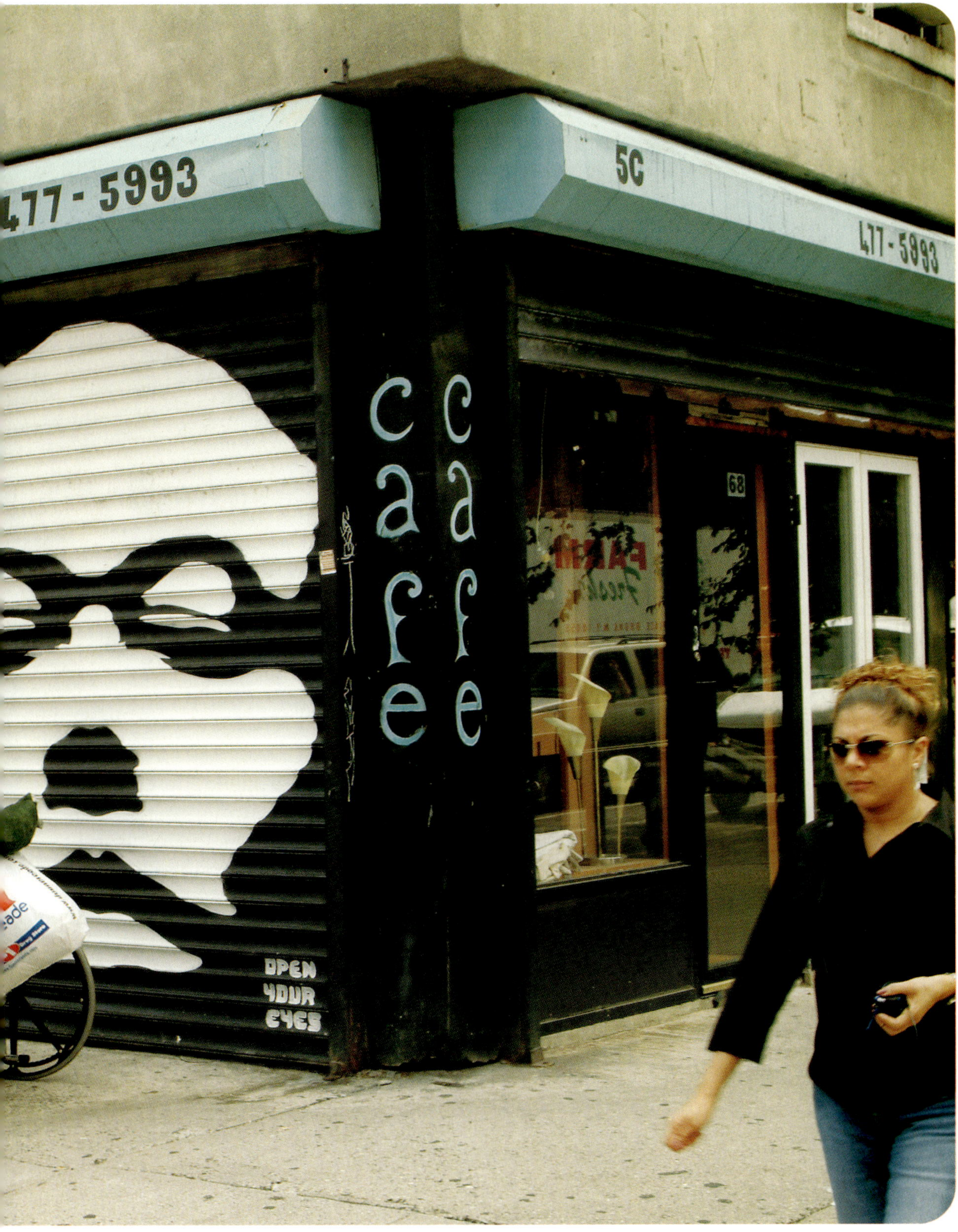
477 - 5993
5C
477-5993
caffe
caffe
68
OPEN
YOUR
EYES

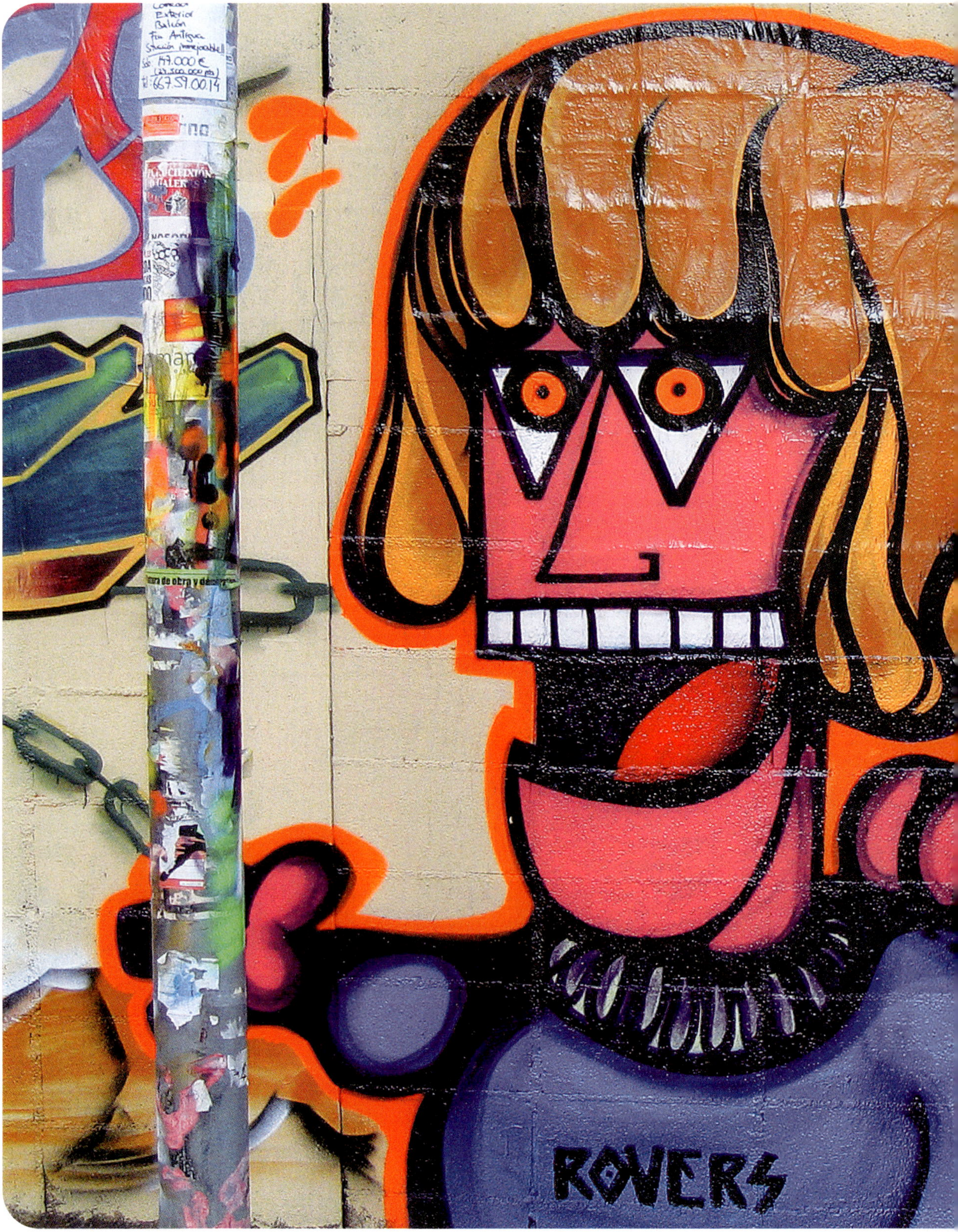
Exterior
Balcón
667.59.00.14
ROVERS

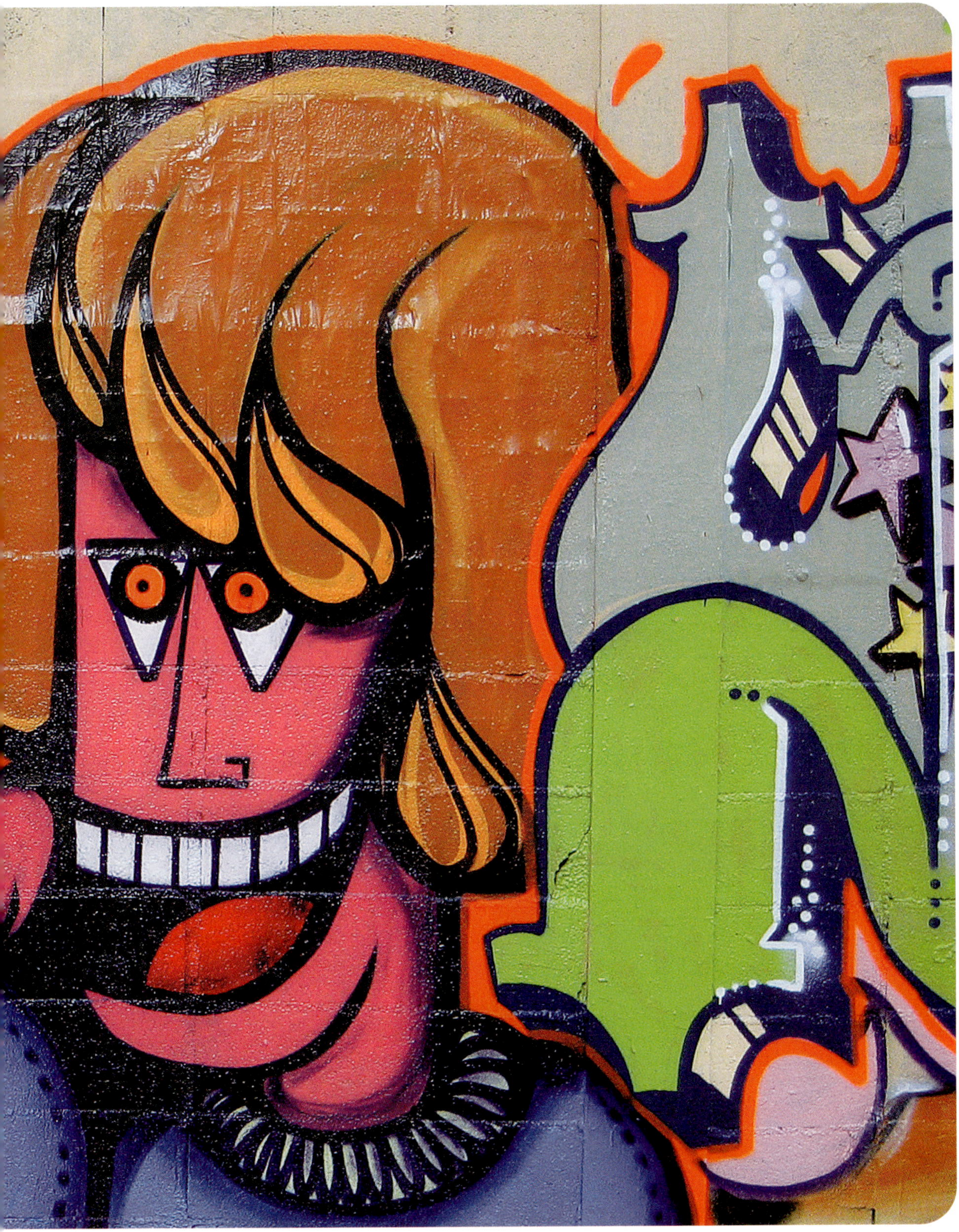

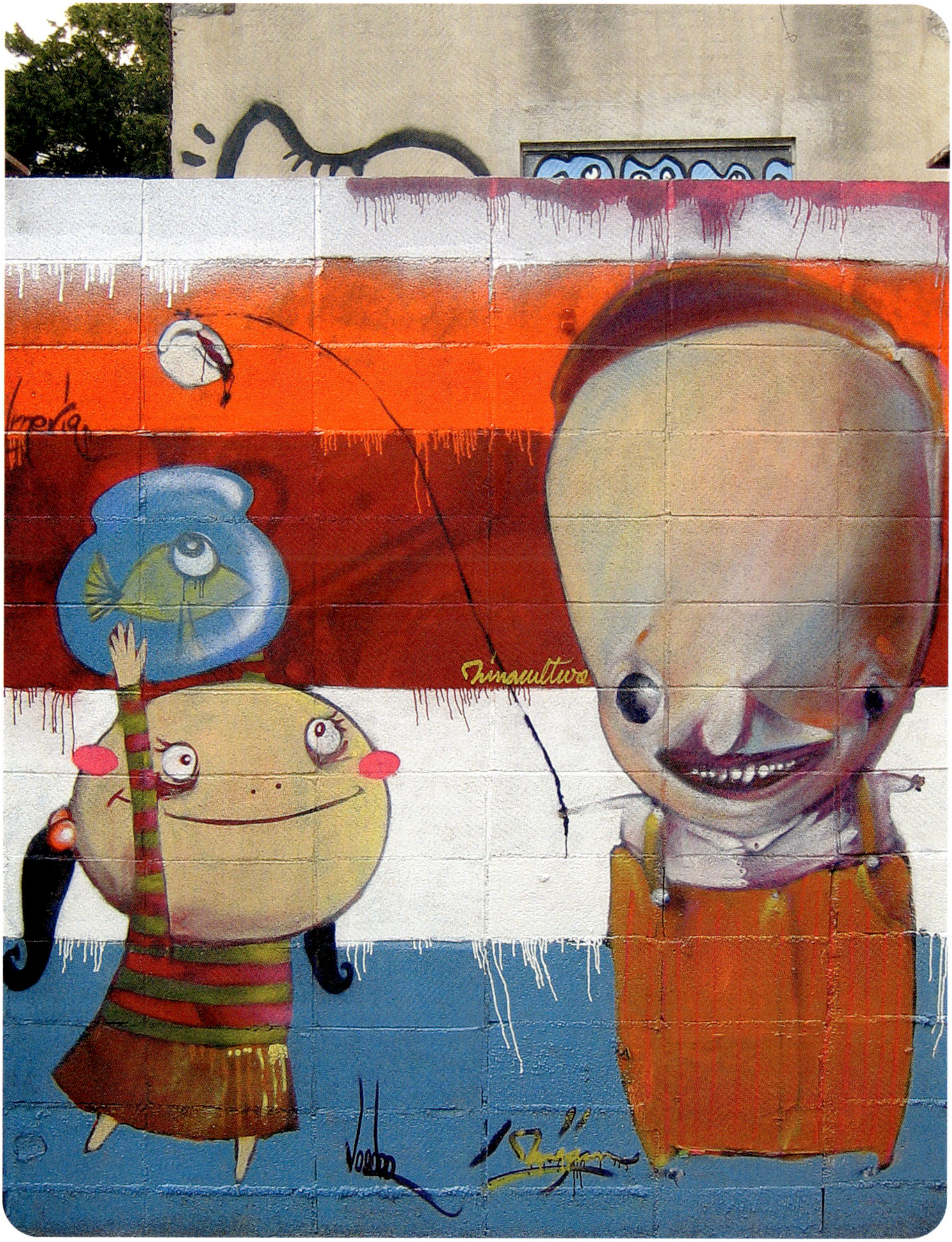

barcelona

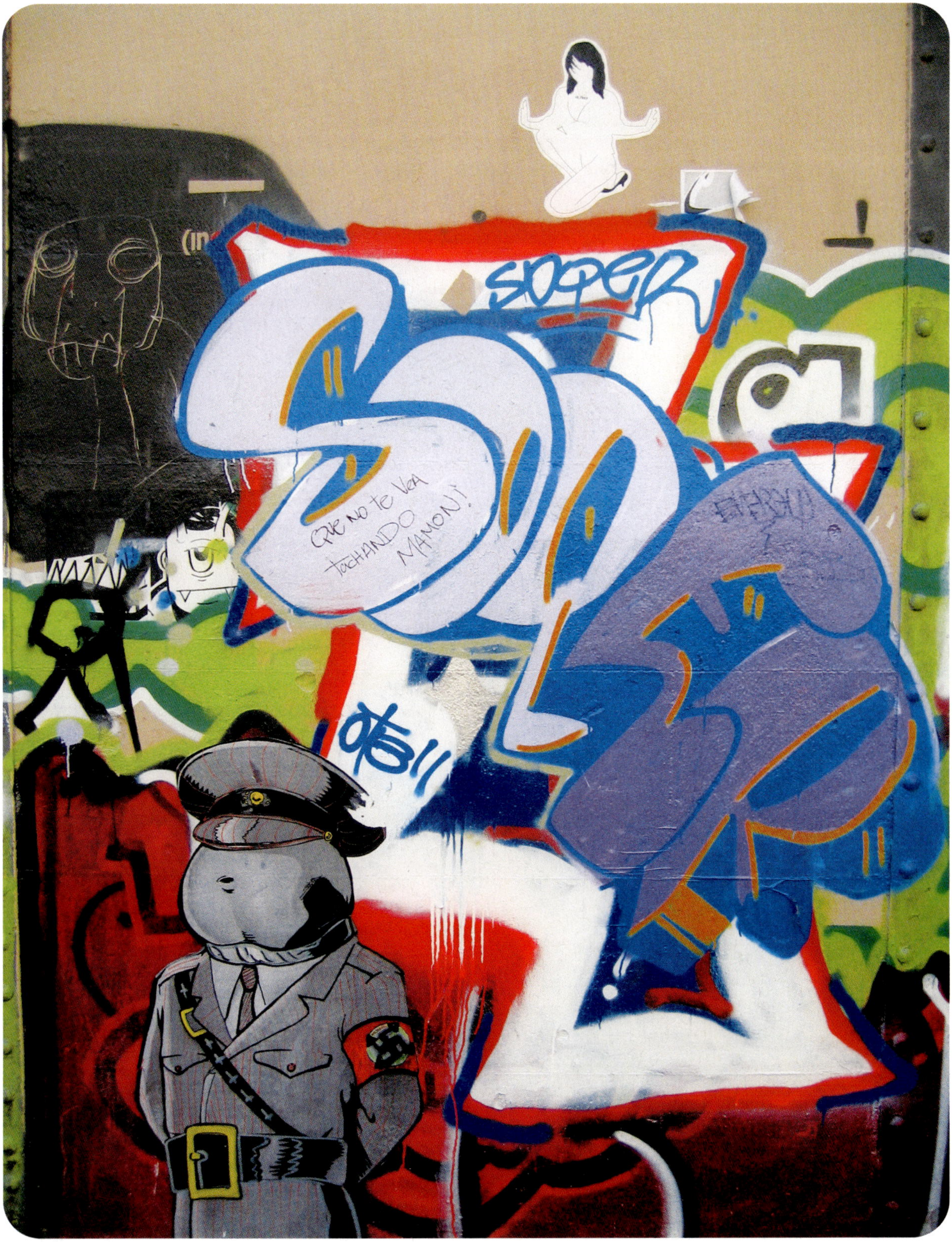
Que no te vea tachando mamon!

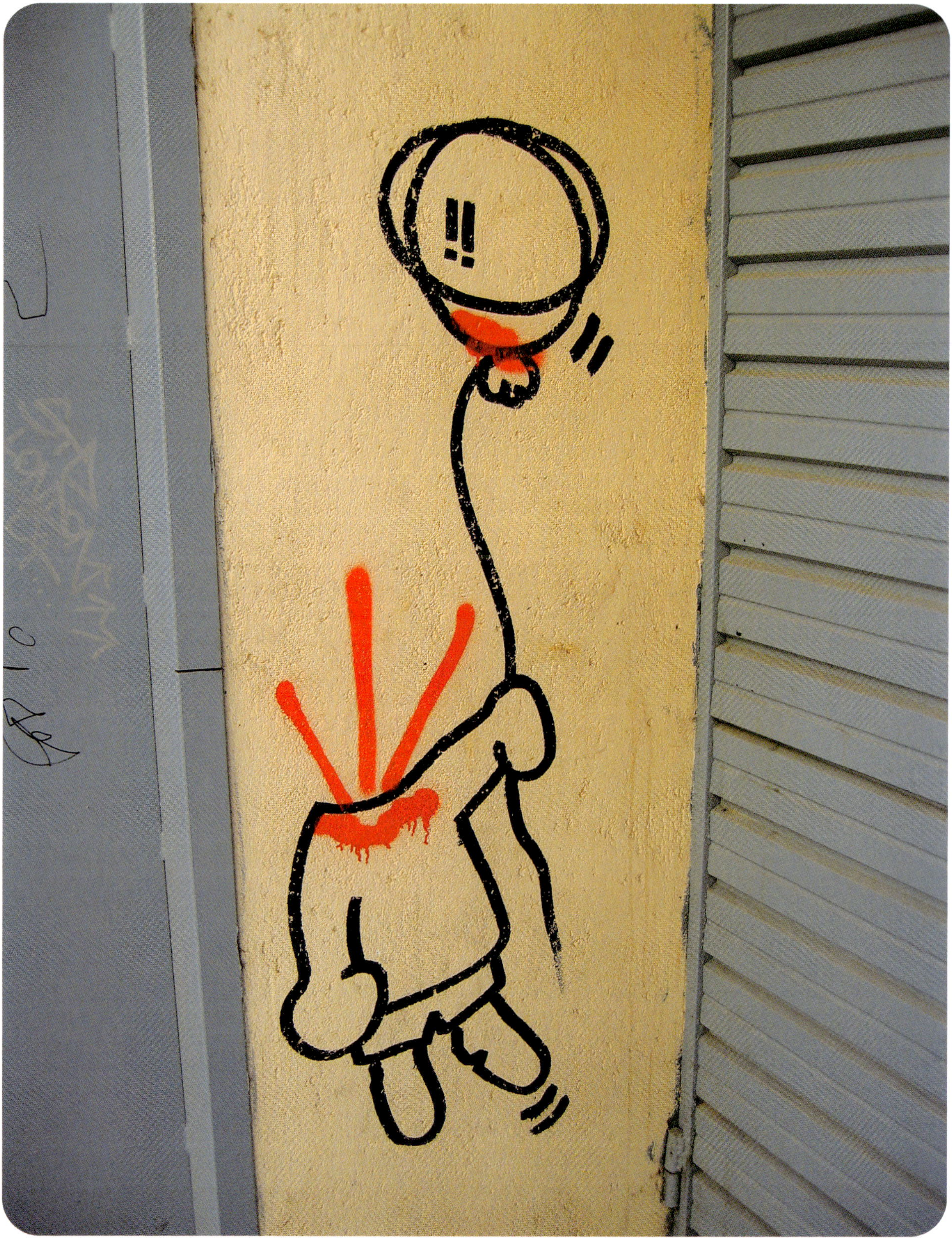

barcelona

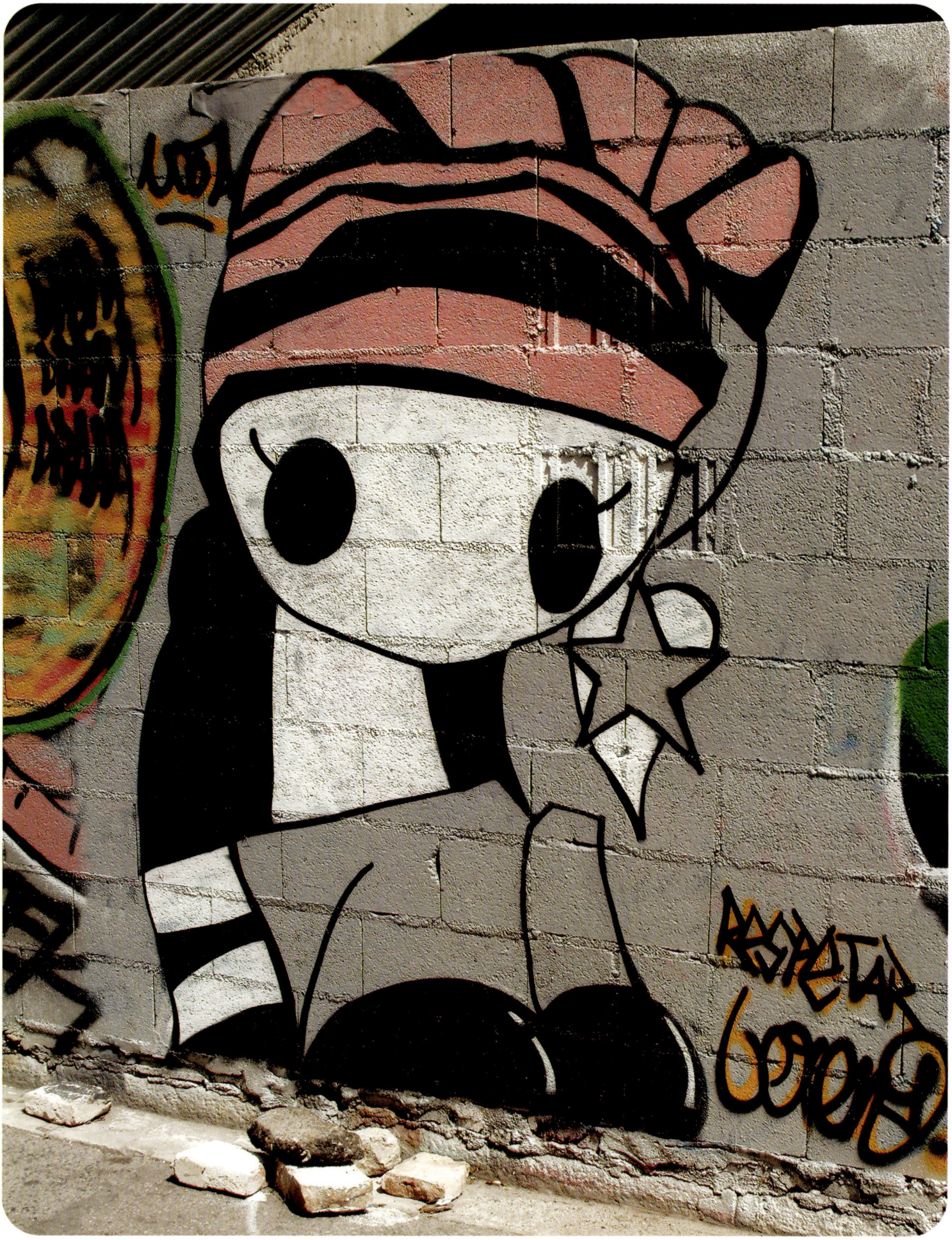

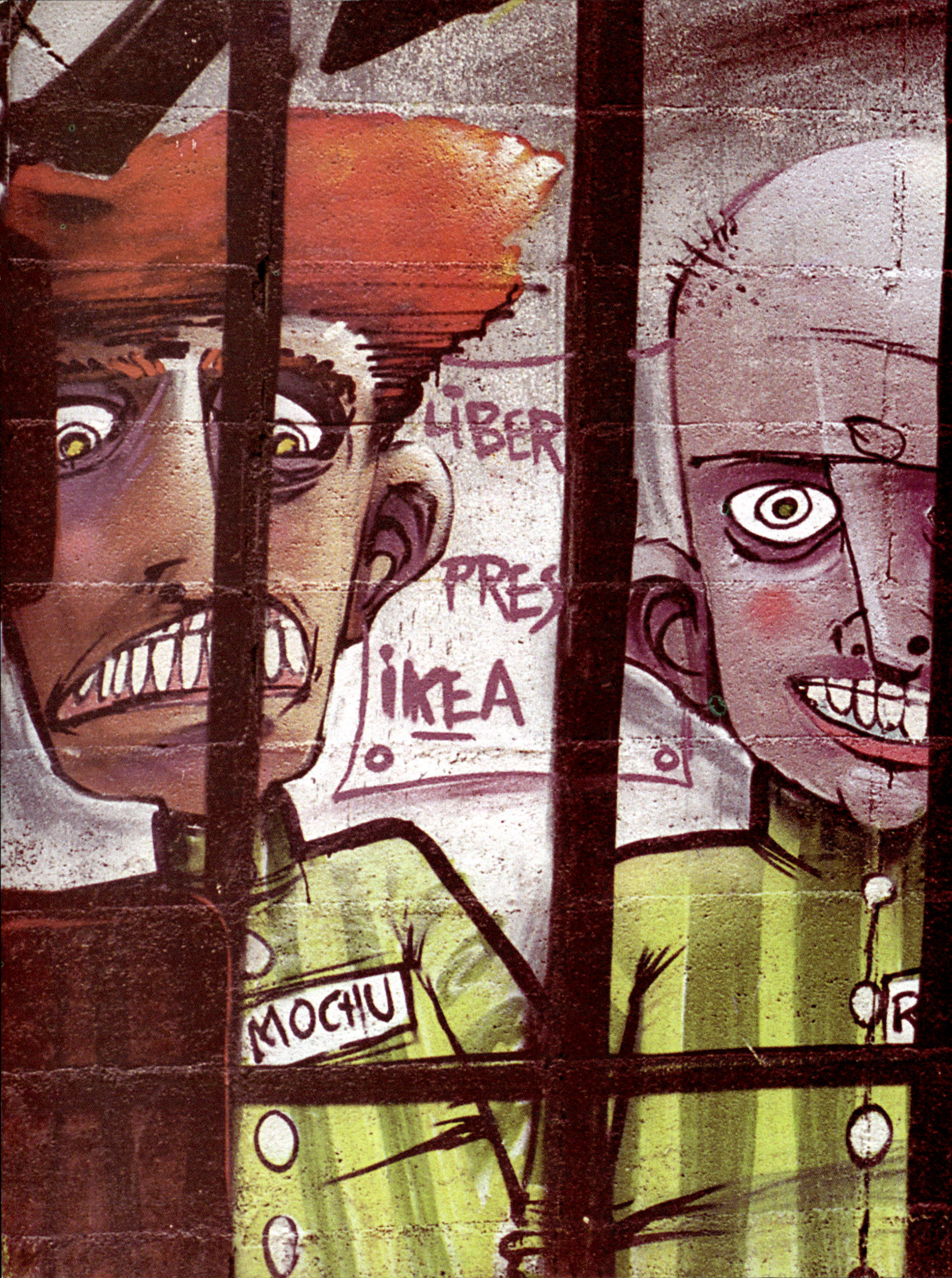
LIBER
PRES
IKEA
MOCHU

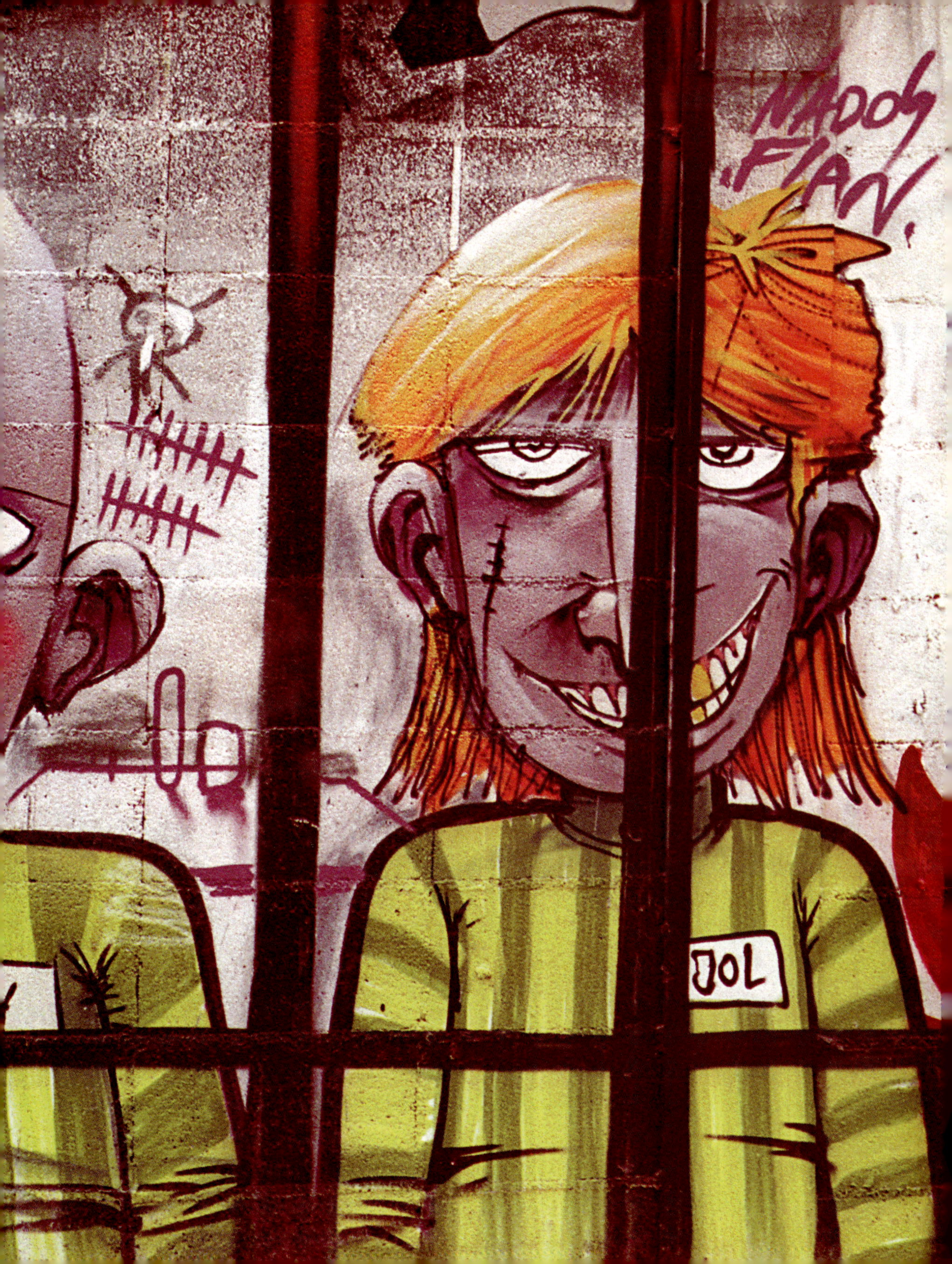
NADOS
FIAN.
JOL

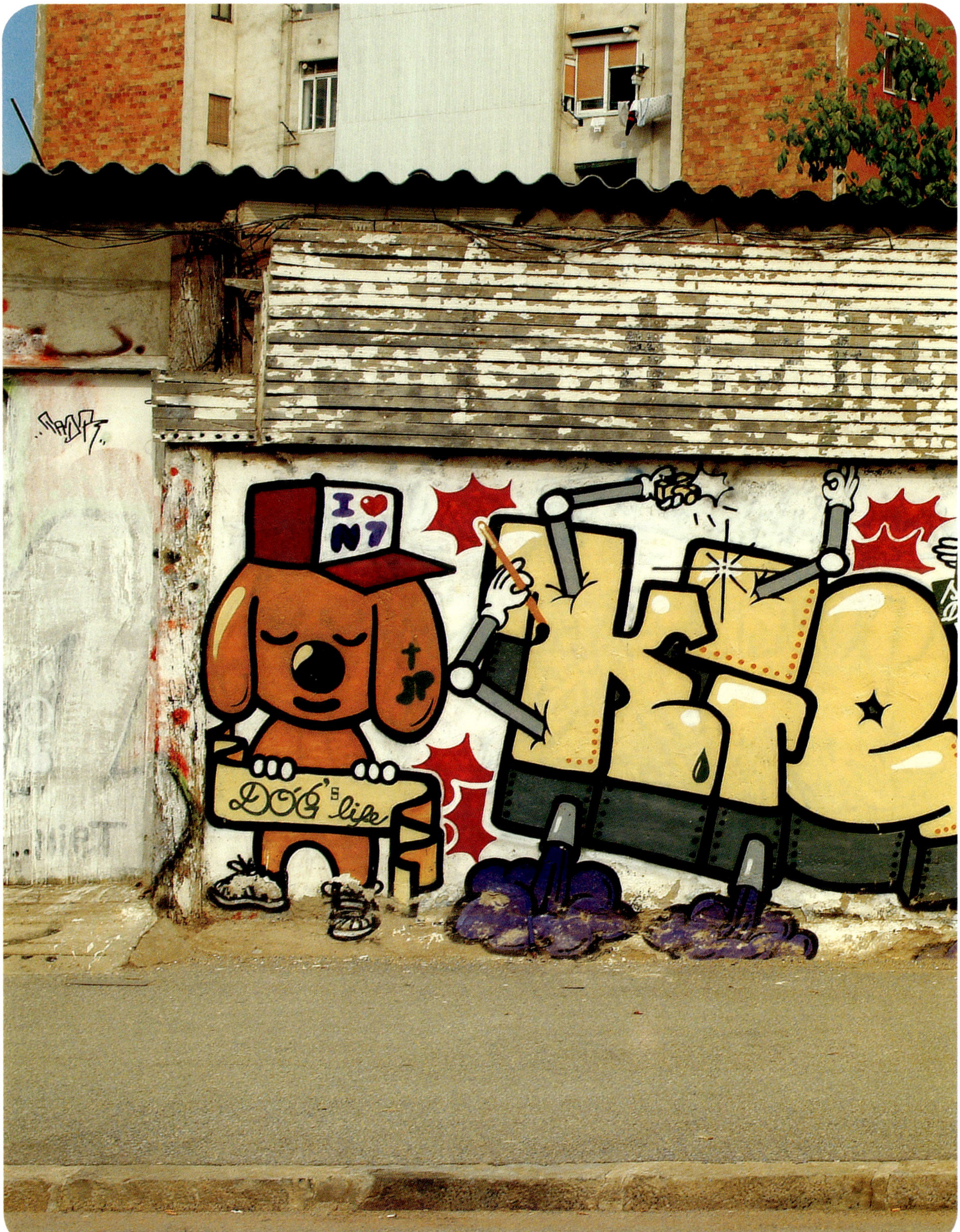
DOG's life

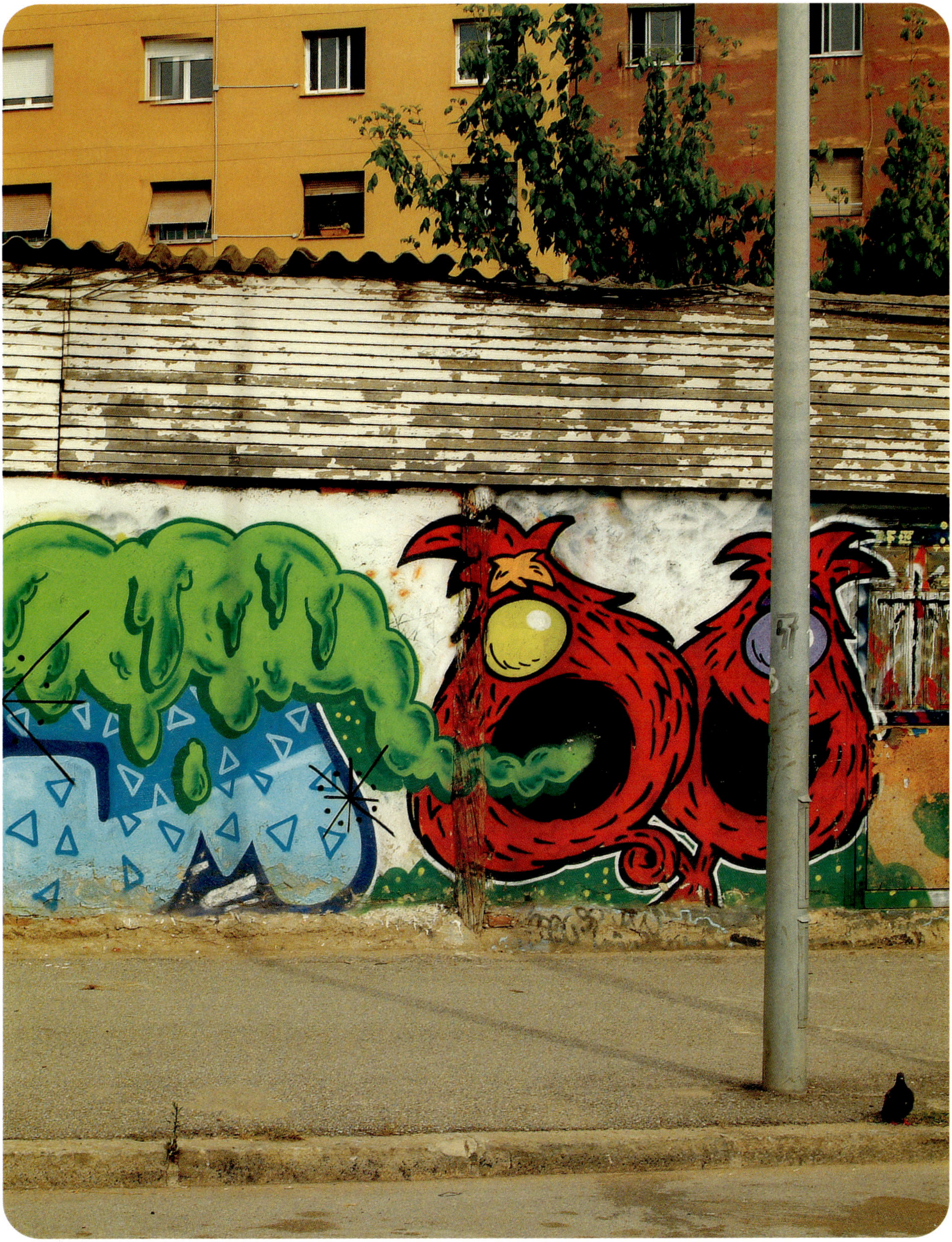

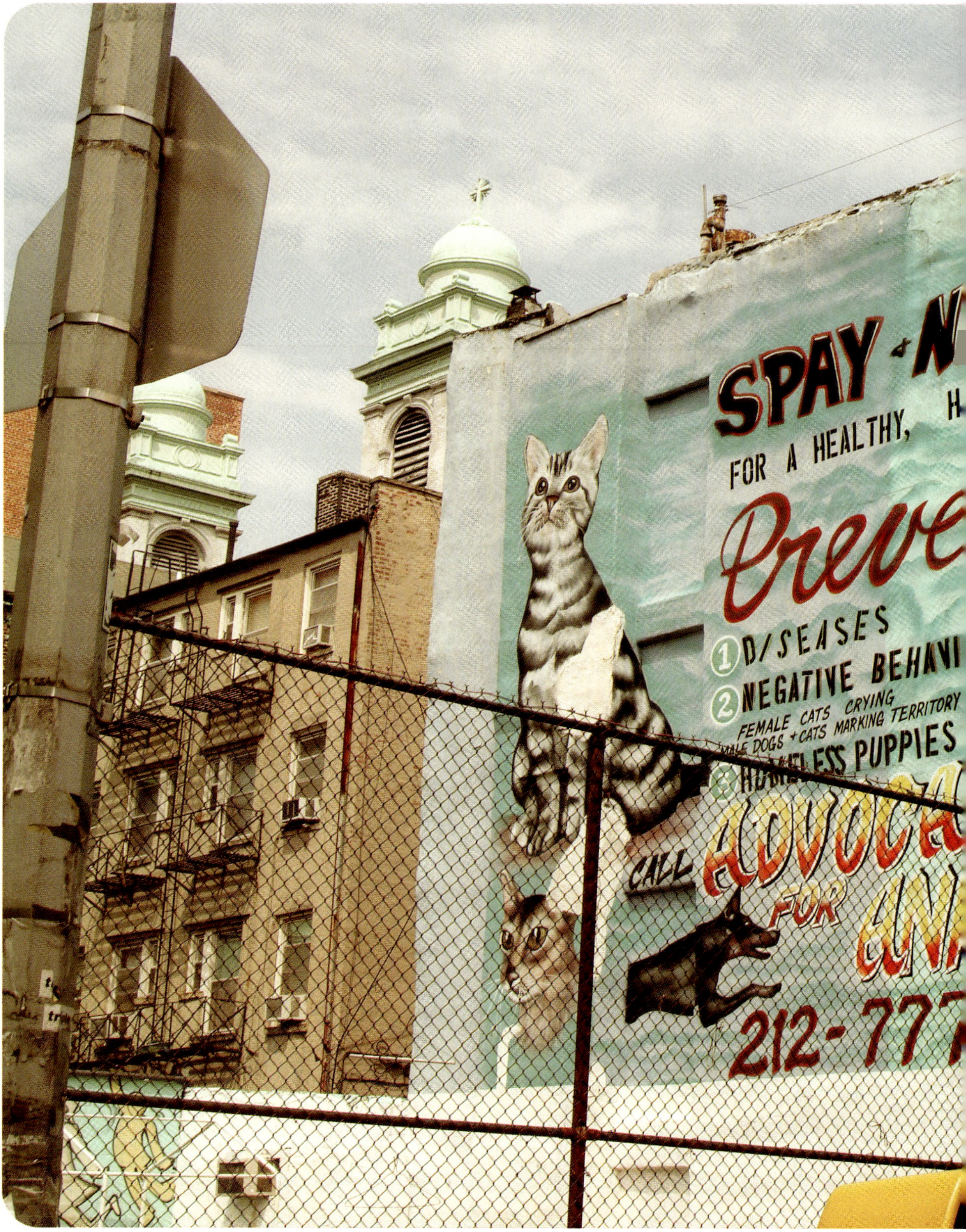
SPAY
FOR A HEALTHY,
1 D/SEASES
FEMALE CATS CRYING
DOGS + CATS MARKING TERRITORY
PUPPIES
CALL
FOR

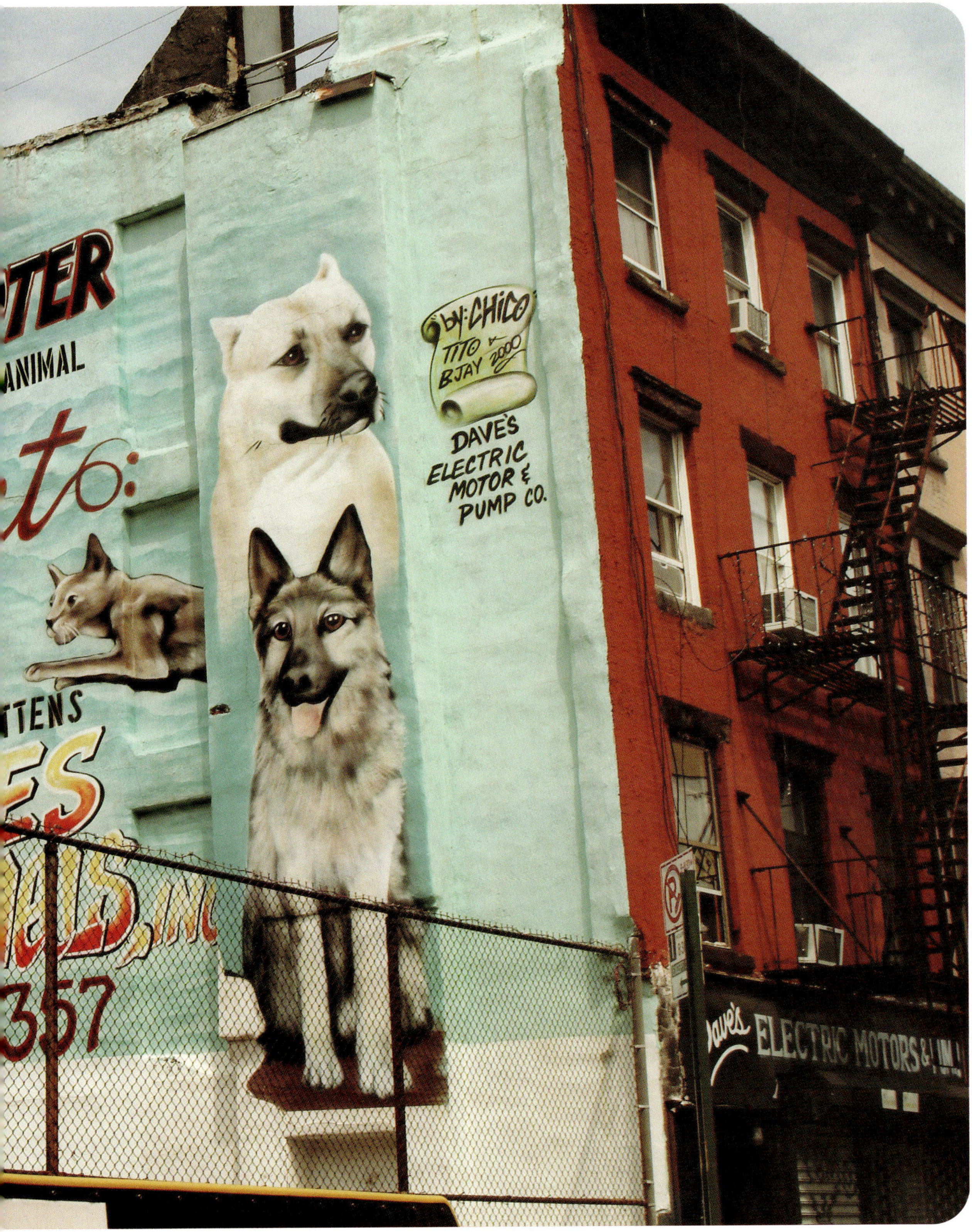
TER
ANIMAL
to:
TTENS
ES
ALS, INC
357
by: CHICO
TITO &
BJAY 2000
DAVE'S
ELECTRIC
MOTOR &
PUMP CO.
Dave's ELECTRIC MOTORS

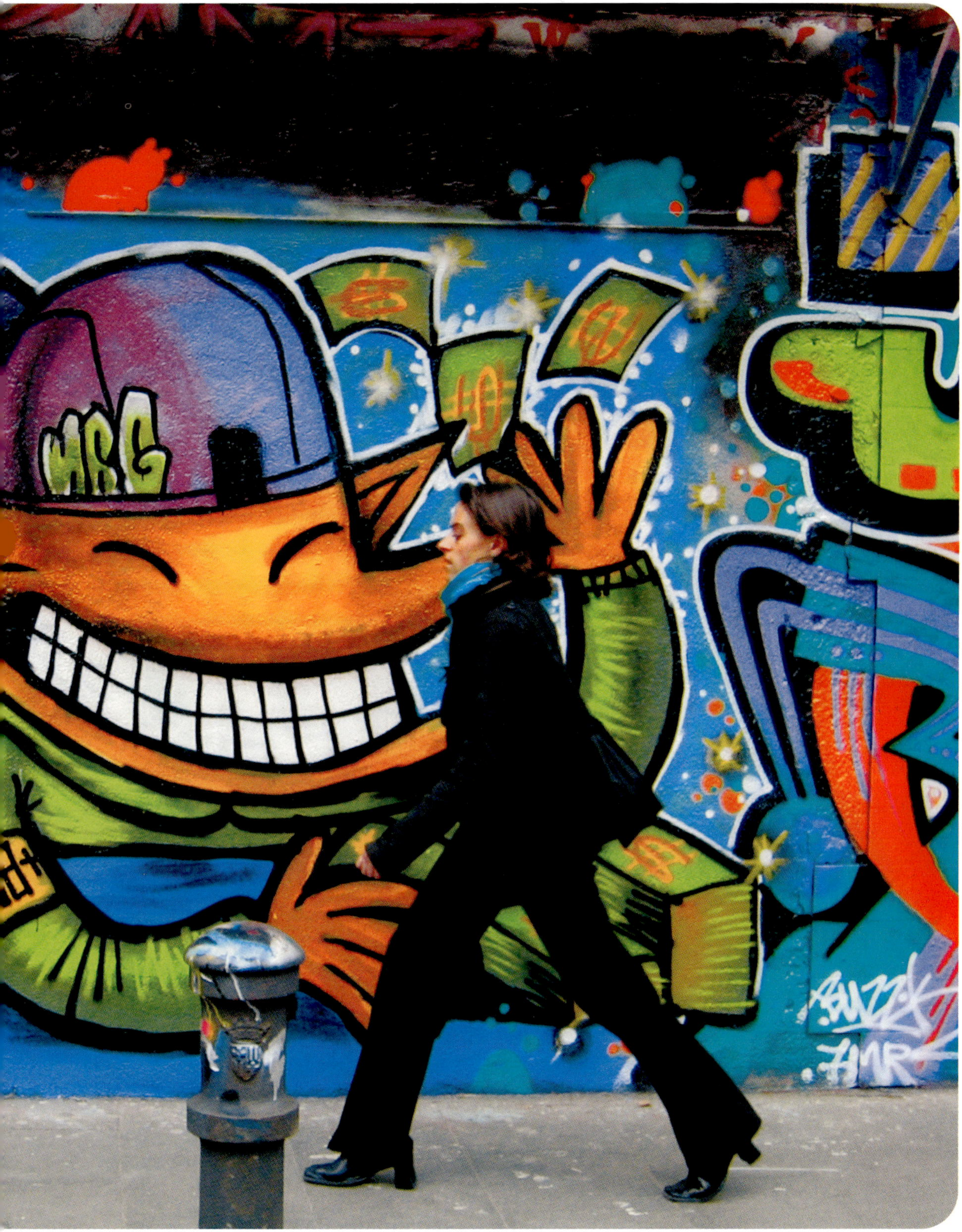

barcelona

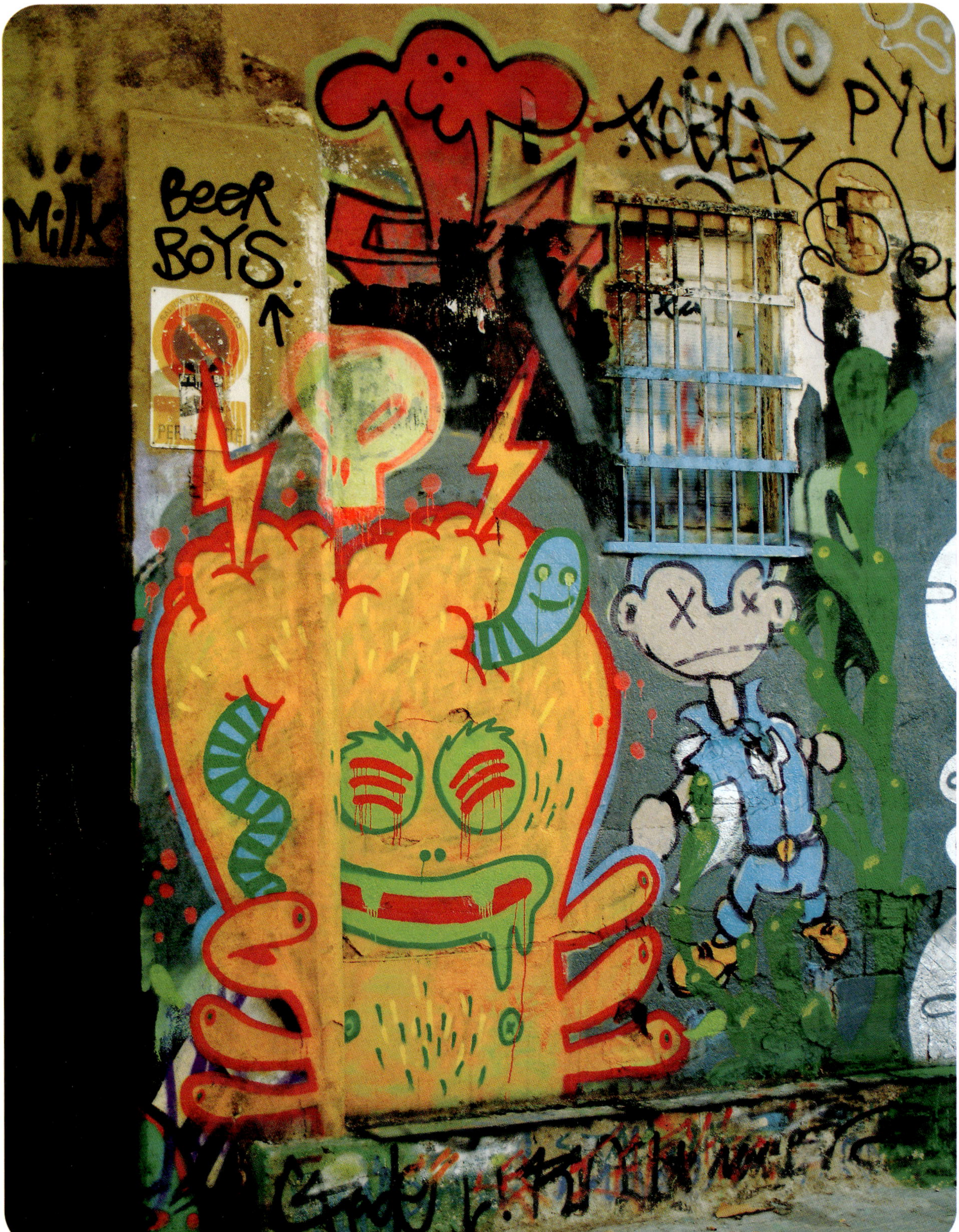

barcelona

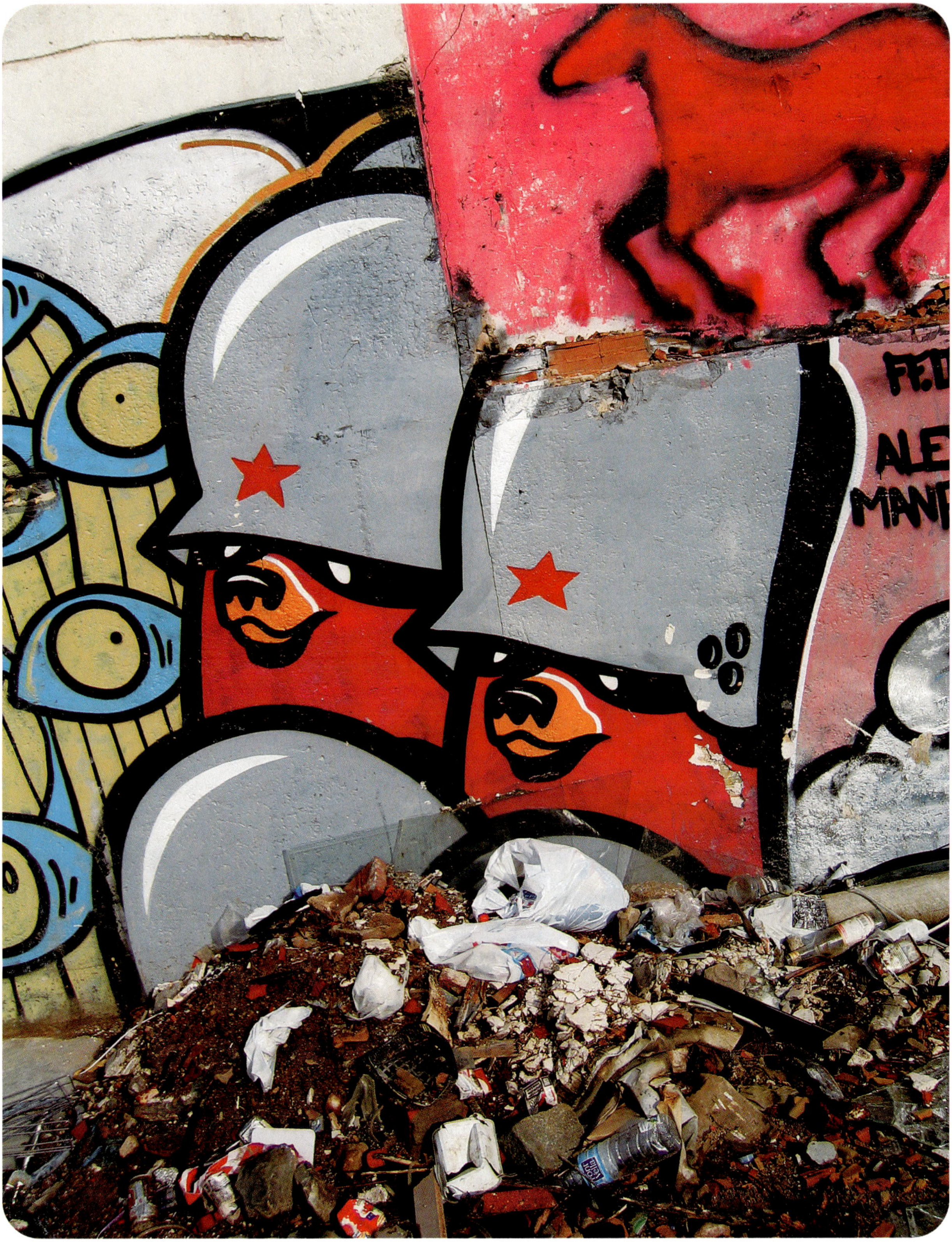

barcelona

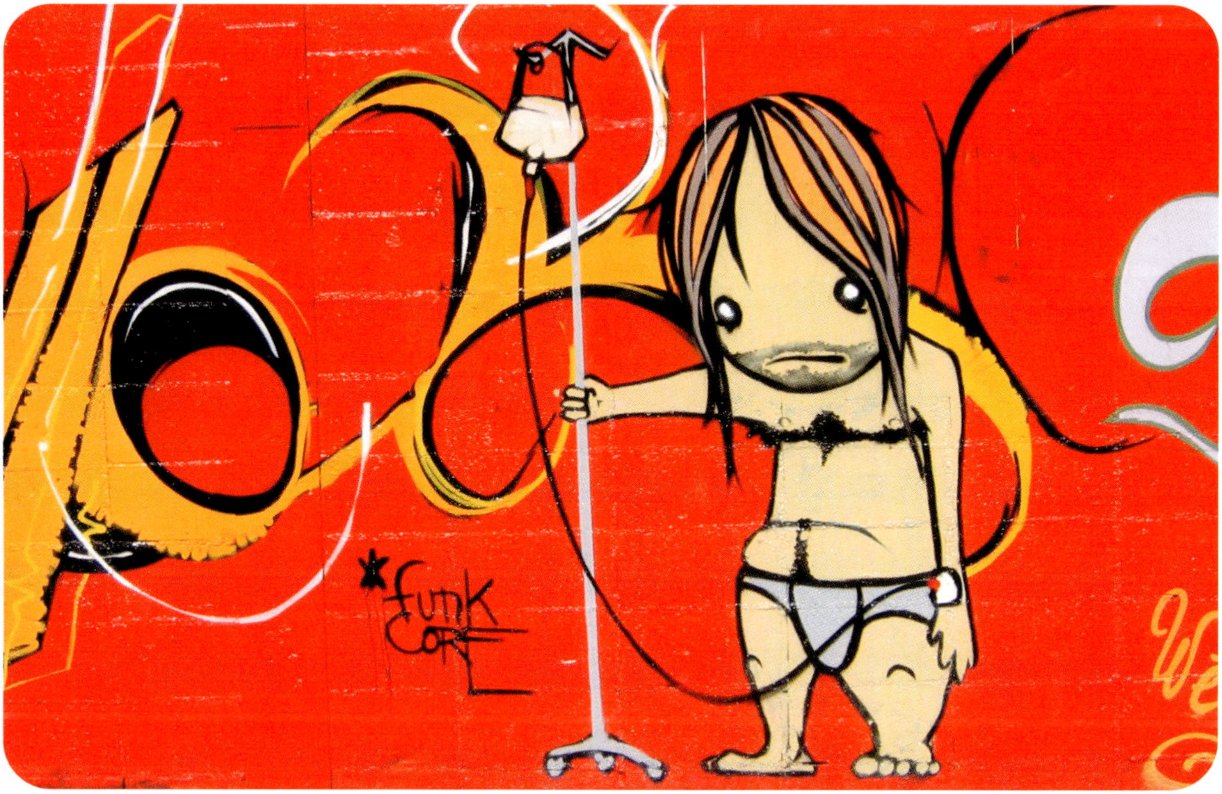
funk
core

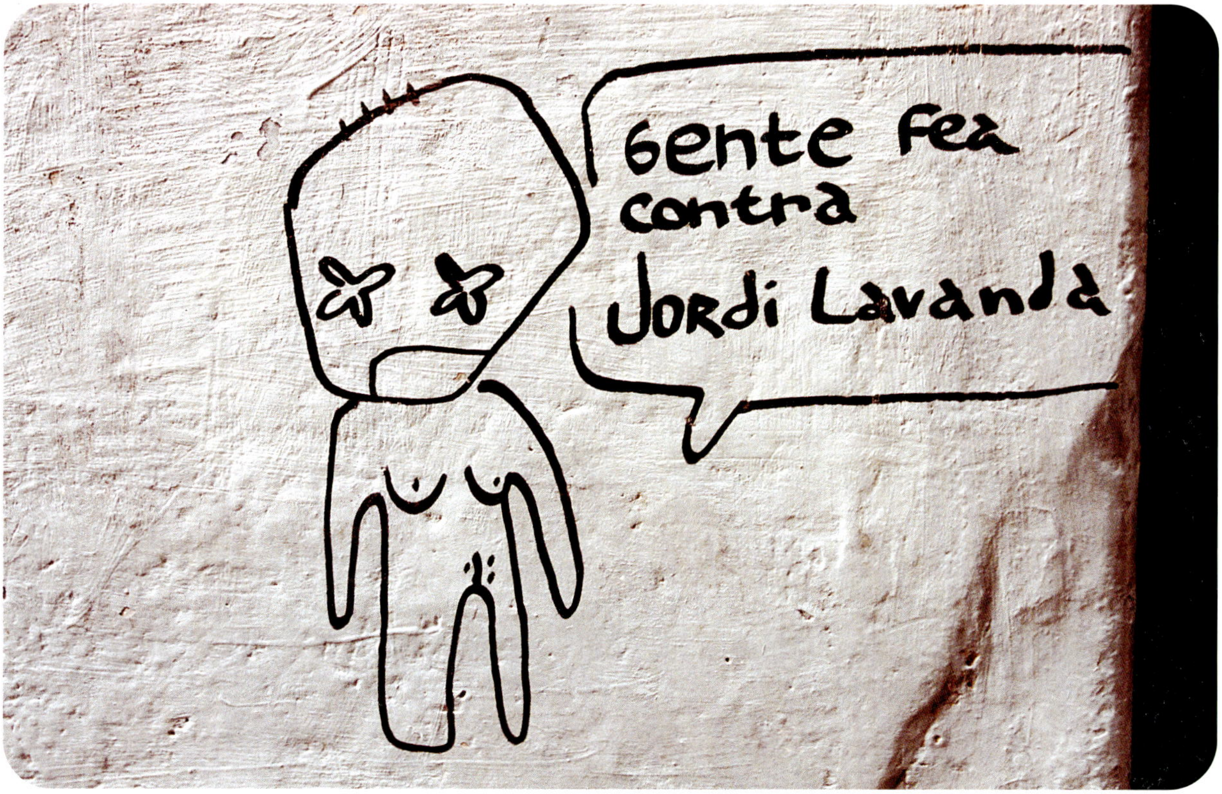
Gente fea contra Jordi Lavanda

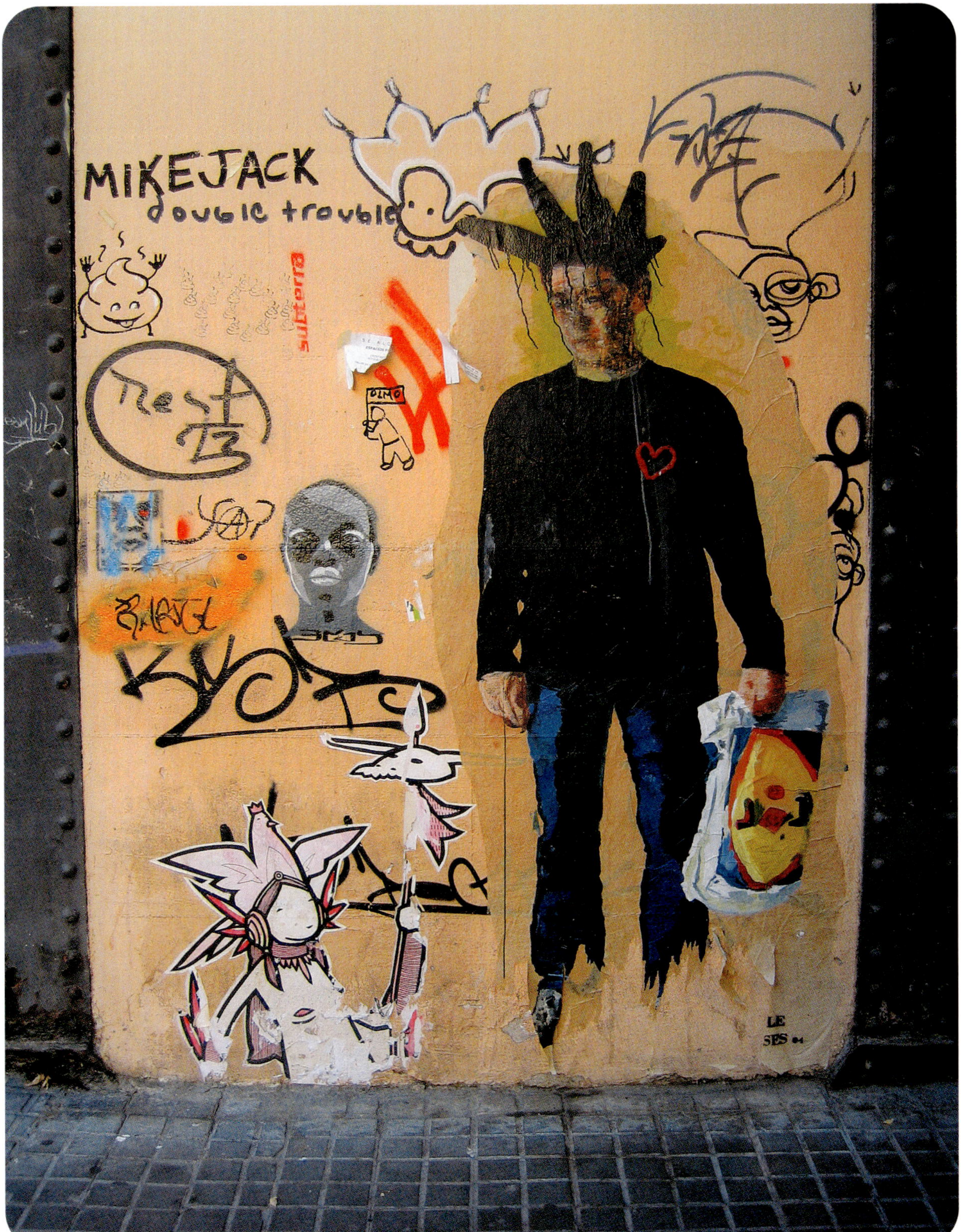

barcelona

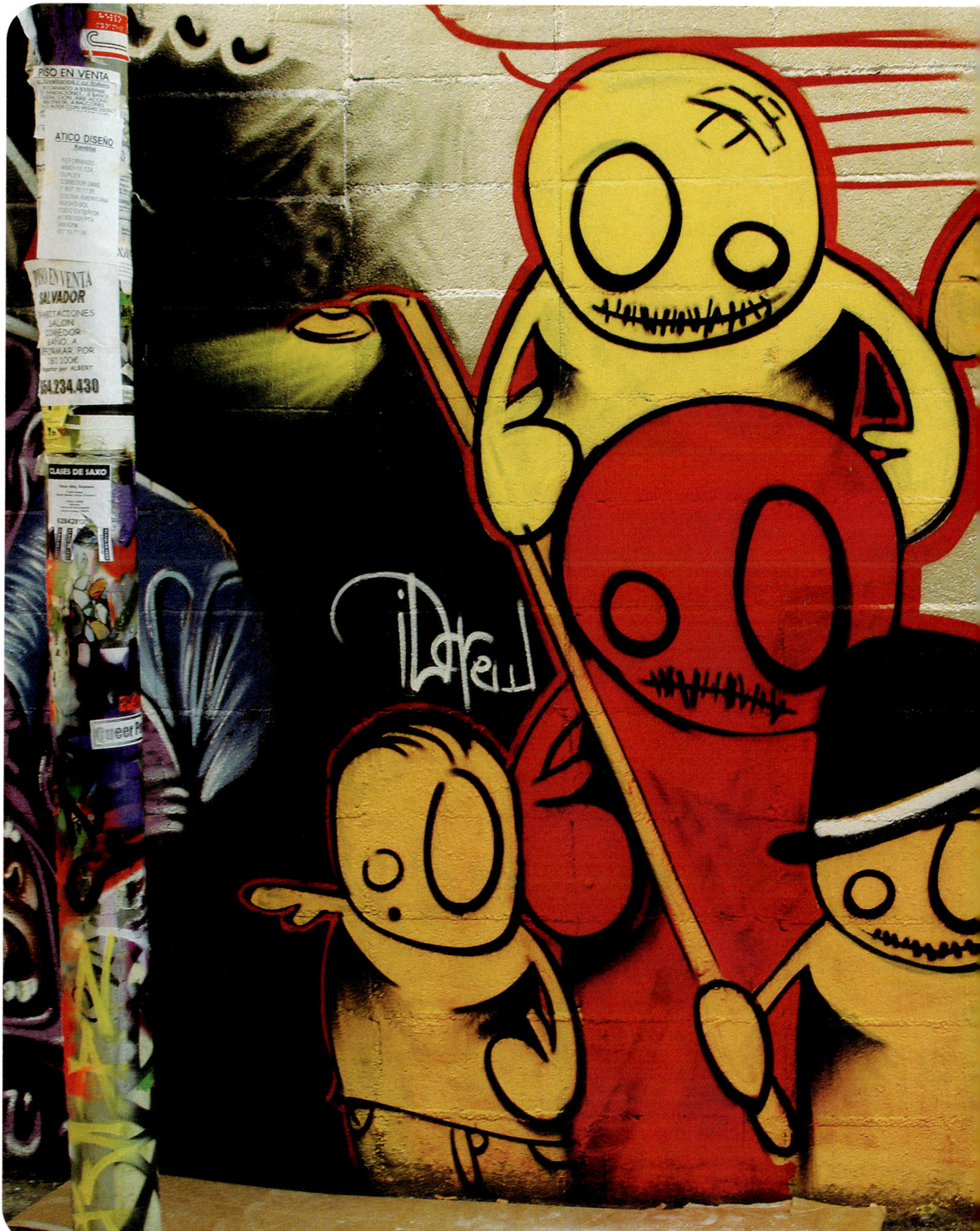
PISO EN VENTA
ATICO DISEÑO
PISO EN VENTA
SALVADOR
CLASES DE SAXO

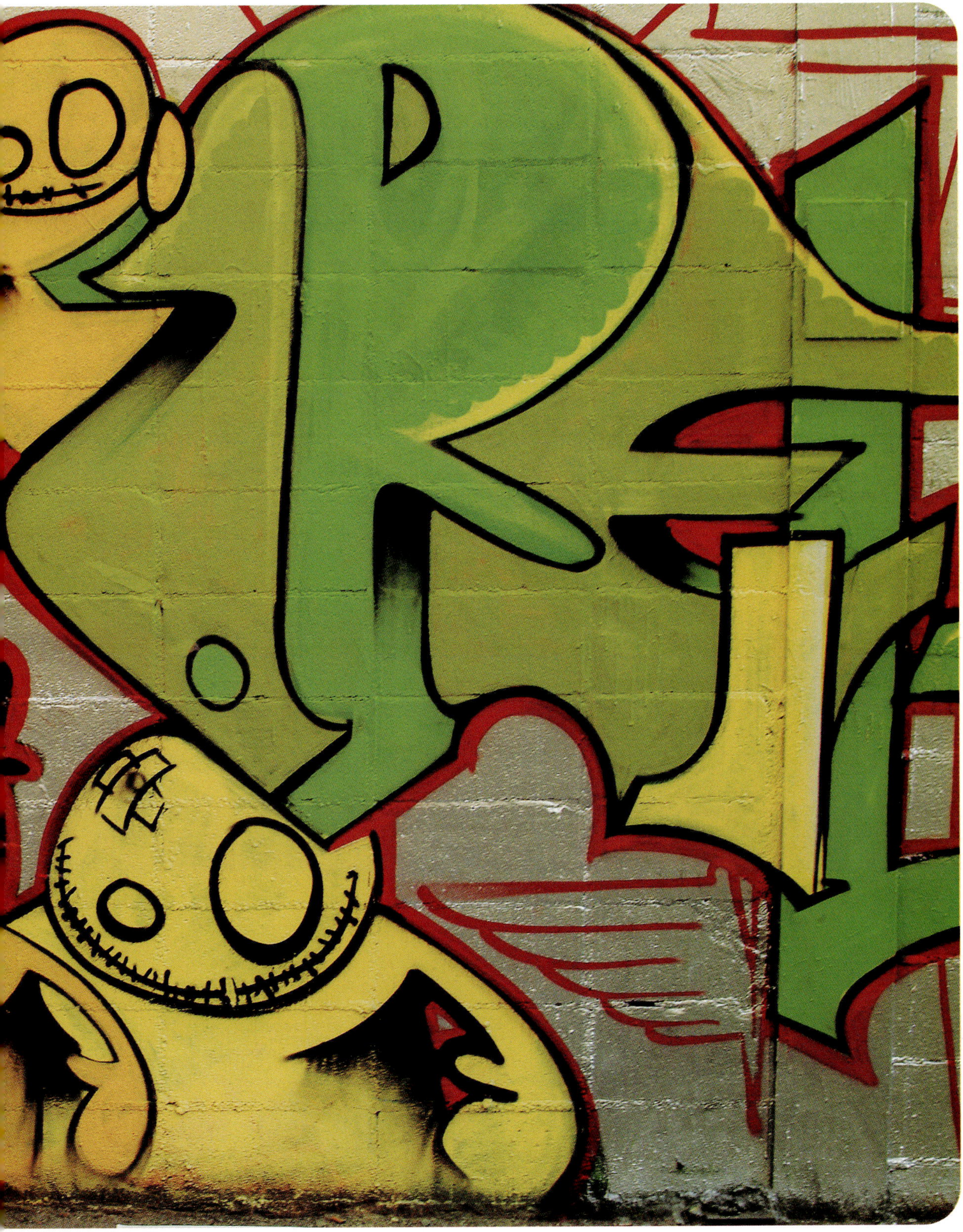

barcelona

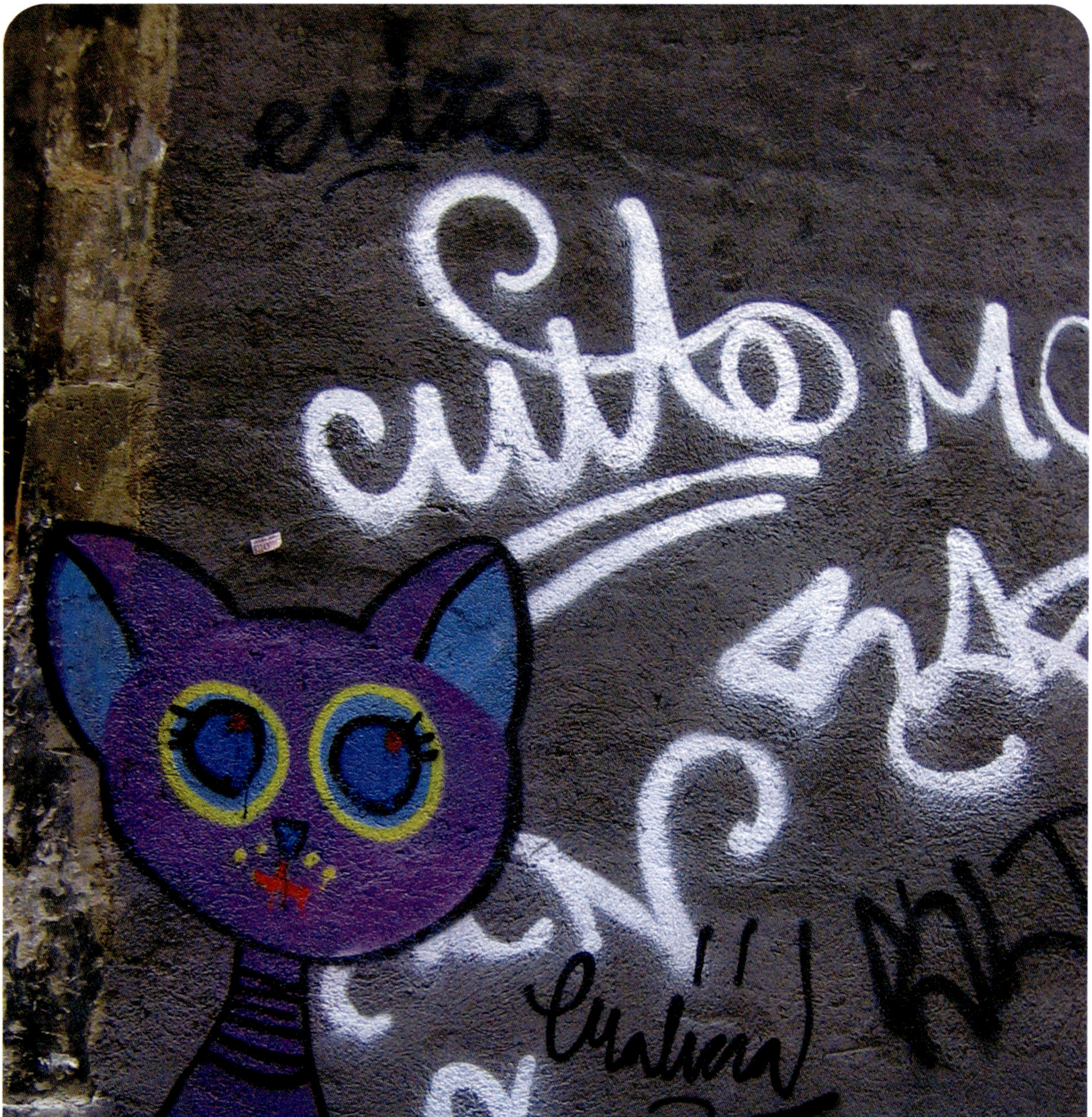

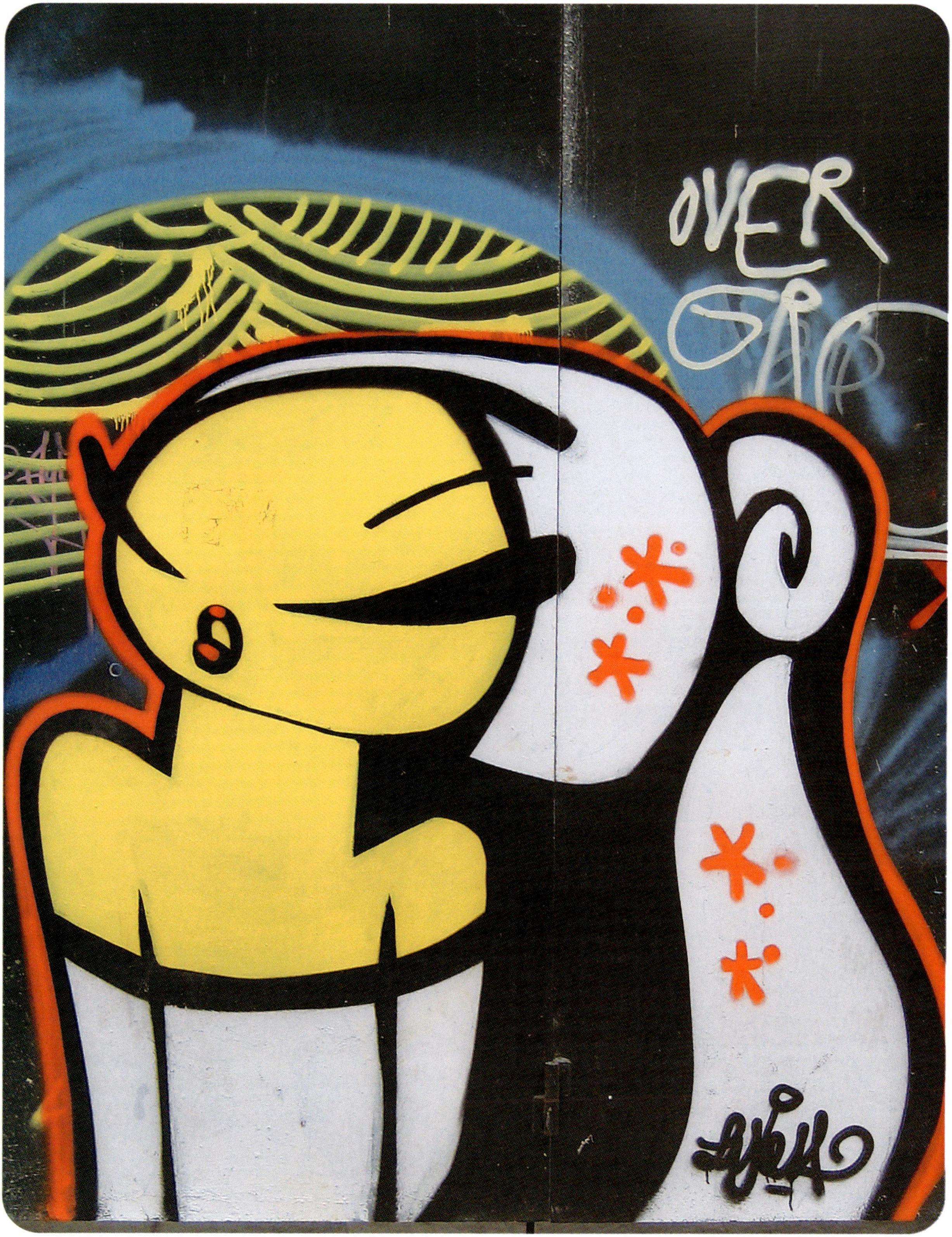

barcelona

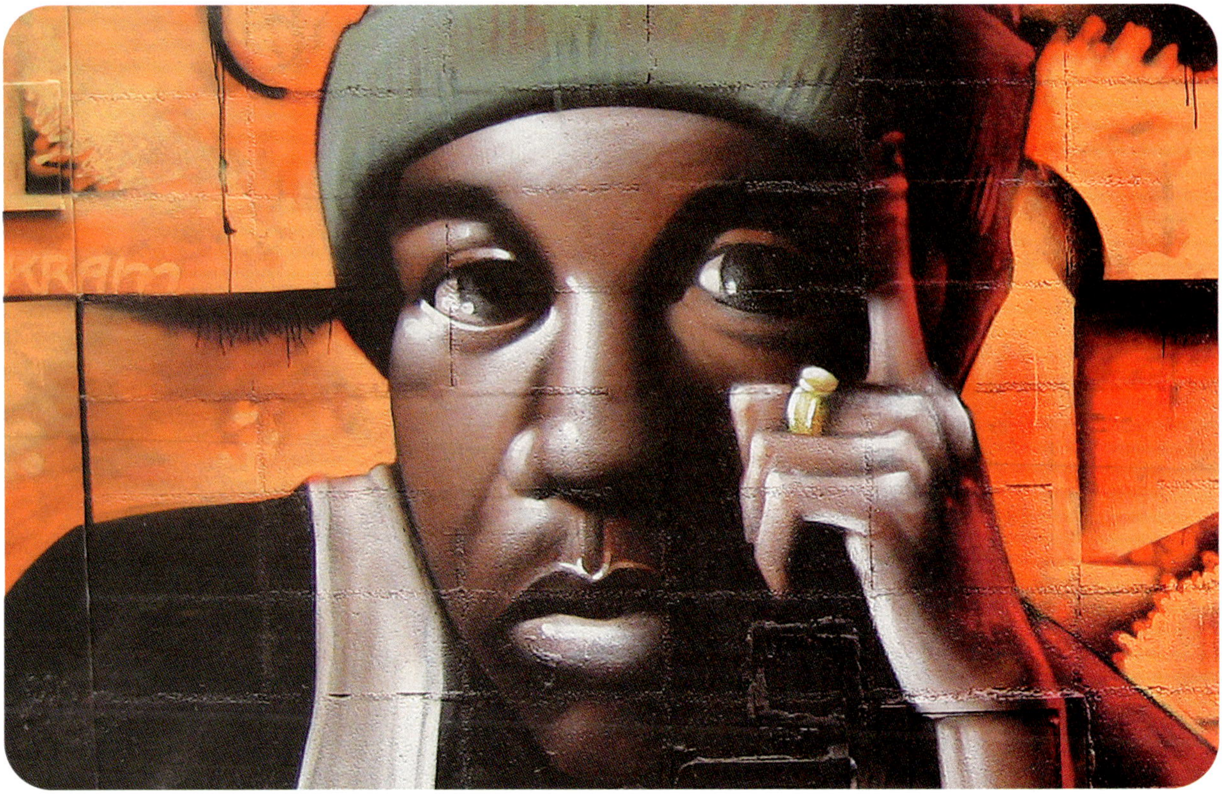

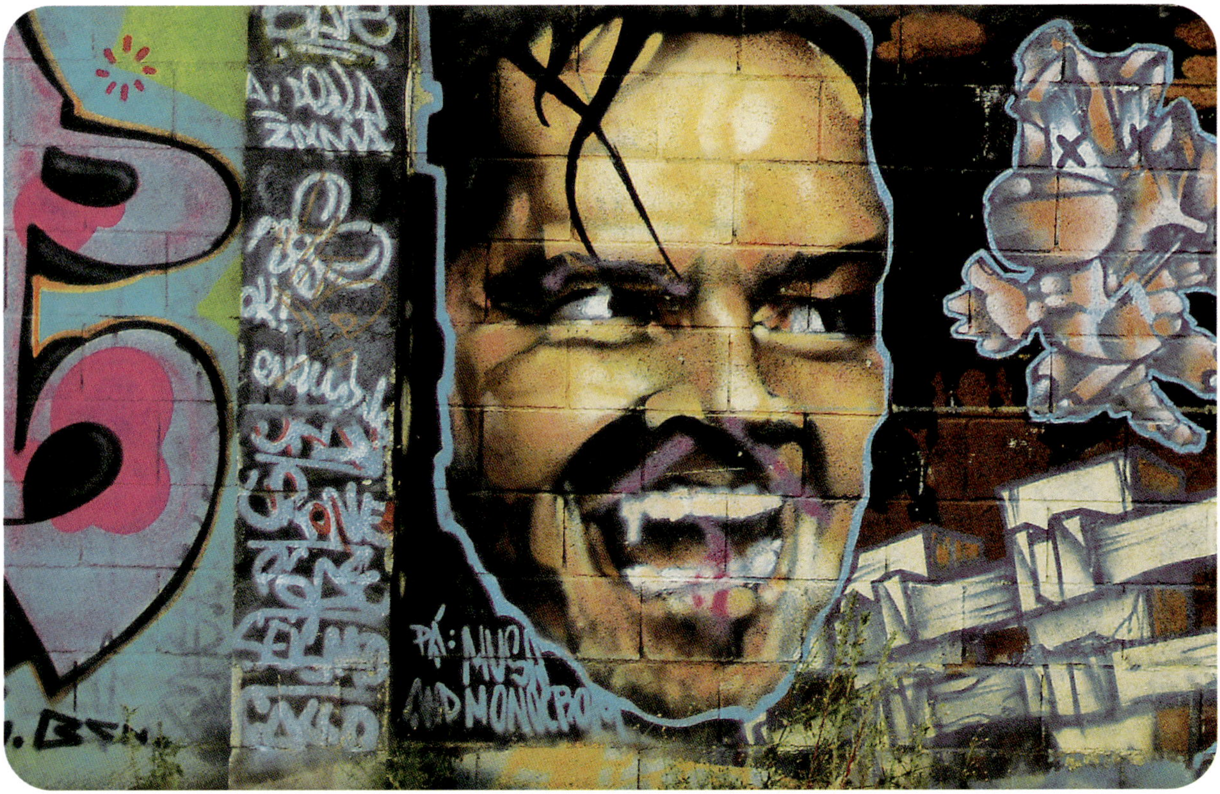

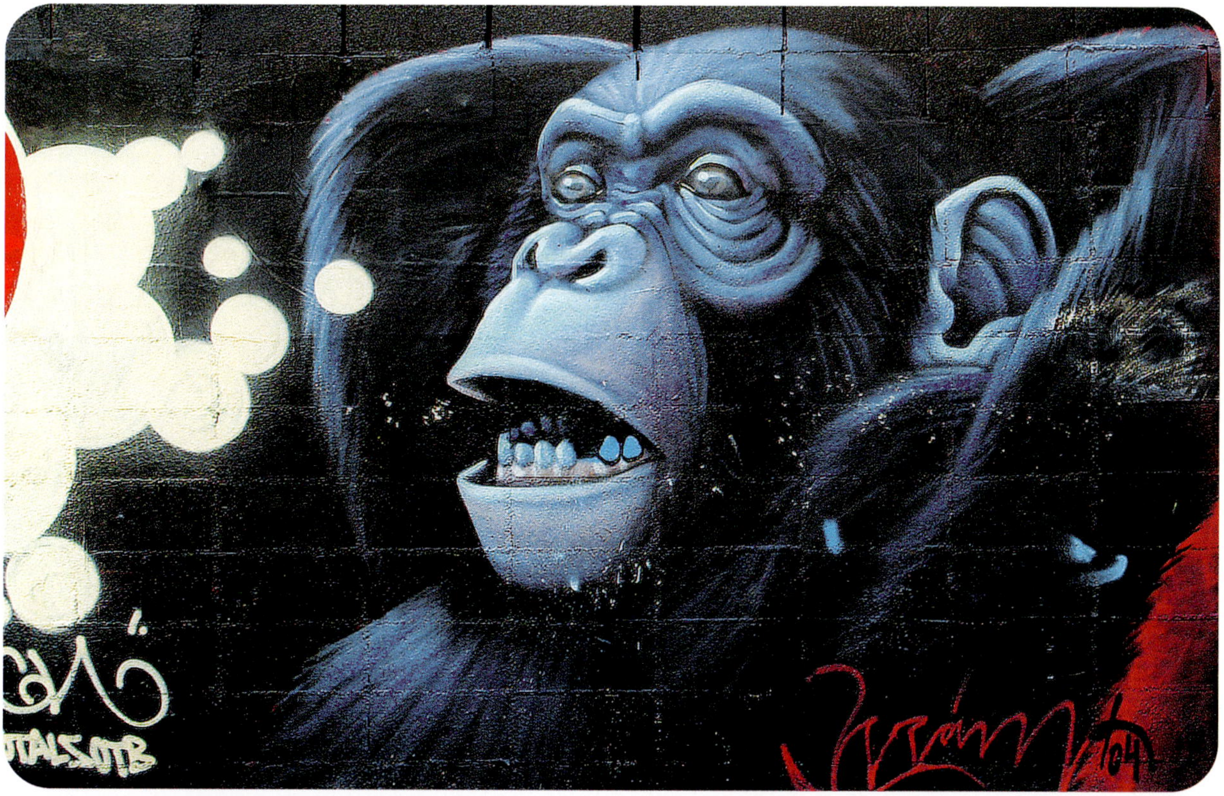

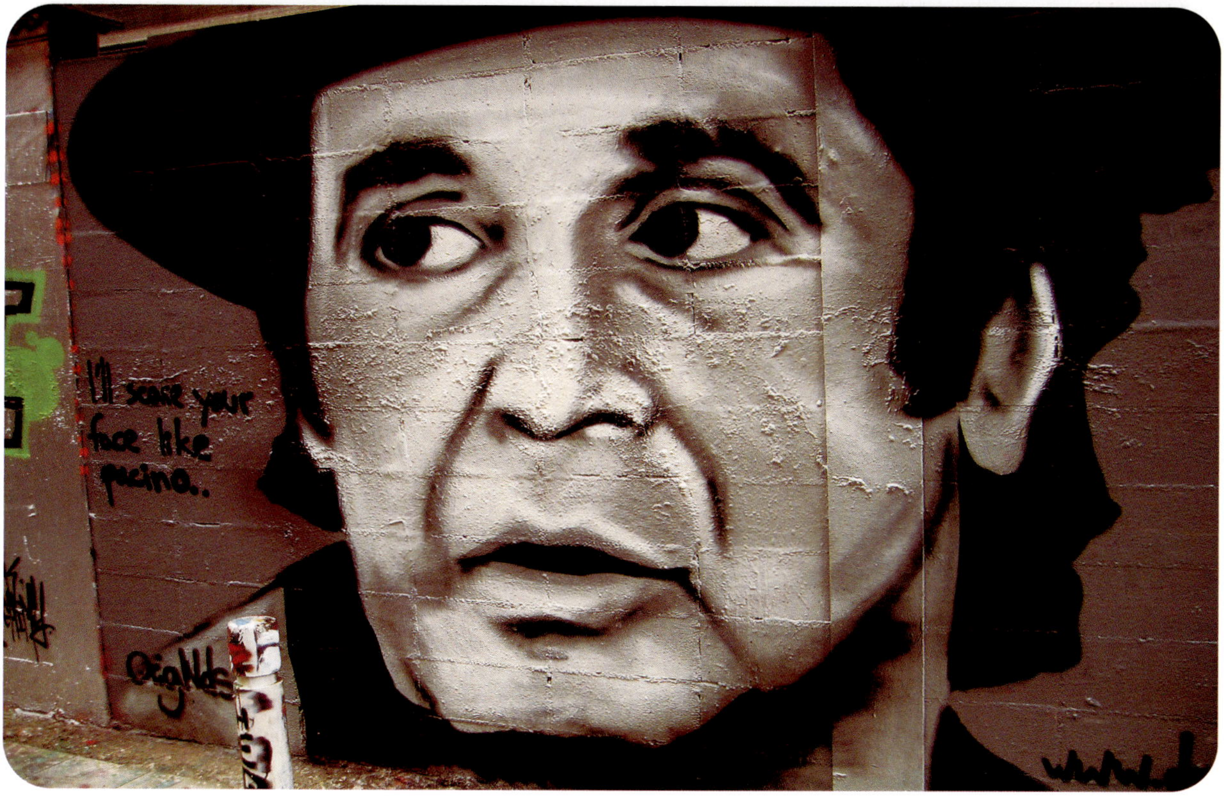
I'll scare your
face like
pacino.

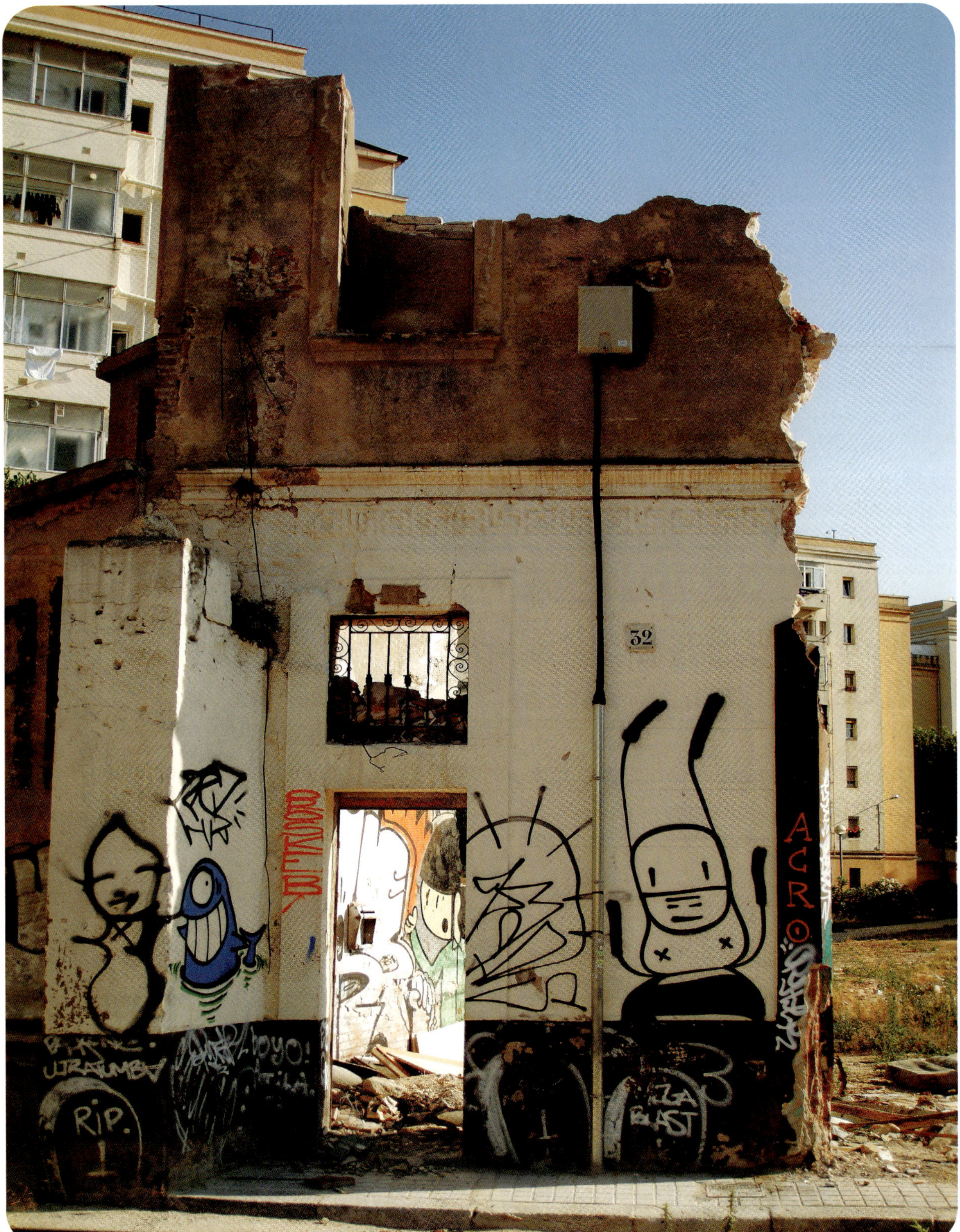

barcelona

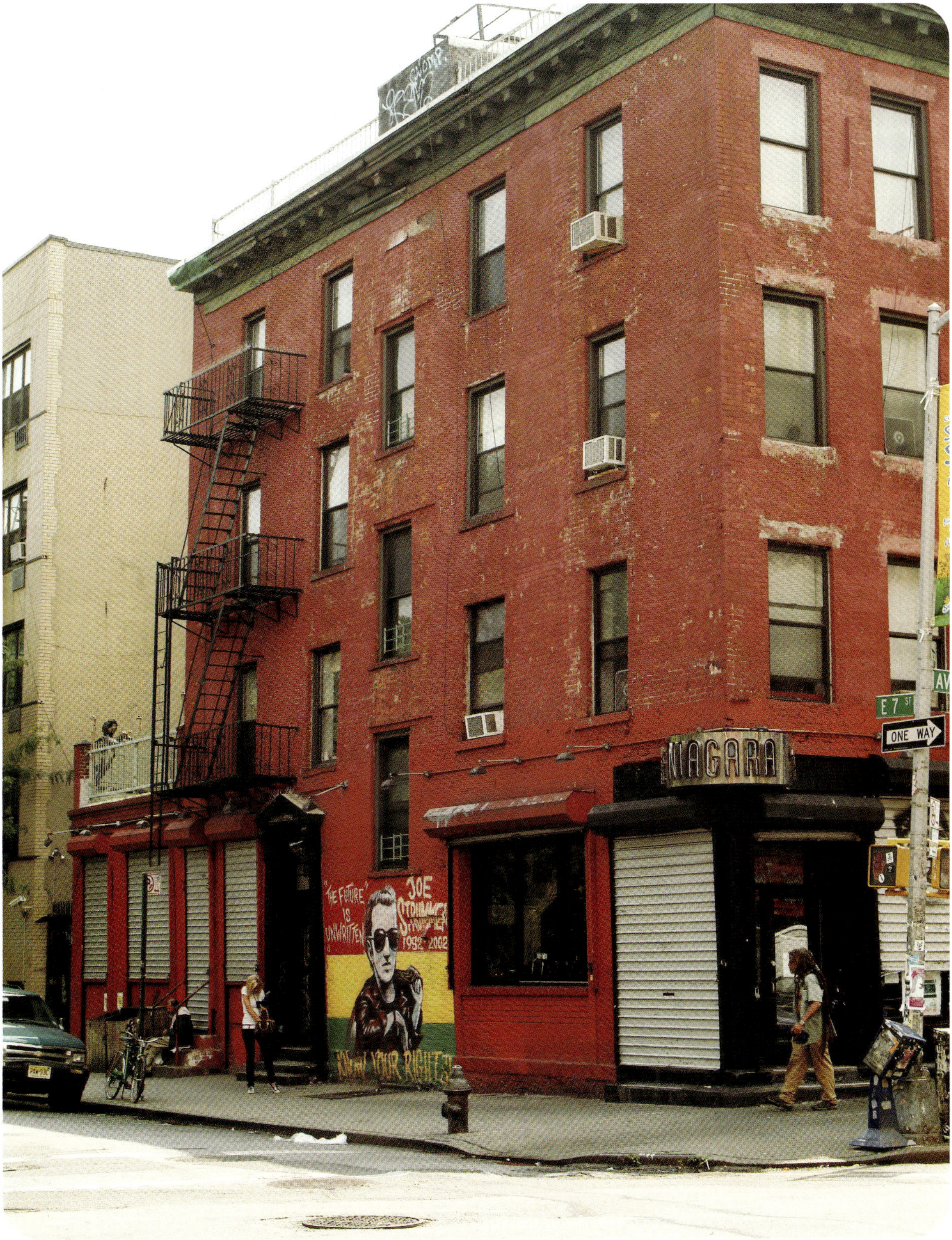
NIAGARA
E 7 ST
ONE WAY
"THE FUTURE" IS UNWRITTEN
JOE STRUMMER
1952-2002
KNOW YOUR RIGHTS

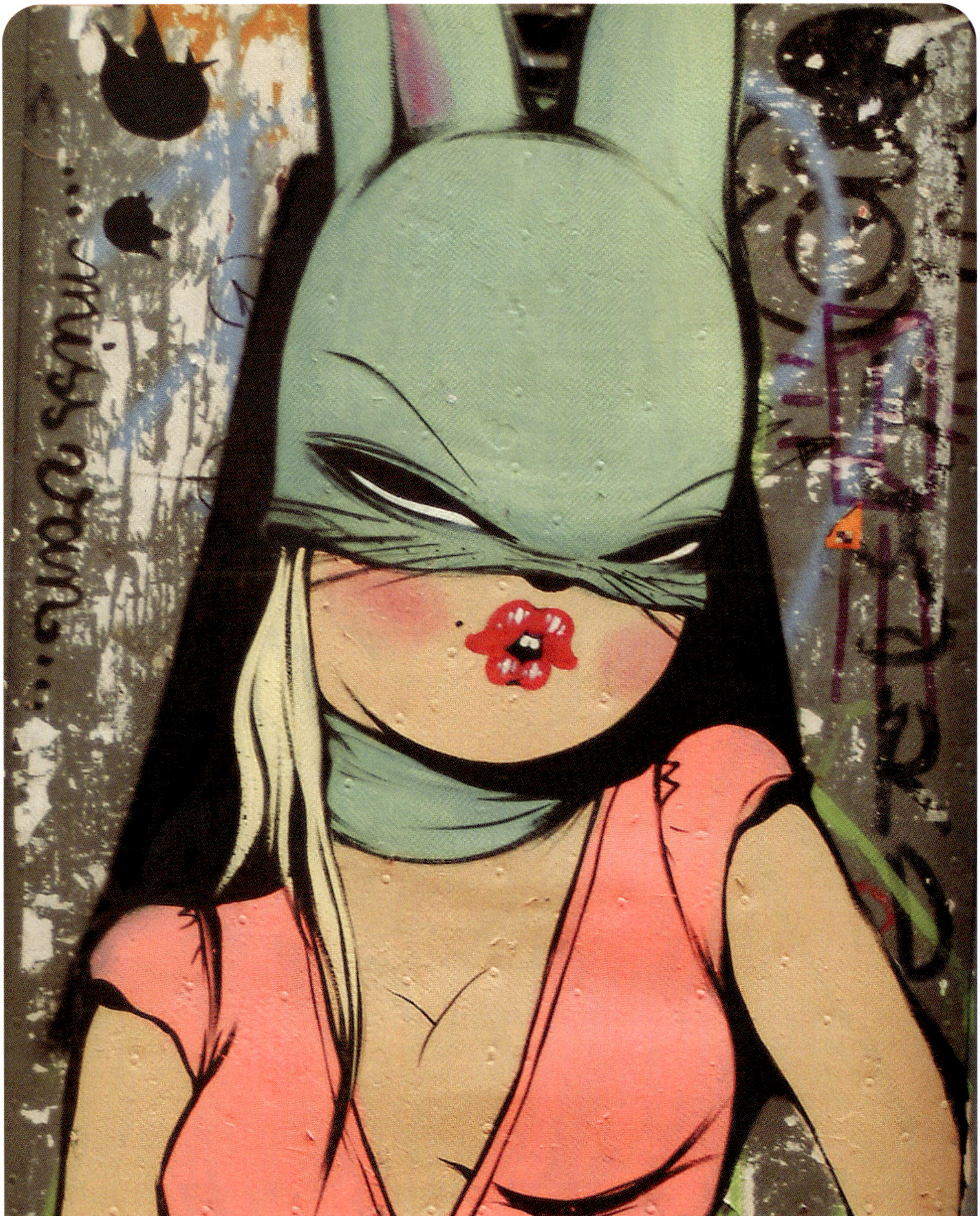

barcelona

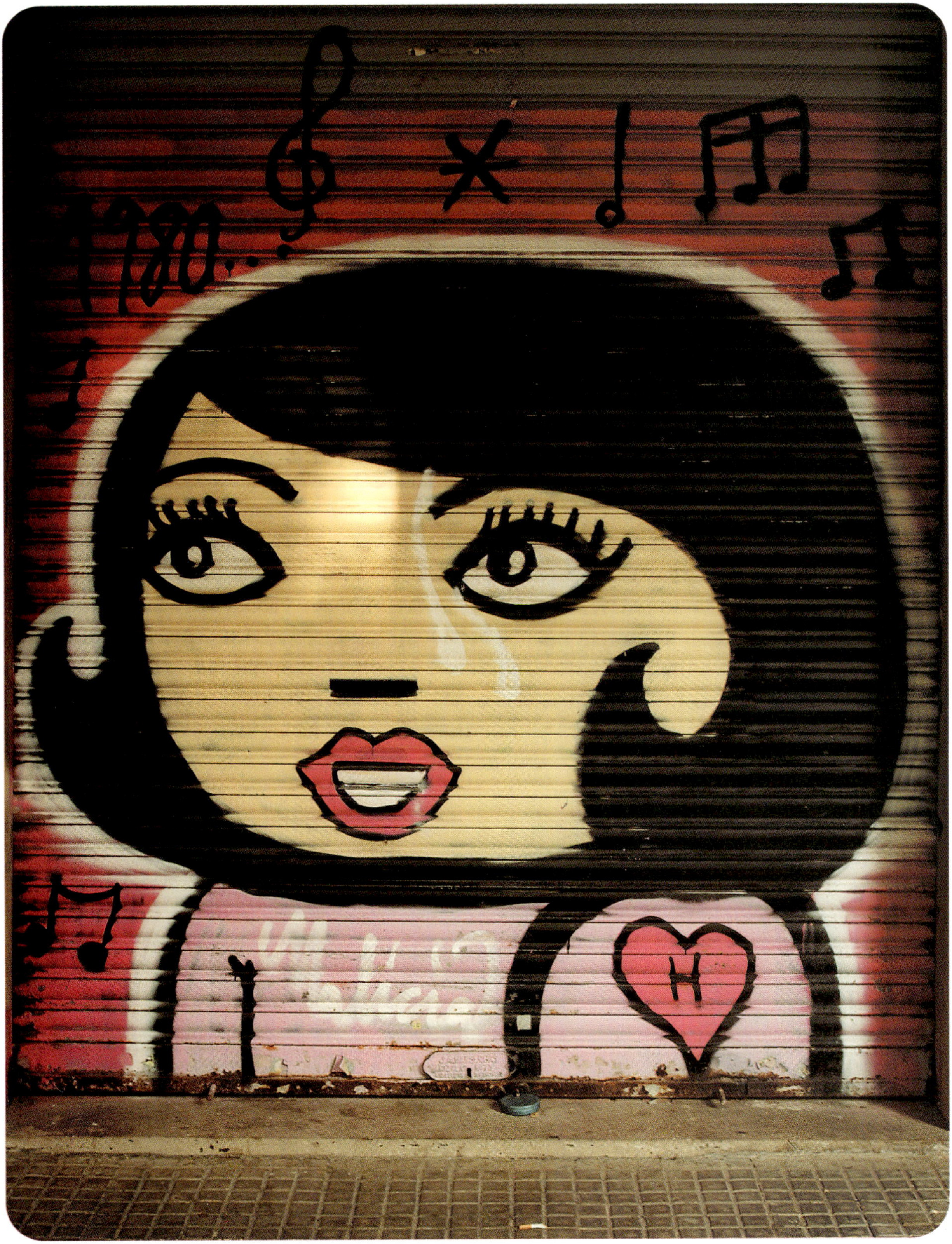

barcelona

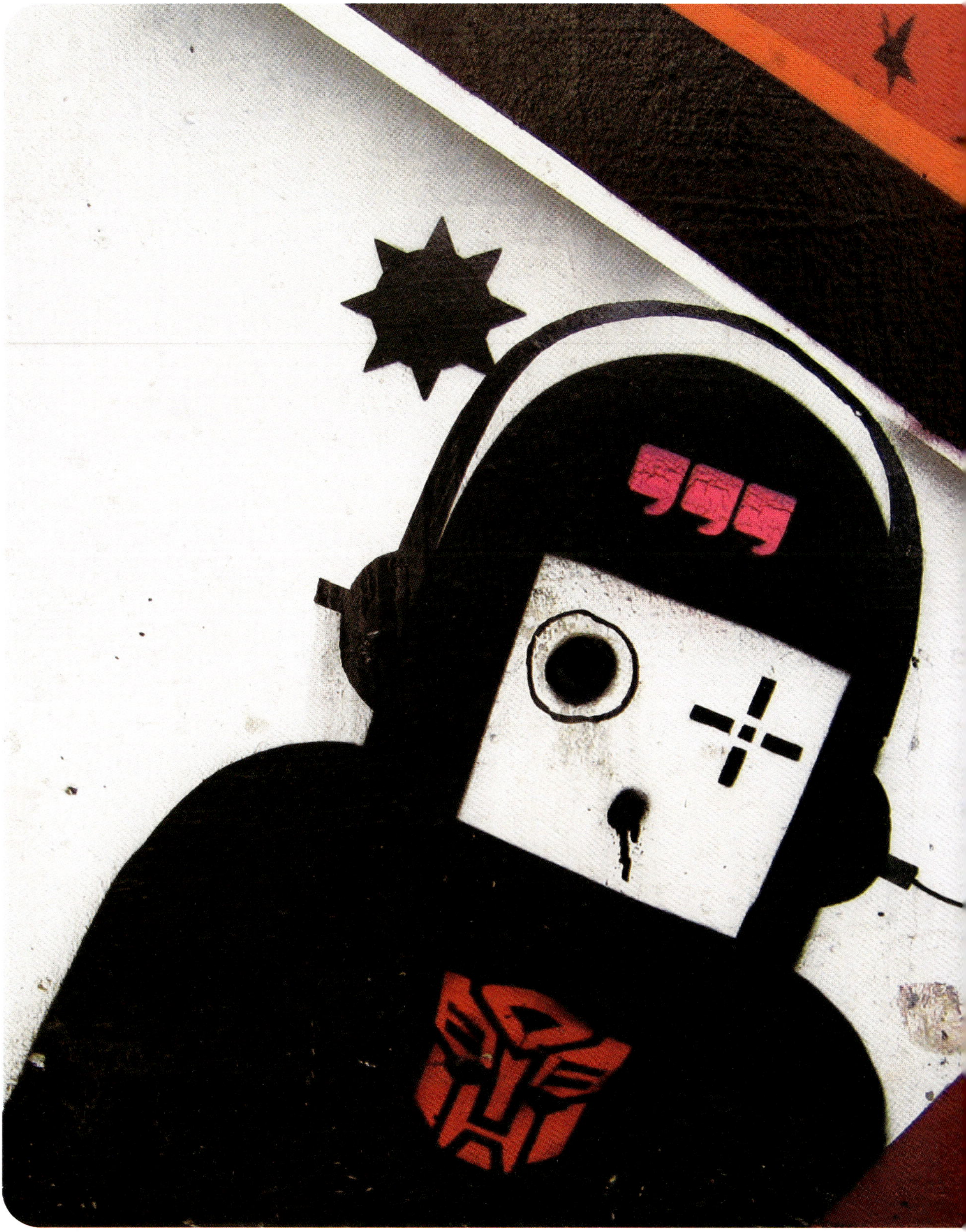

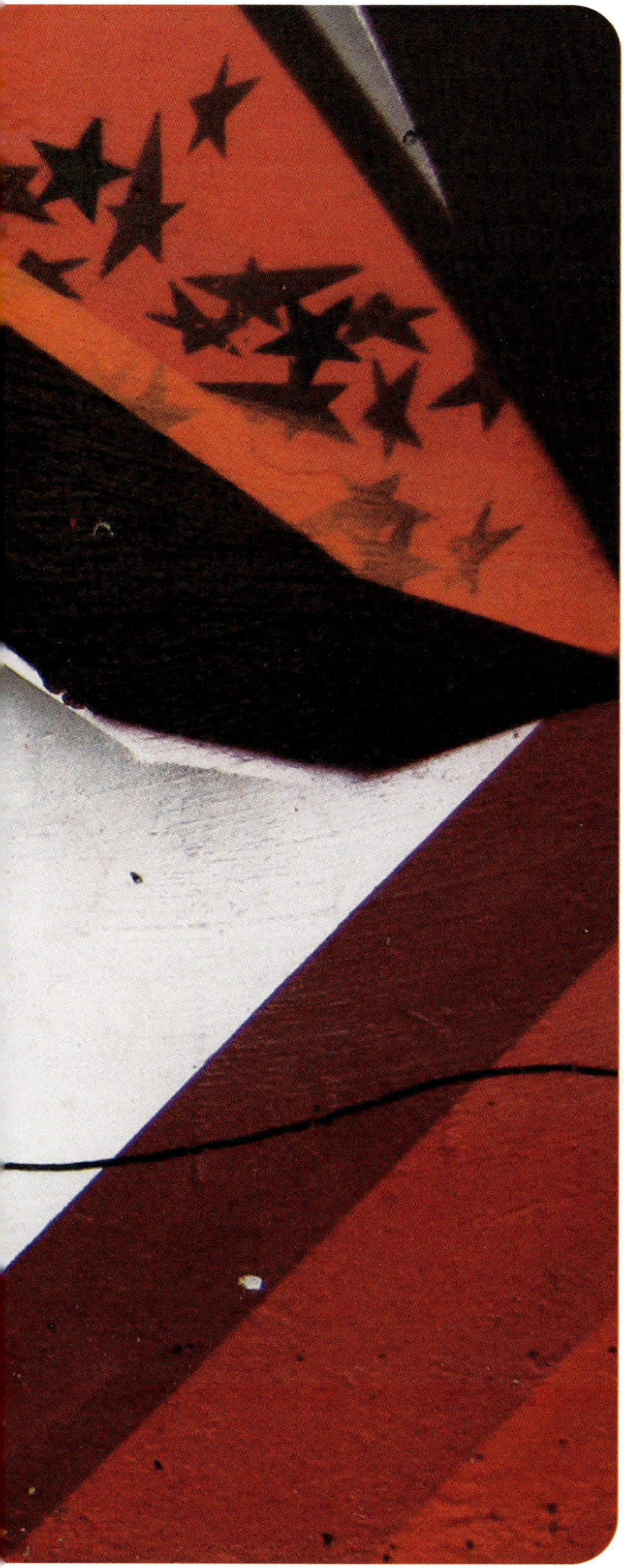

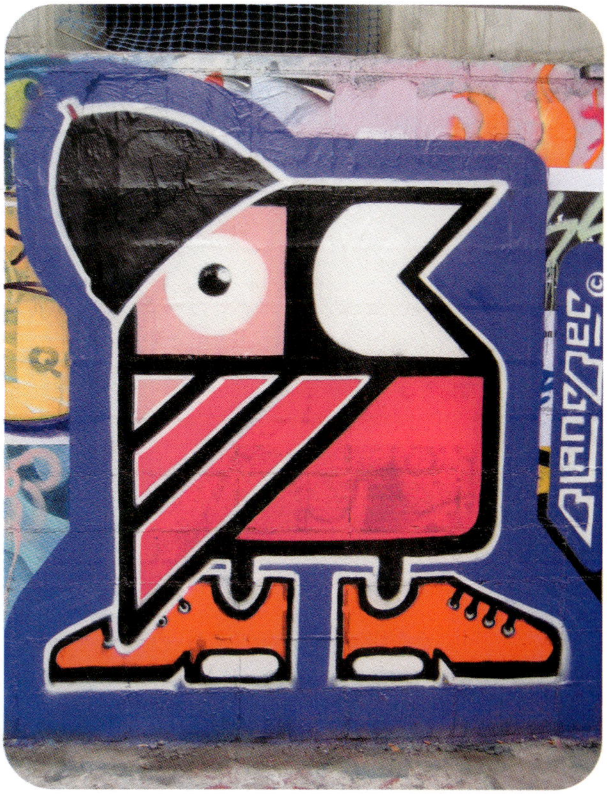

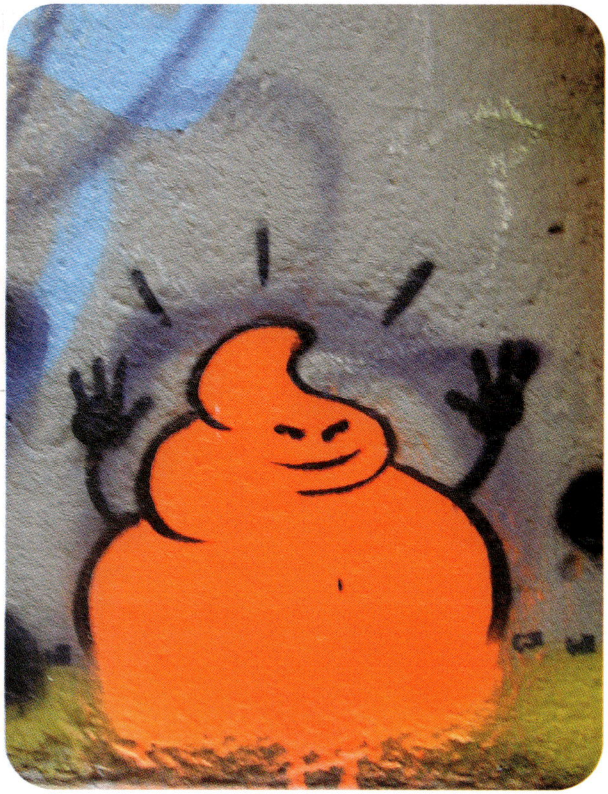

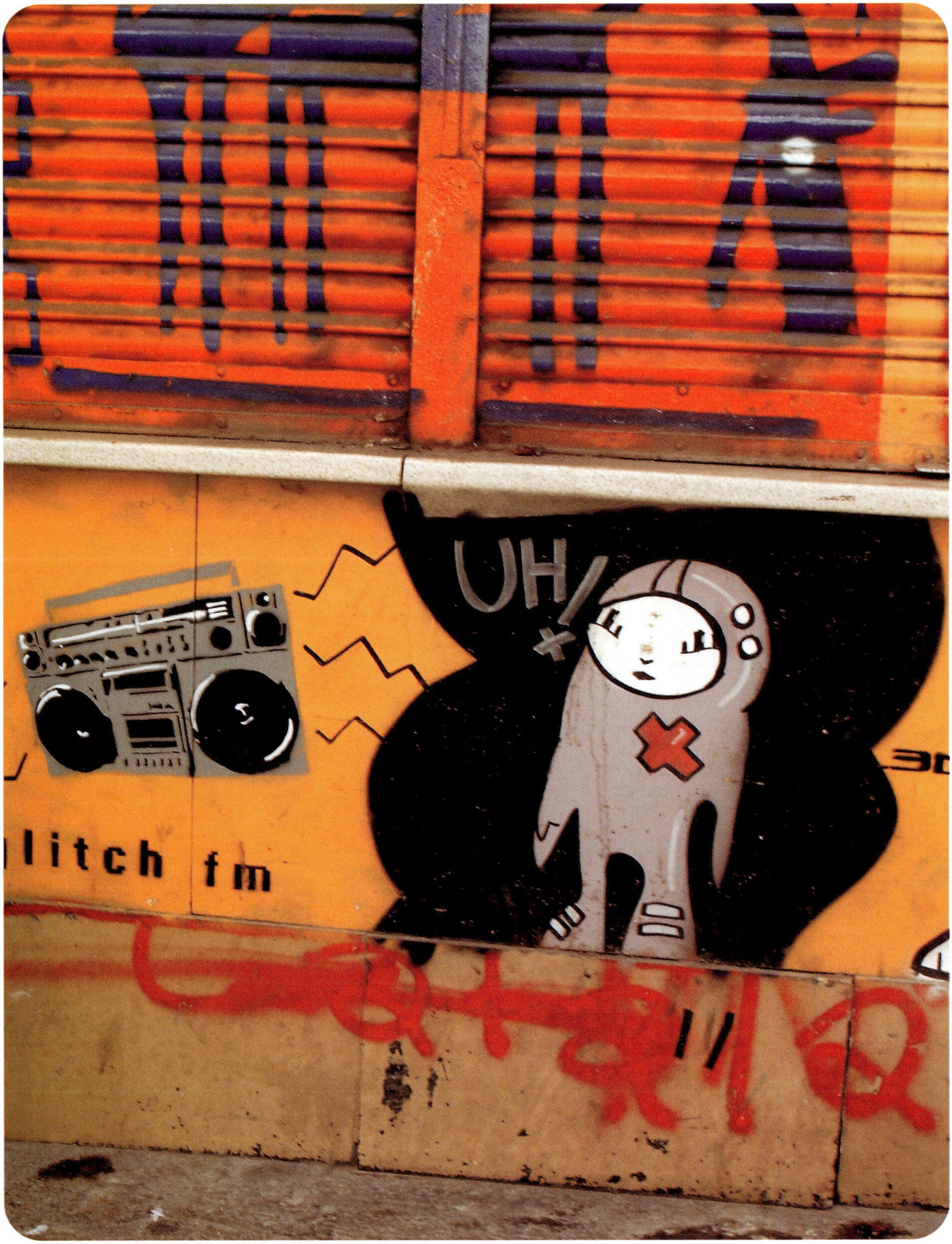
UH!
litch fm

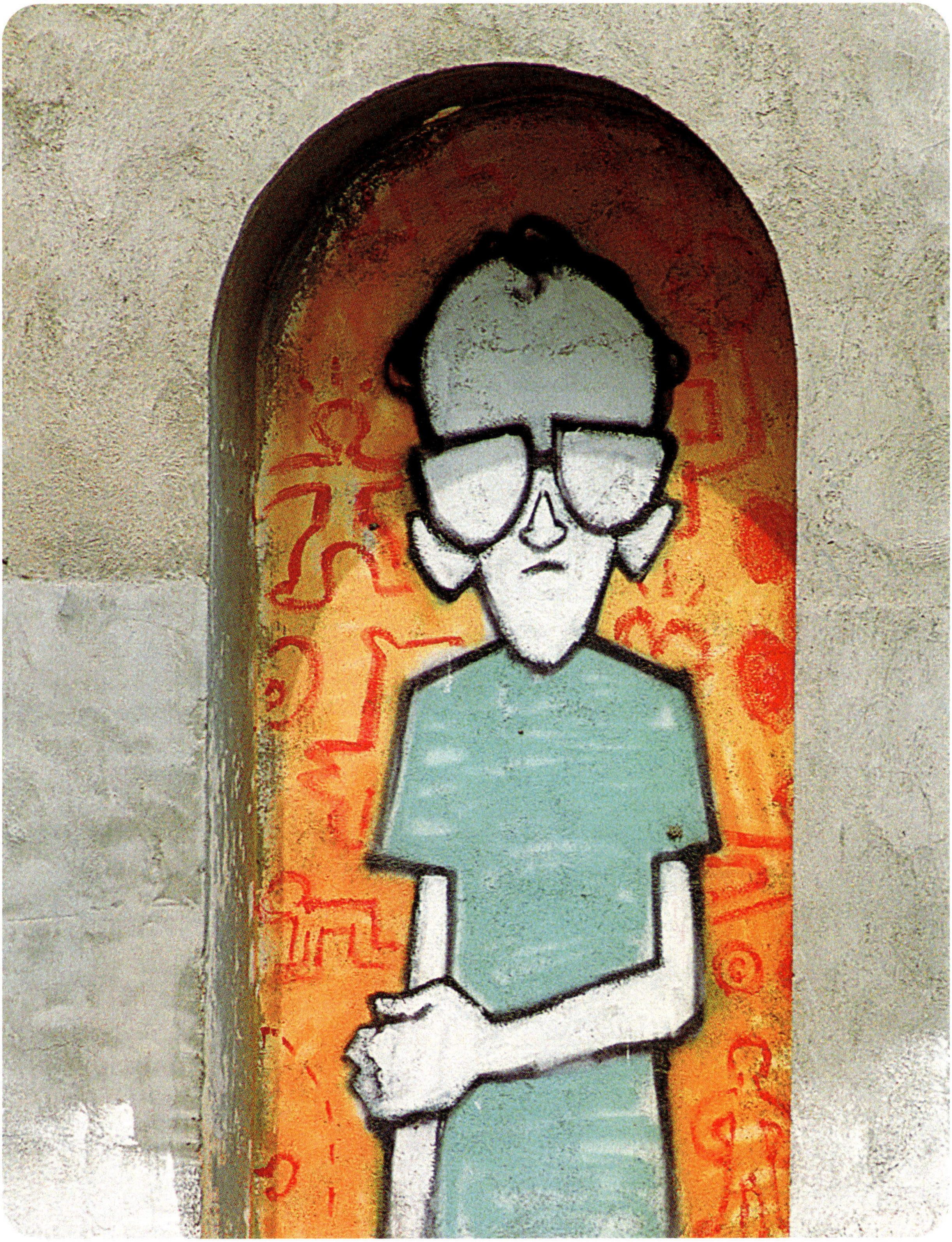

barcelona

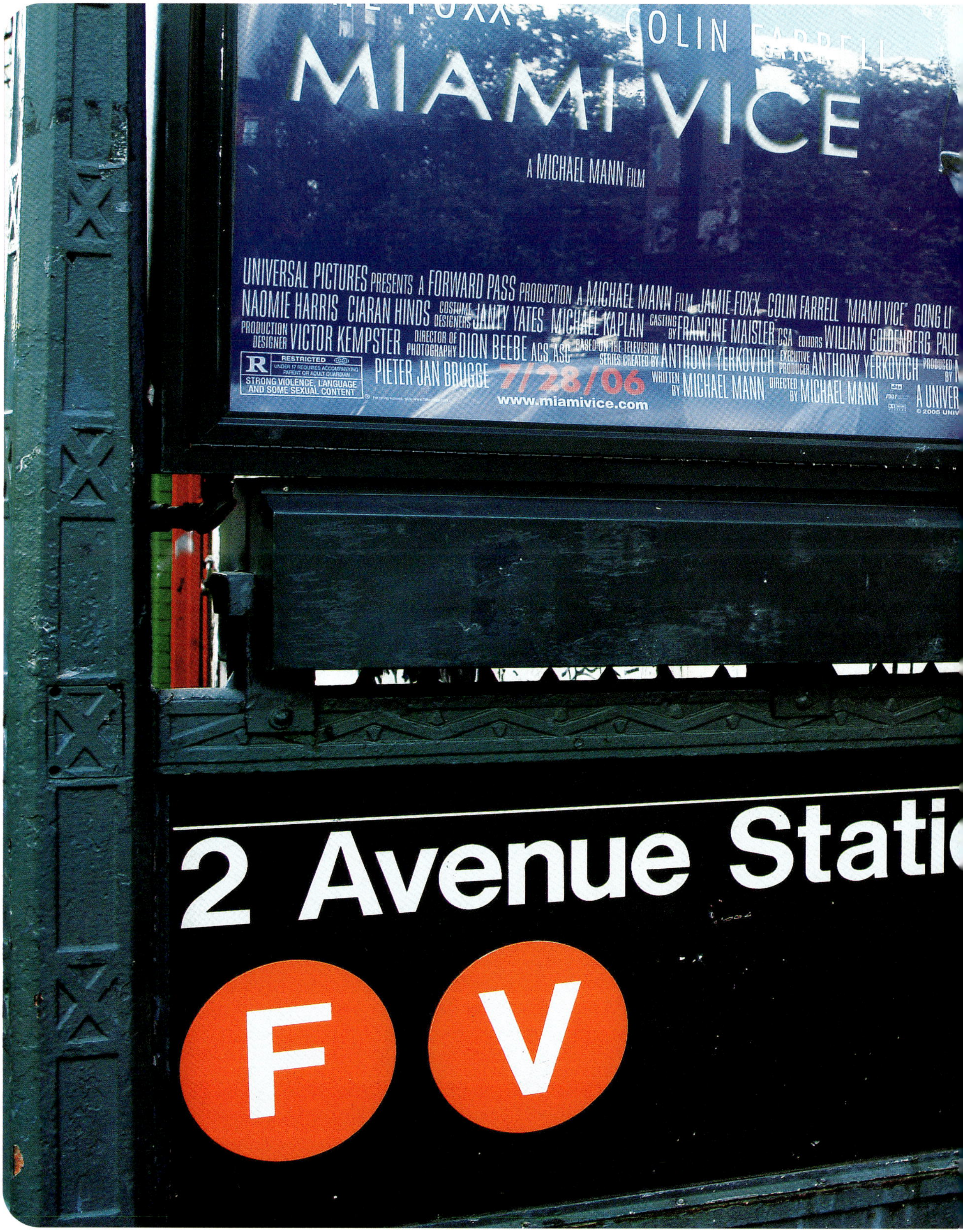
COLIN
MIAMI VICE
A MICHAEL MANN FILM
UNIVERSAL PICTURES PRESENTS A FORWARD PASS PRODUCTION A MICHAEL MANN FILM JAMIE FOXX COLIN FARRELL "MIAMI VICE" GONG LI
NAOMIE HARRIS CIARAN HINDS
PRODUCTION DESIGNER VICTOR KEMPSTER
PIETER JAN BRUGGE
R RESTRICTED
STRONG VIOLENCE, LANGUAGE AND SOME SEXUAL CONTENT
7/28/06
www.miamivice.com
WRITTEN BY MICHAEL MANN DIRECTED BY MICHAEL MANN
2 Avenue Stati
F
V

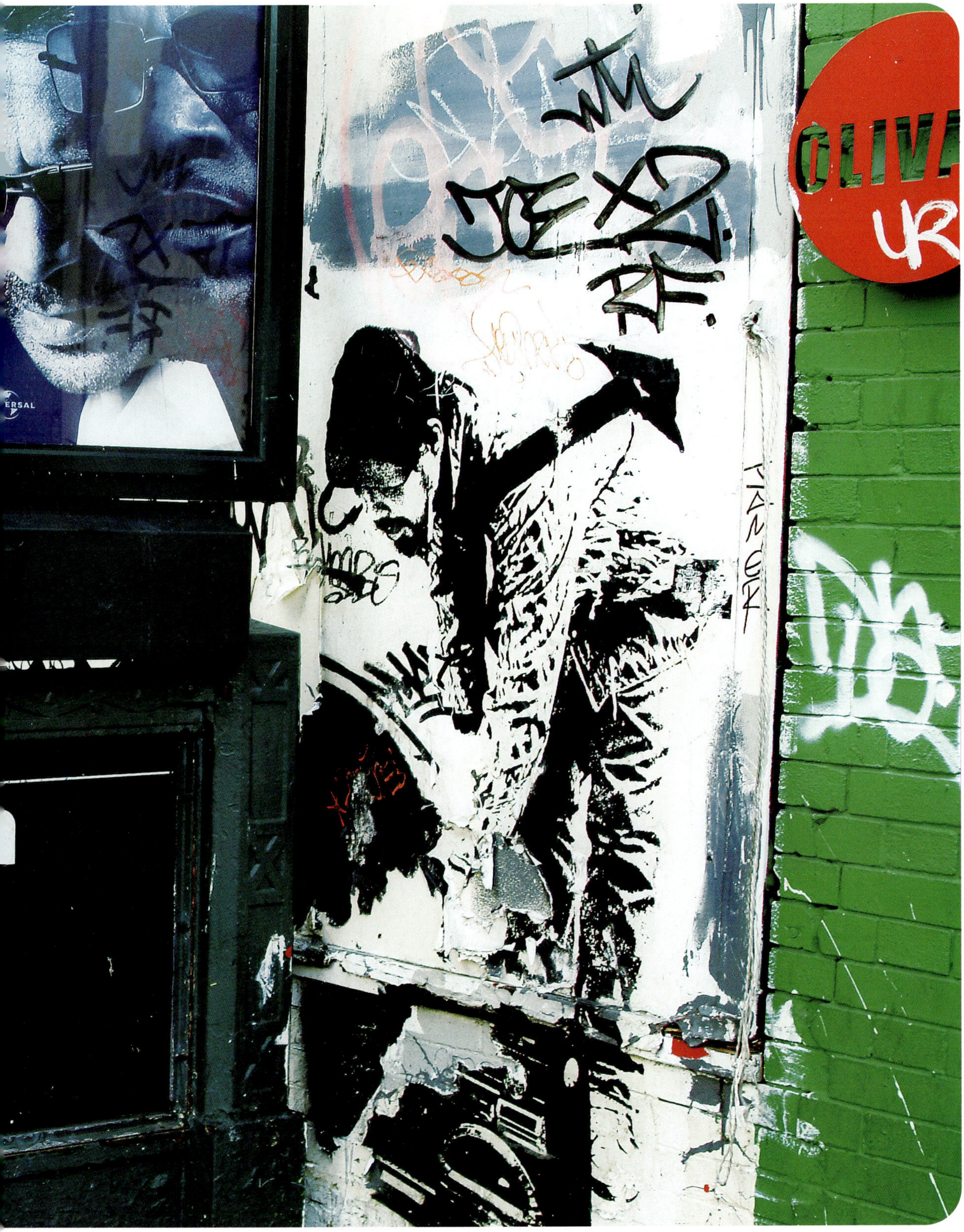
OLIV

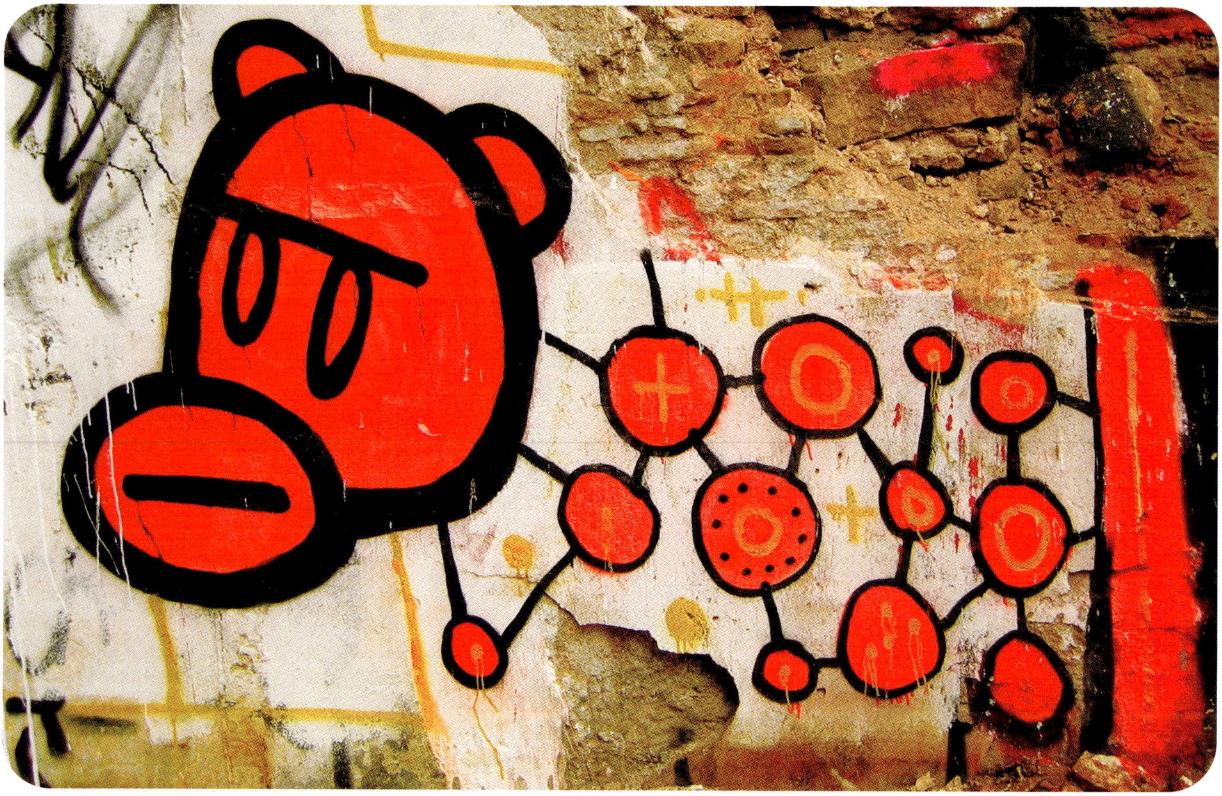

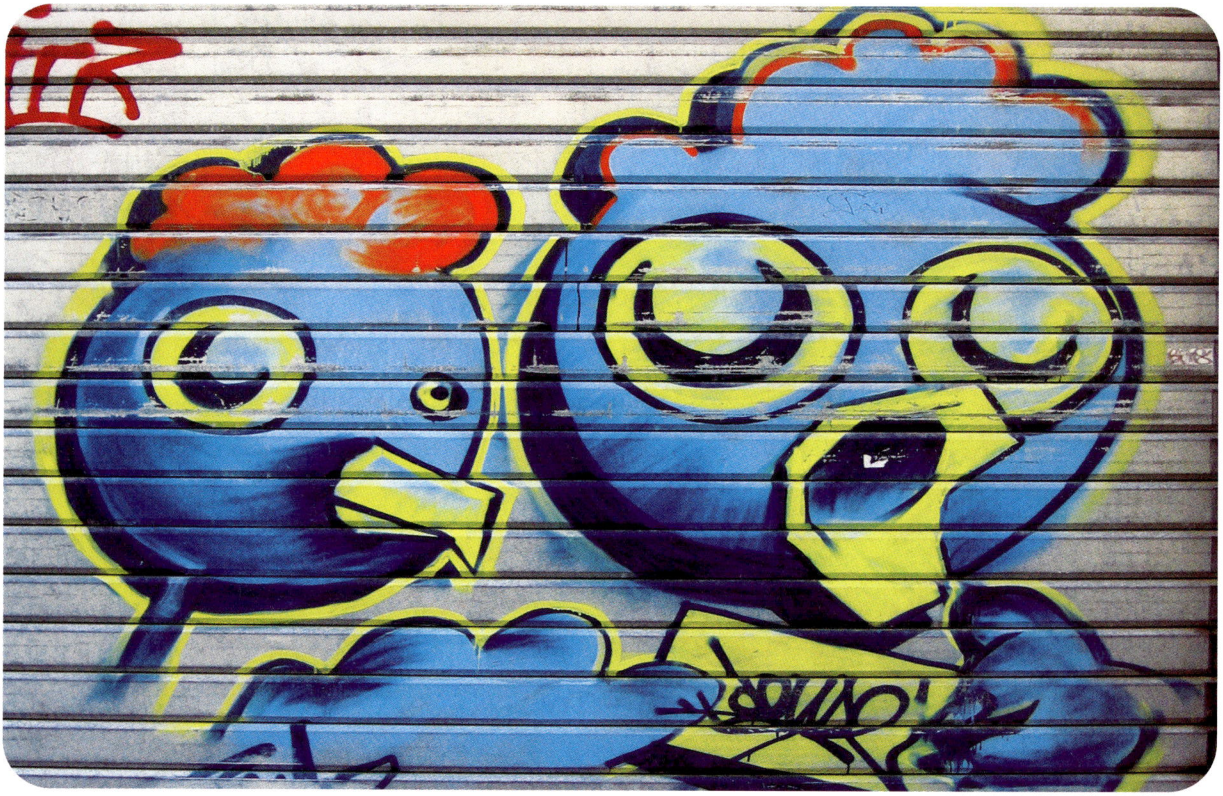

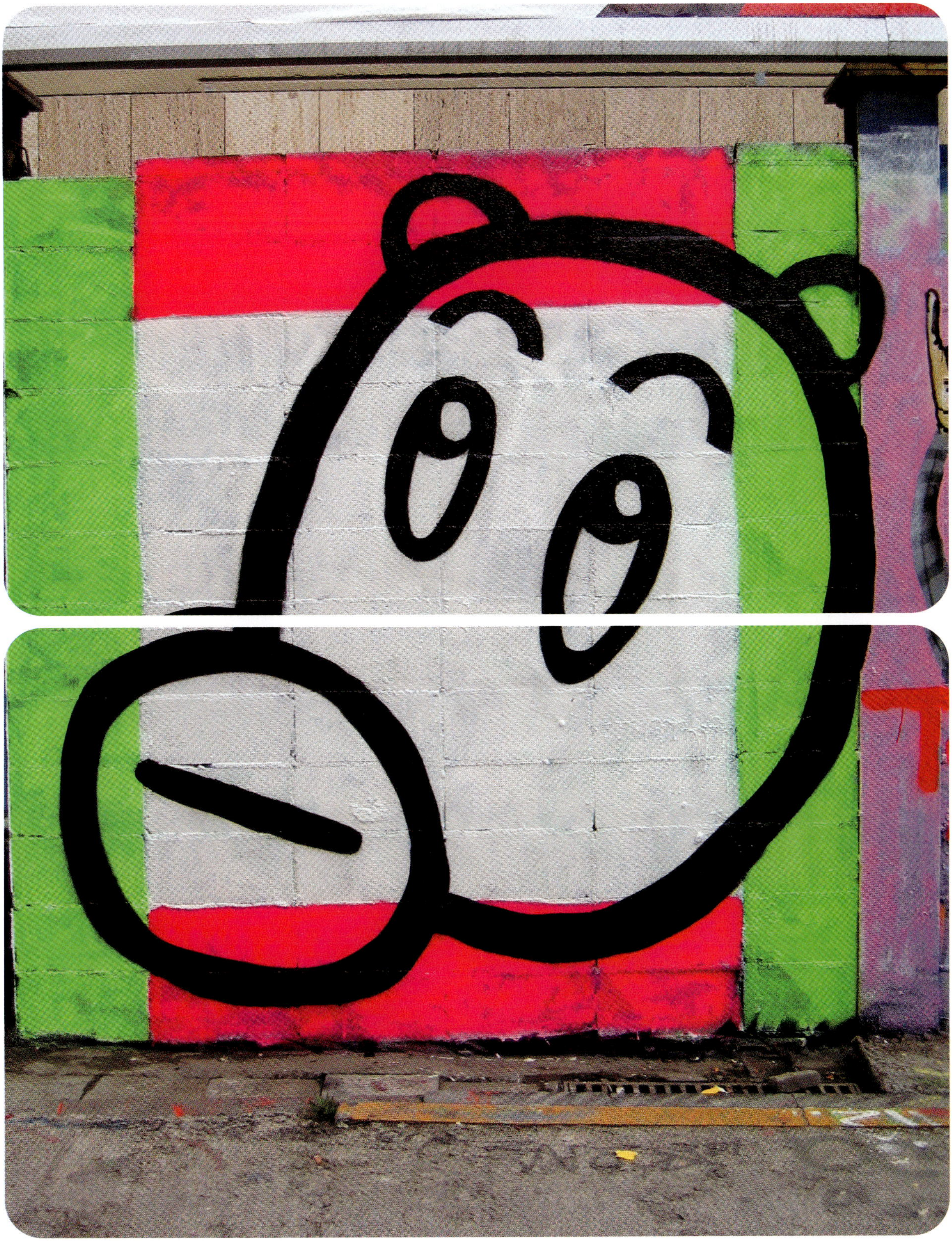

barcelona

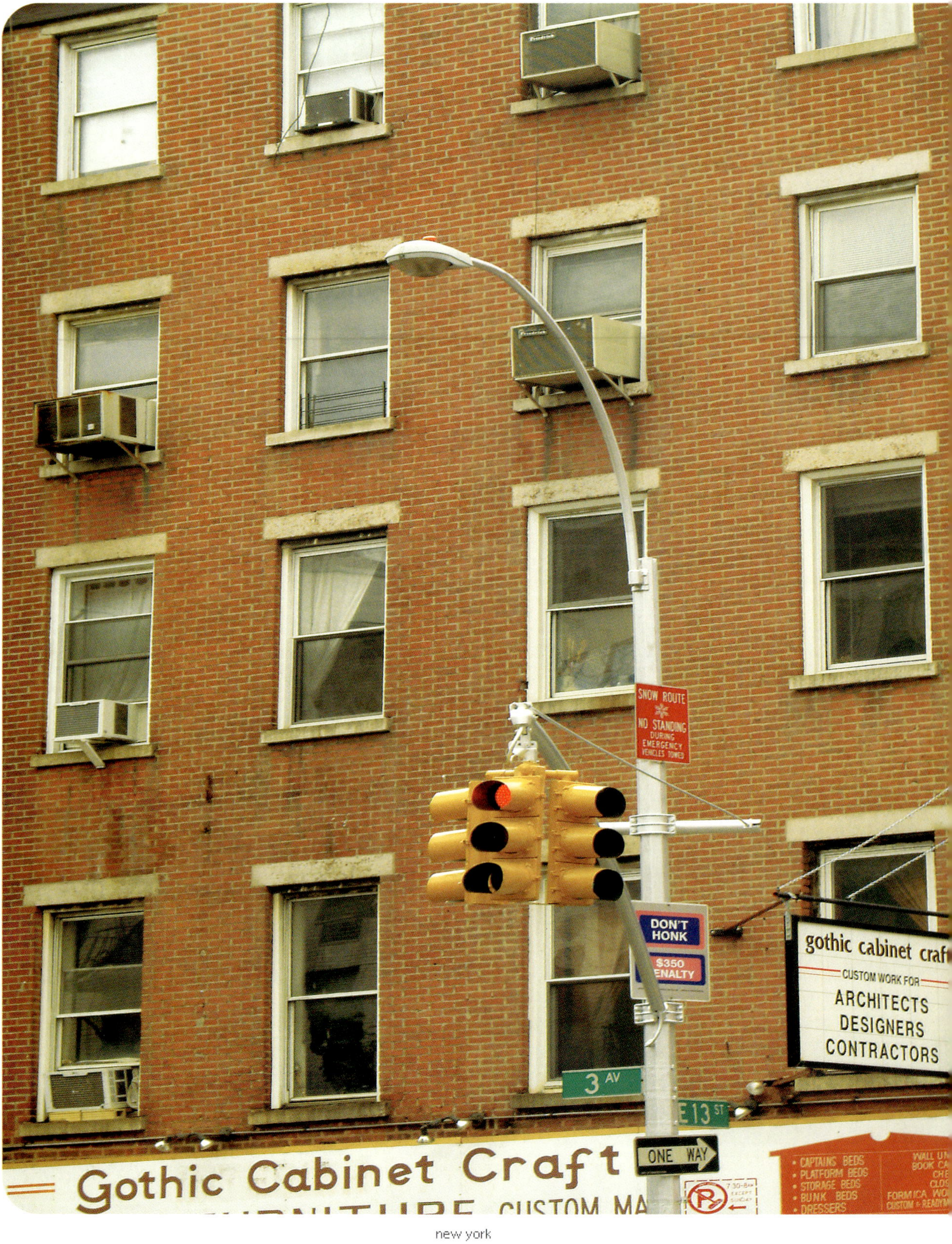
SNOW ROUTE
NO STANDING DURING EMERGENCY VEHICLES TOWED
DON'T HONK
$350
CUSTOM WORK FOR
ARCHITECTS
DESIGNERS
CONTRACTORS
3 AV
E 13 ST
ONE WAY
Gothic Cabinet Craft
CAPTAINS BEDS
PLATFORM BEDS
STORAGE BEDS
BUNK BEDS
DRESSERS

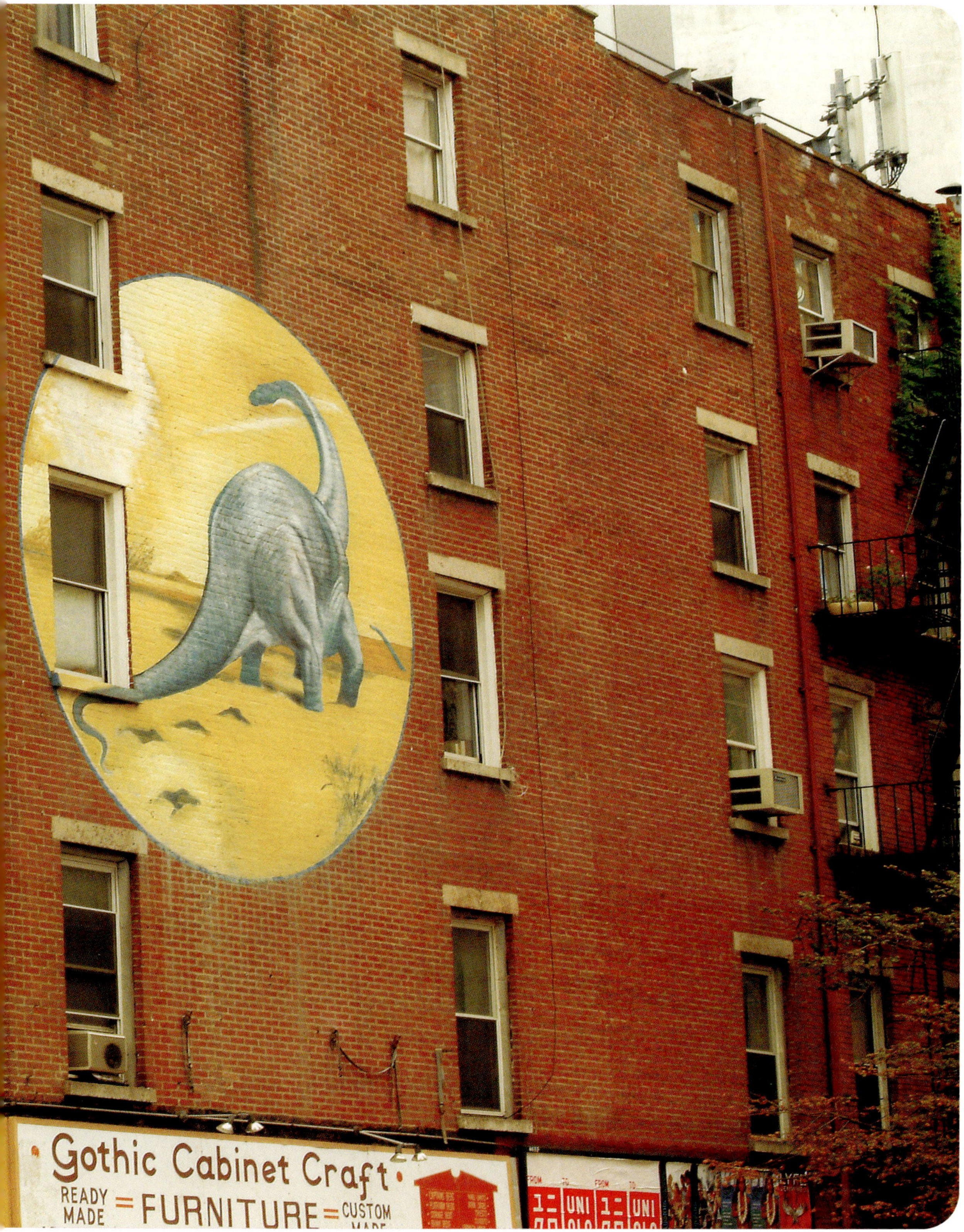
Gothic Cabinet Craft
READY MADE
FURNITURE
CUSTOM

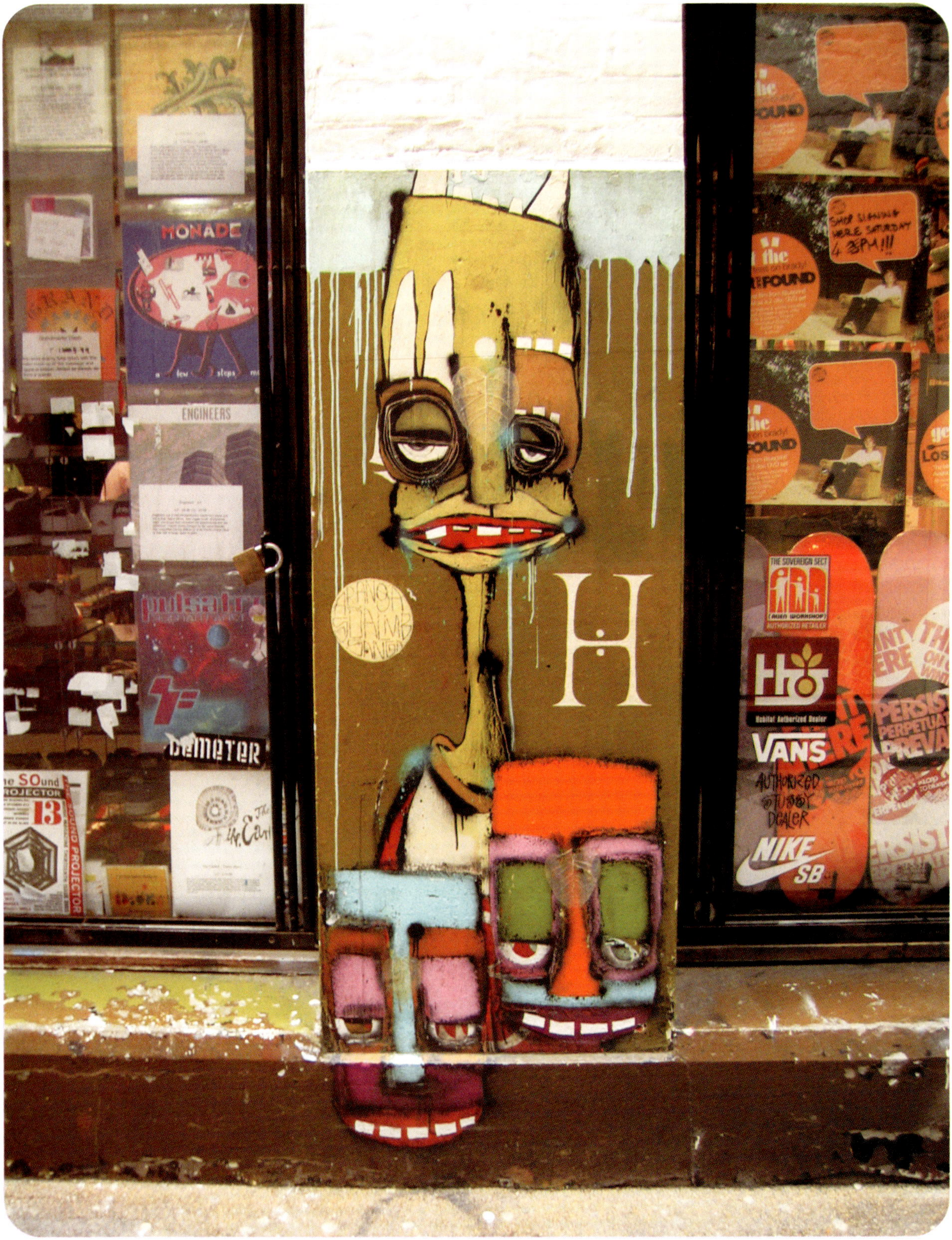
MONADE
ENGINEERS
DEMETER
the SOund PROJECTOR
13
the FOUND
H
THE SOVEREIGN SECT
VANS
AUTHORIZED DEALER
NIKE SB
PERSIST

london

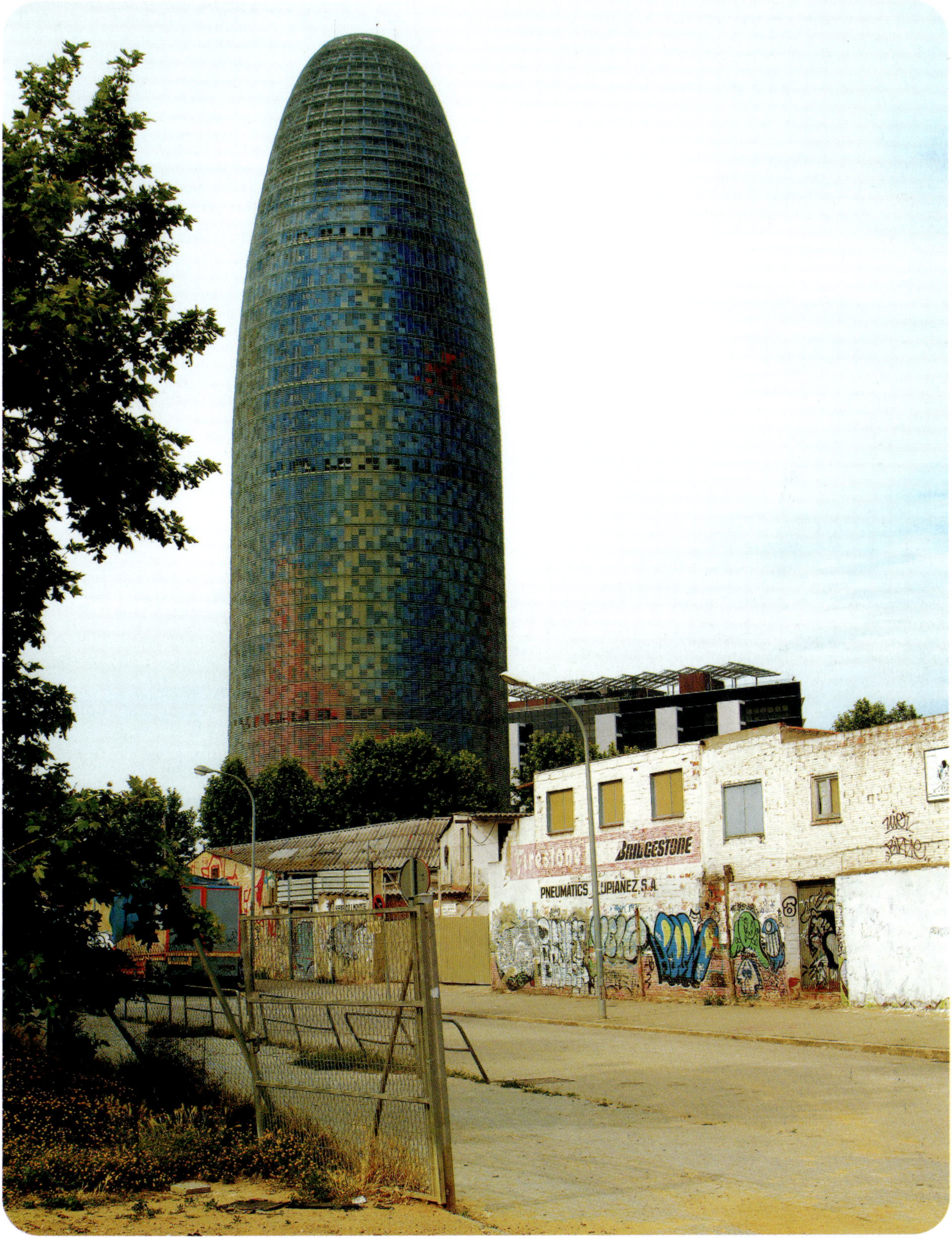

barcelona

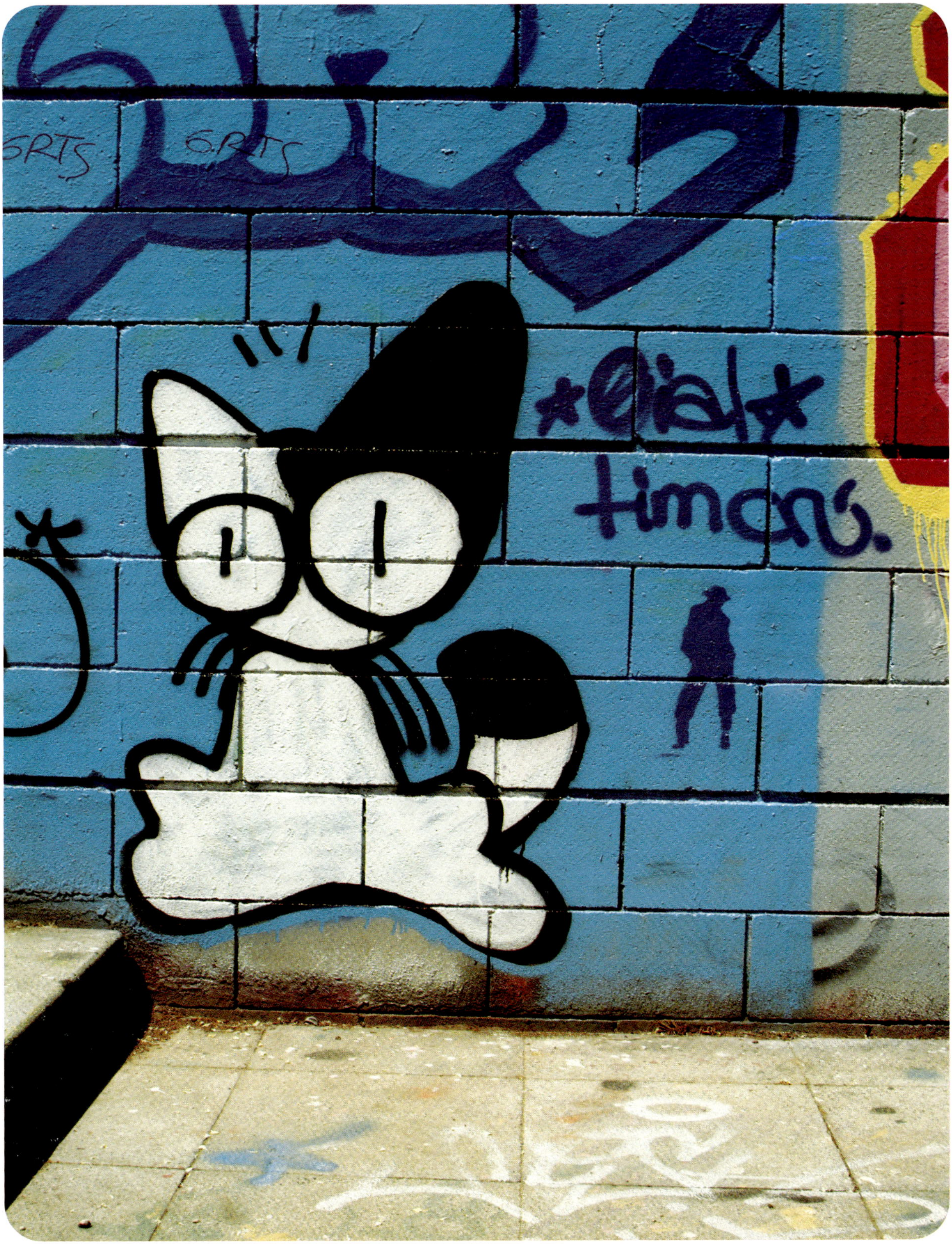
SRTS
SRTS
timons.

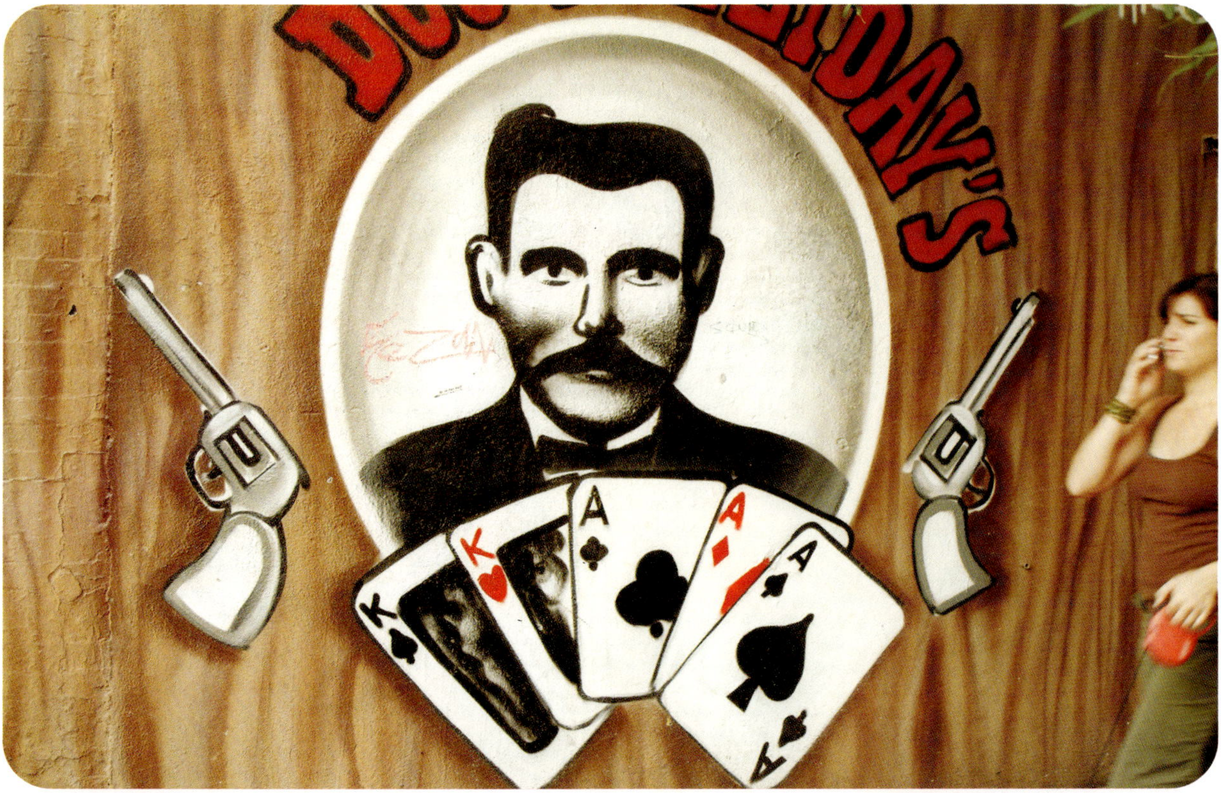
DAY'S

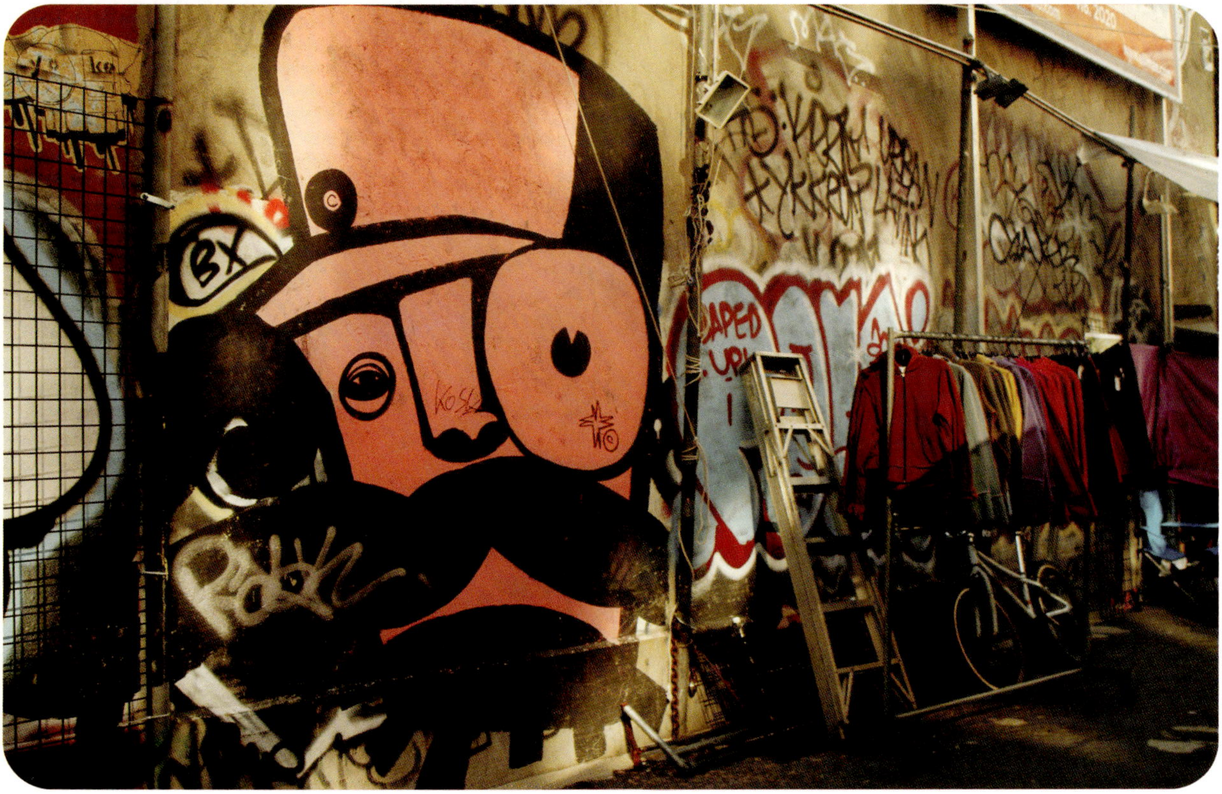

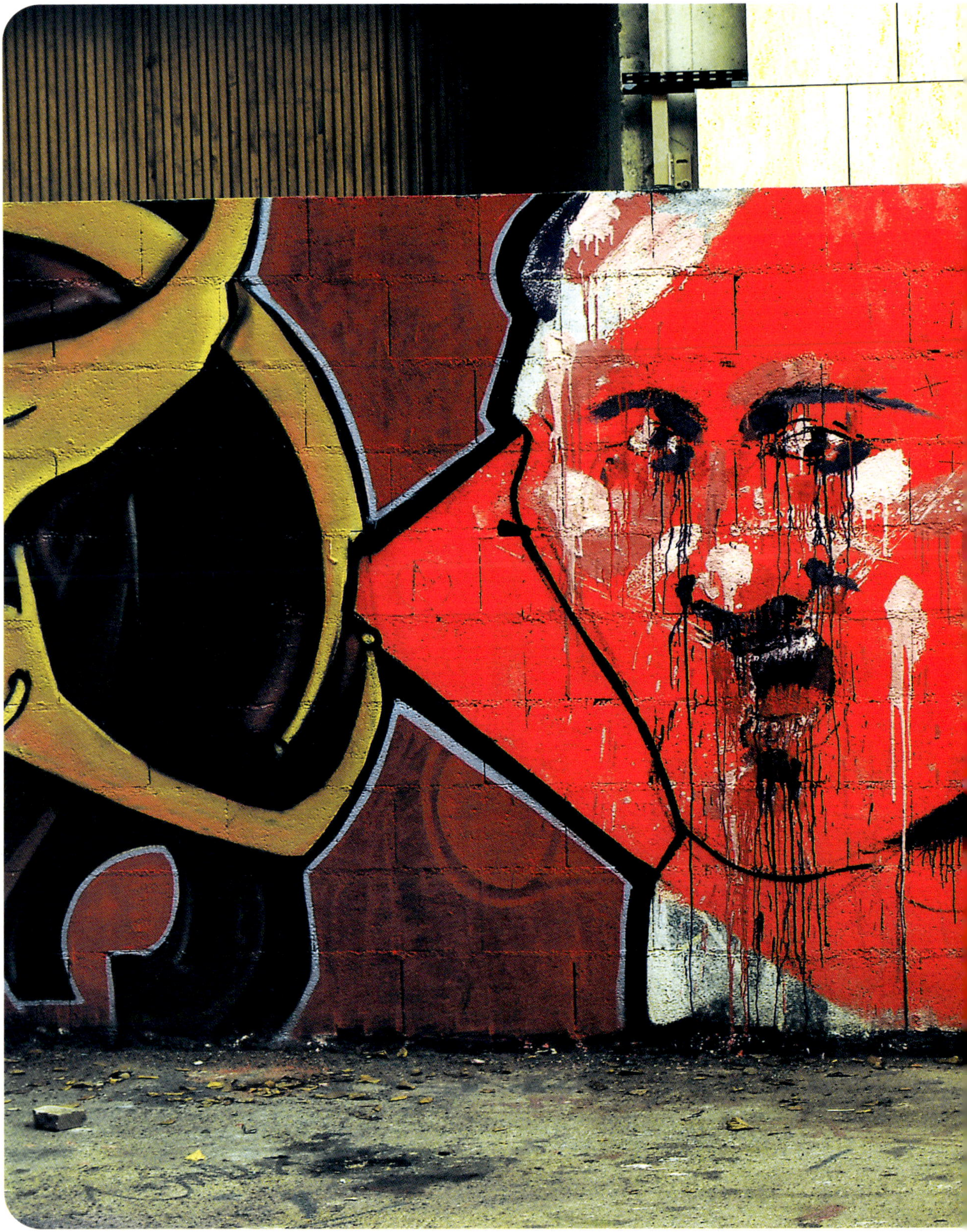

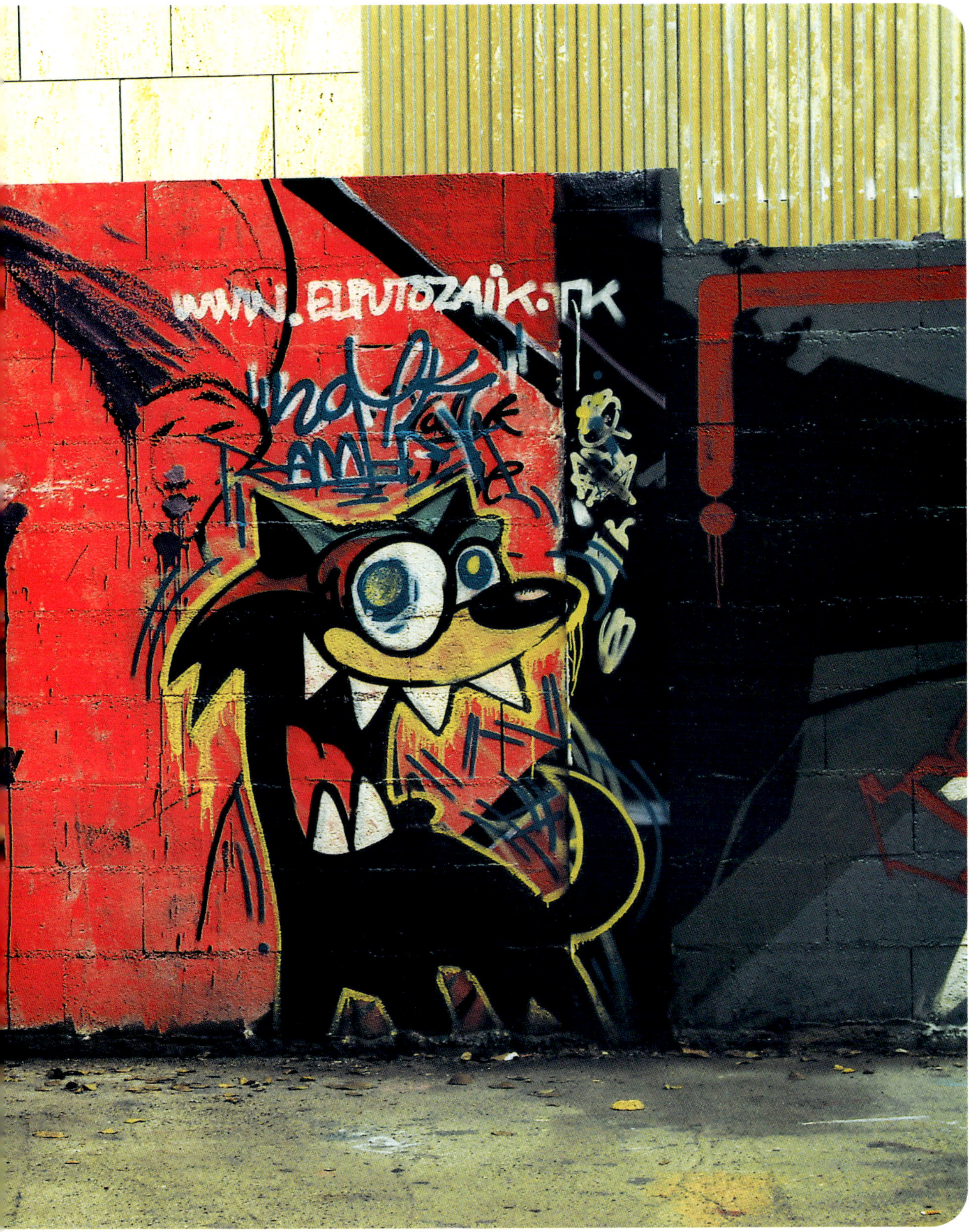
WWW.ELPUTOZAIK.TK

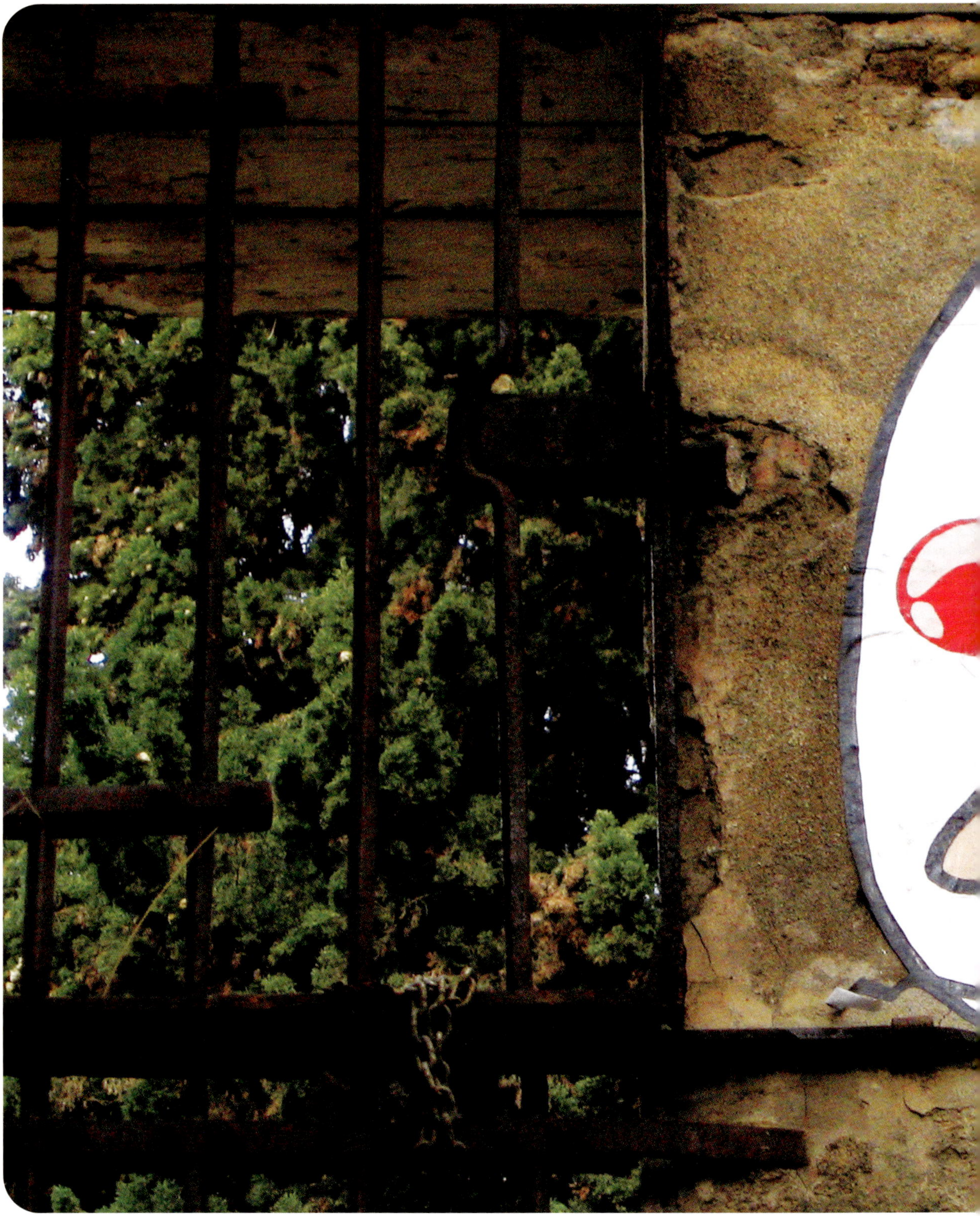

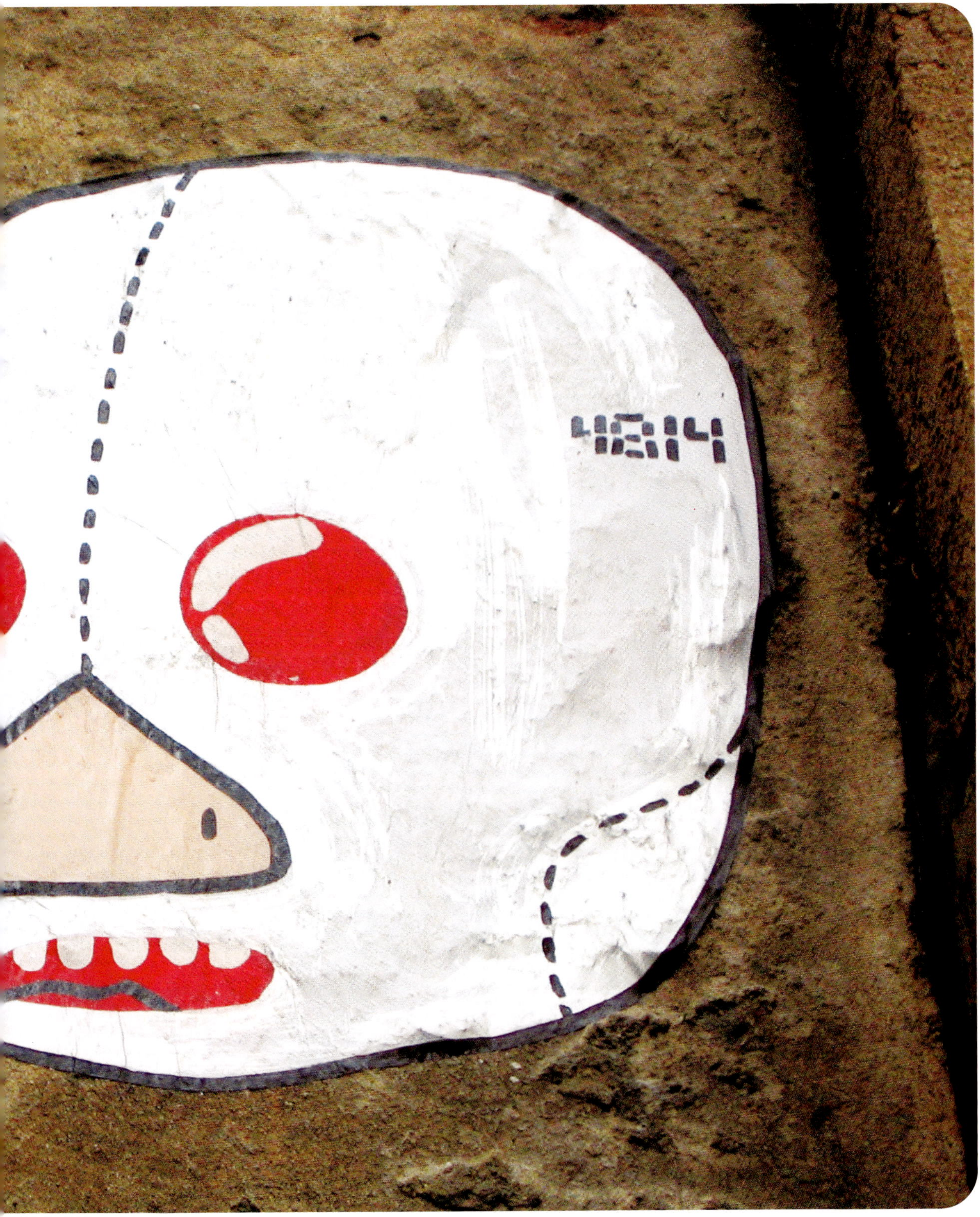

barcelona)))

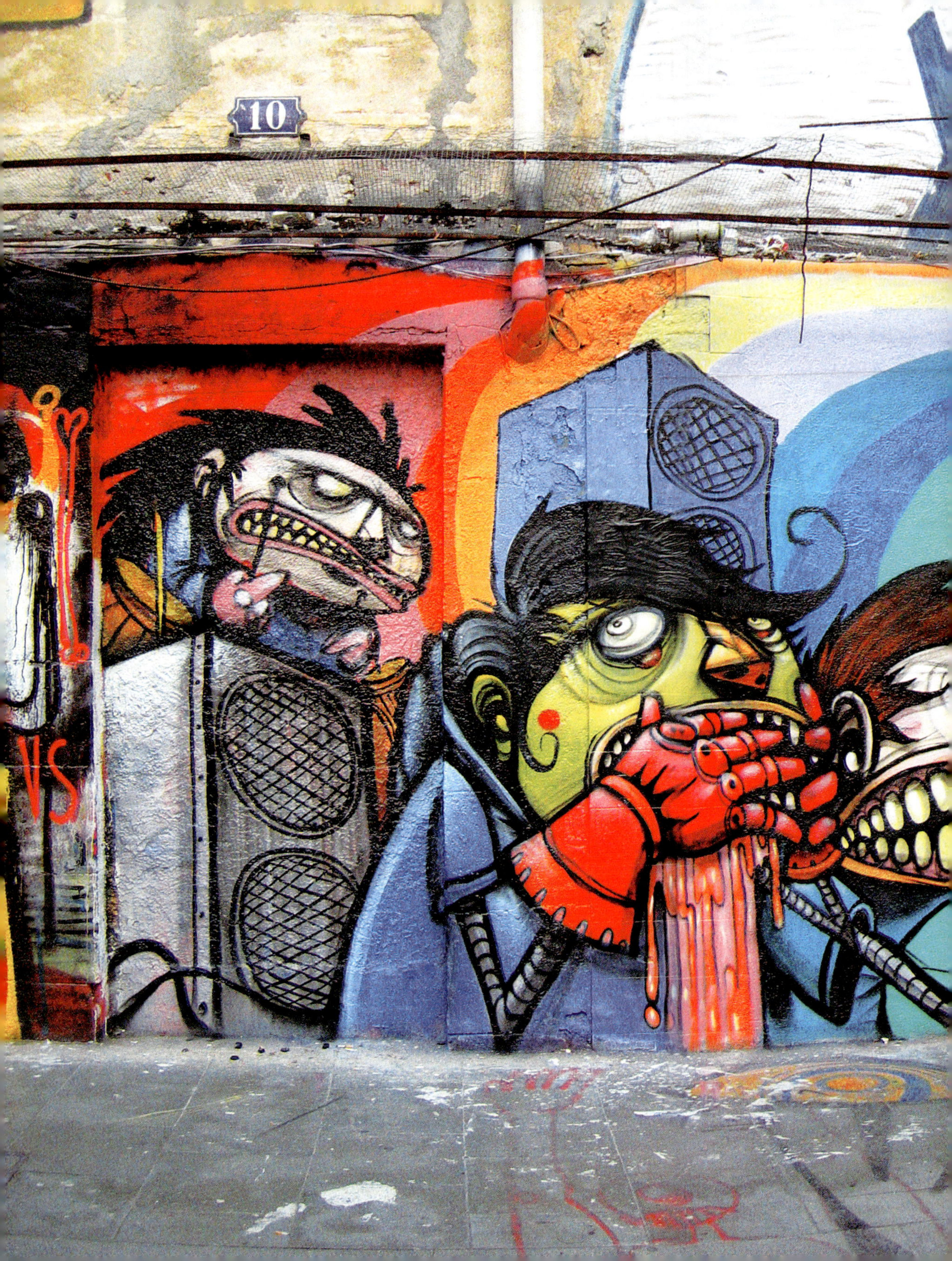
10
VS

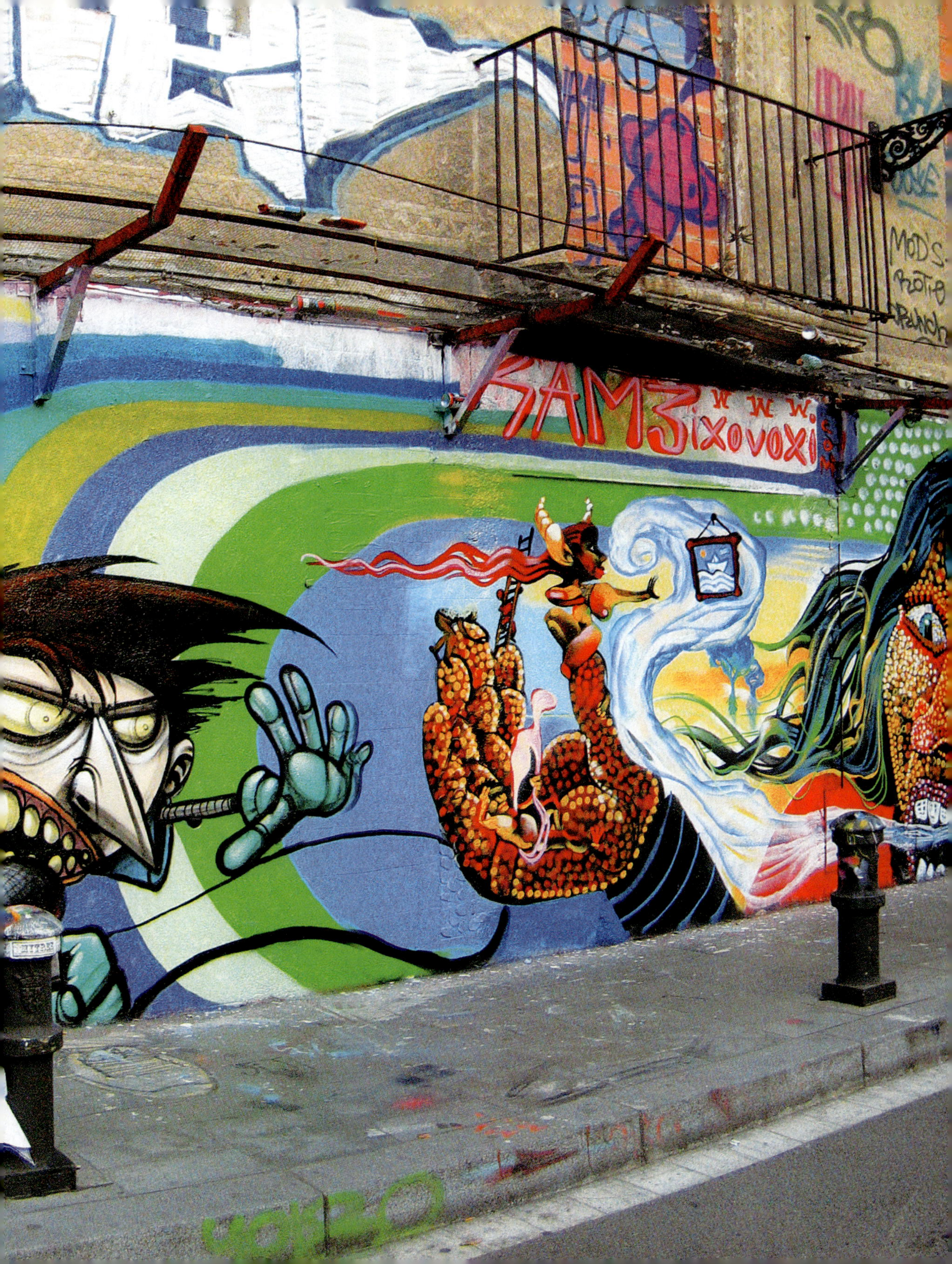
RAM3
www.ixovoxi.com

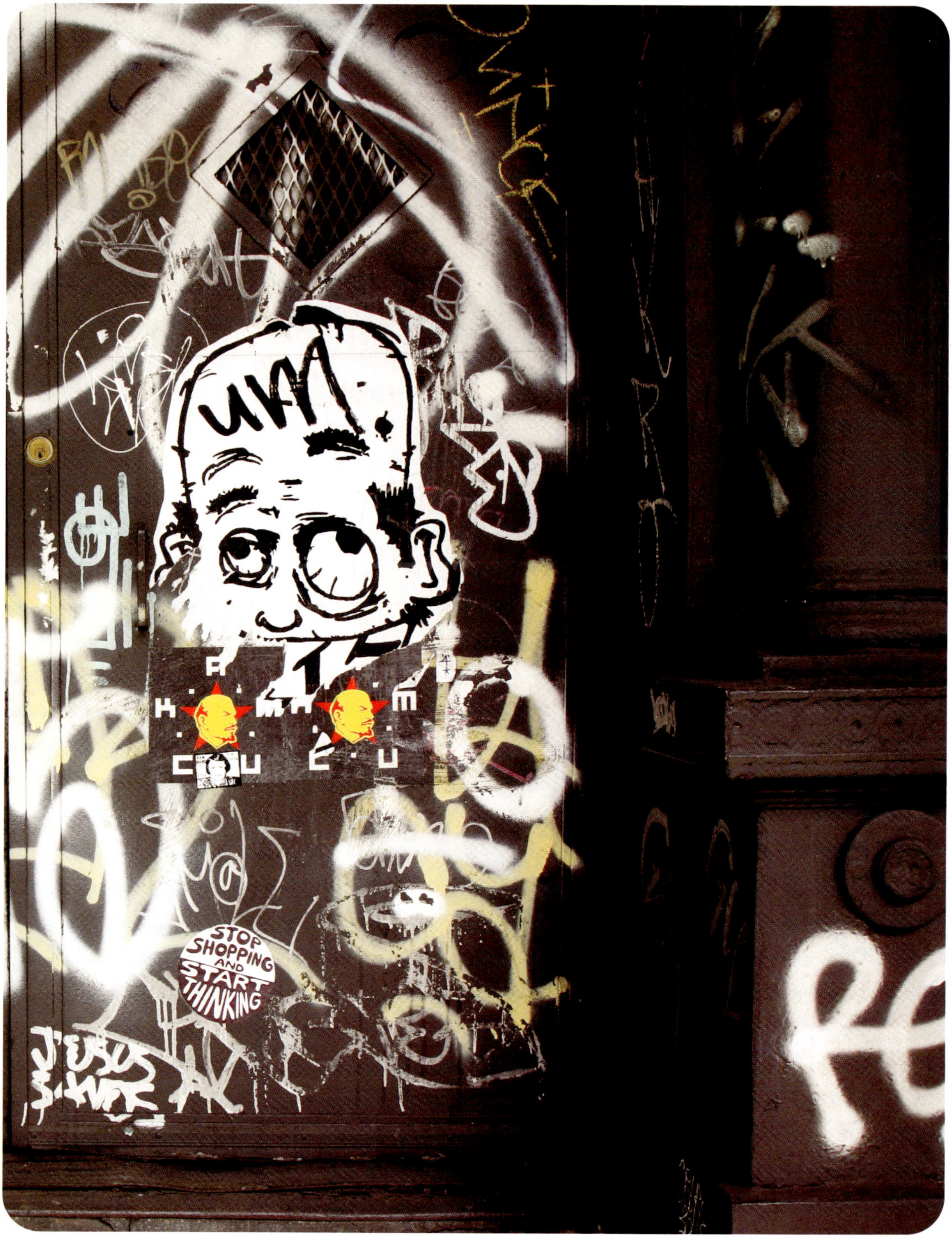
STOP
SHOPPING
AND
START
THINKING

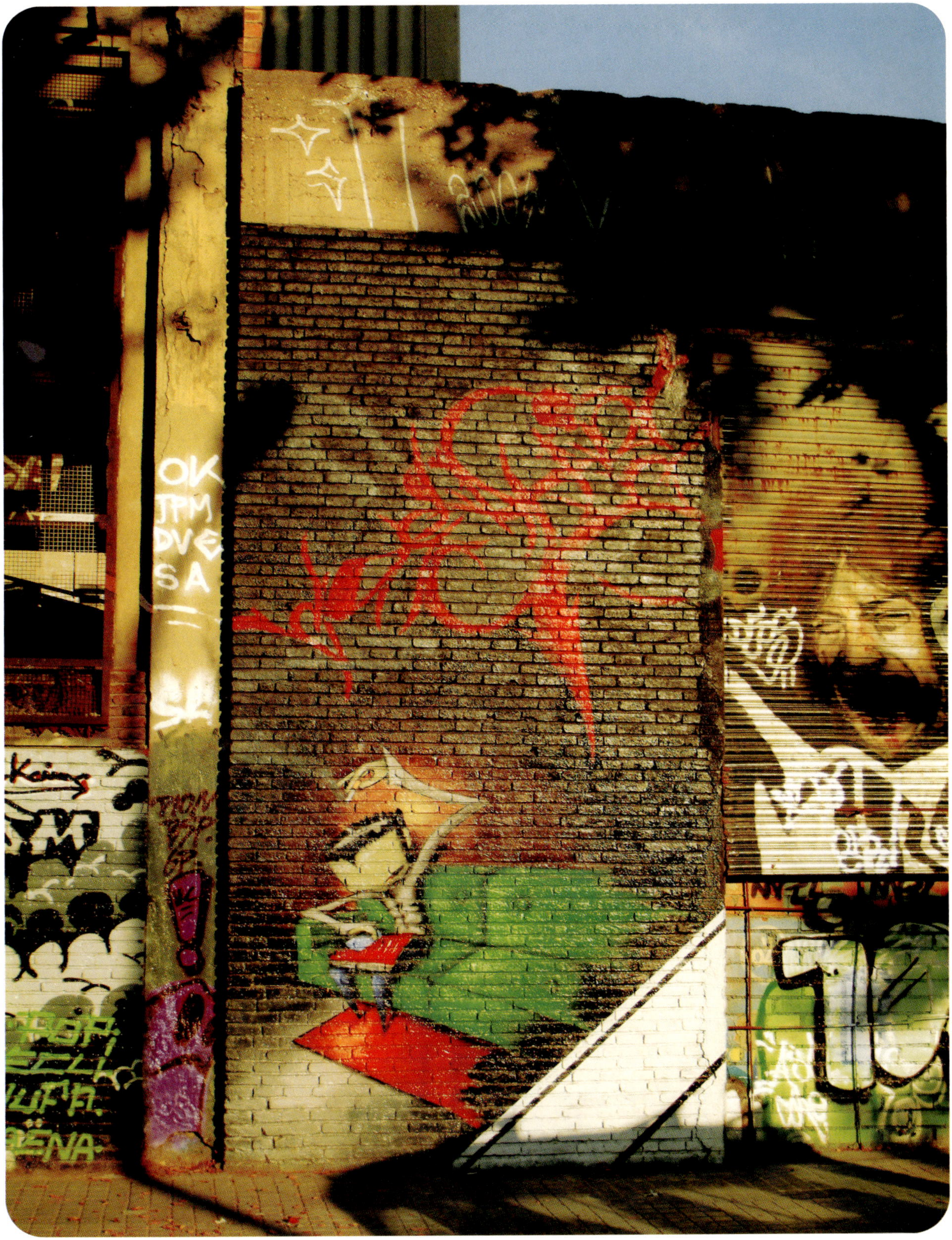

barcelona

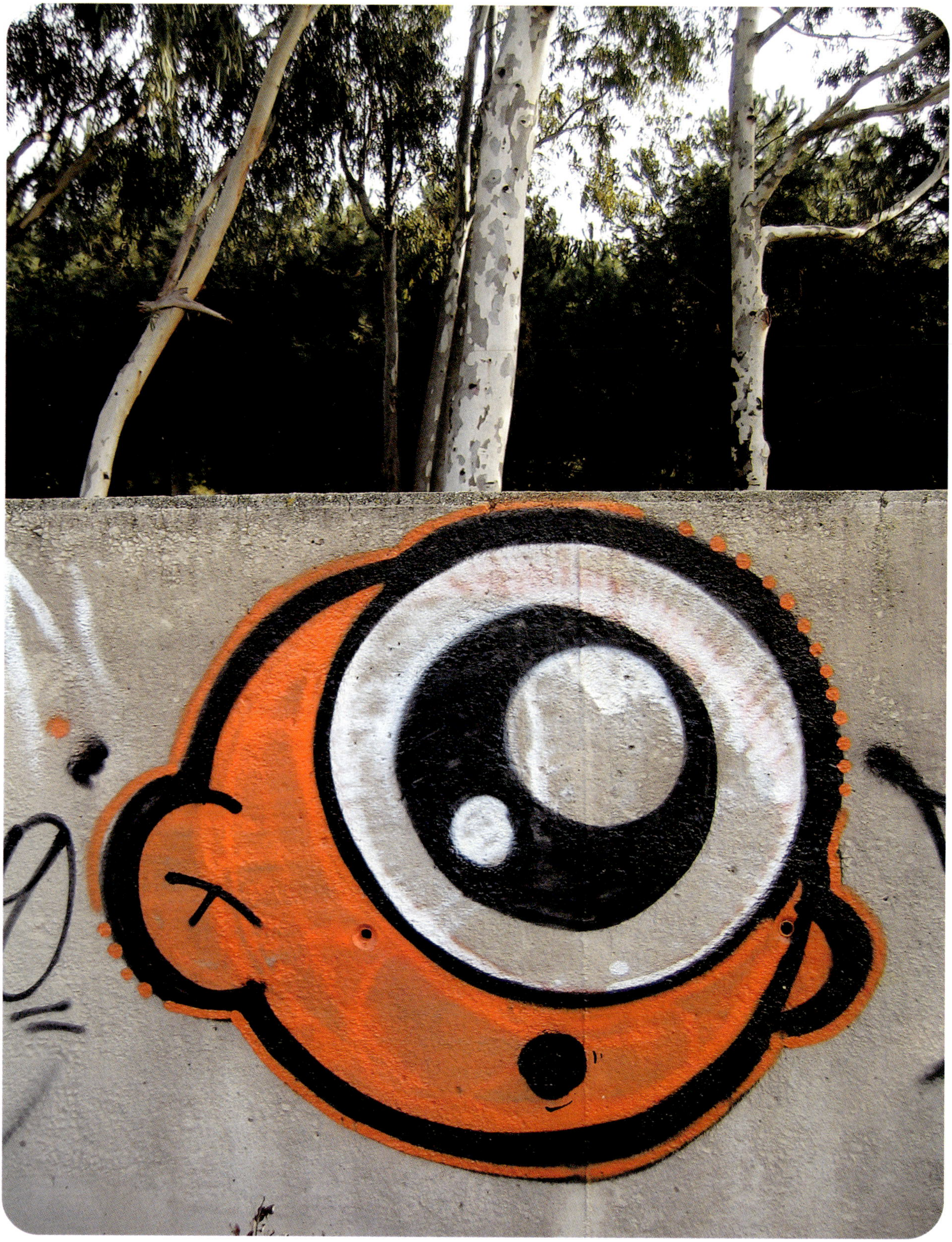

barcelona

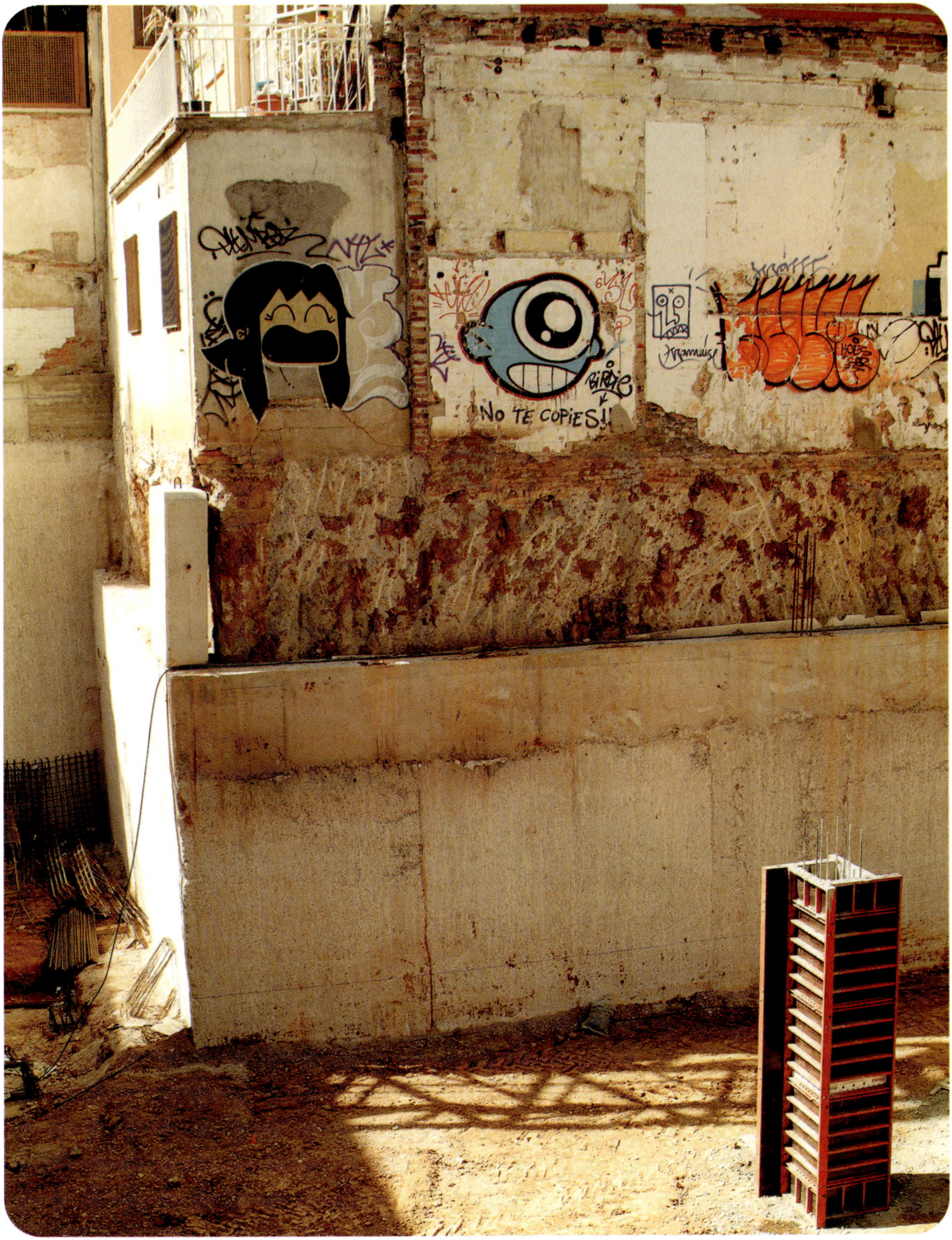

barcelona

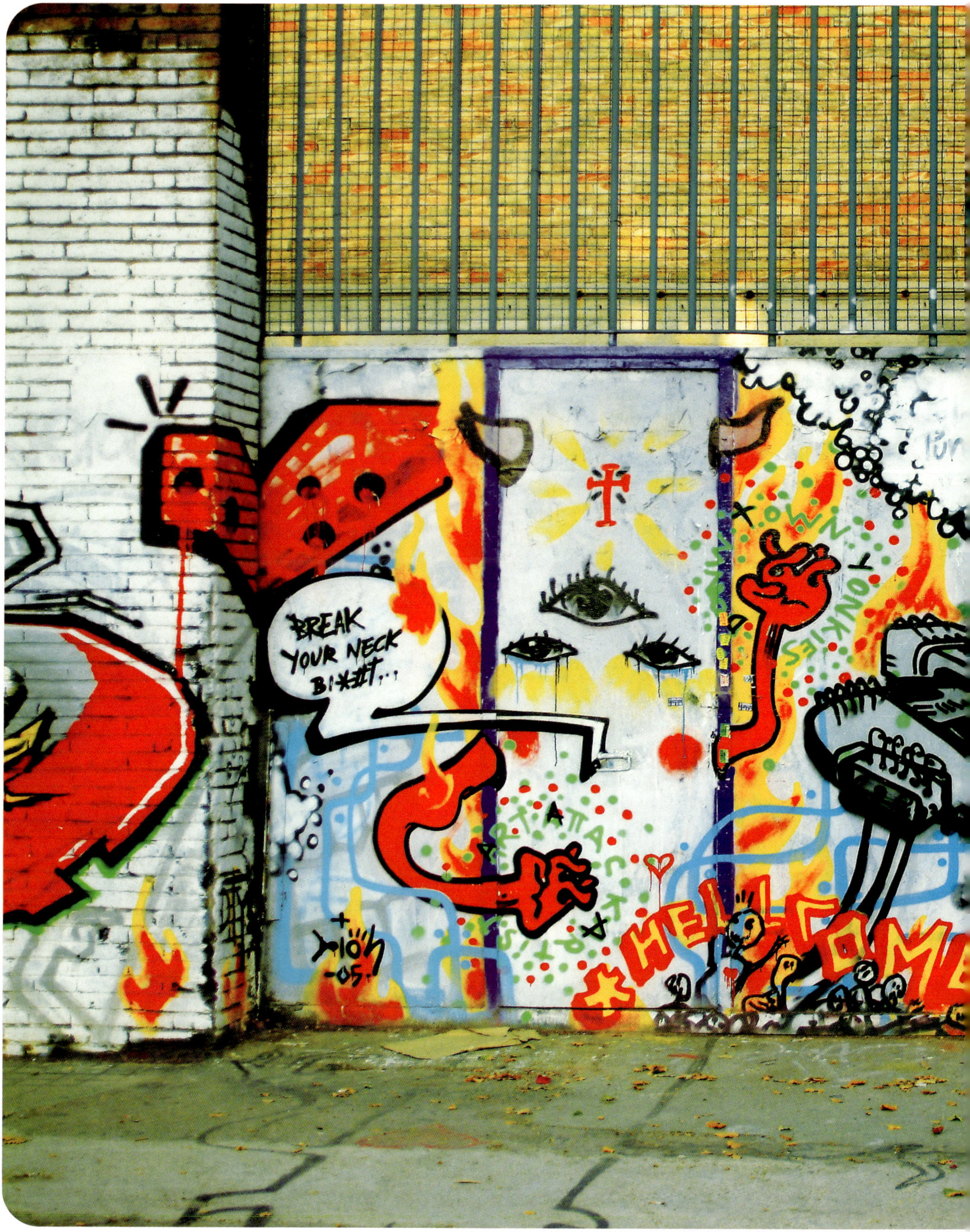
BREAK YOUR NECK BI*#T...
HELLCOM

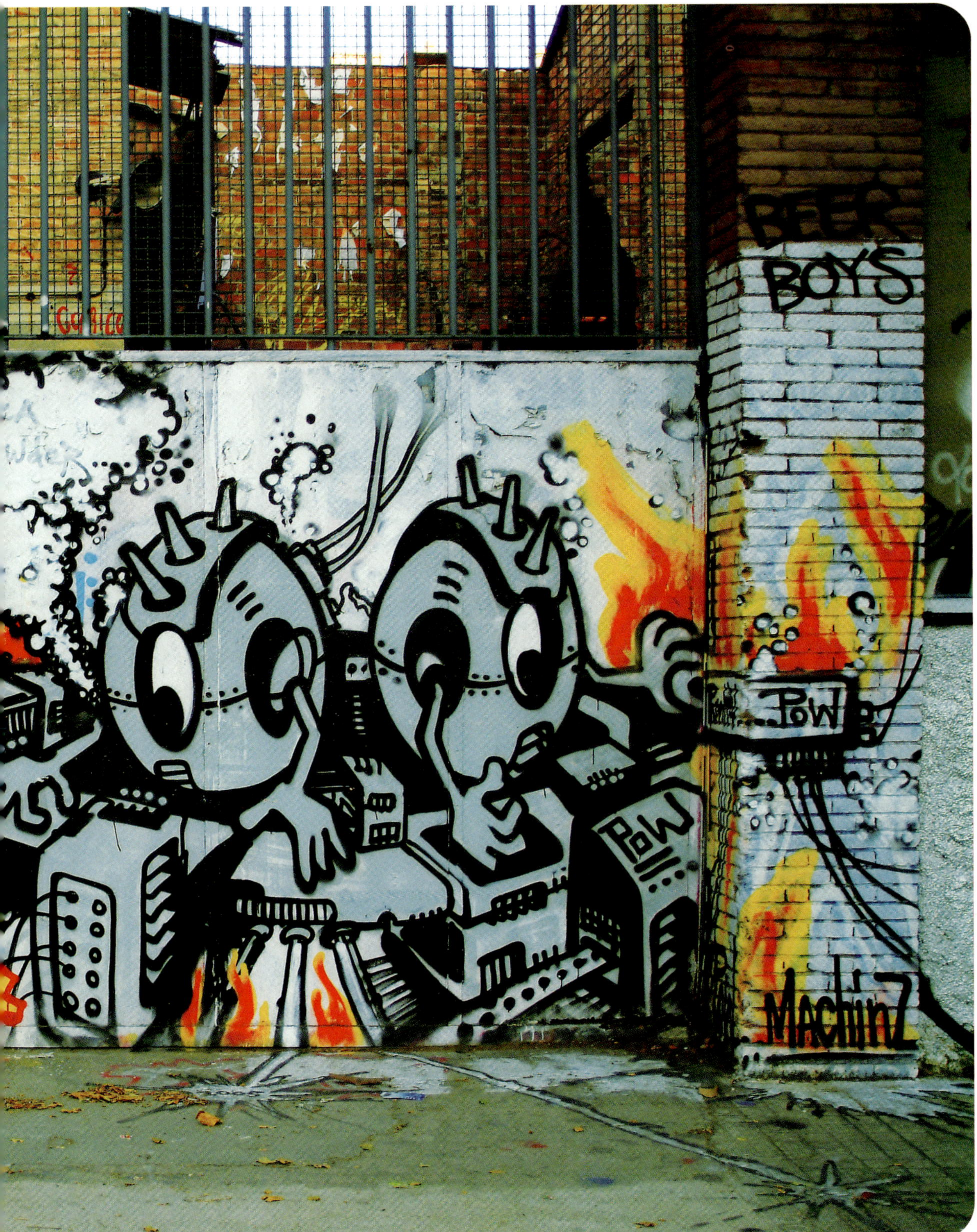
BEER
BOYS
POW
POW
MACHINZ

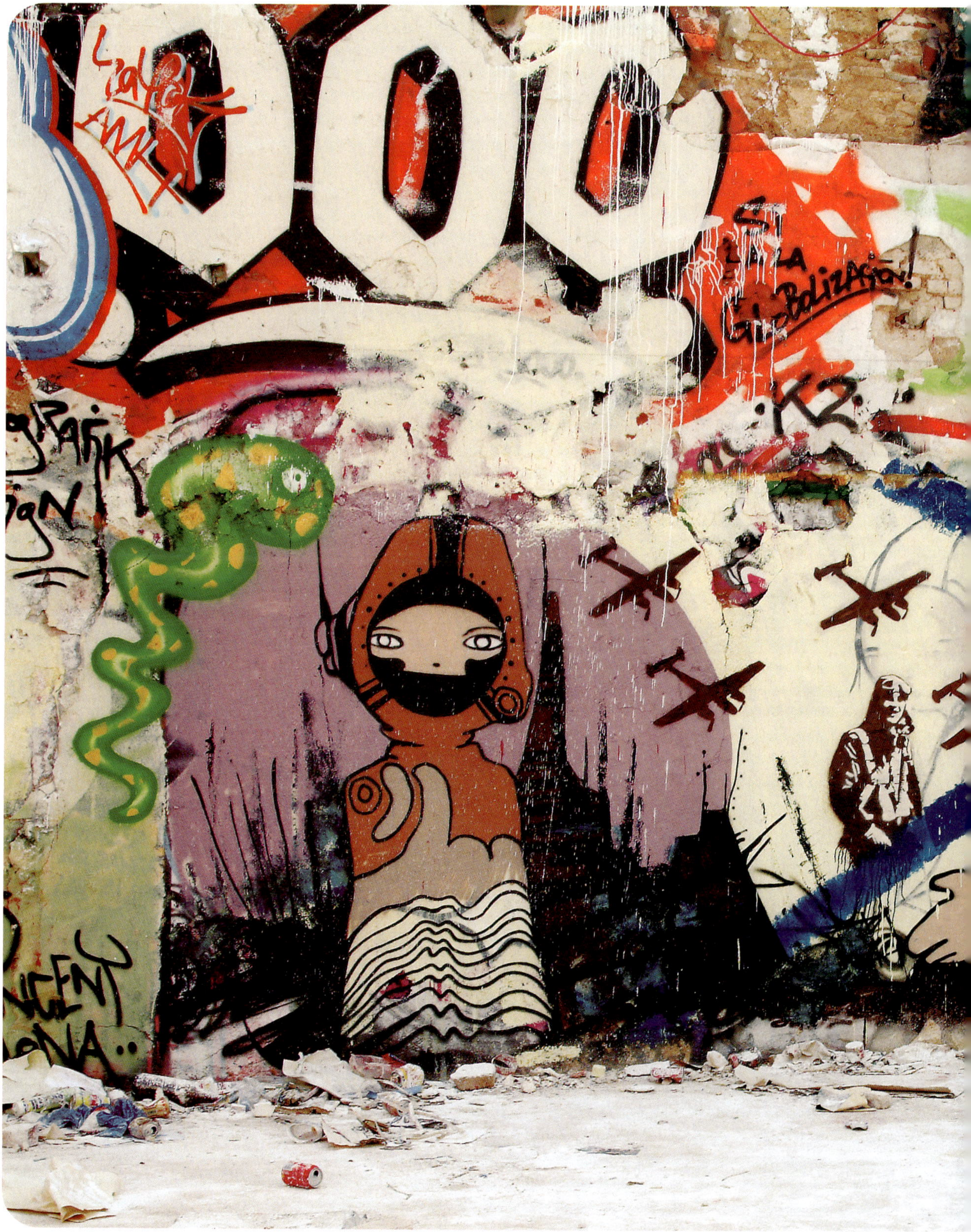

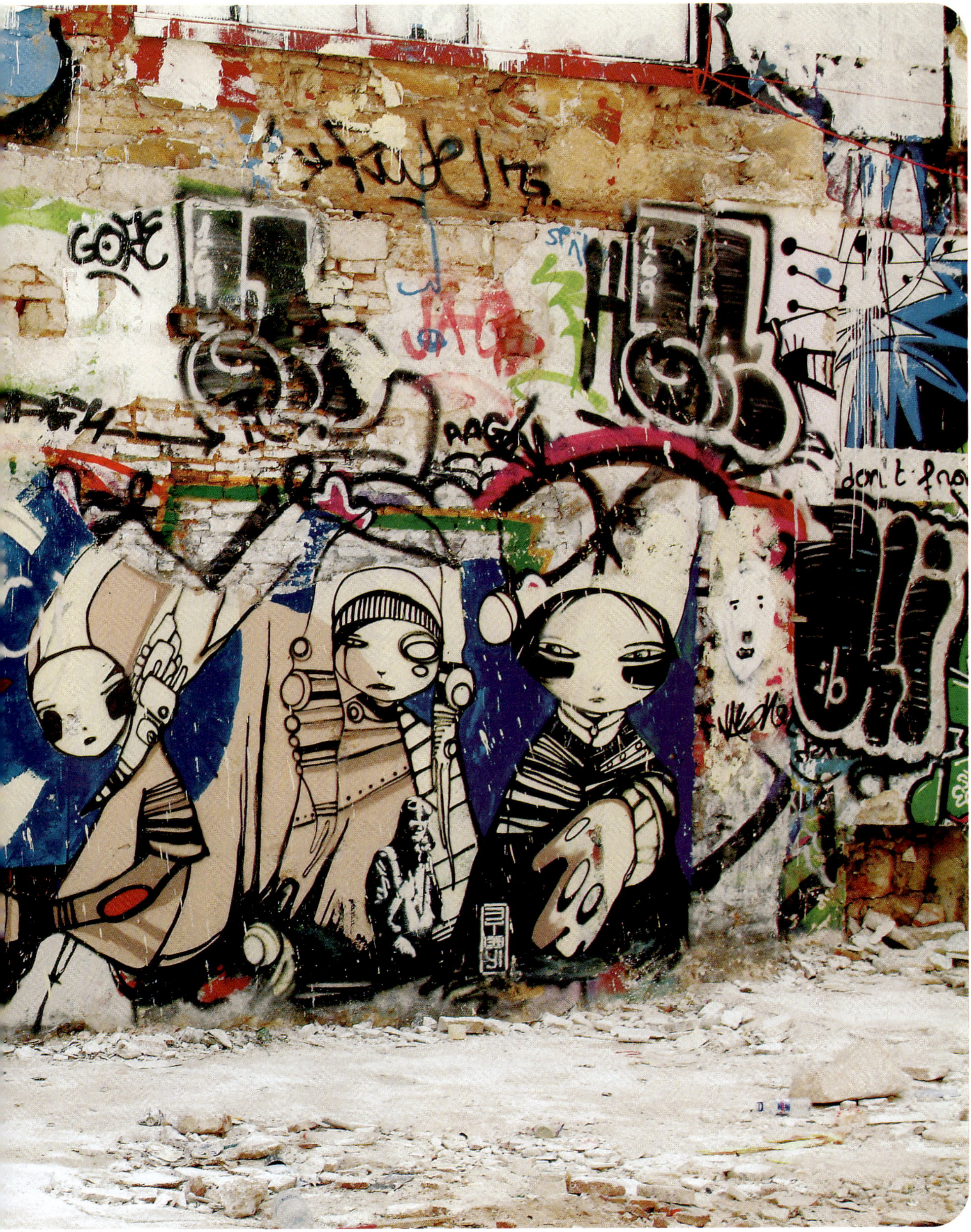

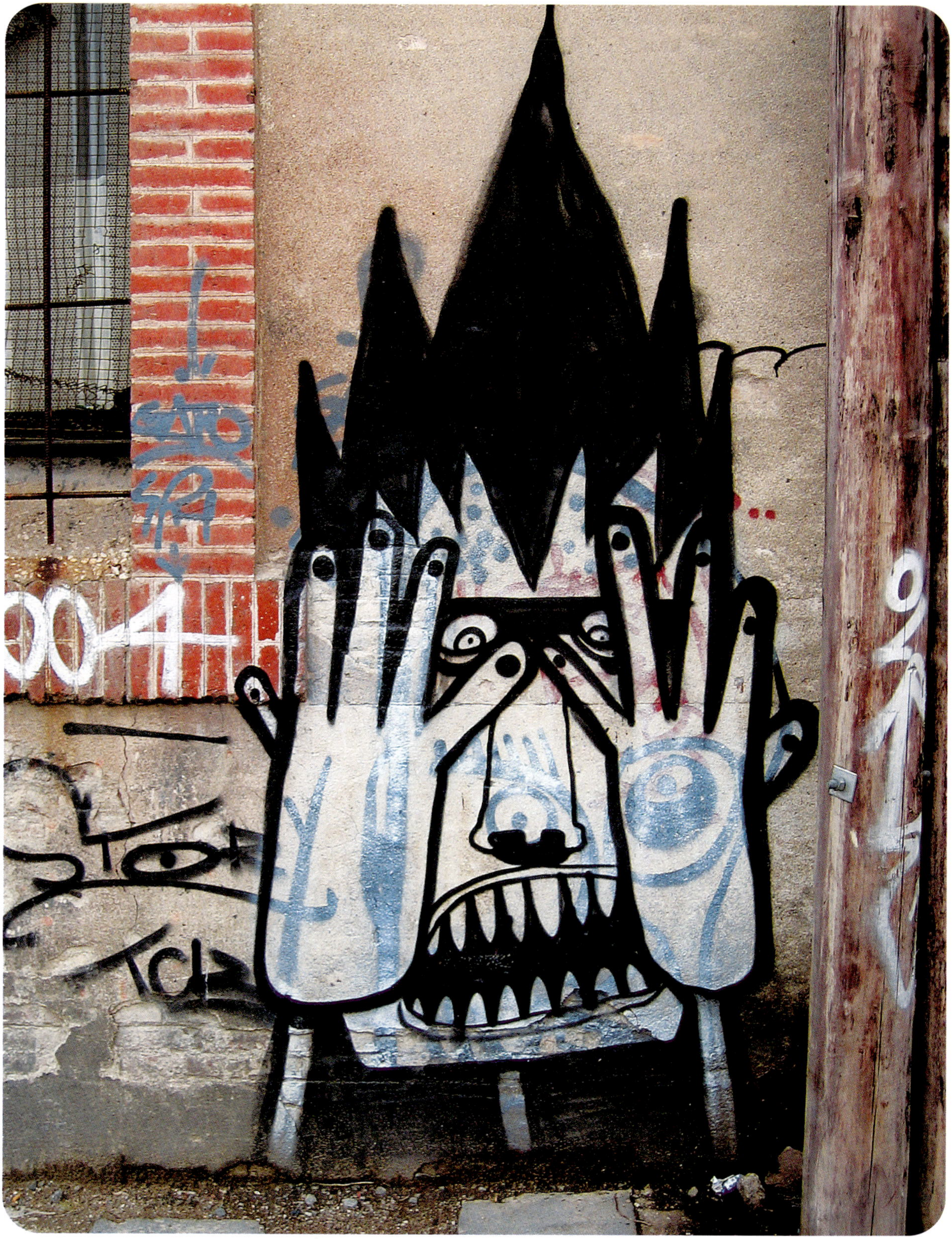

barcelona

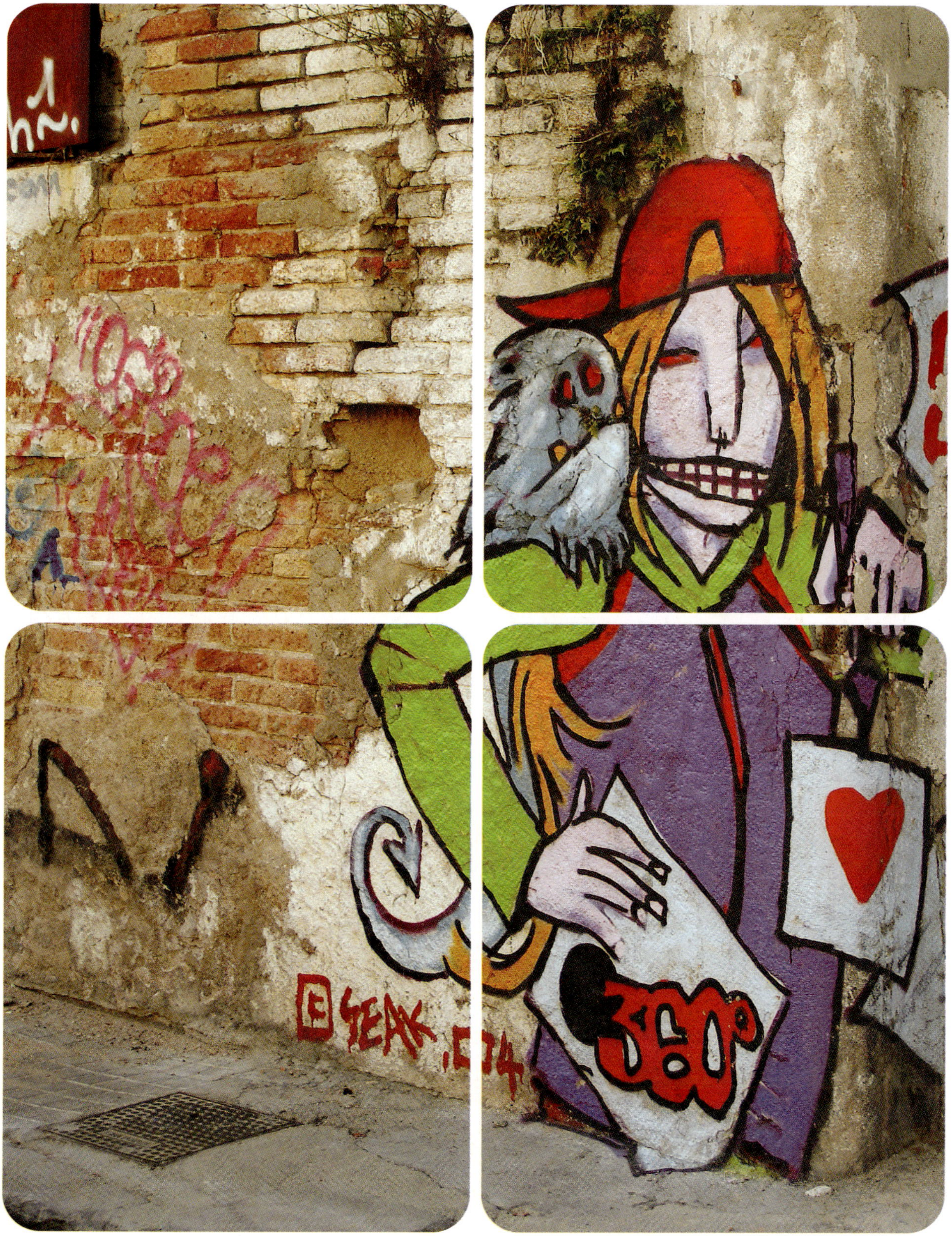

barcelona

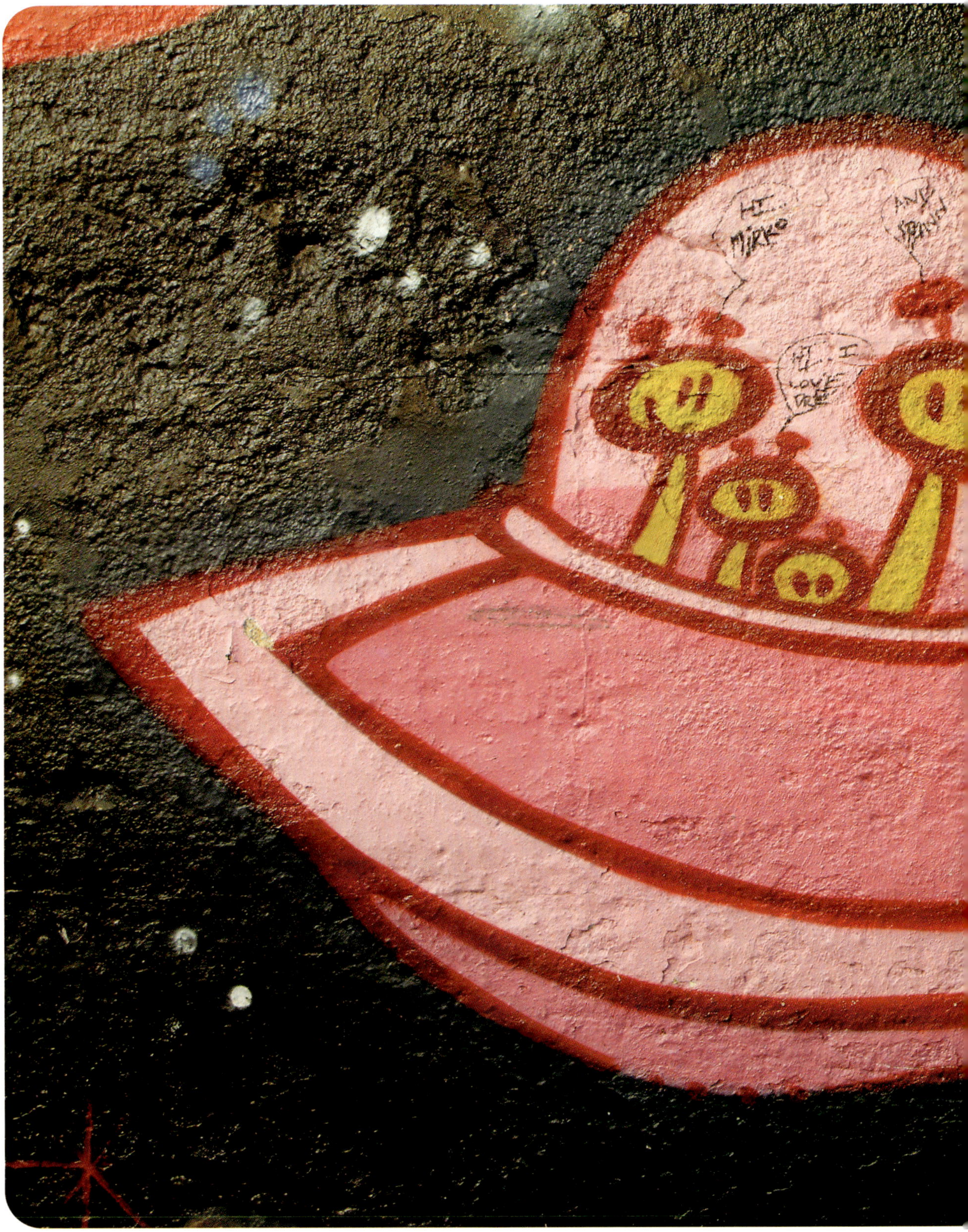
HI..
MIRKO

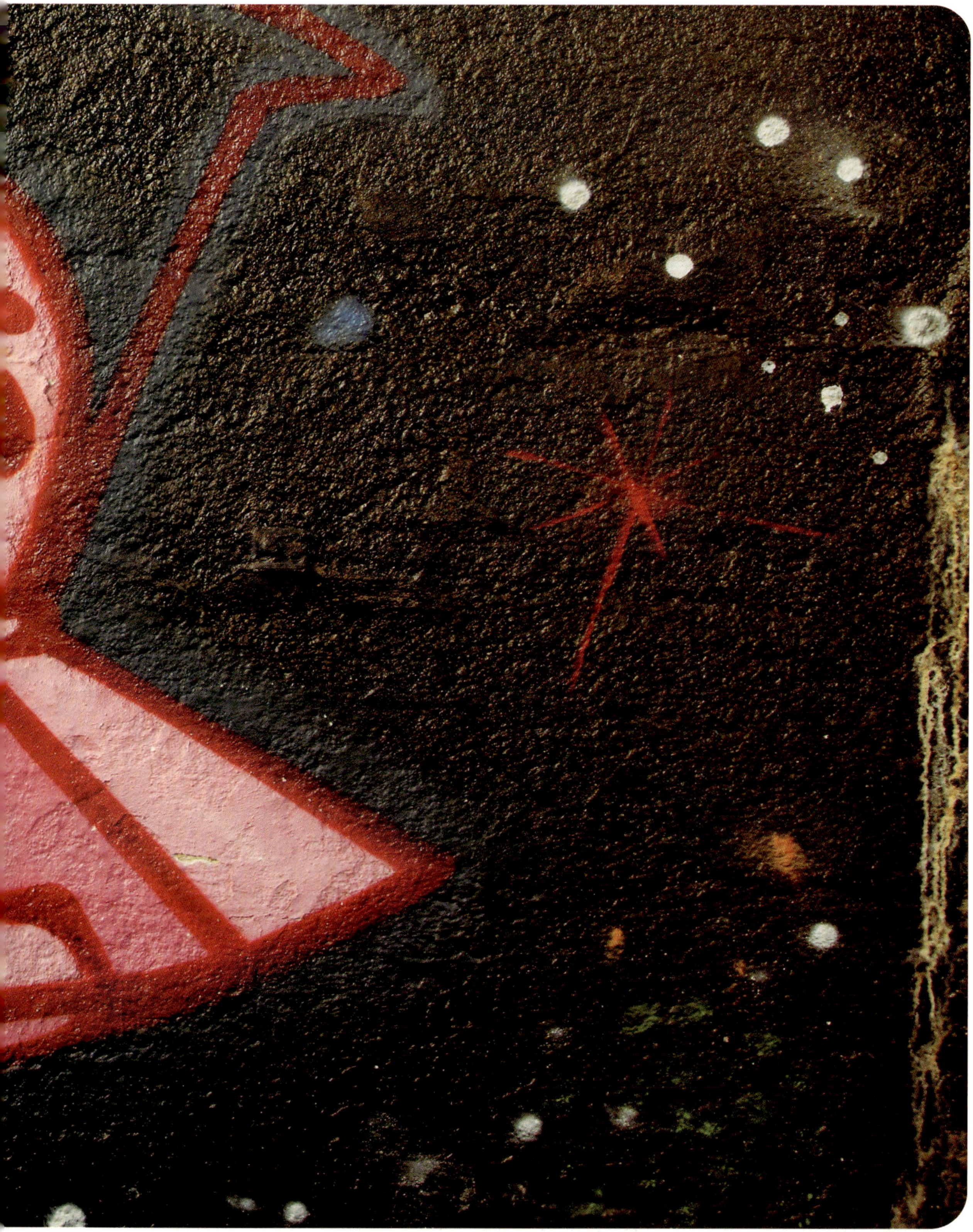

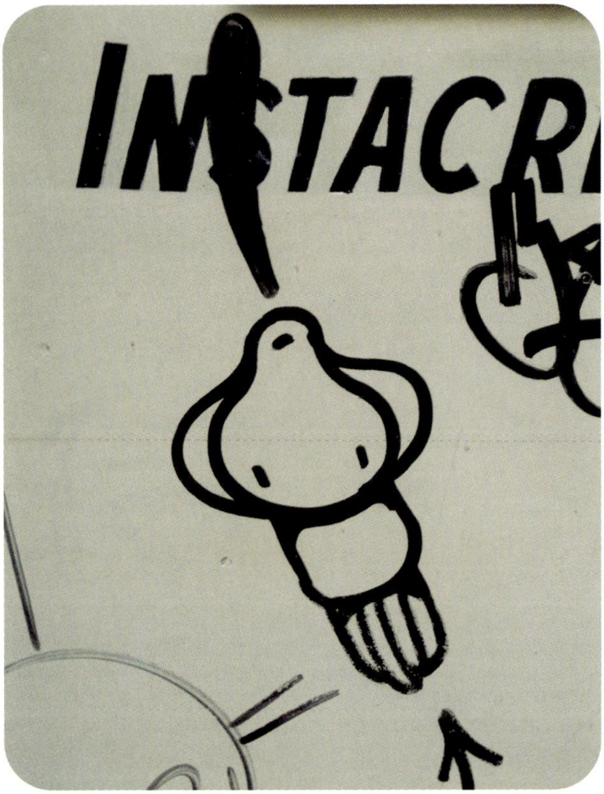
INSTACR

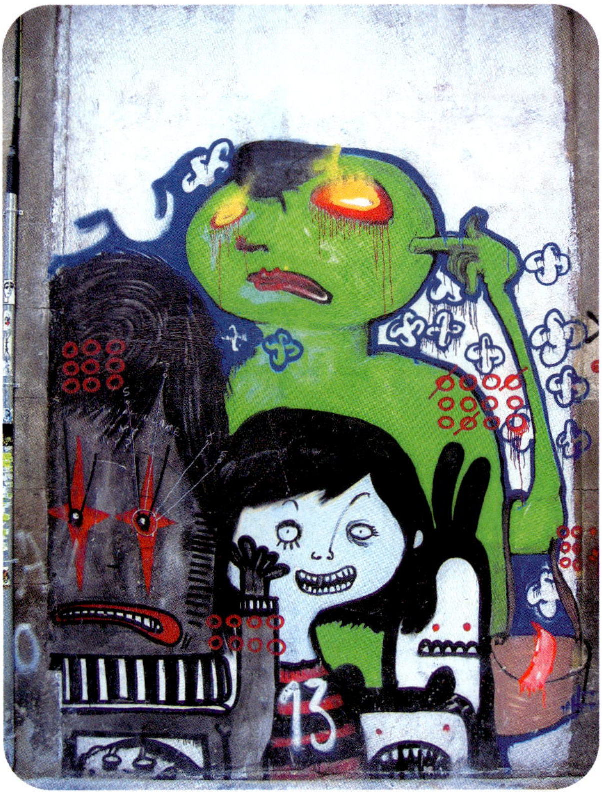
13

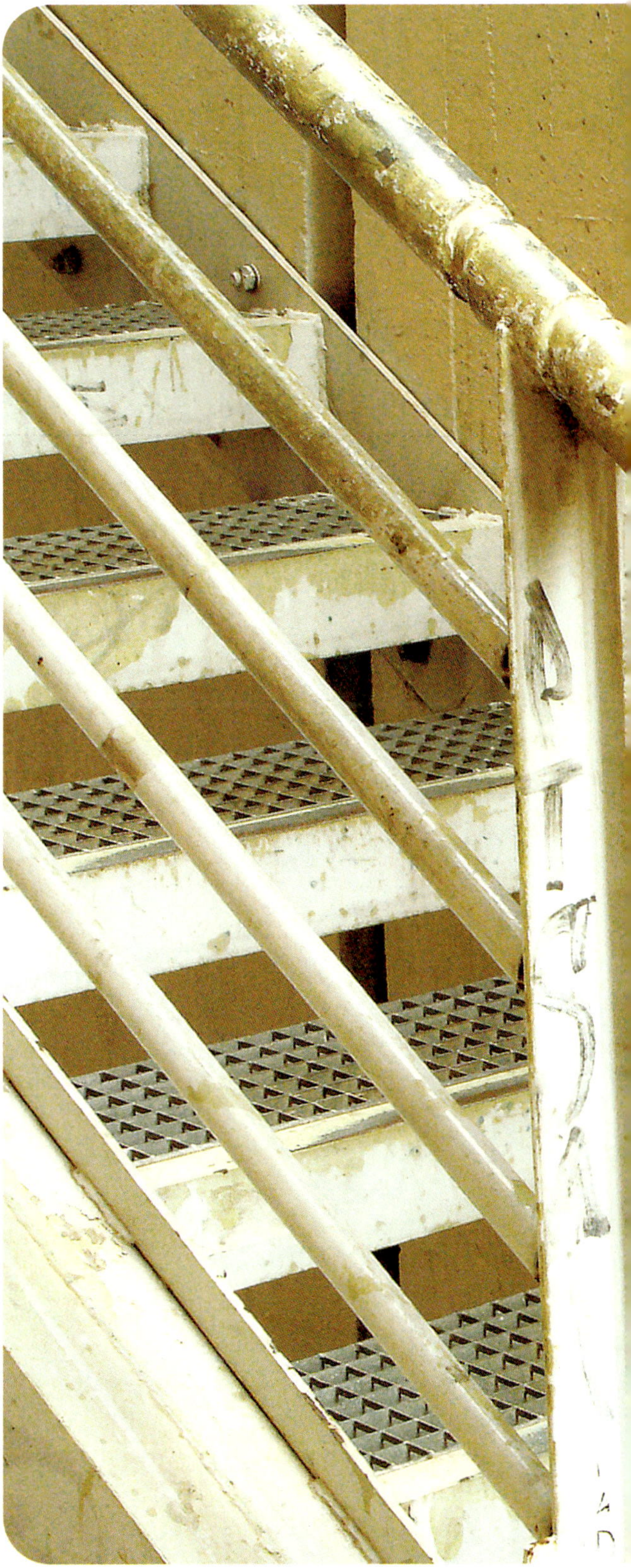

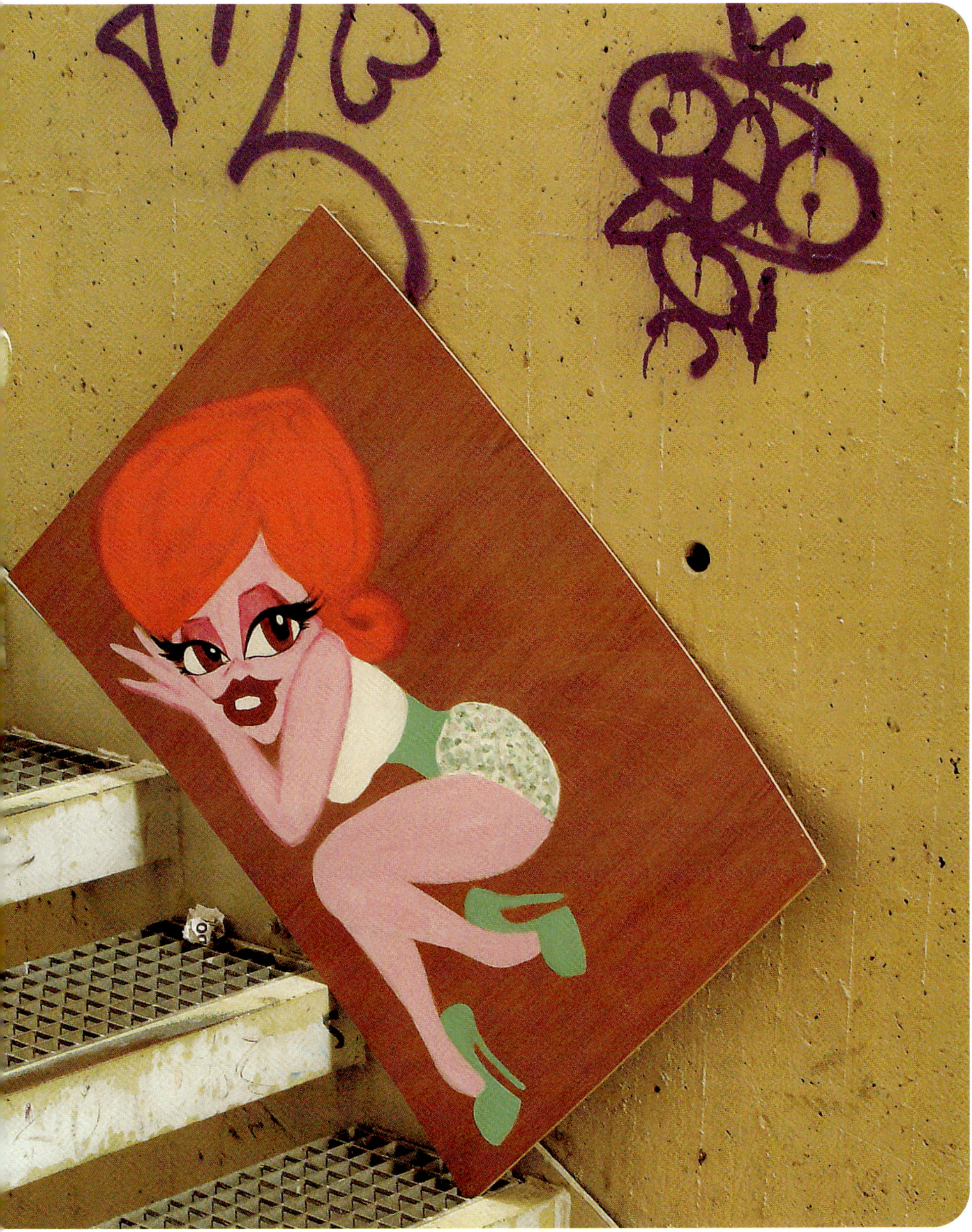

barcelona

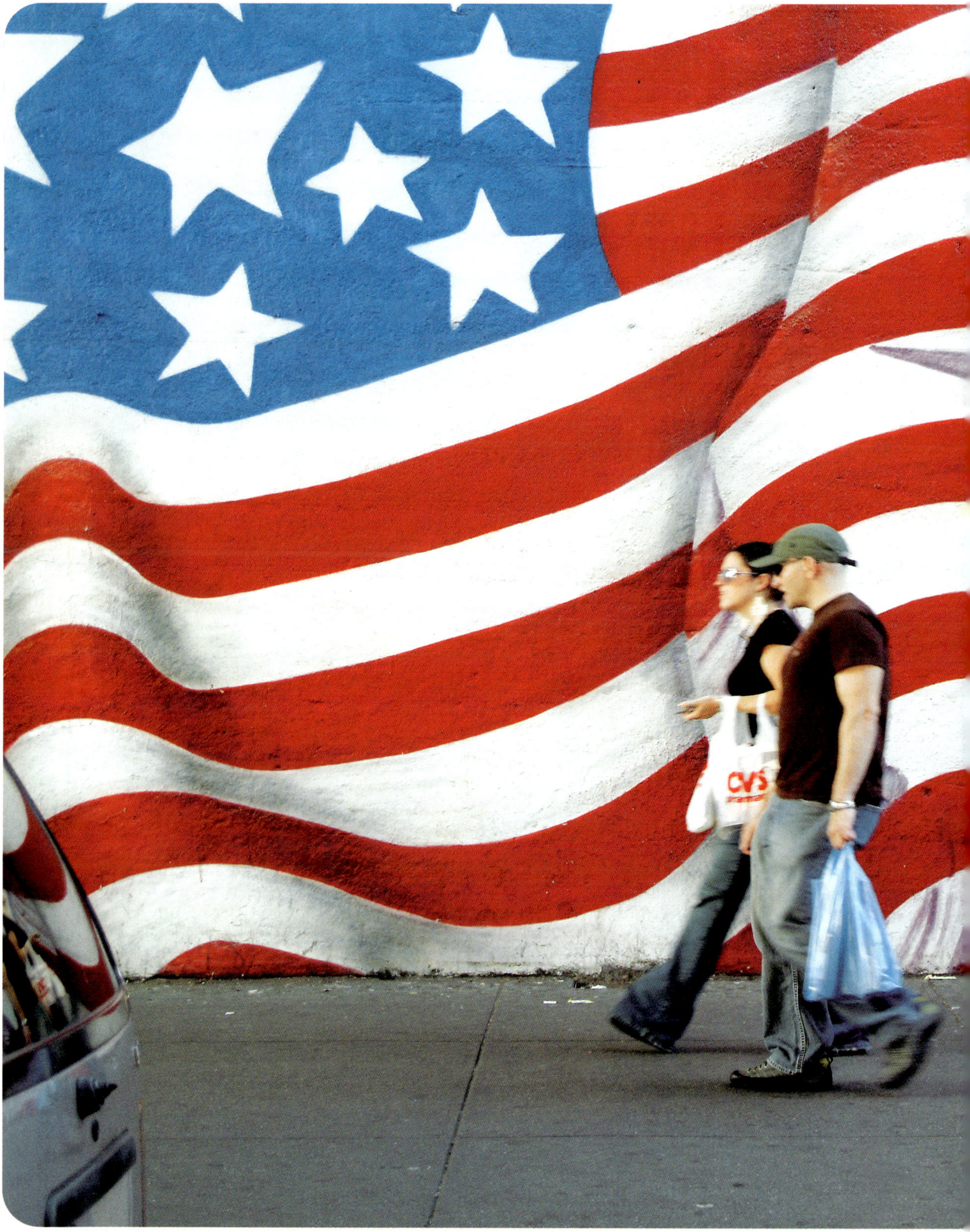
CVS

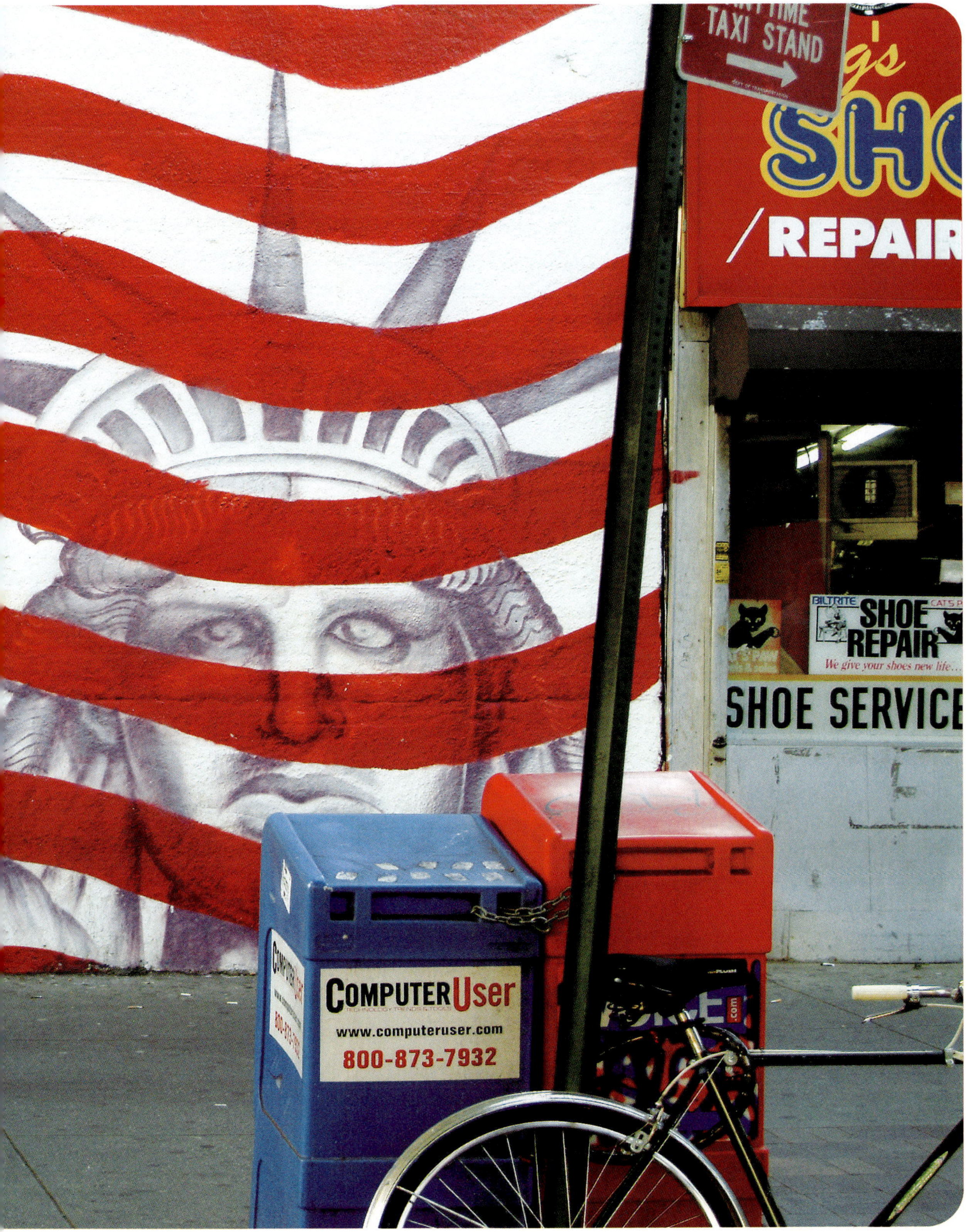
TAXI STAND
REPAIR
BILTRITE
SHOE REPAIR
We give your shoes new life...
SHOE SERVICE
COMPUTER User
www.computeruser.com
800-873-7932

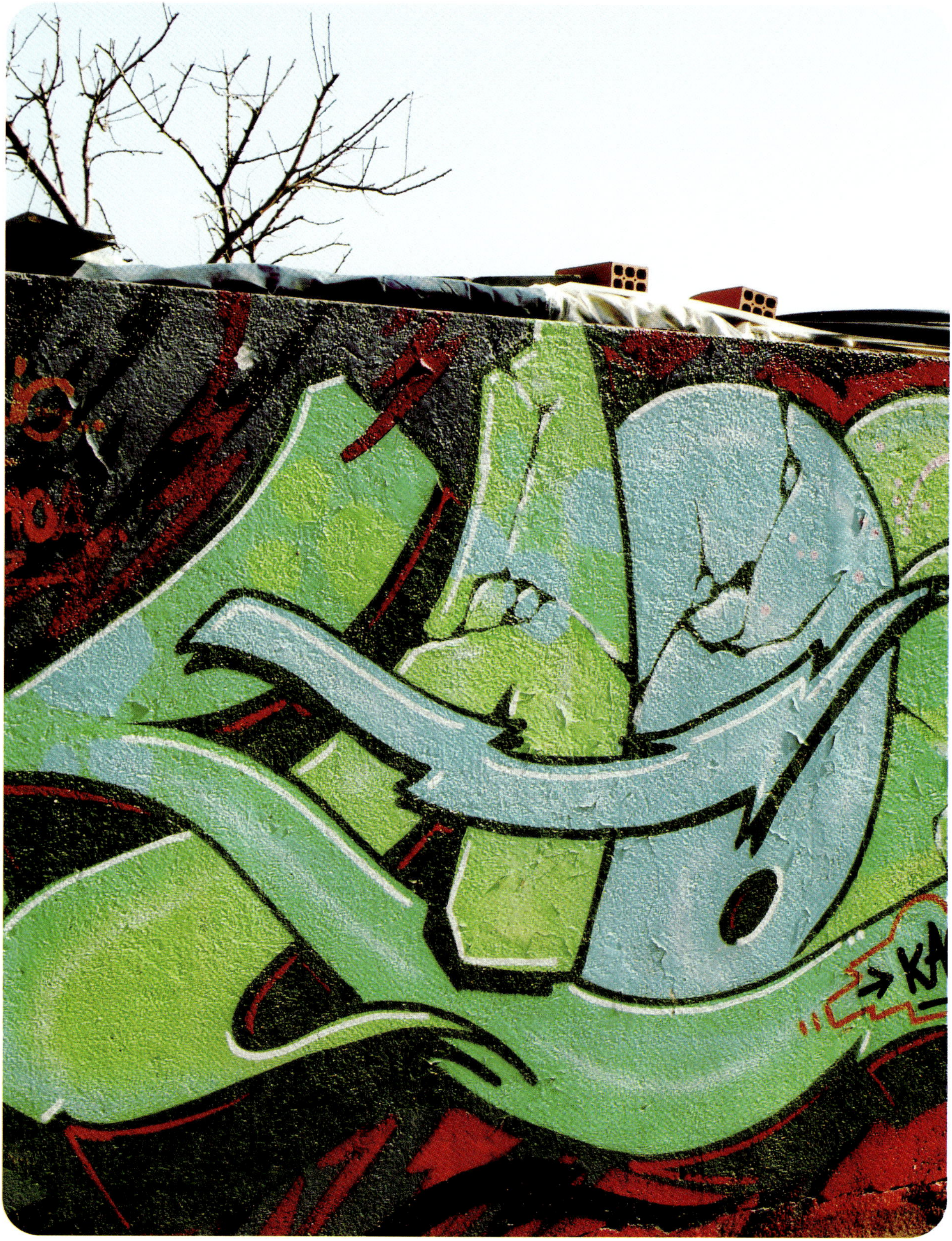

barcelona

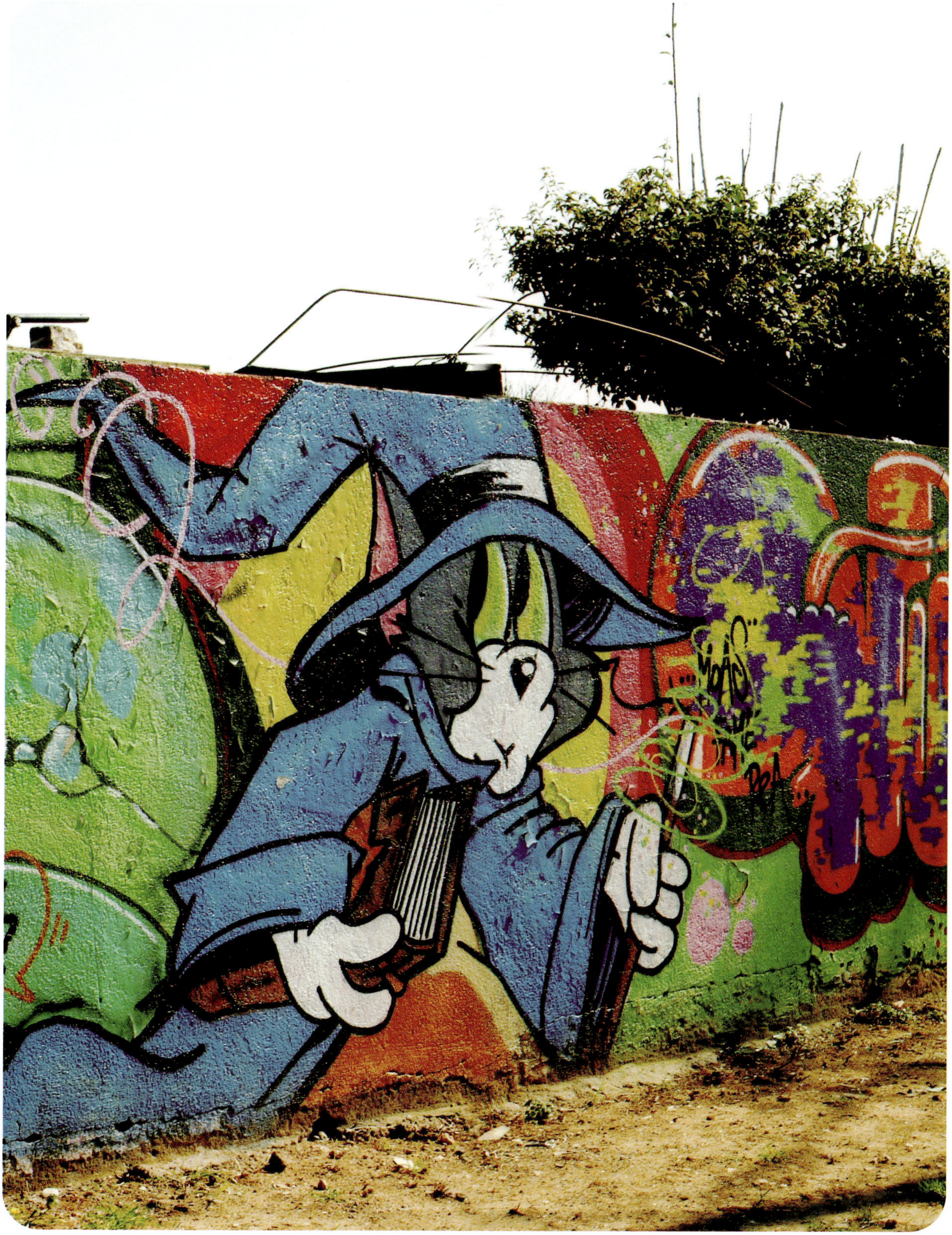

barcelona

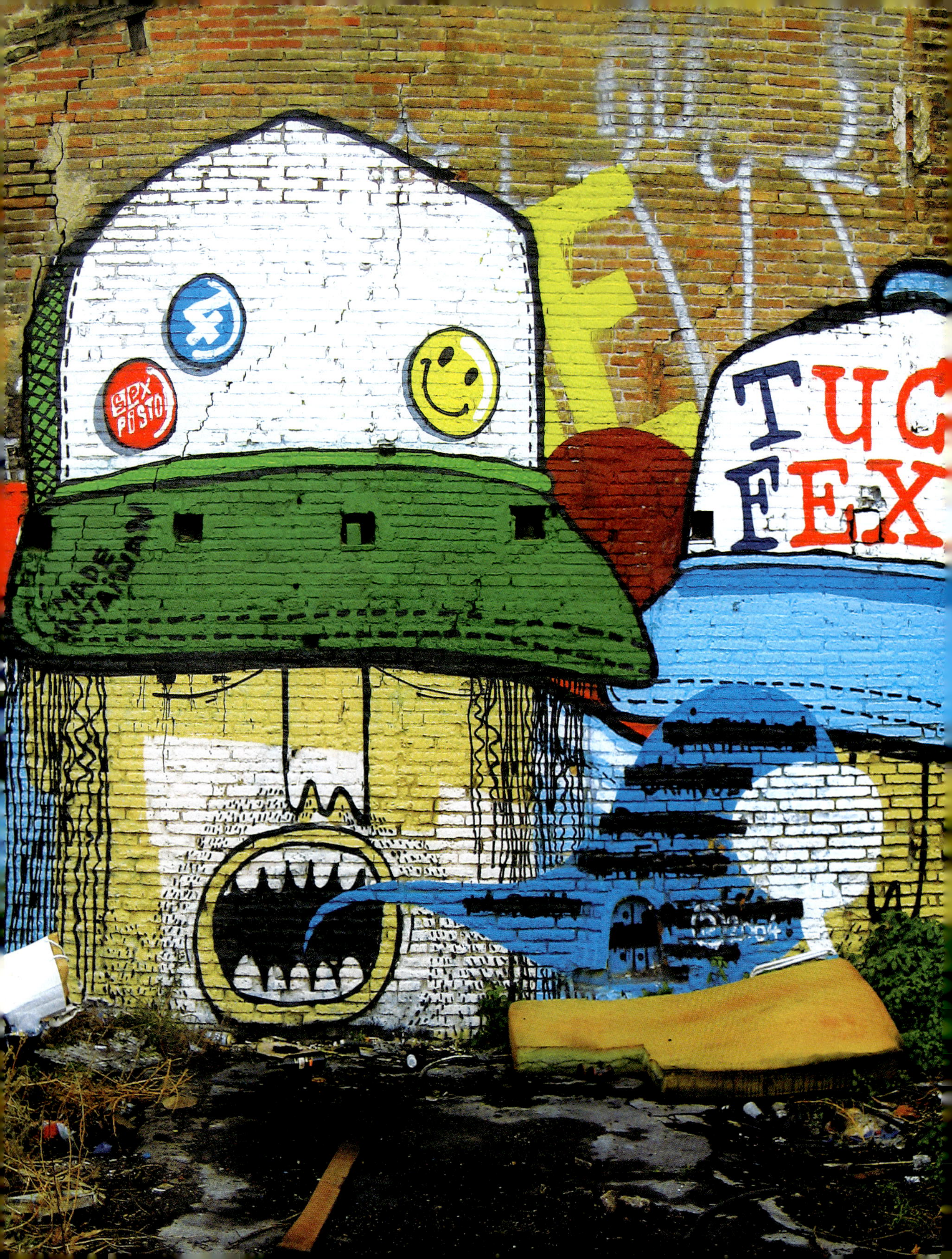
MADE IN TAIWAN
FE.X

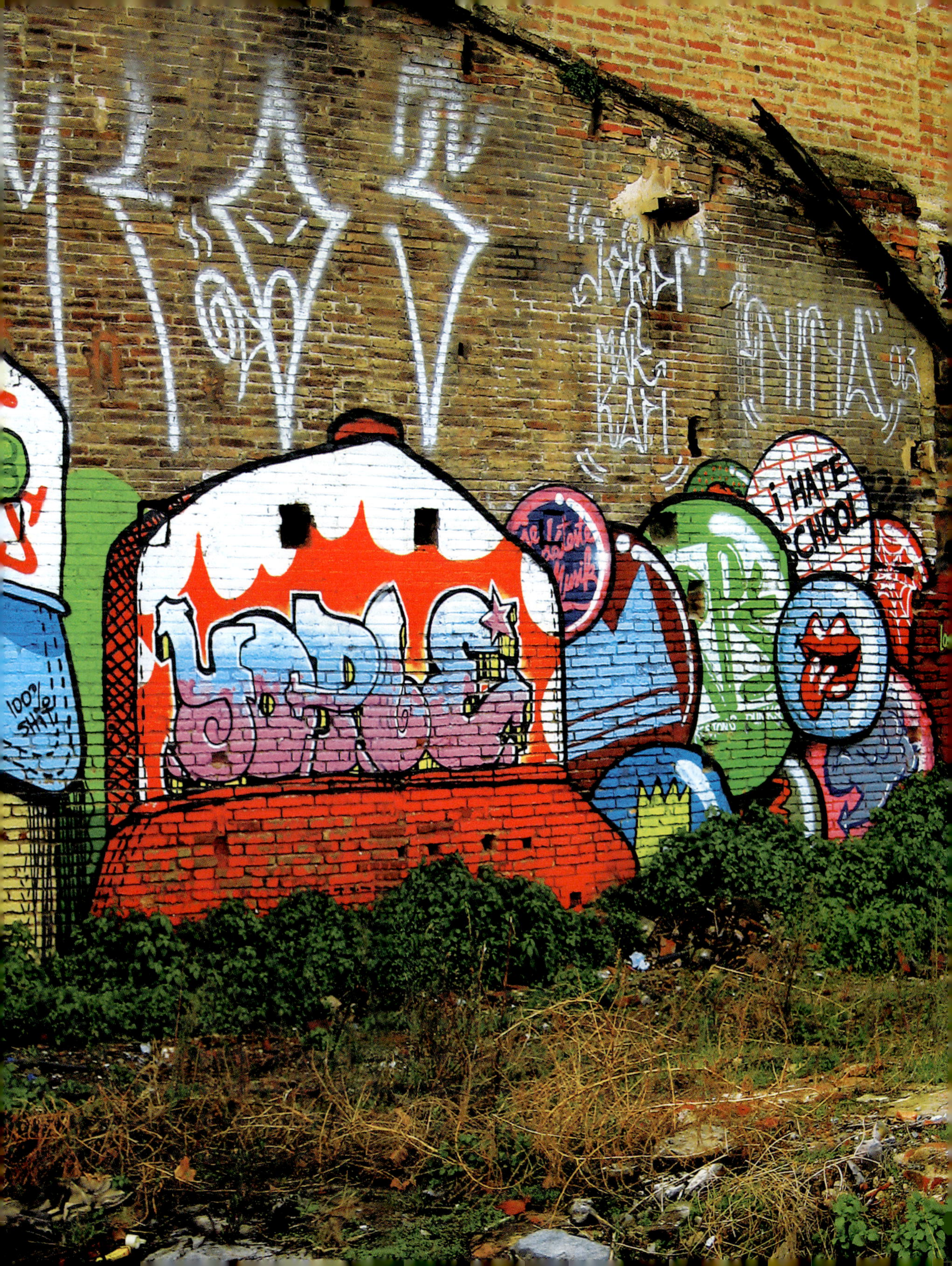
I HATE SCHOOL
100% SHIT